# Adobe Photoshop CS3
# for Photographers

In memory of my mother Marjorie Evening

# Adobe Photoshop CS3 for Photographers

A professional image editor's guide to the creative use of Photoshop for the Macintosh and PC

Martin Evening

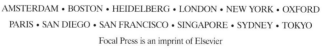

AMSTERDAM • BOSTON • HEIDELBERG • LONDON • NEW YORK • OXFORD
PARIS • SAN DIEGO • SAN FRANCISCO • SINGAPORE • SYDNEY • TOKYO

Focal Press is an imprint of Elsevier

ELSEVIER

Focal Press

Focal Press is an imprint of Elsevier
Linacre House, Jordan Hill, Oxford OX2 8DP, UK
30 Corporate Drive, Suite 400, Burlington, MA 01803, USA

First edition 2007
Reprinted 2007

Notice
No responsibility is assumed by the publisher for any injury and/or damage to persons
or property as a matter of products liability, negligence or otherwise, or from any use
or operation of any methods, products, instructions or ideas contained in the material
herein. Because of rapid advances in the medical sciences, in particular, independent
verification of diagnoses and drug dosages should be made

**British Library Cataloguing in Publication Data**
A catalogue record for this book is available from the British Library

**Library of Congress Cataloging-in-Publication Data**
A catalog record for this book is available from the Library of Congress

ISBN: 978-0-240-52028-5

For information on all Focal Press publications
visit our website at www.focalpress.com

Printed and bound in *Italy*

07 08 09 10   10 9 8 7 6 5 4 3 2

Working together to grow
libraries in developing countries

www.elsevier.com  |  www.bookaid.org  |  www.sabre.org

ELSEVIER      BOOK AID
              International      Sabre Foundation

**Registered Trademarks**
Brand names mentioned in this book are protected by their respective
trademarks and are acknowledged

## Contents

# Contents

## Chapter 3: Configuring Photoshop — 97

# Contents

## Chapter 4: Basic Pixel Image Editing — 133

## Chapter 6: Fine-tuned Image Corrections — 291

## Chapter 7: Image Retouching — 312

## Chapter 8: Layers, Selections and Masking     354

## Chapter 11: Image management     508

## Chapter 12: Color Management     543

## Chapter 15: Automating Photoshop     643

## Index     666

# Foreword

**D**espite its name, Photoshop has not always been a welcome companion amongst the photography set. Much as assembly line automation was seen as the death knell for craftsmen and craftsmanship, at various times, Photoshop was seen as a threat against the skilled photographer. However, a change has recently taken place. Fueled primarily by the advent of digital SLRs with professional features offered at non-professional prices, the confluence of Photoshop and photography, particularly digital photography, has become a certainty. Photoshop is now accepted as a powerful tool in the photographer's arsenal.

But what are veteran shooters and those digital photographers newly minted to make of this brave new world? How can your wealth of darkroom experience be brought to bear on a computer screen and a mouse? Will the sterile environment of technology replace the comforting mess and sickly-sweet chemical smells of fixer and developer? Most importantly, how will you and your photography benefit from the new opportunities offered by Photoshop in its latest incarnation, Photoshop CS3?

Whether you are a long-time traditional film photographer, a newcomer to the 'tradigital' world, or a weekend snapshotter, this book has something to offer. From the broad coverage of the 'Photoshop ways' of performing traditional film and darkroom techniques to new techniques only possible using Photoshop, Martin takes you there and teaches everything step by step. This isn't another 'recipe' book that ignores your skilled eye and assumes all you want to do is paste your head on a supermodel's body. (Of course, Photoshop can do that, but if that is your goal, this is not the book for you.)

Martin understands the photographer's craft isn't always about the creative and artistic side of life. Rest assured, Martin covers the full spectrum of photographic tasks. Important aspects of the workflow of the film photographer moving to digital – scanning and image capture – usually ignored in most other books are covered in depth. Martin also tackles the usually mundane issue of image management within Photoshop CS3, showing how the new Adobe Bridge program can move you well beyond just a 'digital shoebox'.

Viewing Photoshop through the eyes of an experienced photographer takes specialized talent and skills. In this book, Martin effectively shares his experience and expertise both on photography and Photoshop in a thorough and balanced presentation. While this book is also an excellent general Photoshop reference, the focus here is always on photography.

Photoshop can be daunting, photography even more so. To have someone expertly versed in both, presenting his knowledge here in a clean and clear manner, is a real treat.

Marc Pawliger
Senior Director of Engineering, Digital Imaging
Adobe Systems

# Introduction

When I first started using Photoshop, it was a much simpler program to get to grips with compared to what we see today. Adobe Photoshop CS3 has evolved to provide photographers with all the tools they need, and my aim is to provide you with a working photographer's perspective of what Photoshop CS3 can do and how you can make the most effective use of the program.

One of the main selling points of this book is that I work mostly as a professional studio photographer, running a busy photographic business close to the heart of London. On the days when I am not shooting or working on a production I use that time to study Photoshop, write articles and present seminars. And maybe that is one of the reasons why this series of Photoshop books has become so successful, because like you, I too had to learn all this stuff from scratch! I make no grandiose claims to have written the best book ever on the subject. I simply write from personal experience and aim to offer a detailed and comprehensive manual on the subject of digital photography and Photoshop, written by somebody who has first-hand professional experience and a close involvement with the people in San Jose who make the Adobe Photoshop program.

This book was initially aimed at intermediate to advanced users who, as the title suggests, were photographers. But it soon became apparent that all sorts of people were enjoying the book. Over the years I have adapted the content to satisfy the requirements of a broad readership. I still provide good solid professional-level advice, but at the same time I try not to assume too much prior knowledge, and ensure that everything is explained as clearly and simply as possible.

This latest edition has been thoroughly revised to ensure that you are provided with an updated account of everything that is new in Photoshop CS3. As the program has evolved over the years, the book content has had to undergo regular changes in order to reflect the new ways of working. The techniques shown here are based on the knowledge I have gained from working alongside some of the greatest Photoshop experts in the industry – people such as Jeff Schewe and the late Bruce Fraser, who I have regarded as true Photoshop masters. And I've drawn on this information to provide you with the latest thinking of how to use Photoshop to its full advantage. So rather than me just tell you 'this is what you should do, because that's the way I do it', you will find frequent references to how the program works. And these discussions are often accompanied by diagrams that will help improve your understanding of the Photoshop CS3 program.

## Book and DVD contents

The DVD contents are presented in the form of a Photoshop CS3 Help Guide. Load the DVD into your computer and for improved performance copy the contents across to your hard drive. Double click on the start.htm file to launch the DVD contents into your web browser. The Photoshop Help Guide contains movie versions of many of the step-by-step techniques shown in this book, is designed to run on Macintosh and PC systems, and only requires you to install Flash and QuickTime on your computer in order to view them. If you should experience any problems running the disc, please always refer to the FAQ section on the disc or on the website for guidance on how to configure your computer for optimum viewing. Educators may also be interested to know that the images used in the movies are provided on the DVD, along with the relevant extracts from the book in PDF format.

## Photoshop for Photographers website

There is also a website set up to promote this book where you can find many active links (including those mentioned in the book) and Help pages should you encounter problems running the movies from the DVD:
www.photoshopforphotographers.com

### About the images on the disc
You can access most of the images shown in this book, but not all of them. The reason for this is that some of the photographs, especially where models are featured in the picture, do have restricted usages that do not permit me to simply give them away. And some of the other images were kindly released by fellow photographers for use in the book only. So although there are quite a few pictures you can play with, you won't be able to access every photograph you see in this book.

### Rod Wynne-Powell

Over the several editions of this series of books, I have been able to elicit the technical help of Rod Wynne-Powell to check the accuracy of what I have written, and double-check, and sometimes modify, the techniques I have discussed. His enthusiasm and dedication to this task continues to be invaluable – if I am puzzled by some aspect and ask his advice, he will diligently seek out the answer either through his contacts or via the Web, and provide me with a comprehensive reply accompanied by his own evaluation.

I put his name forward to my publishers, Focal Press, when they were considering their forthcoming Workflow series, and he was accepted, so he is now to join their team of authors by writing about the other aspect of many photographers' lives – the operating system that underpins the Mac user's platform for Photoshop, Bridge and Lightroom – Mac OS X. The book is scheduled for publication early 2008 titled *Mac OS X for Photographers* and I wish it every success.

Rod offers training, consultancy and retouching under the banner 'SOLUTIONS photographic' and is able to boast having trained photographers in both France and Italy as well as those from all over the UK, mostly on a one-to-one basis. Rod can be contacted via email, Skype and telephone:

Email: rod@solphoto.co.uk
Skype: rodders63
T: +44(0)1582-725065
M: +44(0)7836-248126

## Acknowledgments

I must first thank Andrea Bruno of Adobe Europe for her suggestion that I write a book about Photoshop aimed at photographers and thank you to all at Focal Press: Marie Hooper, Margaret Denley, Georgia Kennedy, Stephanie Barrett, Lucy Lomas-Walker and Sheri Dean Allen.
None of this would have got started without the founding work of Adam Woolfitt and Mike Laye who helped form the Digital Imaging Group (DIG) forum for UK digital photographers. The production of this book was done with the help of Martin Beuschau, who designed and compiled the DVD, Rod Wynne-Powell, who reviewed the final manuscript and provided help with technical advice and assistance, David Field who provided PC tech edit advice, and Jason Simmons, who came up with the book layout template. Plus a big thank you to my ever helpful personal assistant, Lisa Tebbutt. I must give a special mention to fellow Photoshop alpha tester Jeff Schewe for all his guidance and help over the years (and wife Becky), not to mention the other members of the 'pixel mafia': Katrin Eismann, Seth Resnick, Andrew Rodney and Bruce Fraser, who sadly passed away in December of 2006.

Thank you also to the following clients, companies and individuals: Adobe Systems Inc., Neil Barstow, Steve Broback, Russell Brown, Steve Caplin, Kevin Connor, Chris Cox, Laurie Evans, Tom Fahey, Karen Gauthier, Greg Gorman, Gretag Macbeth, Mark Hamburg, Peter Hince, Thomas Holm, Ed Horwich, Carol Johnson, John Nack, Imacon, Thomas Knoll, MacUser, Bob Marchant, Marc Pawliger, Pixl, Herb Paynter, Paul Pryce, Red or Dead Ltd, Eric Richmond, Addy Roff, Schwarzkopf Ltd, The Smithsonian Institution, Steve Snyder, Martin Soan, Tresemme, Gwyn Weisberg, Russell Williams, Mark Williford and *What Digital Camera*. And lastly, thanks to all my friends and family, my wife Camilla who has been so suppportive over the last year, and especially my late mother for all her love and encouragement.

Martin Evening, April 2007

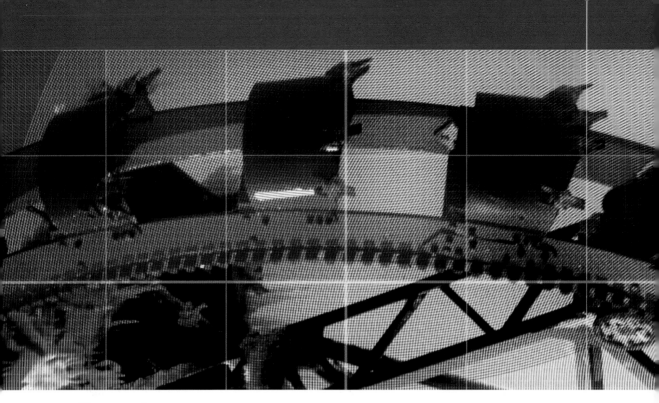

**Chapter 1**

# What's New in Adobe Photoshop CS3

P hotoshop CS3 is now at version 10 of this
phenomenally successful program (well twelfth
actually, if you count versions 2.5 and 5.5). And
it all started almost twenty years ago in late
1987, when Thomas Knoll with his brother John, created
the first prototype version of Photoshop. Photoshop CS3
has come on a long way since then, so much so that even
in a big book like this there is only enough space to cover
the features that are of specific interest to photographers.
In this introductory chapter I have provided a shortlist of
what's new and offered a few brief examples of some of the
things that you can now do in Photoshop and Bridge CS3.

## Pen path appearance

The path outlines that are created when you use the pen tool have now been made slightly bolder and are easier to see on the display. The same also applies when drawing a freehand selection using the lasso tool.

# New interface design

The most immediately noticeable difference in Photoshop CS3 is the new interface design, which is part of a wider strategy to give all the applications in the CS3 creative suite a more unified look and therefore make the interfaces more consistent when switching between applications.

To start with you will notice how the Tools palette is presented in a single column. Now that we are all using bigger displays, there is no real need for the old two column version. You will also notice that the palette well has disappeared from the tool Options bar. The palettes can now be displayed on the left- or right-hand side of the screen grouped into multiple column docking zones and easily hidden or made visible by rolling the mouse to either

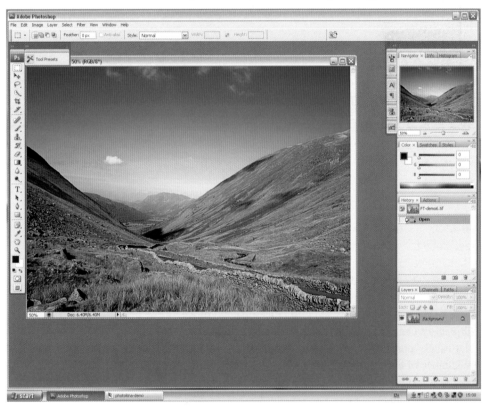

**Figure 1.1** The Photoshop CS3 Windows PC layout.

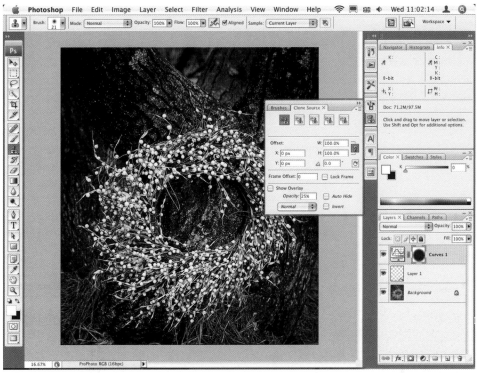

**Figure 1.2** The new Photoshop CS3 Mac OS X layout. In this screenshot the Layers, Channels and Paths palettes were placed in a third column docking zone. You can see here that if I click on a palette icon, this will quickly expand to reveal the normal full size palette.

side of the screen. The main intention here has been to create the most efficient use of screen space when working with the palettes and image documents. Palette docking is easier to accomplish and in the Windows layout in Figure 1.1 you can see how the palettes in the second column from the right have been compressed into tabbed palette mode. All palettes can now be collapsed in this way so that the palettes are represented as icons that graphically indicate the identity of each palette. To collapse a palette docking zone, you just click on the double arrow button at the top of each palette zone and click again to expand the palettes.

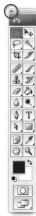

**Figure 1.3** Don't like the single row palette? Well, a click on the double-arrow icon in the Palette tab will allow you to toggle between the single and double row versions of the Tools palette.

## GPU settings

Instead of relying on the Central Processor Unit (CPU) for the graphics processing, some Graphics Processor Units (GPUs) are capable of providing faster graphics rendering. Where a GPU type card is detected, checking the Enable 3D Acceleration box will improve the image display performance. The 3D support will also improve the performance of the brushes. When using a pressure sensitive pen, the brushes response will feel much more sensitive and responsive.

# Performance

Various things have been done to improve the performance. Mac users in particular will benefit from the program being in universal binary, so that Photoshop CS3 is now fully optimized for the latest Macintosh Intel processor computers. Windows users meanwhile will notice faster startup times.

The Photoshop performance preferences offer guidance on how much RAM memory you should ideally allocate to Photoshop. And the scratch disk preferences are now presented in a way that makes it easier to decide which scratch disks are used and in what order of priority.

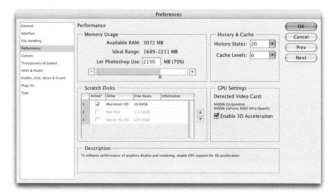

**Figure 1.4** The new Performance preferences dialog, showing the scratch disk and memory allocation.

# Camera Raw 4.0

Camera Raw 4.0 offers several new raw image processing additions that overlap nicely with the Adobe Photoshop Lightroom program (both share the same Adobe Camera Raw processing engine). These include things like the Recovery and Fill Light controls for better tonal editing of the highlight and shadow detail and a Vibrance adjustment for boosting the saturation, but with less risk of clipping (and built-in skin tone color masking).

Dig deeper through the new Camera Raw interface and you will notice how the tabbed panel controls mirror all the adjustments that you will find in the Lightroom program,

This means that you now have the ability to apply what are known as parametric tone Curve adjustments, instead of point tone curve corrections. You can apply hue, saturation and luminance type adjustments (with improved controls over Photoshop's Hue/Saturation) and custom grayscale conversions. Plus you have the ability to correct for red eye in flash photographs, use the retouch tool to spot images and intelligently synchronize the spotting across several images at once. But more importantly, because Lightroom and Camera Raw now share the same controls, settings can be synchronized precisely when you switch between editing an image in Camera Raw via Bridge or Photoshop and editing the same image via Lightroom. The other big change is that you can now set a preference to edit non-raw images such as JPEGs and TIFFs directly, using the Camera Raw dialog.

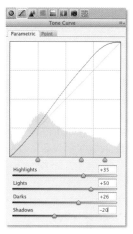

**Figure 1.5** Here are the Camera Raw Tone Curve controls, shown using the Parametric Tone Curve editor mode.

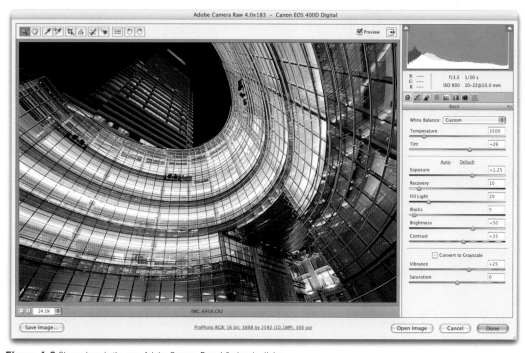

**Figure 1.6** Shown here is the new Adobe Camera Raw 4.0 plug-in dialog, displaying the Basic panel, which features the new ACR controls such as: Recovery, Fill Light and Vibrance adjustments.

## New layer/paint blending modes

It would be nice if the Curves dialog allowed you to control the blending mode from within the dialog itself, so that you could set it to, say, Color or Luminosity. But alas not this time around. However, two new blending modes have been added to the blend menu list. Lighter color is similar to the Lighten mode, except it works on all channels instead of working on a per-channel basis. Darker color is similar to the Darken mode, except it works on all channels instead of working on a per-channel basis. These two new blend modes are quite subtle in the way they work. I have found both to be useful whenever I wish to control the blending of a Curves adjustment so that only the pixels that are made lighter, or the pixels that are made darker, are the ones that get adjusted. These blend modes are often great to use when applying Curves adjustment layers.

# New Curves

With 22 image adjustment methods to choose from, it is hardly any wonder that Photoshop users get confused when trying to decide which image adjustment tool is the best one to use. For photographic work, the only tonal correction tools you ever really needed were Levels and Curves. Photoshop CS3 has at long last merged the functionality of Levels into the Curves dialog. At the bottom of the curve grid are Shadow and Highlight slider controls with Show Clipping controls to help you precisely judge where to set the shadows and highlights endpoints. As with Levels, you can also preview the image in Threshold mode to help judge the endpoints by holding down the ⌥ alt key as you drag on either of these two sliders. In Figure 1.7 you can see the new Curve display options which in this example were configured so that the Curves adjustments made to the individual color channels can be displayed overlaying the main composite channel curve shape.

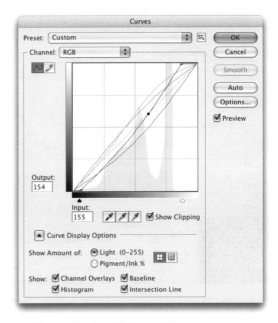

**Figure 1.7** The new Photoshop CS3 Curves dialog.

## New Brightness and Contrast

It may not seem such a big deal, but the Brightness/Contrast image adjustment has been updated so that you can now actually use it safely on photographic images without risk of clipping the highlight or shadow detail. This was always the problem with the old Brightness/Contrast command, even if users were unaware of the harm it could do when being used to adjust photographs. The legacy operating mode is still there if you need the old behavior back.

### Eyedropper options

New eyedropper tool sample size options extend the sample size range. Previously the options included: Sample Point, 3 x 3 and 5 x 5. In addition to this the new sample sizes include: 11 x 11, 31 x 31, 51 x 51, 101 x 101 pixels.

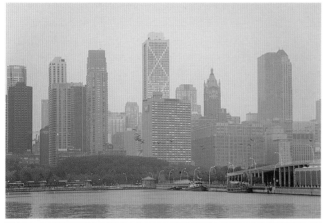

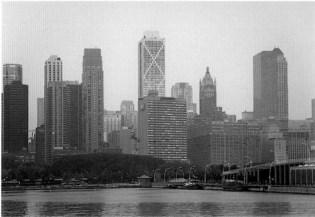

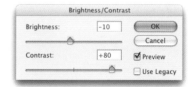

**Figure 1.8** The new, revised Brightness/Contrast image adjustment closely matches the Brightness and Contrast slider adjustments found in the Adobe Camera Raw dialog.

# Black & White adjustments

It is now easier to convert images from color to black and white via a single dialog interface. The new Black & White adjustment is available as a direct image adjustment or as an adjustment layer. The slider settings will allow you to adjust the proportions of the color components that are used to create a black and white conversion and will help you come up with many different types of black and white conversions.

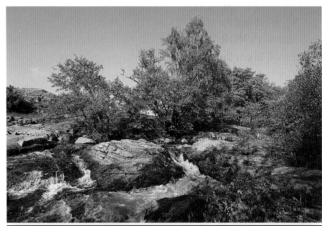

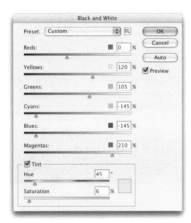

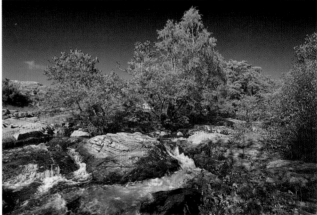

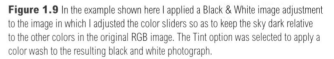

**Figure 1.9** In the example shown here I applied a Black & White image adjustment to the image in which I adjusted the color sliders so as to keep the sky dark relative to the other colors in the original RGB image. The Tint option was selected to apply a color wash to the resulting black and white photograph.

## Align controls

The Edit menu includes an Auto-Align Layers and Auto Blend Layers commands. The Auto-Align command can be used to automatically combine two or more layers and bring them into register with each other using one of the alignment options shown on the right. In the example given below, I wanted to combine the best of the two photographs shown below right, in order to produce a more successful composite image that blended the best of these two pictures. Auto-Align Layers can also be useful for registering misaligned images when working with the Merge to HDR command. The Auto-Blend Layers command takes the auto alignment one stage further and attempts to blend layers together more smoothly by applying layer masks of varying opacity to each layer, evening out any differences in brightness between each of the layers.

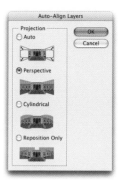

**Figure 1.10** Here are the Auto-Align options for aligning layers. Auto can do a pretty amazing job of automatically registering layers. But in this instance, the Perspective alignment worked best to register the group portraits.

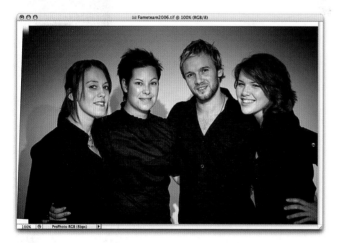

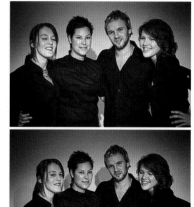

**Figure 1.11** In this example I combined the two images on the right by adding one above the other as a new layer. I then made a shift selection of both layers to temporarily group them. I then went to the Edit menu and chose Auto-Align Layers... and selected the Perspective option from the Auto-Align Layers dialog. This made Layer 1 register in alignment with the Background layer. To merge the images together I added a layer mask filled with black to Layer 1 and painted with white to reveal the girl on the left and blend seamlessly with the layer below.

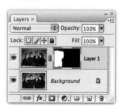

## Automatic Photomerge

The new Align Content processing has also allowed the Photoshop team to update the Photomerge feature such that it can now do a really good job of automatically aligning a group of images, bypassing the need to use the interactive Photomerge layout dialog.

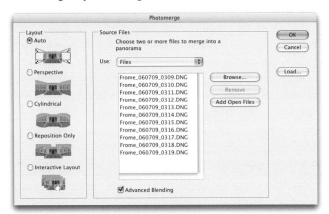

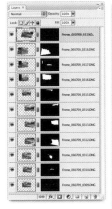

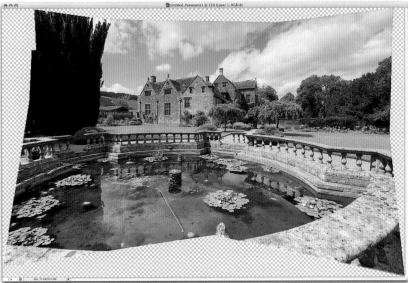

**Figure 1.12** Shown here is the very first attempt at using Photomerge in Auto mode to align a set of 11 photographs, all shot from the same position. I have used Photomerge quite a bit in the past, but the improved accuracy of the results has really been quite impressive.

## Clone Source palette and options

There are a number of new options for both the clone stamp and standard healing brush tools. In the tool Options bar you have clone source options that will allow you to sample from the current layer only or from the current layer and those below only, from all layers (ignoring any adjustment layers) and all layers (including adjustments).

In Figure 1.13, you can see how I switched on the Show Overlay option and adjusted the overlay opacity and blend mode so that when rolling the mouse across the image prior to positioning the destination point, one can predict more accurately how the clone source pixels will register with the pixels in the image below.

### Multi point source cloning

The new Clone Source palette will allow you to select up to five clone source points when working with the clone stamp or standard healing brush tools. This feature won't be of so much interest to retouchers working on stills photographs, but it is something that will be more useful for video and film editors who are retouching multiple frames in a film sequence.

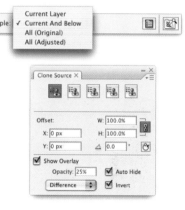

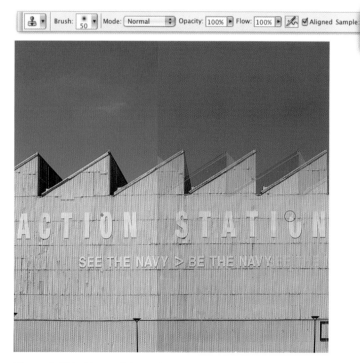

**Figure 1.13** In this example I wanted to sample from the letter 'O' on the left to repair the gap in the letter 'O' on the right. To do this, I switched on the overlay in the Clone Source palette, so that while I rolled the cursor over the image, I could predict where to click to start cloning and make the source letter register with the destination letter.

## Other applied uses of Image Stacks

The technique shown here can also be adapted to merge multiple images shot of the same scene and use the Stacks median rendering to smooth out the differences due to camera noise. Later on in Chapter 5 I have a really good example of how I was able to blend a series of hand-held shots that were taken at dusk using the highest ISO setting on the camera. A Stacks median rendering can do a really good job of removing all the noise and give you smoother detail in the shadows.

## Counting and measuring

The new count tool is probably more useful for scientific applications. When you select the count tool and use it in manual mode, the tool will record each mouse-click as a running count, automatically placing a count number next to each object you click on in the image. For scientists this is a useful way to record and identify cells from a microscope slide. In automatic mode you can click on the Count button in the count tool options to count objects automatically, but to get this feature to work accurately you really need to modify the image appearance first to make the objects more distinct.

Note that Image Stack rendering and the count tool will only be made available in the extended version of Photoshop CS3.

# Blending multiple images with Stacks

Following on from what is new with Auto-Align Layers and Photomerge, there is the Image Stacks feature in Photoshop CS3 which is mainly designed for scientific and forensics use in determining small differences or similarities between a sequence of image frames.

But I have also managed to discover a more creative use for Image Stacks. Later on in the book I will be showing you a step-by-step method (summarized in Figure 1.15) in which I took a series of six pictures where there was always at least one person walking through a scene and I wanted to automatically remove them from the shot. When you see this technique demonstrated it does at first look quite magical, but there is a logical explanation for how the process works. The technique relies mainly on the use of the Auto-Align command to align a chosen set of sample images together and place them within a grouped smart object. After doing a little bit of experimentation I have found that if you record at least five or six exposures, this should provide enough pictures for Photoshop to process in order to work out which pixels appear most frequently at any particular spot in the picture and use the most commonly occurring pixels only to produce the finished blend shown opposite.

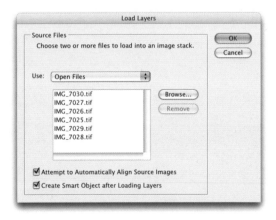

**Figure 1.14** The selected images shown opposite were aligned together as a Smart Object using the Load Files into Stack script from the File menu.

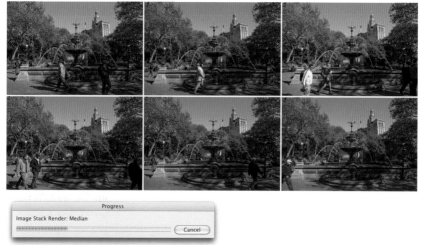

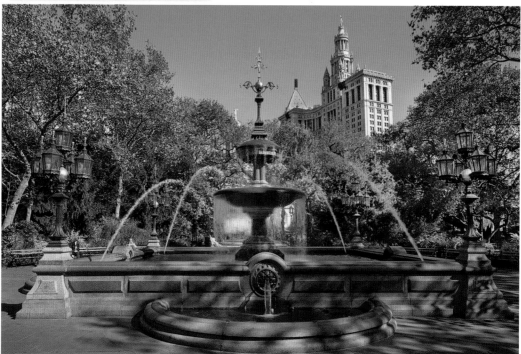

**Figure 1.15** You can use the Image Stack rendering feature in Photoshop CS3 to blend multiple images together and automatically remove varying features (such as people walking through the scene). This finished picture was retouched only slightly, in order to remove a few remaining ghost-like traces from the picture.

## More discoverable

Smart Objects first appeared in Photoshop CS2 but many people never got around to working with them, mainly because the Group into Smart Object command was obscurely hidden in the Layer palette menu and also because it was not easy to open a new image directly as a Smart Object. For example, with CS2 you first had to create an empty new document with the exact pixel dimensions before you could place an image (such as a raw file) as a Smart Object. With Photoshop CS3, you can now place a raw capture file as a Smart Object layer in a single step.

## Editable shadows/highlight

Up until now it has not been possible to edit shadow/highlight adjustments, but you can do so now by using the Convert for Smart Filters command, or when editing an existing Smart Object.

# New Smart Object features

The new Open as Smart Object command makes the Smart Object process a lot more accessible. When you place an image, or convert a layer to become a Smart Object, a range of non-destructive edit options will be at your disposal. As before, you can apply free transform adjustments to Smart Object layers so that you can scale an image layer up or down in size without permanently resizing the layer pixels. But Smart Objects will also now allow you to render images via Stacks (see preceding page) or apply Smart Filters to a Smart Object.

## Smart Filters

When you create a Smart Object, the pixels are always preserved in their original state and as a result of this, Smart Objects can now be used to apply filter effects that are fully editable. This means that when you create a Smart Object (or choose Convert for Smart Filters from the Filter menu), you can select the Smart Object layer, choose a filter effect, and the filter will be applied to a rendered version of the original layer and appear as a Smart Filter layer associated with the same Smart Object layer. This lets you preview the result of any filter effect as applied to the selected layer. If you want to make any further changes, you then have the ability to double-click the Smart Object filter layer to call up the Filter dialog for the filter effect. This will allow you to re-edit the filter settings as many times as you want, add extra filter effects to the Smart Object layer, drag and drop the order in which the filter effects are applied as well as drag and drop them from one Smart Object layer to another. Note that you can also use the ⌥ *alt* key as you drag to copy filter effects between Smart Object layers. Each Smart Object layer will also have a single layer mask, which means that the Smart Filter masking is always applied to all Smart Filter layers. But you can't directly link a layer mask to a Smart Object, although there are a couple of workarounds that will allow you to do so if you wish to move both a Smart Object layer and mask in register. I will be providing tips on these techniques later in the book in Chapter 8.

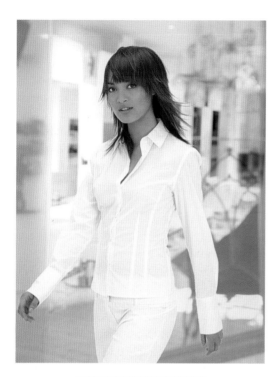

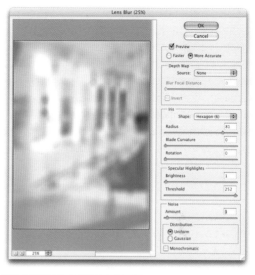

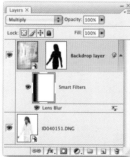

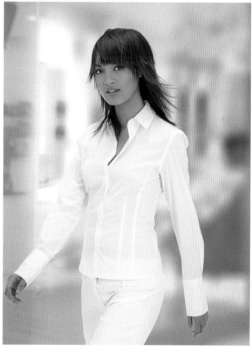

**Figure 1.16** In this example I opened a raw DNG image as a Smart Object and added a normal pixel layer of a backdrop image, which I then converted to become a Smart Object layer. I then added a layer mask to reveal the model on the layer below (see Chapter 8 for instructions on how this was done). Once a layer or group of layers have been converted to a Smart Object, one can then apply Smart Filters. Here, you can see how I applied a Lens Blur filter to the Smart Object and applied a gradient to the Smart Filters mask to reveal some of the unsharpened detail in the original pixel layer.

Client: Indola. Model: Pernille @ Storm.

## Refining layer masks

You can build up a quick selection by repeatedly dragging across the image areas you wish to include in the selection (there is no need to hold down the *Shift* key), but hold down the *⌥* *alt* key to subtract from a quick selection.

# Quick Selections

The quick selection tool is grouped with the magic wand in the Tools palette and takes priority as being the default tool for making magic wand type selections, To make a quick selection you simply drag with the tool to select a sample range of colors from an image, either selecting pixels from a single layer or sampling all layers. From this, Photoshop will calculate a rough selection of pixels that you can further modify by using the refine edge options.

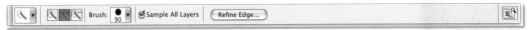

**Figure 1.17** The quick selection tool options.

## Refine selection edges

If you click on the Refine Edge button, you can refine the selection edges using the dialog slider controls. A much better way to use Refine Edge is to convert a selection to a layer mask first and then select Refine Edge... from the Select menu.

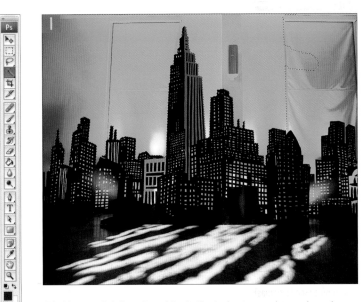

**1** In this example I chose the quick selection tool, set a sample area size and dragged with the quick selection tool to define the areas I wished to include in the selection.

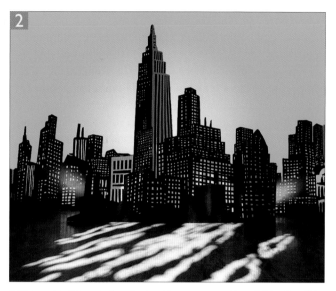

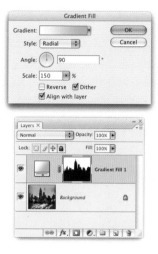

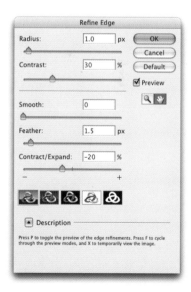

**2** I then moused down on the adjustment layer menu to add a radial Gradient Fill layer using the colors shown here. This single step automatically converted the quick selection into a layer mask.

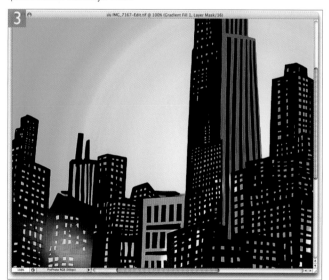

**3** As long as the layer mask is selected, you can fine-tune the mask by going to the Select menu and choosing Refine Edge... In the example shown here, I used ⌘ H / ctrl H to hide the marching ants and was able to preview the Refine Edge adjustments on a layer mask that was actively masking the Gradient Fill layer.

## 3D support

Photoshop allows you to open and work live in Photoshop with 3D files created by programs like Acrobat 3D, 3D Studio Max, and Maya. Supported 3D file formats include .U3D, .3DS, and Sony Collada.

## Extended version only

Only the Extended version includes the measurement tools described here and allows Vanishing Point data to be exported using the DXS format export geometry and planes, and also use the 3SD format to export geometry and textures from an image.

# Vanishing Point 2.0

The Vanishing Point plug-in was an interesting addition to the Photoshop CS2 program, because it allowed you to retouch and place images so that they matched the perspective in the original photograph. Vanishing Point has been updated in CS3 to include some extra new features. Now when you import image data into the Vanishing Point modal dialog you can wrap images around multiple pre-defined plane surfaces. And there is an angle control that can be used for positioning linked planes at angles other than 90°. This means you can define complex geometric surfaces, import an image and paste the image data across more than one plane surface at a time. Plus you can also use the transform tool to rotate a pasted selection before placing it.

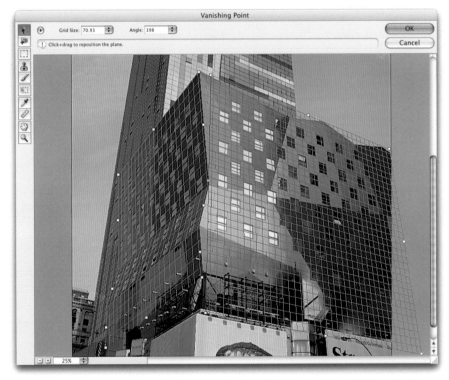

**Figure 1.18** The Vanishing Point 2.0 dialog showing angled plane selections.

# Printing

Printing from Photoshop has been much improved and there are features included in Photoshop CS3 that will most please the professional users.

The Print with Preview has now become the Photoshop Print dialog, from where you can select the printer model to print to, access the system Page Setup dialogs and set the paper orientation. At long last, the preview image is now properly color managed. What you see in the preview is more representative of what the print will look like and will adjust to reflect any changes made to the printer profile selection or rendering intents. If you are using the Print dialog to produce a proof print that simulates a CMYK press setting or proofing device, you can access any pre-saved custom proof condition settings from directly within the Print dialog, plus you can turn the color managed display on or off by checking or unchecking the Match Print Colors checkbox.

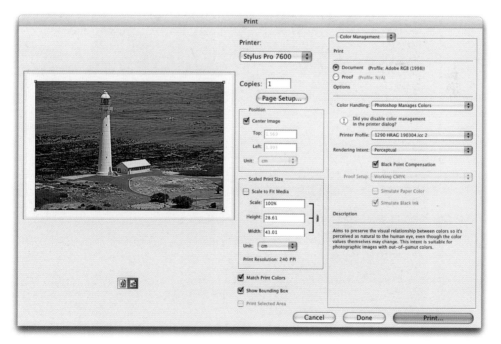

**Figure 1.19** The new Photoshop CS3 Print dialog.

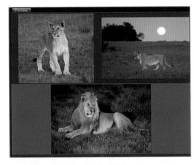

**Figure 1.20** The Bridge 2.0 Preview panel provides accurate color managed previews with smooth rendering and the ability to display a selected group of images at once and has a loupe tool for close-up 1:1 previewing.

# Bridge 2.0

Bridge 2.0 is undoubtedly an improvement, especially as some of the frustrating bugs that were in version 1.0 have now been resolved. The first thing you will notice is the new look interface. The dark gray theme offers better contrast for viewing images and the design layout is flexible enough to allow you to customize the way the panels are laid out almost any way you like. There are some nice refinements in the way the metadata information is displayed and the Preview panel now provides a properly color managed preview of selected images.

The new Filter panel provides extensive image filtering options and file search times have improved, allowing you to filter images with a single mouse-click using criteria such as file type, keywords, image rating and orientation. The Slideshow view mode has also been updated, offering a

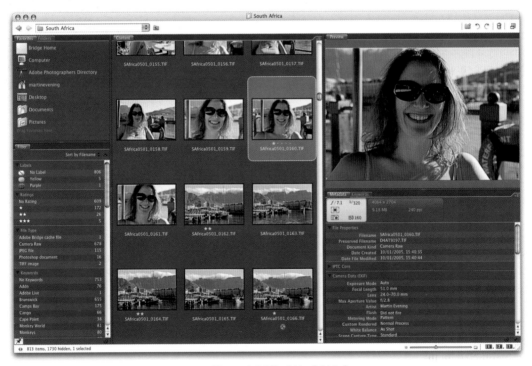

**Figure 1.21** The Bridge 2.0 interface.

choice of slide transitions but with less confusing controls, plus the new ability to zoom into images to check sharpness. Within the Content panel you can organize files better, grouping them into stacks so that they can be quickly expanded or collapsed.

Up until the beginning of 2006, I had been using Bridge 1.0 in conjunction with Camera Raw to manage my digital workflow for everything from capture through to print, using Bridge as my main program for importing, file browser management and as a digital asset manager to manage my image library. As the number of photographs I was shooting each day increased and the library collection grew in size, the task of carrying out all these jobs in Bridge got harder. The main problems with Bridge 1.0 were: that it lacked an automated import procedure, the length of time it took to generate contact sheets and Web photo galleries, plus the awkwardness of inputting metadata. Bridge 2.0 is now better because the thumbnail navigation is faster and the Previews can be made to display a properly color managed preview. But on the other hand, not enough has been done to improve upon these other, more pressing concerns. At the time of writing, the new Photo Downloader plug-in has the potential to offer good automated camera file importing, but unlike other file importers, it fails to provide proper control over the file renumbering. All print outputs have to be processed via Photoshop, which means that the contact sheet generation is still very much reliant on Bridge having to open every image fully via Camera Raw or Photoshop in order to render contact sheet sized images. Other programs, like Adobe Photoshop Lightroom, can generate their contact sheets in a hundredth of the time it currently takes Bridge. The file searching does make Bridge a more effective asset manager, but the metadata input process remains as cumbersome as it was before. Adding custom IPTC metadata or custom keywords can still be a rather slow process, although the Filter panel does now make good use of that metadata information.

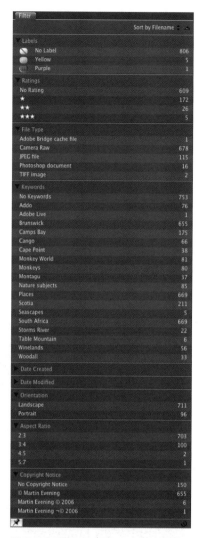

**Figure 1.22** The Bridge Filter panel provides more comprehensive controls for filtering images by.

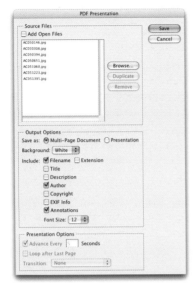

**Figure 1.23** PDF Presentation dialog includes new options.

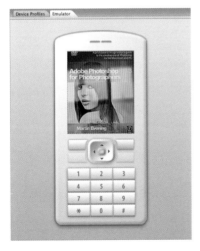

**Figure 1.24** Here is a view of the Emulator panel in Device Central, showing a preview of the book cover, as it might appear on a mobile phone display.

My impression of Bridge 2.0 is that it has certainly improved as an image browser, in that it offers better browsing and some new additional digital asset management features that are worth taking note of. However, for professional-level file imports and full asset management, I suggest you need something like the Photoshop Lightroom program but, for basic image browsing, Bridge 2.0 does offer some useful extra built-in functionality for Photoshop.

## PDF enhancements

The PDF presentation automated plug-in has also been updated. PDF presentations are easier to create out of Photoshop CS3 and let you include extra items in your presentations such as background colors, add filename and extension, title, copyright info, author, description, EXIF info (Exposure F stop and Exposure time), plus annotations (that were in the original file).

And when saving files using the Photoshop PDF format, you can save them using the PDF 1.7 (Acrobat 8 compatible format).

## Device Central

Device Central is a separate application that is included with the Photoshop and Bridge CS3 package that allows you to create and view image files for a variety of mobile devices, such as cell phone devices. You can open Device Central via the File menu in Photoshop, select a particular device and create a new document with the exact pixel dimensions for that device. When you are editing an image you can go to Save for Web and click on the Device Central button where you can use the Emulator panel to preview how an image or design graphic might look on one of the many mobile phone presets supplied.

## Overall impressions

After two years of waiting for this latest upgrade, Photoshop customers might well expect some major new features in this latest release. But at the same time, when new operating systems or computer hardware changes require a revision of the existing code, the task of keeping all the code up to date becomes increasingly harder. This is exactly what happened when Apple decided to adopt the Intel chips for the Mac platform. The Photoshop engineers were obliged to do a complete recompile of all the existing Photoshop code just to keep pace with this change. Consequently, Macintosh users will now be able to appreciate the real benefits of faster Photoshop performance on the latest Intel Mac computers, while PC customers will gain the narrower benefit of improved, faster startup times.

Apart from this, the engineering team have still managed to come up with a larger number of new features. I have highlighted some of my favorites in this introductory chapter. I have not included every new feature because not all these will necessarily be of interest to stills photographers. The new Camera Raw 4.0 plug-in shares the same new image adjustment controls as will be found in the Adobe Photoshop Lightroom program. And as was pointed out, these new Camera Raw controls can now be applied to any image, not just to raw files. Therefore I would say that if you were to buy only Photoshop CS3, then there is actually quite a lot to offer photographers in this upgrade of Photoshop. If on the other hand you intend to buy Lightroom, or will choose to rely on some other third-party program to process and manage your digital captures, then there may be less compelling reasons for you to upgrade.

My own personal view is that I like the new Photoshop CS3 interface design very much. I am also enthused by the new things you can do with features such as the Align Content feature and how this has been implemented to enhance Photomerge, HDR imaging and of course the new Image Stacks processing, which have all featured in

### The Extended version of Photoshop

Photoshop CS3 is sold as Standard and Extended versions. The Extended release includes what are regarded as the advanced features that are designed to meet the needs of dedicated users such as scientists, architects, forensics users and people who regularly work with HDR files in the movie industry. While the Extended version will be sold at a premium price, many of those customers who chose to buy the full Creative Suite package will find that their upgrade will include the Extended version of Photoshop.

this introductory chapter. I would also rate the new Clone Source palette for providing accurate clone control, the Black and White adjustment and new Curves dialog and even Brightness/Contrast, for improved pixel editing. The Refine Edges command has a lot of great potential, especially as you can use it to edit layer masks as well as selections. In my opinion, these new features all provide practical tools for photographic Photoshop users. The only drawback is that things like Image Stacks (which I find really useful) are only available with the Extended version. I am less enthusiastic about Live Filters, because it seems like a lot of overhead in terms of increased file sizes and processing times, for not much gain. And the inability to link a mask to a Smart Object does limit Smart Object functionality. I am also rather lukewarm over Bridge 2.0. During this particular test cycle I could not help but directly compare the usefulness of Bridge 2.0 alongside the new workflow capabilities of Lightroom. None of this personally matters to me so much, because I now mostly rely on using Lightroom to process all the file imports and manage my photographic library collection. I just happen to think that more resources could have been put into redesigning Bridge to make the workflow process easier to manage and faster, rather than adding things like a loupe tool in the Preview panel, which does not necessarily function as well as the zoom controls that are available in other programs. But that said, when you get Photoshop CS3, you will be acquiring the mighty Camera Raw processing plug-in which will now let you process over 150 different raw file formats. Camera Raw 4.0 will definitely be providing a big upgrade here. I think I am being fair in pointing out what I believe to be the shortcomings in this release. But despite these reservations, I do believe Photoshop CS3 still has a lot to offer photographers everywhere.

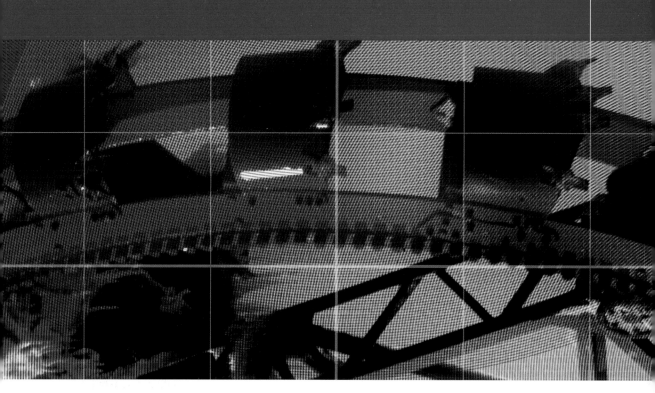

**Chapter 2**

# Photoshop Fundamentals

**B**efore moving on to the practical Photoshop techniques, let's first look at the Photoshop interface. The following pages give an account of the basic Photoshop working area and introduce you to all the different tools and palettes, and give a brief description of their function. You can use this chapter as a reference, as you work through the remainder of the book. If you want to dive straight in, then you can quite easily skip forward to Chapter 4 on Basic Image Adjustments.

### Photoshop CS3 for Photographers

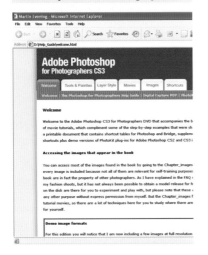

### Macintosh and PC keys

Throughout this book I refer to the keyboard modifier keys used on the Macintosh and PC computers. Where the keys used are the same, such as the *Shift* key, these will be printed in black. Where the keys used are different on each system, I use the Macintosh key first in magenta and the PC equivalent after in blue. So, if the shortcut used is Command (Mac) and Control (PC) this appears abbreviated in the text as: *⌘* *ctrl*. Other keys will be explained as you progress through this and subsequent chapters.

# How to use this book

In writing this book I have tried not to assume too much prior Photoshop knowledge and have structured the chapter order so that it guides you in an order that follows a typical workflow through Photoshop, starting with an introduction to the Photoshop interface through to print output and image management at the end. It is in many ways a personal guide, one that highlights the areas of Photoshop that I find interesting, or those which I feel would be of interest to other photographers. It is not a complete comprehensive guide about everything in Photoshop, but it is one of the most thorough and established books out there; especially designed for photographers.

I should also point out that I have had more than thirteen years' experience of working with Photoshop as a professional photographer. In that time I have had the pleasure of working closely with many of the leading gurus of Photoshop such as Katrin Eismann, Bruce Fraser, Andrew Rodney, Seth Resnick, Jeff Schewe and Rod Wynne-Powell, as well as many of the engineers who build Photoshop. The techniques described in this book have evolved over the time I have been writing this book series and the methods taught in this book reflect the most current thinking about Photoshop.

For this particular version, the book has been re-edited to take into account the changing way photographers use Photoshop, with more emphasis put on the raw image processing favored by digital photographers. In order to keep the page count under control I had to remove large sections of the previous book. But don't despair, not everything has been removed completely! What I have done for this edition has been to produce a *Photoshop CS3 for Photographers Help Guide* to go on the DVD that accompanies the book. Load the DVD into your computer and for improved performance copy the contents across to your hard drive. Double click on the start.htm file to launch the DVD contents into your web browser.

In Figure 2.1 below you can see how the Help Guide should appear in the Bridge window and from there you can then visit the various sub-sections. For example, in the Tool Palettes section you can click on a tool icon to be taken to a page that has a complete, illustrated description of what each tool does. In the other sections, you can find complete descriptions of the Photoshop palettes, image adjustments and a guide to all the keyboard shortcuts in Photoshop. And of course, there are also the movie tutorials, which have always been a popular feature of this book series.

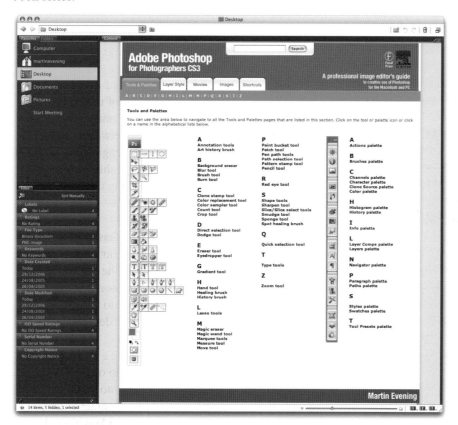

**Figure 2.1** Once installed from the DVD, the Photoshop CS3 for Photographers Help Guide can be accessed via the Favorites panel in Bridge CS3. Click to select a topic such as the Tools and Palettes section shown here and navigate to the subject of interest to learn more about a particular tool or palette.

### Suggested reading order

This book has been deliberately structured to follow a typical digital workflow. If you are new to Photoshop, then I would recommend that you read all of Chapters 2 and 3. And even if you aren't new to the program you may want to glance through the updated Chapter 3 for the latest advice on how to configure your computer system. Chapter 4 describes how to use the classic Photoshop image editing tools; if you are always working with scanned images, this is essential reading. Chapter 5 basically describes the alternative Camera Raw image editing process. If you shoot digitally, this would be a better start point for achieving mostly the same end objective as Chapter 4, although I would still suggest that you read up on the basic pixel image editing techniques, because these will come in use later when you make fine-tuned image adjustments (see Chapter 6). Chapters 7 through to 10 feature various image editing and retouching techniques. Chapter 11 brings everything together with a look at how to manage your images effectively. Chapter 13 is on print output, which will make more sense if you spend at least a little time reading through the color management section in Chapter 12. Chapter 14 provides an overview of Web output and Chapter 15 provides tips on how to work more efficiently and smarter in Photoshop.

### Chapter 2: Photoshop fundamentals

The chapter you are reading now is an introduction to the Photoshop interface and main features such as layers, image resolution and image browsing. It offers a general introduction to how Photoshop works.

### Chapter 3: Configuring Photoshop

How to optimize your computer system, how much RAM and what sort of accessories you need.

### Chapter 4: Basic pixel image editing

This is a good starter chapter for general Photoshop image editing and is particularly aimed at showing you how to prepare scanned images, such as how to remove noise and sharpen pixel images. The basic principles learnt here will be useful whether you shoot film and scan your images or shoot raw.

### Chapter 5: Camera Raw image processing

If you shoot digitally, you will most likely want to shoot in raw mode and this chapter is essential reading on how to prepare digital raw images. This chapter basically shows you the alternative route to image preparation when shooting raw.

### Chapter 6: Fine-tuned image corrections

Regardless of whether you start out with a scanned pixel image or a raw file, this is where the Photoshop workflow starts to converge. This chapter will show you how to apply localized or global image corrections that target specific colors using adjustment layers and advanced image adjustment tools.

### Chapter 7: Image retouching

This is followed by a chapter showing all the various retouching techniques and strategies for removing blemishes and larger objects from a picture, as well as how to retouch in perspective with Vanishing Point.

### Chapter 8: Layers, selections and masking

This lengthy chapter focuses on the use of channels, layers, layer masks and layes styles and how these can be used to combine different image elements, make seamless masks and add special layer effects such as a drop shadow to an image element.

## Chapter 9: Darkroom effects

This chapter shows you how to reproduce darkroom techniques, such as how to create optimum black and white conversions from a color original, how to cross process, fake an infrared effect as well as many other traditional darkroom techniques.

## Chapter 10: Photoshop filters

This chapter explores some of the other filters in Photoshop that rate as useful for photographic retouching work.

## Chapter 11: Image management

These days, most photographers are likely to process many thousands of images. Good image management can help you keep track of your work easily and quickly, and help avoid problems when hardware devices fail.

## Chapter 12: Color management

Everyone needs to know a little about color management. It should be a simple matter of calibrating the monitor and selecting the correct color settings in Photoshop, but somehow life is never that easy! This chapter provides an intermediate level guide to managing color successfully.

## Chapter 13: Print output

This chapter follows on from the previous one, in showing you how to make a perfect print and control the print process, including the all-important output sharpening.

## Chapter 14: Output for Web

Alternatively, you may be more interested in outputting your images for screen display. This chapter covers web image output.

## Chapter 15: Automating Photoshop

The Automating Photoshop chapter shows you some of the ways you can work more efficiently in Photoshop and let the program help you avoid having to do repetitive work.

### Chapters on the DVD

As I mentioned, some of the content that was previously in this book has been removed, but can still be accessed via the Photoshop for Photographers Help Guide on the DVD. Also on the DVD is a whole chapter on digital capture and how digital cameras work, plus a copy of Chapter 12 on color management. These are available as PDF documents which can be read and printed out using the Adobe Acrobat Reader program.

You can load Photoshop on any number of computers, but only a maximum of two installations can be active at any one time. To use any two different machines will involve deactivation and reactivation only, but not a complete install.

# Photoshop installation

Installing Photoshop is as easy as installing any other application on your computer. But make sure that your web browser and any other Adobe programs are closed prior to running the installation setup. After completing your user information and serial number details, you will be faced with a Product Activation option. This has to be selected in order to activate Photoshop. And the reason it is there is to limit unauthorized distribution of the program. The standard license entitles you to use Photoshop on up to two computers, but not both at once.

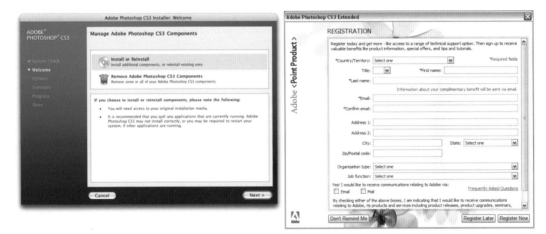

**Figure 2.2** The Photoshop installer procedure will be more or less identical on both Mac and PC systems. As you complete the installation process and are about to start using the program you will be requested to complete a registration form like the one shown above.

## The Photoshop interface

Photoshop CS3 now has a brand new interface which is in keeping with planned integration of all the CS3 suite interface designs. Basically this can make it easier to migrate from using one CS3 program and another when there is a greater level of consistency in the interface design. In Figure 2.3 you can see the default Photoshop layout in which the Photoshop palettes are held in placement zones with the tools palette on the left, the

Options palette running across the top of the screen and all other remaining palettes arranged on the right-hand side of the screen, where they can be docked in various ways to economize on the use of screen space yet remain easily accessible. The default arrangement will present the palettes in a docked mode and over the following few pages we shall look at ways to customize the layout of the interface. For example, you can economize on the space taken up by the palettes by collapsing them into compact palette icons.

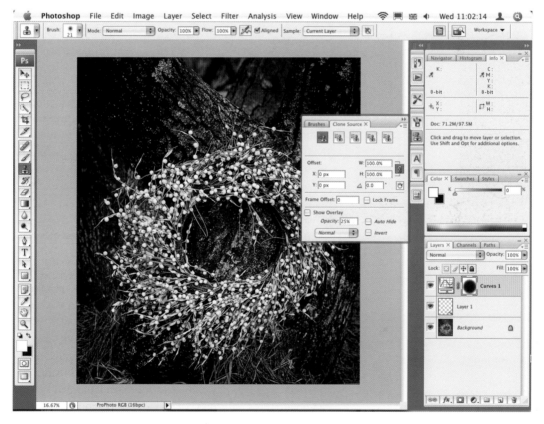

**Figure 2.3** This is the Photoshop CS3 interface showing the default layout for all the palettes. The Options bar is normally positioned at the top of the screen just below the menu bar, but you can also position it at the bottom or even on a second monitor, along with all the other palettes.

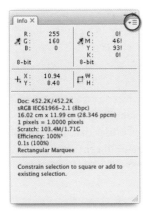

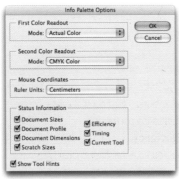

**Figure 2.4** If you mouse down on the Info palette menu (circled), you can open the Info palette options shown here, where you can choose to display which status items you would like to see displayed in the Info palette.

## The image document window

The document window will display extra information about the image in the two boxes located in the status bar at the bottom left of the screen on the PC, and the image window on the Mac. The left-most box displays the zoom scaling percentage, showing the current zoom factor. You can type in a new percentage of any value you like from 0.2% to 1600% up to two decimal places and set this as the new viewing resolution. In the middle is the Work Group Server button, which can be used to check in or check out a document that is being shared over a WebDAV server.

To the right of this is the status information box, which will display one chosen item of information. If you mouse down on the arrow to the right of the box, you will see a list of all the items you can choose to display here, which are described on the page opposite. This window only displays a single item (at a time); if you wish to see several, you can add your choice by ticking the relevant checkboxes in the Info Palette Options. The items that are ticked will then appear in the middle section of the Info palette. In addition to this, you can also choose to enable Show Tool Hints. These appear at the bottom of the Info palette and will change according to any modifier keys you have held down at the time, to indicate extra available options.

If you mouse down in the status box, a page preview will display an outline box of how the image will be scaled and positioned relative to the current Page Setup paper size (also reflecting the settings in Print with Preview). The preview reflects the image dimensions at the current pixel resolution. If you hold down the ⌥ *alt* key while you mouse down on the status information box, this will display the width and height dimensions of the image, along with the number of channels and image resolution. If you hold down the ⌘ *ctrl* key as you mouse down, this will show the image tiling information.

## Title bar proxy icons (Macintosh)

Macintosh users will see a proxy image icon in the title bar. This is dimmed when the document is in an unsaved state and is reliant on there being a preview icon; many JPEGs will not have an icon until they are saved as something else.

To relocate the existing source file and move it to a new location, *ctrl* drag on the proxy icon and drag to a new destination (if you move it to a new disk volume, it will make a copy). To view the file's folder hierarchy and jump to a specific folder location, ⌘ click on the proxy icon.

⌘ click to display the title bar proxy icons (Mac only)

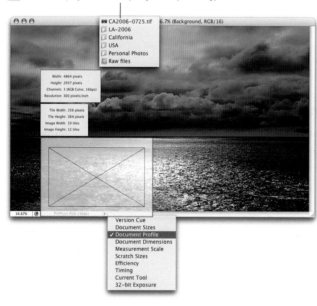

**Figure 2.5** Here is the window layout of a Photoshop document as it appears on the Macintosh. If you mouse down on the arrow icon next to the status information box, you can select the type of information you wish to see displayed there. The status display information can be changed by mousing down on the arrow next to the status information box (the status items are described on the right). Mouse down in the status information box to display a scaled preview showing the size and position the image will print with the current page setup. Hold down ⌥ *alt* key to display the file size and resolution information and hold down ⌘ *ctrl* key to display the image tiling.

**Version Cue**

Current Version Cue status.

**Document Sizes**

The first figure represents the file size of a flattened version of the image. The second, the size if saved including all layers.

**Document Profile**

The profile assigned to the document.

**Document Dimensions**

This displays the physical image dimensions, as would currently be shown in the Image Size dialog box.

**Measurement Scale**

Measurement units (extended version only).

**Scratch Sizes**

The first figure displays the amount of RAM memory used. The second shows the total RAM memory available to Photoshop after taking into account the system and application overhead.

**Efficiency**

This summarizes how efficiently Photoshop is working. Basically it provides a simplified report on the amount of scratch disk usage.

**Timing**

Displays the time taken to accomplish a Photoshop step or the accumulated timing of a series of steps. Every time you change tools or execute a new operation, the timer resets itself.

**Current Tool**

This displays the name of the tool you currently have selected. This is a useful aide-mémoire for users who like to work with most of the palettes hidden.

**32-bit Exposure**

Exposure slider control works in 32-bit mode only.

## Multiple window views

Multiple window views can prove useful if you wish to compare different soft proof views of the same image to get an impression on screen of how the colors in your image might appear in print. See Chapter 12 on Color Management for more about soft proofing in Photoshop.

## Portrait/Landscape tiling

The Window ⇨ Arrange ⇨ Tile options include Tile horizontal for portrait oriented images and Tile Vertical for landscape oriented images. This is designed to allow maximum useful use of the display area when arranging the display of multiple image document windows.

## Managing document windows

You can create a second window view of the image you are working on by choosing Window ⇨ Arrange ⇨ New Window for (document name). The image is duplicated in a second window. For example, you can have one window with the image at a Fit to Screen view and the other zoomed in close-up on a detailed area. Any changes you make can then be viewed simultaneously in both windows. You can also arrange the way all document windows are displayed on the screen. Choose Window ⇨ Arrange ⇨ Cascade to have all cascading down from the upper left corner of the screen, or choose Window ⇨ Arrange ⇨ Tile to have all the currently opened image windows tiled edge to edge. Note that in Photoshop CS or later, when two or more document windows are open, you can synchronize the scrolling and magnification to affect all document windows by depressing the *Shift* key as you scroll or zoom in and out on any window view.

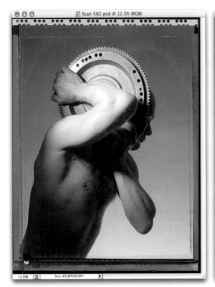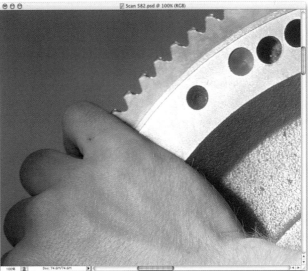

**Figure 2.6** To open a second window view of a Photoshop document, choose Window ⇨ Arrange ⇨ New Window for (document name). Changes applied to the close-up view are automatically updated in the second window view.

Photograph: Eric Richmond.

## Rulers, Guides & Grid

The Grid provides you with a means for aligning image elements to the horizontal and vertical axis (choose View ⇨ Show ⇨ Grid). To alter the grid spacing, go to the General preferences and select Guides & Grid.

Guides can be flexibly positioned anywhere in the image area and be used for the precise positioning and alignment of image elements. Guides can be added at any time, providing the Rulers are displayed. If not, choose View ⇨ Rulers ( ⌘ R  ctrl R ). To add a new guide, mouse down and drag out a new guide from the ruler bar. Release the mouse to drop the guideline in place. If you are not happy with the positioning, select the move tool and drag the guide into the exact required position. But once positioned, it is often a good idea to lock the guides (View ⇨ Lock Guides) to avoid accidentally moving them again.

## 'Snap to' behavior

The Snap option in the View menu allows you to toggle the Snap to behavior for the Guides, Grid, Slices, Document bounds and Layer bounds. The shortcut for toggling Snap to behavior is ⌘ Shift ; ctrl Shift ; . When the Snap to is active and you reposition an image, type or shape layer, or use a crop or marquee selection tool, these will snap to one or more of the above. It is also the case that when Snap is active, and new guides are added with the Shift key held down, the guide will snap to the nearest tick mark on the ruler, or if the Grid is active, to the closest grid line. Objects on layers will snap to position when placed within close proximity of a guide edge. The reverse is also true: when dragging a guide, it will snap to the edge of an object on a layer at the point where the opacity is greater than 50%. Furthermore you can Lock Guides and Clear Guides. If the ruler units need changing, just ctrl right mouse-click on one of the rulers and select a new unit of measurement. If the rulers are visible but the guides are hidden, dragging out a new guide will make any others reappear. You can also position a guide using View ⇨ New Guide... Enter the exact measurement coordinate for the horizontal or vertical axis in the dialog box.

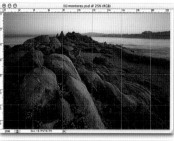

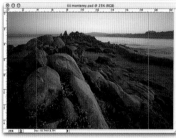

**Figure 2.7** These windows show an image displaying the Grid (top) and Guides (below). To display the Grid, chose View ⇨ Show ⇨ Grid. To position a guide, choose View ⇨ Rulers and drag from either the horizontal or vertical ruler. Hold down the *Shift* key as you drag to make the guide snap to a ruler tick mark (providing View ⇨ Snap is checked). ⌘ H  ctrl H will toggle hiding/showing Extras like the Grid & Guides. Hold down the ⌥ alt key to switch dragging a horizontal guide to dragging it as a vertical (and vice versa).

### Is it on or off?

If a tick mark appears next to an item in the View ⇨ Show menu, it means it is switched on. If you then select the item in the menu and release the mouse, you can switch it off.

### Smart Guides

When Smart Guides are switched on, these can help you align layers as you drag them with the move tool (see page 130).

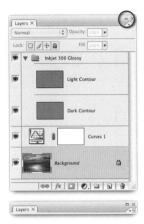

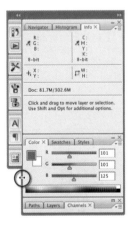

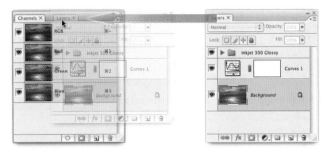

**Figure 2.8** To group palettes, mouse down on the palette tab and with the mouse held down, drag the tab across to another palette or group of palettes and release the mouse once it is inside the other palettes. To remove a palette from a group, mouse down on the palette tab and drag outside the palette group.

**Figure 2.9** Photoshop palettes can be collapsed by clicking on the minus button (Mac) or minimize/maximize button (PC). The Mac button is shown circled above. Clicking this button once will collapse the palette to shrink to the most compact size, according to the number of items present (middle). Clicking again or double-clicking the palette tab will collapse the palette to display the palette tab only (bottom).

**Figure 2.10** When palettes are docked you can adjust the width of all the palettes at once by dragging anywhere along the side edge of the palettes.

# The Photoshop palettes

The Photoshop palettes can be positioned almost anywhere on the screen, but the intention in Photoshop CS3 is for the palettes to reside in a docked layout where the palettes are grouped into column zone areas.

You can position the individual palettes by mousing down on the palette title bar (or palette icon) and dragging them to a new location. A single click on the minus icon (–) in the palette, or indeed anywhere on the palette tab, will collapse a palette into compact mode and clicking on the button or the tab will expand the palette view again. You can also adjust the height and width of a palette by dragging the size box in the bottom right corner.

As is shown in Figure 2.8, palettes can be grouped by mousing down on a Palette tab and dragging it across to another palette. When palettes are grouped this way they are like folders in a file cabinet, just click on a tab to bring that palette to the front of the group. To separate a palette from a group, mouse down on the palette tab and drag it outside of the palette group again.

## Palette docking

The default Photoshop workspace will arrange the palettes in a docked layout a bit like the way the palettes are shown in Figure 2.10, but with the Paths/Layers/Channels palette group expanded to fill the height of the screen.

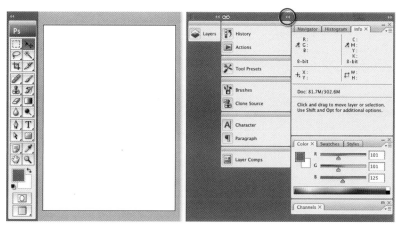

**Figure 2.11** Photoshop palettes can be grouped into columns. When an image document is viewed in Full Screen mode, the document will fill the screen up to the edge of the palette column zone area. You can adjust the width of a palette column by dragging on the bar in the column header and switch from palette icon mode to full palette mode by clicking on the double-arrow button (circled).

In Figure 2.11 I have shown how the palette columns will appear when an image document is displayed in maximized screen mode. In this example, the image document will fill the horizontal space between the Tools palette on the left and the palette columns on the right. I have also shown how you can mouse down on the column bar in the palette header to adjust the column width and highlighted the double-arrow button, which can be used to switch between the icon and full palette modes. As you increase the width of a column, the palette contents will expand and you will get to see the names of the palettes appear next to the icons.

You can rearrange the palette layout by pulling palettes out from a column and placing them anywhere you like on the screen, or drag them to a new position by attaching a palette at the bottom of a column, in the middle, or place it alongside an existing column to create a new palette column. As you do so, a thick blue line will appear along the edge of the column to indicate that if you release the mouse, this is where the palette will attach itself.

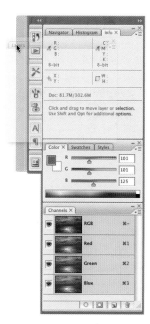

**Figure 2.12** As you reposition a palette and prepare to dock it inside or to the edges of the other palettes, a thick blue line will indicate that when you release the mouse, this is where the palette will attach itself.

## Options palette workspace menu

You can also quickly access saved workspaces via the Workspace menu in the Options palette.

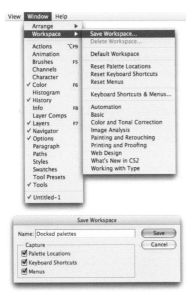

**Figure 2.13** The Save Workspace menu in Photoshop can be used to save custom palette workspace setups. These can be recalled by revisiting the menu and highlighting the workspace name. To remove a workspace, choose Delete Workspace... from the menu.

## Workspace settings

If you are searching for a particular palette and can't find it, the palette may just be hidden. Go to the Window menu and select the palette name from the menu. The *Tab* key (also indicated as →) shortcut will toggle hiding and showing all the palettes. *Tab* *Shift* will toggle hiding/showing all the currently visible palettes except the Tools palette and Options bar. This is useful to remember if all your palettes seem to have disappeared. Try pressing *Tab* and you should be able to view them once again.

If at any time you wish to restore the palette positions, go to the Window ⇨ Workspace menu and select Reset Palette Locations. You can also save the current palette arrangement as a custom workspace by going to the Window menu and choosing Workspace ⇨ Save Workspace... A dialog box will pop up that will ask you to name the workspace and save it. The next time you visit the Window ⇨ Workspace menu you will see the saved workspace appear in the menu listing. This is a real handy feature that can enable you to switch quickly between different custom palette arrangements.

If you want to be extra clever, you can go to the Edit ⇨ Keyboard Shortcuts menu and choose Shortcuts for Application menus: Windows. Scroll down and you will see a list of all the currently saved Workspace presets. You can now assign keyboard shortcuts that will allow you to jump quickly from one workspace setting to another.

If you have a second monitor display, you can arrange for all the palettes to be displayed nestled on the second screen, leaving the main monitor clear to display the whole image.

With Photoshop you can save more than just the palette positions though. You can create custom keyboard shortcuts and customize the layout and coloring of the menu items. You will note that the Save Workspace dialog allows you to include these items in the saved workspace setting and you will note that there are also a number of preset Workspace options that are available for you to try out in the Workspace submenu.

## Customizing the menu options

As the number of features in Photoshop has grown over the years, all the menu choices can be simply overwhelming. This is especially true if you are new to the Photoshop program. If you go to the Edit menu and choose Menus... this will open the Keyboard Shortcuts and Menus dialog, where you can customize the menu options and decide which menu items will be visible and whether to color code certain items to make them more prominent (this is discussed in more detail in Chapter 15). This Customize menu feature is like a 'make simpler' command. You can choose to hide those menu options you never use and apply color coding to make more prominent the menu items you use most often.

But if you go to the Window ⇨ Workspace menu, you can select from a number of pre-configured workspaces that use a combination of palette layout and menu customization options to help make the Photoshop interface more manageable. Photoshop ships with a number of menu customization presets such as: 'What's New in CS3', a 'Basic' and also a 'Legacy Photoshop' workspace preset, which may help you feel more at home when first using CS3. The philosophy behind the use of this feature is: 'everything you do want with nothing you don't want'!

# Image resolution

How can you tell if the files produced by your camera are big enough to meet your needs? And how big a file do you need to make a print at a particular size? These questions come up time and time again. Digital cameras are usually classed according to the number of pixels they can capture. If a CCD chip contains 2000 × 3000 pixel elements, it can be said to capture a total of 6 million pixels, and therefore be described as a 6 megapixel camera. When we talk about the resolution of an image we are principally referring to the number of pixels that are contained in the picture. Basically, every digital image contains a finite number of pixels and the more pixels you have, the more detail the image can contain.

## Mac OS X key fix

The Mac OS X system broke some of the once hallowed rules about not implementing keyboard shortcuts that might conflict with shortcuts in an application designed to run on the Mac system. Mac OS X keyboard shortcuts are now disabled completely since this would only further conflict with the custom keyboard shortcuts in Photoshop. One exception is the ⌘ ⌥ D Feather selection command. This still has to be deselected manually via the Mac OS X System Preferences ⇨ Keyboard & Mouse ⇨ Keyboard Shortcuts.

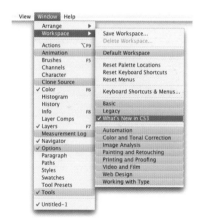

**Figure 2.14** The Custom workspace menu options, which are shown here using the What's New in CS3' setting that color codes all the new menu items in blue.

### Megapixels to megabytes

If you multiply the 'megapixel' size by three you will get a rough idea of the megabyte size of the RGB image output. In other words, a 6 megapixel camera will produce 18 MB RGB images. Quoting megabyte sizes is a less reliable method of describing things because document file sizes can also be affected by the number of layers and alpha channels present and whether the file has been compressed or not. Nevertheless, referring to image sizes in megabytes has become a convenient shorthand when describing a standard uncompressed, flattened TIFF file.

The pixel dimensions of an image are an absolute value. Therefore, a 2400 × 1800 pixel image will contain 4.32 megapixels and this is an absolute measurement of how much information is contained in the image. But a digital image of this size could be printed at 12" × 9" at 200 pixels per inch, or it could be printed at 8" × 6" at 300 pixels per inch. So if you want to know how big an image can be printed, you simply divide the number of pixels along either dimension of the picture by the pixel resolution you wish to print at. This can be expressed clearly in the following formula: number of pixels = physical dimension × (ppi) resolution. In other words, there is a reciprocal relationship between pixel size, the physical dimensions and resolution. If you quote the resolution of an image as being so many pixels by so many pixels, there can be no ambiguity about what you mean.

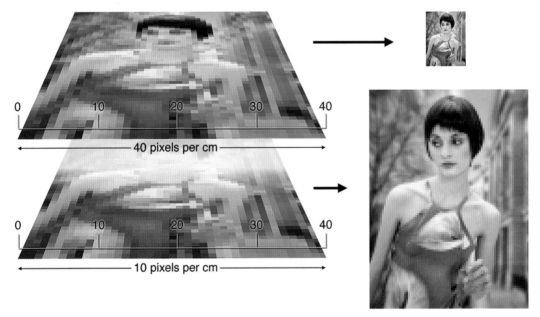

**Figure 2.15** In this diagram you can see how a digital image that is comprised of a fixed number of pixels can have its output resolution interpreted in different ways. For illustration purposes let's assume that the image is 40 pixels wide. The file can be printed big (and more pixelated) at a resolution of 10 pixels per cm, or it can be printed a quarter of the size at a resolution of 40 pixels per cm.

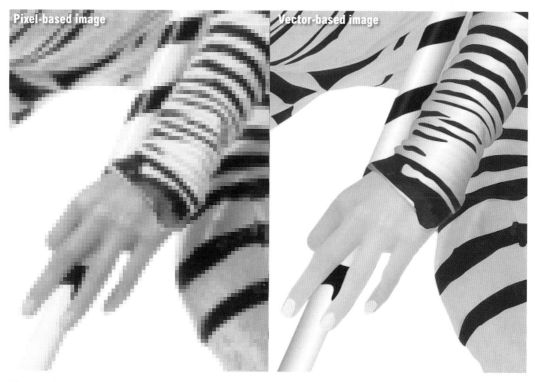

**Figure 2.16** Digital images are made up of a mosaic of pixels. This means that a pixel-based digital image will always have a fixed resolution and is said to be 'resolution-dependent'. If you enlarge such an image beyond the size at which it is meant to be printed, the pixel structure will soon become apparent, as can be seen here in the left-hand close-up view.

But suppose the picture shown opposite originated not as a photograph, but was drawn as an illustration using a program like Adobe Illustrator. If the picture is drawn using vector paths, the image will be resolution-independent. The mathematical numbers used to describe the path outlines shown in the bottom right example can then be scaled to reproduce at any size: from a postage stamp to a billboard poster. As you can see in the comparison shown here, the pixel image starts to break up as soon as it is magnified, whereas the outlines in the vector-drawn image reproduce perfectly smoothly.

'Stalkers' by The Wrong Size. Photograph: Eric Richmond.

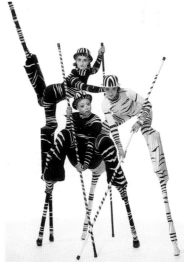

## Photoshop as a vector program

Photoshop is mainly regarded as a pixel-based graphics program, but it does have the capability to be a combined vector and pixel editing program because it also contains a number of vector-based features that can be used to generate images such as custom shapes and layer clipping paths. This raises some interesting possibilities, because you can create various graphical elements like type, shape layers and layer clipping paths in Photoshop and these are all resolution-independent. These 'vector' elements can be scaled up in size in Photoshop without any loss of detail, just as you can do with an Illustrator graphic.

# Pixels versus vectors

Digital photographs are constructed with pixels and as such are resolution-dependent. You can scale up a pixel image, but as you do so, the finite information can only be stretched so far before the underlying pixel structure becomes apparent. Objects created in a program like Adobe Illustrator are defined mathematically, so if you draw a rectangle, the proportions of the rectangle edges, the relative placement on the page and the color it is filled with can all be described using mathematical expressions. An object defined using vectors can be output at any resolution. It does not matter if the image is displayed on a computer screen, or as a huge poster, it will always be rendered with the same amount of detail (see Figure 2.16).

## Terminology

Before proceeding further let me help clarify a few of the confusing terms used and their correct usage when describing resolution.

***ppi: pixels per inch***. This describes the digital, pixel resolution of an image. But you will notice the term 'dpi' is often inappropriately used to describe the digital resolution of film scanners. This is an incorrect use of the term 'dpi' because input devices like scanners produce pixels. They don't produce dots. Only printers can do that! However, it's become quite common now for scanner manufacturers to use the term 'dpi' when they really mean ppi and unfortunately this has only added to the confusion, because you often hear people describing the resolution of an image as having so many dpi. But if you look carefully, Photoshop always refers to the input resolution as being in pixels per inch or pixels per centimeter. So if you have an image that has been captured on a digital camera scanned from a photograph, or displayed in Photoshop, it is always made up of pixels. The pixel resolution (ppi) is the number of pixels per inch in the input digital image.

*lpi: lines per inch*. This is the number of halftone lines or 'cells' in an inch, also described as the screen ruling. The origins of this term go back way before the days of digital desktop publishing. To produce a halftone plate, the film exposure was made through a finely etched criss-cross screen of evenly spaced lines on a glass plate. When a continuous tone photographic image was exposed this way, dark areas formed heavy halftone dots and the light areas formed smaller dots, which when viewed from a normal distance gave the impression of a continuous tone image on the page. The line screen resolution (lpi) is therefore the frequency of halftone dots or cells per inch.

*dpi: dots per inch*. This refers to the resolution of a printing device. An output device such as an imagesetter is able to produce tiny 100% black dots at a specified resolution. Let's say we have an imagesetter capable of printing at a resolution of 2450 dots per inch and the printer wished to use a screen ruling of 150 lines per inch. If you divide the dpi of 2450 by the lpi of 150, you get a figure of 16. Within a matrix of 16 × 16 printer dots, an imagesetter can generate a halftone dot varying in size from 0 to 255, which is 256 print dots. It is this variation in halftone cell size (constructed from the combined smaller dots) which gives the impression of tonal shading when viewed from a distance.

Desktop inkjet printers correctly use the term dpi to describe the resolution of the printer head. Inkjet printers produce an output made up of small dots at resolutions of between 360 and 2880 dots per inch. The inkjet output is not the same as the reprographic process – the screening method used is quite different.

## Confusing terminology

You can see from these descriptions where the term 'lines per inch' originated. In today's digital world of imagesetters, the definition is somewhat archaic, but is nonetheless commonly used. You may hear people refer to the halftone output as 'dpi' instead of 'lpi', as in the number of 'halftone' dots per inch, and the imagesetter resolution referred to as having so many 'spi', or 'spots per inch'. Whatever the terminology I think we can all logically agree on the correct use of the term 'pixels per inch', but I am afraid there is no clear definitive answer to the mixed use of the terms 'dpi', 'lpi' and 'spi'. It is an example of how the two separate disciplines of traditional repro and those who developed the digital technology chose to apply different meanings to these same terms.

## Desktop printer resolution

Inkjet printers use the term 'dots per inch' to describe the output resolution of the printer. The dpi output of a typical inkjet will range from 360 to 2880 dpi. And although this is a correct usage of dpi, in this context the dpi means something else yet again. Most inkjet printers lay down a scattered pattern of tiny dots of ink that accumulate to give the impression of different shades of tone, depending on either the number of dots, the varied size of the dots, or both. The principle is roughly similar to the halftone process, but not quite the same. If you select a finer print resolution such as 1440 or 2880 dpi, you should see smoother print outputs when viewed close up.

The optimum pixel resolution should ideally be the printer dpi divisible by a whole number. So if an inkjet printer head has a resolution of 2880 dpi, the following pixel resolutions could be used: 144, 160, 180, 240, 288, 320, 360. To make large inkjet prints for viewing at a greater distance, use a low pixel resolution. For smaller sized portfolio prints I normally use a 240 or 300 ppi pixel resolution. I doubt very much you will notice any improvement in print quality if you choose a resolution that is higher than this.

## Repro considerations

The structure of the final print output appearance bears no relationship to the pixel structure of a digital image. A pixel in a digital image does not equal a cell of halftone dots on the page. To explain this, if we analyze a CMYK cell or rosette, each color plate prints the screen of dots at a slightly different angle, typically: Yellow at 0 or 90 degrees, Black: 45 degrees, Cyan: 105 degrees and Magenta: 75 degrees. If the Black screen is at a 45 degree angle (which is normally the case), the (narrowest) horizontal width of the black dot is 1.41 (square root of 2) times shorter than the width of the Yellow screen (widest). If we extend the width of the data creating the halftone cell, then multiplying the pixel sample by a factor of 1.41 would mean that there was at least a 1 pixel width of information

## The relationship between ppi and lpi

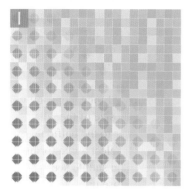

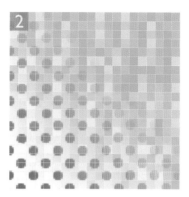

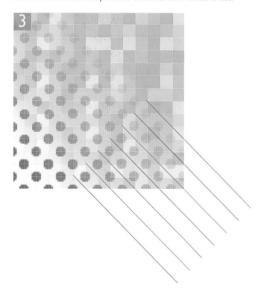

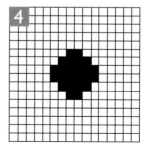

**1** The halftone screen shown here is angled at zero degrees. If the pixel resolution were calculated at ×2 the line screen resolution, the RIP would use four pixels to calculate each halftone dot.

**2** To reproduce a CMYK print output, four plates are used, of which only the yellow plate is actually angled at zero degrees. The black plate is normally angled at 45 degrees and the cyan and magenta plates at less sharp angles. Overlay the same pixel resolution of ×2 the line screen and you will notice that there is no direct relationship between the pixel and line screen resolutions.

**3** There is no single empirical formula that can be used to determine the ideal 'half toning factor'. Should it be ×2 or ×1.5? The black plate is the widest at 45 degrees and the black plate information is usually more prominent than the three color plates. If a half toning factor of ×1.41 (the square root of 2) were used, the pixel resolution will be more synchronized with this angled halftone screen. There is no right or wrong half toning factor – the RIP will process pixel data at any resolution. If there are too few pixels, print quality will be poor. But having more than the optimum number does not necessarily equate to better output, it just means more pixels.

**4** Each halftone dot is rendered by a PostScript RIP from the pixel data and output to a device called an imagesetter. The halftone dot illustrated here is plotted using a 16 × 16 dot matrix. This matrix can therefore reproduce a total of 256 shades of gray. The dpi resolution of the imagesetter, divided by 16, will equal the line screen resolution. 2400 dpi divided by 16 = 150 lpi screen resolution.

## Determining output image size

Image size is determined by the final output requirements and at the beginning of a digital job, the most important information you need to know is:

- How large will the picture appear on the page, poster, etc.?
- What is the screen frequency being used by the printer – how many lpi?
- What is the preferred halftone factor used to determine the output resolution?
- Will the designer need to allow for page bleed, or want to crop your image?

## But we always use 300 ppi!

There is a common misconception in the design industry that everything must be supplied at 300 pixels per inch. This crops up all the time when you are contacting clients to ask what resolution you should supply your image files at. Somehow the idea has got around the industry that everything from a picture in a newspaper to a 48-sheet poster must be reproduced from a 300 ppi file. It does not always hurt to supply your files at a higher resolution than is necessary, but it can get quite ridiculous when you are asked to supply a 370 MB file in order to produce a 30" x 36" print!

with which to generate the black plate. The spacing of the pixels in relation to the spacing of the 45 degree rotated black plate is thereby more synchronized.

For this reason, you will find that the image output resolution asked for by printers is usually at least 1.41 times the halftone screen frequency used, i.e. multiples of ×1.41, ×1.5 or ×2. This multiplication is also known as the 'halftone factor', but which is best? Ask the printer what they prefer you to supply and some will say that the 1.41:1 or 1.5:1 multiplication produces crisper detail than the higher ratio of 2:1. There are other factors which they may have to take into account such as the screening method used. It is claimed that Stochastic or FM screening permits a more flexible choice of ratios ranging from 1:1 to 2:1.

Ideally this information needs to be known before the image is scanned (or captured digitally). Because if you calculate that only 10 MB worth of RGB data will actually be required, there may be no point in capturing more image data than is absolutely necessary. If the printer's specification is not available to you, then the only alternative is to scan or shoot at the highest practical resolution and resample the image later. The downside of this is that large image files consume extra disk space and take longer to process on the computer. If a print job does not require the images to be larger than 10 MB, then you'll want to know this in advance rather than waste time and space working on unnecessarily large files. On the other hand, designers like to have the freedom to take a supplied image and scale it in the design layout program to suit their requirements. So it may seem contrary for me to state that I normally supply my files using a ×2 halftone factor, because that way I know there will always be enough data in the supplied file to allow for a 20% scaling without adversely compromising the final print quality.

## Creating a new document

If you want to create a new document in Photoshop with a blank canvas, go to the File menu and choose New... This will open the dialog shown in Figure 2.17, where you can select a preset setting from the Preset pop-up menu or manually enter new document dimensions and resolution in the fields below. When you choose a preset setting, the resolution will adjust automatically depending on whether it is a preset used for print or computer screen type work. You can change the default resolution settings for print and screen in the Units & Rulers Photoshop preferences dialog. The Advanced section lets you do extra things like choose a specific profiled color space. After you have entered custom settings in the New Document dialog these can be saved by clicking on the Save Preset... button. In the New Document Preset dialog shown below you will notice that the options will allow you to select which attributes will be included in the saved preset.

## Pixel Aspect Ratio

The Pixel Aspect Ratio is there to aid multimedia designers who work in stretched screen formats. So, if a 'non-square' pixel setting is selected, Photoshop will create a scaled document which will preview how a normal 'square' pixel Photoshop document will actually display on a stretched wide screen. And the title bar will add [scaled] to the end of the file name to remind you that you are working in this special preview mode. When you create a non-square pixel document the scaled preview can be switched on or off by selecting the Pixel Aspect Correction item in the View menu.

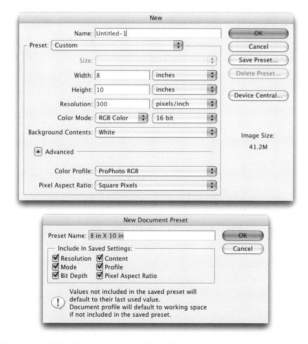

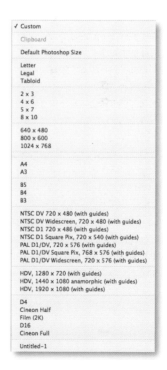

**Figure 2.17** The New document and New Document Preset dialogs.

## Resolution and viewing distance

In theory the larger a picture is printed, the further away it is meant to be viewed and the pixel resolution should not have to alter in order to achieve the same perception of sharpness. There are limits though, below which the quality will never be sharp enough at normal viewing distance (except at the smallest of print sizes). It also depends on the image subject matter – a picture containing a lot of mechanical detail will need more pixels to do the subject justice and be reproduced successfully. If you had a picture of a softly lit cloudy landscape, you could quite easily get away with enlarging a small image through interpolation, beyond the normal constraints.

## Altering the image size

The image size dimensions and resolution can be adjusted using the Image Size dialog. The dialog will normally open with the Resample Image box checked. This means that as you enter new pixel dimension values, measurement values or adjust the resolution, the overall image size will adjust accordingly. As you adjust one set of units you will see the others adjust simultaneously. When Resample Image is unchecked, the pixel dimensions will be grayed out and any adjustment made to the image will not alter the total pixel dimensions, only the relationship between the measurement units and the resolution. Remember the rule I mentioned earlier: the number of pixels = physical dimension × (ppi) resolution. You can put that rule to the test here and use the Image Size dialog as a training tool to better understand the relationship between the number of pixels, the dimensions and the resolution. The Constrain Proportions checkbox links the horizontal and vertical dimensions, so that any adjustment is automatically scaled to both axis. Only uncheck this box if you wish to squash or stretch the image while adjusting the image size.

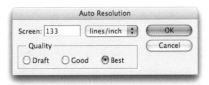

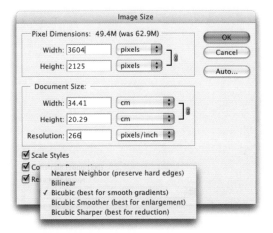

**Figure 2.18** To change the image output dimensions but retain the resolution, leave the Resample box checked. To change the image output dimensions with a corresponding change in resolution, leave the Resample box unchecked. Click on the Auto button to open the Auto Resolution dialog. This will help you pick the ideal pixel resolution for repro work based on the line screen resolution.

## Image interpolation

Image resampling is also known as interpolation and Photoshop can use one of five methods when assigning approximated values for any new pixels that are generated. The interpolation options are located next to the Resample Image checkbox.

***Nearest Neighbor*** is the simplest interpolation method, yet I use this quite a lot, such as when I want to enlarge a screen grab of a dialog box for this book by 200% and I don't want the sharp edges of the dialog boxes to appear fuzzy.

***Bilinear interpolation*** will calculate new pixels by reading the horizontal and vertical neighboring pixels. It is fast, and perhaps that was an important consideration in the early days of Photoshop, but I don't see there is much reason to use it now.

***Bicubic interpolation*** provides better image quality when resampling continuous tone images. Photoshop will read the values of neighboring pixels vertically, horizontally and diagonally, to calculate a weighted approximation of each new pixel value. Photoshop intelligently guesses the new pixel values, by referencing the surrounding pixels.

### When to interpolate?

I consider 'interpolating up' an image in Photoshop to be preferable to the interpolation methods found in basic scanner software. Digital files captured from a scanning back or multishot digital camera are extremely clean and, because there is no grain present, it is usually possible to magnify a digitally captured image much more than you would magnify a scanned image of equivalent size. There are other third-party programs that claim to offer improved interpolation, but there appears to be little evidence that you will actually gain any major improvements in image quality over and above what you can achieve using Photoshop.

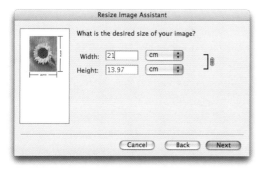 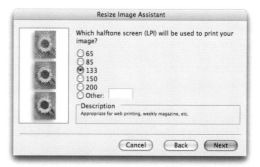

**Figure 2.19** If Image Size is proving too confusing, the Resize Image Assistant is on hand to help guide you. This wizard is located in the Help menu and can be used to resize images both for print and for the Web.

## Planning ahead

Once an image has been scanned at a particular resolution and manipulated, there is no going back. A digital file prepared for advertising usage may never be used to produce anything bigger than a 35 MB CMYK separation, but you never know. It is safer to err on the side of caution and better to sample down than have to interpolate up. It also depends on the manipulation work being done. Some styles of retouching work are best done at a magnified size and then reduced. Suppose you wanted to blend a small element into a detailed scene. To do such work convincingly, you need to have enough pixels to work with to be able to see what you are doing. For this reason some professional retouchers will edit a master file that is around 100 MB RGB or bigger even. Another advantage of working with large file sizes is that you can always guarantee being able to meet clients' constantly changing demands, although the actual resolution required to illustrate a glossy magazine double-page full-bleed spread is probably only around 40–60 MB RGB or 55–80 MB CMYK. Some advertising posters may even require smaller files than this, because the print screen on a billboard poster is that much coarser. When you are trying to calculate the optimum resolution you cannot rely on being fully provided with the right advice from every printer. Sometimes it will be necessary to anticipate the required resolution by referring to the table in Figure 2.21. This shows some sample file size guides for different types of print job.

## Bicubic interpolation methods

The Photoshop bicubic interpolations are improved and more accurate than before, especially with regard to the downsampling of images. And if you need to apply an extreme image resize either up or down in size, I suggest that you consider using the Bicubic Sharper or Bicubic Smoother interpolation methods.

*Bicubic Smoother* is the ideal choice if you wish to make an image bigger. In my view it is not a good idea to use Bicubic Sharper when interpolating an image up in size, because although Bicubic Smoother will result in (as the name suggests) a smoother interpolation enlargement. it is better to use Bicubic Smoother followed by a sharpening action at the end, which should be dictated by the type of print output you wish to make.

*Bicubic Sharper* should be used when you want to reduce the pixel resolution more accurately; for example, if you have a high resolution digital capture of detailed machinery and want to make a duplicate copy but at a much lower pixel resolution. If you reduce the image size using Bicubic Sharper the scaled down image will retain more detail and sharpness.

## Step interpolation

Some people might be familiar with the step interpolation technique, where you gradually increase or decrease the image size by small percentages. This is not really necessary now because you can use Bicubic Sharper or Bicubic Smoother to increase or decrease the image size in a single step. Some people argue that for really extreme image size changes they prefer to use a 10% step method.

Unsharp masking should always be applied last as the file is being prepared for print. This is because interpolating after sharpening will enhance the image artifacts introduced by the sharpening process.

| Pixel size | Megapixels | MB (RGB) | MB (CMYK) | Inches 200 ppi | Centimeters 80 ppc | Inches 300 ppi | Centimeters 120 ppc |
|---|---|---|---|---|---|---|---|
| 1600 x 1200 | 2 | 6 | 7.5 | 8 x 6 | 20 x 15 | 5.5 x 4 | 13.5 x 10 |
| 2400 x 1800 | 4.3 | 12.5 | 16.5 | 12 x 9 | 30 x 22.5 | 8 x 6 | 20 x 15 |
| 3000 x 2000 | 6 | 17.5 | 23.5 | 15 x 10 | 37.5 x 25 | 10 x 6.5 | 25 x 17 |
| 3500 x 2500 | 8.75 | 25 | 33.5 | 17.5 x 12.5 | 44 x 31 | 11.5 x 8.5 | 29 x 21 |
| 4000 x 2850 | 11.4 | 32.5 | 43.5 | 20 x 14 | 50 x 36 | 13.5 x 9.5 | 33.5 x 24 |
| 4500 x 3200 | 14.4 | 41 | 54.5 | 22.5 x 16 | 56 x 40 | 15 x 10.5 | 37.5 x 27 |
| 5000 x 4000 | 20 | 57 | 76 | 25 x 20 | 62.5 x 50 | 16.5 x 13.5 | 42 x 33.5 |

**Figure 2.20** The above table shows a comparison of pixel resolution, megapixels, megabyte file size and output dimensions at different resolutions, both in inches and in centimeters.

| Output use | Screen ruling | x1.5 Output resolution | MB Grayscale | MB CMYK | x2 Output resolution | MB Grayscale | MB CMYK |
|---|---|---|---|---|---|---|---|
| A3 Newspaper single page | 85 lpi | 130 ppi | 3 | 12.5 | 170 ppi | 5.5 | 21.5 |
| A3 Newspaper single page | 120 lpi | 180 ppi | 6 | 24 | 240 ppi | 10.5 | 42.5 |
| A4 Magazine mono single page | 120 lpi | 180 ppi | 3 | na | 240 ppi | 5.3 | na |
| A4 Magazine mono double page | 120 lpi | 180 ppi | 6 | na | 240 ppi | 10.6 | na |
| A4 Magazine single page | 133 lpi | 200 ppi | 3.7 | 14.8 | 266 ppi | 6.5 | 26.1 |
| A4 Magazine double page | 133 lpi | 200 ppi | 8 | 29.6 | 266 ppi | 13 | 52.2 |
| A4 Magazine single page | 150 lpi | 225 ppi | 4.7 | 18.7 | 300 ppi | 8.3 | 33.2 |
| A4 Magazine double page | 150 lpi | 225 ppi | 9.4 | 37.4 | 300 ppi | 17 | 66.4 |

**Figure 2.21** Here is a rough guide to the sort of file sizes required to reproduce either a mono or CMYK file for printed use. The table contains file size information for output at multiples of x1.5 the screen ruling and x2 the screen ruling.

## Converting raw data into pixels

A large number of readers will probably be using a digital camera to capture their photographs and will find themselves presented with a choice between capturing in JPEG or raw mode. Whichever way you look at it, all images are captured as raw data and the raw information has to be converted at some stage into an RGB pixel image that Photoshop can work with.

All digital cameras have an on-board processor that will interpret the raw capture data and render it as a pixel image. This process will usually take into account the camera white balance settings, along with any other custom settings that dictate things like sharpness, levels clipping, color mode and noise reduction, etc. If you shoot using the camera's JPEG mode, you will be letting the camera decide on-the-fly how the conversion is to be carried out and the capture file output will be a fully-rendered pixel image saved using the JPEG format. If your camera output is a JPEG or a TIFF image, there is not much else you need to know about raw data right now and you can get straight down to the business of editing your images in Photoshop.

When you edit a pixel image, your starting point will always be a fixed pixel original. There are a number of ways in Photoshop that you can edit such a picture non-destructively, by using layers and adjustment layers or Smart Objects even. But your options will always be constrained by the nature of the original pixel image. Plus, adding more layers can greatly increase the overall file size.

But if you choose to shoot in raw mode, the possibilities are endless. The raw data is just that: it is the raw image data that was captured by the sensor and the only thing that is fixed in the raw file is the ISO setting that was used to capture the photograph. The raw image is therefore like a digital negative just waiting to be developed and you can have complete control over how the image is processed, whereas if you shoot using the JPEG mode, you will be letting the camera make all the raw process editing decisions for you.

The Adobe Camera Raw plug-in has evolved over several versions of Photoshop now and provides a lot of powerful features with which to process raw image files from selected cameras and convert them into pixel images that Photoshop can work with. The Camera Raw plug-in provides true non-destructive image editing because the raw file is never modified. The edits you make via the Camera Raw plug-in are effectively instruction edits that are saved as metadata to a central database and can also be saved locally to XMP sidecar files (or in the case of DNG and other non-proprietary files saved to the file itself). This marks a radical shift in direction from the pixel-based image editing that Photoshop built its reputation on, and in Chapter 5 you can read all about all the new features in the Camera Raw 4 plug-in.

If I want to preserve all the information from one of my Canon EOS 1Ds Mk II camera captures as a 16-bit TIFF file, the file would end up being almost 100 MB in size (and that is before adding extra layers). A raw master file by comparison will be no bigger than 15 MB (less if converted to DNG) and every time I edit the raw file, the edit instructions can be stored in just a few kilobytes of extra data. Raw image processing is now just as important as pixel imaging (some would argue it is even more so) and it is not just in the realm of Photoshop. There are now many other programs that will allow you to edit almost exclusively with raw images. The new Adobe Photoshop Lightroom program will let you edit and manage both raw and non-raw images. Capture One is another raw image processor that is popular with photographers and Apple's Aperture which, like Lightroom, is primarily a workflow tool for digital photographers.

How do we describe this raw image processing? Do we call it raw editing, instruction set editing, metadata editing? Whatever it is called, Raw offers photographers a greater level of control over how they process their images and encourages us to keep our images in their raw state longer, before it is necessary to render them as pixel images to be worked on in Photoshop.

**Before there was Camera Raw**

Deferred pixel processing isn't such a new concept. Some of you may remember the Live Picture program, which used proxy images to apply the image edits and stored these as instructions which could later be used to render a final output image.

Any late-breaking information plus access to on-line help and professional tips are all easily accessible within Photoshop. If you click on the PS icon in the Tools palette, this will open the Adobe On-line... dialog (which is also available in the Help menu).

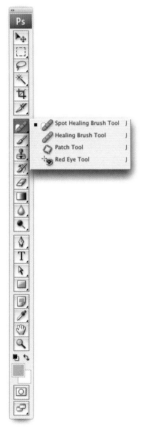

**Figure 2.22** Where tools are marked with a triangle in the bottom right corner, if you mouse down on the tool you will see all the other tools that are nested in that particular group.

# Photoshop CS3 Tools palette

The Tools palette layout contains 60 separate tools. Double-clicking any tool will automatically display the Tool options palette (if it happens to be hidden) and from there you can select individual options for that tool (see page 58).

Many of the tools listed in the Tools palette have a triangle in the bottom right corner of the tool icon, which indicates that there are extra tools nested in a tool group. If you mouse down on the tool icon, this will reveal the list of tools (see Figure 2.22) and you can click on any of the tools in the list to make it the new default tool for that group.

You will notice that each tool or set of tools will have an associated keyboard shortcut. This is displayed whenever you mouse down to reveal the nested tools or hover with the cursor to reveal the tool tip info; you can use these to quickly select a tool without having to always use the Tools palette to select the tool you wish to use. For example, pressing **C** on the keyboard will activate the crop tool and pressing **J** will select whichever of the healing brush group of tools is currently selected in the Tools palette. Where more than one tool shares the same keyboard shortcut, you can cycle through these other tools by holding down the **Shift** key as you press the keyboard shortcut. But if you prefer to restore the old behavior whereby repeated pressing of the key would cycle the tool selection, go to the Photoshop menu, select Preferences ⇨ General and deselect the Use Shift Key for Tool Switch option (personally, I prefer using the shift key method). You can also **⌥** **alt**-click the tool icon in the Tools palette to cycle through the grouped tools.

There are specific situations when Photoshop will not allow you to use certain tools and displays a prohibit sign (⊘). For example, you might be editing an image in 32-bit mode where only some tools can be used to edit the image. Clicking once in the image document window will call up a dialog explaining the exact reason why you cannot access or use a particular tool.

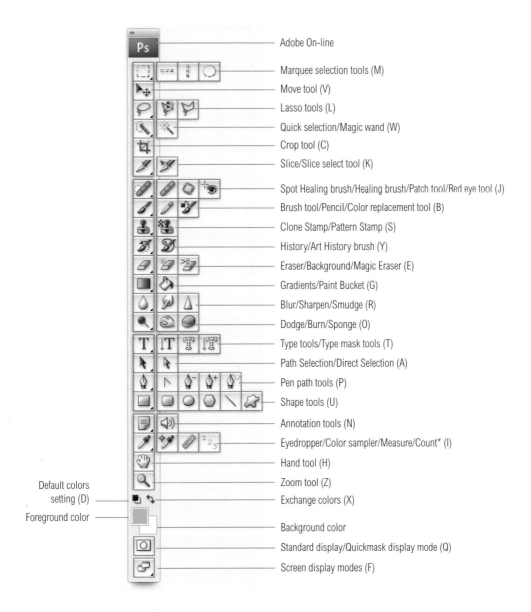

Adobe On-line

Marquee selection tools (M)

Move tool (V)

Lasso tools (L)

Quick selection/Magic wand (W)

Crop tool (C)

Slice/Slice select tool (K)

Spot Healing brush/Healing brush/Patch tool/Red eye tool (J)

Brush tool/Pencil/Color replacement tool (B)

Clone Stamp/Pattern Stamp (S)

History/Art History brush (Y)

Eraser/Background/Magic Eraser (E)

Gradients/Paint Bucket (G)

Blur/Sharpen/Smudge (R)

Dodge/Burn/Sponge (O)

Type tools/Type mask tools (T)

Path Selection/Direct Selection (A)

Pen path tools (P)

Shape tools (U)

Annotation tools (N)

Eyedropper/Color sampler/Measure/Count* (I)

Hand tool (H)

Zoom tool (Z)

Exchange colors (X)

Background color

Standard display/Quickmask display mode (Q)

Screen display modes (F)

Default colors setting (D)

Foreground color

**Figure 2.23** The Tools palette with keyboard shortcuts shown in brackets. Note that the count tool is only available in the extended version of Photoshop CS3.

## Hovering tool tips

In order to help familiarize yourself with the Photoshop tools and palette functions, help dialog boxes will pop up after a few seconds whenever you leave a cursor hovering over any one of the Photoshop buttons or tool icons (see Show Tool Tips in the General Preferences). A brief description is included in the box and tools have their keyboard shortcuts written in brackets.

## Options palette

The Options palette will normally appear at the top of the screen, snapped to the main menu. This is a convenient location for the Options palette, and you will soon appreciate the ease with which you can make changes to any options with minimal mouse navigation movement. The Options palette can be unhooked, by dragging the gripper bar (on the left edge) away from the top of the screen. As was mentioned earlier on page 38, you can use the _Shift_ _Tab_ shortcut to toggle hiding the palette stack only, keeping just the Tools palette and Options palette visible.

The individual Options palette settings for some of the tools are shown throughout the rest of this chapter. To reset a tool or all tools, _ctrl_ right mouse down on the tool icon on the left and choose Reset Tool or Reset All Tools. Quite often you will see 'tick' and 'cancel' icons on the right-hand side of the Options palette. These are there so that you can OK or cancel a tool that is in a modal state. For example, you might be using the crop tool and are about to accept or cancel the crop but, after a while, you may find it easier to use the E key to OK or the _esc_ key to cancel a tool operation such as a crop.

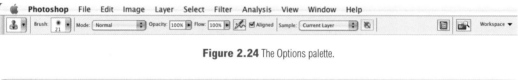

**Figure 2.24** The Options palette.

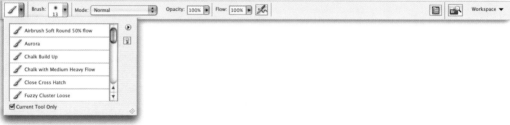

**Figure 2.25** Here is a view of the Options palette, where I had moused down on the arrow next to the Brush tool icon to reveal the Tool Presets menu.

## Tool Presets palette

Many of the Photoshop tools will offer a range of possible tool options. Tool Presets will allow you to store multiple saved tool settings, which can be accessed via the Options palette (as shown in Figure 2.25), or via the Tool Presets palette shown in Figure 2.26.

With Tool Presets you can access any number of tool options very quickly and this will save you the bother of having to reconfigure the Options palette settings each time you use a particular tool. For example, you might find it useful to save crop tool settings for different image dimensions and pixel resolutions, so that you can access these without having to reconfigure the Options palette every time. And likewise, you might like to store pre-configured brush preset settings, rather than have to keep adjusting the brush shape and attributes. To save a new tool preset, click on the New Preset button at the bottom of the Tool Presets palette and to delete a preset, click on the Trash button.

If you mouse down on the Tool Presets options, you can use the menu shown in Figure 2.27 to manage the Tools Presets. In Figure 2.26 the Show All Tool Presets option was selected which meant that all the tool presets were displayed at once. This can be useful, because clicking on a preset will simultaneously select the tool and the preset at the same time. But most people will find the Tool Presets palette easier to manage when the Show Current Tool Only option is selected.

You can use the Tool Presets options to save or load preset settings. For example, if you create a set of custom presets, you can share these with other Photoshop users by choosing Save Tool Presets... to create a saved set of settings for a particular tool. Another thing that may not be immediately apparent is the fact that you can also use the Tool Presets to save type tool settings. This again is useful, because you can save the font type, font size, type attributes and font color settings all within a single tool preset. This feature can also be really handy if you are working on a web or book design project.

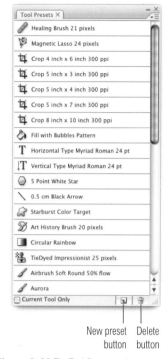

New preset    Delete
button        button

**Figure 2.26** The Tool Presets palette.

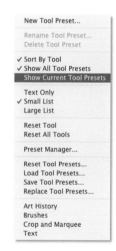

**Figure 2.27** The Tool Presets options.

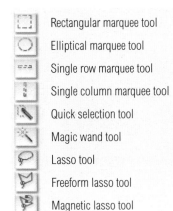

Rectangular marquee tool

Elliptical marquee tool

Single row marquee tool

Single column marquee tool

Quick selection tool

Magic wand tool

Lasso tool

Freeform lasso tool

Magnetic lasso tool

## Selection tools

In Photoshop the usual editing conventions apply: pixels can be cut, copied and pasted just as you would when working with text in a word processing document and mistakes can be undone by using the Edit ⇨ Undo command or by selecting a previous history state via the History palette.

The Photoshop selection tools can mainly be used to define a specific area of the image that you wish to modify, or have copied. The use of the selection tools in Photoshop is therefore like highlighting text in a word processor program in preparation to do something with the selected content. In the case of Photoshop, you might want to make a selection to define a specific area of the image, so that when you apply an image adjustment or a fill, only the selected area will be modified. Alternatively, you might use a selection to define an area you wish to copy and paste, or define an area of an image that you want to copy across to another image document as a new layer.

The marquee selection tool options include the rectangular, elliptical and single row/single column selection tools. The lasso tool can be used to draw freehand selection outlines and has two other modes: the polygon lasso tool, which can draw both straight line *and* freehand selections plus the magnetic lasso tool, which is like an automatic freehand lasso tool that is able to auto-detect an edge you are trying to trace.

The quick selection tool is a new addition in Photoshop CS3 and, like the magic wand tool, it can be used to make selections based on pixel color values; however the quick selection tool is a little more sophisticated than the standard magic wand and hence the new default tool in this particular tool grouping. For full descriptions of these and other tools mentioned here don't forget to install the *Photoshop CS3 for Photographers Help Guide* that is available on the DVD.

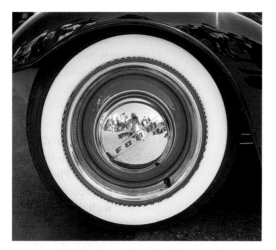 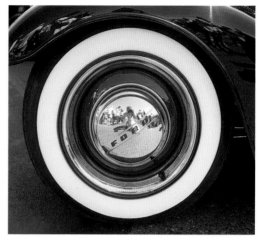

**Figure 2.28** A selection can be used to define a specific area of an image that you wish to work on. In this example, I made an elliptical marquee selection of the inner tire wheel and followed this with an image adjustment to desaturate the red color.

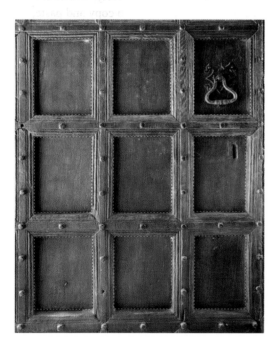 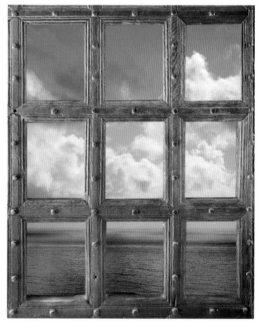

**Figure 2.29** In this example I used the rectangle marquee tool to marquee one of the inner panels and followed this by holding down the *Shift* key to select more panels with the rectangular marquee. I deleted the selected areas and placed the cut-out image as a layer above a seascape image (see Figure 2.44 for an example of how Photoshop layers work).

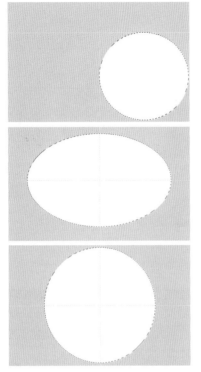

**Figure 2.30** These composite screenshots show Quick Mask views of selections created by dragging out from the center with _Shift_ held down (top), with ⌥ _alt_ held down (middle) and _Shift_ ⌥ _Shift_ _alt_ (bottom).

## Modifier keys

Macintosh and Windows keyboards have slightly different key arrangements, hence the double sets of instructions throughout the book, where the ⌘ key on the Macintosh is equivalent to the _ctrl_ key on a Windows keyboard (because Windows PC computers don't have a Command key) and the Macintosh ⌥ key is equivalent to the _alt_ key in Windows. In fact, on most Macintosh keyboards the Option key is labeled 'Alt' anyway.

Windows users (and Mac users with a 'Mighty Mouse') can use the right mouse button to access the contextual menus (Mac users can also use the _ctrl_ key to access these menus) and, finally, the _Shift_ key which operates the same on both Mac and PC computers.

These keys are referred to as 'modifier' keys, because they modify tool behaviors. If you hold down the _Shift_ when drawing a marquee selection this will constrain the selection to a square or circle. If you hold down ⌥ _alt_ when drawing a marquee selection it will center the selection around the point where you clicked on the image. And if you hold down _Shift_ ⌥ _Shift_ _alt_ when drawing a marquee selection, this will constrain the selection to a square or circle and center the selection around the point where you first clicked. The Spacebar is also a modifier key, in that it allows you to reposition your selection midstream.

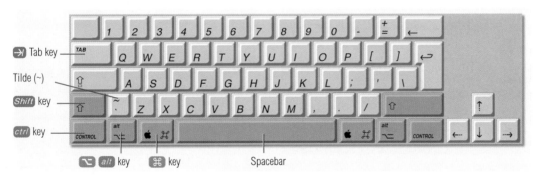

**Figure 2.31** The modifier keys on a Macintosh keyboard and their Windows PC equivalents are indicated in brown. The other keys commonly used in Photoshop are the Tab and Tilde keys, shown here in blue.

After you have created an initial selection, the modifier keys will behave differently. If you hold down the *Shift* key as you drag with the marquee or lasso tool, this will add to the selection (holding down the *Shift* key and clicking with the magic wand tool also adds to an existing magic wand selection). If you hold down the ⌥ *alt* key as you drag with the marquee or lasso tool, this will subtract from the selection (holding down the ⌥ *alt* key and clicking with the magic wand tool also subtracts from the existing selection). And the combination of holding down the *Shift* ⌥ *Shift* *alt* keys together whilst dragging with a selection tool (or clicking with the magic wand) will create an intersection of the two selections.

The modifier keys can also be used to modify the options that are available in Photoshop. For example, if you hold down the ⌥ *alt* key as you click on the marquee tool in the Tools palette you will notice how this cycles through the tools available in this group. And whenever you are in a Photoshop dialog box it is also worth exploring what happens to the dialog buttons when you hold down the ⌥ *alt* key. You will often see the button names change to reveal more options.

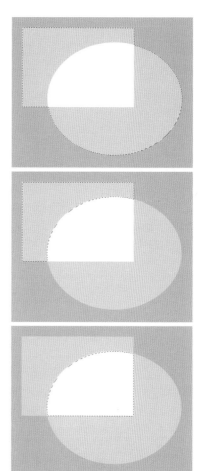

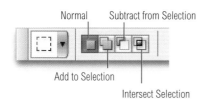

Normal    Subtract from Selection

Add to Selection

Intersect Selection

**Figure 2.33** The Options bar has four modes of operation for each of the selection tools: Normal; Add to Selection; Subtract from Selection; and Intersect Selection. You can also achieve these same operating modes by using the modifier keys as you work with a tool in Normal mode.

**Figure 2.32** These composite screenshots show Quick Mask views of selections modified after the first stage. The top view shows an elliptical selection combined with a rectangular selection with *Shift* held down, adding to a selection. The middle view shows an elliptical selection combined with a rectangular selection with ⌥ *alt* held down, which will subtract from the original selection. The bottom view shows an elliptical selection combined with a rectangular selection with *Shift* ⌥ *Shift* *alt* held down, which will result in an intersected selection being made.

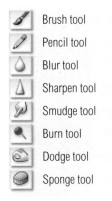

Brush tool

Pencil tool

Blur tool

Sharpen tool

Smudge tool

Burn tool

Dodge tool

Sponge tool

**Brush size limits**

The standard brush presets in Photoshop range from a single pixel to a 2500 pixel-wide brush, with varying degrees of softness.

# Painting tools

The next set of tools I want to focus on is the painting tools. These include: the brush tool, pencil, blur, sharpen, smudge, burn, dodge and sponge tools. The painting tools are used to add or edit the pixel information in an image. If you want to keep your options open you may want to do all your painting work on a separate new layer, and you can do this with all the above tools except for the eraser tools. But in some instances you may need to adjust the sample options so that you sample the layers below or all layers.

When you select any of the above tools, the first thing you will want to do is to choose a brush size, which you can do by going to the Brush Preset Picker (the second item from the left in the Options palette), select a brush, then double-click on the chosen preset to close the Brush Preset Picker. Normally you will be able to choose from many different shapes and sizes of brushes and you can also use the Master Diameter and Hardness sliders to modify these brush size/shape characteristics.

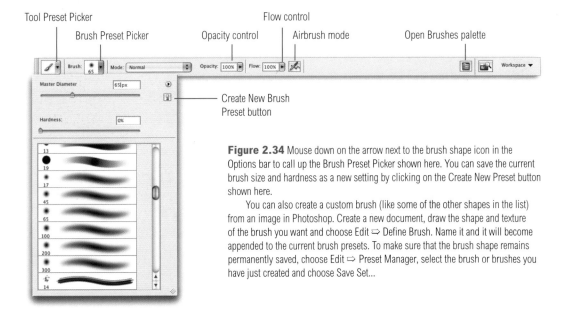

Tool Preset Picker

Brush Preset Picker

Opacity control

Flow control

Airbrush mode

Open Brushes palette

Create New Brush Preset button

**Figure 2.34** Mouse down on the arrow next to the brush shape icon in the Options bar to call up the Brush Preset Picker shown here. You can save the current brush size and hardness as a new setting by clicking on the Create New Preset button shown here.

You can also create a custom brush (like some of the other shapes in the list) from an image in Photoshop. Create a new document, draw the shape and texture of the brush you want and choose Edit ⇨ Define Brush. Name it and it will become appended to the current brush presets. To make sure that the brush shape remains permanently saved, choose Edit ⇨ Preset Manager, select the brush or brushes you have just created and choose Save Set...

## On-the-fly brush changes

Instead of visiting the Brush Picker every time you want
to adjust the size or hardness of a brush, you will find it is
much quicker to use the square bracket keys as described in
Figures 2.35 and 2.36 to make these on-the-fly changes.

If you *ctrl* right mouse-click in the image you are
working on, this will open up the Brush Preset menu,
directly next to the cursor. Click on the brush preset you
wish to select and once you start painting, the Brush Preset
menu will close (or alternatively, use the *esc* key). Note
that if you are painting with a Wacom stylus you can close
this pop-up dialog by lifting the stylus off the tablet and
squeezing the double-click button. If you *ctrl* *Shift*-click
right mouse *Shift*-click in the image while using a brush
tool, this will open the blending mode list. These blend
modes are like rules which govern how the painting pixels
are applied to the pixels in the image below. For example,
if you paint using the Color mode, you can apply color
only to an image. And if you click on the Edit Brush...
menu item this will once more reveal the Brush Preset list.

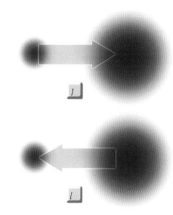

**Figure 2.35** There is no need to visit the
Brush or Tool presets each time you want to
change the size of a brush. Use the right square
bracket key *]* to make a brush bigger and the
left square bracket key *[* to make it smaller.

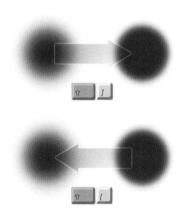

**Figure 2.36** Combine the square bracket keys
with the Shift key on your keyboard and you can
use the *Shift* *]* to make a brush edge harder
and *Shift* *[* to make a brush edge softer.

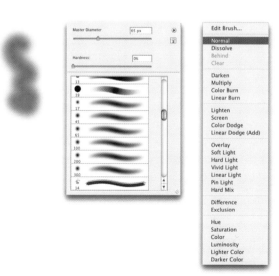

**Figure 2.37** When using any of the paint tools in Photoshop, a *ctrl* right
mouse-click will open the Brush Preset menu, while a *ctrl* *Shift*-click or right
mouse *Shift*-click will reveal the brush blending modes list shown here.

## Brushes palette

So far we have looked at the Brush Preset options which are used to determine the brush shape and size. The Brushes palette, however, is used to define the brush attributes. The brush attributes include things like how the opacity of the brush is applied when painting. And if you are using a pressure sensitive pen stylus, there are additional options in the Brushes palette that will enable you to link the pen pressure of the stylus to how much paint opacity will be applied. You can switch this behavior on or off and determine things like how the paint opacity and flow will be controlled by the pen pressure or the angle of tilt of the pen. The following section explains in more detail how these settings work.

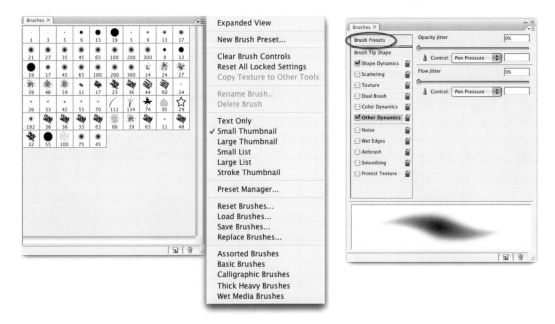

**Figure 2.38** If you open the Brushes palette, the default view will just list the various brush shapes. If you go to the Brushes palette menu options and click on Expanded View, this will reveal the extra brush options shown in the second palette view. When Brush Presets is selected (circled) the brush shapes list will remain in the right-hand section of the Brushes palette. But if you click on one of the brush attributes in the list, the right-hand section will change to reveal the options settings. Specific brush panel settings can be locked by clicking on a Lock button.

### Brushes palette options

The following notes and tips on working with the Brushes palette will apply to most, but not all of the painting tools.

The Jitter controls will introduce randomness into the brush dynamics behavior. Increasing the opacity jitter means that the opacity will still respond according to how much pen pressure is applied, but there will be a built-in random fluctuation to the opacity that will vary even more as the jitter value is increased. The flow setting governs the speed at which the paint is applied. To understand how the brush flow dynamics work, try selecting a brush and quickly paint a series of brush strokes at a low and then a high flow rate. When the flow rate is low, less paint will be applied, but more paint will be applied if you increase the flow setting, apply more pressure, or paint more slowly. Other tools like the dodge and burn toning tools use the terms Exposure and Strength. Essentially these have the same meaning as the opacity controls.

The Shape Dynamics can be adjusted to introduce jitter into the size angle and roundness of the brush. And the scattering controls will enable you to produce broad, sweeping brush strokes with a random scatter. The Color Dynamics let you introduce random color variation to the paint color. The foreground/background color control can be useful as this will let you vary the paint color between the foreground and background color, according to how much pressure is applied (see Figure 2.39). The Dual Brush and Texture Dynamics can introduce texture and more interactive complexity to the brush texture (it is worth experimenting with the Scale control in the Dual Brush options). The Texture Dynamics utilize a choice of blending modes for different effects and of course you can add a custom texture of your own design, direct from the Pattern presets.

Photoshop no longer has a separate airbrush tool. Instead, all the brush tools have an Airbrush mode button in the Options palette.

### Pressure sensitive control

The Wacom™ Intuos range includes some pens that have a thumbwheel control and in Photoshop you can exploit all of these responsive built-in Wacom features to the full via the brush dynamics settings. You will notice that as you alter the brush dynamics settings, the brush stroke preview below will change to reflect what the expected outcome would be if you had drawn a squiggly line that faded from zero to full pen pressure (likewise with the tilt and thumbwheel). This visual feedback is extremely useful as it allows you to experiment with the brush dynamics settings in the Brushes palette and learn how these will affect the brush dynamics behavior.

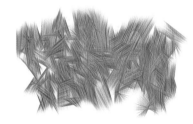

**Figure 2.39** In this example, I selected the Aurora brush preset and experimented with the pen tilt settings for things such as the size and angle in the Shape Dynamics settings. I then set turquoise as the foreground color and purple for the background. I used a pen pressure setting to vary the paint color from foreground to background. I created the doodle in this image by twisting the pen angles as I applied the brush strokes.

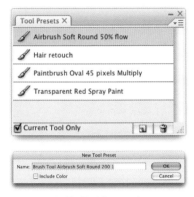

Figure 2.40 The Tool Presets palette.

## Brush tool presets

When you have finished tweaking the Brushes palette dynamics and other settings, you can save a combination of the brush preset shape/size setting, the Brushes palette attribute settings plus the brush blending mode (and brush color even) as a single Brush tool preset. To do this, go to the Tool Presets palette and click on the New Preset button at the bottom (see Figure 2.40). Or, you can mouse down on the Tool Preset Picker in the Options palette and click on the New Brush setting button. Give the brush shape a name and click OK to append it to the current list. Once you have save a brush tool preset, you can access it at any time via the Tool Presets palette or the Tool Preset menu in the Options palette.

## Tools for filling

The various shape tools and line tool are of more use to graphic designers for creating things like buttons or adding vector shapes to a design layout. In Figure 2.41, you can see an example of how a custom vector shape had been added on top of a gradient fill layer.

The paint bucket tool is like a combination of a magic wand selection combined with an Edit ⇨ Fill with foreground color command. As much as I try to ignore the paint bucket, people keep coming up with ways to prove me wrong. Recently, photographer Stuart Weston showed me how he used the paint bucket tool to add small filled patches of color to a large composite fashion image. The final image looked really good!

The gradient tool should be of more interest to photographers. You can also use the Adjustment layer menu to add a solid or Gradient Fill layer to an image, and Gradient Fill layers can be applied in this way to create gradient filter type effects (see pages 468–469). But you will also find that the gradient tool comes in use when you want to edit the contents of a layer mask. For example, you can add a black to white gradient to a layer mask to apply a gradient fade to the layer opacity.

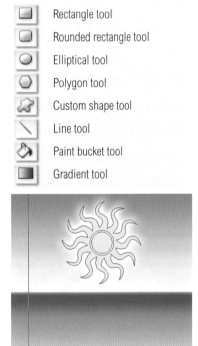

Rectangle tool
Rounded rectangle tool
Elliptical tool
Polygon tool
Custom shape tool
Line tool
Paint bucket tool
Gradient tool

Figure 2.41 In this example I filled the background using a linear gradient tool and the sun was added as a custom shape layer.

## Tools for drawing

If you want to become a good retoucher, then at some stage you are going to have to bite the bullet and learn how to use the pen tools. The marquee, lasso and magic wand selection tools are fine for making approximate selections, but the pen tools are essential for all those other times where you need to create precision selections and masks.

The pen tool group includes the main pen tool, a freeform pen tool (which in essence is not much better than the lasso or magnetic lasso tools) and modifier tools to add, delete or modify path points. There are several examples coming up in Chapter 8 where I will show you how to use the pen tools to draw a path.

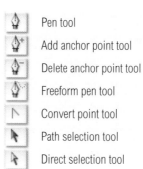

Pen tool

Add anchor point tool

Delete anchor point tool

Freeform pen tool

Convert point tool

Path selection tool

Direct selection tool

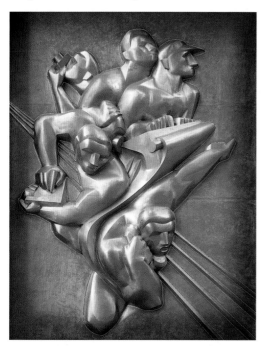

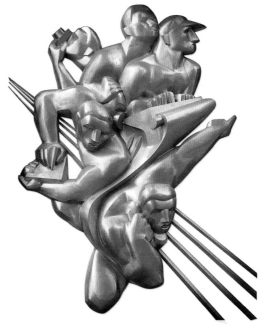

**Figure 2.42** If you need to isolate an object or create a cut-out like the one shown here, the only way to do so is to use the pen and pen modifier tools to draw a path outline. You see, with a photograph like this, there is very little color differentiation between the object and the background, and it would be very difficult for an auto masking tool to accurately predict the edges in this image. I timed myself and it took me between 8-9 minutes to draw the path outline that was used to create the cut-out shown on the right.

Crop tool

 Move tool

 Eraser

 Magic eraser

 Background eraser

 Clone stamp

 Pattern stamp

 Spot healing brush

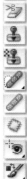 Healing brush

 Patch tool

 Red eye tool

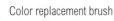 Color replacement brush

## Image editing tools

The line-up of editing tools has changed quite a bit from the early days of Photoshop. You have a crop tool that can be used to trim pictures or enlarge the canvas area.

The eraser tools are still there should you wish to erase the pixels directly, although these days it is more common to use layer masks to selectively hide or show the contents of a layer. The background eraser and magic eraser tools do offer some degree of automated erasing, but I would be more inclined to use a tool such as the Extract command from the Filter menu, or the new quick selection tool even for this type of masking.

The clone stamp tool has been around since the beginning of Photoshop and is an essential tool for all types of retouching work. You can use the clone stamp to sample pixels from one part of the image and paint with them in another. The clone stamp tools were joined recently by the healing brush and patch tool which work almost exactly the same as the clone stamp, but cleverly blend the pixels around the edges of where the retouching is applied, to produce almost flawless results. The patch tool functions exactly like the healing brush except it uses a selection to define the area to be healed. And the spot healing brush is rather clever because you don't even need to set a sample point, you simply click and paint over the blemishes you want to remove.

Providing you use the right flash settings on your camera it should be possible to avoid red eye occurring in your portrait photographs. But for all those times when the camera flash leaves your subjects looking like beasts of the night, the red eye tool provides a fairly basic and easy way to auto-correct such photographs. And the color replacement brush is kind of like a semi-smart color blend mode painting tool which analyzes the area you are painting over and is useful for making quick and easy color changes without the need to create a selection mask first.

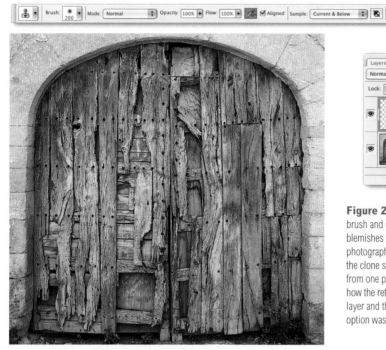

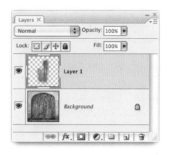

**Figure 2.43** I mostly use the healing brush and clone stamp tools to retouch small blemishes or to remove sensor dust marks from photographs. In this example I have shown how the clone stamp tool can be used to paint detail from one part of an image onto another. Note how the retouching is applied to an empty new layer and the Sample: 'Current & Below' layers option was selected in the Options palette.

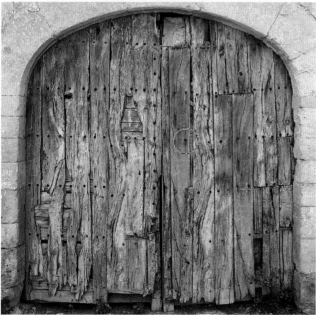

## Blending modes

Photoshop image layers can be made to blend with those underneath using any of the 25 different blending modes. Layer effects/styles allow you to add effects such as drop shadows, gradient/pattern fills or glows to any layer. Custom styles can be loaded from and saved to the Styles palette. You will find some of the sub-menu options for layers are duplicated in the Layer main menu.

## Working with Layers

Photoshop layers allow you to build and edit an image using multiple layered sections. A layer can be an image element, such as a duplicate of the background layer, a copied selection made into a layer, or another Photoshop document that has been copied across to an existing document. Or, it can be a text vector shape layer. Adjustment layers are like image adjustment instructions that are applied in a layer form. Layers can be placed together in groups, which makes the layer organization easier to manage and you can apply masking to the contents of a layer with either a pixel layer mask or a vector mask. There are plenty of examples throughout this book where I will be showing you how to use layers.

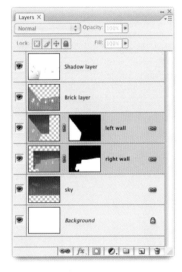

**Figure 2.44** Note that in Photoshop CS2 onwards, layer linking is controlled via a Link button at the bottom of the palette.

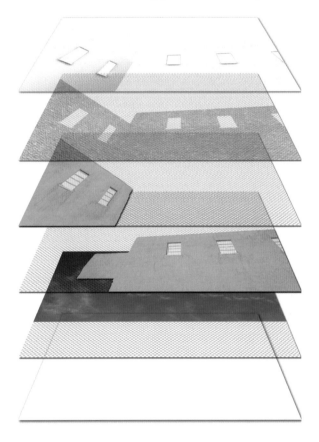

## Automating Photoshop

Why spend more time than you have to performing repetitive tasks, when Photoshop is able to automate many of these processes for you? For example, the Actions palette will let you load and save Photoshop actions, which are basically recordable Photoshop scripts. In Figure 2.45 you can see a screen shot of the Actions palette displaying an expanded view of the Default Actions set. As you can see from the action descriptions, these will perform automated tasks such as adding a vignette or creating a wood frame edge effect. OK, these are not exactly the sort of actions you would use everyday, but if you go to the palette fly-out menu and select Load Actions... you will be taken to the Photoshop CS3/Presets/Photoshop Actions folder. Here you will find lots of useful actions that would be worth installing. If someone sends you a Photoshop action, then all you have to do is just double-click it and this will automatically install the action in the Actions folder and if Photoshop is not running at the time, this step will also launch the program as well.

To run an action, you will usually need to have a document already open in Photoshop and simply press the Play button. It is also quite easy to record your own custom actions, and once you get the hang of doing this you can progress to using the File ➪ Automate ➪ Batch... function to apply a recorded action to a batch of images, as well as converting actions into droplets, which are like self-contained batch action operations. In Chapter 15 I will explain in more detail how to automate Photoshop using Actions, batch processes and droplets.

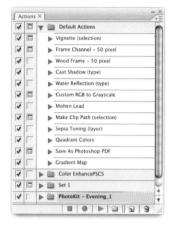

**Figure 2.45** The Actions palette.

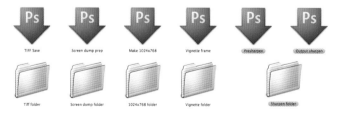

**Figure 2.46** With Photoshop droplets you can apply a batch action operation by simply dragging and dropping a file or folder onto a droplet.

## Nudging layers and selections

The keyboard arrow keys can be used to nudge a layer or selection in 1 pixel (10 pixels with the *Shift* key also held down) increments. A series of nudges count as a single Photoshop step in history and is undone with a single undo or step back in history.

## Move tool alignment options

The move Options palette now also integrates the alignment options that were previously only listed in the Layer menu. To find out more about layer alignment and distribution, refer to page 398.

## Move tool

The move tool can perform many functions such as moving layer contents, directly moving layers from one document to another, copying layers, applying transforms, plus selecting and aligning multiple layers. In this respect the move tool might be more accurately described as a move/transform/alignment tool. The Transform mode is apparent whenever the Show Bounding Box is checked (initially a dotted bounding box appears around the object). And when you mouse down on the bounding box handles, the Options palette will change to display the numeric transform controls.

The move tool can also be activated at any time when another tool is selected by holding down the ⌘ *ctrl* key (except for the slice, slice select, hand, pen tool or path selection tools). Holding down the ⌥ *alt* key while the move tool is selected will let you copy a layer or selection contents. Therefore it is useful to remember that using the ⌥ *alt* key plus ⌘ *ctrl* (the move tool shortcut) will let you make a copy of a layer or selection contents when any other tool is selected (apart from those I just listed).

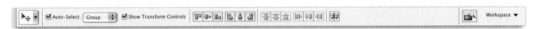

**Figure 2.47** The move Options palette.

## Group or layer

There is a menu item in the move tool Options palette that will allow you to choose between Group or Layer auto-selection. When Layer is selected, Photoshop will auto-select individual layers. When Group is selected, Photoshop will auto-select whole layer groups.

## Layer selection using the move tool

When the move tool is selected, dragging with the move tool will move the layer or selection contents (the cursor does not have to be centered on the object or selection, it can be anywhere in the image window). When the Auto-Select Layer option is switched on, the move tool will auto-select the uppermost layer containing the most opaque image data below the cursor. This can be useful when you have a large numbers of image layers stacked up. The move tool also makes multiple layer selection possible, because when the move tool is in the Auto Select Layer mode you can marquee drag with the move tool from outside the canvas area to select multiple layers, the same way as you make a marquee selection using the mouse cursor to select multiple folders or documents in the Finder.

It is also worth noting that if you have the move tool selected and the Auto Select Layer option is currently unchecked, holding down ⌘ *ctrl* will temporarily invert the state of the move tool to Auto Select Layer mode.

Where you have many layers that overlap, remember there is a Contextual mode for the move tool that will help you target specific layers (use *ctrl* right mouse-click to access the Contextual layer menu). Any layer with an opacity greater than 50% will show up in the contextual menu, allowing you to select a specific layer beneath the cursor point with greater precision.

### Align/Distribute layers
When several layers are linked together, you can click on the align and distribute buttons in the Options bar as an alternative to navigating via the Layer ⇨ Align Linked and Distribute Linked menus (see Chapter 9 for more about the Align and Distribute commands).

### Layer selection shortcuts
Note that the move tool selection will not select locked layers. So if you use the Auto Select layer mode to marquee drag across the image to make a layer selection, the background layer will not be included in the selection. You can also at any time use the ⌘ ⌥ A *ctrl* ⌥ A shortcut to select all layers.

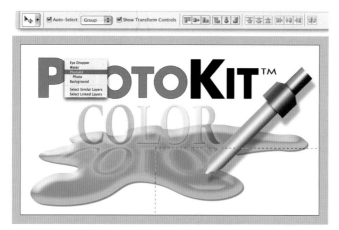

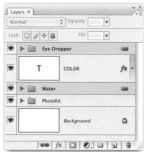

**Figure 2.48** When the move tool is selected and the Auto Select Layer box is checked, you can marquee drag with the move tool from outside of the canvas area inwards to select specific multiple layers. When the Auto Select Layer option is deselected, you can hold down ⌘ *ctrl* to temporarily switch the move tool to the Auto Select Layer mode.

Hand tool

Zoom tool

Eyedropper

Color sampler

Measure tool

Count tool

Notes tool

Audio annotation tool

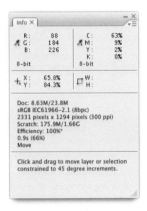

Figure 2.49 The Info palette showing an eyedropper color reading, a measurement readout plus two color sampler readouts below.

### Zoom shortcuts

Another zoom shortcut is ⌘ + ctrl + (Command-click the ═ key) to zoom in and ⌘ − ctrl − (next to the ═ key) to zoom out.

# Navigation and information tools

When you are viewing an image in close-up, you can select the hand tool and drag to scroll the image on the screen. To zoom in on an image, either click with the zoom tool to magnify, or drag with the zoom tool, marqueeing the area you wish to magnify. This combines a zoom and scroll function in one (in Normal mode, a plus icon appears inside the magnifying glass icon). To zoom out, hold down the ⌥ alt key and click (the plus sign is replaced with a minus sign). And holding down the Spacebar at any time will access the hand tool. Holding down the Spacebar and then the ⌘ ctrl key calls up the zoom tool (except when you are editing text). Holding down the Spacebar+⌥ alt calls up the zoom out tool. The hand and zoom tools also have another navigational function. Double-click the hand tool to make the image fit to screen and double-click the zoom tool to magnify the image to 100%.

The eyedropper tool can be used to measure pixel values directly from a Photoshop document – these values will be displayed in the Info palette, as shown in Figure 2.49. The color sampler tools can be used to place up to four color samplers in an image for persistent measurement of the pixel values. This is useful for those times when you need to closely monitor the pixel values as you make adjustments to an image. The measure tool can be used to measure distance and angles in an image and again, this data is displayed in the Info palette. The count tool is new to Photoshop CS3, but is only available in the extended version and is perhaps more useful to those working in areas like medical research where you can use the count tool to count the number of cells in a microscope image.

The notes tool is really handy for adding sticky notes to an open image in Photoshop. I use this tool quite a lot at work. Whenever a client calls me to discuss a retouching job, I will open the image, click next to the area that needs to be worked on and type in notes to describe what further retouching needs to be done. The audio annotation tool is a sound recording equivalent of the notes tool.

## History

The History feature was introduced in Photoshop 5.0 and
back then it was considered a real breakthrough feature,
because for the first time Photoshop offered multiple undos
during a single Photoshop editing session. History can
play a really important role in the way you use Photoshop.
I thought here would be a good opportunity for me to
describe this feature in more detail and explain how history
can help you use Photoshop more efficiently.

As you work on an individual image, Photoshop
will record a history of image states as steps which can
be viewed in the History palette. If you want to reverse
a step, you can still use the conventional Edit ⇨ Undo
command ( ⌘ Z  ctrl Z ), but if you visit the History
palette, you can go back as many stages in the edit process
as you have saved history steps. The history steps can also
be saved as Snapshots, which will temporarily prevent
them from 'slipping off the radar' and becoming deleted
as more history steps are created. One can look at the
history as a multiple undo feature in which you can reverse
through up to 1000 image states, but it is actually a far
more sophisticated tool than just that. For example, there
is a non-linear history option for multiple history path
recording and a history source column that allows you to
select a history state to sample from when working with
the history brush. Painting from history can save you from
tedious workarounds like having to duplicate a portion
of the image to another layer, retouching this layer and
merging back down to the underlying layer again.

### The History palette

The History palette displays the sequence of Photoshop
states recorded during a Photoshop session and its main
purpose is to let you manage and access the history states
recorded by Photoshop. To revert to a previous state, drag
the slider up the list of history states or, alternatively, you
can click directly on a specific history state. In Figure 2.50,
I carried out a simple one-step undo by clicking on the one
but last history step.

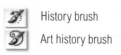

History brush

Art history brush

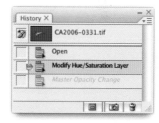

**Figure 2.50** A previous history state can be
selected by clicking on the history state name in
the History palette. When the History palette is set
to its default configuration, you will notice how the
history states that appear after the one selected
will be dimmed. If you have moved back, and then
you make further edits to the image, the history
states after the selected history state will be
deleted. You can change this behavior by selecting
Allow Non-linear History in the History palette
options (see history settings pages 76–77).

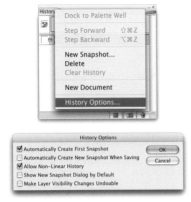

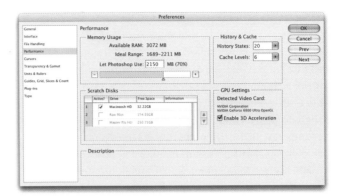

**Figure 2.51** The number of history states can be set via the Performance section of the Photoshop preferences dialog.

**Figure 2.52** The History Options are accessed via the History palette fly-out menu. These will allow you to decide the snapshot settings. I usually prefer to check the Allow Non-Linear History option, because this enables me to use the History feature to its full potential (see page 80).

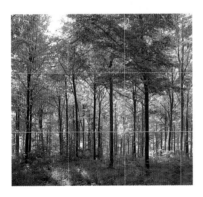

**Figure 2.53** This picture shows the underlying tiled structure of a Photoshop image. In this example we have a width of four tiles and a height of three tiles. This is the clue to how History works as economically as possible. The History stores the minimum amount of data necessary at each step in Photoshop's memory. So if only one or two tile areas are altered by a Photoshop action, only the data change for those tiles is recorded.

## History settings and memory usage

The number of recorded histories can be set in the Photoshop Performance preferences (see Figure 2.51). When the maximum number of history states has been reached, the earliest history state at the top of the list will be discarded. Note that if you reduce the number of history states allowed, via the preferences, any subsequent action will immediately cause all earlier states beyond this new limit to be discarded. To set the options for the History palette, mouse down on the fly-out menu and select History Options... I'll come on to the snapshot settings shortly, but at this stage you may want to consider enabling non-linear history. This will allow you to select a previous history state, but instead of undoing those steps between the earlier state and the latest, and deleting them, non-linear history will allow you to shoot off in a new direction and still preserve all the original history states. Make Layer Visibility Changes Undoable is a recent addition and this simply makes switching layer visibility on or off a recordable step in history.

The History cleverly makes use of the image tiling to limit any unnecessary drain on memory usage. Conventional wisdom would suggest that any multiple undo feature is bound to tie up vast amounts of scratch disk space to store all the previous image states. However, proper testing of History indicates that this is not really the case. It is true that a series of global Photoshop steps may cause the scratch disk usage to rise, but localized changes will not. You can observe this for yourself by monitoring the scratch disk usage over a number of Photoshop steps. This is because every Photoshop image is made up of tiled sections. When a large image is in the process of redrawing you may see these tiles rendering across the screen. Photoshop's History memorizes the changes that take place in each tile only. If a brush stroke takes place across two image tiles, only the changes taking place in those tiles are updated. When a global change takes place such as a filter effect, the whole of the image area is updated and the scratch disk usage will rise accordingly. A savvy Photoshop user will want to customize the History feature to record a reasonable number of histories, while at the same time being aware of the need to change this setting if the history usage is likely to place too heavy a burden on the scratch disk. The Figure 2.54 example demonstrates that successive histories need not consume an escalating amount of memory. After the first adjustment layer, successive adjustment layers have little impact on the scratch disk usage (only the screen preview is being changed). Clone stamp tool cloning and brush work affect changes in small tiled sections. Only the Flatten Image and Unsharp Mask filter which are applied at the end add a noticeable amount to the scratch disk usage.

The Purge History command in the Edit ⇨ Purge menu provides a useful way to keep the amount of scratch disk memory used under control. If the picture you are working with is exceptionally large, then having more than one undo can be both wasteful and unnecessary, so you should perhaps consider restricting the number of recordable history states. On the other hand, if multiple history undos are well within the scratch disk memory limits of your system, then make the most of them. And remember, History is not just there as a mistake correcting tool, it has great potential for mixing composites from previous image states.

| History stages | Scratch disk |
|---|---|
| Open file | 793 MB |
| Levels adjustment | 884 MB |
| 16 bit to 8 bit | 938 MB |
| Healing brush | 968 MB |
| Healing brush | 980 MB |
| Healing brush | 992 MB |
| Marquee selection | 974 MB |
| Feather selection | 990 MB |
| Inverse selection | 1006 MB |
| Add adjustment layer | 1050 MB |
| Flatten image | 1100 MB |
| Unsharp mask filter | 1160 MB |

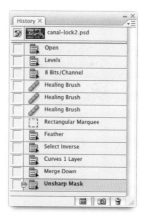

**Figure 2.54** The accompanying table shows how the scratch disk usage will fluctuate during a typical Photoshop session. The opened image was 63 MB in size and 1300 MB of memory was allocated to Photoshop. The scratch disk overhead is always quite big at the beginning of each Photoshop session, but notice how there is little proportional increase in scratch disk size with each added history state.

## Art history brush

The art history brush is something of an oddity. It is a history brush that allows you to paint from history but does so via a brush which distorts the sampled data. It can be used to create impressionist type painting effects. You can learn more about this tool from the Photoshop CS3 for Photographers Help Guide that can be installed from the DVD.

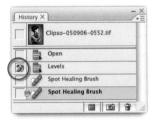

**Figure 2.55** A previous history state can be selected as the source for the history brush by going to the History palette and clicking in the empty space to the left of the history state you want to paint from using the history brush.

## History brush

The history brush can be used to paint from a previous history state. To do this you don't change the current history state, but instead you set a source history state for the history brush, by clicking a box in the column next to the history state you wish to sample from. In Figure 2.55 you can see how I set the Levels history state as the history source. The small history brush icon indicates which history state (or snapshot) is currently being used as the source. I was then able to paint with the history brush from this previous history state. The history brush therefore allows you to selectively restore the previously held image information as desired. In the Figure 2.55 example I was using the history brush to paint over the areas where I had applied the healing brush, in order to restore those parts of the picture to the Levels adjusted history state.

## Use of history versus undo

As you will have seen so far, the History feature is capable of being a lot more than a repeat Edit ⇨ Undo command. Although the History feature is described as a multiple undo, it is important not to confuse Photoshop History with the role of the Undo command. For example, there are a number of Photoshop procedures that are only undoable with the Edit ⇨ Undo command, like intermediate changes made when setting the shadows and highlights in the Levels dialog. Plus there are things which can be undone with Edit ⇨ Undo that have nothing to do with the history. If you delete an action or delete a history, these are also only recoverable using Edit ⇨ Undo. The Undo command is toggled and this is because the majority of Photoshop users like to switch quickly back and forth to see a before and after version of the image. The current combination of Undo commands and history has been carefully planned to provide the most flexible and logical approach. History is not just an 'oh I messed up. Let's go back a few stages' feature, the way some other programs work; it is a tool designed to ease the workflow and allow you more creative options in Photoshop.

## Snapshots

To create a snapshot, click on the Snapshot button at the bottom of the palette. Snapshots are stored above the divider and this records the image in its current state and prevents this version of the image from being overwritten for as long as the document is open and being edited. The default operating mode stores a snapshot of the opening image state. You can choose not to store an opening image this way if you prefer or take more snapshots at any time to add to the list. This feature is useful if you have an image state that you wish to temporarily store and not lose as you make further image changes. There is no real constraint on the number of snapshots that can be stored, and in the History palette options you can check to automatically generate a new snapshot each time you save (which will also be time-stamped). You can also click the Duplicate image button (next to the Snapshot button) to create a duplicate image state and save this as a separate file.

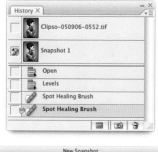

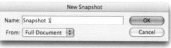

**Figure 2.56** To record a new snapshot, click on the New Snapshot button at the bottom of the History palette. This will record a snapshot of the history at this stage. If you ⌥ alt-click the button, there are three options: Full Document, which stores all layers intact; Merged Layers, which stores a composite; and Current Layer, which stores just the currently active layer. Note if you have the Show New Snapshot dialog by Default turned on in the History palette options, the New Snapshot dialog appear directly, without you having to ⌥ alt-click the New Snapshot button. The adjacent New Document button will create a duplicate image of the active image in its current history state.

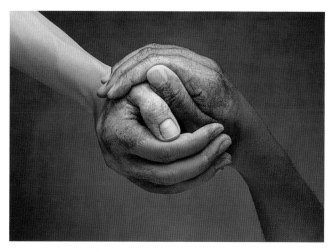

**Figure 2.57** Photographer Jeff Schewe has had a long standing connection with the Adobe Photoshop program and its development. The origins of the History feature can perhaps be traced back to a seminar where he used the Globe Hands image shown here to demonstrate his use of the Snapshot feature in Photoshop 2.5. Jeff was able to save multiple snapshots of different image states in Photoshop and then selectively paint back from them. This was all way before Layers and History were introduced in Photoshop. Chief Photoshop Engineer Mark Hamburg was suitably impressed by Jeff's technique and the ability to paint from snapshots became an important part of the History feature. Everyone had been crying out for a multiple undo in Photoshop, but when History was first introduced in Photoshop 5.0 it came as quite a surprise to discover just how much the History feature would allow you to do.

## Non-linear history

Non-linear history enables you to branch off in different directions and recombine effects without the need for duplicating separate layers. Non-linear history is not an easy concept to grasp. The best way to think about non-linear history is to imagine each history state having more than one 'linear' progression, allowing the user to branch off in different directions instead of as a single chain of events in Photoshop. You can take an image down several different routes, whilst working on the same file in a single Photoshop session. Snapshots of history branches can be taken and painted in with other history branches without the need to save duplicate files.

Non-linear history requires a little more thinking on your part in order to monitor and recall image states, but ultimately makes for more efficient use of the available scratch disk space. And overall, I find it useful to have this switched on all the time, regardless of whether I need to push non-linear to its limits or not. To see some practical examples of how to use this and other History features in a typical Photoshop retouching session, see Chapter 7.

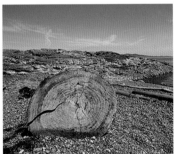 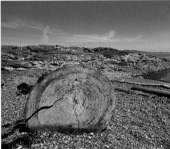 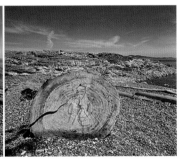

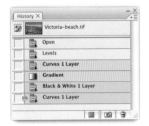

**Figure 2.58** The Non-linear history option allows you to branch off in different directions and simultaneously maintain a record of each history path up to the maximum number of history states that can be allowed. Shown here are three history states: a Levels adjusted version, another with a sky gradient and lastly a toned monochrome version (I colored the history states in the History palette to make the illustration clearer).

# Preset Manager

The Preset Manager manages all your presets from within the one dialog. It keeps track of: brushes, swatches, gradients, styles, patterns, layer effect contours and custom shapes. Figure 2.59 shows how you can use the Preset Manager to edit a current set of Custom Shapes. You can append or replace an existing set of presets via the Preset Manager options. The Preset Manager can also be customized to display the preset information in different ways. In Figure 2.60 I used a Large List to display thumbnails of the gradient presets.

## Loading presets

If you double-click any Photoshop setting that is outside the Photoshop folder, it will automatically load the Photoshop program and append the preset to the Preset Manager settings.

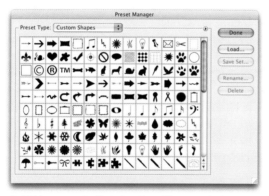

**Figure 2.59** You can use the Photoshop Preset Manager to load custom settings or replace them with one of the pre-supplied defaults. Presets include: Brushes, Swatches, Gradients, Styles, Patterns, Contours and Custom Shapes.

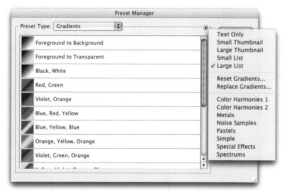

**Figure 2.60** Apart from being able to load and replace presets, you are able to choose how the presets are displayed. In the case of Gradients, it is immensely useful to be able to see a thumbnail preview alongside the name of the gradient.

The Bridge work space can be customized and there are already a number of work space presets ready to load which are available from the Window ⇨ Workspace menu. The palettes can be grouped together in different ways and the palette dividers dragged so that if you wish, the preview panel can fill the Bridge interface more fully.

**Return to Photoshop**
Most of the time you will probably click on the Bridge button in Photoshop to launch Bridge and return to Photoshop every time after you have opened a file. But you can also toggle between the two programs when you are not opening images by using: ⌘ *Shift* O *ctrl* *Shift* O. This will take you to Bridge and using the same shortcut while in Bridge will return you to the last used application.

# Adobe Bridge CS3

Bridge is designed to provide you with an integrated way to navigate through the folders on your computer and provide compatibility with all the Creative Suite applications. The Bridge interface will allow you to inspect images in a folder, make decisions about which ones you like best, rearrange them in the content panel, hide the ones you don't like and so on. At the simplest level you can use Bridge to quickly review the images in a folder and open up the ones you wish to work with in Photoshop. At a more advanced level, you can perform batch operations, share properties between files by synchronizing the metadata information, apply Camera Raw settings to a selection of images and use the Filters panel to fine-tune your image selections. It is very easy to switch back and forth between Photoshop and Bridge and one of the key benefits of having Bridge operate as a separate program is that Photoshop is no longer fighting with the processor when you use Bridge to perform image browsing tasks.

## The Bridge interface

Bridge can be accessed from Photoshop by choosing File ⇨ Browse... or by clicking on the Open Bridge button which is always present in the Photoshop Options palette (you can also set the Photoshop preferences so that Bridge launches automatically as you launch Photoshop). Bridge will initially open a new window pointing to the last visited folder of files. You can have multiple Bridge windows open at once. This is very useful if you want to manage files better by being able to drag them from one folder to another more easily. It also saves having to navigate back and forth between different folders. To make multiple Bridge windows more manageable, you can click on the Compact mode button in the top right corner to toggle shrinking/expanding the Bridge windows.

It makes sense to resize the Bridge window to fill the screen and if you have a dual monitor setup you can always arrange to have the Bridge window (or windows) displayed on the secondary monitor. Image folders can be

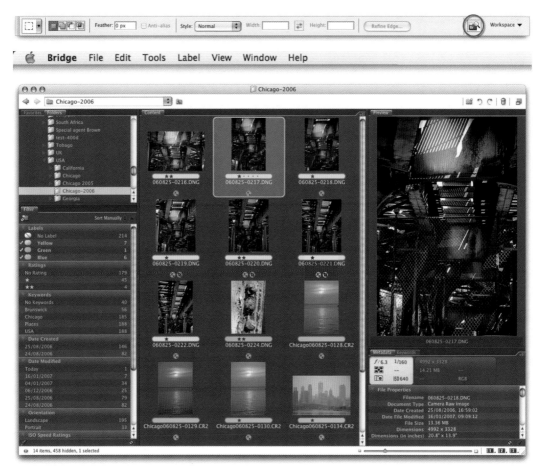

**Figure 2.61** The Bridge CS3 interface consists of three column zones which are used to contain the Bridge panel components. This will allow you to customize the Bridge layout in any number of ways. For a complete overview of the components that make up the Bridge interface please refer to page 510.

selected via the Folders or Favorites panels and the folder contents viewed in the Content panel area as thumbnail images. When you click on a thumbnail, an enlarged view of individually selected images can be seen in the Preview panel and images can be opened by double-clicking on the thumbnail. The Bridge window can remain open after you open an image without compromising Photoshop's performance.

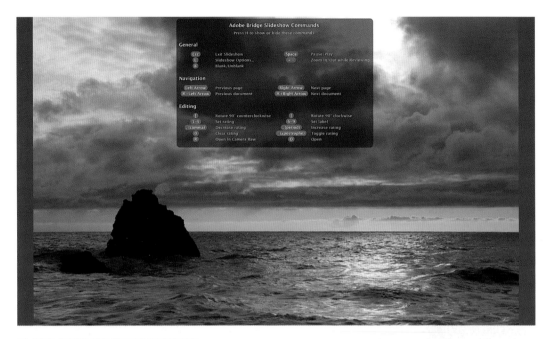

## Saving from raw files

If you save an image opened up from a raw file original, Photoshop will by default suggest you save it using the Photoshop native file format. You are always forced to save it as something else and never to overwrite the original raw image. Most raw formats have unique extensions anyway like .crw or .nef. But Canon did once decide to use a .tif extension for some of their raw file formats (so that the thumbnail would show up in their browser program). The danger here was that if you overrode the Photoshop default behavior and tried saving an opened Canon raw image as a TIFF, and you also ignored the warning you were about to overwrite the original image, you did run the risk of losing the original raw file!

**Figure 2.62** You can use the Bridge application View ⇨ Slideshow mode to display all selected images in a slideshow form. You can make all your essential review and edit decisions with this easy-to-use interface. Press the **H** key to call up the Slideshow shortcuts shown here.

## Opening and saving images from Bridge

The Bridge interface offers you an easy way to open images up in Photoshop. All you have to do is select a thumbnail and double-click to open it. Or you can choose File ⇨ Open from the main Bridge menu. If you are opening a raw or DNG image, the file will automatically open via the Camera Raw dialog shown in Figure 2.63. And if you are opening multiple raw images from Bridge you will see a filmstrip of thumbnails down the left hand side of the Camera Raw dialog. But there is also a preference setting in Bridge CS3 that will allow you to open up JPEG and TIFF images via Camera Raw as well. The advantages of using Camera Raw are discussed in depth in Chapter 5 and I would say that the main benefits are that any edits you apply in Camera Raw are non-permanent and this latest version in CS3 represents a huge advance in raw processing. But for now, you can often choose just to click on the Auto button in Camera Raw (circled at the top in Figure 2.63) and then click on the Open Image button without concerning yourself too much just yet with what all these controls do. Because when the default settings in Camera Raw are set to Auto, these will automatically optimize the image settings for you. This should give you a good image to start working with in Photoshop and the beauty of working with Camera Raw is that you never overwrite the original master raw file (but do see the warning in the sidebar on page 84 about saving raw files). If you don't like the auto settings Camera Raw is giving you, then it is relatively easy to adjust the tone and color sliders to improve upon the auto adjustment settings.

**Full Screen mode**

If you click on the Full Screen mode button in Camera Raw, you can quickly switch the Camera Raw view to Full Screen mode.

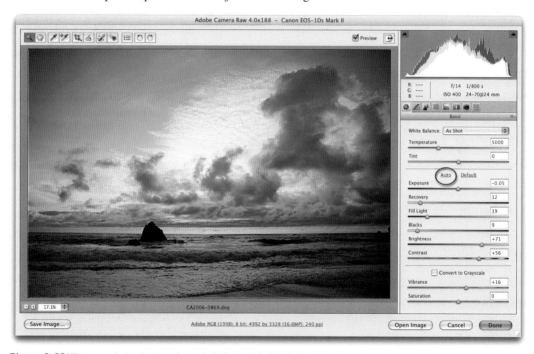

**Figure 2.63** When you select a single raw image in Bridge, and double-click to open, you will be faced with the Camera Raw dialog shown here. Use the sliders in the Basic panel section to fine-tune the tones and colors. If you are not sure how to use these yet, then click on the Auto button (circled) and click Done to OK the adjustments or click Open Image to open the Camera Raw processed image in Photoshop.

## Corrupt files

There are various reasons why a file may have become corrupted and refuses to open. This will often happen to images that have been sent as attachments and is most likely due to a break during transmission somewhere, resulting in missing data.

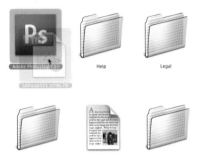

**Figure 2.64** When files won't open up directly in Photoshop the way you expect them to, then it may be because the header is telling the computer to open them up in a different program instead. To force open an image in Photoshop, drag the file icon on top of the Photoshop application icon or an alias or shortcut thereof, such as an icon placed in the dock or on the desktop.

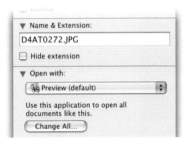

**Figure 2.65** The header information in some files may contain information that tells the operating system to open the image in a program other than Photoshop. On a Macintosh go to the File menu and choose File ⇨ Get Info and under the 'Open with' item, change the default application to Photoshop. On a PC you can do the same thing via the File Registry.

## When files won't open

You don't have to use Bridge to open an image of course. You can open up a file from anywhere on your computer. If an image file is in a file format that Photoshop recognizes, if you double-click, it will open in Photoshop. And if the program is not running at the time, this action will also launch Photoshop as well.

If you use Bridge as the main interface for opening your files in Photoshop then there should be very few times where an image file will fail to open. But if you try to open a file outside of Bridge, there are a few things to watch out for. Every document file on your computer will contain a header section which among other things tells the computer which application should be used to open it with. For example, Microsoft Word documents all have a familiar blue letter icon and Excel spreadsheets, a green cross. Photoshop will recognize nearly all image type documents regardless of the application they may have originated from. But sometimes you will see an image file with an icon for another specific program, like Macintosh Preview, or Internet Explorer. If you double-click these files, they will open in these respective programs. To get around this, use Bridge to open everything. Or, you can use the File ⇨ Open command from within Photoshop. Or, you can drag a selected file or files to the Photoshop program icon or a shortcut or an alias of the program icon. In each of these cases you are overriding the computer operating system reading the file header and forcing the file to open in Photoshop.

Yet there are times when even these methods will fail too and this points to one of two things. Either you have a corrupt file, in which case the damage is most likely permanent. Or, the file extension has been wrongly changed. It says .psd, but is it really a PSD? Is it possible that someone has accidentally renamed the file with an incorrect extension? In these situations, the only way to open it will be to use the Photoshop File ⇨ Open command and navigate to locate the mis-saved image (and then I suggest, resave to register a correct file format).

## Save often

Do you remember the bit at the end of the movie *Stand by Me* where the author shuts down the computer at the end of writing his book? Every computer literate person in the theater wanted to shout 'No, don't. Save first!' It goes without saying that you must always remember to save, often while working in Photoshop. Thankfully you don't come across many crashes when working with the latest operating systems for Macintosh and PC. But that doesn't mean you should relax too much. Saving a file is fairly easy, but there are still some pitfalls to be aware of.

Choosing File ⇨ Save will always create a safe backup of your image, but as with everything else you do on a computer, make sure you are not overwriting the original with an inferior modified version. There is always the danger that you might make permanent changes such as a drastic reduction in the image size, accidentally hit Save and lose the original in the process. But before you close a file you can always go back a step or two in the History palette and resave the image in the state it was in before it was modified.

When you save an image in Photoshop, you are either resaving the file (which will overwrite the original) or forced to save a new version using the Photoshop file format. The determining factor will be the type of file format the image was in when you opened it and how it has been modified in Photoshop. Some of the different file formats are discussed over the next few pages, but the main thing to be aware of is that some file formats will restrict you from being able to save things like layers, pen paths or extra channels. If, for example, you open a JPEG format file in Photoshop and modify it by adding a pen path, you can choose File ⇨ Save and overwrite the original without any problem. But if you open the same file and add a layer or an extra alpha channel, you won't be able to save it as a JPEG any more. This is because although a JPEG file can contain pen paths, it cannot contain layers or additional channels, so it has be saved using a file format that is capable of containing these extra items.

### History saves

Alas, it is not possible to save a history of everything you did to an image, but if you go to the Photoshop preferences you can choose to save the history log information of everything that was done to the image. This can record a log of everything that was done during a Photoshop session and be saved to a central log file or saved to the file's metadata.

The other thing you can do is go to the Actions palette and click to record an action of everything that is done to the image. The major downfall here is that Actions cannot record everything. So for example you cannot record brush strokes within an action.

### Version Cue

Version Cue was first introduced as a component of the original Adobe Creative Suite and is included when you buy a complete Creative Suite set of applications. If you have Version Cue, you can enable it by choosing Preferences ⇨ File Handling and select the checkbox next to Enable Version Cue Workgroup Management. Do this and you will have a choice between using the OS Save or the Adobe Save dialogs. The latter will allow you to make use of the Version Cue features where you can share files with other users over a network and prevent others from over-writing an image file that is already open and in the process of being edited by another user.

### The 'save everything' file formats

There are four main file formats that can be used to save everything you might add to an image such as image layers, type layers, channels and also support 16-bits per channel. These are: TIFF, Photoshop PDF, the large document format, PSB and lastly the native Photoshop file format, PSD. I always favor using the PSD format when saving master RGB images.

### Quick saving

As with all other programs, the keyboard shortcut for saving a file is: ⌘ S
ctrl S . If for some reason you should wish to force Photoshop to save without showing the Save dialog, then use: ⌘ ⌥ S ctrl alt S .

I won't go into lengthy detail about what can and can't be saved using each format. But basically, if you modify a file and those modifications can be saved using the file format the original was in, that's what Photoshop does. If the modifications applied to an image mean it can't be saved using the original file format then it will always default to using the PSD (Photoshop document) format, but could still be saved using TIFF or PDF. PSD is a good format with which to save any master image, since PSD files can contain anything you add in Photoshop and it offers good, lossless file compression, which can ultimately help you save valuable disk space.

### Save As... and Save a Copy

But what if you want to save the image in the original format without saving all the layers, etc. Or, if you want to save an image as a duplicate? When you choose File ⇨ Save, you can force Photoshop to save in the original file format still, by selecting the file format you want to

**Figure 2.66** If you have Version Cue installed and it is enabled in the Photoshop preferences, the Save As dialog will display the standard OS Save dialog mode as shown here, but you will also be able to click on the Use Adobe Dialog button to use the Adobe Save dialog, where you can access the Version Cue features. If the file format you choose to save in won't support all the components in the image such as layers, then a warning triangle will alert you that when you save this document, the layers will not be included. Note that the Mac OS dialog shown here can be collapsed or expanded by clicking on the downward pointing disclosure triangle to toggle the expanded folder view.

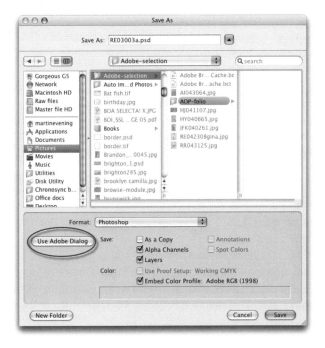

save in from the Format menu list. When you do this the incompatible features will be automatically removed and the image flattened if necessary. The Save dialog will indicate with a warning triangle that certain items will not be saved when you do this.

## File formats

Photoshop supports nearly all current image file formats. And for those that are not supported, you will find some specialized file format plug-ins are supplied as extras on the Photoshop application DVD. Choosing which format to output your images to should be determined by what you want to do with that file and the list can then be further narrowed down to a handful of recognized formats that are appropriate to your needs. You may want to choose a format that is intended for prepress output, or screen-based publishing, or maybe you wish to use a format that is suitable for image archiving only.

### *Photoshop native file format*

The Photoshop file format is a universal file format and therefore a logical choice when saving and archiving your master files since the Photoshop (PSD) format will recognize and contain all known Photoshop features. But so too will the TIFF and PDF file formats. However, there are several reasons why I find it preferable to save the master images using the PSD format. Firstly, it helps me to distinguish the master, layered files from the flattened output files which I usually save as TIFFs. But more importantly, when you have layered images, saving with the PSD format is faster and more efficient compared to using TIFF.

Adobe InDesign and Adobe GoLive enable you to share Photoshop format files between these separate applications so that any changes made to a Photoshop file will be automatically updated in the other program. This modular approach means that most Adobe graphics programs are able to integrate with each other quite easily.

**Maximum compatibility**

Only the Photoshop, PDF, PSB and TIFF formats are capable of supporting all the Photoshop features such as vector masks and image adjustment layers. But for Photoshop format documents to be completely compatible with other programs (especially Photoshop Lightroom), you must ensure you have 'Maximize PSD and PSB Compatibility' checked in the Photoshop File Handling preferences. The reason for this is because Lightroom is unable to read layered PSD files that don't include a saved composite saved within the file. If PSD images fail to be imported into Lightroom, it is most likely because they were saved with this preference switched off.

## TIFF image compression options

An uncompressed TIFF is about the same size as shown in the Image Size dialog box. The TIFF format in Photoshop offers several compression options. LZW is a lossless compression option. Data is compacted and the file size reduced without any image detail being lost. Saving and opening will take longer when LZW is utilized, so some bureaux will request that you do not use it. ZIP is another lossless compression encoding that like LZW is most effective where you have images that contain large areas of a single color. JPEG compression is a lossy compression method and is described more fully in Chapter 15.

## Save Image Pyramid

The Save Image Pyramid option will save a pyramid structure of scaled-down versions of the full resolution image. TIFF pyramid-savvy DTP applications (there are none I know of yet) will then be able to display a good quality TIFF preview, but without having to load the whole file.

## PSB (Large Document Format)

The PSB file format is provided as a special format for those who need to save files that exceed the normal 30,000 × 30,000 pixel dimensions limit in Photoshop. The PSB format has instead an upper limit of 300,000 × 300,000 pixels. This implies that you can create huge-sized files. But the only photographic application I can think of where you might need such a large file would be if you were creating a long panoramic image. Even so, a lot of applications and printer RIPs cannot handle files greater than 2 GB anyway. But there are exceptions, such as ColorByte's ImagePrint and Onyx's PosterShop. For this reason the 30,000 × 30,000 limit has been retained for all existing file formats in Photoshop, where the TIFF specification is limited to 4 GB and the native Photoshop PSD format limit is 2 GB maximum size. You also have to bear in mind that only Photoshop CS or later is capable of reading the PSB format.

## TIFF (Tagged Image File Format)

The main formats used for publishing work are TIFF and EPS. Of these, TIFF is the most universally recognized, industry-standard image format, but this does not necessarily imply that it is better, because the PDF file format is also gaining popularity for DTP (desktop publishing) work. TIFF files can readily be placed in QuarkXpress, InDesign and any other DTP or word processing document. The TIFF format is more open though and unlike the EPS format, you can make adjustments within the DTP program as to the way a TIFF image will appear in print.

Labs and output bureaux generally request that you save your output images as TIFFs, as this file format can be read by most other imaging computer systems. If you are distributing a file for output as a print or transparency, or for someone else to continue editing your master file, it will usually be safer to supply the image using the TIFF format. TIFFs saved using Photoshop 7.0 or later will support alpha channels, paths, image transparency and all the extras that can normally be saved using the native PSD and PDF formats. Labs or service bureaux that receive TIFF files for direct output will normally request that a TIFF file is flattened and saved with the alpha channels and other extra items removed. For example, earlier versions of Quark Xpress had a nasty habit of interpreting any path that was present in the image file as a clipping path.

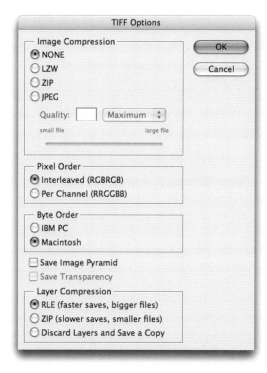

**Figure 2.67** The TIFF save options can be customized. If an open image contains alpha channels or layers, the Save dialog in Figure 2.66 will indicate this and you can keep the necessary options checked to preserve these in a TIFF save. If the File Saving preferences have Ask Before Saving Layered TIFF Files switched on, a further alert dialog will warn you after clicking OK to the TIFF options the first time you save an image as a layered TIFF.

## Pixel order

The Photoshop TIFF format has traditionally saved the pixel values in an interleaved order. So if you were saving an RGB image, the pixel values would be saved as clusters of RGB values like the following sequence: RGBRGBRGB. All TIFF readers are able to interpret this pixel order. The Per channel pixel order option will save the pixel values in channel order. All the red pixel values are saved first, followed by the green, then the blue. So the sequence is more like: RRRGGGBBB. Using the Per channel order can provide faster read/write speeds and better compression. Most third-party TIFF readers should support Per channel pixel ordering, but there is a very slim chance that some TIFF readers won't.

## Byte order

The byte order can be made to match the computer system platform the file is being read on. But there is no need to worry about this since I know of no examples where this can cause compatibility problems.

## Layer compression

If there are layers present in the image, compression options can be applied separately to the layers. RLE stands for Run Length Encoding and provides the same type of lossless compression as LZW. The ZIP compression is another form of lossless compression. Or alternatively you can choose Discard Layers and Save a Copy, which will save a copy version as a flattened TIFF.

## PDF versatility

The PDF format in Photoshop is particularly useful for sending Photoshop images to people who don't have Photoshop, but do have Adobe Reader™ on their computer. If they have a full version of Adobe Acrobat they will even be able to conduct a limited amount of editing, such as changing a text layer slightly. Photoshop is also able to import or append annotations from Adobe Acrobat.

## Photoshop PDF

The PDF (Portable Document Format) is a cross-platform file format that was initially designed to provide an electronic publishing medium for distributing documents without requiring the recipient to have a copy of the program that originated the document. Acrobat enables others to view documents the way they are meant to be seen, even though they may not have the fonts used to compile that document. All they need is the free Adobe Reader program.

Adobe PDF has now gained far wider acceptance as a reliable and compact method of supplying pages to printers, due to its ability to embed fonts, compress images and its color management features. It is now becoming the native format for Illustrator and other desktop publishing programs. But it is also gaining popularity for saving Photoshop files, because it can preserve everything that a Photoshop (PSD) file can. Adobe Reader™ and its predecessor Acrobat Reader™ are free, and easily obtained from the Adobe website. But the full Adobe Acrobat™ program is required if you want to distill page documents into the PDF format and edit them. Best of all, Acrobat documents are small in size and can be printed at high resolution. I can create a document in InDesign and export it as an Acrobat PDF using the Export command. Anyone who has installed the Adobe Reader program can open a PDF document I have created and see the layout just as I intended it to be seen, with the pictures in full color plus text displayed using the correct fonts. The Photoshop PDF file format can be used to save all Photoshop features such as Layers, with either JPEG or lossless ZIP compression and is backwards compatible in as much as it will save a flattened composite for viewing within programs that are unable to fully interpret the Photoshop CS3 layer information. On pages 94–95 I have shown and described all the PDF Save dialog options.

## *PDF security*

The PDF security options allow you to restrict file access to authorized users only. This means that a password will have to be entered before an image can be opened in either Adobe Reader, Acrobat or Photoshop. And you can also introduce a secondary password for permission to print or modify the PDF file in Acrobat. Note: this level of security only applies when reading a file in a PDF reader program. You can only password protect the opening of a PDF file in a program like Photoshop. Once opened, it will be fully editable. Even so, this is still a useful feature to have. The PDF security allows you to prevent some unauthorized first level access to your images. There are two security options: 40-bit RC4 for lower-level security and compatibility with versions 3 and 4 of Acrobat and 128-bit RC4, for higher security using Acrobat versions 5–7. However, because the PDF specification is an open-source standard, some other PDF readers are able to by pass these security features and can quite easily open a password-protected image! So the security features are not totally infallible, but marginally better than using no security at all.

### Placing PDF files

The Photoshop Parser plug-in enables Photoshop to import any Adobe Illustrator, EPS or generic single/multi-page PDF file. Using File ⇨ Place, you can select individual pages or ranges of pages from a generic PDF file, rasterize them and save to a destination folder. Use File ⇨ Place to extract all or individual image/vector graphic files contained within a PDF document as separate image files (see Figure 2.68).

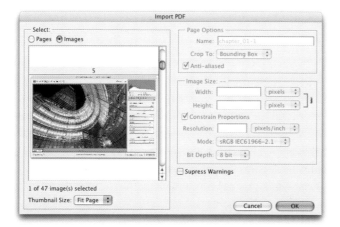

**Figure 2.68** If you try to open a generic Acrobat PDF from within Photoshop by choosing File ⇨ Open or File ⇨ Place, you will see the Import PDF or Place PDF dialog shown here. This will allow you to select individual or multiple pages or selected images only and open these in Photoshop or place them within a new Photoshop document.

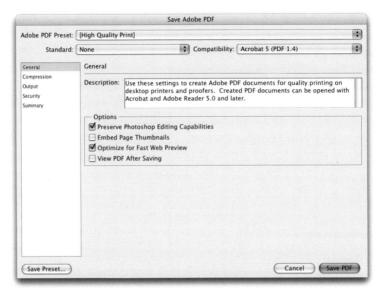

**Figure 2.69** You can start by selecting a PDF preset setting before you save, or configure the settings, starting with the General options. In most situations you will want to preserve the ability to edit the saved PDF image again in Photoshop and improve the performance of PDFs on web servers. If you want to preview the PDF in Adobe Acrobat afterwards, then check View PDF After Saving.

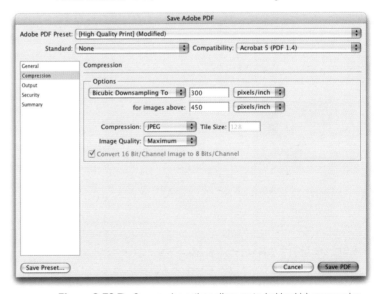

**Figure 2.70** The Compression options allow you to decide which compression method (if any) should be used.

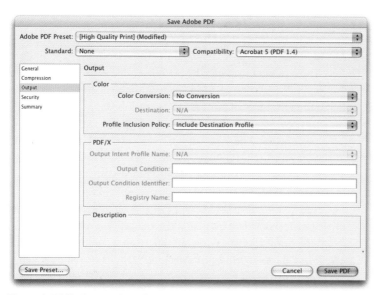

**Figure 2.71** The Output options allow you to set document level color management policies. So, for example, you could save an RGB file with a Convert to Destination policy and set the destination space below.

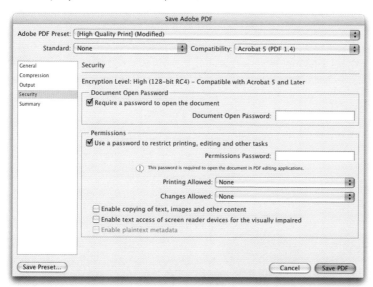

**Figure 2.72** The Security options will be linked to the version compatibility you have selected, but essentially allow you to restrict access by requiring a password to open the document and have a separate password to restrict edit changes or document printing.

### ATWs

Being a member of the team that makes Photoshop has many rewards. But one of the perks is having the opportunity to add little office in-jokes in a secret spot on the Photoshop splash screen. It's a sign of what spending long hours building a new version of Photoshop will do to you! The instructions for how to access these are described in the main text.

### Photoshop code names

Nearly every version of the Photoshop beta program has traditionally been named after a music track or a movie. Past honored music artists have included: Adrian Belew, William Orbit and Lou Reed.

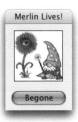

**Figure 2.73** Can you find Merlin?

# Easter eggs

We'll round off this chapter with some of the hidden fun items in Photoshop. If you drag down from the system or Apple menu to select About Photoshop... The splash screen reopens and after about 5 seconds the text starts to scroll telling you lots of stuff about the Adobe team who wrote the program, etc. Hold down ⌥ *alt* and the text will scroll faster. And last, but not least, a special mention to the most important Photoshop user of all.... Now hold down ⌘ *ctrl* *alt* and choose About Photoshop... and you will see the Red Pill beta test version of the splash screen. In case you are interested, Red Pill is a reference to the movie *The Matrix* where choosing the red pill will change your perception forever. Wow, all this from a computer program! For what its worth I fell asleep both times I tried to watch *The Matrix* and gave up after episode 2. When the credits have finished scrolling, carefully ⌥ *alt*-click in the white space above the credits, but below the image to see what are known as Adobe Transient Witticisms appearing one at a time above the credits. Another thing you can do when the alternative splash screen is in view is to take a screen shot of it and process the screen capture in Levels, cranking the shadow input levels all the way to the right to reveal a special tribute message. If you want to see another Easter egg, go to the Layers palette, hold down ⌥ *alt* and choose Palette Options from the palette submenu.

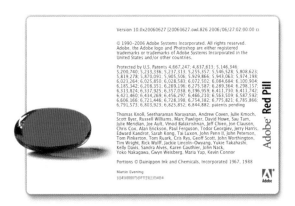

**Figure 2.74** The Red Pill splash screen.

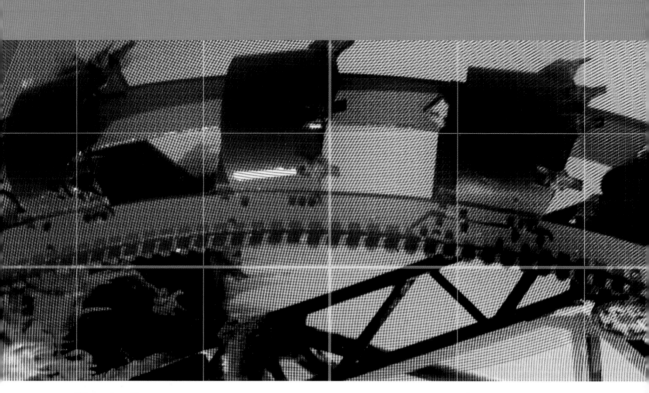

**Chapter 3**

# Configuring Photoshop

I n order to get the best performance out of Photoshop, you need to ensure that your computer system has been optimized for image editing work. When I first began writing the 'Photoshop for Photographers' series of books, it was always necessary to guide readers on how to buy the most suitable computer for Photoshop work and what hardware specifications to look for. These days I would suggest that almost any computer you can buy is capable of running Photoshop and can be upgraded later to run the program faster. As always, I try to avoid making distinctions between the superiority of the Macintosh or PC systems. If you are an experienced computer user, you know what works best for you and I see no reason to evangelize my preference for using a Mac. Throughout my computer career, it's what I have grown up

## 64-bit processing support

64-bit processing is now the new standard for the latest computer hardware. Photoshop CS and CS2 were partly able to take advantage of this on the Macintosh G5 system. Photoshop CS2 and CS3 offers more extensive support. If you are running Mac OS X 10.3 or higher, you can now allocate up to 4 GB (less whatever the operating system frameworks take up, so effectively up to 3.5 GB). If you are running Windows 2000 or the regular version of Windows XP, you can still only allocate up to 2 GB. If you are running Windows XP 64-bit edition you can allocate 4 GB (minus a very small amount for the operating system). Some people have asked why Photoshop CS3 is not fully optimized for 64-bit processing and the answer is that at this stage there were still rather limited advantages to be gained from doing so and only a few users running the right OS system on the right computer with the right drivers would have seen any appreciable performance increase. This is something that we will most likely only see in the next version of Photoshop. For more information on this subject, check out Scott Byer's Adobe blog:
http://blogs.adobe.com/scottbyer/

## RAM upgrades

It is well worth while making sure you have as much RAM installed as possible in your computer. Photoshop is able to make use of up to 4 GB of RAM memory. The RAM figures quoted here are the minimum recommended amounts. I would advise installing at least 2 GB RAM if you can.

with and it feels like home. The same arguments apply if you're a Windows PC user. And apart from anything else, once you have bought a bunch of programs, you are kind of locked into using that particular system. If you switch, it means facing the prospect of buying most of your favorite software packages all over again.

# What you will need

Today's entry level computer will contain everything you need. Here is a guide to the system requirements for Macintosh and Windows machines:

## Macintosh

Photoshop CS3 will run on a Power PC G4, G5 or any of the latest Intel-based Macs running Mac OS 10.3 or later including Leopard (10.5). Minimum RAM requirement is 320 MB and Photoshop CS3 will require an estimated 1.5 GB of hard disk space. You will also need a monitor with at least 1024 x 768 pixel resolution driven by a 16-bit graphics card with at least 64 MB video RAM and a CD/DVD drive. All the current range of Apple Macintosh computers are capable of meeting these requirements, although with some of the older G4 and G5 computers you may need to upgrade the RAM memory and graphics card.

## Windows

Photoshop CS3 will run on Pentium 4 processors or similar powered Xeons. Core 2, Core 2 Duo and Xeon multi-core processors will also be suitable, as will AMD 64 processors. Use Windows XP Service Pack 2 or Vista. Minimum RAM requirement is 320 MB and will require an estimated 650 MB of hard disk space. You will also need a monitor with at least 1024 x 768 pixel resolution driven by a 16-bit graphics card with at least 64 MB video RAM and a CD drive. Almost any new PC system you buy should have no trouble meeting these requirements. But if you have an older computer system, do check that you have enough RAM memory and a powerful enough graphics card.

## The ideal computer setup

Your computer working environment is important. Even
if space is limited there is much you can do to make your
work area an efficient place to work in. Figure 3.1 shows
a general view of the office area from where I run the
business and do all my Photoshop work and, as you can
see, it allows two operators to work simultaneously. The
desk unit was custom built to provide a large continuous
worktop area with good cable management in order to
minimize the number of stray leads hanging all over the
place. The walls are painted neutral gray with paint I was
able to get from a local hardware store, and when measured
with a spectrophotometer is almost a perfect neutral color.
The under shelf lighting uses cool fluorescent strips that
bounce off behind the displays to avoid any light hitting

### Chip acceleration

Upgrading the processor chip is the most
dramatic way you can boost a computer's
performance. But not all computers will allow
you to do this. If you have either a daughter
card slot or some other processor upgrade
slot then you will be able to upgrade your old
computer and give it a new lease of life. The
upgrade card may also include an increase
of backside cache memory to further
enhance performance. The cache memory
stores frequently used system commands
and thereby takes the strain away from the
processor chip allowing faster performance
on application tasks.

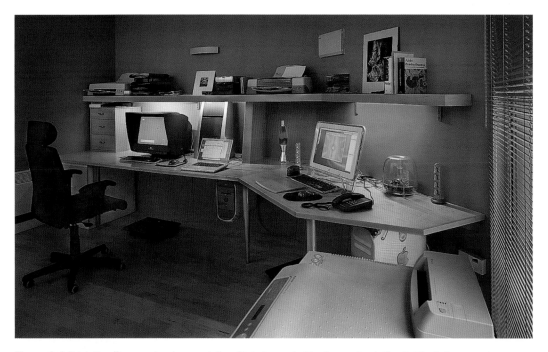

**Figure 3.1** This is the office area where I carry out all my Photoshop work. It has been custom built so that the desk area remains as
clear as possible. The walls are painted neutral gray to absorb light and reduce the risk of color casts affecting what you see on the monitor
screens. The lighting comes from daylight balanced tubes which backlights the monitor screens. I usually have the light level turned down
quite low, in order to maximize the monitor viewing contrast. And yes, it really did used to look this tidy once!

## Chip speed

Microchip processing speed is expressed in megahertz, but performance speed also depends on the chip type. A 2 GHz Pentium class 4 chip is not as fast as a 2 GHz Intel Duo Core processsor. Speed comparisons in terms of the number of megahertz are only valid between chips of the same series. Many of the latest computers are also enabled with twin processing. And another crucial factor is the bus speed. This refers to the speed of data transfer from RAM memory to the CPU (the central processing unit, i.e. the chip). CPU performance can be restricted by slow system bus speeds so faster is better, especially for Photoshop work where large chunks of data are always being processed.

the screens directly. The window is north facing, so I never have any problems with direct sunlight entering the room and what daylight does enter the office can be controlled with the venetian blind. It is also important to choose a chair that is comfortable, ideally one with arm rests and adjustable seating positions so that your wrists can rest comfortably on the table top. The monitor should be level with your line of view or slightly lower.

Once you start building an imaging workstation, you will soon end up with lots of electrical devices. While these in themselves may not consume a huge amount of power, do take precautions against too many power leads trailing off from a single power point. Cathode ray tube monitors are vulnerable to damage from the magnets in an unshielded speaker or the electrical motor in an inkjet printer. Just try not to position any item other than the computer too close to a CRT monitor screen. Interference from other electrical items can cause problems too. To prevent damage or loss of data from a sudden power cut, place an uninterruptible power supply unit between your computer and the mains source. These devices will also smooth out any voltage spikes or surges in the electricity supply.

## Choosing a display

The display is one of the most important components in your entire kit. It is what you will spend all your time looking at as you work in Photoshop. You really do not want to economize by buying a cheap screen that is unsuited for graphics use. There are two types of display that you can buy: cathode ray tube (CRT) monitors and liquid crystal displays (LCDs). A cathode ray tube fires electrons from its red, green and blue guns to produce a color image as the electrons strike the colored phosphor screen. CRTs have been around a long time and they remain popular with high-end graphics users. This is because most CRT displays make it possible to manually adjust the calibration of the display (see page 103) so that you can achieve a nice, neutral-looking output and there is less further adjustment required with the monitor profile. So ideally, the monitor profile will simply fine-tune the image to appear correctly on the calibrated CRT. But because CRT displays are analog devices, they are prone to fluctuate in performance and output. This is why you must always calibrate a CRT monitor regularly. The hardware controls of a CRT will typically allow you to adjust the contrast, brightness and color balance of the display output. The more expensive CRT monitors such as the Barco Calibrator have built-in self-calibrating tools. These continually monitor and regulate the output from the moment you switch the device on. A 22" CRT display is a big and bulky piece of equipment, whereas the light, slim-line design of a flat panel LCD screen will occupy less desk space. LCDs range in size from the screens used on a laptop computer to big 30" desktop displays. An LCD contains a translucent film of fixed-size liquid crystal elements that individually filter the color of a backlit, fluorescent light source. Therefore, the only hardware adjustment you can usually make is to adjust the brightness of the backlit screen. You can calibrate the brightness of the LCD hardware but that is about all you can do. The contrast is fixed, but it is usually more contrasty than a typical CRT monitor, which is not a bad thing when doing Photoshop work for print output.

Because LCDs are digital devices they tend to produce a more consistent color output. They still need to be calibrated and profiled, but the display's performance will remain fairly consistent over longer periods of time. On the other hand, there will be some variance in the image appearance depending on the angle from which you view the screen. The brightness and color output of an LCD will only appear to be correct when the screen is viewed front on. And this very much depends on the design of the LCD display. The worst examples of this can be seen on ultra-thin laptop display screens. But the evenness of the output from a 23" Apple Cinema display and other desktop LCD screens is certainly a lot more consistent.

**Using a second display**

If you are able to run two displays from your computer, then you might want to invest in a second, smaller screen and have this located beside the main display and use it to show the Photoshop palette windows and keep the main screen area clear of palette clutter. To run a second display you may need to buy an additional PCI card that provides a second video port.

**Floating windows**

In the past, PC users were restricted by the limits of the Photoshop application window. This is now resolved in two ways. Firstly, because Bridge is now a separate application, it is no longer constrained to working in Photoshop, as we were with the File Browser. And secondly, Photoshop has a floating windows feature in the PC version which lets you move document windows outside the bounds of the application window.

### Video cards

The graphics card in your computer is what drives the display. It processes all the pixel information and converts it to draw a color image on the screen. An accelerated graphics card will enable your screen to do several things. It will allow you to run your screen display at higher screen resolutions, hold more image screen view data in memory and it will use the monitor profile information to finely adjust the color appearance. When more of the off-screen image data remains in memory the image scrolling is enhanced and this provides generally faster screen refreshes. In the old days, computers were sold with a limited amount of video memory. If you were lucky you could just about manage to run a small screen in millions of colors. If you buy a computer today the chances are that it will already be equipped with a good, high performance graphics card, easily capable of doing all of the above. These cards will contain 128 MB (or more) of dedicated memory. There is probably not much advantage to be gained in fitting anything other than this (unless you have a very large LCD screen) because the top of the range graphics cards are mostly optimized to provide faster 3D games performance rather than providing a better 2D display.

It is interesting to speculate what displays will look like in the future. BrightSide Technologies (www.brightsidetech.com) has developed an LCD display which uses a matrix of LED lights instead of a fluorescent light source to pass light through the LCD film. These displays have an incredible dynamic range and are capable of displaying a 16-bit per channel image with an illumination range that makes an ordinary 8-bit display look dull and flat by comparison. We may one day have display technologies that are able to get closer to simulating the dynamic range of natural light. These will be great for viewing computer games and video, but for Photoshop print work we will mostly want to have the display we are looking at match our expectations of what can be reproduced on a print.

### Display calibration and profiling

We now need to focus on what is the most important aspect of any Photoshop system: getting the monitor to correctly display your images in Photoshop at the right brightness and neutralized to avoid introducing color casts. This basic setup advice should be self-evident, because we all want our images in Photoshop to be consistent from session to session and match in appearance when they are viewed on another user's system. There are several ways that you can go about this. At a bare minimum you will want to calibrate the monitor display so that the contrast is turned up to maximum, that the brightness is consistent with what everyone else would be using and that neutral grays really do display as gray on the screen. As I mentioned earlier, CRT displays will fluctuate in performance all the time. So before you calibrate a CRT monitor, it should be left switched on for at least half an hour to give it a chance to warm up properly and stabilize. A decent CRT monitor will have hardware controls that allow you to adjust the brightness and the color output from the individual color guns so that you can easily correct for color shifts and reset the gray balance of the output. However, the life-span of a CRT is about three years and as these devices get older they will lose their brightness and contrast to the point where they can no longer be successfully calibrated or be reliable enough for Photoshop image editing.

The initial calibration process should get your display close to an idealized state. From there, you can build a monitor profile which at a minimum describes the black point, white point and chosen gamma. The black point describes the darkest black that can be displayed so that the next lightest tone of dark gray is just visible. The white point information tells the video card how to display a pure white on the screen that matches the specified color temperature. For a CRT displays I suggest you use D65/6500. For LCD displays I suggest you select the native white point. And lastly the gamma. This tells the video card how much to adjust the midtone levels compensation. Note that the gamma you choose when creating a monitor profile does not affect how light or dark an image will be displayed in Photoshop. The monitor profile gamma only affects how the midtone levels are distributed. Whether you use a Mac or PC computer, you should always choose a gamma of 2.2 when building a monitor profile. If you use a measuring instrument (see Figure 3.3) to accurately calibrate and profile the display, you can build a monitor profile that will contain a lot more detailed information about how the screen is able to display a broad range of colors.

Basically, the calibration process should reset your hardware to a standardized output. Next, you build a monitor profile that describes how well the display actually performs after it has been calibrated. A good CRT monitor will let you manually adjust the color output of the individual guns (smart monitors like the Sony Artisan and Barco Calibrator do this automatically). If the screen is more or less neutral after calibration there is less further adjustment required to get a perfectly profiled display. The monitor profile sends instructions to the video card to fine-tune the display. If these adjustments are relatively minor, you are making full use of the video card to describe a full range of colors on the screen. If you rely on video card adjustments to calibrate the display as well, then the

### Prolonging the life of a CRT display

A CRT display will typically provide three years of good use before the tube starts to fade and calibration becomes difficult, although using a screen saver will help prolong the life of a CRT. A CRT monitor display will usually have hardware controls that allow you to configure the alignment of the image. It is suggested that you carefully configure the alignment so that you don't have the display image filling the entire area of the CRT screen. Use the hardware controls to reduce the width and height slightly so that you have, say, a quarter inch unused border around the display viewing area.

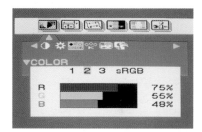

**Figure 3.2** This is a screen shot showing the hardware monitor controls for the LaCie Electron Blue III CRT display. The hardware controls enable me to adjust the output of the individual guns that control the red, green and blue color of the display. I adjust these settings as part of the display calibration process to make the screen neutral before building the monitor profile.

### Eizo ColorEdge

Eizo have established themselves as offering the finest quality LCD displays for graphics use. The ColorEdge CG221 is the flagship model in the range. Capable of providing uniform screen display from edge to edge, it encompasses the Adobe RGB gamut and comes with ColorNavigator calibration software that can be used with Gretag MacBeth calibration devices. This display is more expensive than most, but is highly prized for its color fidelity.

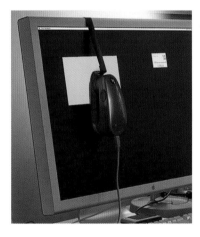

**Figure 3.3** The Gretag Macbeth Eye-One is a popular spectrophotometer that can be used to accurately measure the output from the monitor display to both calibrate the output and, using the accompanying Eye-One software, measure color patches and build an ICC profile for your display.

video card is having to make bigger adjustments and the color output may suffer as a result. For example, with a CRT display you can use the monitor hardware controls to regulate and neutralize the color output via the video card. Not all CRT monitors are capable of doing this and LCD displays certainly don't. The only adjustment you can make on an LCD monitor is to adjust the brightness. This is not to say that all LCD screens are unsuitable devices for graphics work. The lower grade LCD displays such as those used on laptop computers are not really good enough for Photoshop color work. But the higher grade LCD screens will feature relatively good viewing angle consistency, are not too far off from providing a neutral color and D65 white balance and won't fluctuate much in performance. As with everything else in life, you get what you pay for. If you are not going to invest in a calibration/ measuring device, your best option with an LCD is to load a canned profile for your monitor and keep your fingers crossed. It will sort of work and is better than doing nothing. But I do urge you to consider buying a monitor and calibration device as a complete package.

### *Calibration hardware*

Let's now look at the practical steps for calibrating and profiling the display. First, get rid of any distracting background colors or patterns on the computer desktop. And consider choosing a neutral color theme for your operating system. The Mac OS X system has a graphite appearance setting especially there for Photoshop users! If you are using a PC, try going to Control Panels ⇨ Appearance ⇨ Themes, choose Display and click the Appearance tab. Click on the active and inactive window samples and choose a gray color for both. If you are using Windows XP, try choosing the silver color scheme. This is all very subjective of course, but personally I think these adjustments improve the system appearances.

The only reliable way to calibrate and profile your display is by using a hardware calibration system. Some displays, such as the LaCie range can be bought with a

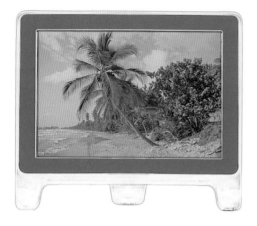

1 An uncalibrated and unprofiled monitor cannot be relied on to provide an accurate indication of how colors should look.

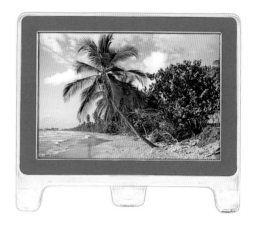

2 The calibration process simply aims to optimize the display for gray balance, contrast and brightness.

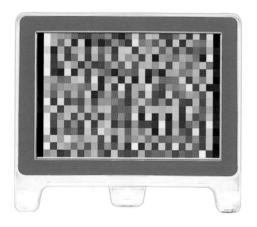

3 The profiling process records at a minimum the black point, white point, and gamma. With the right software, the profiling process will also measure how a broad range of colors is displayed. Recording this extra color information is the only way you can truly produce an accurate profile.

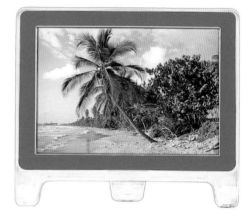

4 To create a profile of this kind you need a colorimeter device. A calibrator such as the Gretag Macbeth Eye-One Display 2 or Eye-One Photo with the Eye-One Match 3.0 or Profile Maker 5 Professional software will produce the most accurate results.

## Color managing the print output

This leaves the question of how to profile the print output. Well, getting custom profiles built for your printer is a good idea, and this topic is covered in some detail in Chapter 12. However, calibrating and building a profile for your display is by far the most important step in the whole color management process. Get this right and the canned profiles that came with your printer should work just fine. You should already be seeing a much closer match between what you see on the display and what you see coming out of your printer. But without doubt, a custom print profile will help you get even better results.

bundled hardware calibrator, but there are many other types of stand-alone calibration packages to consider. The ColorVision Monitor Spyder and Spyder2Pro Studio are affordable, and are sold either with PhotoCal or the more advanced OptiCal software. The Monitor Spyders are colorimeter devices and can be used to measure the output from a CRT or LCD monitor display. The X-Rite is also a good system and comes with the easy-to-use Monaco OPTIX software.

CRT measuring devices generally use rubber suckers to attach to the screen, but to measure an LCD display, a weighted strap is used to counterbalance the instrument so it just rests against the LCD screen. Whatever you do, don't try attaching anything with rubber suckers to an LCD screen, as you will completely ruin the surface of the display! My personal preference is the Gretag Macbeth Eye-One system, which is available in several different packages. The Eye-One Photo measuring device is an emissive spectrophotometer that can measure all types of displays and build printer profiles as well when used in conjunction with the ProfileMaker 5 or Eye-One Match 3.0 software. The Eye-One Display 2 device is a low cost colorimeter device and is designed for measuring both CRT and LCD displays. If all you are interested in is calibrating and profiling a computer display, there is no great advantage in choosing a spectrophotometer over the more economically priced colorimeter devices. But whatever you do, I do advise you to include a calibrator/software package with any display purchase.

### Do you want good color or just OK color?

Let me summarize in a few paragraphs why you should pay special attention to how your images are displayed in Photoshop and why good color management is essential.

The choice of an LCD or CRT display can be a matter of individual choice. Although Sony, Eizo, Viewsonic, Phillips and NEC still appear to be selling CRTs, I have a personal preference for using LCDs. Once you have chosen a good display you need to consider how you are going to calibrate and fine-tune it. This is crucial and if it is done right it will mean you can trust the colors you see on the screen. You are going to be spending a lot of time looking at the display as you work in Photoshop and you will naturally want to see print results that match what you saw on the screen. In the long run you are going to save yourself an awful lot of time and frustration if you calibrate and profile the screen properly from the start. Not so long ago, the cost of a large screen, plus a decent video card, would have cost a small fortune and monitor display calibrators were specialist items. These days, a basic monitor calibration and profiling device can cost about the same as an external hard drive, so I would urge anyone setting up a computer system for Photoshop to put a monitor display calibrator high on their spending list. A standard colorimeter like the Eye-One Display 2 from Gretag MacBeth is easy to set up and use and all the necessary software will be supplied to enable you to calibrate and build a profile for your monitor.

All the monitor display calibrator products I have tested will automatically place a profile for your monitor in the correct folder in your system and you are then ready to start working straight away in Photoshop with a properly calibrated display. Once you are in Photoshop you need to make sure you are using the right color settings for your workflow: see page 110 for instructions on how to check if you are using the right settings for a photography setup. Once that is done, the Color Settings will remain set until you change them. And after that, all you need to worry about is making sure that the calibration and profiling for your display is kept up to date. If you are using a CRT type display, this should probably be done about once a week. If you are using an LCD type display, the profiling is just as important, but regular calibration will not be quite so critical. Checking once a month will probably be enough.

Color management does not have to be intimidatingly complex and nor does it have to be expensive. So the question is, do you want good color or simply OK color? Or, to put it another way, can you afford not to?

**Gamma setup**

When you utilize a calibration device the calibrating software will want to ask you which gamma you will be using. Now quite often you are told that PC users should use a 2.2 gamma and Macintosh users should use a 1.8 gamma. But a 2.2 gamma is the ideal gamma setting to use regardless of whether you are on a Mac or a PC. You can build a correct monitor profile using a 1.8 gamma option, but 2.2 is closer to the native gamma of most displays. I once asked an engineer why they still included it as an option in their software and he replied that it's only there to comfort Mac users who have traditionally been taught to use 1.8. So now you know.

**Display luminance**

The target luminance will vary according to which type of display you are using. A typical modern LCD display will have a luminance of 200 candelas $M^2$ or more at the maximum luminance setting, which is way too bright for image editing work in subdued office lighting conditions. And with older CRT monitors you may be lucky to reach the desired target of 100 candelas $M^2$ (a sure sign that the display is due for retirement). A target of around 140 candelas $M^2$ is ideal for a desktop LCD monitor display.

## White point setup

The other puzzling question concerns the white point. You will sometimes be urged to choose a 5000 K whitepoint for print work. My advice is to always use 6500 K instead. Most displays run naturally at a white point of 6500 K. Some people regard 5000 K as being the correct value to use for CMYK proofing work. But in reality, the whites on your display will appear too yellow at this setting. 6500 K may be cooler than the assumed 5000 K standard, but 6500 K will give much better contrast on your display and your eyes always adjust naturally to the colors on the display, the same way as your eyes adjust normally to fluctuations in everyday lighting conditions. The apparent disparity of using one white point for the lightbox and another for the display is not something you should worry about.

With LCD displays it is not possible to physically adjust the whitepoint, so it is better to select the native white point option when calibrating an LCD display. Again, remember that colors are perceived relative to the white point and the eye will compensate naturally from the white point seen on the display to the white point used by an alternative viewing light source.

## Calibration using a third-party calibrator

The following steps show an example of how to use the Eye-One Match 3.0 software with a Gretag MacBeth monitor calibration device.

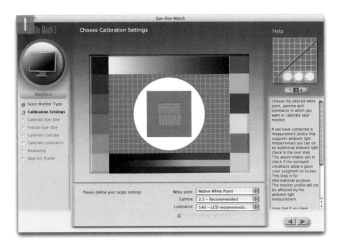

**1** I like using Eye-One Match 3 because it is easy to set up and use. The initial screens will ask what type of device you which to profile. In this case, I wanted to calibrate and profile an LCD display. I set the white point to Native, the Gamma to 2.2 and the luminance to 140 candelas $M^2$, the recommended target setting for desktop LCD displays.

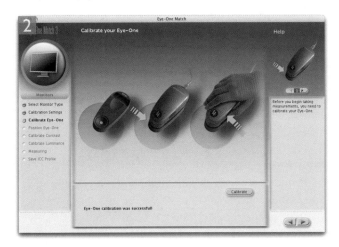

**2** Eye-One Match will then ask you to calibrate the device (placing it on the base unit to measure the white tile) before hanging the device onto the screen.

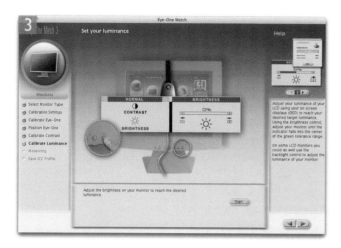

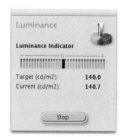

**3** You will then be asked to set the contrast to maximum (skip this step if calibrating an LCD) and then adjust the brightness, by starting with the brightness controls dimmed right down. Eye-One Match will measure the display as you gradually increase the brightness and indicate when you have reached the target luminance setting you set at the beginning.

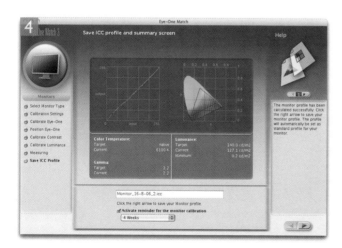

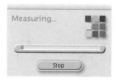

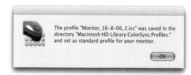

**4** When you proceed to the next step, Eye-One Match will automatically sense the placement position of the calibration device and start measuring a sequence of colors from the display and, once it has completed doing this, generate a monitor profile named with today's date. All you have to do is click OK to establish this as the new monitor profile to use, replacing any previous monitor profile. You might also want to set a reminder for when the next monitor profile should be made. If you are using an LCD, once every 4 weeks should be just fine.

**Old monitor profiles**

Do you really need to hang on to old monitor profiles? I recommend that you purge the Colorsync Profiles folder on your system of older monitor profiles to avoid confusion. All you really need is one good up-to-date profile for your display.

### Synchronizing the Color Settings

I recommend people look at the region settings and if these do not suit exactly, then make the necessary changes and save these as a custom user setting. Once this is done, open Bridge (if you have not done so already and synchronize the Color Settings there). If you are using other programs in the Creative Suite this will ensure that the same color settings are used in all the other programs, such as InDesign. Finding this later can be a real problem, and is so easy to avoid.

## Color management settings

One of the very first things you should do after installing Photoshop is to configure the color management settings. The default Photoshop color settings are configured using a general setting for the region you live in, which will be: North America, Europe or Japan. If you are using Photoshop for design work or photography, you will want to follow the prompt that Photoshop is giving you here. Go to the Edit menu and select Color Settings. This will open the dialog shown in Figure 3.4. Next, go to the Settings menu and select one of the prepress settings. The individual prepress settings only differ in the default RGB to CMYK conversions that they use, and which you should choose will depend on the geographical area you are working in. So if you live and work in the US, choose North America Prepress 2 and you will be fine with that setting. Please note that adjusting the prepress settings will change the RGB working space from sRGB to Adobe RGB. This is a good thing to do if you intend editing RGB photographs in Photoshop. But it is not enough just to change the RGB workspace setting on its own. The prepress settings

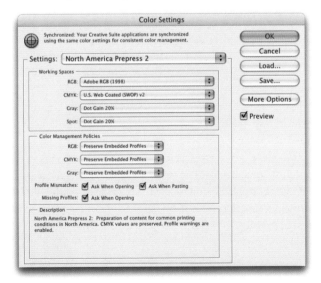

**Figure 3.4** The Photoshop Color Settings. All the Photoshop color settings can be managed from within this single dialog.

will also adjust the policy settings to preserve embedded profiles and ignore profile mismatch warnings. This will minimize the number of times you are shown the profile mismatch warning dialog when working with image files that are in different color spaces.

You don't need to worry too much more about the ins and outs of Photoshop color management just yet, but as your Photoshop knowledge increases you will definitely want to read in more detail about the color management system in Chapter 12 and also Chapter 13 on how to print output.

## Extras

An internal 24× or faster CD-ROM drive is standard issue these days. Other things to buy could include a second hard drive to use as a scratch disk plus a removable media storage device such as the Iomega Zip drive or a CD writer, although a lot of computers are sold with a CD drive that functions as a CD writer and DVD writer too. You need these to back up your main hard disk and store all your image documents. It is tempting to accumulate lots of image files on the computer hard drive, but you have to ask yourself what would happen if your computer got stolen or that hard drive failed. Removable disks are ideal for transferring documents off-site. Print shops should be able to satisfactorily read Mac and PC format files whether supplied on ZIP, CD or DVD. USB 2 and FireWire 800 (IEEE 1394) are the latest connection standards for peripheral devices. You can have up to 127 USB devices linked to a single computer and you can plug and unplug USB devices while the machine is switched on. USB 2 is the latest standard and has many advantages for those in a PC working environment. USB 1.0 is slow, but it's fine for connecting control devices such as the mouse, Wacom tablet and printer. FireWire has the potential to provide fast data transfer rates of 100 MB+ per second (faster still with FireWire 800). So use FireWire wherever possible to connect devices that rely on fast data transfer such as hard drives, CD writers, digital cameras and scanners.

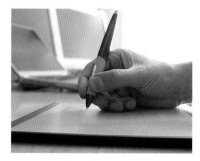

**Figure 3.5** Wacom™ pad and pen.

### Graphics tablets

I highly recommend you get a digitizing graphics tablet. This is pressure responsive and is easier to draw with and can be used alongside the mouse as an input device. Bigger is not necessarily better. Some people like using the A4 sized tablets, others find it easier to work with an A5 or A6 tablet from the Wacom™ Intuos™ range, which now features a cordless mouse and switchable pens. You don't have to move the pen around so much with smaller pads and these are therefore easier to use for painting and drawing. Once you have experienced working with a pen, using the mouse will seem like trying to draw while wearing boxing gloves! The ™ Cintiq™device is a combination of LCD monitor and digitizing pen pad. This radical new design will potentially introduce a whole new concept to the way we interact with the on-screen image. I don't know if it is going to be generally seen as the ideal way of working with photographs, but there are those who reckon it makes painting and drawing a more fluid experience.

## Backup strategies

For a more detailed look at how to back up your files, please refer to Chapter 11 on image management.

## Backing up image data

The solution I use is to archive important data on primary and backup hard drives and maintain a further backup archive using DVD disks. The cost of hard disk storage space is so cheap that this is now an easily affordable solution. It means I can access important files more easily while I am working on the computer, and I am using the one method of disk storage which has so far remained relatively unchanged over the years and therefore has more chance of continuing to be supported in the future. For a basic studio setup I would recommend storing all your archive images and work in progress images on an external drive and carry out scheduled backups to a secondary hard drive of matching size that can be stored off-site or kept in a fire proof safe.

For extra backup, I like to archive my files to removable media. In the lifetime of the Photoshop program we have seen many different systems come and go. Floppies, Syquests, Magneto Opticals... the list goes on. And although you can still obtain devices capable of reading these media formats, the question is, for how long? And what will you do in the future if a specific hardware device fails to work? The introduction of recordable CD/DVD media has provided a reasonably consistent means of storage since, for at least 10 years now, nearly all computers have been able to read CD and DVD discs. DVD drives have evolved to provide much faster read/write speeds. DVD media may be able to offer increased storage space in the future, and we are already seeing bigger disc media storage systems such as Blu-ray Disc and HD-DVD. So how long will CD and DVD media remain popular and be supported by future computer hardware? More to the point, how long will the media discs themselves last? It is estimated that aluminium and gold CD discs could last up to 30 years, or longer, if stored carefully in the right conditions such as at the right temperature and away from direct sunlight. DVD discs that use vegetable dyes may have an even shorter life-span.

# Photoshop preferences

The Photoshop preferences are located in the Edit menu in Windows and the Photoshop menu in OS X. The preferences let you customize the various Photoshop functions. A new preference file is generated each time you exit Photoshop and deleting or removing this file will always force Photoshop to reset all its preferences. The preference file is stored along with other program settings in the system level Preferences folder (Mac) or Registry folder (PC): C:/Documents and Settings/Current User/ Application Data/Adobe/Photoshop/10.0/Adobe Photoshop CS3 Settings.

## General preferences

When you open the preferences you will first be shown the General preferences. I suggest you leave the Color Picker set to Adobe (unless you have a strong attachment to the system Color Picker). And leave the image interpolation set to Bicubic. If you need to override this setting then you can do so in the Image ⇨ Image Size dialog.

The Automatically Launch Bridge option will ensure Bridge is always launched in the background and ready for immediate use. Check Auto-Update Open Documents

## Resetting the preferences

If you hold down ⌘ ⌥ Shift ctrl alt Shift during startup cycle, this will pop a dialog box that allows you to delete the current Photoshop preference file.

## Resetting dialogs

The Reset All Warning Dialogs will reset things like the profile mismatch warning messages. These dialogs contain a Don't Warn Me Again checkbox – if you had pressed any of these at any time, and wished to restore them, click here. The Reset All Tools in the Options bar will reset the tool behavior.

## Back up the preference file

After setting up the preferences, create a duplicate of the Photoshop preference file and store it within easy reach. Having access to a clean preference file can speed resetting the Photoshop settings should the working preference file become corrupted.

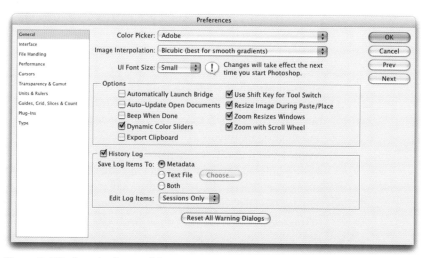

**Figure 3.6** The General preferences dialog.

### Customizing the UI Font Size

LCD computer displays are getting bigger all the time and are only really designed to operate at their best when using the finest resolution setting. This can be great for viewing photographs, but the downside is that the application menu items are getting smaller and smaller. The UI (user interface) Font Size option allows you to customize the size of the smaller font menu items in Photoshop so that you don't have to strain your eyes too hard to read them. For example, when using a large LCD screen, the Medium font size option will make it easier to read the smaller font menu items from a distance.

if you are share files that are open in Photoshop but have been updated by another application. Only check the Beep When Done box if you want Photoshop to signal a sound alert when tasks are complete. The Dynamic Color Sliders option ensures that the colors change in the Color palette as you drag the sliders, so keep this selected. Unchecking the Export Clipboard box will save time when you exit Photoshop to launch another program, but if you really need the ability to paste clipboard contents to another program then leave it on, but otherwise I suggest you switch it off. The Use Shift Key for Tool Switch answers the needs of users who wish to disable the Shift key modifier for switching tools in the Tools palette with repeated keyboard strokes. The Resize Image During Paste/Place is useful if you want pasted or placed items to be automatically scaled to match the size of the image you are pasting/placing them in. Check the Keyboard Zoom Resizes Windows if you want the image window to shrink to fit whenever you use a keyboard zoom shortcut like ⌘ − ctrl − or ⌘ + ctrl + . And lastly, there is the Zoom Scroll Wheel option which among other things will enable you to zoom in and out via the scroll wheel if you have one on your mouse. Holding down *Shift* will constrain the zoom to the usual percentage increments.

The History log is useful if you wish to keep track of everything that has been done to an image. The History Log options will let you save the history log directly in the image file metadata, to a saved text file stored in a pre-configured folder location, or both. The edit log items can be recorded in three modes. Sessions will record which files are opened and closed and when. The Concise mode will record an abbreviated list of which tools or commands were applied, again with times. Both these modes can provide basic feedback that could be useful in a studio environment to monitor time spent on a particular project and calculate billing. The Detailed mode records everything, such as the coordinates used to make a crop. This mode can be useful, for example, in forensic work.

## Interface

Regarding what I said earlier about removing distracting colors from the interface, the Use Grayscale Toolbar Icon option will remove the blue color from the Photoshop icon in the Tools palette. The Display Color Channels in Color option is a somewhat redundant feature as this does not really help you visualize the channels any better. If anything it is a distraction and is best left unchecked. Photoshop allows you to create custom menu settings and use colors to highlight favorite items, but this feature aspect can be disabled by unchecking the Show Menu Colors item. When the Show Tool Tips option is checked you will see tool tips displayed a few seconds after you roll over most items in the Photoshop interface. Tool tips are an excellent learning tool, but can become irritating after a while. The Auto-Collapse Icon Palettes option will allow you to open palettes from Icon mode and auto collapse them back to Icon mode again as soon as you start editing the image. And if you would like Photoshop to always remember the last used palette layout, check the Remember Palette Locations box (the Reset Palette Locations to Default option is also located under the Window menu, as are the saved Workspace settings).

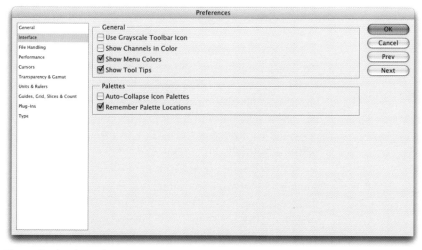

**Figure 3.7** Interface preferences.

### Economical web saves

There are times though when you don't need previews. Web graphic files should be uploaded as small as possible without a thumbnail or platform specific header information (Save for Web defaults to removing previews). I usually upload files to my server in a raw binary format, which strips out the previews and other file resource information anyway.

### Restart to activate preferences

Some of the Photoshop preferences will only take effect after you quit and restart the program. For example, the Scratch Disk preference settings will only come into effect after a restart, and the same is true of other preferences such as the Prefer Adobe Camera Raw for JPEG files preference setting.

## File Handling

You will normally want to include image previews when you save a file. It is certainly useful to have image thumbnail previews that are viewable in the system dialog boxes although the Bridge program is capable of generating large thumbnails regardless of whether a preview is present or not. You can also choose to save a Windows and Macintosh thumbnail with your file, to enable better cross-platform compatibility. Appending a file with a file extension is handy for keeping tabs on which format a document was saved in and is also very necessary when saving JPEG and GIF web graphics that need to be recognized in an HTML page. If you are exporting for the Web, you may want to check the Use Lower Case box for appending files. But instances of where servers trip up on upper case naming are fairly rare these days.

### File compatibility

Now that Camera Raw is able to edit JPEG images as well as raw files, you can set a preference to automatically open Camera Raw every time you open a JPEG image. This is only useful if you shoot in JPEG mode and wish to use Camera Raw to process the JPEG masters without actually editing the master files (because Camera Raw records all the edits as separate instructions). And you can set a preference to always launch Adobe Camera Raw as your favored raw processor when opening a proprietary raw file. Some cameras may embed an sRGB profile tag in the EXIF metadata of a JPEG capture file, where the image profile isn't actually a correct sRGB profile. If you check the Ignore EXIF profile tag, Photoshop will ignore this particular part of the metadata and read from the embedded profile data instead.

A TIFF format file saved in Photoshop 6.0 or later can contain all types of Photoshop layer information and a flattened composite is always saved in a TIFF. If you place a layered TIFF image in a page layout, only the flattened composite will be read by the program when the page is finally converted to print. Some people argue that there are specific instances where a layered TIFF might trip up a print production workflow, so it might be safer to never save layers in a TIFF if you don't know for certain where your files will be printed. When the Ask Before Saving Layered TIFF Files option is checked, Photoshop will present you with an option to either flatten or preserve the layers when saving a layered image as a TIFF. If this is unchecked, then the layer information will always be saved with a composite and there will be no warning dialog.

However, standard Photoshop PSD files created in Photoshop CS3 are never going to be 100% compatible if they are likely to be read by someone using an earlier version of Photoshop. This has always been the case with every upgrade of the program. Setting the Maximize PSD and PSB Compatibility to 'Always' will allow you to do the same thing as when saving a flattened composite with a TIFF. This option will ensure that a flattened version of the image is included with the saved Photoshop file and the safe option is to always keep this checked. For example, if you create a Smart Object layer in Photoshop CS2 or CS3, the Photoshop file will not be interpreted correctly when read by Photoshop CS or earlier, unless you maximize the compatibility of the saved PSD. In these circumstances, if

### Version Cue

The Enable Version Cue Workgroup File Management relates to the use of Adobe Version Cue. This option caters for those working in a networked environment and where they are sharing working on image files with other Photoshop users. When a user 'checks out' a file, only he or she can edit it. The other users who are sharing your files will only be able to make edit changes after the file has been checked back in. This precautionary file management system means that other users cannot overwrite your work while it is being edited.

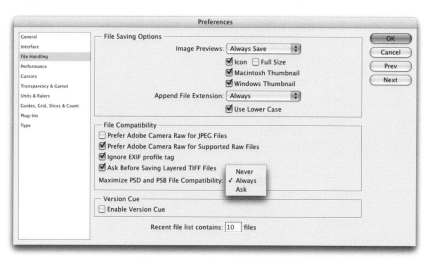

**Figure 3.8** The File Handling preferences.

### Recent File list

The Recent File list refers to the number of image document locations remembered in the Photoshop File ⇨ Open Recent submenu. I usually like to set this number to remember the last 10 opened images. But you may wish to set this higher.

Photoshop is unable to interpret an image, it will present an alert dialog. This will warn that certain elements cannot be read and offer the option to discard these and continue, or to read the composite image data. Discarding the unreadable data will allow another user to open your image, but when opened, it will be missing all the elements you added and most likely look very different from the file you intended that person to receive. But if they click the Read Composite Data button, and a composite was saved, the image will open using a flattened composite layer which does look the same as the image you created and saved. If no composite was created, they will just see a white picture and a multi-language message saying that no composite data was available.

Adobe InDesign allows you to place Photoshop format (PSD) files in a page layout but, if you do so, the Maximize Backwards Compatibility option must be checked in the General preferences (to generate a flattened composite). If you use layered TIFF, PSD (or Photoshop PDF) format files in your page layout workflow, you can modify the layers in Photoshop and the page design image will immediately be updated. This way you don't run the risk of losing synchronization between the master image that is used for Photoshop edits and a flattened version of the same image that is used solely for placing in the layout.

If you want to 'round trip' your images this way, TIFF is the more universally recognized file format. The downside is that you may end up with bloated files and these can significantly increase the file transmission times. If you are archiving layered Photoshop images, the most efficient option could be to save using the native PSD format and have Maximize PSD File Compatibility set to 'Never'. But such economies can come at a price. Maximizing PSD compatibility will make image load quicker in Bridge (and other file browser programs) and Adobe Lightroom is only able to read layered PSD files that have this option turned on. If there is no saved composite, Lightroom won't be able to import it.

## Performance

The Performance preferences section lets you configure all the things in Photoshop that will influence how efficiently Photoshop is able to run on your computer. The memory usage can now be set using a sliding percentage scale and you will notice how Photoshop provides a hint as to what the ideal range should be for your particular computer. The History & Cache preferences are now placed here too. The default number of History States is 20. You can set this to any number you like from 1–1000, but remember that the number of histories you choose will have a bearing on the scratch disk usage. The image cache settings affect the speed of screen redraws. Setting a higher number can help if you often work with very large images in Photoshop.

In the Scratch Disks section you can nominate up to four hard drives as scratch disks. Note how you now get to see more information about each disk used and can drag to rearrange them in order of priority (I'll be discussing memory and scratch disk usage over the next few pages). Checking the Enable 3D Acceleration option in the GPU Settings will allow Photoshop to make full use of the graphics processor memory on GPU enabled graphics cards.

### GPU settings

Photoshop is able to detect the graphics card used by your computer and if it has a built-in Graphics Processor Unit (GPU) capability, the Enable 3D Acceleration box will be shown. This feature will give you the option to take advantage of the GPU performance on the graphics card. In many instances this should lead to an improvement in graphics performance, but cannot be guaranteed. This is because with some of the more recent computers, or soon to be released Intel chip computers, the Central Processor (CPU) may actually offer the fastest graphics performance.

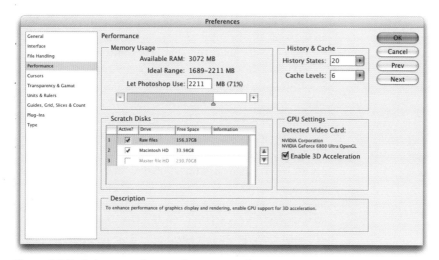

**Figure 3.9** The Performance preferences, where you can configure the Memory usage, History, Cache, Scratch Disks and GPU settings.

## RAM memory upgrades

Most PCs and Macs use DIMMs (Dual In-line Memory Modules). The specific RAM memory chips may vary for each type of computer, so check carefully with the vendor that you are buying the right type for your machine. RAM memory used to cost a small fortune, but these days the price of RAM is almost inconsequential. If you have four RAM slots on your machine, you should easily be able to install 4 × 512 MB RAM or 4 × 1 GB RAM memory chips, which will give you 2 or 4 GB of installed RAM.

## Move don't copy

To copy selections and layers between documents, use drag and drop actions with the move tool. This will save on memory usage and at the same time preserve the current clipboard contents.

## Virtual memory tricks

The Apple Macintosh and Windows operating systems are able to make efficient use of memory using their own virtual memory management systems. The Windows VM file should be set to at least 1.5 times your physical memory size. There are some software utilities that claim to double your RAM, but these will conflict with Photoshop's virtual memory and should not be used.

# RAM memory and scratch disks

The amount of RAM memory you have installed is a key factor that will determine how efficiently you can work in Photoshop. Adobe recommend for Photoshop CS3 that you allocate a minimum of 320 MB RAM memory, which means that if you allow an additional 128–256 MB of RAM for the operating system, you will need to have at least 512 MB of RAM installed in your computer. If you also take into account the requirements of other programs and the likelihood of newer operating systems needing even more memory, it is perhaps safer to suggest you will need a minimum of 1GB RAM memory in total.

Each time you launch Photoshop a certain amount of RAM memory will be set aside for use by the application, and this will depend on the amount set in the Performance preferences as a percentage of the total amount of RAM that is available to Photoshop. The figure you see in the Performance preferences is the RAM reserved for Photoshop imaging use, although the RAM you set aside for Photoshop will be shared by other applications when it is not actively being used by Photoshop, and don't forget that you will need to allow RAM memory to run Adobe Bridge at the same time as Photoshop.

How much RAM is available to Photoshop will depend on the total amount of RAM memory installed. Photoshop CS3 is a 32-bit application that is designed to work on computers with 32-bit or 64-bit processors running 32-bit or 64-bit operating systems. If you run Photoshop on a 64-bit computer that has 4 GB or more of RAM installed, a maximum of 3 GB will be allocated to Photoshop for handling image data. When you go to the Performance preferences, the total available RAM will be displayed in the Memory Usage section and below this you will see the recommended percentage of memory to allocate to Photoshop. On a Windows system the default setting is 50% and on a Mac it will be 70%. Although the memory assigned to Photoshop is freed up whenever Photoshop is not running, if the memory is set too high Photoshop may end up competing with the operating system for memory and this will slow performance.

## Enhancing memory and performance

The Performance preferences will provide a guide for the ideal RAM setting for your computer and what the upper limit should be, but you can always try allocating 5% above the recommended amount of memory, relaunch Photoshop and closely observe the Efficiency readout in the status bar or Info palette. Monitor the Efficiency readout: anything less than 100% will indicate that Photoshop is running short of RAM memory and having to make use of extra scratch disk space. But if you allocate too high a percentage, this will also compromise efficiency. The trick is to find the optimum percentage before you see a drop in performance. You might find the speed test described in the sidebar is a useful tool for gauging Photoshop performance.

If you have more than 4 GB memory installed (up to 6 GB on Windows and 8 GB on Mac OS X), the RAM above 4 GB can also be used by the operating system as a cache for the Photoshop scratch data. So although you can't allocate this extra memory directly, installing extra memory can boost Photoshop's performance.

Photoshop stores data such as recent history states and clipboard data in its memory on the scratch disk. Copying a large selection to the clipboard also uses up a lot of the scratch disk memory. Should you experience a temporary slowdown in performance you might want to purge Photoshop of any excess temporarily held data in the memory. To do this, choose Edit ⇨ Purge ⇨ Undo, Clipboard, Histories or All.

## Scratch disks

Photoshop utilizes free hard disk space as an extension of RAM memory and makes use of all the available free hard disk as specified in the Scratch Disks section as 'virtual memory'. When you launch Photoshop it will check to see how much hard disk space is free for scratch disk usage and it is worth noting here that should you for any reason have less scratch disk space than RAM memory space, the RAM memory will be restricted by the amount of scratch disk space that is available.

### Speed and efficiency test

To help evaluate the performance efficiency of your computer setup, there is a really useful weblink to a site hosted by a company called Retouchartists.com: retouchartists.com/pages/speedtest.html. From there you can download a test file which contains a sample image and a Photoshop action that was created by Alex Godden. All you have to do is time how long it takes for the action to complete, to gauge and compare how fast your computer is running. And then you can compare your speed test results with others.

## Scratch disk usage and history

The scratch disk usage will vary according to how many history states you have set in the History and Cache section and also how you use Photoshop. Generally speaking, Photoshop will store a version of each history state, but it does not always store a complete version of the image for each history state. As was explained in Chapter 2, the History feature only needs to save the changes made in each image tile. So if you carry out a series of brush strokes, the history will only store changes made to the altered image tiles. For these reasons the scratch disk usage will increase as you add more history states, but in practice the usage does not increase in large chunks, unless you were to perform a series of global filter changes.

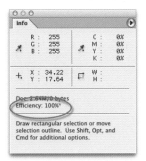

**Figure 3.10** You can monitor how efficiently Photoshop is running by adjusting the Info palette options to display an Efficiency readout. If the efficiency reading drops below 100% this means that Photoshop is having to rely on the designated scratch disk as a virtual memory source.

The primary scratch disk should ideally be one that is separate to the disk running the operating system and Photoshop. If you partition the main disk volume and designate an empty partition as the scratch disk, this will serve no useful purpose because the disk drive head will simply be switching back and forth between different sectors of the same disk as it tries to do the job of running the computer system and providing scratch disk space. For optimal image editing, at least 4 GB of free hard disk space is recommended, but ideally you want a scratch disk with at least 20–40 GB of free space, and the disk used should be as free as possible of fragmentation.

Photoshop always makes the most efficient use of real RAM memory and tries to keep as much RAM as possible free for memory intensive calculations. Low-level data like the 'last saved' version of the image is stored in the scratch disk memory giving priority to the current version and last undo versions being held in RAM. Normally, Photoshop uses all the available free RAM as buffer memory in which to perform real-time calculations and mirrors the RAM memory contents on the scratch disk. Photoshop does this whenever there is a convenient opportunity to do so. For example, after you open a new image you may notice some disk activity as Photoshop writes from the RAM memory buffer to the scratch disk. Photoshop then continually looks for ways to economize the use of RAM memory, writing to the hard disk in the background whenever there are periods of inactivity. Scratch disk data is also compressed when it is not in use (unless the optional plug-in extension that prevents this has been loaded at startup).

When Photoshop exhausts its reserves of RAM memory, it is forced to use the extra space on the scratch disk as a source of virtual memory and this is where you often start to see a major slowdown in efficiency. When the Efficiency indicator drops below 100% this means that the RAM buffer is full and Photoshop is now relying exclusively on the hard disk scratch disk space as a memory reserve.

## Scratch disk performance

With all this reliance on the scratch disk (or multiple scratch disks) to read/write data from the RAM memory buffer, the hard disk performance of the scratch disk plays an important role in maintaining Photoshop efficiency. There is provision in Photoshop for as many as four scratch disks. Each individual scratch file created by Photoshop can be a maximum of 2 GB and Photoshop can keep writing scratch files to a scratch disk volume until it becomes full. When the primary scratch disk runs out of room to accommodate all the scratch files during a Photoshop session, it will then start writing scratch files to the secondary scratch disk and so on. This makes for more efficient and faster disk usage.

## *Interface connections*

Most modern Macs and PCs have IDE, ATA or SATA drives as standard. A fast internal hard disk is adequate for getting started. But for better performance results, you should really install a second internal or external hard drive and have this dedicated as the primary scratch disk (make this the number one scratch disk in the Performance preferences). Your computer will most likely have the choice of a USB or FireWire connector for linking external devices. USB 2 offers a much faster connection speed than the old USB 1. FireWire (IEEE 1394) has many advantages over the older SCSI interface. First of all FireWire is a lot faster and secondly, it will often allow you to hot swap a drive between one computer and another. This is particularly useful when you wish to shuttle very large files around quickly. With the advent of FireWire 800 we are now seeing an appreciable improvement in data transfer speeds. FireWire drives are still IDE drives with a bridge to the FireWire standard, and since the Oxford Chipset came out, they have been able to enhance the throughput closer to the theoretical limit. Internal SCSI connections often use SCSI 2, which provides a quicker data transfer standard. Note that it is the data transfer and not data access time that is the measure of disk speed to look out for.

### Assigning scratch disks at startup

If you keep the `⌘` `⌥` `ctrl` `alt` keys held down at the beginning of the Photoshop startup cycle, you can first choose the location of the Additional Plug-ins Folder, followed by a prompt to assign the scratch disks.

### Hard drive spindle speeds

Most desktop computers use internal drives which run at 7200 rpm and you can easily find spare internal drives that run at this speed or faster. There are drives that even run at 10,000 rpm, but these are hard to come by and expensive. Laptop computers usually have slower hard drives fitted as standard (typically 5400 rpm). If you are working regularly from a laptop, you should notice quite a difference if you use just a standard external drive running at 7200 rpm as the primary scratch disk.

### Oxford Chipset

The most common Oxford Chipset is the 911, but 924 is even faster, and can be found in the very reliable Wiebetch drives.

## Software RAIDs

It used to be the case that software-created RAIDs such as the one included with the Mac OS X Disk Utilities program were a lot slower than a dedicated system. The read/write speeds from a software RAID will still be slower than a true dedicated RAID system since a software RAID will be stealing some of your computer processor cycles, but these days the speed loss is not so bad as it used to be. A software-driven internal striped RAID 0 can bring about a 45% increase in disk access speed. Overall I recommend that if you do choose to go down the internal RAID route, you include a RAID controller.

## RAID scratch disks

A striped RAID disk setup will offer the fastest scratch disk option. RAID stands for Redundant Array of Independent Disks. A simple way to explain RAID is that it allows you to treat multiple drives as a single drive volume to provide either increased data integrity, capacity, transfer rates or fault-tolerance compared to a single volume. And how it does this depends on the RAID level you choose. You will need a minimum of two disks to configure a RAID system and most off-the-shelf RAID solutions are sold as a bay dock that can accommodate two or more drives with a built-in RAID controller. A RAID disk can usually be connected via internal SCSI or an external FireWire 400/800 connection.

## RAID 0 (striping)

With a RAID 0 setup, two or more drives are striped together to create a single large volume drive. So for example, if two 200 GB drives are striped using a RAID 0 setup you will end up with a single 400 GB volume. RAID 0 is useful where you require fast hard drive access speeds, because the drive access speed will increase proportionally to the number of drives that are added. So if you have a 2 x 200 GB drive RAID 0 system, the hard drive access speed should be two times that of a single 400 GB drive. This is why a RAID 0 setup is ideal for Photoshop scratch disks.

## *Internal RAID*

You can fit an internal RAID system with a do-it-yourself kit consisting of two internally mounted drives and a RAID controller card. It should not be too challenging to install yourself, but if you are in any doubt about whether you are capable of doing this then you should get a qualified computer specialist to install the system in your computer. The advantage of an internal RAID is that it is always there whenever you turn the computer on and is an economical solution compared to buying an external RAID drive setup. Most PC tower computer systems should have plenty of free hard drive bays, which will make it fairly easy for

you to install internal RAID. The older G4 Macintosh
computers will allow you to fit two extra drives to form
a striped RAID 0 which can be managed by an internally
mounted PCI slot controller card. Note that the latest G5
desktops only have room to fit one extra drive. So a Quad
G5 computer will only suit an internal mirrored RAID
1 or a striped RAID 0 setup, which is not much use for
Photoshop work. But if you get one of the WiebeTECH G5
Jam Plus kits, this will allow you to install up to four extra
drives and includes a RAID controller card.

A RAID setup will definitely speed up the time it
takes Photoshop to read and write data to the scratch
disk. However, if you have more hard drives running
simultaneously this will mean more power consumption,
which in turn will generate more heat and possibly more
noise too. The extra heat may cause problems for the
cooling system in your computer and may put extra strain
on the internal power supply unit.

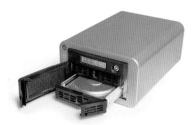

**Figure 3.11** A RAID system drive setup
contains two or more drives linked together that
can provide either faster disk access or more
secure data backup.

### *External RAID*

External RAID hard drive units are not overly expensive
and you can easily buy a ready assembled bay dock with a
couple of drives and a built-in RAID controller hardware
that can be configured for RAID 0. The speed will be
governed not just by the number of drives making up the
RAID but also by the speed of the cable connection. Some
RAID systems still use wide SCSI and require a SCSI card
to connect to the computer. More often these days they will
connect via Firewire 400/800 or SATA, which may again
require a special card in order to connect to the computer
(for now). Computers in the future are more likely to
support SATA as standard.

## Image Cache

The image cache settings affect the speed of screen redraws. Whenever you are working with a large image, Photoshop uses a pyramid type structure of lower resolution cached versions of the full resolution picture. Each cached image is a quarter scale version of the previous cache level and is temporarily stored in memory to provide speedier screen previews. Basically, if you are viewing a large image on screen in 'Fit to screen' display mode, Photoshop will use a cache level that is closest to the fit to screen resolution to provide a screen refresh view of any edit changes you make at this viewing scale. The cached screen previews can provide you with faster screen redraws and larger images will therefore benefit from using a higher cache level. A higher setting will provide a faster screen redraw, but at the expense of sacrificing the quality of the preview. This is because a lower resolution cache preview is not as accurate as choosing to view the image at Actual Pixels.

### Cache pyramid structure

You may sometimes notice how the layered Photoshop image on screen is not completely accurate at anything other than the 100% magnification – this is the image cache at work, it is speeding up the display preview at the expense of accuracy. If you have to work on an image at a less than 100% magnification, then do make sure the magnification is a wholly divisible number of 100%. In other words, it is better to work at 50%, 25% or 12.5% magnification, rather than at 66% or 33%. Note also that the number of cache levels chosen here will affect the structure of a 'Save Image Pyramid' TIFF file.

## Cursors

The painting cursor can be displayed as a painting tool icon, a precise crosshair or with the default setting, which is an outline of the brush shape at its 'most opaque' size in relation to the image magnification. In Photoshop CS2 and CS3 you can choose to display a Full Size brush tip, representing the entire outer edge reach of a soft edged brush, although it is debatable whether this improves the appearance of the painting cursors or not. The Show Crosshair in Brush Tip option will allow you to additionally display a crosshair inside the brush size cursor. For Other Cursors, the Standard option will represent other tools using the tool icon. I suggest you change this to the Precise setting, because this will make it easier for you to target the placement of these tools.

The *Caps Lock* key can be used to toggle the cursor display. When the standard paint cursor is selected, *Caps Lock* will toggle between standard and precise. When the precise or brush size paint cursor option is selected, *Caps Lock* will toggle between precise and brush size. When standard cursor mode is selected for all other cursors, *Caps Lock* will toggle between the standard and the precise cursor.

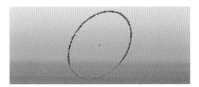

**Figure 3.12** This is an example of the brush cursor using the Full Size Brush Tip mode with Show Crosshair in Brush Tip.

### Brush opacity and cursor size

When the Normal brush tip is selected, the brush cursor size will represent the boundary of the brush shape up to where the brush opacity is 50% or denser in opacity. The full size cursor will represent the complete brush area size.

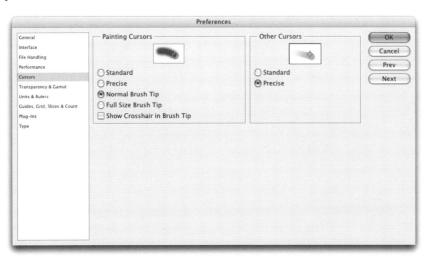

**Figure 3.13** The Display & Cursors preferences.

## Removing the checkerboard

I had an email recently from a reader who wanted to know how to get rid of the transparency checkerboard pattern. If you go to the preferences shown here you can select different grid sizes and colors, but you can also select None. When None is selected the transparent areas will be displayed as solid white.

## Color Picker gamut warning

The Gamut warning can also be invoked independently of the image in Photoshop's Color Picker dialog. The default overlay color is a neutral gray at 100% opacity, but I suggest reducing the opacity to make the gamut warning appear as a transparent overlay.

## Transparency & Gamut

The Transparency settings determine how the transparent areas in an image are represented on the screen. If a layer contains transparency and is viewed on its own with the background layer visibility switched off, the transparent areas are normally shown using a checkerboard pattern. The display preferences let you decide how the checkerboard grid size and colors are displayed. The Gamut Warning will alert you in advance to any colors that will be out of gamut after a conversion is made from, say, the RGB Color mode to whichever color space is currently loaded in the View ⇨ Proof Setup menu. So, if you are working on an image in RGB mode and you choose View ⇨ Gamut Warning, Photoshop will highlight these out-of-gamut colors with a color overlay. The gamut warning is, in my view, a rather crude instrument for determining whether colors are in gamut or not, since a color that is only slightly out will be highlighted as strongly as a color that is hugely out of gamut. A good quality graphics monitor using a Custom proof setup view mode is a much more reliable guide.

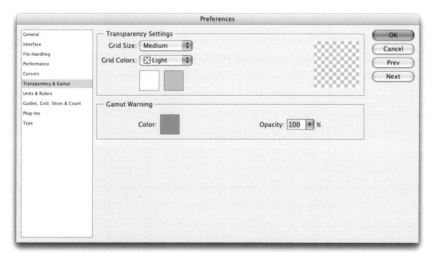

**Figure 3.14** The Transparency display settings are editable. You have a choice of Transparency display settings: None, Small, Medium or Large grid pattern, and a choice of different grid colors.

## Units & Rulers

You can use this preference section to set the Ruler measurement (inches or centimeters, etc.) and type of units used. The measurement units can also be changed via the Info palette submenu or by *ctrl* right mouse-clicking a ruler to open the contextual menu. You can also double-click the ruler bar as a shortcut for opening the preference window shown below. The New Document Preset Resolution options allow you to decide what pixel resolution should be the default for screen display or print output work when you select a preset size from the File ⇨ New Document dialog. The Print Resolution setting is the more useful as this always has an important bearing on the size that an image will print. The Screen Resolution has typically always been 72 ppi. But there is no real significance to whatever resolution is set here for an image that is destined to appear in a web page design. Web browser programs are only concerned with the physical number of pixels an image has. The resolution setting actually has no relevance.

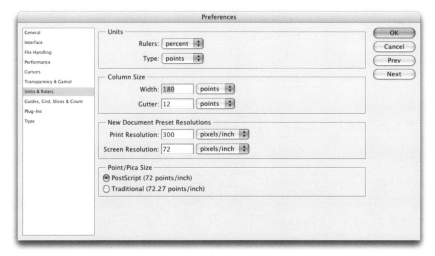

**Figure 3.15** Ruler units can be set in pixels, inches, cm, mm, points, picas or as a percentage. The percentage setting is ideal for recording actions that you wish to apply proportionally at any image size.

## Ensuring preferences are saved

Once you have configured your preferences and got everything set up just the way you want, it is a good idea to Quit and restart Photoshop, as this will then force Photoshop to save these preferences to the preference file.

## *Guides, Grid & Slices*

These preferences let you choose the colors for the Guides, Smart Guides and Grid. Both Grid and Guides can be displayed as solid or dashed lines, with the added option of dotted lines for the Grid. The number of Grid subdivisions can be adjusted to suit whatever project you are working on and the Slice options include Line Color style and whether the Slice numbers are displayed or not.

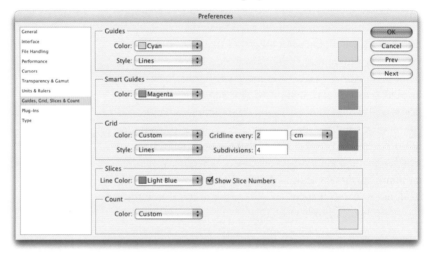

**Figure 3.16** The Guides, Grid & Slices preferences.

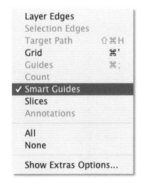

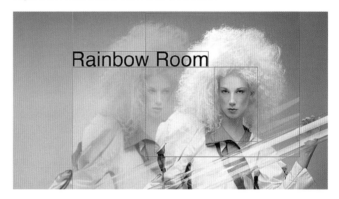

**Figure 3.17** The View ⇨ Show menu options include Layer Edges. When this is selected the currently selected layer or layers will be indicated with a rectangular color edge border. The Smart Guides option is useful as a visual aid for aligning layer elements. The Smart Guides (shown here in pink) will flash on and off to indicate when a layer element is aligned to other layers in the image.

## Plug-ins

The Plug-ins folder will automatically be recognized by
Photoshop so long as it resides in the same application
folder. But you can also choose an Additional Plug-ins
Folder that may be located in another application folder
(such as Adobe Photoshop Elements) so these can in effect
be shared with Photoshop. To do this click on the Choose...
button to locate the additional folder. If you install any
third-party plug-ins that pre-date Photoshop CS3, they
may possibly incorporate a hidden installation process that
looks for a valid Photoshop serial number in the older style,
consisting of letters and numbers. To be honest, this change
in serial number formats happened such a long time ago,
it is unlikely you will need to bother with this. But if you
experience this type of problem, just remember that you
can enter your old Photoshop serial number in the Legacy
Serial Number box.

   If you keep the ⌘ ⌥ *ctrl* *alt* keys held down at the
beginning of the Photoshop startup cycle, this will pop a
Navigation dialog that will let you point to the location of
the Additional Plug-ins Folder.

### Accessing the JPEG 2000 plug-in

The JPEG 2000 file format plug-in is not
installed as part of the regular Photoshop
installation, but it will be installed in the
Bridge Plug-ins folder. So if you click the
Additional Plug-ins Folder checkbox and
click on the Choose button and navigate to
the Bridge Plug-ins folder, you will be able
to save images out of Photoshop using the
JPEG 2000 file format after you relaunch
Photoshop.

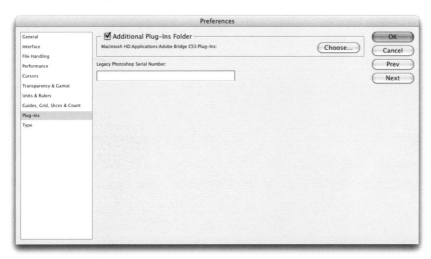

**Figure 3.18** The Plug-ins preferences.

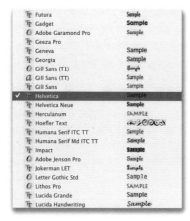

**Figure 3.19** Photoshop presents the font lists using a WYSIWYG menu listing.

## Type preferences

We could all do with smart quotes I guess, but the smart quotes referred to here are a preference for whether the text tool uses vertical quotation marks or rounded ones that are inverted at the beginning and end of a sentence. The Show Asian Text Options is there for Asian users, to enable the Chinese, Japanese and Korean text options in the Character palette. The Show Font Names in English option is of more significance for non-English language users. If they are using a regionalized version of Photoshop they will see an option for displaying font names in their native language. The Enable Missing Glyph Protection option will switch on automatic font substitution for any missing glyph fonts (those swirly graphic font characters).

The Type tool Options palette also provides a WYSIWYG menu listing of all the available fonts when you mouse down on the Font Family menu (see Figure 3.19). The Font Preview Size menu will determine the font sizes used when displaying this list and this menu item should not be confused with the UI Font Size preference that is in the General preferences section.

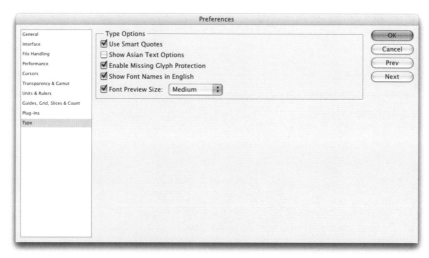

**Figure 3.20** The Type preferences.

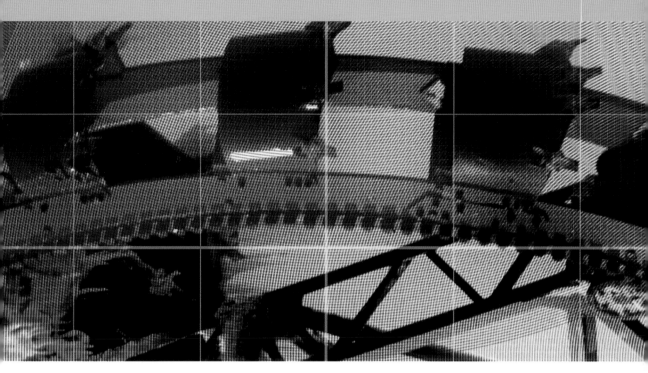

**Chapter 4**

# Basic Pixel Image Editing

**T**he aim of this chapter is to introduce you to the basic Photoshop image adjustments. Since this is what you are going to be doing to every picture you edit in Photoshop, it is worth spending some time understanding the underlying principles of what the adjustment tools do.

When I first started writing about Photoshop, one could assume that most images would have been brought in from a scanner and had originated as rendered pixel images. These days, a lot of photographers will be shooting digitally and therefore may be starting out with a raw capture file. In this chapter I am going to focus on basic pixel image processing only and in the following chapter I will be showing you the alternative way to process camera capture images, using Camera Raw.

In the main body text I refer to 'rendered pixels'. I use this to describe pixel images after they have been converted from the raw capture state. This includes images that are scanned as well as images that have been captured with a digital camera. This is because all digital images are captured using an analog sensor of some kind. The analog signal is processed to form a raw digital image that can be saved as a raw file or converted into a fixed pixel image by interpreting the raw data in a specific way. Once a capture image has been rendered as a pixel image you cannot revert to the raw data version unless you have access to the raw data in a raw file. This is a key benefit of shooting in raw mode because preserving the raw capture data as it comes off the camera will allow you to interpret it in many different ways before you fix the raw data as a pixel image.

# Image capture and file output

All digital images will have been captured via a sensor of some kind. If you use a film scanner, the sensor device will pass across the surface of the film or print to read the image and record the image capture data. The scanner software will preview the capture data and allow you to make some basic adjustments before exporting it as a rendered pixel image. A scanner will usually export such files as TIFF images.

If you use a digital camera, the camera will record the light hitting the sensor and convert this into a digital capture file that can be processed in one of two ways. If the camera is set to TIFF or JPEG mode, the camera will use an on-board processor (which is like a mini-computer) to automatically calculate how best to interpret the raw capture data and render it as a fixed TIFF or JPEG pixel image output. If the camera is set to raw mode, it will instead save the unprocessed raw data as a raw output file and this will give you the flexibility to make all the post-capture adjustments later and override the camera auto processing settings.

The images you bring into Photoshop therefore fall into two categories. Rendered pixel images are what most of us are familiar with and these include: file outputs from a scanner, images that have been captured digitally from a camera using the TIFF or JPEG setting and, basically, any image that is not a raw file. Such images can be opened directly into Photoshop and edited directly within the program. The amount of editing that is required will depend on how well the images have been optimized. But in most cases you will need to use the adjustment tools described in this chapter to fine-tune your images, and the techniques discussed here should be regarded as essential foundation skills for Photoshop image editing. Because, however, you bring your images into Photoshop, you will at some point need to know how to work with the basic image editing tools like Levels and Curves, such as when adding adjustment layers to an image.

In the case of raw images your choices are more open. You could use the raw processing software that came with the camera, or you could use one of the main independent raw processing programs such as Capture One from Phase One, Apple Aperture, Bibble or dcRaw. But since this is a book about Photoshop I will be focusing later on how to use Adobe Camera Raw that is bundled with Photoshop CS3. This is the same raw processing engine that is used by Adobe Photoshop Lightroom and the latest Camera Raw provides full compatibility with most of the develop settings in Lightroom.

If you intend bringing your images in via Camera Raw, it can be argued that the Photoshop image adjustment tools are unnecessary, because Camera Raw will provide you with all the tools you need to produce perfectly optimized images. You can save Camera Raw adjustments to disk or open Camera Raw processed images as rendered pixel images in Photoshop. If you shoot digitally, I recommend you use the raw mode and suggest you carry out all the initial image editing in Camera Raw rather than in Photoshop, and would advise you to follow the instructions outlined in Chapter 5 for optimizing raw images. However, you will still find that the information contained in this chapter is important, because it will teach you how to use the basic editing tools. These are the things that every Photoshop user should be aware of and need to use when applying things like localized corrections. So, for now, let's look at basic pixel image editing techniques.

## Scanner software

If you are scanning in images you will mostly be limited to working with the software that was supplied with the scanner. I recommend that you use the scanner software to optimize the image to a minimum standard in which the levels are just about beginning to clip the shadows and highlights. Some scanner software will allow you to add sharpening or noise reduction. But you may prefer to bypass these built-in scanner controls, because you can also apply such corrections in Photoshop.

### Adobe Photoshop Lightroom

The Adobe Photoshop Lightroom program is designed as a raw processor and image management program for photographers. As mentioned in the text, it uses the exact same Adobe Camera Raw color engine that is used in Photoshop CS3, which means that raw files that have been adjusted in Lightroom can also be read and opened via Photoshop. However, Lightroom has the advantage of offering a full range of workflow modules designed to let you edit and manage raw images all the way from the camera import stage through to print and web output.

### WYSIWYG image editing

If you want true WYSIWYG editing (what you see is what you get), it is important that you follow the instructions laid out in the previous chapter on how to calibrate the display and configure the color settings. Do this and you will now be ready to start editing your photographs with confidence.

## Interpreting an image

A digital image is nothing more than a lot of numbers and it is how those numbers are interpreted in Photoshop that creates the image you see on the display. We can use our eyes to make subjective judgements about how the picture looks, but we can also use the number information to provide useful and usable feedback. The Info palette is your friend. If you understand the numbers, it can help you see the fine detail that your eyes are not sharp enough to discern. And we now have the Histogram palette, which is a godsend to geeks who just love all that statistical analysis stuff, but it is also an excellent teaching tool. The Histogram palette will make everything that follows much easier to understand.

## Digital camera histograms

Some digital cameras provide a histogram display that enables you to check the quality of what you have just shot. This too can be used as an indication of the levels captured in a scene. However, the histogram you see displayed is often based on a JPEG capture only. If you are shooting in JPEG mode, that's what you are going to get. But if you prefer to shoot using raw mode, the histogram will not provide an accurate guide to the true potential of the image you have captured. See Chapter 11 for more about digital capture and shooting in raw mode.

## The image histogram

The histogram is a bar chart that graphically represents the shades of tone (described as Levels) that make up a digital photograph. A basic 8-bit per channel grayscale image has a single channel and uses 256 shades of gray to describe all the shades of tone from black to white. Black has a levels value of 0 (zero) and white has a levels value of 255. And all the numbers in between represent the shades of gray going from black to white. The histogram is like a graph with 256 increments, each representing how often a particular levels number (a specific gray color) occurs in the image. If a picture contains mostly a lot of grays with number values of between 30 and 130 levels, you will expect to see a peak around the 30–130 levels point of the histogram graph. Figure 4.1 shows a typical histogram and how the appearance of the graph relates to the tonal structure of a photographic image.

Now let's look at what that information can tell us about a digital image. The histogram show us the distribution of tones in an image. A high-key photograph will have lots of peaks towards the right of the graph and a low-key photograph will have lots of peaks to the left. And most importantly, it shows the positioning of the shadow and highlight points. When you apply a tonal correction using Levels or Curves, the histogram provides a visual clue that helps you judge where the brightest highlights and deepest shadows should be. And the histogram also tells you something about the condition of the image you are editing. If the bars are bunched up at either end of the histogram, this suggests that the highlights or shadows are most likely clipped and that when the original photograph was scanned or captured it was effectively under- or overexposed. Unfortunately, if the levels are clipped at either end of the scale you can't restore the detail that has been lost. And if there are gaps in the histogram, this will most likely indicate a poor quality scan or that the image had previously been heavily manipulated.

The histogram can therefore be used to check the quality of an image at the beginning of an edit session. If it looks particularly dreadful then maybe you should

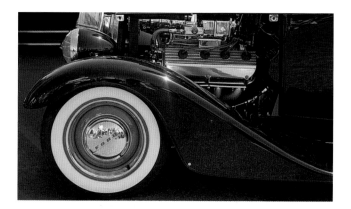

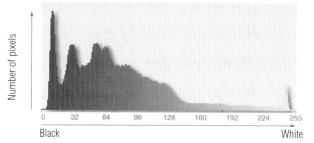

**Figure 4.1** Here is an image histogram that represents the distribution of tones from the shadows to the highlights. Because this photograph mostly contains dark shades of gray you will notice that the levels are predominantly located to the left end of the histogram. The height of each bar in the histogram indicates the frequency of pixels occurring at each level point.

try rescanning the picture. But must one be so absolutely pixel-correct about always obtaining a smooth histogram? Any image editing you do will inevitably degrade the image. Because after a picture has been manipulated the histogram will always look less smooth than it was at the beginning. If you are preparing a photograph to go to a print press, you would be lucky to detect more than 50 levels of tonal separation from any single ink plate. So the loss of a few levels at the completed edit stage does not necessarily imply that you have too little digital tonal information from which to reproduce a full-tonal range image in print. But appreciate that if you begin with a bad-looking histogram, the image is only going to be in a worse state after it has been retouched, so start with the best image scan or capture. And in particular watch out for any signs of clipping.

## The Histogram palette

There has always been a histogram in the Levels dialog and there is now also a Histogram palette, which gives you even more feedback when working in Photoshop. With the Histogram palette, you can continuously observe the impact your image editing has on the image levels. You can also check the histogram while making curves or any other type of image adjustment. The Histogram palette only provides an approximate representation of the image levels. To ensure that the Histogram palette is giving an accurate representation of the image levels, it is advisable to force Photoshop to update the histogram view, by clicking on the Refresh button at the top of the palette.

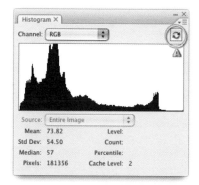

**Figure 4.2** The warning triangle in the Histogram palette indicates that you need to click on the Refresh button above to update it.

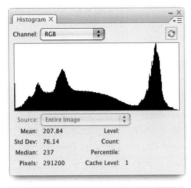

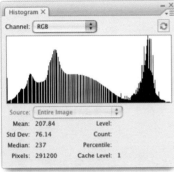

**Figure 4.3** The histogram at the top is from an image in 8-bits per channel mode that started out in 16-bits per channel mode but where the levels were expanded using a Levels and a Curves adjustment. The histogram below is of the same image after the same adjustments had been applied as before, but the image was in 8-bits per channel mode throughout. As you can see, if you keep a picture in 16-bits per channel mode at the initial stages while you apply Levels and Curves adjustments, more of the levels data will be preserved.

# 16-bits per channel support

Most of the techniques described in this book have been carried out on files that originated from a 48-bit RGB color original file (an image made up of three 16-bit color channels). Most scanners and professional digital cameras are able to capture more than 8 bits per channel. And if an imported image contains more than 8 bits per channel data, it will be opened in Photoshop in 16-bits per channel mode. A 24-bit color image will have only 256 data points in each of its 8-bit per color channels, whereas a 16-bit per channel image in Photoshop can have up to 32,768 data points per color channel (because in truth, Photoshop's 16-bit depth is 15 bit +1). This gives you a lot more levels of tone to play around with, especially when using Levels or Curves adjustments where you are stretching these levels to expand and fill a wider tonal range, as well as when you are modifying the contrast or altering the color balance.

Some have argued that 16-bit image editing is a futile exercise because no one can tell the difference by looking at an image that has been edited in 16 bit compared to one that has been edited in 8 bit. Well, perhaps, but I personally believe this to be a foolish argument. For a start, if you can capture a picture in 16 bit why not make use of all that extra tonal information, even if it is only to make your primary Levels and Curves edits? After that you switch to do everything else in 8-bit per channel mode. If you look at Figure 4.3, this shows two histogram displays which compare the result of making Levels and Curves edits to an image in both 8-bit per channel and 16-bit per channel modes. You may save a second or two by making these corrections in 8-bit mode, but is that saving worthwhile when you see how much data will become lost? The second point is you never know what the future has in store. On pages 176–179 we shall be looking at Shadow/Highlight adjustments. This feature exploits the fact that a deep-bit image can contain lots of hidden levels data which can be exploited to reveal more image detail than was possible before. It will work with 8-bit images too, but you get better results if you scan or capture in 16-bit per channel mode.

Photoshop offers extensive support for 16-bit mode editing. You can crop, rotate, make all the usual image adjustments and use all the Photoshop tools and work with layers in 16-bit mode, in grayscale, RGB, CMYK and Lab Color modes. But only a few filters are available including the new Lens Correction and now also the Liquify filter. Wherever possible, I always aim to begin my editing with a file that has been scanned or captured using high-bit data and brought into Photoshop in 16-bit per channel mode. I will crop the picture and apply a Levels and Curves adjustment to get the picture looking good on the screen and then and only then will I consider converting the image to 8-bits per channel mode. But since Photoshop also allows you to work using layered images in 16 bit, I will keep the image in this mode for as long as I can. You may not feel the need to use 16 bits per channel all the time for every job, but I would say that for critical jobs where you don't want to lose an ounce of detail, it is essential to make all your preliminary edits in this mode.

## 16-bit and color space selection

For a long time now Photoshop experts such as myself have advocated editing in RGB using a conservative gamut color space such as Adobe RGB (if you want to read more about RGB color spaces then you will need to read Chapter 13 on color management). Although 16-bit editing is not new to Photoshop, it is only since the advent of Photoshop CS that it has been possible to edit more extensively in 16 bit. And one of the advantages this brings is we are no longer limited to using a relatively small gamut RGB work space to edit in. It is perfectly safe to use a large gamut space such as ProPhoto RGB when you are editing in 16-bits per channel mode because there are 128 times as many data points in each color channel compared to when you are editing in a standard RGB space such as ColorMatch or Adobe RGB. In practice, I still use Adobe RGB as my main color space, but I sometimes start editing my captures or scans in 16-bit ProPhoto RGB and convert to 8-bit Adobe RGB afterwards.

### Where did the extra levels go?

If you have a keen knowledge of math, you will notice that Photoshop uses only 32,768 levels out of a possible 65,536 levels when describing a 16-bit mode image. This is because having a tonal range that goes from 0 to 32,767 is more than adequate to describe the data coming off any digital device. And also because from an engineering point of view, 15-bit math calculations give you a midpoint value. Most digital compacts and digital SLRs claim a bit depth of 12 bits per channel. High-end cameras are realistically capable of capturing up to 14 bits per channel. So the true figure of 15 bits per channel when editing in Photoshop's 16-bit per channel mode is still more than adequate for now.

### Displaying deep-bit color

It is hard to appreciate a significant difference between 8-bit per channel and 16-bit per channel editing when all you have to view your work on is an 8-bit per channel display. But screen display technology is rapidly improving and in the near future we will see the introduction of flat screen displays that use a combination of LEDs and LCDs, capable of displaying images at greater bit depths and at a higher dynamic range. Sunnybrook Technologies have shown an early prototype and the difference is remarkable. In the future, such displays will enable you to see the images you are editing in greater tonal detail and over a much wider dynamic range, should you wish to do so.

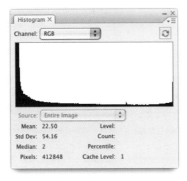
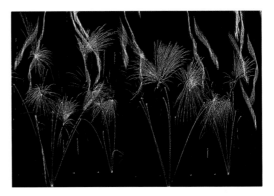

**Figure 4.4** If the levels are bunched up towards the left, this is a sign of shadow clipping. But in this example we probably want the shadows to be clipped in order to produce a rich black sky.

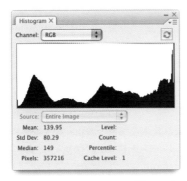
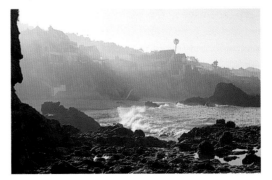

**Figure 4.5** If the levels are bunched up towards the right, the highlights may be clipped. But in this image I wanted the brightest areas of the sky to burn out to white.

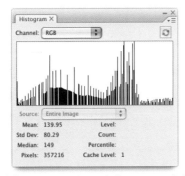
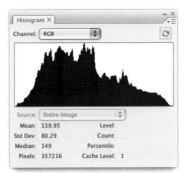

**Figure 4.6** A histogram with a comb-like appearance indicates that either the image has already been heavily manipulated or an insufficient number of levels were captured in the original scan.

**Figure 4.7** This histogram shows that the image contains a full range of tones, without any shadow or highlight clipping and no gaps between the levels.

## Levels adjustments

When you open an image in Photoshop your main objective will probably be to make an inkjet print, convert the image to CMYK or add it to a website. And the first thing you will want to do is adjust the tonal range so that the photograph has a nice full range. If it is destined for the web, your only concern will be how light or dark you want to make it, so that it appears OK on a typical PC display. If it is going to print then you may be aware of the fact that the shadow point should be adjusted to compensate for the printing process. But you shouldn't let any of this concern you too much, because the shadow point is always adjusted automatically in Photoshop when you choose a print profile in the print driver (as described in Chapter 14) or when you convert the image from RGB to CMYK. If you are optimizing an RGB image for output, all you need to worry about is making sure that the blacks go to black and the whites go to white. We are now going to look at a few different ways to make a tonal correction in Photoshop. We will begin with some black and white images. I deliberately chose to start with some monochrome photographs, because it makes the interpretation of the histogram simpler.

### When levels have to be set manually

You should be aware that some repro companies operate what is known as a closed-loop system where they edit files in CMYK and do not use a profiled workflow. This is something that will affect high-end repro users of Photoshop and if this is the case, then you will need to target the shadows manually according to the conditions of the printing press. The same is also true if you are editing a grayscale file in Photoshop that is going to press. These prepress examples are covered later on in the chapter.

### Exposure image adjustment

The Exposure adjustment, introduced first in Photoshop CS2, was included as an image adjustment for specialist users doing compositing work with HDR images (see pages 286–290). You can use it to adjust normal images, but that is not its real purpose.

Input shadows slider     Gamma slider     Input highlights slider

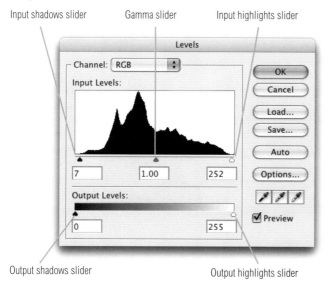

Output shadows slider     Output highlights slider

**Figure 4.8** The Photoshop Levels dialog. The Input sliders are just below the histogram display and you use these to adjust the input shadows, highlights and gamma (the relative image brightness between the shadows and highlights). Below these are the Output sliders and you can use these to set the output shadows and highlights. It is best not to touch these unless you are retouching a prepress file in grayscale or CMYK, or you deliberately wish to reduce the output contrast for some reason.

**1** The monochrome photograph shown here was in fact in RGB mode (because this allowed me to demonstrate the full range of Levels adjustment options). And the Histogram palette displays a histogram of the composite RGB channel. The contrast could be improved by expanding the levels so that the histogram displays a fuller range of tones going from black to white. To improve the tonal range, I chose Image ⇨ Adjustments ⇨ Levels.

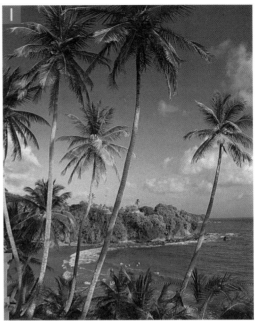

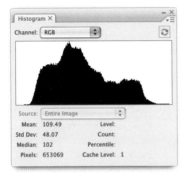

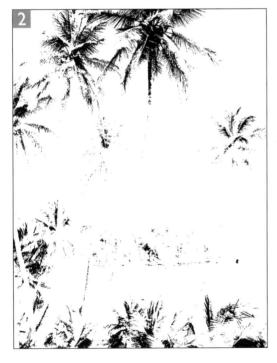

**2** As I dragged the highlight and shadow Input sliders in the Levels dialog, I could decide where the new shadow and highlight endpoints should be. One way of doing this is to simply look at the histogram in the Levels dialog and drag the Input sliders inwards until they meet either end of the histogram. But you can get a better idea of where to set the endpoints by switching to Threshold display mode. I held down the ⌥ *alt* key as I dragged the Shadow slider inwards and the image in the document window then appeared posterized. This threshold view enables you to discern more easily where the darkest shadows are in the picture. Drag in too much and you will clip all the shadow detail. The view shown opposite is too extreme, so I would want to back off from here, otherwise the shadows would become too clipped.

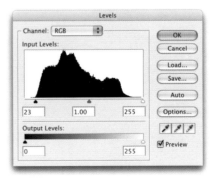

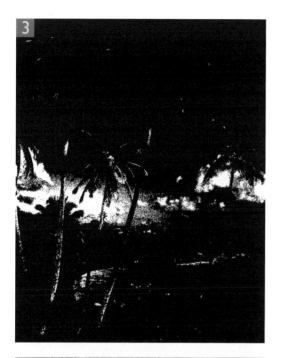

**3** I now wanted to adjust the highlights. The same technique can be applied here as well. I held down the ⌥ *alt* key as I dragged the Highlight slider to the left. The Threshold mode display started off completely black and the lightest highlights appeared first as I dragged inwards. As before, the view shown here was too extreme so I would want to back off a bit and search for the lightest highlight point without the risk of clipping too much of the highlight detail.

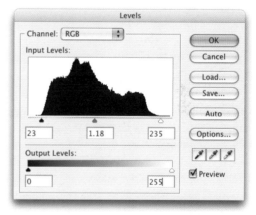

**4** All that remained now was to compensate the lightness of the picture, which was achieved by dragging the Gamma slider (which is the middle Input slider). Dragging to the right made the image relatively darker, and dragging to the left made it relatively lighter. The final image shown here has a full contrast range and the correct brightness.

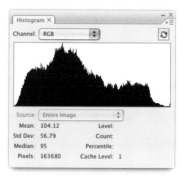

## Automatic Levels compensation

Figure 4.9 shows an example of what an image histogram looks like after it has been optimized in Photoshop. This is accompanied by two more histogram views that show how the histogram would look after the image has been converted to make an inkjet print or converted to CMYK color. Notice how the histogram shape changes and in particular how the shadow point is adjusted inwards after the image has been converted. This is because Photoshop will automatically calculate the shadow point compensation for you (advanced users who use the Convert to Profile command in the Image ⇨ Mode menu should remember to always check the Black Point Compensation checkbox).

## Levels after a conversion

So far you have seen how the Levels histogram can be used to help you visualize the tonal range of an image from the shadows to the highlights. By using the Levels dialog in conjunction with the histogram you can optimize the contrast precisely so that the darkest pixel in the image goes to black and the lightest pixel goes to white. And in the majority of instances it really should be as simple as that. But there are instances when you will want to hold back on the highlights slightly and these are discussed over the following few pages. The only other times when you need to give special consideration to setting the shadows to anything other than level 0, and the highlights to level 255, are when you are required to edit a CMYK or grayscale file which is destined to go to a printing press.

Sometimes you come across advice that the shadows in an RGB image should be set to something like 20, 20, 20 (the Red, Green, Blue RGB values) and the highlights should be set to 245, 245, 245. And the reason given for this is because anything darker than a 20, 20, 20 shadow value will reproduce in print as a solid black. Well, if you follow these instructions you will certainly get to see the shadow detail, but your prints may have much lighter shadows than is really necessary. In the early days of Photoshop it was necessary to make this kind of compensation when you were setting the levels. But for some time now, Photoshop has had a built-in mechanism which automatically compensates the shadow point for you whenever you convert an RGB image to CMYK or produce a desktop print output (see Chapter 14: Output for the Web). Not only that, but Photoshop is able to compensate the shadow point by the exact amount for each different type of output. So when you are setting the shadows, just keep it simple: use 0, 0, 0 and let Photoshop automatically calculate the best optimized shadow point for you during the conversion to the output color space.

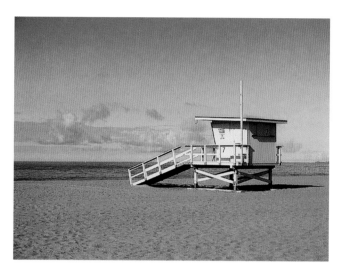

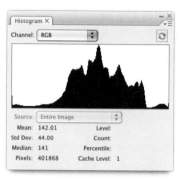

Original histogram – Adobe RGB

**Figure 4.9** The histogram appearance usually changes after a mode or profile conversion. For example, when you use the Print with Preview dialog to convert an RGB file to a print output space, the shadow tones are automatically made a little lighter so as to render the best shadow detail on the paper. The same thing happens when you make a CMYK conversion, but the black point will probably shift in even more. If you see a box called Black Point Compensation, leave it checked. Photoshop automatically compensates the black point to suit your CMYK conversion. Do not attempt to deliberately make the shadows lighter beforehand when you are editing an image in RGB.

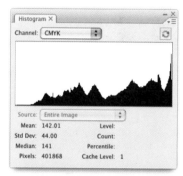

CMYK setting used for this book

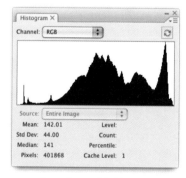

Epson Heavyweight Matte paper

And what about the highlight points? Will Photoshop automatically convert these for you as well? The answer here is no, the highlights have to be set manually and it really is dependent on the image as to what is the best highlight point setting to use. The problem here is that if you make the highlights go all the way to 255, 255, 255, the levels may be so high that the image highlight tones within the 240–255 range will all print as pure white. With certain types of image this will cause problems and you will want to make sure your brightest tones are no lighter than, say, 245. And other times you will have photographs where you don't need to preserve all the highlight detail. We will be looking at two examples of setting the highlights shortly, but first, let's look at one of the exceptional cases where you may be required to fine-tune the endpoints manually.

## Resetting the image adjustments

If you want to reset the settings in any of the Image adjustment dialog boxes, hold down the ⌥ alt key – the Cancel button changes to Reset. The Auto button will set the clipping points automatically (the Auto settings are covered in Chapter 5).

## *Fine-tuning the endpoints*

You can also use the black point and white point tools in the Levels or Curves adjustment dialogs to assign specific pixel values independently to the shadows and the highlights. Normally you can rely on the image mode conversion to adjust the shadow points. But there are certain situations where it is desirable to fine-tune the endpoints manually yourself. Targeting and assigning the endpoints in this way is important if you are working on grayscale images that are destined for print in a book, magazine or a newspaper. And it may also be necessary if the image is already in CMYK mode but without an embedded profile, where you know what the press output should be. Instead of relying on profiles to do the conversion, you can assign a shadow point that is higher than 0% and assign a highlight point that is slightly darker than 100%. You usually do this when you wish to ensure that the highlight detail will be adequately preserved. It can also be useful as a means of color correcting an image and removing a color cast from the shadows or highlights in an image. In between the black point and white point tools is the gray point tool which can be used to assign a target gray color to the midtones (this and other methods of color correction will be dealt with more thoroughly in the next chapter).

Let's now run through the basic steps for assigning a highlight and shadow point via the black point and white point tools. But before you do anything else, select the eyedropper tool in the Tools palette and go to the eyedropper Options bar and set the Sample Size to 3 × 3 Average. You can use the black point and white point tools with their default settings to simply assign a highlight point of 100% and a shadow point of 0%, but in the example shown on the page opposite I demonstrate how to assign specific target values to the black point and white point tools, so that you can map specific parts of the image to new pixel values. This method allows you to decide exactly where the highlight and shadow points should be.

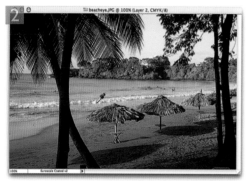

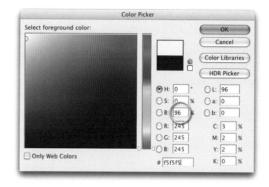

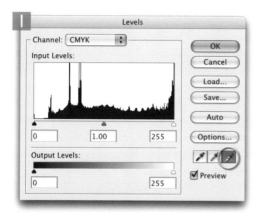

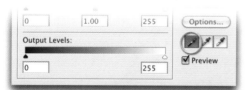

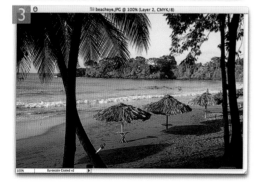

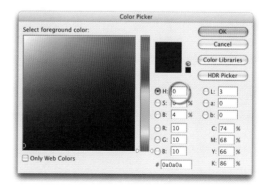

**1** I double-clicked the highlight eyedropper icon in the Levels dialog box and set the highlight target value to match that of the press. A brightness setting of 96% as shown here is OK for most printing situations.

**2** I studied the image and looked for the shadow and highlight points. The previously described Threshold mode technique is a good way of finding out where these are. I zoomed in on the image and clicked on the area I wanted to assign as the highlight target point. This should be a subject highlight, not a specular highlight such as a reflection or glare.

**3** Next I set the shadow point. I double-clicked the shadow eyedropper icon and set a brightness setting of 4% (or higher, depending on the press) in the text box as the target brightness. After that, with the shadow eyedropper still selected, I zoomed in on the image to identify and clicked on the darkest shadow point. The Gamma slider could be adjusted the same way as in the last example to adjust the relative image brightness.

## Setting the highlights

As you aim to expand the tonal range, you want to make the lightest point go to white so the whites do not look too dull. But at the same time you don't want the highlights to look burnt out either. Setting the highlight point is very often a subjective decision and where you set the white point is really dependent on the nature of the image. In most cases you can use the basic Levels adjustment Threshold mode technique to locate the highlight point and set the endpoint accordingly and not worry about losing any highlight detail. But if the picture you are editing contains a lot of delicate highlight information then you will want to be careful to set the highlight point to somewhere slightly less than pure white on the levels scale. This is because a pixel value that is close to maximum white, when converted to a printing process, may blow out to white as well. But what if the image contains bright specular highlights, such as highlight reflections off metal? Specular highlights do not contain any detail, so you therefore want these to print to paper white. If you don't, then the image will print a lot duller than is necessary.

## Specular Highlights

When you are using a Levels adjustment to set the highlights you have to examine the image and ask yourself if the highlight detail matters or not. Some pictures will contain subtle highlight detail while others may look like the photograph below in Figure 4.10, where the highlights consist of what is referred to as 'specular' light reflecting off a shiny metal surface. In a case like this the last thing you need to concern yourself with is preserving the detail. You can safely drag the Input highlight slider inwards to clip the highlights and thereby force these specular highlights to print as pure white. Because there is no actual detail in these highlights, there is nothing worth preserving anyway. By forcing the specular highlights to the maximum white you are safely enhancing the image contrast.

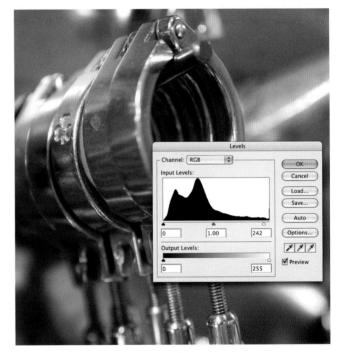

Figure 4.10 The highlights in this image contain no detail. There is no point in limiting the image contrast by setting the highlight to anything less than the maximum white possible. One can safely afford to clip the highlights in this image without losing important image detail.

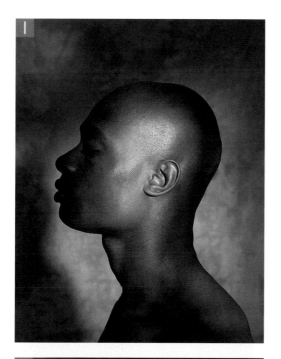

**1** If you are too cautious about setting the endpoints for the shadows and highlights and do not make full use of the tonal range, this can lead to a dull print output. There are times when you will want to make use of rich blacks and bright paper whites to reproduce a full contrast image. The subject shown here contains specular highlights. In other words, it contains highlights that have no detail. If I were to assign these 'specular' highlights a white point of 243, and the shadow point 12, the printed result will look needlessly dull and flat.

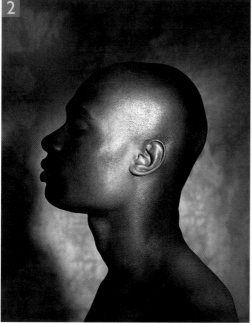

**2** The brightest portions of the image are the shiny skin reflections and I can safely let these areas burn out to white, because they do not contain any significant image detail. I assigned the brightest area in the highlights (where there is detail) as the white point and let the specular highlights print to paper white. The adjusted version shown here benefits from a wider tonal scale making full use of the press and at the same time retains important highlight detail where it matters.

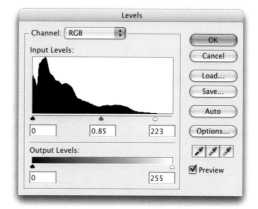

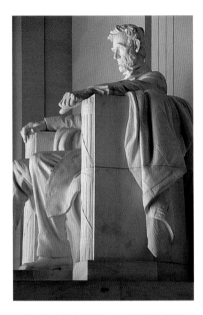

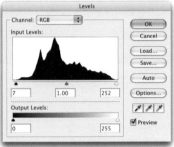

Figure 4.11 The highlights in this picture contain a lot of important detail. So you really want to avoid clipping the highlights too much. It is important to ease off slightly more than usual when setting the highlights. This will avoid you running the risk of losing important highlight information in the final print.

## Preserving the highlight detail

So the lesson we have learnt so far is that one has to be very careful when judging where to set the highlight point. If you don't drag the Levels highlight slider in far enough, you will get dull highlights. But if you drag the highlight slider in too far then you risk losing important highlight detail. The photograph in Figure 4.11 is a good example of an image requiring careful attention to preserve all the highlight detail. In most cases you will want to use the threshold analysis method described on pages 142–143 to detect the highlight point and use your informed judgement to decide whether to drag the Input highlight slider in further, leave it where it is (where the highlights just start to clip) or drag it out ever so slightly.

## Cut-outs against a white background

Subjects photographed or cut out against a white background are another special case deserving careful treatment. Ideally you want the white background to print as pure white on the paper, but not at the expense of losing image detail in important highlight areas elsewhere in the photograph. When preparing such a cut-out, the levels should first be adjusted with consideration for the subject only. The background should be adjusted separately without compromising the tonal range of the subject. The accompanying example suggests one strategy to achieve this. I made a feathered selection of the background, filled it with white and then used the history brush to paint the edge detail back in. Graphic designers may sometimes use a clipping path to create the cut-out. A clipping path is a designated pen path saved in an EPS or TIFF file format that is used to mask an image when placed in a page layout program. If I was preparing a clipping path of the model in the following step-by-step, I would do everything the same, but make the clipping path a few pixels beyond the model's outline, so that the tonal transition to pure white is preserved.

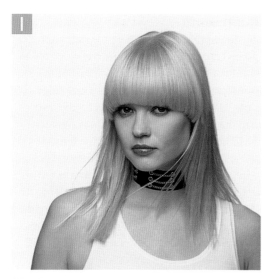

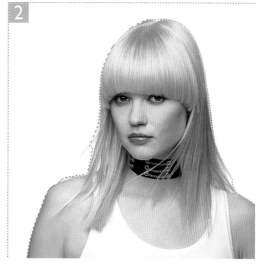

1 The above image required special attention to ensure the background went to pure white. Yet I did not want to blow out the highlights on the white shirt or on the model's blonde hair.

2 A Levels adjustment was applied to make the highlights go as light as possible on the shirt, but without losing any detail. But the background still needed to go whiter. I made a quick selection of the background area, feathered the selection by 2–4 pixels and filled this with white.

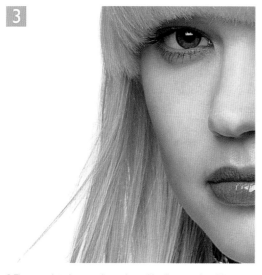

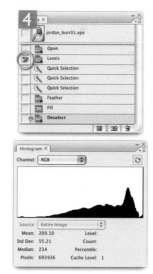

3 There needs to be a gentle tonal transition between the white cut-out and the edges of the subject. If not, the edge detail will become lost in print. I deselected the selection and set the history source against the original history state (see the circled history state icon in the History palette) and carefully painted around the subject edges, especially around the fine strands of hair, to restore detail.

4 If we check the final histogram you can see a slight gap between where the highlight tones of the subject tail off and the white background cuts in.

Client: Jordan Burr. Model: Vivi @ M&P.

## Are Curves all you need?

I have very much become a firm believer in trying to make Photoshop as simple as possible. There are 22 different items listed in the Image Adjustments menu and of these I reckon that you can achieve almost all the image adjustments you need by using just Curves and Hue/Saturation. Although Curves can replace the need for Levels, I do still like to use the Levels dialog, because it is nice and simple to work with. There are also a lot of tutorials out there that rely on the use of Levels.

And as if Photoshop were not complicated enough already, you are very likely to come across lots of suggestions on ways to tonally adjust images by different means. And you know what, in most cases these techniques can often be summarized with a simple single Curves adjustment. It's just that it can sometimes actually work out quicker (and feel a lot more intuitive) to use a slightly more convoluted route. Let me give you an example of what I mean. There is an example on page 472 that shows you how to use Gradient Fill layers to map the colors and tones in a photograph. Essentially, you can describe these adjustments as a curve. But the gradient mapping method is more easy to follow. In Photoshop there is always more than one way to achieve a particular effect. But to quote Fred Bunting: there are those techniques that are 'more interesting than relevant.'

## Curves adjustments

Any image adjustment that can be done in Levels can also be done using Curves, except with Curves you can accurately control the tonal balance and contrast of the master composite image as well as the individual color channels. You can also target specific points on the tone curve and remap the pixel values to make them lighter or darker and adjust the contrast in that tonal area only.

Figures 4.12 and 4.13 show the new Photoshop CS3 Curves dialog in which you have the same controls as usual but with some new added features. The default RGB units are measured in brightness levels from 0 to 255, where the linear curve line represents the tonal range output against the input, ranging from 0 in the bottom left corner to 255 levels top right. The vertical axis represents the output values and the horizontal axis the input values. In the two figure illustrations shown here, the Curve Grid options have been expanded. As you can see the RGB default mode for curves uses the Light setting, which shows unit values of 0–255 and the CMYK default mode uses the Pigment/Ink option to display the units (this is preferable for repro users who prefer to see the output values expressed as ink percentages of 0–100%). Alongside that are the grid view options which allow you to switch between 25% and 10% increments. Note that you can also toggle the Curves dialog grid display mode by ⌥ *alt*-clicking in the graph area; the finer grid allows for more accurate tweaking.

If you check the Histogram box, you can see a 'cached' histogram displayed in the curves grid area, which is just like the one shown in Levels. The Baseline option will let you see a standard reference line to compare your curve movements against. And the Intersection Line option will temporarily preview intersection lines as you mouse down on a curves point. The reason this is there is so that you can more easily reference a curve point against the outline of the histogram. Also new is the Presets menu at the top. As you save Curve settings, these saved settings can now be readily accessed via the pop-up Presets menu.

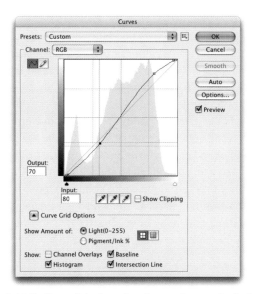

**Figure 4.12** The Curves dialog is an alternative way of representing the input and output levels, in which the levels' relationship is plotted as a graph. In this example, the two ends of the curve have been dragged in as you would in Levels, in order to set the optimum shadow and highlight points. You can control both the lightness and the contrast of the image by adjusting the shape of the curve.

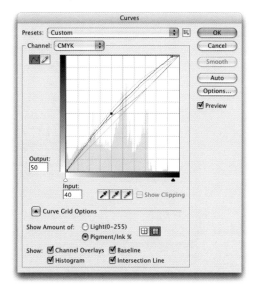

**Figure 4.13** If you ⌥ *alt* -click anywhere inside the grid area the grid units will switch from 25% to 10% increments.

## Threshold mode preview

The Curves input sliders work exactly like the ones in Levels. You can preview the shadow and highlight clipping by holding down the ⌥ *alt* key as you drag on the shadow and highlight sliders circled in the Curves dialog shown in Figure 4.14.

## *Using Curves in place of Levels*

You can adjust the shadow and highlight levels in Curves exactly the same way as you can using Levels. In the Curves dialog you have an Input shadows and an Input highlights slider. You can drag these sliders inwards to clip the shadow and highlight levels. If you select the shadow or highlight curves point and move these points up or down, you can adjust the Output levels for the shadows or highlights. In Levels you adjust the relative brightness of the image using a single Gamma slider. In the Curves dialog you can add a single curve point and move it left to lighten or right to darken. The added advantage of this is that you can add many more curve points and this will allow you to make more fine-tuned tone adjustments.

**Figure 4.14** The Levels and Curves dialog settings shown here will both apply an identical adjustment to an image. In the Levels dialog I moved the shadows and highlight Input levels sliders inwards. You will notice that the Curves dialog has an identical pair of sliders with which you can map the shadow and highlight input levels. In the Levels dialog I moved the Gamma slider to the right, to darken the midtones. In the Curves dialog you can add a point midway along the curve and drag this to the right to achieve an identical kind of 'gamma' midtone adjustment.

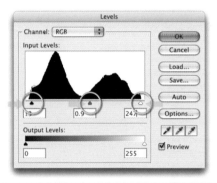

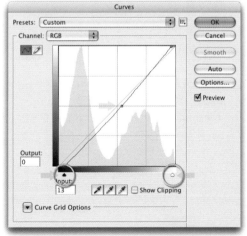

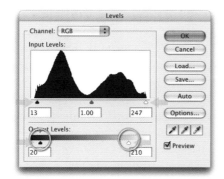

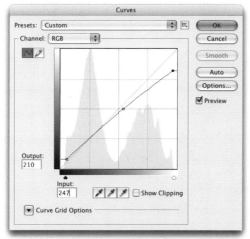

Figure 4.15 The Levels and Curves dialog settings shown here will also apply identical adjustments. In the Levels dialog I kept the input levels the same and adjusted the output levels to produce an image where the optimized levels were mapped to a levels range of 20–210. In the Curves dialog you can see the highlight point is selected and the curve point has been moved downwards to show a corresponding output value of 210 (the same value entered in the Levels output levels).

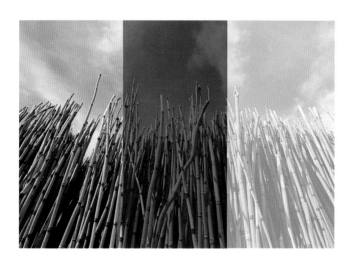

Figure 4.16 Setting the output levels to something other than zero is not something you would normally want to do, except for those times where you specifically want to dull down the tonal range of an image. In the example shown here, the left section shows standard optimized levels, the middle section shows the same image with reduced highlight output levels and the right section shows the image with reduced shadow output levels.

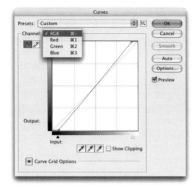

**Figure 4.17** The Levels and Curves adjustments shown in this chapter all take place in the composite channel. When you choose Levels or Curves, the default setting enables you to simultaneously correct all the color channels that make up the composite color image. If you mouse down on the Channel menu, you can select an individual color channel to edit. This is how you can use Curves to make color adjustments.

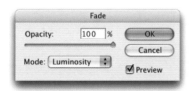

**Figure 4.18** After you apply a Levels or Curves adjustment, try choosing Fade Curves... from the Edit menu. This will pop a dialog like the one shown here. Mouse down on the Mode menu and select Luminosity. When you select Luminosity the Curves adjustment will only affect the luminance, and the color and saturation will be unaffected.

## Using Curves to improve contrast

An initial Levels, or Curves adjustment, as described on the previous pages, should be all that is required to achieve a picture where the tonal range from the shadows to highlights has been optimized quite nicely. But there are often times where you may wish to modify the contrast further. Curves will let you do this without compromising the shadow and highlights you set previously.

Take a look at the photograph shown in Figures 4.19–4.21. These three examples demonstrate how you can use a Curves adjustment to manipulate the contrast. In Figure 4.19, only the shadows and highlights have been optimized. In Figure 4.20, two curve points have been added to create a steep 'S' shape curve. Where the curve shape is steepest, this will increase the contrast in the tones, and in this example, more contrast has been added to the midtones. In Figure 4.21, two curve points have been added, to create a shallow 'S' shape curve. In this example you will notice that there is a decrease in contrast in the midtone areas, where the curve is at its shallowest.

When you first start using Curves try to get used to working with no more than two or three points at a time. As you develop your Photoshop skills you can try adding more points. But as you do so, take care to maintain a nice smooth curve shape. Adding more points, especially if they are set too close together, can induce a sharp kink in the curve which can produce an unwanted solarized look.

## Curves luminance and saturation

A Normal mode Levels or Curves adjustment will always adjust both the luminance and color. This will be particularly evident when you apply a contrast increasing curve, as this will increase both the luminance contrast and color contrast. It can therefore be handy to separate out a curves adjustment such that it applies either a luminance or color adjustment only and one way you can do this is by using the Edit ⇨ Fade command and changing the blend mode. Setting the blend mode to Luminosity will cause the

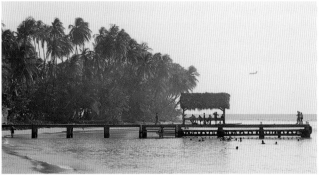
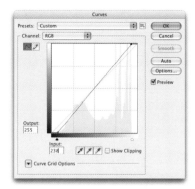

**Figure 4.19** This is a normal landscape view with no Curves adjustment.

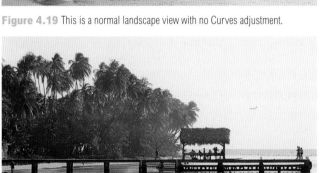
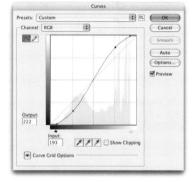

**Figure 4.20** You can increase the contrast in this image by adding two or more curve points and creating an 'S'-shaped curve as shown in the accompanying Curves dialog.

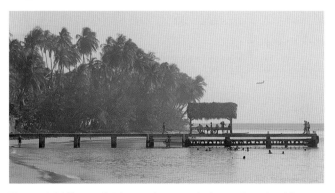
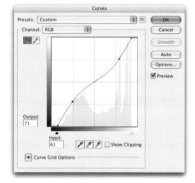

**Figure 4.21** You can also decrease the contrast in the same image by adding two or more curve points and creating an 'S'-shaped curve in the opposite direction as shown in the accompanying Curves dialog.

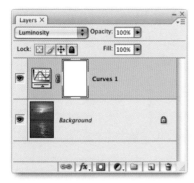

Figure 4.22 Another alternative is to apply an image adjustment such as a Curves adjustment as an adjustment layer and change the blend mode from Normal to something else, like Luminosity or Color.

last applied Curve adjustment to adjust the tone luminance only, while setting the blend mode to Color will cause the last applied Curves adjustment to adjust the color values only. Applying a curve in Color mode is useful when using individual Curve channel adjustments to manipulate the color only (as shown later) and you only want to affect the color and do want to preserve all the luminance information. Another method you could use is to apply all your tone corrections using adjustment layers and change the layer blend mode there. I will be discussing the use of adjustment layers later on in Chapter 6.

### Saving and loading curves

Curve settings can be saved by clicking on the Save/Load button circled in Figure 4.23. When you save a preset, the saved preset will then be accessible via the preset file list menu that appears at the top of the Curves dialog.

Figure 4.23 You can save any image adjustment as a reusable setting by clicking on the Save/Load button in the Curves dialog. This will pop the Save dialog shown below. You can save curve settings wherever you like, but I prefer to keep them in a custom folder, such as a Curves folder added inside the Photoshop application folder. Once a curves setting has been saved, it will appear listed in the Curves preset file list. Pre-existing curve settings can be added by going to the Save/Load button and selecting Load Preset... Note that a curve setting must by identified with the .acv extension; you can only load a curves setting if it has an .acv extension.

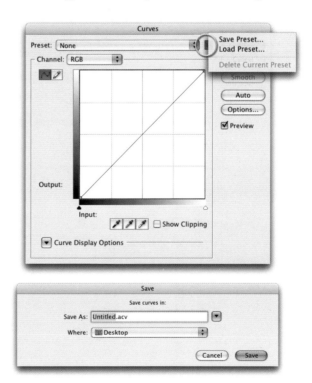

### *Curve presets*

At the top of the Curves dialog is the Preset menu. This will comprise of a list of presets that you have already saved, plus a number of Custom Curve presets that shipped with the program. Among these are some fairly straight forward settings such as curve settings to make an image lighter or darker and also several contrast settings. These are useful as starting point settings and you can run through the Presets menu selecting the various curve settings just to see how they will affect the look of an image. And there are also some more ambitious curve settings that aim to apply a cross process style effect or convert a color negative scan to make a positive image. In my opinion, these are a bit hit or miss and over the page I have demonstrated how if you want to convert a color negative scan to make a positive it would usually be necessary to create a specific custom curve setting for different types of color neg emulsion. In all honesty, if you are going to scan color negatives, then you are probably going to be better off using the scanner software settings to do the conversion for you.

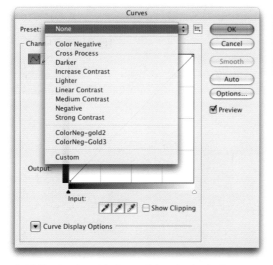
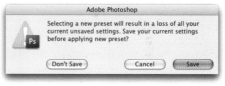

**Figure 4.24** Here is a view of the Curves dialog, showing the Custom curves menu. Note that if you create a manual curves setting and then select a preset, the warning dialog shown here will alert you that the current settings will become lost.

**1** If you use Photoshop to convert a color negative to make a positive, you could try selecting the Color Negative preset from the Curves dialog. However, when doing so, you can't always expect a successful conversion.

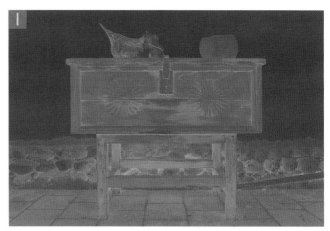

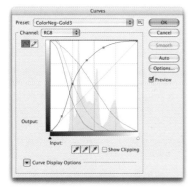

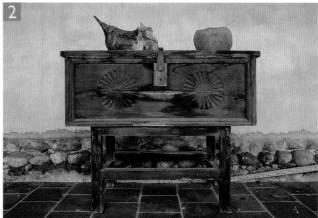

**2** In most instances it will be necessary to adapt the shape of the curve in the composite and individual color channels (as shown below) in order to achieve an optimum conversion.

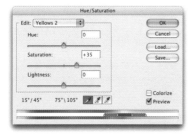

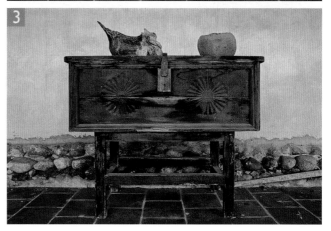

**3** In the bottom example I added a saturation boost to the image. Because of the extreme nature of such adjustments, it is better to work on an image that was scanned in 16-bits per channel.

## Manipulating portions of a curve

Following on from this basic introduction to curves contrast corrections, let's now look at how one might approach improving the contrast in a less standard type of image like the one shown in Figure 4.26. In this example I wanted to increase the contrast overall, but I mostly wanted to increase the contrast in the shadow to midtone range. But at the same time I did not want to lose any of the highlight detail.

If you look at the shape of the curve in the example shown here, you will notice that I placed a curve point at the top end of the curve to anchor the highlights and I then added three more points to the curve to create a steep curve 'S' shape which would add contrast in the desired tonal area. When you compare the before and after, note how the tonal detail in the highlight area has been preserved and the increased contrast elsewhere has produced a more contrasty looking photograph and brought out more detail where it matters most.

### Accurate point placement

If you wish to place a point on the curve that corresponds with an exact tonal value in the picture you are editing then all you have to do is move the cursor outside of the Curves dialog and mouse down inside the document window. As you do so, you will notice a hollow circle appear, hovering on the curve. If you ⌘ *ctrl*-click on the image a point will be added to the curve.

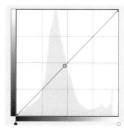

Figure 4.25 When the cursor is dragged over the image, a hollow circle will indicate where the tone value is on the curve.

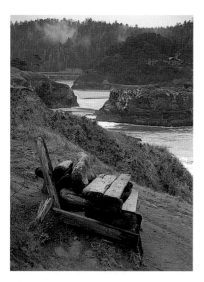 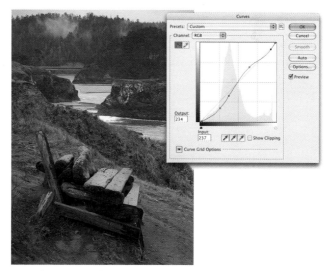

Figure 4.26 Careful manipulation of the curve points will enable you to create irregular-shaped curves that enhance the contrast at different portions of the tonal scale.

## Mask adjustments

The one time when you may find it useful to use the legacy style Brightness/Contrast image adjustment is when you want to edit the contents of an image layer mask. The crudeness of the Brightness and Contrast adjustments can actually be beneficial when you want to force the mask highlight areas to go to white or black.

## Improved Brightness and Contrast

For as long as Photoshop has been around, there has been an adjustment control called Brightness/Contrast. For years now many authors and experts have done their best to discourage people from using this adjustment control, because of the potential harm it could do to your pictures. Yet so many people continued to use it, oblivious to the fact that it was never intended for photographic use.

Well, all that has changed in Photoshop CS3, because the new default behavior is designed to match the Brightness and Contrast sliders found in Camera Raw (see the following chapter). The new Brightness/Contrast adjustment, unlike its predecessor (see Figure 4.27 below), always preserves the shadow and highlight endpoints and constrains the tone shifts within these limits. The old legacy behavior is available still as a extra option within the Brightness/Contrast. The main reason for retaining this old style behavior is to maintain compatibility with legacy images where an old style Brightness/Contrast adjustment has been applied as an adjustment layer.

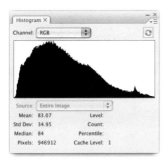
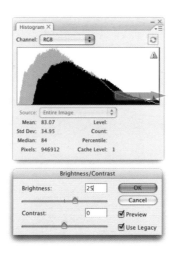
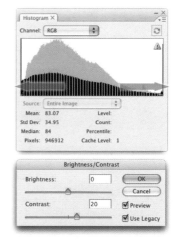

**Figure 4.27** The Histogram palette allows me to demonstrate why the legacy Brightness/Contrast image adjustment is such a poor tool to use for photographic tonal correction The histogram on the left shows the normal histogram. If you use the Brightness slider to increase the Brightness, all you are doing is shifting all the tones lighter and the highlight detail will immediately become clipped. If you try to increase the Contrast, then the tones are stretched in both directions so that both the shadows and highlights become clipped.

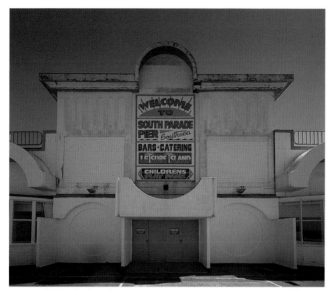
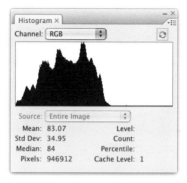

**1** The before version here is of a photograph that needed an extra boost to brighten the colors more.

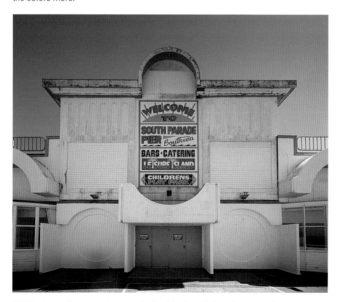
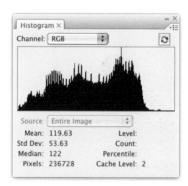
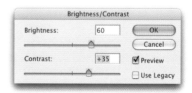

**2** This shows the same photograph after I had applied a Brightness/Contrast adjustment to raise both the Brightness and Contrast. Notice how the histogram in the corrected version is able to now preserve the full tonal range from the shadows to the highlights.

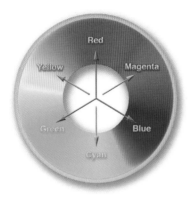

Figure 4.28 The Variations dialog displays color balance variations based on the color wheel model. Here you see the additive primaries (red, green, and blue) and the subtractive primaries, (cyan, magenta, and yellow) placed in their complementary positions on the color wheel. Red is the opposite of cyan; green is the opposite of magenta; and blue is the opposite of yellow. Use these basic rules to gain an understanding of how to correct color.

# Color corrections

We shall now look at using the image adjustment controls to adjust the colors in an image. Again, almost everything you want to do to edit the color in a flattened pixel image can be done using just Levels, Curves and Hue/Saturation. But before we get into how these should be used, we should take a quick look at the Variations interface, because this is a good starting point for understanding how color correction works; you can see how this relates to the color wheel diagram shown in Figure 4.28. This makes Variations a good learning tool for beginners, because all the basic image editing tools are combined in a single interface. I would not advise using Variations as a general tool for color correction because Variations is doing nothing more than providing a Levels style Gamma slider control for the overall brightness and individual color channels. Anything you do using Variations can be done more simply using Levels and more accurately using Curves. And although you have a Saturation control, the Hue/Saturation adjustment has more versatile controls. The same goes for the Color Balance image adjustment. This too is simply offering you another way to apply Levels style adjustments.

Figure 4.29 The Variations interface will enable you to modify the color of the shadows, highlights or midtones separately. For example, clicking on the More Red thumbnail image will cause the red variant to shift to the center and readjust the surrounding thumbnail previews accordingly. Clicking on the More Cyan thumbnail will restore the central preview to its original color balance. In this respect, Variations is just like the Color Balance adjustment, but you also have built in the saturation adjustments and a lighter or darker option. And you can save or load a previous Variations adjustment setting. Variations may be a crude color correcting tool, but it is nonetheless a useful means by which to learn color theory.

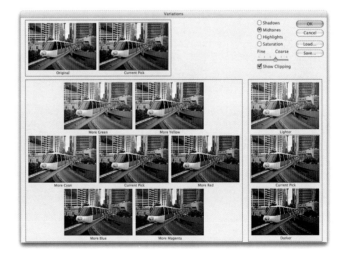

## Basic color balancing with Levels

You can correct color casts in an image by adjusting the Input and Output sliders for the individual color channels in the Levels dialog. To edit a channel, go to the pop-up menu next to where it says 'Channel', mouse down and choose a color channel to edit. Let's say you have a picture which looks too blue and you want to add more yellow. Go to the Channel menu and select the Blue channel. Increasing the Blue channel gamma (moving the middle Input slider to the left) will make the image more blue. And conversely, decreasing the gamma in the Blue channel will make the image more yellow. Another way to neutralize midtones in the Levels or Curves dialog box is to select the gray eyedropper and click on an area in the image that should be a neutral gray. The levels will automatically adjust the gamma setting in each color channel to remove the cast. Levels may be adequate enough to carry out basic image corrections, but does not provide you with much control beyond reassigning the highlights, shadows and midpoint color values. The best tool to use for color correction is Curves. This is because you can change the color balance and contrast with a degree of precision that is not available with all the other image adjustments.

## Color corrections in RGB

You will note that the instructions for all the color corrections described in this chapter are done using the RGB color mode. This is because RGB is a more versatile color mode for photographers to work in. There are further reasons why I recommend this particular workflow, which I will discuss in more detail in Chapter 12.

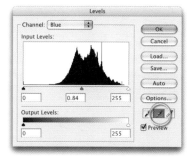

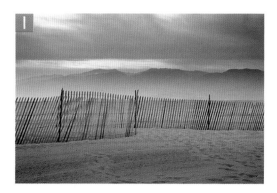

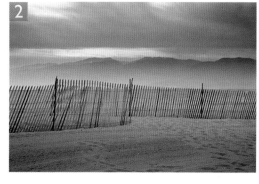

**1** With a photograph like this it is not necessarily a bad thing to have a color cast, but let's say we wanted to apply a basic color correction to the photograph to make it more yellow.

**2** I went to the Image menu and chose Adjustments ⇨ Levels. I selected the Blue channel from the Channel menu and moved the Input gamma slider to the right. This decreased the gamma in the Blue channel and made the midtones in the photograph more yellow.

## PhotoKit Color gray balancing

I was the project manager for a Pixel Genius plug-in called PhotoKit Color 2. PhotoKit Color 2 contains a set of gray balancing effects which provide effective automatic color balancing with most images. The RSA Neutralize is especially good at the automatic removal of heavy color casts. www.pixelgenius.com/color/

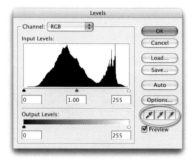

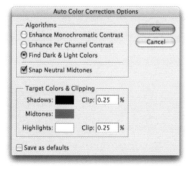

**Figure 4.30** The Auto image adjustments discussed here and shown on the page opposite can also be accessed when you click on the Options... button in the Levels or Curves dialogs. If Snap Neutral Midtones is selected, Auto Color will also neutralize these. You can customize the Clipping values to set how much the highlights and shadow tones are clipped by the image adjustment.

## Auto adjustments

The Image ⇨ Adjustments menu contains three auto image adjustment tools: Auto Levels, Auto Contrast and Auto Color. These are designed to provide automated tone and color correction.

The Auto Levels adjustment works by expanding the levels in each of the individual color channels, to fully optimize them. This per-channel levels contrast expansion will always result in an image that has fuller tonal contrast. But it may also change the color balance of the image as well. Auto Levels can produce improved results, but sometimes not. So if you want to improve the tonal contrast without affecting the color balance of the photograph then try using the Auto Contrast adjustment instead. This will carry out a similar type of auto image adjustment as Auto Levels, except it will optimize the contrast by applying an identical Levels adjustment to all the color channels.

Lastly, there is the Auto Color adjustment. This provides a combination of Auto Contrast to enhance the tonal contrast, combined with an auto color correction which maps the darkest colors to black and the lightest colors to white.

If you open the Levels or Curves dialogs you will see an Options... button at the bottom. Click on this and you will see the Auto Color Correction Options shown in Figure 4.30. The algorithms listed here match the auto adjustments. Enhance Per Channel Contrast is the same as Auto Levels. Enhance Monochromatic Contrast is the same as Auto Contrast and Find Dark & Light Colors is the same as Auto Color. But notice there is also a Snap Neutral Midtones option. When this is checked, a gamma adjustment is applied in each color channel which aims to correct the neutral midtones as well as the light and dark colors. A clipping value can be set for the highlights and shadows and this will determine by what percentage the endpoints get automatically clipped.

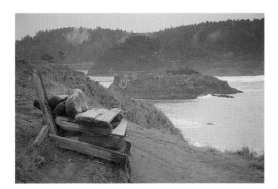

Before

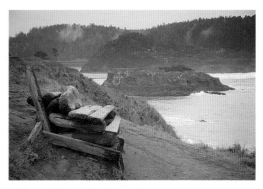

Auto Levels (Enhance Per Channel Contrast)

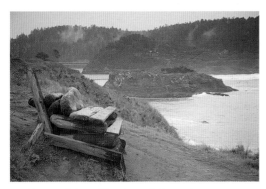

Auto Contrast (Enhance Monochromatic Contrast)

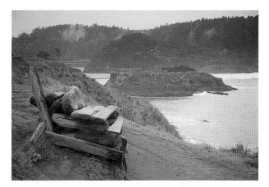

Auto Color (Find Dark & Light Colors + Snap Neutral Midtones)

**Figure 4.31** These photographs show the three auto adjustment methods (with the equivalent descriptions, as they are also described in the Levels and Curves dialogs).

Auto Levels optimizes the shadow and highlight points in all three color channels. This will generally improve the contrast and color balance of the image. Auto Contrast will apply an adjustment across all three channels that will increase the contrast, but without altering the color balance. The Auto Color option will map the darkest and lightest colors to a neutral color. (If the swatch colors shown in Figure 4.30 have been altered, you may see a different result.) And lastly, an Auto Contrast adjustment followed by a PhotoKit Color RSA (Rule Seeking Algorithm) Gray Balance Fine effect has been applied.

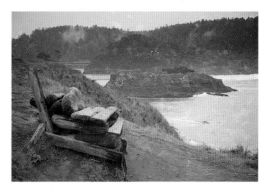

Auto Contrast + PhotoKit Color RSA Gray Balance Fine

## Color correction with Levels or Curves

Of all the color correction methods described so far, Auto Color provides the best automatic one-step tone and color correction method. But if you prefer to do your color corrections manually, then I would recommend you forget Variations and Color Balance and explore using Levels or Curves color channel adjustments. Earlier I showed you how to set the highlight and shadow points in Levels and how to use a gamma adjustment to lighten or darken the image. To keep things simple I used a monochrome photograph. But let's now take things one stage further and use this technique to optimize the individual color channels in an RGB color image.

I have shown here how you can use the Threshold mode analysis technique to discover where the shadow and highlight endpoints are in each of the three color channels and use this feedback information to set the endpoints. This is a really good way to locate the shadows and highlights and set the endpoints at the same time. Once you have corrected the highlight and shadow colors, all the other colors will usually fall into place and the photograph won't require any further color correction.

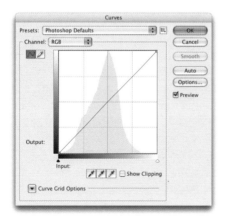

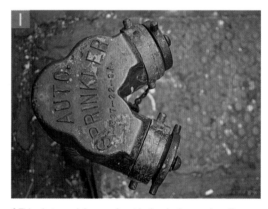

**1** This photograph has a red cast in the shadows and a yellow cast in the highlights. The first step is to go to the Image ⇨ Adjustments menu and choose Curves...

168

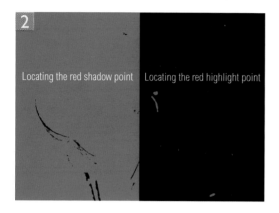

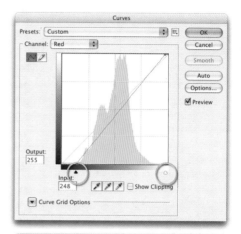

**2** I went to the Channel menu and selected the Red channel and adjusted the Shadow and Highlight input sliders until the red shadow and highlight points were set just to the point where they started to clip. If you hold down the ⌥ *alt* key as you do this you will see the Threshold display mode shown here which will help you locate the shadow and highlight points more easily. I then repeated these steps with the Green and Blue channels until I had adjusted the shadow and highlight points individually in all three color channels.

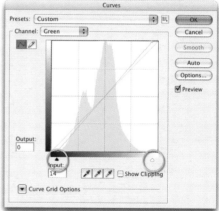

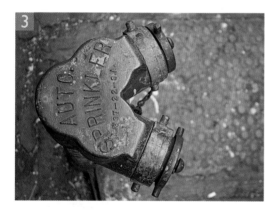

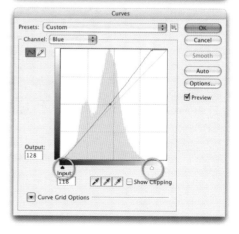

**3** This technique of adjusting the color channels one by one will help you remove color casts from the shadows and highlights with a lot of precision. The trick is to use the Threshold mode display as a reference tool to indicate where the levels start to clip in each channel and consider backing off slightly, so that you leave some headroom in the composite/master channel to make general refinements to the Curves adjustment, ensuring that the highlights do not blow out (as discussed earlier). Finally, I added and adjusted a midpoint in the Blue channel to add a little more yellow.

## Finding a neutral RGB value

If you are editing an image in RGB mode and using one of the standard RGB color spaces such as Adobe RGB, sRGB, ColorMatch RGB or ProPhoto RGB you can use the eyedropper or color sampler tools to match the RGB values (see Figure 4.32).

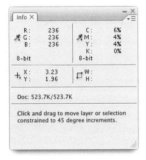

**Figure 4.32** The Info palette can be used to read color information which helps determine whether the colors are neutral or not regardless of any monitor inaccuracies. Equal Red, Green and Blue values will always mean a color is neutral.

## Precise color correction using Curves

The Levels adjustment technique is quite effective in correcting the color at the shadows, highlights and midtones. And, in fact, the Auto Color image adjustment is doing exactly the same thing, but doing so automatically. And since Auto Color adjustments can be done in both Levels and Curves, we can just as easily apply the image adjustment made in the last example as a curve.

So, if Levels enables you to make precise color corrections, then Curves must surely enable you to make even more precise color corrections. As a general rule, once you have corrected for a cast in the highlights and then the shadows, everything else mostly falls into place. And a further tweak to the midtones is maybe all you need. But there are still plenty of situations where you might wish to exploit the full potential of a Curves adjustment in order to gain the maximum amount of control over the way you modify the colors in an image to improve the color appearance. Let's look at how to make a Curves adjustment based on a sample analysis of the colors in an image.

To add a new color value as a control point on the curve, ⌘ *ctrl*-click inside the document window and you will see a control point appear on the corresponding portion of the curve. If you hold down ⌘ *Shift* *ctrl* *Shift* and click in the document window, control points will be automatically added to all three color channels at once. So when adding control points to color correct the white shirt image example that follows on pages 172–173, I ⌘ *Shift* *ctrl* *Shift*-clicked on top of each of the color sampler points to add these as control points in all three color channels in the Curves dialog. When you are editing the points in the Curves dialog, use *Shift*-click to select multiple points. As you adjust one control point the others will move in unison. To deselect all the points, use ⌘ *D* *ctrl* *D*. When a single point is selected you can select the next point using *Tab* *ctrl* *Tab* right mouse and you can select the previous point by using *Tab* *Shift* *ctrl* *Tab* *Shift* right mouse.

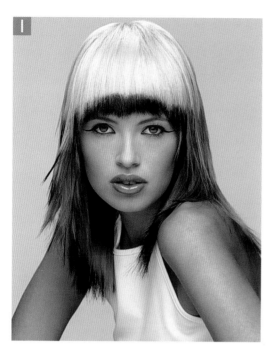

**1** This photograph has a cold blue cast that is particularly noticeable in the backdrop, which should be a neutral gray. I went to the Image ⇨ Adjustments menu and chose Curves... this opened the Curves dialog and I was able to get rid of the cast in stages by adjusting the shape of the curve in the individual color channels.

**2** This shows you the curves corrected version. The main Curves dialog allows you to make tonal corrections to the composite color channel (in this case, the RGB composite channel). I first selected the Red color channel from the Channel menu and added a couple of control points to the curve to adjust the color balance for the midtones and highlights. I then went to the Blue channel and added two points to the curve, this time to correct the color for the shadows and highlights in the Blue channel. I applied these corrections based on appearance and what would make the image look right. The next example illustrates how you can carry out a more accurate, measured correction.

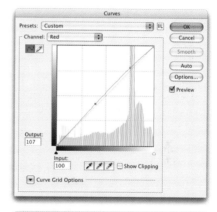

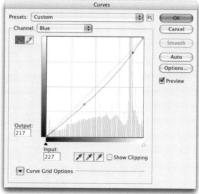

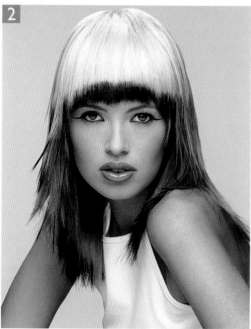

Client: Anita Cox Salon.

1 Whenever you have something white photographed against a white or gray background, any color cast will be extremely noticeable. In this example I selected the color sampler tool and clicked on the image at three different places on the model's white jacket. With each click I positioned a new persistent color sampler readout and the readout values are displayed in the Info palette. The intention here was to measure the color at different points of lightness so that these measurements could be used to calculate a precise Curves adjustment.

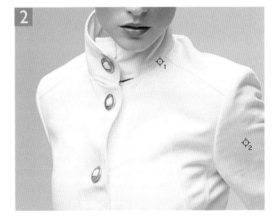

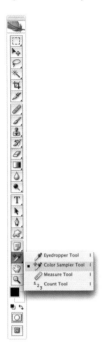

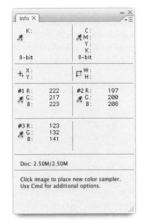

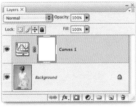

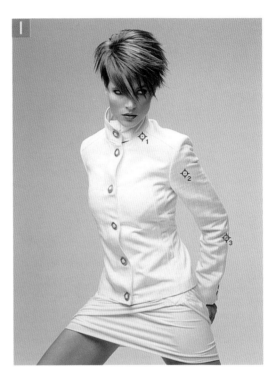

2 The color sample points can be repositioned as necessary by dragging on them with the color sampler (you can access the tool while in an image adjustment dialog, by holding down the *Shift* key). Once the color sampler readouts were in place, it was time to add a Curves adjustment layer above the Background layer. With the Curves dialog open, I zoomed in to get a close-up view of the jacket where the points had been placed and ⌘ *Shift* *ctrl* *Shift*-clicked on top of each of the sampler points. This added a corresponding curve control point to the individual RGB channel curves. When I inspected the Red, Green and Blue channels in the Curves dialog I could see three points had been added in each channel.

Client: Alta Moda. Model: Nicky Felbert @ MOT.

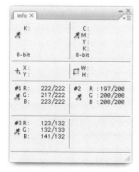

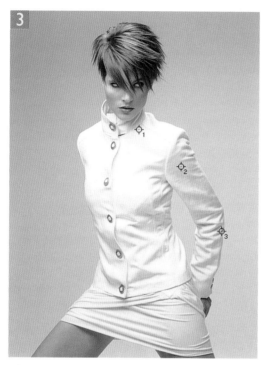

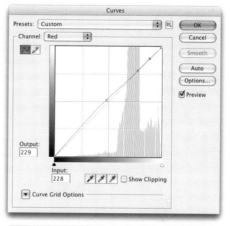

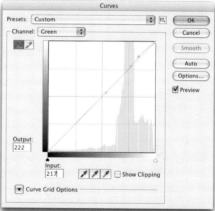

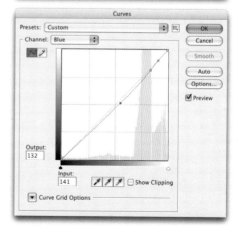

3 Here is an example of the Curves adjustment that was made to the three channels using the information provided in the Info palette. The first RGB readout figure indicates the original input value. At each point I would look at the numbers and decide which of these represented the median value. I would then adjust the points in the other two channels so that the other two output values matched the median value. One can manually drag the point or use the keyboard arrows to balance the output value to match those of the other two channels. Note that *Shift*+arrow key moves the control points in multiples of 10.

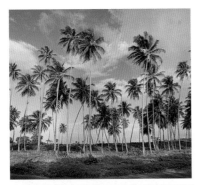

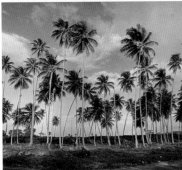

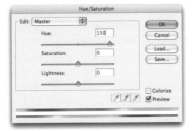

Figure 4.33 This is an extreme example of how a Hue/Saturation adjustment can be used to radically alter the appearance of a photograph. As you move the Hue slider left or right the colors in the image will be mapped to new values. You get an indication of this transformation by looking at the two color ramps at the bottom of the dialog. The top one represents the original 'input' color spectrum and the lower ramp represents how those colors will be translated as output colors.

## Hue/Saturation

The Hue/Saturation dialog controls are based around the HSB (Hue, Saturation, Brightness) color model, which is basically an intuitive form of the Lab Color model. When you select the Hue/Saturation image adjustment you can alter these components of the image globally. Or, you can selectively apply an adjustment to a narrow range of colors. The two color spectrum ramps at the bottom of the Hue/Saturation dialog box provide a visual clue as to how the colors are being mapped from one color to another. The hue values are based on a 360 degree spectrum. Red is positioned mid-slider at 0 degrees. All other colors are assigned numeric values in relation to this. So cyan (the complementary color of red) can be found at either minus 180 or +180 degrees. Adjusting the Hue slider only will alter the way color in the image will be mapped to a new color value. Figure 4.33 shows an extreme example of how the colors in a normal color image would be mapped by a Hue adjustment only. As the Hue slider is moved you will notice the color mapping outcome is represented by the position of the color spectrum on the lower color ramp. Saturation adjustments are easy enough to understand. A plus value will boost saturation, a negative value will reduce the saturation. Outside the Master edit mode, you can choose from one of six preset color ranges with which to narrow the focus of the Hue/Saturation adjustment. Once you have one of these color ranges selected, you can then sample a new color value from the image window, and this will center the Hue/Saturation adjustments around the sampled color. *Shift*-click in the image area to add to the color selection and *alt*-click to subtract colors (see page 175).

When the Colorize option is switched on, the hue component of the image is replaced with red (Hue value 0 degrees), Lightness will remain the same at 0% and Saturation at 25%. Some people recommend this as a method of obtaining a colored monochrome image, but there are better ways of achieving this, which are outlined later in Chapter 9 on Darkroom Effects.

174

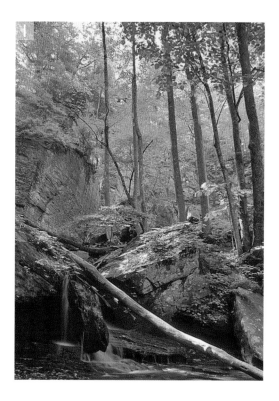

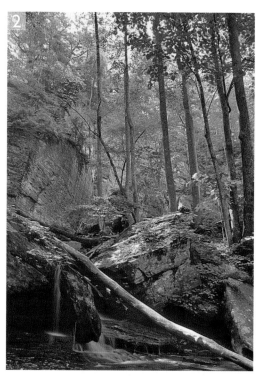

**1** The Edit menu in the Hue/Saturation dialog box defaults to the Master setting, and any adjustments will affect all the colors in an image. If you mouse down on the Edit menu you can narrow the Hue/Saturation adjustment to specific colors. If I select Greens, I can enhance or subdue the saturation of the green color component of the image. And I can shift the green colors so that they become either more yellow or more cyan.

**2** As you can see, if I move the Hue slider to the left, I can make the green leaves turn more yellow and rapidly change the seasonal appearance of the photograph. You can also be very specific as to which colors are selected. In this example I clicked on the standard eyedropper in the Hue/Saturation dialog and clicked on a leaf in the picture to set this as the target green color to change (the two vertical markers creating the gap in the middle of the sliders represent the chosen color range to modify. The spaces defined by the outer triangular markers represent the fuzziness drop-off either side of the color selection. I then added to the color range selection by selecting the Add to Sample eyedropper (circled) and clicked to add more color sample points to the Hue/Saturation adjustment color range.

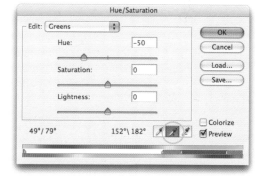

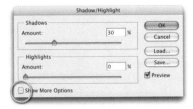

Figure 4.34 The Shadow/Highlight adjustment dialog shown here in basic mode. Checking the Show More Options box will reveal the Advanced mode dialog shown below in Figure 4.35.

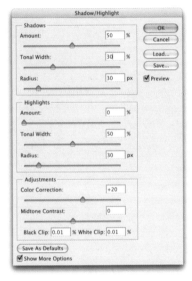

Figure 4.35 The Show More Options mode Shadow/Highlight dialog contains a comprehensive range of controls. I would advise you to always leave this box checked.

## Correcting shadow and highlight detail

The Shadow/Highlight image adjustment enables you to reveal more detail in either the shadow or highlight areas of a picture. Shadow/Highlight is a great image adjustment tool to use whenever you have useful tonal information but it is just too compressed to be seen properly. It can be used to perform wonders on most images, not just those that desperately require corrections to recover detail in the shadows and highlights.

The Shadow/Highlight image adjustment tool makes adaptive adjustments to an image, and it works much in the same way as our eyes do when they automatically compensate and adjust to the amount of light illuminating a subject. The Shadow/Highlight adjustment works by looking at the neighboring pixels in an image and making a compensating adjustment based on the average pixel values within a given radius. In Advanced mode, the Shadow/Highlight dialog has various controls which allow you to make the following fine-tuning adjustments.

### Amount

This is an easy one to get to get to grips with. The default Amount setting is 50%. Increase or decrease this to achieve the desired amount of highlight or shadow correction. I find this default setting does tend to be rather annoying, so I usually try setting the slider to a lower amount or zero and click on the Save As Defaults button to set this as the new default setting for every time I open Shadow/Highlight.

### Tonal Width

The Tonal Width determines the tonal range of pixel values that will be affected by the Amount set. A low Tonal Width setting will narrow the adjustment to the darkest or lightest pixels only. As the Tonal Width is increased the adjustment will spread to affect more of the midtone pixels as well.

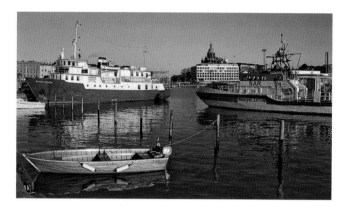

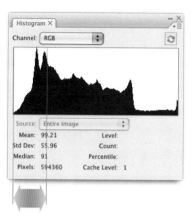

## Radius

The Radius setting basically governs the pixel width of the area that is analyzed when making an adaptive correction. Let's concentrate on what would happen when making a shadow correction. If the Shadow Radius is set to zero, the result will be a very flat-looking image. You can increase the Amount to lighten the shadows and restrict the Tonal Width, but if the Radius is low or is set to zero, Photoshop will have very little 'neighbor pixel' information to work with when trying to calculate the average luminance of the neighboring pixels. So if the sample Radius is too small, the midtones will also become lightened. If the Radius setting is set too high, this will have the effect of averaging all of the pixels in the image and likewise the lightening effect will be distributed such that all the pixels will get the lightening treatment, not just the dark pixels. The optimum setting to use is dependent on the image content and the area size of the dark or light pixels. The optimum pixel Radius width should be about half that amount or less. In practice you don't have to measure the pixel width of the light and dark in every image to work this out. Just be aware that after you have established the Amount and Tonal Width settings, you should adjust the Radius setting making it larger or smaller according to how large the dark or light areas are. There will be a 'sweet spot' where the Shadow/Highlight correction is just right.

**Figure 4.36** The Tonal Width slider determines the range of levels the Shadow/Highlight adjustment is applied to. So, for example, if the Shadow adjustment Tonal Range is set to 50, then the pixels which fall within the darkest range from level 0 to level 50 will be adjusted.

## Radius halos

As you make an adjustment to the Radius setting you will sometimes notice a soft halo appear around sharp areas of contrast between dark and light areas. This is a natural consequence of the Radius function and is most noticeable when you are making dynamic changes to the image. Aim for a Radius setting where the halo is least noticeable or apply a Fade... adjustment after applying the Shadow/Highlight adjustment. If I am really concerned about reducing halos, I sometimes use the history brush to selectively paint in a Shadow/Highlight adjustment.

**1** In this photograph of young Lillian, her face is quite dark because she is backlit by the sun. But with a little help from the Shadow/Highlight adjustment, I can bring out more detail in her face and darken the sky.

**2** I went to the Image menu and chose Adjustments ⇨ Shadow/Highlight. I set the Amount to 36% and raised the Tonal Width to 60%. The Radius adjustment is now crucial because this determines the distribution width of the Shadow/Highlight adjustment. As you can see in this step, if I set the Radius to zero, the result will look incredibly flat.

**3** The other alternative is to take the Radius setting up really high. But this too can diminish the Shadow/Highlight adjustment effect. The simple way to approach setting the Radius is to realize that the optimum setting is area size related and it will fall somewhere midway between these two extremes. In the end, I went for a high Radius setting of 124 pixels for the shadows and 165 pixels for the highlights. This was because I was correcting large shadow and large highlight areas and these settings appeared to provide the optimum correction for this particular photograph.

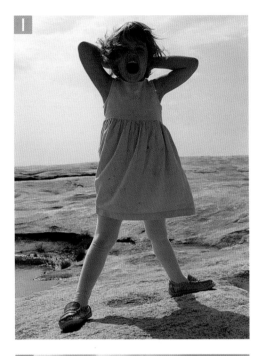

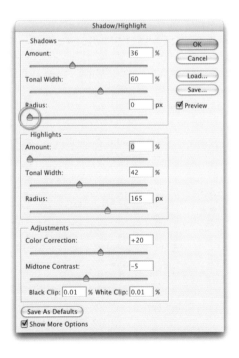

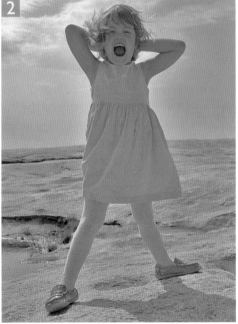

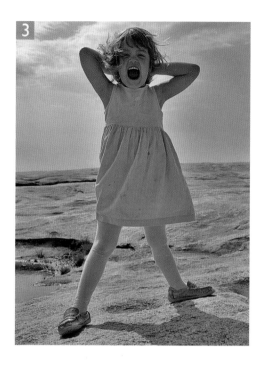

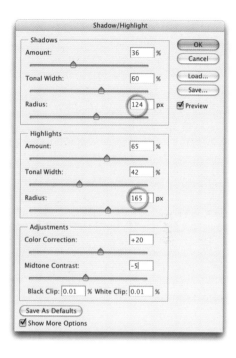

## Color Correction

As you correct the highlights and the shadows, the
color saturation may unexpectedly change. This can be
a consequence of using the Shadow/Highlight to make
extreme adjustments. The Color Correction slider will let
you compensate for any undesired color shifts.

## Midtone Contrast

Even though you may have paid careful attention to getting
all the above settings optimized just right so that you target
only the shadows or highlights (or both), the midtone areas
may still get affected and you can lose some contrast. The
Midtone Contrast slider control lets you restore or add
more contrast to the midtone areas.

### CMYK Shadow/Highlight adjustments

You may notice that the Shadow/Highlight
adjustment performance is improved and
you can now use Shadow/Highlight in
CMYK color as well.

### Adobe Camera Raw adjustments

Shadow/Highlight can work great on a lot
of images, but now that Camera Raw can
be used to edit JPEG and TIFF images
as well as raw files, you may like to
explore using the Recovery and Fill Light
adjustments described on pages 258–259.
In many cases you will find that Recovery
and Fill Light work better.

179

## Pros and cons of Smart Filters

The appeal of Smart Filters is that you can apply any filter non-destructively to an image in Photoshop. But this flexibility comes at the cost of larger file sizes (4 to 5 times bigger), a slower workflow switching between the Smart Object and parent documents and longer save times, at least this has been my experience when working with a fairly fast computer with lots of RAM memory. But this is not the first time we have come across speed problems like this: some Photoshop techniques are a little ahead of themselves and we have to wait for the computer hardware to become faster before we can use them comfortably.

While Smart Filtering does offer true non-destructive filtering, it is a technique you probably want to use sparingly. In this book I have highlighted a few of the situations where Smart Filters may offer some benefit, such as when blurring a background layer, or using the midtone contrast technique shown on pages 184–185.

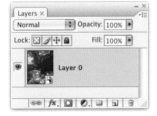

# Smart Filters

This is perhaps a good time to introduce the Smart Filters feature in Photoshop CS3, which will allow you to apply most filter adjustments non-destructively. And as shown here, also apply a Shadow/Highlight adjustment non-destructively. In the following steps I have provided a brief introduction to working with Smart Filters. Smart Filters are essentially filter effects that are applied to a Smart Object, and the process always starts with you converting a layer or group of layers to a Smart Object, or selecting a layer and choosing Convert for Smart Filters.

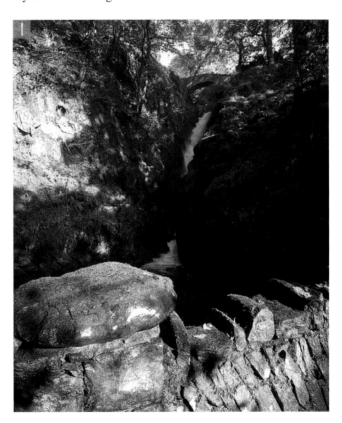

1 To apply a Shadow/Highlight adjustment as a non-destructive smart filter, the Background layer (or a group of layers) must first be converted to a Smart Object. To do this I went to the Filter menu and chose: Convert for Smart Filters. This converted the Background layer to a normal, Layer 0 layer.

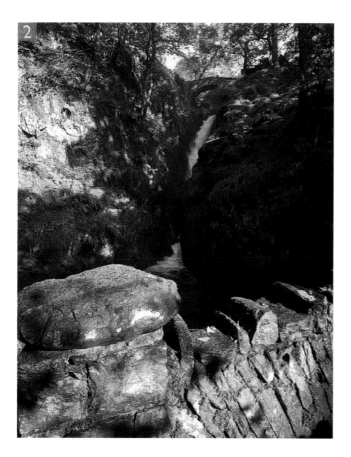

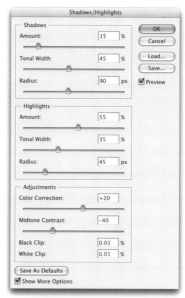

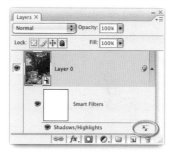

**2** I then went to the Image menu and chose Adjustments ➪ Shadows/Highlight and applied the settings shown here. As you can see, I used the Shadows/Highlight adjustment to bring out more detail in the shadows. If you check the Layers palette you will notice that the Shadows/Highlight adjustment has added a Smart Filter layer to the layer stack. You can now click the eye icon to switch the effect on or off. And when I double-clicked on the Smart Filter blend options button (circled), this opened the Blend Options dialog shown here, which allowed me to adjust the opacity of the Smart Filter adjustment.

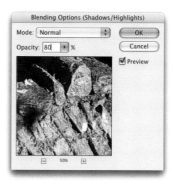

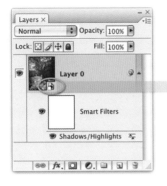

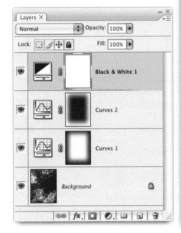

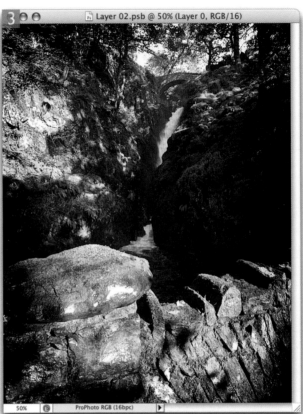

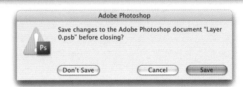

3 I was then able to double-click on the Smart Object icon in the Layers palette and open the Smart Object layer in a new document window. This image document is the original image without the Shadow/Highlight adjustment and I could now edit this document as one would do normally. If you look at the Layer palette for the Smart Object you will notice that I added a Curves adjustment layer to apply some localized lightening to the center of the image and a second adjustment layer to apply a darkening vignette to the edges of the photograph and, finally, a Black & White adjustment layer to convert the image to monochrome. That pretty much completed all the work I wanted to carry out on the Smart Object. When I closed the document window a dialog box prompted me to save it, which you must do in order to save the Smart Object adjustments back to the parent document.

# Improving the midtone contrast

The technique described over the next few pages was shown to me by Jeff Schewe (who also shot the Antarctica pictures I used here), and Jeff in turn has credited Mac Holbert of Nash Editions as the person who actually devised this really clever way of improving the midtone contrast in a photograph. The technique relies on the use of the High Pass filter applied using the Overlay blend mode, to add halo edges specifically to the midtone areas of the picture. This is really a kind of soft edge, midtone sharpening technique and it is particularly useful when applied to subjects like landscapes, and can be used to help bring out more detail when making a print.

**Nash Editions**

Nash Editions is based in California, and was founded in 1990 by Mac Holbert and Graham Nash to provide a specialist fine-art digital printing service. They were the original pioneers of fine-art inkjet printing.

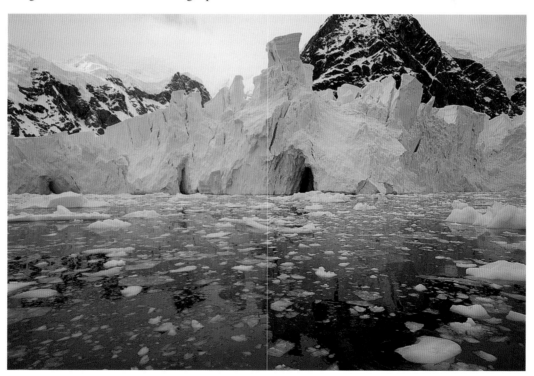

**Figure 4.37** The photograph shown here nicely illustrates the benefits of the midtone contrast technique described over the next few pages. The left half shows the before version and the right half how the image detail looks so much sharper and more contrasty in the midtone areas.

Photograph: Jeff Schewe.

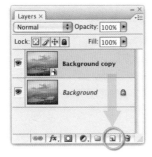

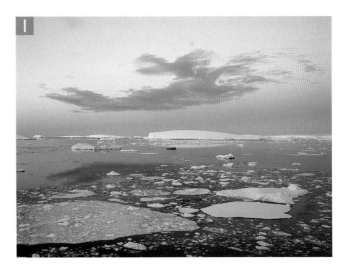

1 In this example I wanted to demonstrate how the medium contrast technique could be applied to a photograph using a Smart Filter technique. You are not supposed to have to duplicate the Background layer in order to use Smart Filter layers, but in this instance it was necessary because the Smart Filter blending options are not yet as comprehensive as one would like. I began by dragging the Background layer to the New Layer button to make a copy and went to the Filter menu and chose: Convert for Smart Filters.

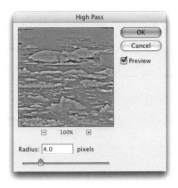

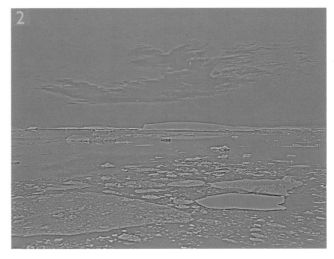

Photograph: Jeff Schewe.

2 With the Background copy layer selected (which is now a Smart Object), I went to the Filter menu and chose Other ⇨ High Pass. It does not matter too much at this stage what value is used since I was able to re-edit this setting later at Step 4.

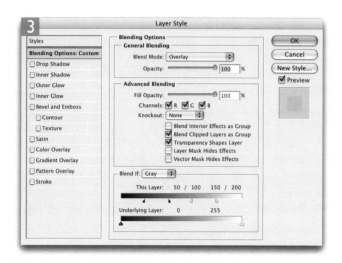

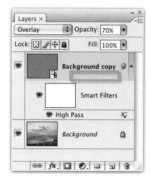

3 Now that I had applied the High Pass filter, I needed to change the layer blend mode setting to Overlay. To do this I double-clicked on the Background copy layer, targeting the blank space area (this is the area within the green box and not the thumbnail or the layer name itself). I set the blend mode to Overlay and at the same time, went to the Blend If options at the bottom and adjusted the This Layer sliders so that they were split as shown above: 50/100 150/200. To set the sliders like this, you have to hold down the ⌥ alt key to split them apart.

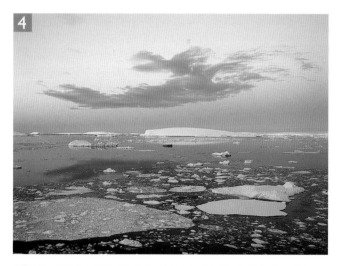

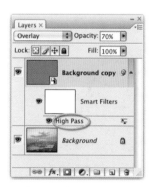

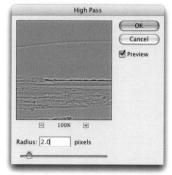

4 The layer blend changes will cause the filter layer to blend with the layer below, adding a radius halo around the midtone areas of the photograph only. It is at this final stage that you might want to double-click the High Pass filter layer in the Layers palette (circled) to reopen the Filter dialog and fine-tune the filter setting.

# Removing noise from an image

This next section deals with image noise and the inter-related issues that surround image sharpening. All images are likely to suffer from some degree of noise, but the amount of noise present in an image is likely to vary according to a number of factors, such as whether the image was scanned from film or whether it was shot digitally. The noise we see in scans from film originals will mainly be down to the actual film grain in the film emulsion (especially if a photograph was shot using 35mm film), but it can also be due to noise that is generated by the scanning process itself. Scanned image noise will also vary according to whether it came from a color neg or chrome, and what specific film emulsion was used. With photographs that were shot digitally, it will vary depending on the camera sensor, and what ISO setting the photograph was shot at.

Photoshop offers several strategies for reducing image noise. If you process images via Camera Raw, you can use the Noise Reduction slider to reduce the noise in pictures that have been shot at a standard or moderate ISO speed with a modern digital camera (this is described in the following chapter). In Photoshop itself there is the Reduce Noise filter and this is also fairly good at processing digital captures or scanned images. The tools in Photoshop work well enough for the majority of pictures where there isn't a huge amount of noise to conquer. But whenever you have to apply major noise reduction, this will inevitably lead to some softening of the image detail, unless you incorporate counter steps to preserve the all-important edges in the picture. Let's look at the two main noise reduction techniques that are available in Photoshop, starting with a noise removal method for scanned images that feature a lot of noticeable film grain.

## Reducing film grain noise

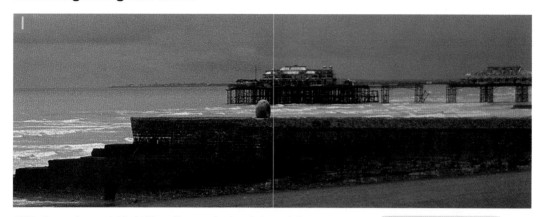

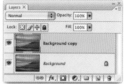

**1** This shows a close-up detail of a 35mm film scan, showing a before and after version of the image. The left half shows the unsharpened image before noise reduction was applied and the right half shows the image after noise reduction. Rather than run the noise reduction on the original image, it is best to make a copy of the Background layer first and then run the noise reduction steps on this layer only.

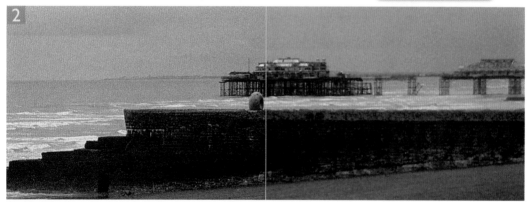

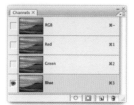

**2** And here is how the noise reduction was done. The technique involves selecting each of the RGB color channels and applying multiple passes of the Despeckle filter, which is located in the Filter ⇨ Noise submenu. In this example, I applied two passes of Despeckle to the Red and the Green channel, and four passes to the Blue channel (because the Blue channel is usually the noisiest). Although the noise reduction will soften the image, you can now proceed to sharpen the picture using one of the sharpening techniques described later, but without further enhancing the noise in the original scan. And remember, because the noise reduction has been applied to a copy layer, you have the ability to fade the opacity of the layer or mask the layer contents to restore more of the original version of the image.

## Reduce Noise filter

The Reduce Noise filter uses a method of smart noise reduction that can remove noise from an image without destroying the edge detail in the picture. Overall, the Reduce Noise filter is a useful one shot filter that is better at reducing the noise in images that originated as digital captures, rather than reducing film grain noise from scanned 35mm images. The Reduce Noise filter is mainly designed to target the twin problems of digital luminance noise, which is like a very fine speckly grain, and color noise, which is commonplace with digital captures shot at

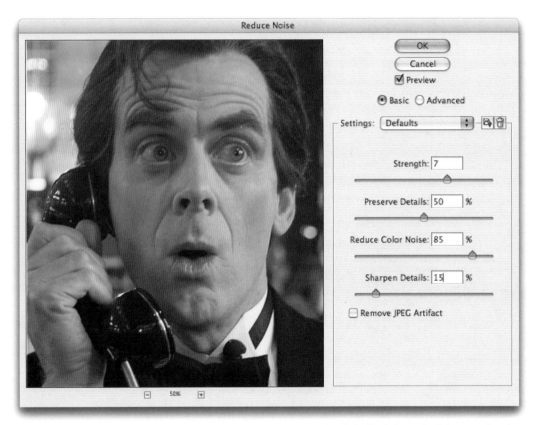

**Figure 4.38** Here is the Reduce Noise filter being used to help remove the noise from a digital capture of 'Special Agent' Russell Brown, which was shot at 1250 ISO. The Reduce Noise filter helped get rid of most of the noise artifacts.

high ISO settings. The problem with this filter is that it is quite memory intensive, so be prepared for a wait while it performs its calculations. And although it can appear quite effective at removing heavy noise, if you have to apply extreme settings, you can end up with an enhanced noise pattern after you have sharpened the image.

In Basic mode you can simply adjust the strength of the noise reduction and then use the controls below to modify the noise filtering, and these should be adjusted in the order they are displayed. The Strength slider adjusts the amount of noise reduction that is applied, while the Preserve Details slider will help preserve the edge luminance information. The luminance noise reduction will appear strongest when you set Preserve Details to zero %. But as you increase Preserve Details, more edge detail (and often more noise) will become visible. Below that is the Reduce Color Noise slider, which will allow you to separately control the color noise suppression.

After you have adjusted all of the above settings, it is highly likely that the image will have suffered some loss in sharpness. The Sharpen Details slider will allow you to dial back in some detail sharpness. But I would urge caution here, because adding too much sharpening can simply introduce more artifacts.

### Advanced mode noise reduction

In Basic mode you can only adjust the Reduce Noise settings so that they affect the overall strength and preservation of image detail. When the Advanced mode button is checked you can apply the noise reduction adjustments on a per channel basis. This can be useful if you wish to apply differential noise reduction to individual channels. As in the film grain noise removal example, the Blue channel is usually the noisiest so it can therefore be a good idea to apply more reduction to this channel and less to the Red and Green channels where the noise is not such a major problem.

**Color bleed caution**

There are times when you may want to crank up the Color Noise Reduction to 100%, in order to remove as much of the noise artefacts as possible. But be aware that too much Color Noise Reduction can sometimes cause colors to bleed badly and cause too much softening of the image.

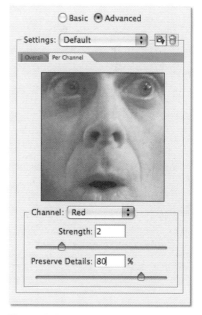

Figure 4.39 A close-up view of the Reduce Noise filter settings in Advanced mode.

## Record as an action

To save repeating all the steps shown here, each time you want to reduce the noise in a photograph, I suggest you record these steps as a Photoshop action.

## *Targeted noise reduction*

The following steps are derived from a technique described by Bruce Fraser in his book: *Real World Sharpening with Adobe Photoshop CS2*, published by Peachpit. These steps show you how to mask a Reduce Noise filter layer so that the edge detail is preserved from the softening effect of the noise reduction process.

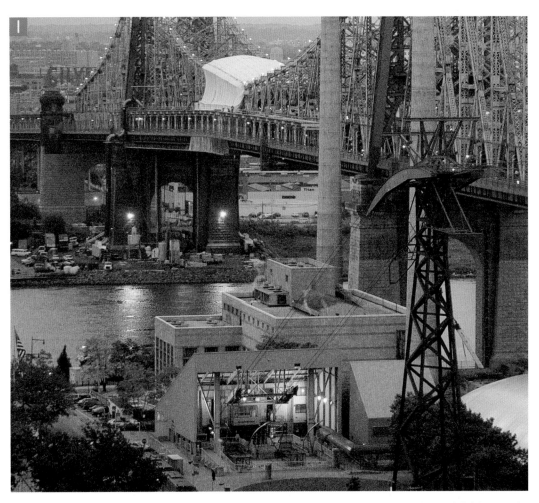

1 Here is a close-up view of an underexposed and unsharpened digital capture that was shot at 400 ISO. You can clearly see a lot of luminance noise and color noise in this picture.

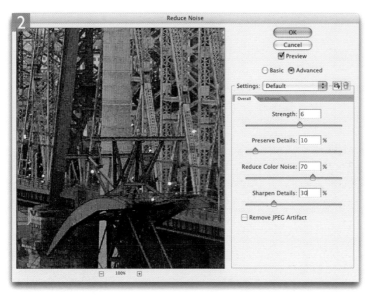

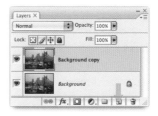

2 The first step is to make a duplicate copy of the Background layer. You can do this by dragging the Background layer down to the New Layer button. I then applied the Reduce Noise filter, adjusting the settings so as to remove as much of the luminance and color noise as possible. You have to be careful to not set the Reduce Color Noise setting too high, as this can cause strong colors (such as the red crane featured here) to bleed slightly.

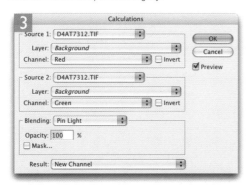

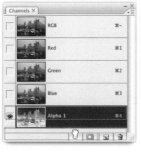

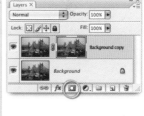

3 I now wanted to create a protection mask for the Background copy layer that would help preserve more of the edge detail. I chose Image ⇨ Calculations and configured the dialog as is shown here. I was basically creating a New alpha channel that was a blend of the Red and Green channels, using the Pin Light blend mode. The Alpha 1 channel appeared in the Channels palette and I dragged this to the Make New Selection button to load as a selection and clicked on the Add Layer Mask button (circled) in the Layers palette to convert this active selection into a layer mask for the Background copy layer.

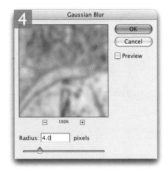

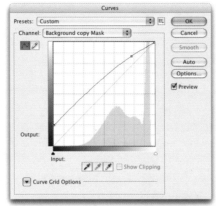

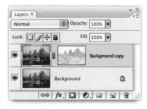

4 The mask was now ready for editing. I went to the Filter ⇨ Stylize menu and chose Find Edges. This was then followed by a Gaussian Blur filter of between 3–5 pixels and a Curves adjustment, which lightened it slightly. The idea here is that darker shades of gray in the layer mask will hide the layer contents and the lighter areas of the mask will allow more of the layer to be revealed.

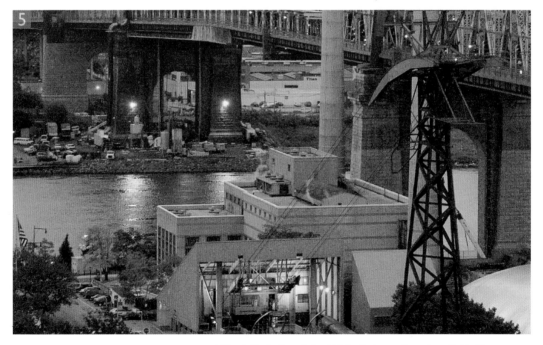

5 Here is the final result, in which the Background copy layer that had been processed using the Reduce Noise filter is masked by a layer mask that hides the edges more and keeps them from being filtered.

## JPEG noise removal

You can also use the Reduce Noise filter to smooth out
JPEG artifacts. If you have a heavily compressed JPEG
image, the Reduce Noise filter can certainly help improve
the image smoothness. But I reckon you can use the
Reduce Noise filter in this mode to improve the appearance
of GIF images as well. Of course you will need to convert
the GIF image from Indexed Color to RGB mode first. But
once you have done this you can use the Reduce Noise
filter adjustments to help get rid of the banding by taking
the Preserve Details slider down to zero % and raising the
Sharpen Details to a higher amount than you would be
advised to use normally.

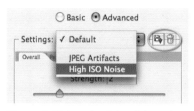

**Figure 4.40** Accessing Reduce Noise settings.

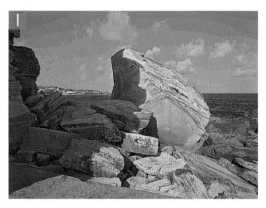

**1** The Reduce Noise filter has a Remove JPEG Artifact option
that can be useful if you wish to improve the appearance of an
image that has suffered from over-heavy JPEG compression. But
it can also help rescue a GIF image where a lot of the color levels
information has been lost in the conversion to Indexed Color mode.

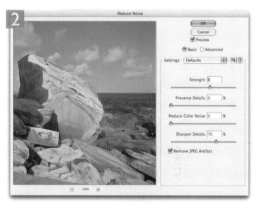

**2** A GIF image will have to be converted to RGB mode first. You
can then apply the Reduce Noise filter. In this example I checked
the Remove JPEG Artifact box. To remove the color banding, the
Preserve Details had to be set to 0%. To make the image sharp
again I increased the Sharpen Details to 70%.

### *Saving Reduce Noise settings*

Favorite Reduce Noise settings can be saved by clicking on
the Save Changes to Current Settings button. And Reduce
Noise settings can be deleted by clicking on the trash icon
next to it.

## Removing moiré patterns

Camera noise and moiré problems can sometimes arise when you shoot digitally. Moiré is becoming less of an issue now that the pixel resolutions are getting larger. But if you do see a moiré problem arise at the shooting stage, try changing the camera distance from the subject. This can often cure the problem in advance. I would also advise applying a layer mask to the blurred layer and selectively painting in the blurred layer. The following technique was shown to me by Thomas Holm of Pixl in Denmark.

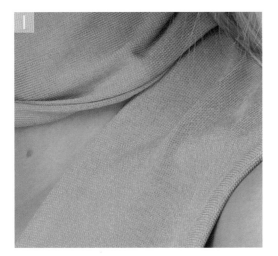

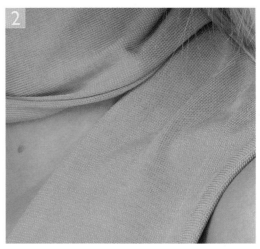

1 In this digitally captured photograph, there is a moiré pattern visible on the fabric of the dress.

2 To remove the moiré pattern, I copied the Background layer, changed the blend mode to Color and applied the Gaussian Blur filter to this layer. For this particular image a blur radius of 12 pixels was required to eradicate the moiré. Note that when you use a Color blending mode, it is only color information that is blurred – the luminosity (the detail information) will remain unaffected.

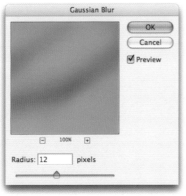

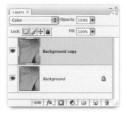

## Image sharpening

It is an unavoidable fact that image detail will progressively become lost at critical stages of the digital image making process. Without corrective sharpening, a printed image will appear softer than expected.

This is by no means a new phenomenon or one that is unique to digital imaging. The problems begin as soon as you focus the subject in your viewfinder and press the shutter release. The first variable is the camera lens. Most photographers are all too aware that cheaper inferior lenses will produce less sharp pictures, but the film emulsion can also influence the sharpness, as can the quality of the digital sensor and the number of photosites on the sensor chip. And if you are shooting film, then you will have to scan a chrome transparency, negative or photographic print made with a darkroom enlarger (which involves yet another optical step). Therefore, even if you use the finest quality lenses and digital equipment, it is inevitable that the capture/scanning process will lead to some image degradation and an apparent loss of sharpness before you even bring the photograph into Photoshop and start editing it.

The other problem concerns the loss of sharpness at the output stage. Whenever you make a print output you are usually converting an image that is made up of pixels into an image that is made up of ink dots on paper. Translating pixels into an image that is printed via a mechanical process will inevitably incur even more loss of sharpness.

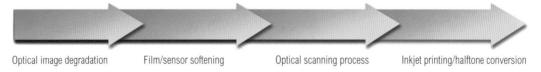

Optical image degradation    Film/sensor softening    Optical scanning process    Inkjet printing/halftone conversion

**Figure 4.41** The above diagram maps out the path to blurry destruction for photons that enter a camera lens and are eventually interpreted as printer's ink on the page. At each of the above stages either a little or a lot of detail will become lost.

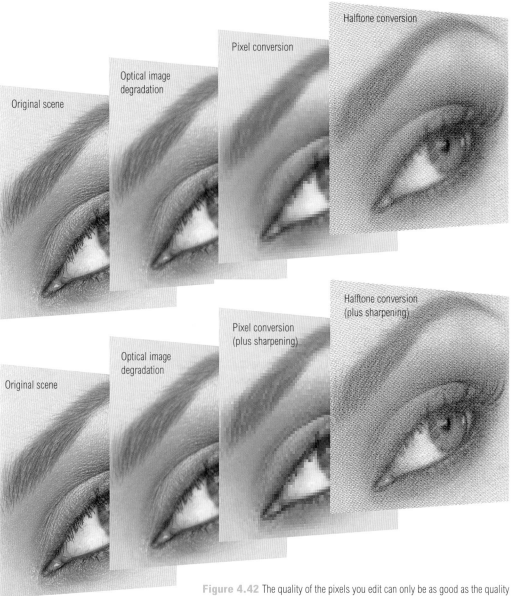

**Figure 4.42** The quality of the pixels you edit can only be as good as the quality of the lens used on the camera, the number of pixels captured and the quality of the camera sensor or scanning device. Even the finest recorded images will benefit from some sharpening to adjust for a loss in sharpness. More sharpening losses will occur when outputting the image as a halftone print or inkjet. Further sharpening in Photoshop is therefore recommended before you make any type of output.

## Sharpening solutions

Over the years various strategies have evolved. For example, some film scanning devices are set up to automatically sharpen scanned images so that they can go straight to a printing press. To some extent this is fine if all you are concerned with is preparing images to go to print in a publication. The downside of this one-step sharpening approach is that because the sharpening is so heavy-handed, the pictures will be more difficult to retouch. Plus the sharpening will usually be calculated for a specific print output size and this also raises more limitations as to what else you can do with photographs that are scanned this way.

If you shoot digitally and capture anything other than a raw file, the camera's built-in software will apply a small amount of sharpening in order to make the output files look acceptably sharp. Of course, nobody wants to see blurry pictures from their expensive cameras, but it is important to realize that an unsharpened 'soft' capture file is not necessarily the sign of a bad camera or scanner. For example, all raw digital files will look soft in appearance until they have been sharpened, which is why raw processing software such as Adobe Camera Raw has a Sharpen slider. The question is, how much sharpening does an image need and when is the best time to apply the sharpening? Because there are several competing considerations that need to be taken into account here.

### *Multipass sharpening*

Noted author and imaging expert Bruce Fraser (who sadly passed away in 2006), concluded that there really are no one-shot sharpening solutions that can sharpen an image to address the deficiencies in the softness of the original image and sharpen the image ready for print output. As a result, Bruce came up with the notion of multipass sharpening, where sharpening is applied to the image at the beginning stages to take into account the source origin of the image. This is then followed by a further sharpening to optimize for the image content. And finally an output sharpening must be applied before making a print.

### Origins of unsharp masking

Unsharp masking sounds like a contradiction in terms, because how can unsharpening make a picture sharper? The term in fact relates to the reprographic film process whereby a light, soft, unsharp negative version of the image was sandwiched next to the original positive during exposure. This technique was used to increase the edge sharpness on the resulting plate. The Photoshop Unsharp Mask (USM) filter reproduces the effect digitally and you have a lot of control over the amount of sharpening and the manner in which it is to be applied.

## Turning off the auto sharpening

Wherever possible, use an unsharpened original as your master and apply any sharpening as necessary in Photoshop. Do check the settings in the camera capture or scanner software carefully because a lot of manufacturers like to sneak in some unsharp masking even when they tell you everything is set to zero. If you find this is happening, check to see if you can turn off the sharpening completely in the scanner software.

## Capture sharpening

The first step is to apply an initial corrective sharpening to each image before you start any retouching. The aim here is to compensate for the loss of sharpness which occurs naturally during the photographic process. This is what we call capture sharpening, and there are various ways you can achieve this. If you are happy with the amount of sharpness that is automatically applied by your scanner or digital camera, then you won't need any more sharpening at this stage. But if you prefer, you can disable any sharpening in your camera or scanner software and apply the presharpening in Photoshop instead. One should recognize of course that not all methods of scanning and capture are the same and not all film emulsions or digital camera types and resolutions are the same either. And different amounts of sharpening will be required in order to attain a standard level of sharpness where each image appears sharp enough to look good on the computer display you are using.

## Sharpening for output

What you see on the screen will not exactly match the printed result. The process of converting a digital image to a halftone plate and from there to ink on the page (or making an inkjet print) inevitably incurs a further loss of sharpness. For this reason it is always necessary to 'sharpen for print'. This means that if you are preparing a picture to appear in print, you should apply an extra amount of sharpening, beyond that which makes the image look good on the computer display. Sharpening for output should be done at the end of a Photoshop session and after the image has been resized to the final print size. It therefore makes sense to keep a master version which you can make copies from as requested and always apply the final unsharp masking on a resized copy of the master. I shall be covering sharpening for output towards the end of this book in Chapter 13. But for now, we shall concentrate on the image capture sharpening processes.

## Unsharp Mask filter

The only sharpening filters you ever need are the Unsharp Mask (USM) and the Smart Sharpen filter. Sharpen and Sharpen More are preset filters that have none of the flexibility associated with the Unsharp Mask filter. While unsharp masking may make a picture look sharper, this apparent sharpening is achieved at the expense of introducing artifacts into the image that will permanently degrade the picture and possibly emphasize any noise that is present. Furthermore, if you oversharpen an image before carrying out color adjustments and any retouching, the sharpening artifacts can become even more noticeable afterwards. So the main aim when using the Unsharp Mask filter is to increase the apparent sharpness and at the same time try to minimize the amount of artifacting that can be introduced by the sharpening process. And we do this by refining how the Unsharp Mask filter is applied. Namely, through the use of the Luminance blend mode so that only the luminance information gets sharpened, and at a more advanced level, through the use of an edge mask, similar to the one used with the Reduce Noise filter. Let's begin by looking at the three controls in the Unsharp Mask filter dialog and what they do.

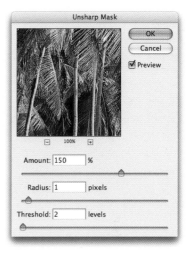

**Figure 4.43** The Unsharp Mask filter dialog.

### *Amount*

The Amount setting controls the intensity of the sharpening. This is a really simple one to understand. The higher the percentage (up to 500%) the greater the sharpening effect will be. The correct amount to apply will vary depending on the state of the image or the type of press output. Generally speaking, I would typically apply an amount between 50 and 200% for a capture sharpening (experience will help you make the right judgement on screen as to what the correct amount to use should be). Here is a good tip: try setting the Amount value really high to begin with. Try to find out which Radius and Threshold settings work best at this high Amount setting and then reduce the Amount percentage to an appropriate level.

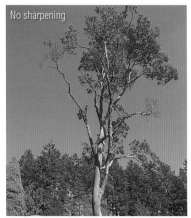

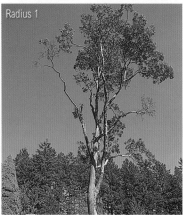

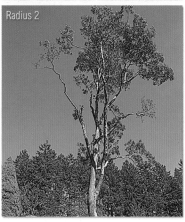

### Radius

The Amount setting controls the level or intensity of unsharp masking, but the Radius and Threshold settings affect the distribution of the sharpening effect. The Radius setting controls the width of the sharpening effect and the ideal setting will depend very much on the subject matter and also the size of your output. Use a Radius of between 0.4 and 1 for capture sharpening and use a Radius between 1.0 and 2.0 when sharpening for inkjet or halftone output. As the Radius setting is increased you will notice how the edges are emphasized more when a wider radius is used. Figure 4.44 demonstrates the impact increasing the Radius can have on the edge sharpness.

### Threshold

The Threshold setting controls which pixels will be sharpened based on how much the pixels to be sharpened deviate in brightness from their neighbors. Higher Threshold settings apply the filter only to neighboring pixels which are markedly different in tonal brightness, i.e. edge outlines. At lower settings more or all pixels are sharpened including areas of smooth continuous tone. If the Threshold setting is 4, for example, and there is a difference of fewer than four levels of tone between any two neighboring pixels, they won't be sharpened. If there are more than four levels of tone difference between them they will be sharpened. Raising the Threshold setting will therefore enable you to sharpen edge contrast, but without sharpening scanner noise artifacts or film grain (the things you don't want to make sharper). For this reason, scans made from 35 mm film originals usually benefit from being sharpened with a higher Threshold setting than would need to be applied to a 120 film scan. The Threshold setting is most critical when preparing a scanned film image. As a general rule, use a Threshold of between 0 and 10.

**Figure 4.44** These pictures demonstrate the effect of increasing the Unsharp Mask filter Radius size and have been treated as follows: no sharpening (top). Amount 200% Radius 1, Threshold 0 (middle). Amount 200% Radius 2, Threshold 0 (bottom).

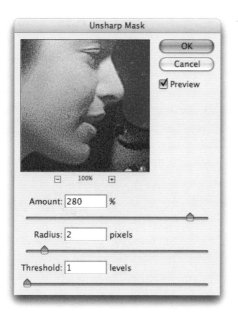

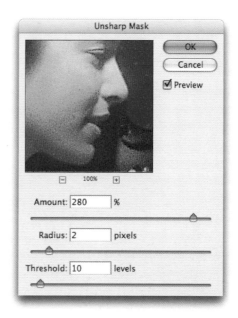

**Figure 4.45** This photograph taken of musicians underwater was shot through a scratched glass porthole. As a result of these environmental conditions, the picture was already quite soft in appearance and therefore needed a lot of extra sharpening. But the problem with doing that is that at a low Threshold setting, the high Amount and Radius also emphasized the film grain. Increasing the Threshold to 10 solved the problem. The photograph was made to appear sharper but without sharpening too much of the film grain.

Photograph by Eric Richmond.

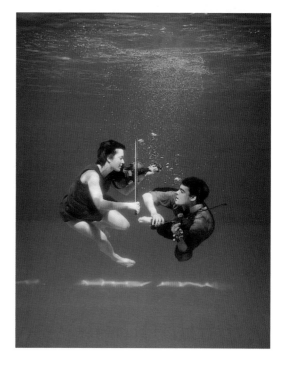

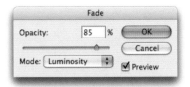

Figure 4.46 Unsharp masking can produce chromatic artifacts in some areas of the image. Luminance sharpening can help when you want to avoid overemphasizing the color noise artifacts in an image. Apply an Edit ⇨ Fade command and change the blending mode to Luminosity. This has the same effect as converting an image to Lab mode and sharpening the Luminosity channel only, but is less destructive (and faster).

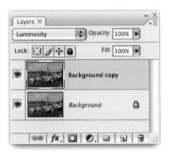

Figure 4.47 The other alternative is to make a copy of the Background layer first, set the layer blend mode to Luminosity and then sharpen the layer using the Unsharp Mask filter. And here is another advantage: if you set the layer opacity to 66% before you sharpen, you can judge what would be the best sharpness to apply at the 66% Opacity setting and then have the freedom to increase or decrease the sharpening strength after you have applied the filter.

## Luminance sharpening

Unsharp masking on its own is a fairly blunt instrument to work with and as I pointed out earlier, in order to get the best results from the Unsharp Mask filter, we need to look at ways to fine-tune its application. Since we only want to sharpen the detail in the image, the main thing we want to do is to restrict the effect of the Unsharp Mask filter to the luminance information only.

The artifacts caused by unsharp masking can sometimes be avoided by filtering the luminance information in the image only. After you have applied an Unsharp Mask filter, go immediately to the Edit menu, choose Fade Filter and change the blend mode to Luminance. You can make the initial unsharp masking amount a little stronger than is required and use the Fade Opacity slider to adjust the sharpening effect to achieve the desired result. Or, you can duplicate the Background layer, set the layer blend mode to Luminosity and apply the Unsharp Mask filter to this layer.

After the last edition of this book was published I was taken to task by some readers for ignoring certain Lab color mode techniques. These omissions were deliberate, and it is not because I have an anti-Lab mode agenda. If I were writing this book fifteen years ago, I too would be telling you to convert the image from RGB to Lab color mode and apply the Unsharp Mask filter to the Lightness channel, because that is how we did things back then. But we are not living in 1992 any more. Photoshop has for a long time now had layers, which means that in my opinion (and that of most other experts) we don't need to go through the procedure of converting an image from RGB to Lab mode and back to RGB again in order to target the image luminosity when sharpening. For one thing, if you are editing an 8-bit per channel image, the conversion from RGB to Lab and back again is unnecessarily destructive. Although there is a small difference between sharpening the Lightness channel of an image in Lab mode compared to a luminosity sharpen, the difference is slight compared to the greater gain that is achieved through targeting the luminance detail only using the methods I just described.

## Sharpening for the image source

If you don't wish to explore any further, then I recommend you stick with the simple Fade ⇨ Luminosity technique. If you do want to refine the presharpening process, then I recommend you follow the steps shown here and use the Actions palette to record these steps. You will then have a simple action that can be applied to any image that needs presharpening.

Let's now look at how to use the Unsharp Mask filter with the Luminance blend mode to apply a presharpening layer that is tailored to the source image. By this I mean that you choose a sharpen setting that is most suited to the image file source. We shall assume that where there was any noise in the original, this has first been removed using one of the noise reduction methods described earlier. The following steps are based on the advanced techniques described by Bruce Fraser in his *Real World Sharpening with Adobe Photoshop CS2* book.

### Sharpening the midtones

In Step 2 of the following action, I show how to adjust the Blend If sliders. The reason for including this extra step is to restrict the sharpening so that it affects the midtones only. This is because we need to concentrate the sharpening where it is needed most and we want to avoid clipping the shadows and highlights.

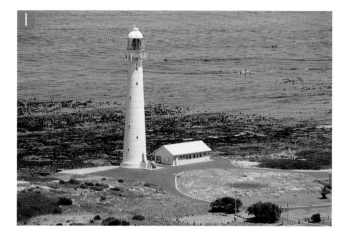

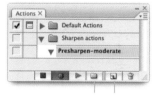

Create new set    Create new Action

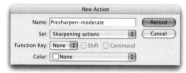

1 Here is an image that was processed from a raw capture shot using the Canon EOS 1Ds Mk 1 camera. The file was processed using Adobe Camera Raw with the Detail Sharpen slider set to zero and with the Color Noise Reduction set to 25%. Before doing anything to the image, I went to the Actions palette, clicked on the Create new set button to create a new Action set and then clicked on the Create new Action button to open the New Action dialog shown here. I named the action Presharpen–moderate and clicked on the Record button to begin recording.

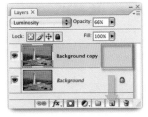

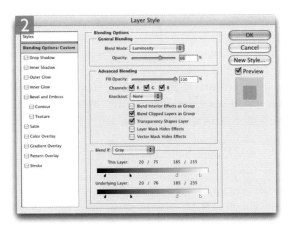

## Splitting the arrows

To split the Blend if arrows as shown in Step 2, hold down the ⌥ alt key to separate the slider into two halves.

2 The first step is to make a copy of the Background layer, which can be done by dragging the Background layer to the New Layer button in the Layers palette. I set the layer opacity to 66% and changed the layer blend mode to Luminosity. I then double-clicked on the layer (targeting the area inside the green box area) to open the Layer Style options dialog. Now for the tricky part. The Blend if sliders (including the This Layer and the Underlying Layer sliders) have to be adjusted as follows: Minimum black: 20, Maximum black: 75, Minimum white: 185, Maximum white: 235.

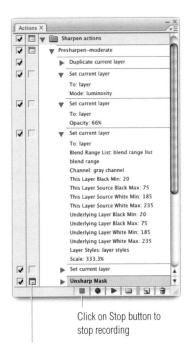

Click on Stop button to stop recording

Click in the space next to the Unsharp Mask step to insert a pause in the action

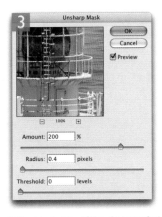

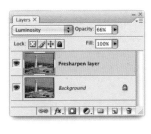

3 After I had clicked OK to the Layer Style dialog, I was now ready to sharpen the layer. Note that if you are recording these steps as an action, you might want to rename the Background copy layer, as I have done here. I applied the Unsharp Mask filter to the new layer using the settings shown here. I used a low Radius value because the original image came from an 11 megapixel digital camera. At this point I clicked on the Stop button to stop the Action recording. But there is one more thing you can do that might prove useful. If you click on the box next to the final Unsharp Mask step, you can insert a pause in the action that will open the dialog allowing you to modify the settings each time you replay the action.

## Which sharpen settings to use

The Sharpen for image source technique offers some significant advantages over the ordinary method or Lab mode method of sharpening. You gain all the main benefits of Lab mode Lightness channel sharpening, but without the need for a double mode conversion from RGB mode to Lab and back again. Secondly, the Unsharp Mask step is applied at the very end, rather than at the middle stage. And lastly, the sharpening is applied on a layer at 66% opacity, and this will allow you to modify the final sharpness, to make it stronger or weaker.

The Sharpen for image source technique is actually intended as a preliminary sharpening step where you sharpen the image according to the size of the source file and what type of image the source file is. The steps I have just shown are intended for presharpening an image from an 11 megapixel or greater digital capture file and the final Unsharp Mask settings you should use will vary according to the file source type. For example, with digital capture images the Amount and Threshold settings should remain the same. But with a 6 megapixel camera, use a Radius of 0.6 pixels. With an 8 megapixel camera use a Radius of 0.5 pixels and with an 11 megapixel camera or higher, use a Radius of 0.4 pixels.

Over the next few pages we shall look at the second stage presharpening where we sharpen for the image content. To summarize, Sharpen for image source is about sharpening for the file size and source type. Sharpen for content is about choosing the best sharpening routine based on whether the image contains lots of detail where the fine edges need a lot of emphasis, or whether the image contains soft flat areas of detail (such as skin tones), where it would be more appropriate to leave these areas unsharpened and sharpen the areas of higher contrast only.

All the presharpening techniques shown here are based on just a few of the recipes recommended by Bruce Fraser in his book (see side panel).

**Real World Sharpening**

It should be pointed out that these examples represent just a few of the more common presharpening routines from among the many that are discussed in Bruce Fraser's book. The full title is *Real World Sharpening for Adobe Photoshop CS2*, by Bruce Fraser, available from Peachpit Press.
ISBN number: 0-321-44991-6.

**A simpler option**

If the techniques described over the next few pages appear too complex, you could simply adopt the Sharpen for image source technique as a complete presharpening routine and adapt the Unsharp Mask settings at the end to suit your needs and visually check to see if the image looks sharp enough on the screen.

## Sharpening for fine to moderate edges

This next stage takes the presharpening process one stage further and shows you how to additionally presharpen an image where the image contains fine to moderate edge detail, such as the details on the building and the sea waves.

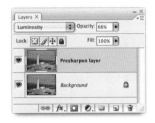

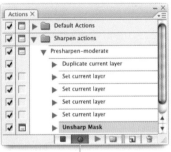

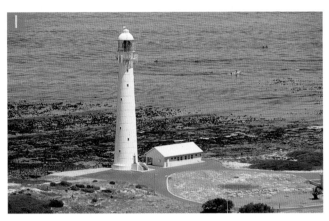

1 Here is the same image as was processed in the previous example, where we had reached Step 3. The object now is to apply a second pass sharpen to complete the presharpening process but, in doing so, take into account the image content. This particular photograph had a lot of fine edge detail on the lighthouse, so I applied an edge sharpening technique for fine to moderate edges. But before all that, I went to the Actions palette, selected the action I had recorded up until Stage 3 and pressed the Record button to resume recording the action.

Click on Record button
to resume recording

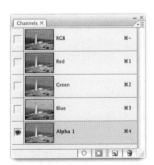

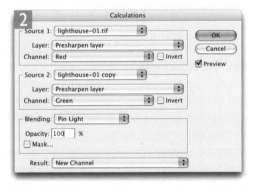

2 This step is identical to the one used to prepare an edge mask for the Noise Reduction technique. I chose Image ⇨ Calculations and configured the dialog as shown here. I was basically creating a new alpha channel that was a blend of the Red and Green channels, using the Pin Light blend mode.

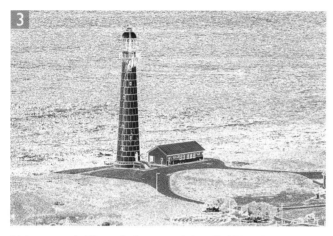

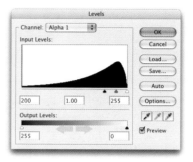

**3** I then went to the Filter ⇨ Stylize menu and chose Find Edges. This was followed by a Levels adjustment using the settings shown here. The Levels adjustment increased the contrast and emphasized the edges more. Note that with this adjustment, I swapped the Output levels so that the shadow output switched from 0 to 255 and the highlight output switched from 255 to 0. This Output levels switch is the same as choosing Image ⇨ Adjustments ⇨ Invert.

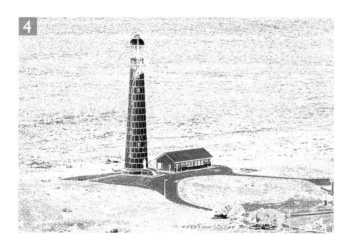

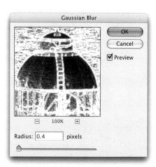

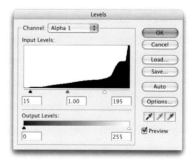

**4** I then went to the Filter menu and chose Blur ⇨ Gaussian Blur and applied a small 0.4 Radius Blur to the channel. The blur amount used here is quite critical, because this stage is very much tailored to the content of the image, where I wanted to emphasize the narrow edge detail of the lighthouse. If I was presharpening an image with softer edges, I might apply a larger Radius Blur. This was followed by applying the Levels adjustment shown here.

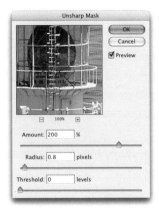

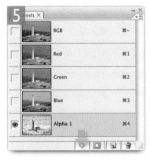

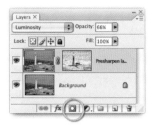

**5** For the next step, I dragged the Alpha 1 channel down to the Make Selection button to load as a selection and then clicked on the Add layer mask button in the Layers palette to convert the active selection into a layer mask that masked the 'Presharpen layer'. And now, it is very important to click on the Presharpen layer image thumbnail to make it active (instead of the layer mask) and apply the Unsharp Mask filter, using the settings shown here. If the layer mask appears in the Unsharp Mask filter preview, you will know you have forgotten to target the actual layer.

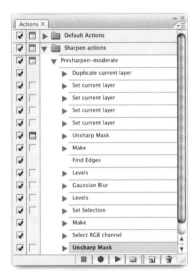

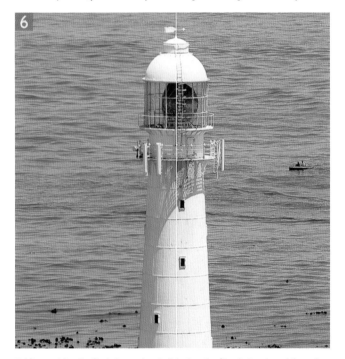

**6** After applying the final sharpening, I clicked on the Stop button to end the action recording. And here is the finished image, shown with the unsharpened version on the left and the presharpened version on the right. Note that the combined pictures shown here have been further sharpened for print output at 300 ppi.

## Sharpening for smooth edge content

The following steps show the basic method for sharpening images where the image content mostly features soft edges, such as this portrait of myself taken by my wife, Camilla. The intention here is to generate a very soft wide edged mask, through which to apply the final Unsharp Mask.

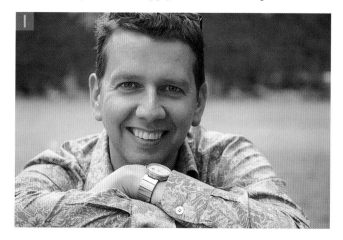

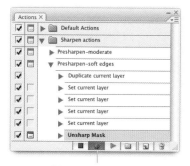

Click on Record button
to resume recording

1 Here is an image that predominantly has soft edge detail. As in the previous example, the image was initially processed using the first pass steps, as described on pages 203–204. You can see in the Actions palette that the action steps are currently at the same point as they were at the beginning of the moderate edge content action. I pressed the Record button to begin recording this new action.

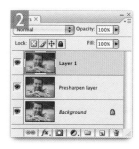

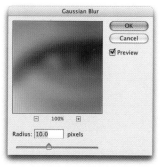

2 The steps for sharpening an image with soft edge content are slightly more complicated than those used for an image with fine to moderate edge content. The first step is to add a new layer filled with a merged copy of the image. I use this step a lot in all my retouching, so it is worth memorizing. The keyboard shortcut is: ⌘ ⌥ Shift E (Mac) ctrl alt Shift E (PC). I then applied a 10 pixel Gaussian Blur to the new merged copy layer.

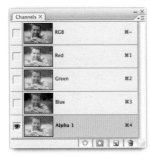

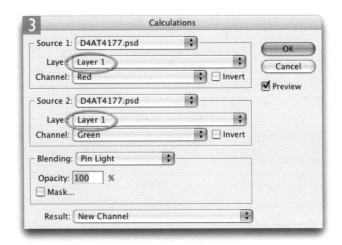

3 With this new blurred layer selected, I then chose Image ⇒ Calculations and used the same settings as before. But note that the Layer section should point to this new blurred layer: Layer 1. I clicked OK to create a new alpha channel.

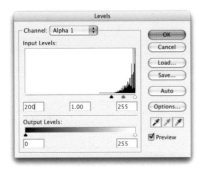

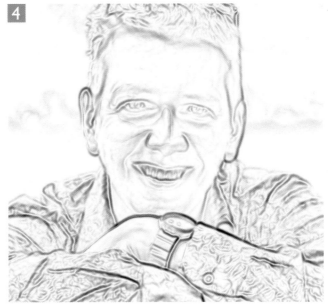

4 The following steps all take place on the new alpha channel and these steps are now more or less similar to those used in the moderate edges technique. I began by going to the Filter menu and choose Stylize ⇒ Find Edges. This was followed by applying the Levels adjustment shown here.

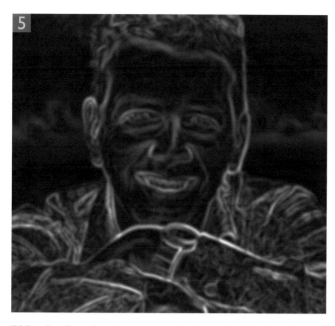

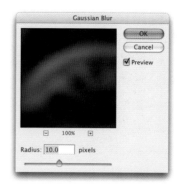

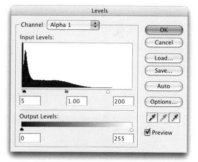

**5** I then chose Image Invert to create a negative image of the Alpha channel and followed this with a 10 pixel Gaussian Blur, to soften the edges more. I then followed this with the Levels adjustment shown here, which added more contrast to the channel mask.

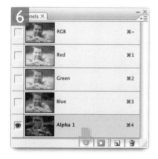

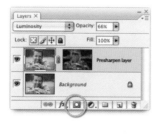

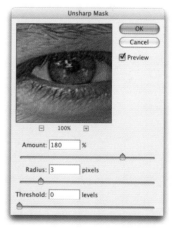

**6** The mask was now ready for use. I went to the Channels palette and dragged the Alpha 1 channel down to the Make Selection button (you can now delete the channel after loading it as a selection). I then clicked on the Add layer mask button in the Layers palette to convert the active selection into a layer mask that masked the Presharpen layer. The merged copy layer was no longer required, so I deleted the Layer 1. And I also made sure the image thumbnail (not the mask) was selected in the Presharpen layer. I then applied the Unsharp Mask filter using the settings shown here. The Radius was deliberately set to a wide setting. But remember that the Unsharp Mask filter is being applied here through a wide edges layer mask.

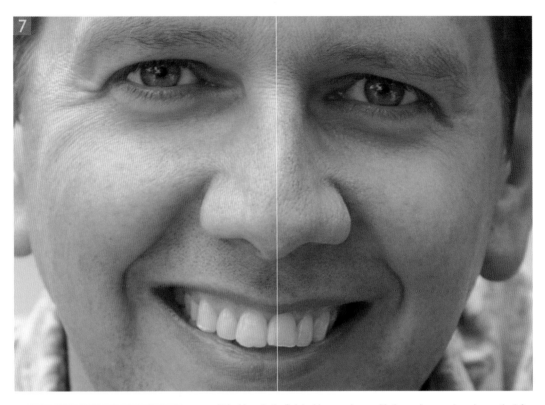

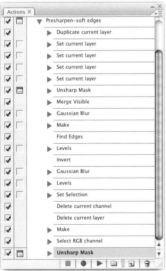

**7** And here is the finished image, shown with the unsharpened version on the left and the presharpened version on the right. Note that the combined pictures shown here have been further sharpened for print output at 300 ppi.

After applying the final sharpening, I clicked on the Stop button to end the action recording. In the Actions palette you can see all the additional steps that had been recorded and how I placed pauses next to the two sharpening stages: the first one was at the first pass presharpen stage and the second at the second pass presharpen stage at the end. As I mentioned earlier, one of the advantages of having the presharpen layer set to 66% is that you can increase the sharpening easily (as well as reduce it) by adjusting the opacity of the layer. In this example, I increased the opacity to 100% in order to make the sharpening difference more obvious.

## Presharpening summary

In these few pages I have tried to distill some of the key benefits of a multi pass presharpening workflow. At the very least I would advise you to use a Luminosity fade when applying the unsharp mask filter. But I would also recommend you to record the preliminary sharpening steps shown on pages 203–204 as an action that can be replayed on other images. The secondary Sharpen for content techniques are also worth using and I have so far shown two distinct methods: one for images with fine to moderate edges and one for images with soft edge detail. If you follow the instructions shown here, you can create two basic actions that can then be applied in many sharpening situations. Remember, the Unsharp Mask settings used for the initial sharpen are determined by the source. The settings used in the subsequent sharpening are dependent on the image content.

## Third-party sharpening plug-ins

As you can see, there is a lot more to sharpening than meets the eye. The Unsharp Mask filter in Photoshop is perfectly capable of giving good results and these can be further enhanced using some of the selective sharpening tips I have described here. But there are also some third-party plug-in solutions available that offer an alternative to the Unsharp Mask filter. For example, there is a product called PhotoKit Sharpener from Pixel Genius, a company I am personally involved with. But all credit goes to fellow Pixel Genius member and author Bruce Fraser, who devised this special set of Photoshop sharpening effects that are designed to apply just the right amount of image sharpening for all different types of film and digital file formats. Bruce's sharpening routines incorporate all the techniques discussed here in this chapter, and then some. They include import sharpening for a multitude of film types and digital captures, output sharpening for inkjet printers or repro, and creative sharpening layers for selective image sharpening. A demo version of PhotoKit Sharpener is on the CD and can also be downloaded from the Pixel Genius website: www.pixelgenius.com.

### Actions assumptions

The Photoshop action recordings I have described so far were all carried out on a flattened image with just a single Background layer. Since presharpening is the first thing that you do to an image, I thought it would be OK to assume that one did not need to make the action any more complex than the examples shown here.

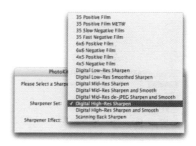

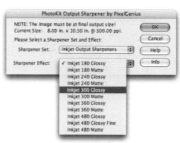

**Figure 4.48** The Pixel Genius PhotoKit Sharpener automated plug-in that is able to apply sharpening routines in stages for capture selective (painting in on a layer) and output sharpening. The sharpening routines are each customized to provide the optimum amount of sharpening for these different tasks.

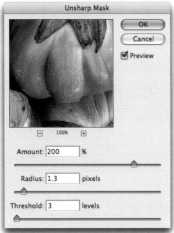

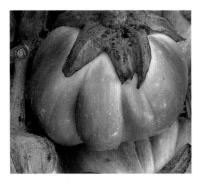

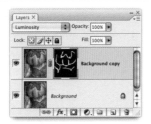

Figure 4.49 This illustrates one way of applying unsharp masking to a picture. I copied the Background layer and applied an aggressive amount of unsharp masking to the layer. I then ⌥ alt-clicked on the Add Layer Mask button at the bottom of the Layers palette to add a layer mask that 'hides all'. With the layer mask active, one can paint in the sharpness using a brush, with white as the foreground color.

## Selective sharpening

There is another type of sharpening that we should look at and that is selective sharpening. You see, although most presharpening methods should be all you need in order to get a nice sharp looking picture, there are some images that could always do with an extra sharpening boost, to add emphasis to key areas of a photograph.

Selective sharpening can sometimes be useful as an added step, just after the capture sharpening, and there are several ways you can sharpen an image selectively. Forget using the sharpen tool because it is too harsh a tool to work with. In the Figure 4.49 example I created a duplicate of the Background layer (or you could create a new empty layer and fill this with a merged snapshot of the current image). I set the blend mode to Luminosity and applied an aggressive sharpen using the Unsharp Mask settings shown here. Next, I added a layer mask, filled with black. This will hide the contents of the sharpened layer, but by selecting the brush tool, and with white as the foreground color, one can then paint to reveal just those parts of the sharpening layer where you want to see sharpening.

The trick here is to use the brush tools to paint delicately and precisely so that you minimize revealing too many artifacts, because you don't want to end up making these more noticeable than they are already. The selective sharpening method described here is quite basic. You could also use the midtone contrast technique described on pages 183–185 to add some sharpening contrast and then mask the layer and paint the effect in selectively. If you use a Smart Filter layer you have the added control of adjusting the High Pass filter settings. Or you could also use the Smart Sharpen filter that I describe next to correct for blurryness in an image and apply this selectively.

By the way, anti-aliased text and other graphic artwork should never be sharpened. Photoshop vector objects are on separate layers anyway and will be processed separately by a PostScript RIP when rendered in print. If you do ever need to render any of the shape or type layers, try to keep them on their separate layers and only sharpen the bitmapped image data.

## Smart Sharpen filter

The Smart Sharpen filter does a good job of sharpening an image. It incorporates better edge detection and can improve the appearance of blurry images without introducing any unwanted halos. I consider this to be more useful as a tool for corrective sharpening rather than as a tool for general sharpening. The main reason why I think this is because it runs very slowly compared to the Unsharp Mask filter. In my opinion the refined presharpening steps shown on the previous pages will produce smoother sharpening results in less time. But in all other respects, the Smart Sharpen can be a great tool for selectively sharpening images that need special treatment.

When you start using Smart Sharpen you will want to mainly concentrate on using the Amount and Radius slider controls to adjust the effect. There are three blur removal modes: Gaussian Blur removal is more or less the same method as that used in the Unsharp Mask filter. The Lens Blur method is the most useful though since it enables you to counteract optical lens blurring. And lastly, Motion Blur removal, which can be effective at removing small amounts of Motion Blur from an image.

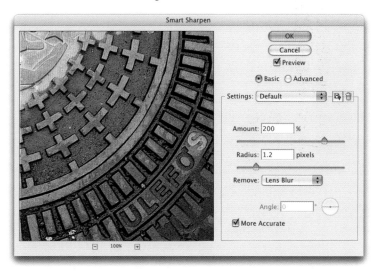

**Figure 4.50** The Smart Sharpen filter dialog, shown here in Basic mode.

## Saving the Smart Sharpen settings

You can save Smart Sharpen settings as you work by clicking on the save settings icon circled below in Figure 4.51, and call these up via the Settings menu at a later time.

## Advanced Smart Sharpen mode

In Advanced mode you will get to see two additional tabbed sections marked Shadow and Highlight. The controls in these sections act like a dampener on the main smart sharpening effect. The Fade Amount slider will selectively reduce the amount of sharpening in either the shadow or highlight areas. This is the main control to play with as it will have the most initial impact in reducing the amount of artifacting that may occur in the shadow or highlight areas. Below that is the Tonal Width slider and this operates in the same way as the one in the Shadow/Highlight image adjustment: you use this to determine the tonal range width that the fade is applied to. These two main sliders allow you to subtly control the smart sharpening effect. The Radius also works in a similar way to the Radius slider in the Shadow/Highlight adjustment and is used to control the area width of the smart sharpening.

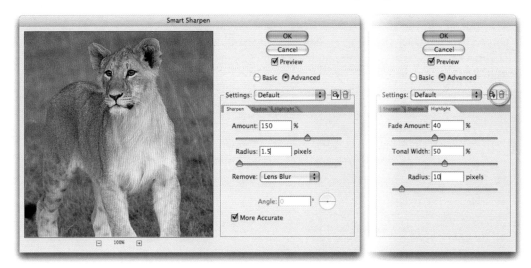

**Figure 4.51** In this photograph I set the Smart Sharpen filter to Advanced mode and applied an Amount of 150% at a Radius of 1.5 using the Lens Blur mode with the More Accurate box checked. Once I had chosen suitable settings for the main Smart Sharpen, I clicked on the Shadow and Highlight tabs and used the settings in these sections to decide how to limit the main sharpening effect. A high Fade Amount setting will fade the sharpening more and the Tonal Width determines the range of tones that are to be faded. And lastly, there is the Radius slider, where you can enter a Radius value to set the scale size for the corrections.

## Removing Motion Blur

The Motion Blur mode can be used to correct for mild camera shake or small amounts of subject movement in a photograph. When Remove Motion Blur is selected, the trick here is to get the angle in the dialog to match the angle of the Motion Blur in the picture and adjust the Radius and Amount settings to optimize the Motion Blur correction. If you want to achieve optimum results with any of these sharpening modes, then do check the More Accurate option below. This will increase the time it takes the filter to process the image. If you want to get the very best results, then I suggest you leave this checked.

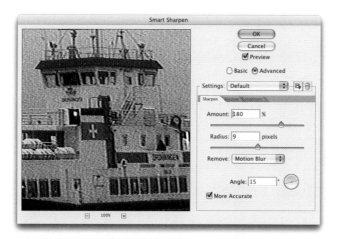

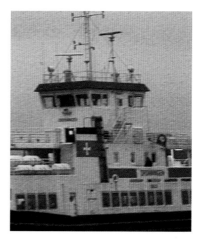

Figure 4.52 The Motion Blur method of smart sharpening is reasonably good at improving sharpness where there is just a slight amount of camera shake or subject movement. I initially set the Amount, Radius and Angle to achieve the most effective sharpening and in Advanced mode went to the Highlight panel to adjust the Fade and Tonal Width settings so as to dampen the sharpening effect on the highlights. This helped achieve a slightly smoother-looking result.

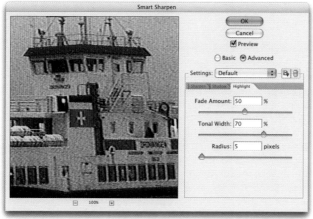

## Front Image cropping

If you want a crop to match the dimensions and resolution of a document that is already open in Photoshop, click on that document to make it active. Then click on the Front Image button in the Crop Options bar. This will load the document dimensions and resolution into the Crop Options settings. Now select the image you wish to crop and as you drag with the crop tool, the aspect ratio of the front image will be applied. When you OK the crop, the image size will be adjusted to match the front image resolution.

## Cropping

The image you are editing will most likely require some kind of crop, either to remove unwanted edges or to focus more attention on the subject. Select the crop tool from the Tools palette and drag to define the area to be cropped. To zoom in on the image as you make the crop, you may sometimes find it useful to use the zoom tool shortcut: Spacebar followed by holding down the ⌘ *ctrl* and marquee drag over the area you want to magnify. To zoom out, use ⌘ *0* *ctrl 0*, which is the shortcut for View ⇨ Fit To Window. You can then zoom back in again to magnify another corner of the image to adjust the crop handles.

If the crop tool does not behave as expected try clicking on the Clear button in the tool Options bar. This will reset the tool. In the normal default mode the crop tool will allow you to set any rectangular-shaped crop you like and merely trim away the unwanted pixels without changing the image size or resolution.

Crop tool presets    Swap height and width    Crop resolution    Load foreground image dimensions and resolution

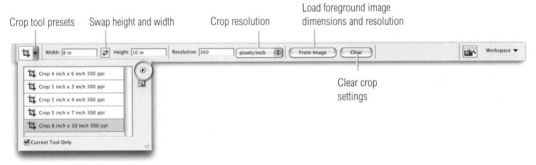

Clear crop settings

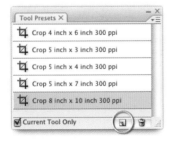

**Figure 4.53** Here are the primary options for the crop tool that are in the tool Options bar. If you mouse down on the triangle button next to the crop tool you will see a list of any preloaded crop tool presets. If none are visible click on the triangle button there (circled) or go to the Tool Presets palette to load the Crop and Marquee.tpl preset. New individual custom presets can be added by clicking on the New Preset button in the Tool Presets palette (circled). To set a custom crop, enter the crop unit dimensions in the Width and Height boxes followed by: mm, cm, in or px to denote the unit dimension type. In this example the crop tool has been set to a fixed crop of 8 inches wide by 10 inches tall at a resolution of 300 pixels per inch. If you click on the button between the Width and Height boxes, you can swap these dimensions. Clicking on the Clear button will clear the current crop options.

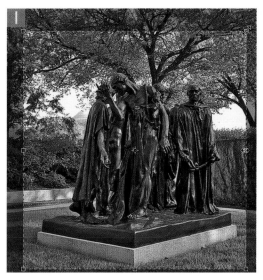

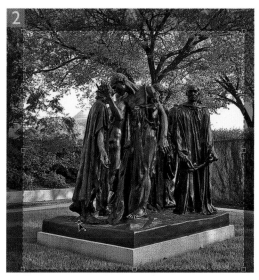

**1** I selected the crop tool and dragged across the image to define the crop area. The cursor can then be placed above any of the eight handles in the bounding rectangle to readjust the crop.

**2** Dragging the cursor inside the crop area will allow you to move the crop. You can also drag the crop bounding box center point to create a new central axis of rotation.

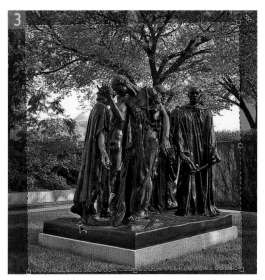

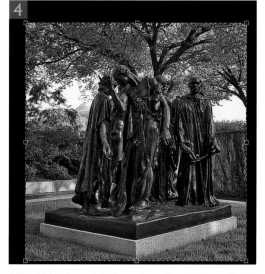

**3** You can mouse down outside the crop area and drag to rotate the crop around the center point (which can even be positioned outside the crop area). You normally do this to realign an image that has been scanned slightly at an angle.

**4** The shield color and shade opacity can be anything you like. In this example I increased the shading opacity to 100% to produce a completely opaque shield. You can even use ⌘ H ctrl H to hide the bounding box completely and still be able to drag the corners or sides of the crop to make adjustments.

## Fixed aspect ratio crops

One of the big advantages of using the rectangular marquee tool to make a selection crop is that you can set a fixed aspect ratio for the crop in the marquee tool options (see Figure 4.55).

## *Selection-based cropping*

You can also make a crop that is based on an active selection by simply choosing Image ⇨ Crop. Where the selection has an irregular shape, the crop will be made to the outer limits of the selection and the selection will be retained. The practical advantages of this is that you might want to ⌘ *ctrl*-click a layer to make a selection based on a single layer and then execute a crop (as described in Figure 4.56 below).

Shade cropped area    Shade color    Enable perspective cropping    Apply crop

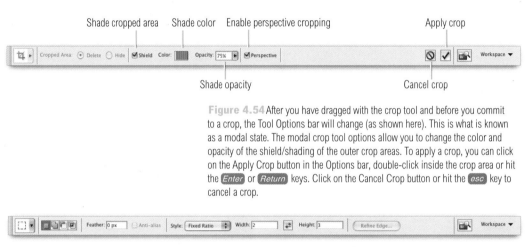

Shade opacity    Cancel crop

**Figure 4.54** After you have dragged with the crop tool and before you commit to a crop, the Tool Options bar will change (as shown here). This is what is known as a modal state. The modal crop tool options allow you to change the color and opacity of the shield/shading of the outer crop areas. To apply a crop, you can click on the Apply Crop button in the Options bar, double-click inside the crop area or hit the *Enter* or *Return* keys. Click on the Cancel Crop button or hit the *esc* key to cancel a crop.

**Figure 4.55** If you select the rectangular marquee tool you can use the Constrain Aspect Ratio option to make a proportional crop without altering the image resolution or dimension units. Enter the desired proportions in the Width and Height boxes, drag the marquee selection tool across the image to define the area to be cropped and chose Image ⇨ Crop.

**Figure 4.56** Sometimes it is quicker to make a crop from a selection instead of trying to precisely position the crop tool. In the example shown here, if we want to make a crop of the box containing the letter D, the quickest solution would be to ⌘ *ctrl*-click on the relevant layer in the Layers palette and then choose Image ⇨ Crop.

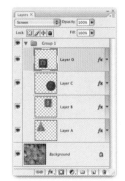
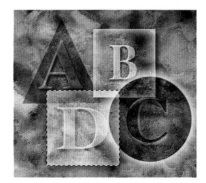

220

## Perspective cropping

With Photoshop's crop tool you can crop and correct any converging verticals or horizontal lines in a picture with a single crop action. In the Figure 4.57 example, we might wish to remove the converging verticals or 'keystone' effect in the photograph of the buildings. If you check the Perspective box, you can accurately reposition the corner handles on the image to match the perspective of the buildings and then apply the crop to straighten the lines that should be vertical. This tweaking adjustment can be made even more precisely if you hold down the *Shift* key as you drag a corner handle. This will restrict the movement to one plane only. I find the perspective crop tool is useful when preparing photographs of flat copy artwork as it enables me to always get the copied artwork perfectly square.

**Disable edge snapping**

Edge snapping can be very distracting when you are working with the crop tool. But this can easily be disabled in the View ➯ Snap To submenu (or by using the 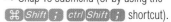 shortcut).

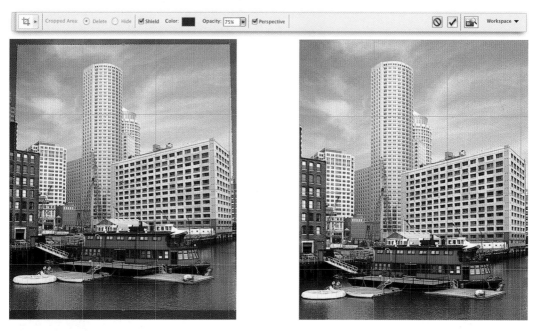

**Figure 4.57** The crop tool is great for correcting the perspective in a photograph. Once a crop is in progress you are then able to check the Perspective box in the Options bar and move the corner handles independently. By using this method, you will find it much easier to zoom in and gauge the alignment of the crop edges against the converging verticals in the photograph. It helps here to switch on the Grid display (go to the Window menu and choose Show ➯ Grid).

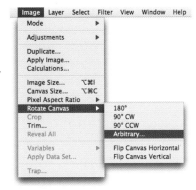

**Figure 4.58** The Image ⇨ Rotate menu including the Arbitrary option which is described below in Figure 4.59.

## Image rotation

If an image requires rotating you can use the Image ⇨ Rotate controls to orientate your picture the correct way up or flip it horizontally or vertically even. More likely you will want to make a precise image rotation, especially if the horizon line is not perfectly straight. You can correct a wonky image by making a rotated crop with the crop tool. Or, by making an angle measurement with the measure tool followed by an arbitrary rotation as described below.

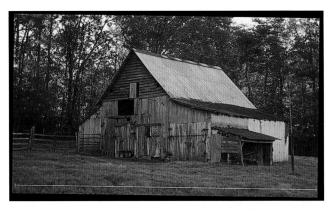

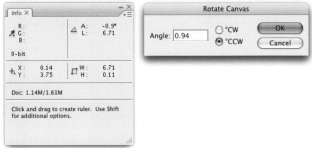

**Figure 4.59** When an image is opened up in Photoshop, you may discover that a scanned original is not perfectly aligned. Although the crop tool will allow you to both crop and rotate at the same time, there is another more accurate way of correcting the alignment. Select the measure tool from the Tools palette and drag along what should be a vertical or hoizontal edge in the photo. After doing this, go to the Image menu and select Rotate Canvas ⇨ Arbitrary... You will find that the angle you have just measured is already entered in the Angle box. Choose to rotate either clockwise or counterclockwise and the picture will then be accurately rotated so that it appears to be perfectly level (although Photoshop usually manages to auto-select the correct direction to rotate in).

## Canvas size

The Image ⇨ Canvas size lets you enlarge the image canvas area, extending it in any direction. This is useful if you want to extend the image dimensions in order to place new elements. If you check the Relative box you can enter the unit dimensions you want added to the current image size. The pixels that are added will be filled using the current background color but you can also choose other fill options from the Canvas Size dialog (see Figure 4.60). It is also possible to add to the canvas area without using Canvas Size. You can use the crop tool as an 'add canvas tool' by dragging beyond the document boundaries (see the instructions in Figure 4.61 below).

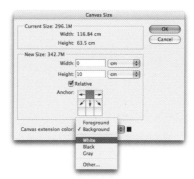

Figure 4.60 To add extra pixels beyond the current document bounds use the Canvas Size from the Image menu. In the example shown here, the image is anchored so that pixels will be added equally left and right and to the bottom of the image only. The relative box is checked and this allows you to enter the number of units of measurement you wish to add 'relative' to the current image size.

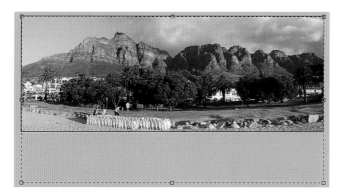

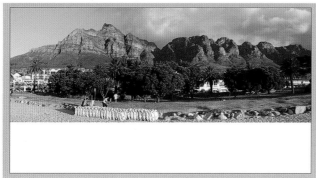

Figure 4.61 To use the crop tool as canvas size tool, first make a full frame crop, release the mouse and then drag any one of the bounding box handles outside of the image and into the canvas area. Double-click inside the bounding box area or hit *Enter* to add to the canvas size, filling with the background color.

## Background layers and big data

If your image contains a Background layer and you want to preserve the data on this layer after making a 'hide' crop, you must first double-click the Background layer to promote it to a normal layer. If you don't take this step you will still be deleting everything on this layer when you crop.

## Big data

The Photoshop, PDF and TIFF formats all support 'big data'. This means that if any of the layered image data extends beyond the confines of the canvas boundary, it will still be saved as part of the image when you save it, even though it is no longer visible in the image. If you have layers in your image that extend outside the bounds of the canvas, you can expand the canvas to reveal all of the big data by choosing Image ⇨ Reveal All. But remember, you will only be able to reveal the big data again providing you have saved the image using the PSD, PDF or TIFF format. When you crop a picture using the crop tool, you can delete or hide the layered big data by selecting either of these radio buttons in the modal crop Options bar (see below).

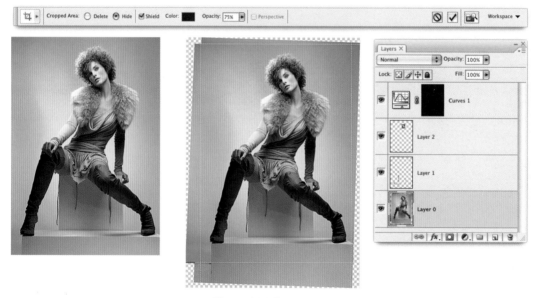

**Figure 4.62** The cropped version of this picture contains several layers which when expanded using the Image ⇨ Reveal All command show all the hidden 'big data' extending outside of the cropped view. The Hide option in the crop tool options enables you to preserve the pixels that fall outside the selected crop area instead of deleting them. Note also how the Background layer has been converted to a normal Photoshop layer (Layer 0). This is essential if you wish to preserve all the information on this layer as big data.

Client: Rainbow Room. Model: Nicky Felbert @ MOT.

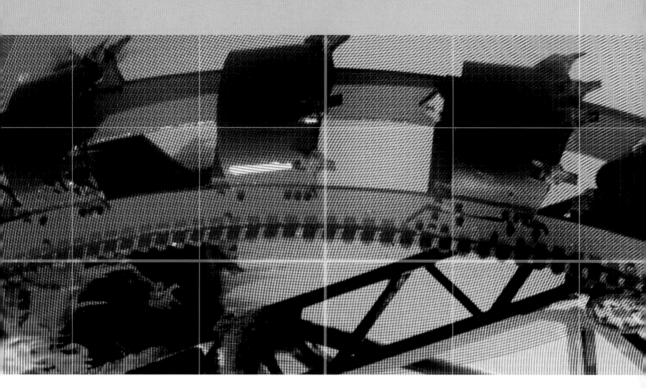

Chapter 5

# Camera Raw Image Processing

There are now two ways to process most images in Photoshop. The basic image adjustments I just described will probably play a core role in your everyday use of Photoshop and understanding how Photoshop is used to edit images. The Camera Raw image processing route represents a new and better way to optimize your images in the early stages. And now that Camera Raw can be used to process JPEG, TIFF and Photoshop files (those with saved composite images), Camera Raw provides a powerful and compelling alternative to the usual Photoshop image editing tools. In fact, if you could apply the Camera Raw adjustments locally via adjustment layers, I might probably stop using the conventional image adjustments all together! But first, let's look at the origins of Camera Raw and typical raw capture workflows.

225

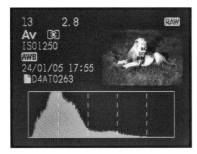

## Raw versus JPEG

If you are shooting with a professional back, digital SLR, or an advanced compact digital camera, you will almost certainly have the capability to shoot using the camera's raw format mode. The advantages of shooting in raw as opposed to JPEG mode are not always well understood. If you shoot in JPEG mode the files are compressed by varying amounts and this file compression will enable you to fit more captures on a single card. Some photographers assume that shooting in raw mode simply provides you with uncompressed images without JPEG artifacts and the trade-off with this is that fewer captures can be stored. But there are some more important reasons why capturing in raw mode is better than shooting with JPEG.

## From light to digital

Let's begin by looking at the way the CCD or CMOS chip in your camera converts the light hitting the sensor into a digital image. In order to digitize the information, the signal must be processed through an analog-to-digital converter (ADC). The ADC measures the amount of light hitting the sensor at each photosite and converts the analog signal into a binary form. At this point, the raw data simply consists of image brightness information coming from the camera sensor. The raw data must then be converted somehow and the raw conversion method used can make a huge difference to the quality of the final image output. Most cameras will have an on-board microprocessor that is able to convert the raw data into a readable image file, which in most cases will be a JPEG type format. The quality of a digital image is primarily dependent on the lens optics used to take the photograph, the recording capabilities of the CCD or CMOS chip and the analog-to-digital converter. But it is the raw conversion process that matters most. If you choose to process the raw data on your computer instead, you have much greater control than is the case if you had let your camera automatically guess which were the best raw conversion settings to use.

## Raw is the digital negative

You can liken capturing in raw mode to shooting with negative film, and the great thing about negative film is that it doesn't matter if someone makes a bad print, because you can always make an improved print from the original negative. When you shoot raw, you are recording a master file that contains all the color information that was captured at the time of shooting. To carry the analogy further, shooting in JPEG mode is like taking your film to a high street photo lab, throwing away the negatives and scanning from the prints. If you shoot using JPEG, the camera is deciding automatically at the time of shooting how to set the white balance and the tonal corrections, often clipping the highlights and shadow detail in the process. These days, everything I shoot is captured in raw mode (unless I am using a small compact camera for fun or I am not concerned about preserving fine image quality). The difference in what can be achieved from a raw file compared to a JPEG is quite incredible and only goes to show that even on the more sophisticated digital compacts, it is well worth saving the raw data and making the conversion later, at your leisure, on the computer.

## Raw conversion software

Cameras that are capable of shooting in raw mode will usually come supplied with the software to process the raw data, make custom white balances, tonal corrections and save out as TIFF files that can be read by Photoshop or other image editing programs. The camera-supplied software programs are often disappointingly slow, but there are programs such as Capture One from Phase One that have proved popular with raw shooters. The raw conversion is very important and therefore the photographer must feel confident that the software they use is up to the task of making an optimum interpretation of the raw data. If you hang out on any of the photography Internet forums, it is quite obvious that this subject stirs the emotions of raw shooters just as much as the PC versus Mac debates have done in the past. My personal view is that when anyone

## White balance and tone correction

The most important camera capture setting is the white balance. If you shoot JPEG, the on-board processor will create a file with a fixed white balance based on the camera's preference settings, which might be set to apply a predetermined white balance or use an auto setting. When you shoot using raw mode it does not matter which settings the camera uses, you can decide on the most appropriate white balance setting to use later when you convert the image on your computer. For example, Adobe Camera Raw enables you to apply an optimum white balance for any lighting situation.

## Third-party raw converters

The other software programs that can read the raw camera data include: Bibble: www.bibblelabs.com, FotoStation: www.fotostation.com, Apple's Aperture, Capture One from Phase One and of course now, Adobe Photoshop Lightroom.

## Whose data is it anyway?

If photographers think it is a good thing for the industry to move towards a standardized raw file format, then the DNG format deserves to succeed. It will also encourage other software manufacturers to support DNG and give the camera user even more choice. The only sticking point appears to be those camera manufacturers who have adopted a protective stance about the raw file processing. One gets the impression that there is a certain amount of irritation within some camera companies whenever outsiders have managed to 'crack the code' and successfully reverse engineered their proprietary raw file formats. One manufacturer once went so far as to devise a method of encryption that would defeat any attempts to make the file format more widely accessible. Photographer and Photoshop expert Jeff Schewe raised an important point here: 'After I have taken a photograph and captured an image as a raw file, whose data is it? It's my damn data, and not anyone else's!' Which neatly brings us back to the whole raison d'être of the DNG file format, which is to make raw shooting more accessible for all. The opportunity is there for everyone to gain. Photographers have a new file format that will enable them to archive their raw captures with confidence for the future. If the camera manufacturers support the new DNG format they will make their customers happy too. But the real choice will be down to the consumer. They will decide which camera choice to make and support for DNG should be regarded as an important decision when making future purchases of camera equipment.

invests a lot of their time and reputation in using a specific workflow they will inevitably become very defensive when someone tells them they are using the wrong raw processing software and software program 'X' is the only one you should use. I don't believe there are necessarily any image quality differences between what can be processed in one program and another and it is mainly a matter of knowing how to use the adjustment controls to their full advantage in the software you prefer using. In the case of Adobe Camera Raw the criticisms I have read have usually been based on incomplete testing. Besides which, Photoshop CS3 now features an update to Camera Raw where the raw image processing options now include new controls such as Recovery, Fill Light and Vibrance sliders in the Basic panel as well as controls for Hue, Saturation and grayscale conversions.

## DNG file format

In the slipstream of every new technology there follows the inevitable chaos of lots of different new standards competing for supremacy. Nowhere is this more evident that in the world of digital imaging. In the last ten years or so, we have seen many hundreds of digital cameras come and go along with other computer technologies such as Syquest disks and SCSI cables. And I have probably encountered well over a hundred different raw format specifications. It would not be so bad if each camera manufacturer had adopted a raw format specification that could be applied to all the cameras they produced. Instead we have seen raw formats evolve and change with each new model that has been released. And those changes have not always been for the better.

The biggest problem is that with so many types of raw format being developed, how reliable will a raw format be for archiving your images? Ten years ago Adam Woolfitt and myself conducted a test report on a range of professional and semi-professional digital cameras. Wherever possible, we shot using raw mode. I still have the CD of master files. If I want to access those images today, in some cases I am going to have to track down a computer running Mac OS 8.6 in order to load the camera manufacturer software required to read the data! If that is a problem now, what will the situation be like in 60 years' time?

It is the proprietary nature of all these formats that is the central issue here. At the moment, all the camera manufacturers appear to want to devise their own brand of raw format and therefore if you want to access the data from a raw file, you are forced to use their brand of software to do so. Now while the camera manufacturers are excellent at designing fantastic hardware, the raw processing software they have produced has mostly been quite basic. Just because a company is good at building digital cameras, it does not follow that they are going to be good at designing graphics software to read the raw data.

## The DNG solution

Fortunately there are third-party companies who have devised ways of processing some of these raw formats. So you are not always limited to using the software that came with the camera. Adobe is the most obvious example here of a company who offers a superior alternative. At the time of writing, Camera Raw will recognize raw formats from over 150 different cameras. The new DNG (digital negative) file format specification has come about partly as a means of making Adobe's life easier for the future development of Camera Raw and making Adobe Photoshop compatible with as many cameras as possible. DNG is a well thought out file format that is designed to accommodate the many specification requirements of all today's cameras and is also flexible enough to adapt to future technologies. Because it is an open standard, the specification is freely available for anyone to develop and to incorporate into their software or camera system. It is therefore hoped that the camera manufacturers will adopt the DNG file format more widely and that the DNG format will be offered as the main raw file format, or at least offered as an alternative choice on the camera.

**Support the petition!**

If you agree that a common raw format standard would be beneficial to the photographic industry and would like to let the manufacturers know this, then you can register your feelings by going to www.rawformat.com and signing the DNG petition. You might also like to visit the www.openraw.org site where you can join the Open Raw discussion group and read the results of their 2006 raw survey.

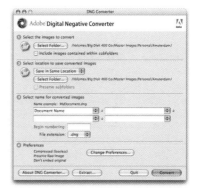

Figure 5.2 Adobe has made the DNG converter program available for free, which can be downloaded from their website: www. adobe.co.uk/products/dng/main.html. The DNG converter is able to convert raw files from any camera currently supported by Camera Raw for Photoshop into DNG files. The advantage of doing this is that you can start making backups of your raw files in a file format that will preserve all the data in your raw captures and archive them now in a format that has a greater likelihood of support in the future.

## DNG adoption

Over the last few years DNG has been adopted by many of the mainstream software programs such as iView (now Microsoft Expression), Capture One, Portfolio and Photo Mechanic. And at the time of writing, Hasselblad, Leica, Samsung and Ricoh cameras all support a DNG raw capture format option.

This will bring several advantages. If DNG is adopted there will be less risk of your raw image files becoming obsolete, as there will be ongoing support for the DNG standard despite whatever computer operating system or platform changes take place in the future. Whenever a new camera is released, the DNG format will allow the raw files to be immediately accessible, assuming the camera is enabled to provide DNG raw files.

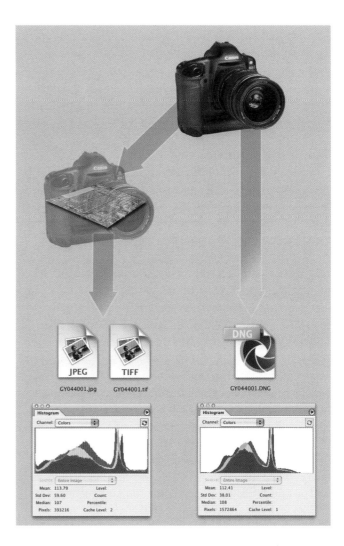

**Figure 5.3** If you shoot using the JPEG or TIFF mode on your camera, the raw conversion is carried out on-the-fly using the camera's on-board computer. All the important tonal editing decisions such as the white balance, the highlight exposure, shadow point and contrast will be decided for you by the camera and permanently fixed in the resulting JPEG or TIFF image. When you shoot using JPEG or TIFF, the camera is immediately discarding up to 88% of the image information captured by the sensor. This is not as alarming as it sounds, because as you know from experience, you don't always get a bad photograph from a JPEG capture. But consider the alternative of what happens if you shoot using a raw mode capture. In the simplified raw workflow shown here, the raw file is saved to the memory card without being processed by the camera. This allows you to work with all 100% of the image data captured by the sensor and you can edit the image later on your computer. The histograms at the bottom illustrate the advantage this can bring. With a JPEG capture you may permanently clip the shadows and highlights. With raw, you will often be able to recover a lot more tonal detail.

# Getting raw images into Photoshop

There was a time, not so long ago, when one would simply scan a few photographs, put them in a folder and double-click to open them up in Photoshop. These days most photographers are working with large numbers of images and it is therefore important to be able to import and manage those images efficiently. When Photoshop 7 came along, Adobe introduced the File Browser, which was like an alternative open dialog interface incorporated within Photoshop that offered a superior way to manage your images, allowing you to preview and manage multiple images at once. The File Browser was superseded by the Bridge program in Photoshop CS2. As image browser programs go, Bridge's main advantage is that you have ready access to Photoshop to open up single or multiple images and apply batch operations directly from within the program. If you compare Bridge with other browser programs, it has enough basic functionality to suit many photographers' needs, although it has to be said that Bridge does not yet provide the full functionality that professional photographers have come to rely on in other programs.

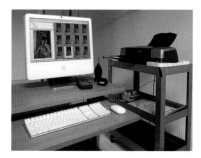

Figure 5.4 Here is a typical studio setup where I have an iMac computer stationed close to the actual shooting area, ready to process the captured images from the shoot. With the setup shown here I can either import camera card images via a Firewire card reader or shoot tethered.

## Image ingestion

The first thing we should look at is how to get images from the camera and on to the computer ready to work on. This process is sometimes referred to as 'image ingestion'. It's not a particularly pretty phrase, but it is how some like to describe the process. Bridge CS3 features a Photo Downloader utility program that makes the downloading process much easier to carry out than in the earlier version of Bridge. Over the next few pages I have outlined all the steps that are required when working with the Photo Downloader. For comparison purposes I have followed this up with an example of how to use the new Adobe Photoshop Lightroom program, because this is the method I actually use when bringing photographs into the computer for Photoshop editing.

## *Importing images via Photo Downloader*

EOS_DIGITAL

**1** The process begins by inserting a camera card into the computer via a Firewire or USB 2.0 card reader. The card should then mount on the desktop or appear in the My Computer window as a new mounted volume.

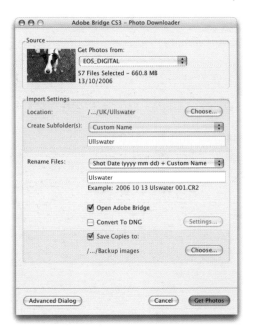

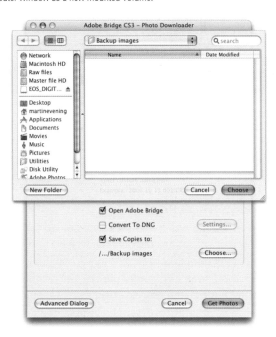

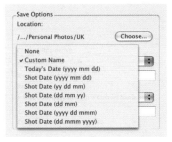

Figure 5.5 The subfolder naming options.

**2** Now launch Bridge 2.0 and choose File ➭ Get Photos from Camera... This will open the Photo Downloader dialog shown here, where you can start by selecting where to download the files from, in this instance, the EOS_Digital camera card. Next, choose a location to download the photos to. Here I selected a master folder that was used to contain all my UK location images. And then I selected 'Custom Name' from the Create Subfolder(s) menu (see Figure 5.5) and typed in a name for the shoot import. This name was appended to the Location setting to complete the file path. I then checked the Save Copies to: box and clicked on the Choose... button to locate a backup folder to save the files to.

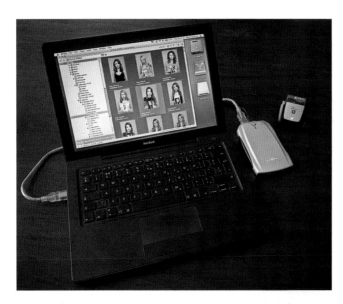

## Backup insurance

Your camera files are vulnerable to loss for as long as they remain in one location only, especially if they only exist on the camera card, which can easily get lost or the data might be corrupted. This is why it is always a good idea to get your camera files off the card and stored on a computer hard drive as soon as possible. Not only that, it is also a good idea to make a backup of the camera files as you do so. Note that Bridge will apply the settings setup in the Photo Downloader to the files that are copied to the main folder location. But, the files copied to the backup location will be plain clone copies of the original camera files. The backup copy files will not be renamed as are the main import files. This is a good thing because should you make a mistake during the rename process you always retain a backup version of the files just as they were named when captured by the camera.

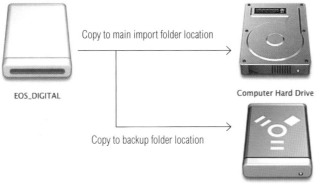

EOS_DIGITAL

Copy to main import folder location

Computer Hard Drive

Copy to backup folder location

Backup Hard Drive

3 Lets review the import settings set so far. The camera card contained the images I wished to import and the Photo Downloader settings have so far been configured to make a main copy to the primary disk location, which in this instance would be the computer hard drive, and at the same time make a backup copy of all the images to a secondary location (in this case, a backup hard drive). With the setup shown here, I can use the Photo Downloader to make renamed copies of the files to the principal drive/folder location and, if desired, convert the files to DNG as I do so. The backup files are like an insurance policy against both a drive failure and also any file renaming mixups. With this setup I will always have at least two copies of each image stored on my system. After the downloading is complete, it will be safe to delete the originals on the card.

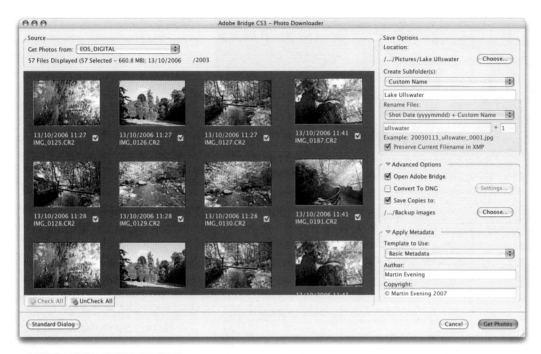

Do not rename files
Today's Date (yyyymmdd)
Shot Date (yyyymmdd)
Shot Date (yyddmm)
Shot Date (ddmmyy)
Shot Date (ddmm)
Shot Date (yyyyddmmm)
Shot Date (ddmmmyyyy)
Custom Name
Shot Date (yyyymmdd) + Custom Name
✓ Shot Date (yyddmm) + Custom Name
Shot Date (ddmmyy) + Custom Name
Shot Date (ddmm) + Custom Name
Shot Date (yyyyddmmm) + Custom Name
Shot Date (ddmmmyyyy) + Custom Name
Custom Name + Shot Date (yyyymmdd)
Custom Name + Shot Date (yyddmm)
Custom Name + Shot Date (ddmmyy)
Custom Name + Shot Date (ddmm)
Custom Name + Shot Date (yyyyddmmm)
Custom Name + Shot Date (ddmmmyyyy)
Same as Subfolder Name

**Figure 5.6** Here are the options for the Rename Files menu, highlighted in the dialog above.

4 If you click on the Advanced dialog button in the bottom left corner you will see an expanded version of the Photo Downloader dialog. This will allow you to see a grid preview of all the images on the card you are about to import from and the tabbed options at the bottom will allow you to decide whether to include all the pictures or just a few specific images. You can do this by clicking on the Check All or Uncheck All tabs, or clicking on the individual image checkboxes.

There are several options for the Rename Files section (which are shown in Figure 5.6). Which you should choose will depend on which convention works best for you. This is a topic I will explore in greater detail in the Image Management chapter. Here I selected to rename using the shoot date followed by a custom shoot name. You can see how the renaming will work by inspecting the Example filename below where you will note that the imported files will be automatically renumbered starting from the start number entered here. If you check the Preserve Current Filename in XMP, this will give you the option to use the Batch Rename feature in Bridge to recover the original filename at a later point. This is useful should you ever need to recover the original file names.

The Advanced Options will let you decide what happens to the imported images after they have been renamed. Naturally you will most likely want Bridge to default to previewing the folder with the images as they are being imported, so do check the Open Adobe Bridge option.

In the Apply Metadata section you can choose a pre-saved metadata template (see Chapter 11) and enter your author name and copyright information. This data will then be automatically embedded as metadata in the files as they are imported.

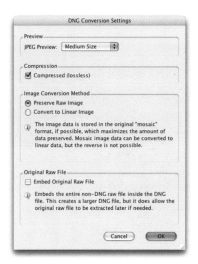

**DNG compatibility**

The DNG file format is an open standard file format for raw camera files. There are now quite a few raw processor programs that can read DNG, including Photoshop and Lightroom of course. I personally feel quite comfortable converting my raw files to DNG and then deleting the original camera raw files, and I don't see the need to embed the original raw file data in the DNG file, since this will only increase the file size unnecessarily. However, if you do feel it is essential to preserve complete compatibility, embedding the original raw file data will allow you to extract the original native raw file from the DNG at some later date. The advantage of this is complete compatibility with the camera manufacturer software. The downside is that you will more than double the size of your DNG files.

**5** The Convert to DNG option can be used to convert raw images to the DNG file format as they are imported. For some people it can be useful to carry out the conversion straight away, but this will add to the time it takes to import all the pictures. If you click on the Settings... button for the DNG option this will open the DNG Conversion Settings dialog shown here. For reasonably fast imports select the Medium size JPEG Preview option. This will generate a standard size preview for the imported pictures – there is no point in generating a full size preview just yet since you may well be changing the camera raw settings soon anyway. Check the Compressed option for smaller file sizes (note that this is lossless compression and does not risk degrading the image quality). I recommend that you preserve the raw image data and don't convert. This will keep the raw data in the DNG in its original state. And lastly, you can choose to embed the original raw data (along with the DNG data) in the DNG file.

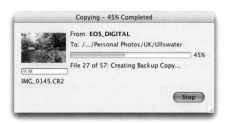

**6** After I clicked on the Get Photos button in the Photo Downloader dialog, the images started to download from the card and to the Save Options location folder. The progress dialog shown here tells you how the download process is proceeding.

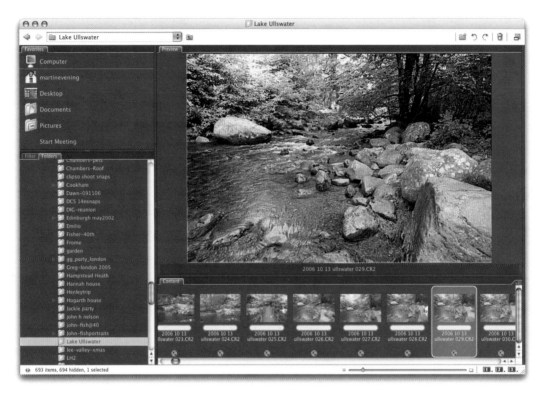

## Deleting camera card files

It isn't really necessary to delete the files from the camera card first, because formatting a card in the camera will delete everything that is on the card anyway. Formatting the card is good housekeeping practice as this will help guard against future file corruptions occurring with the card. However, I find that if you are in the midst of a busy shoot it is preferable to get into a routine of deleting the files before you put the card back in the camera. Otherwise I am always left with the nagging doubt: 'have I downloaded all the files on this card yet? Is it really safe to delete everything on this card?'

**7** Because the Open Adobe Bridge option had been selected, once the download was complete, Bridge opened a new window to display the downloaded and renamed files.

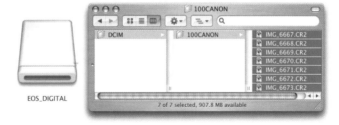

**8** All that remains now is to clear the files from the current card and prepare it for reuse in the camera. I normally like to locate all the files on the card and physically send them to the Trash or Recycle Bin and delete them there and then. And then when I put the card back in the camera I will reformat the card to permanently clear the card of any data before shooting a fresh batch of pictures with that card.

## *Tethered shoot imports*

It is possible to shoot in tethered mode with Bridge, but it all depends on the capabilities of your camera and whether it has a suitable connection socket and the software that will allow you to download files directly to a computer. Bridge CS3 on its own offers no tethered shoot ability, because if Bridge were able to do so, there would have to be tethered support for at least all the 150 cameras that Camera raw supports. Enabling full tethered shoot functionality is difficult enough to do for one camera type. Some software programs, such as Capture One and Bibble, do offer tethered shooting with a range of popular digital SLR cameras. For some people this is justification enough for spending the extra money to shoot tethered. However, many cameras, and especially the digital SLR cameras, will most likely come with some kind of software that will allow you to hook your camera up to the computer via an appropriate cable such as Firewire or USB 2. If your camera has the software to let you download files directly to the computer, then Bridge can monitor that folder and this will give you a next best solution to a dedicated software program that is designed to operate in tethered mode. The only drawback to shooting tethered is that the camera must be wired up to the computer and you don't have the complete freedom to wander around with the camera. If you have a wireless communication device then it may be possible to shoot in a direct import mode to the computer, without the hassle of a cable. But at the time of writing, wireless shooting isn't particularly speedy when shooting raw files with a typical digital SLR.

Over the next few pages I have described a method for shooting in tethered mode with a Canon EOS camera, using the Canon Viewer program that ships with most of the Canon EOS digital cameras (the Canon Rebel range of cameras will ship with the Canon EOS Utility program, which is fairly similar). Both these programs will enable you to download camera files as they are captured, to a designated watched folder. Nikon owners will find that Nikon Capture includes a Camera Control component that

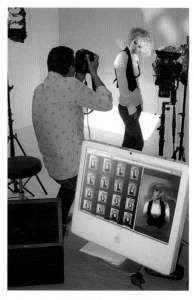

**Figure 5.7** Here is a photograph taken of myself at work in the studio, shooting in tethered mode.

allows you to do the same thing as the Canon software and establishes a watched folder to download the images to. The latest version of Nikon Capture supports all the D Series cameras as well as the Nikon Coolpix 8700. Alternatively, you might want to consider buying Bibble Pro 4.7 software from Bibble Labs (www.bibblelabs.com). Bibble Pro costs a lot less than Nikon Capture. It enables tethered shooting with a wide variety of digital cameras and, again, allows you to establish a watched folder for the downloaded images.

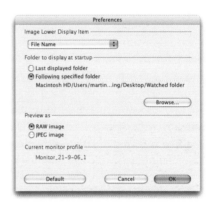

EOS Viewer Utility

1 To begin with, launch EOS Viewer utility and click the Preferences button. Click on the Browse... button to select a watched folder to download the tethered captures to and click OK. You will need to quit and then relaunch the program for the new folder location to be recognized.

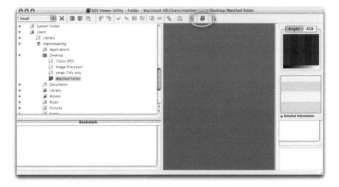

2 Back in the main EOS Viewer program, make sure the camera is tethered to the computer correctly and is switched on. Click on the Connect to Camera button in the EOS Viewer control bar (circled) and this will launch the EOS Capture utility program.

EOS Capture

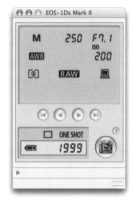

3 Once the EOS Capture dialog appears on the screen you can now use the camera as normal by pressing the shutter release, or alternatively you can use the EOS Capture utility to capture pictures remotely by clicking on the blue Camera button in the dialog.

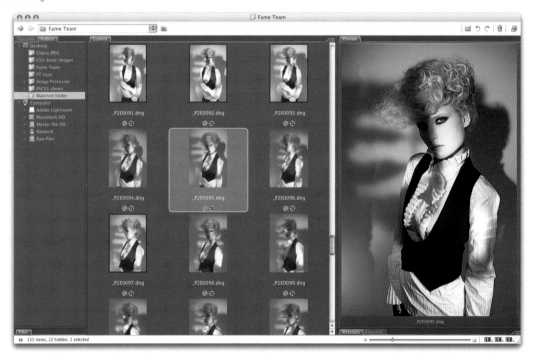

4 As you start shooting, the EOS Viewer utility will bring the camera files directly into the Watched folder you selected in Step 1. You will need to point Bridge at the same Watched folder as was configured in the EOS Viewer preferences to see the pictures appear in Bridge directly.

Client: Fame Team. Model: Jagna @ Profile.

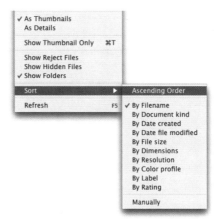

**5** Of course, if you are shooting continuously in the studio or location with such a setup, then you will most likely wish to see the newest pictures appear first at the top of the content area In the Bridge window. To enable this, go to the View menu and highlight the Ascending Order item in the Sort menu so that files are now sorted in reverse order with the most recent appearing first.

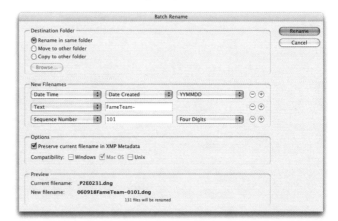

**6** This method of file importing, while quicker than having to keep downloading cards, won't necessarily allow you to rename the files. Or at least with the setup I have shown here it wasn't possible to do so. The camera software you use may be different. But in this example, after I had finished shooting, it was necessary for me to go to the Tools menu in Bridge and choose Batch Rename. This opened the dialog shown here, where I configured the rename settings (renaming in the same folder). With the Batch Rename in Bridge CS3, if you add more files to this folder and want to rename them, the rename settings will be sticky and the start number will auto adjust to begin consecutively from the last renamed file onwards. When the shoot is complete you will need to move all the files from the Watched folder and empty it ready to start a fresh tethered shoot to the same Watched folder.

## Importing images via other programs

As you will see in Figure 5.8, of all the various methods for importing images, there is no one program that can do everything perfectly. But of these, I would say that Capture One is the only program capable of ticking most of the boxes (as long as your camera is supported). ImageIngester is a great little utility that can provide a fast and robust import workflow and the standard version for Mac and PC is currently available to download for free.

Ever since Adobe Photoshop Lightroom made its first appearance as a beta product, I have been using Lightroom in the studio and on location and now use Lightroom all the time to import images from cards as well as for shooting in Tethered mode. I have now stopped using Bridge completely at the import stage. Although Lightroom is a separate program that would need to be bought separately, I thought I should at least show the workflow I personally use for bringing images into the computer, ready to be worked on in Photoshop, and also explain why I feel this is a better program to work with.

### ImageIngester™ program

The ImageIngester™ program designed by Marc Rochkind is aimed at photographers who shoot digitally, who use a raw workflow, and need to ingest hundreds of images from a typical shoot. You can download the basic ImageIngester program for free from the following link: www.basepath.com/ImageIngester/.
An ImageIngester Pro version is on the cards, but at the time of writing I cannot confirm if this will be sold as a product.

| | Direct integration with Bridge | File renaming | Full auto renumbering | Secondary backup of data | Convert to DNG | Import settings saved for concurrent imports | Tethered shooting | Preview and pre-selection of import files |
|---|---|---|---|---|---|---|---|---|
| Photo Downloader | ✗ | ✗ | | ✗ | ✗ | ✗ | | ✗ |
| Tethered shooting via Bridge | ✗ | | | | | | ✗* | |
| DNG Converter | | ✗ | ✗ | | ✗ | ✗ | | |
| Lightroom Import Photos | | ✗ | ✗ | ✗ | ✗ | ✗ | | ✗ |
| Lightroom Auto Import | | ✗ | ✗ | | | ✗ | ✗* | |
| Image Ingester Standard | | ✗ | ✗ | ✗ | ✗ | ✗ | | |
| Capture One | | ✗ | ✗ | ✗ | ✗ | ✗ | ✗ | |

Figure 5.8 In this table I have compared the features available using some of the various methods that are available when importing camera images into the computer. As you can see, there is no one perfect solution out there that will let you do everything, although the external programs such as Lightroom, Image Ingester and Capture One offer the most complete feature set in a single package.

* In these instances, tethered shooting is only possible if done in conjunction with a camera manufacturer's import software.

## *Importing images via Lightroom*

EOS_DIGITAL

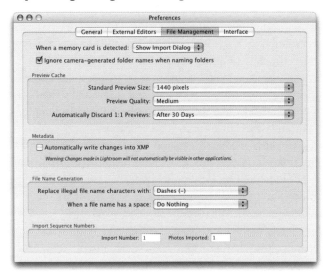

**1** The Lightroom preferences are located in the Lightroom menu. If you select the Show Import Dialog option for when a memory card is detected, Lightroom will automatically launch the Import Photos dialog each time a memory card is inserted.

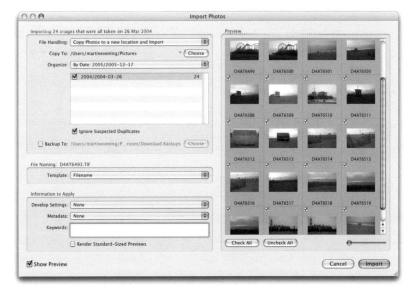

**2** Lightroom automatically opened the Import Photos dialog. If Show Preview is checked you can quickly scroll through the thumbnails of all the images you are about to import and choose which ones to import.

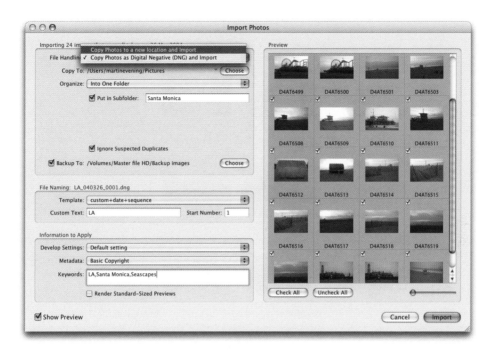

**3** If importing from a camera card, the quickest option is to select the Copy files to a new location and import option. Alternatively you can select the Copy Photos as Digital Negative (DNG) and import option. This will make a duplicate copy of all the images on the memory card and convert them to DNG. At this stage I usually prefer to organize the imported images into a single named folder and ignore any suspected duplicates. I then check the Backup To option and choose a folder to store backups of the files as they are imported.

The File Renaming section makes use of file renaming templates such as the one shown in Figure 5.9 . Below this you can enter a custom text for use in the file renaming plus a start number for the numbering sequence.

You can apply a pre-created Develop setting (a Lightroom camera raw image adjustment) at this pre-import stage. Once you have configured the import settings, click Import to start copying the images to the computer.

Information that might be considered important such as your copyright and contact information can be added by selecting a pre-created metadata template from the Metadata menu and information that relates specifically to the image collection you are about to import can be entered using custom keywords. As you type in the first few letters of a keyword, Lightroom will try to auto-complete a name for you and pop a menu of possible keywords. This will help you avoid spelling mistakes and be consistent in your keywording.

And lastly, Render Standard-Sized Previews will slow down the import process since it forces Lightroom to render previews of the images using the selected Develop setting before displaying them in Lightroom.

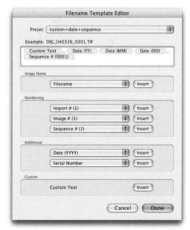

**Figure 5.9** The Filename Template Editor offers far more versatile options for creating file renaming templates. And, more importantly, Lightroom keeps track of files as they are imported and will auto-update the renumbering until you next change the Import Photos settings.

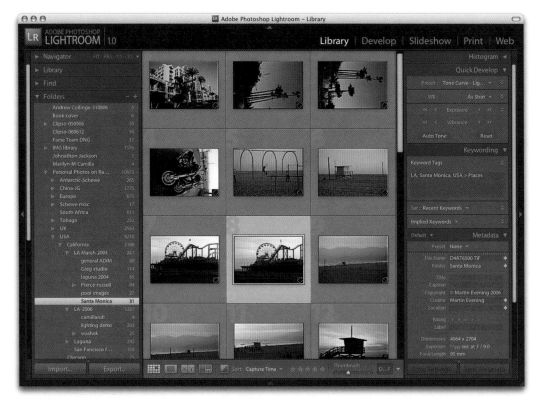

### The Adobe Photoshop Lightroom book

If you want to find out more about Lightroom, I have written a complete guide about this new program called simply: *The Adobe Photoshop Lightroom Book*, published by Adobe Press. ISBN-13: 978-0321385437.

**4** As the images are imported the thumbnails will start to appear one by one in the content area and you will also see the import progress shown in the Status indicator in the top left corner. The progress bar will give you an indication of how long it will take to complete the import process. You should not normally encounter any problems when importing files from a camera card, but if you choose the Copy Photos as DNG option, you will be alerted to any corruptions in the files as they are imported. Once you have successfully imported all the images across to the computer and backup drive (if applicable) you can now safely delete all the images that were on the card, eject the camera card and prepare it for reuse.

After the files have been imported into Lightroom, the imported images will appear listed in the Folders section of the Library module. The Folders panel displays all the images that have been imported so far into Lightroom using the same hierarchy structure as the folders that are found in the system folder organization. Moving files or folders in Lightroom is exactly the same as moving files or folders at the system level or via Bridge. One of the main features of Lightroom is that master files are always preserved as the original files, and Develop module edits in Lightroom are applied in the form of metadata instructions (just like Camera Raw). To open pictures from Lightroom into Photoshop, you create an edit copy of the master either with or without Lightroom adjustments and edit these in Photoshop, just as you would when opening a file from Bridge, and save back to the folder.

# Basic Camera Raw image editing

Camera Raw was originally designed for processing raw images from cameras Camera Raw supported. Camera Raw has kept pace with nearly all the latest raw camera formats in the compact range and digital SLR market, but only supports a few of the higher-end cameras such as the Leaf systems and latest Hasselblad H2 and H3 cameras (which now support the DNG format).

Camera Raw has changed quite a lot in this version CS3 release. And because the raw processing engine is the same as that now used in Lightroom, it shares nearly all of Lightroom's new raw processing features. If you want to get the best quality images from your camera, then you should always shoot raw. But you can now use Camera Raw described here to process TIFF, JPEG and PSD images as well (providing the PSD file has been saved with a flattened composite). The advantages of this are that Camera Raw editing is now available for a wider range of file formats and the edits you make in Camera Raw are applied in the form of metadata instructions and the files themselves are never modified. So the techniques described in this following section of the book can apply equally to most images, including camera JPEGs and scanned TIFFs. Because the image adjustment controls in Camera Raw 4 are the same as those in Lightroom 1.0, I personally favour using either Lightroom or Camera Raw over Photoshop when making all the major tonal image adjustments, and not just at the import stage either. The color and black and white controls in Lightroom and Camera Raw 4 are incredibly versatile and in some cases more intuitive as well. So if I have an image where I wish to convert it to black and white or apply a creative coloring effect, I am often more inclined to open the fully edited Photoshop image up in Camera Raw and use the adjustment controls there rather than use the image adjustment tools that are in Photoshop. The other advantage this brings is that the edits made in Camera Raw do not add appreciably to the file size apart from the addition of a few extra kilobytes to store the Camera Raw editing instructions.

## Camera Raw support

Camera Raw won't 'officially' interpret the raw files from every digital camera. But Adobe is committed to providing intermittent free Camera Raw updates that will always include any new camera file interpreters as they become available. Now understand that while not all raw camera file formats are supported, this is in no way the fault of Adobe. Certain camera manufacturers have in the past done things like encrypt the white balance data, which makes it difficult for anyone but themselves to decode the raw image data. But there are now over 150 different raw formats supported by Camera Raw.

## Camera Raw as default for JPEG

If you want Camera Raw to be the default image editor for JPEG images, there is a 'Prefer Adobe Camera Raw for JPEG files' option in the Photoshop File Handling preferences. When this is checked, double-clicking a JPEG image 'should' always default to opening the JPEG image via Camera Raw (but you will need to reboot Photoshop for this to come into effect). But if only it were that simple! See the sidebar on the following page: 'Opening JPEGs via ACR in Bridge'.

## Closing Bridge as you open

If you hold down the ⌥ alt key as you double-click to open a raw image, this will close the Bridge window as you open the Camera Raw dialog.

## Opening JPEGs via ACR in Bridge

As well as the Photoshop File Handling preference 'Prefer Adobe Camera Raw for JPEG files', there is also a Bridge Thumbnails preference 'Prefer Adobe Camera Raw for JPEG and TIFF Files'. When this Bridge preference option is checked, thumbnails generated in Bridge will instruct Bridge to open JPEG and TIFF images via Camera Raw. But any thumbnails that were generated while this option was switched off will mean that these JPEG and TIFF images will not open in Camera Raw, but open via Photoshop instead (even though you had the 'Prefer Adobe Camera Raw for JPEG files' switched on in the Photoshop File Handling preferences). One way to resolve this is to make sure that both options in Photoshop and Bridge are checked and use the Tools ⇨ Cache ⇨ Purge Cache command to clear the thumbnail cache settings for a particular folder. This action will zap any previously generated thumbnail cache settings and force Bridge to generate new thumbnails, and these thumbnails will have the desired preference of opening the JPEG and TIFF files via Camera Raw. And in case you are wondering, this is my attempt to provide a simplified summary of the official guidelines on Bridge/Photoshop Camera Raw JPEG/TIFF file opening.

# Working with Camera Raw and Bridge

The mechanics of how Photoshop and Bridge work together are made as simple as possible so that you can open single or multiple images or batch process images quickly and efficiently. Figure 5.10 summarizes how the linking between Bridge, Photoshop and Camera Raw works.

Central to everything is the Bridge window interface, where you can browse, preview and make selections of which images you want to process. The way most people are accustomed to opening images is to select the desired thumbnail icon (or icons) and either double-click, use the File ⇨ Open command, or the ⌘ O ctrl O shortcut. The way things are set up in Bridge, all of the above methods will open the selected raw image (or images) via the Camera Raw dialog hosted by Photoshop (if the image is not a raw file, it will open in Photoshop directly). Alternatively, you can use File ⇨ Open in Camera Raw... or use the ⌘ R ctrl R shortcut to open the images via the Camera Raw dialog. In these instances, Bridge will host Camera Raw and allow you to perform batch processing operations in the background without compromising Photoshop's performance. If the 'Double-click edits Camera Raw Settings in Bridge' option is deselected in the General Bridge preferences, *Shift* double-clicking will allow you to open an image or multiple selection of images in Photoshop directly, bypassing the Camera Raw dialog.

Opening single raw images via Photoshop will be quicker than opening them via Bridge. Opening multiple images via Photoshop will take about the same time, but Photoshop will consequently be tied up managing the Camera Raw processing. The advantage of opening via Bridge is that Bridge can process large numbers of raw files, while freeing up Photoshop to perform other tasks. And you can toggle between the two programs. So for example, you can be processing an image in Camera Raw while you switch to viewing another image in Photoshop for comparison with the one you are editing in Camera Raw.

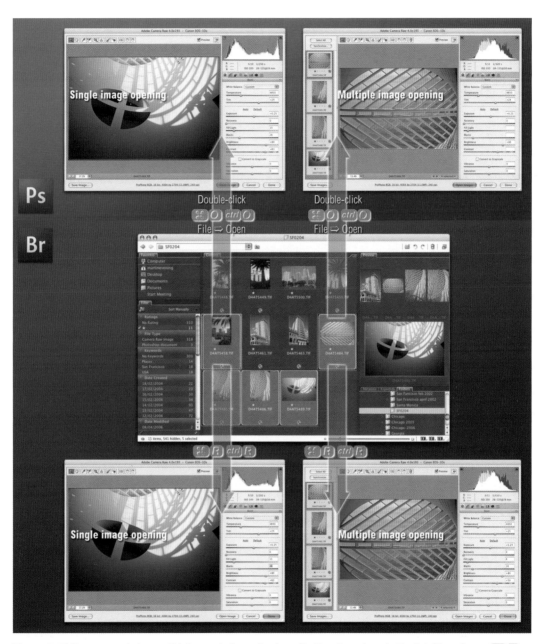

Figure 5.10 You can open single or multiple images via Camera Raw hosted by Photoshop using a double-click, File ⇨ Open or ⌘ O ctrl O. Photoshop is ideal for processing small numbers of images. If you use ⌘ R ctrl R, Bridge will host the single or multiple Camera Raw dialog. Opening via Bridge is better suited for processing large batches of images in the background.

## Camera Raw tools

### 🔍 Zoom tool (Z)

Use as you would with the normal zoom tool to zoom in or out the preview image.

### ✋ Hand tool (H)

Use as you would with the normal hand tool to scroll an enlarged preview image.

### ✒ White balance tool (I)

The white balance tool is used to set the White Balance in the Adjust controls.

### 🎯 Color sampler tool (S)

This allows you to place up to nine color sampler points in the preview window.

### 🔳 Crop tool (C)

The crop tool will apply a crop setting to the raw image which will only be applied to the Bridge thumbnail/preview or when the file is opened in Photoshop. It has a submenu of Aspect Ratio Crop presets to which you can add custom crop ratios.

### 📐 Straighten tool (A)

You can drag with the straighten tool along a line that is meant to be horizontal or vertical for Camera Raw to apply a 'best fit', straightened crop.

### 🩹 Retouch tool (B)

Use to remove sensor dust spots and blemishes from a picture.

### 👁 Red eye removal tool (E)

For removing red eye from portraits shot using on-camera direct flash.

### ☰ ACR preferences (⌘ ctrl–K)

Opens the Adobe Camera Raw preferences dialog.

### ↺ Rotate counterclockwise (L)

Rotates the image 90° counter clockwise.

### ↻ Rotate clockwise (R)

Rotates the image 90° clockwise.

## General controls for single file opening

When you open a single image, this will reveal the dialog shown in Figure 5.11. The status bar will show which version of Camera Raw you are using and the make of the camera for the file you just opened. In the top left section you have the Camera Raw tools, which I have listed on the left. Below that is the image preview area where the zoom setting can be adjusted via the pop-up menu at the bottom. The initial Camera Raw dialog displays the Basic panel control settings. In this mode the Preview checkbox will allow you to toggle previewing any global adjustments made in Camera Raw. Once you start selecting any of the other panels, the Preview will toggle showing only the changes that have taken place within that particular panel. As you carry out these adjustments, the histogram view can help you gauge where to set the clipping points. The histogram graph represents the output histogram of an image and is calculated based on the RGB output space selected in the Workflow options. The shadow and highlight triangles in the histogram display will help indicate the shadow and highlight clipping and, as either of these get clipped, the triangles will light up with the color of the channel or channels that are about to be clipped. If you click on these, they will display a color overlay (blue for the shadows, red for the highlights) to indicate which areas in the image are being clipped. At the bottom we have the Show Workflow Options. Click on this to open the Workflow Options shown in Figure 5.12. The destination color space should ideally match your RGB workspace setting configured in the Photoshop color settings. I would suggest setting the bit depth to 16-bits per channel, as this will ensure that the image bit depth integrity is maintained when the image is opened up in Photoshop. The file size setting will let you open the image using smaller or larger pixel dimensions than the default capture file size (these size options are indicated by + or − signs). The Resolution field lets you set the file resolution in pixels per inch or per centimeter. Note that the value selected has no impact on the pixel dimensions.

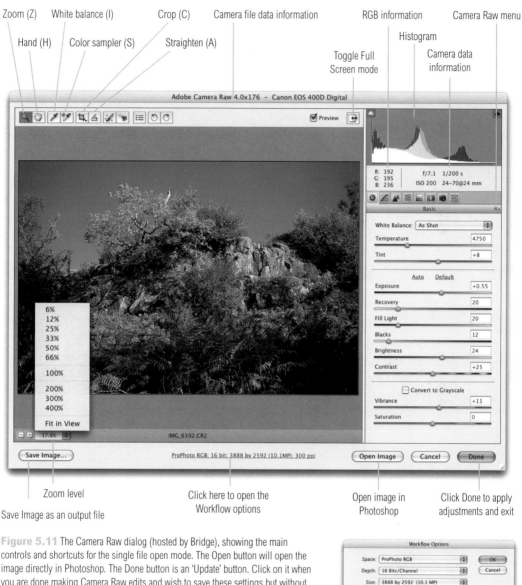

Zoom (Z)    White balance (I)    Crop (C)    Camera file data information    RGB information    Camera Raw menu

Hand (H)    Color sampler (S)    Straighten (A)    Histogram    Camera data information

Toggle Full Screen mode

Adobe Camera Raw 4.0x176 – Canon EOS 400D Digital

R: 192    f/7.1   1/200 s
G: 195    ISO 200   24-70@24 mm
B: 236

Basic

White Balance: As Shot

Temperature    4750
Tint    +8

Auto    Default

Exposure    +0.55
Recovery    20
Fill Light    20
Blacks    12
Brightness    24
Contrast    +25

Convert to Grayscale

Vibrance    +11
Saturation    0

6%
12%
25%
33%
50%
66%
100%
200%
300%
400%
Fit in View

17.8%    IMG_6392.CR2

Save Image...    ProPhoto RGB: 16 bit; 3888 by 2592 (10.1MP); 300 ppi    Open Image    Cancel    Done

Zoom level    Click here to open the Workflow options    Open image in Photoshop    Click Done to apply adjustments and exit

Save Image as an output file

Figure 5.11 The Camera Raw dialog (hosted by Bridge), showing the main controls and shortcuts for the single file open mode. The Open button will open the image directly in Photoshop. The Done button is an 'Update' button. Click on it when you are done making Camera Raw edits and wish to save these settings but without opening the image. In Figure 5.12 I point out the option to open images in Photoshop as Smart Objects. But you can also hold the *Shift* key when clicking 'Open Image' to open images as Smart Objects in Photoshop on an individual basis.

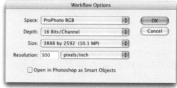

Workflow Options

Space:    ProPhoto RGB    OK
Depth:    16 Bits/Channel    Cancel
Size:    3888 by 2592  (10.1 MP)
Resolution:  300    pixels/inch

Open in Photoshop as Smart Objects

Figure 5.12 The workflow options let you set the color space and pixel dimensions. Plus, an option to open in Photoshop as a Smart Object.

249

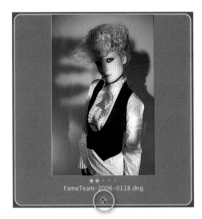

## Histogram and RGB space

The RGB space that is selected in the Workflow options will be reflected in the appearance of the preview image and also influence the histogram display. It can be interesting to compare the effect of different output spaces when editing a raw capture image.

**Figure 5.14** When you click on the Save Images... button you have the option of choosing a folder destination to save the image to and a Batch File Naming dialog so you can customize the file naming as you do so. In the Format section you can choose the file format. For example, when choosing the new DNG format, you can select the desired file format options. A save operation from Camera Raw will always auto-resolve any naming conflicts so as to avoid overwriting any existing files in the same save destination. This is important if you wish to save multiple versions of the same image as separate files. Holding down the [⌥] _alt_ key will bypass the Save dialog shown here.

# General controls for multiple file opening

The multiple image Camera Raw dialog will appear whenever you open multiple images from Bridge. In the default Bridge settings mode, double-click, File ⇨ Open or [⌘][O] [ctrl][O] will open Camera Raw via Photoshop and File ⇨ Open in Camera Raw... or [⌘][R] [ctrl][R] will open Camera Raw via Bridge.

The multiple image dialog contains a filmstrip of the selected images running down the left-hand side of the dialog. You can select individual images by clicking on the thumbnails in the filmstrip, or you can use the Select All button to select all the images. Make a continuous selection using the _Shift_ key or a discontinuous selection using the [⌘] _ctrl_ key when making custom selections from the Filmstrip. Once you have made a selection you can then navigate using the navigation buttons to progress through the images and apply Camera Raw adjustments to the individual selected images. The Synchronize... button will then allow you to synchronize the Camera Raw settings adjustments across all the images that are currently selected, based on the current 'most selected' image, which will be the thumbnail highlighted with a blue border. Click on the Synchronize... button and a sub dialog will then let you choose which of the Camera settings you want to synchronize. You can learn more about how to copy and paste and synchronize Camera Raw settings on page 285.

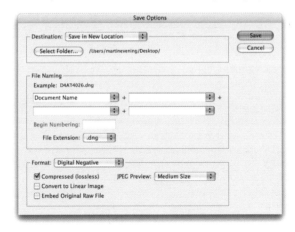

Select all images

Synchronize Camera
Raw settings

Retouch tool (R)

Remove red
eye tool (E)

Rotate tools

Camera Raw preferences
⌘ ctrl–K

Mark for delete (X)

Preview

Warning triangle warns that the preview image
has not refreshed completely yet

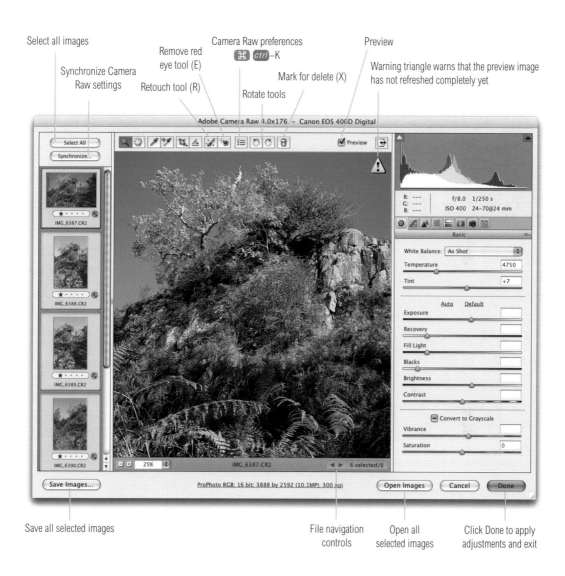

Save all selected images

File navigation
controls

Open all
selected images

Click Done to apply
adjustments and exit

**Figure 5.15** Here is a view of the Camera Raw dialog in the multiple file open
mode, highlighting more of the Camera Raw tools and controls. The Save option
allows you to save a raw file as DNG, TIFF, PSD or JPEG files. The file save
processing is then carried out in the background, allowing you to carry on working
in Bridge or Photoshop (dependent on which program is hosting Camera Raw at the
time). And if you hold down the ⌥ alt key as you click on the Save... button, you
can bypass the Save dialog box, which is really handy if you want to add file saves
to a queue and wish to continue making more edit changes in this or the single view
Camera Raw dialog (see Figure 5.11).

## Deleting images

As you use Camera Raw to edit your shots, the *Delete* key can be used to mark images to be sent to the trash later. This will place a big red X in the thumbnail and can be undone by hitting *Delete* again.

## Image browsing with Camera Raw

In multiple view mode, the Camera Raw dialog can also be used as a magnified view image browser. You can match the magnification and location across all selected images to check and compare details, inspect them in a sequence and apply ratings to selected images.

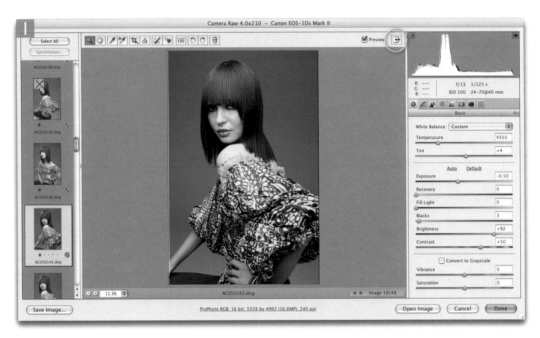

## Selecting rated images only

If you *⌘* *ctrl*-click on the Select All button, this will select the rated images only. This means that you can use the ratings to first select the images you are interested in editing and then use the above shortcut to make a quick selection of just these images.

1 If you have a large folder of images to review with a sequence of images, the Camera Raw dialog can be configured to provide a synchronized magnified view of all the selected pictures. The dialog is shown here in a compacted mode, but you can click on the Full Screen mode button (circled) to expand the dialog to fill the screen.

2 I clicked on the first image in the sequence and clicked on the Select All button. I then used the zoom tool to magnify the image. This action will synchronize the zoom view display for all selected images in the Camera Raw dialog. You can also use the hand tool to synchronize the scroll location for all the images.

3 Once this has been done you can deselect the thumbnail selection and then start inspecting the photographs. This can be done by clicking on the file navigation controls or by using the ← → keyboard arrow keys to progress through the images one by one. You can then mark your favorite pictures by using the usual Bridge shortcuts: *⌘* *>* *ctrl* *>* will progressively add more stars to a selected image; *⌘* *<* *ctrl* *<* will progressively decrease the number of stars.

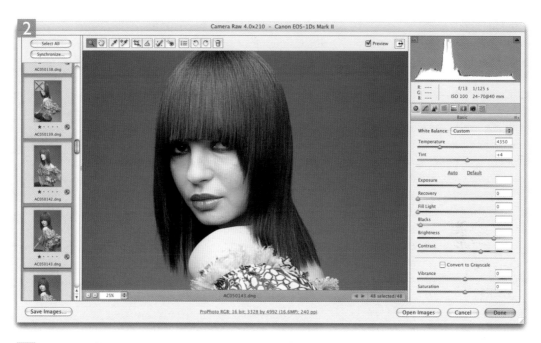

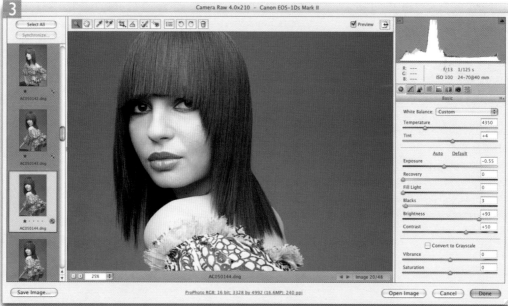

Client: Anita Cox. Model: Jennifer Muller @ Nevs.

## Auto tone adjustments

Camera Raw has the useful ability to apply auto tone corrections. Just click on 'Auto' any time you want to auto correct an individual image, or use the ⌘ U ctrl U shortcut. You can also have Auto set as a Camera Raw preference (see Figure 5.16). When this is checked, any image that has not been processed in Camera Raw yet will automatically have the auto tone setting applied to it. But any images you have previously edited using Camera Raw will remain as they are.

Auto tone works really well on most images, such as outdoor scenes and natural lit portraits. But it works less well on photographs that have been shot in the studio using controlled lighting. In these instances it can be something of a nuisance and is best left switched off.

## Camera Raw preferences

The Camera Raw preferences can be opened by choosing Bridge CS3 ⇨ Camera Raw Preferences... clicking on the Open Preferences button in the Camera Raw dialog, or using the ⌘ K ctrl K shortcut while in the Camera Raw dialog. Let's look at the General section first. I suggest you have the Camera Raw image settings saved as sidecar '.xmp' files. If the XMP data cannot be stored internally within the file itself (such as is the case with a DNG file), this will force the image settings to be stored locally, accompanying the files. The image sharpening can be applied to the previews only, should you wish to preview your adjustments with sharpening turned on, but without actually sharpening the output. The reason for this is because you might want to use a third-party sharpening program in preference to Camera Raw's sharpening.

In the Default Image Settings section, you can set various behaviors. When 'Apply auto tone adjustments' is switched on, Camera Raw will automatically apply an auto tone adjustment to all new images it encounters. The 'Apply auto grayscale mix when converting to grayscale' refers to the HSL/Grayscale controls, where Camera Raw

## Camera Raw cache size

The Preview cache is used to store all the thumbnail and preview data as compressed images in a central location. Bridge and Camera Raw use this data to populate the previews. If you have enough free hard disk space available, you may want to increase the size limit for the cache, or choose a new location to store the central preview cache data.

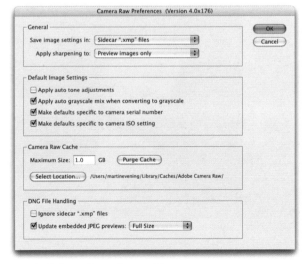

Figure 5.16 Camera Raw preferences dialog.

will apply an auto slider grayscale mix adjustment when converting a color photograph to black and white (the auto slider settings are in fact determined by the white balance setting). The next option allows you to make any default settings camera-specific. Basically, there is an option in the Camera Raw options menu that will allow you to save a particular set of Camera Raw settings as a new default setting to be used every time Bridge or Camera Raw encounters a new image. This option will make these settings specific to the camera serial number. This can be particularly useful for ensuring that the correct Camera Calibrate panel settings are applied automatically, based on the serial number of the camera used. Similarly, the 'Make defaults specific to camera ISO setting' will allow you to save a default setting for specific ISO values. This means that when you adjust the Detail panel settings, these can also be saved as the default settings for a particular ISO setting. And when both this and the previous option are checked, you can effectively have in Camera Raw, multiple default settings that will take into account the combination of the camera model and ISO setting.

## Basic panel controls

The Basic controls are best approached and adjusted in the order you find them. The white balance refers to the color temperature which essentially describes the warmth or the coolness of the lighting conditions. Tungsten lighting has a low warm color temperature, while daylight has a higher, more blue color temperature. If you choose to shoot in raw mode it does not matter how you set the white point settings at the time of shooting, because you can decide later which is the best white balance setting to use. The white balance setting will normally default to using the 'As Shot' white balance setting embedded in the raw file metadata at the time the image was taken. This might be a fixed white balance setting that is used on your camera or it could be an auto white balance made at the time the picture was shot. If this is not correct, you can try mousing down on the White Balance pop-up menu and select a

### DNG file handling

Camera Raw and Lightroom will embed the XMP metadata in the XMP header space of a DNG file. Therefore there is no need to use sidecar files to read and write XMP metadata when sharing files between these two programs. However, some third-party programs may create sidecar files for DNG files and the DNG preferences can be set to ignore 'xmp' sidecar files when reading DNGs. If this is checked, Camera Raw will not be side tracked by data in sidecar files that accompanies a DNG file unless, of course, you want Camera Raw to read this data.

DNG files contain embedded previews that will represent how an image will look with the current applied Camera Raw settings. When the Update embedded JPEG preview is checked, this will force the previews in all DNG files to be rebuilt based on the current Camera Raw settings, overriding previously embedded previews.

### Camera Raw white balance

Camera Raw was designed by Thomas Knoll, one of the original creators of the Photoshop program. Thomas has cleverly used two profile measurements, one made under tungsten lighting conditions and another done using daylight balanced lighting, and used these to calculate the white balance adjustment between these two white balances and then extrapolated the data to calculate the white balance going to extremes either side of these measured values.

## Color temperature

In the world of traditional color photography we basically had just two color temperature choices when choosing a film emulsion: daylight and tungsten. Daylight film for outdoor photography and studio flash was rated at 5500 degrees Kelvin and Tungsten at 3200 degrees Kelvin. These absolute values would rarely match the lighting conditions you were shooting with, but they would enable you to get roughly close to the appropriate color temperature of the light you were using in either a daylight/strobe lighting or indoor/tungsten light setting. One could then fine-tune the color temperature by using filters over the camera lens or color gel filters over the lights themselves.

preset setting that correctly describes the white balance that should be used. Alternatively, you can simply adjust the Temperature slider to make the image appear warmer or cooler and adjust the Tint slider to balance the white balance green/magenta tint bias. But the easiest way to do this is to select the white balance tool and click on an area that is meant to be an off-white color (you will notice that as you move the tool across the image, the RGB values will be displayed just below the histogram).

The image tonal adjustment controls are next. These allow you to make further adjustments to the way the raw image data will be interpreted when it is converted and opened in Photoshop. It is important to note here that with raw files, the raw data exists in a linear gamma space. This is because camera sensors have a linear response to light and the unprocessed raw files exist in what is referred to as a 'linear gamma space'. Human vision interprets light in a non-linear fashion, so one of the main things a raw conversion has to do is to apply a large gamma correction to the original image data to make the correctly exposed,

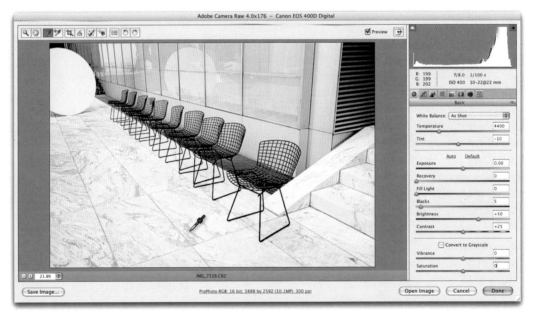

Figure 5.17 Setting a white balance with the white balance tool.

raw image look correct, the way our eyes would expect to perceive the scene in an image (see Digital exposure on pages 260–261). So the preview image you see in the Camera Raw dialog presents a gamma corrected preview of the raw data, while the adjustments you apply in Camera Raw are in fact being applied to the raw linear data. The reason I mention this is to illustrate one aspect of the subtle but important differences between the tonal edits that can be made in Camera Raw to raw files and those that are applied in Photoshop where the images have already been 'gamma corrected'. Note that in the case of non-raw files, Camera Raw has to temporarily convert the image to a linear RGB space to carry out the calculations.

The Exposure slider is used to set the overall brightness, so that the photograph looks 'correctly exposed'. Unlike previous versions of Camera Raw, you don't have to worry about setting the exposure too bright or clipping the highlights, because the Recovery slider can be used to help preserve details in the highlights. If you hold down the ⌥ [alt] key as you drag the Recovery slider you will get to see a Threshold mode preview, which can often make it easier to determine the optimum setting. The Blacks slider is a little less critical, but again I find it useful to hold down the ⌥ [alt] key to obtain a threshold mode preview display to help determine the point where the shadows just clip. The Fill Light kind of (but not exactly) matches the behavior of the Shadow amount slider in the Shadow/ Highlight image adjustment dialog. Dragging Fill Light to the right will add more lightness to the dark tone areas lightening the shadows. You can overdo things, because if you apply too much Fill Light you may knock back the contrast too much. The primary goal is to apply a first step tonal correction to set the overall brightness, the highlight clipping, the shadow point and shadow tone detail. From here you can either use the Basic panel Brightness and Contrast sliders to modify the photograph, or use the Tone Curve panel controls which, in my view, offer a more versatile method for fine-tuning the image tone contrast.

## Highlight recovery

The Camera Raw Recovery slider cleverly utilizes the highlight detail in whichever channels contain the best recorded highlight detail and thereby boosts the detail in the weakest highlight channel. There are limits as to how far you can push a Recovery adjustment, but one may be able to recover as much as a stop of overexposure. Camera Raw can sometimes use extra tricks such as ignoring digital gain values used to create higher ISO captures.

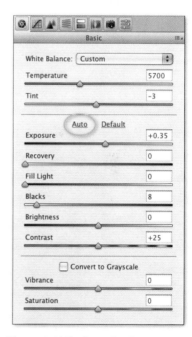

**Figure 5.18** The Camera Raw Basic panel controls. Clicking Auto will apply an auto adjustment and clicking Default will apply the default Camera Raw settings (which will differ according to whether you are editing a raw or non-raw image). ⌘ U ctrl U can also be used to apply an Auto setting.

# Basic image adjustment procedure

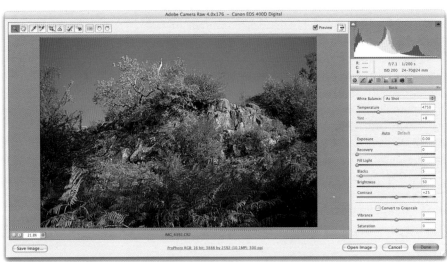

**1** This shows a raw image as viewed in the Camera Raw dialog, using the default settings in the Basic panel. One way to quickly optimize an image is to click on the Auto button. If you want to reset all the settings you can do so by double-clicking on the individual sliders, or by clicking on the Default button.

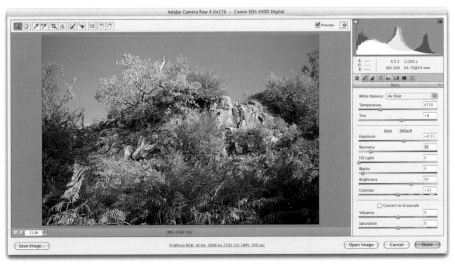

**2** In this example I adjusted the Exposure to make the photograph look lighter and achieve what looked like the best visual brightness. You don't have to worry about blowing out the highlight detail, because you can use the Recovery slider to restore any highlight detail that may be clipped (but without destroying the exposure effect).

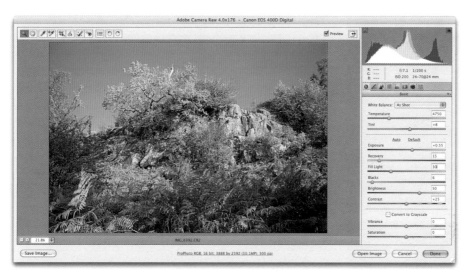

3 The next step was to optimize the shadows. I used the Blacks slider to set the
clipping point for the shadow detail and after that I used the Fill Light slider to
lighten the darker areas of the photograph such as the bracken in the foreground.
Note that as you adjust the Recovery and Blacks sliders, you can hold down the
⌥ alt key as you drag to see a threshold view of the image, which can help you
determine how far to drag to set the correct amount of clipping.

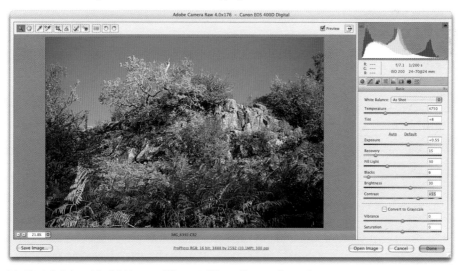

4 And last of all, I used the Brightness and Contrast sliders to fine-tune the tonal
balance of the photograph. It is important that you use the Basic adjustment
controls in the order suggested here, instead of adjusting the Brightness first and
then tweaking the Exposure afterwards.

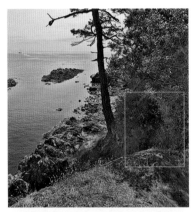

**Normal exposure**

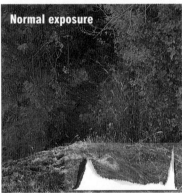

**- 1.5 stop exposure**

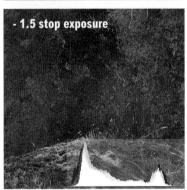

Figure 5.19 This shows the difference
the exposure can make in retaining shadow
information. The darker the exposure, the fewer
discreet levels the CCD chip can capture and this
can result in poor compromised shadow detail.

## Digital exposure

Digital shooting requires a whole new approach when determining the optimum exposure setting compared to shooting with film. Most digital cameras such as digital SLRs and even the raw enabled compacts are capable of capturing 12 bits of data, which is equivalent to 4096 recordable levels per color channel. As you halve the amount of light that falls on the chip sensor, you potentially halve the number of levels that are available to record an exposure. Let us suppose that the optimum exposure for a particular photograph at a given shutter speed is f16. This exposure will make full use of the chip sensor's dynamic range and consequently the potential is there to record up to 4096 levels of information. If one were then to halve the exposure to f22, you would only have the ability to record up to 2048 levels per channel. It would still be possible to lighten the image in Camera Raw or Photoshop to create an image that appears to have similar contrast and brightness. But, and it's a big but, that one stop exposure difference has immediately lost half the number of levels that could potentially be caught by using a one stop brighter exposure. The image is now effectively using only 11 bits of data per channel instead of 12. This is true of digital scanners as well. Perhaps you may have already observed how difficult it can be to rescue detail from the very darkest shadows, and how these can end up looking very posterized. Have you also noticed how much easier it is to rescue highlight detail compared to shadow detail when using the Shadow/ Highlight adjustment? This is because far fewer levels will be available to define the light information recorded in the darkest areas of the picture and these levels can easily become stretched further apart as you try to lighten the shadows. This is why posterization is always much more noticeable in the shadows. And it also explains why it is important to target your digital exposures as carefully as possible so that you make the brightest exposure possible, but without the risk of blowing out the highlight detail.

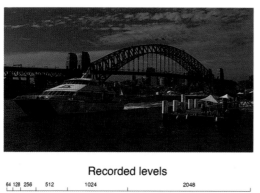

### Recorded levels

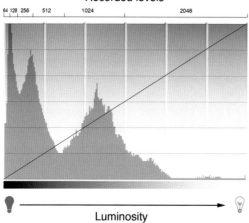

Luminosity

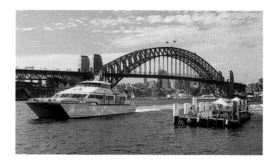

### Recorded levels

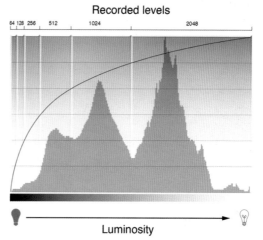

Luminosity

**Figure 5.20** If you inspected the images your camera captured as raw files, they would look something like the image shown top left. Notice that the image is very dark, it is lacking in contrast and the levels (representing the tonal information) in the histogram appear to be mostly bunched up to the left. During the raw conversion process, a gamma curve correction is applied when converting the linear data so that the processed image matches the way we are used to viewing the relative brightness in a scene. The picture top right shows the same image after a basic raw conversion.

A consequence of this is that the more brightly exposed areas will preserve the most tonal information and the shadow areas will end up with fewer levels. A typical CCD sensor can capture up to 4096 levels of tonal information. Half these levels will be recorded in the brightest stop exposure range and the recorded levels are effectively halved with every stop decrease in exposure. The digital camera exposure is therefore quite critical. Ideally, you want the exposure to be as bright as possible so that you make full use of the Levels histogram, but at the same time be careful to make sure the highlights don't get clipped.

### Camera histograms

The histogram that appears on a compact camera or digital SLR screen is unreliable for anything other than JPEG capture. This is because the histogram you see there is usually based on the camera-processed JPEG and is not representative of the true raw capture. The only way to check the histogram for a raw capture file is to open the image via a raw processing program such as Camera Raw.

## Negative vibrance and saturation

Not all of us want to turn our photographs into super-colored versions of reality. You can use the Vibrance and Saturation sliders to apply negative adjustments too. If you take the Saturation down to −100, this will convert an image to monochrome. This used to be how one went about making black and white renderings from Camera Raw (you can now use the HSL/Grayscale panel instead). But negative Saturation and Vibrance adjustments can be used to produce nice pastel-colored renderings.

## *Vibrance and Saturation*

A Vibrance slider has been added to the Camera Raw basic controls and this can apply what are described as non-linear color saturation adjustments, which means colors that are already brightly saturated in color remain relatively protected when you boost the vibrance, compared to the colors that are not so saturated, which receive a greater saturation boost. The net result is a Saturation control that allows you to make an image look more colorful, but without the attendant risk of clipping those colors that are saturated enough already. Try opening a photograph of some brightly colored flowers and compare the difference between a Vibrance and a Saturation adjustment. You should notice how extreme Saturation adjustments will soon cause the brighter colors to clip. The other thing that is rather neat about the Vibrance control is that it has a built-in skin tone protection filter which does quite a good job of not letting the skin tones increase in saturation as you move the slider to the right. In Figure 5.21, I boosted the Vibrance to +45, which boosted the colors in the dress, but without giving the model an unnaturally 'vibrant' suntan.

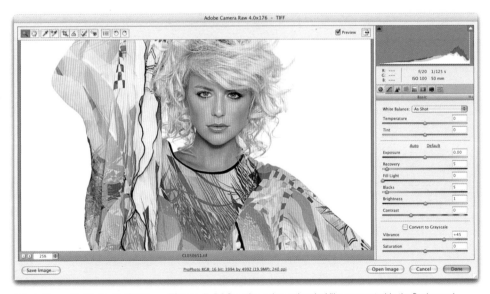

Client: Clipso. Model: Carina @ FM     **Figure 5.21** Boosting colors using the Vibrance control in the Basic panel.

## Tone Curve panel

The Curve panel control is a fine-tuning control that is applied to the image in combination with the initial adjustments made in the Adjust panel controls. In the Point Curve editor mode, the default setting uses a Medium Contrast curve, which applies a moderate increase in contrast that arguably matches the default contrast applied by most cameras when they carry out their on-board processing to produce a JPEG image. So this default setting combined with the auto settings will probably produce the 'snappiest' looking results. But it is just a default and it is quite simple to turn the curve off by setting it to Linear and this can become your new default. The Parametric Curve editor mode provides a new mechanism for editing the tone curve shape where, instead of clicking to add points and dragging them, you use the slider controls to control the curve shape; judging from responses so far, photographers generally find this method much more intuitive to work with.

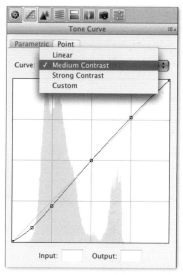

**Figure 5.22** The Tone Curve panel, shown here in Point Curve editor mode and displaying the basic ACR Curve preset settings.

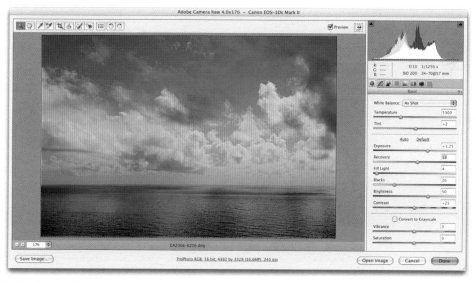

1 In this first example, the image tones were adjusted using the Basic panel controls to produce an optimized range of tones that were ready for further enhancement. I could have used the Brightness and Contrast sliders next, but the Tone Curve panel provides a simple yet effective interface for manipulating the contrast and brightness.

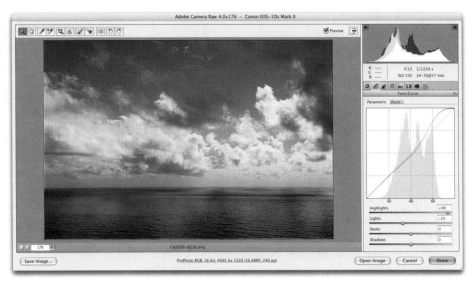

**2** Over in the Tone Curve panel I selected the Parametric curve option and by dragging the Highlights slider to the right and reducing the Lights slider a little, I was able to increase the contrast in the sky.

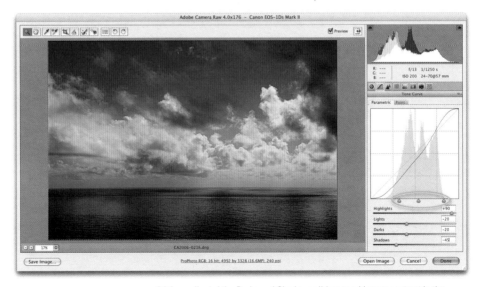

**3** I then adjusted the Darks and Shadows sliders to add more contrast in the dark regions of the photograph. But in addition to this I fine-tuned the scope of adjustment for the Tone Curve sliders by adjusting the positions of the three tone range split points (circled).

## *Image effects using the Point Curve editor*

If you switch to the Point Curve editor mode, you can edit the curve shape manually. This makes it possible to edit previously applied point curve settings, but you can also use the point curve to create special effects like the black and white solarization effect shown below.

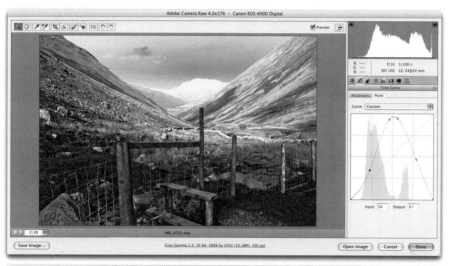

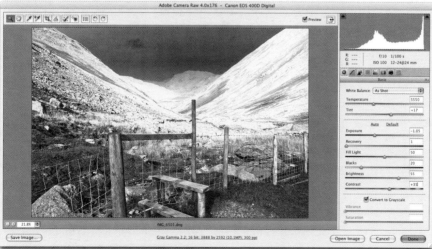

**Figure 5.23** In this example, I created an inverted 'V' curve shape via the Point Curve in the Tone Curve panel. I then switched to the Basic panel and used the tone controls there to further modify and vary the effect.

## Other Noise Reduction methods

I would recommend that you also consider using the Reduce Noise filter in Photoshop as a method for reducing heavy image noise artifacts.

## Camera Raw JPEG sharpening

If you shoot using the JPEG mode, your camera will have already sharpened the capture data. And in general, if you are opening a JPEG or TIFF image via Camera Raw it would be safe to assume that the image should have already been presharpened. Now in Camera Raw it is always possible to sharpen any image, but in the case of JPEGs and other non-raw images, the default setting is wisely set to zero. This is because in nearly every case only you should decide when to apply Camera Raw sharpening. It is not something you want to see applied by default.

## Detail panel

The Detail settings allow you to make improvements to the smoothness and sharpness of the raw conversion and compensate for any color noise. To make a proper judgement when using any of the Detail slider controls, you should preview the image at 100%.

I sometimes prefer to leave Camera Raw processed images unsharpened and carry out the presharpening in Photoshop (as described in the previous chapter). But even if you don't intend to sharpen in Camera Raw, it is nonetheless useful to see sharpening applied to the preview images in Camera Raw as this will help you make better judgements when making tonal and contrast edit adjustments. If you mouse down on the small triangle next to the Camera Raw settings you can open the Camera Raw preferences shown back in Figure 5.16 and set the sharpening so that it is applied to the preview images only and then leave the Detail Sharpness setting at 25%.

Mind you, I have grown to appreciate the Camera Raw sharpening as a basic capture sharpening method and reckon it is worth promoting to readers as a simpler way to presharpen images. The single slider control in Camera Raw is certainly a simpler concept to get to grips with!

Whenever you shoot using a high ISO setting on the camera, you will almost certainly encounter noise and the Luminance and Color Noise Reduction can be used to improve the appearance of images that suffer from such noise artifacts. The Luminance slider can be used to smooth out the physical clumpiness of the noise artifacts while the Color Noise Reduction can soften the color and get rid of the colored speckles. The noise will vary a lot from camera to camera, so it is hard to give out any specific settings advice. Figure 5.24 shows the settings used on a fairly grainy capture that was shot using the camera's maximum 400 ISO setting. For the most part you can safely set the Color Noise Reduction to maximum, but not if the photograph you are editing contains a lot of blue information, such as an underwater photograph. As you can see in Figure 5.25, too much color noise reduction can significantly soften the edge detail in a photograph.

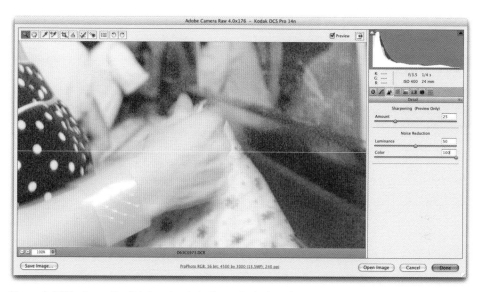

Figure 5.24 The Camera Raw Detail panel controls. The preview is shown here divided in two. The top half shows the before image and the bottom half the preview with the Luminance Smoothing and Color Noise Reduction applied.

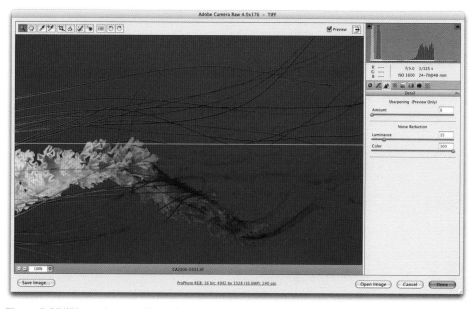

Figure 5.25 With an underwater subject such as this, you should be wary of applying excessive noise reduction. In the bottom half view you can see how this can lead to blurring of the image detail.

## More about Stacks

Stacks is new to Photoshop CS3 and is one of my favorite features for photographers. But unfortunately it is only available as part of the extended version of Photoshop CS3. Check out the tutorial on pages 398–401 in which I demonstrate how to remove groups of people who have walked in front of the camera during a set of exposures that were taken of a still-life scene.

## Removing noise using multiple exposures

Here is a technique that makes use of the Stacks feature in Photoshop CS3 to merge a set of identical exposures and obtain a smoother-looking image.

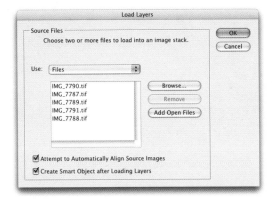

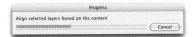

**1** I started by going to the File menu and chose Scripts ⇨ Load Files into Stack and browsed to select a set of five images that had been shot at identical exposures where I had simply hand held the camera and fired off a short sequence. Note, these particular photographs were all shot at a high ISO setting in twilight conditions and were Camera Raw processed TIFFs without any noise reduction. I checked the Align Source images and Create Smart Object options and clicked OK.

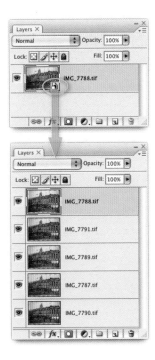

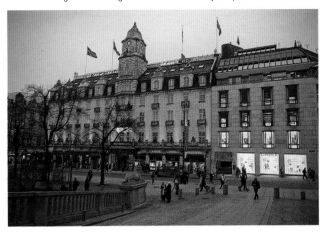

**2** The selected images opened as a single image document grouped together as a single Smart Object. If I were to double-click on the Smart Object icon (circled), this would open the Smart Object in a separate document window and allow me access to all the individual layers, which wasn't necessary in this case (but would be if you wanted to edit any of the individual layers).

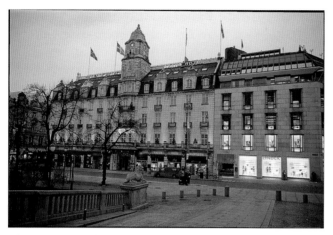

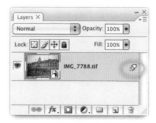

**3** Back in the original Smart Object document, I went to the Layer menu and chose Image Stacks ⇨ Image Stack Rendering ⇨ Median. The processing may take a little while, depending on the size and number of layers, plus bit depth. Once completed, you will notice how the Smart Object layer has a 'stacks' icon (circled) indicating that the Smart Object has been rendered using the Stacks feature.

### Median versus Mean

If you are processing a series of still-life captures, then a Mean stacks rendering can remove more noise than Median. For example, if you were processing astronomy pictures, you would want to use a Mean rendering.

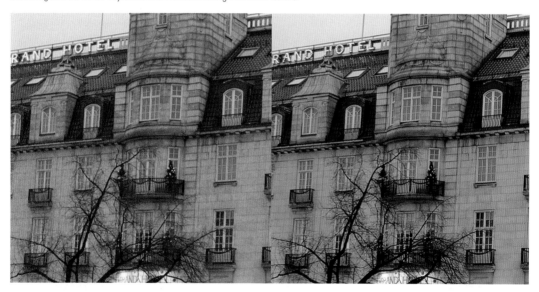

**4** Here is a comparison showing a close-up view of a single exposure on the left and a rendered version on the right where the five separate exposures were merged to produce a smoother noise-free image. The Median rendering was used here because it analyzes the pixel values from the lowest to the highest that occur at any one point and picks the middle value, thereby eliminating nearly all of the noisy pixels that were present on each of the separate layers.

## HSL color controls

The choice of color ranges for the HSL sliders is really quite logical when you think about it. We may often want to adjust skin tone colors, but skin tones aren't red or yellow, but are more of an orange color. And the sea is often not blue but more of an aqua color. Basically, the hue ranges in the HSL controls are designed to provide a more applicable range of colors for photographers to work with.

## HSL/Grayscale panel

The HSL/Grayscale panel is a new addition to Camera Raw 4. The HSL controls provide eight color sliders with which to control the Hue, Saturation and Luminance. These controls are similar to the Hue/Saturation adjustment in Photoshop, but in many ways better, because from my experience I find that the controls are more predictable in their response. For example in Figure 5.26, I used the Luminance controls only to darken the blue sky and add more contrast between the clouds and the sky, plus I lightened the grass and trees slightly. Do this in Hue/Saturation and you will find that the blue colors will tend to lose saturation as you darken the luminosity. You will also notice that the slider colors have departed from the traditional additive and subtractive primary colors of red, green, blue, plus cyan, magenta, yellow, rather that match the color model used in conventional color tools. The color controls in the HSL panel are based on colors that are of more actual relevance when editing photographic images.

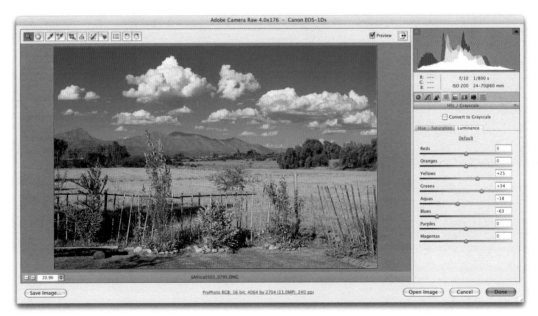

**Figure 5.26** In this example, the HSL/Grayscale panel was used to add more cloud contrast to the sky by darkening the Aquas and Blues sliders.

## Camera Raw black and white conversions

If you check the Convert to Grayscale box, Camera Raw will make a black and white, 'Grayscale Mix' version of the image, which is produced by blending the image's color data to produce a monochrome rendering of the original. Clicking 'Auto' will apply a custom setting that is based on the white balance setting used in the Basic panel, and if you click 'Default', this will reset all the sliders to zero. You can also manually drag the sliders to make certain colors in the color original lighter or darker. And the beauty of this is that the overall tone brightness and contrast will not fluctuate much as you do this. This makes it easy to experiment with different slider combinations. If you want the sky to be darker, you would do as I did in Figure 5.27 and drag the Aquas and Blues sliders to the left. I would also suggest that you switch over to the Basic and Tone Curve panels to make continued adjustments to the white balance and tone controls as this can have a strong bearing on the outcome of the grayscale conversion.

## Grayscale Mix tips

You might also like to try adjusting the Vibrance or Saturation before you click on the Convert to Grayscale box, as this can help produce stronger contrast results. You might also like to experiment with an alternative grayscale mix technique, where you set all the HSL Saturation sliders to −100 and then adjust the HSL Luminance sliders. This method offers a different type of slider response and you may prefer the results you get. You will also have full interactive control with the Vibrance and Saturation where, interestingly, a negative vibrance can actually enhance a Darken Luminance adjustment.

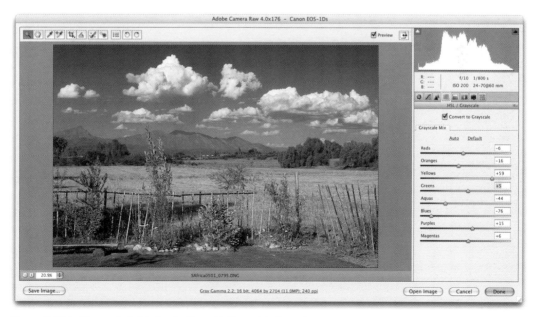

**Figure 5.27** In this example, I clicked on the Convert to Grayscale button and made some custom slider adjustments to increase the sky contrast.

271

## Color image split toning

Although the Split Toning panel appears to be an extension of the Grayscale Mix, the Split Tone controls are just as useful for working on color images. Later in this book I will be describing how to create a color cross processing effect in Photoshop, but the Split Toning controls described here can produce identical results, but with much less hassle. In fact I would say that there are quite a few Photoshop tips and tricks where Camera Raw is taking away the mystery of how to use Photoshop and making everything simpler and easier to accomplish directly within Camera Raw.

## Split Toning panel

After you have used the HSL/Grayscale panel to convert a photograph to black and white, you can the use the Split Toning panel to colorize the image. The controls in this panel will allow you to apply one color to the highlights, another color to the shadows and then use the Saturation sliders to adjust the intensity of the colors. This is how you create a basic split tone color effect. There is also the Balance slider, which will allow you to adjust the midpoint of the split tone. For example, in Figure 5.28, the photograph I was applying the split tone to was a high-key image and it was therefore more appropriate to offset the Balance slider so that the blue shadow tone would register more in the shadows. Without such an adjustment the shadow color would have barely registered. The HSL/Grayscale and Split Tone controls are incredibly versatile. Bear in mind these will work equally well with non-raw images and make the new Black and White image adjustment in Photoshop almost completely redundant.

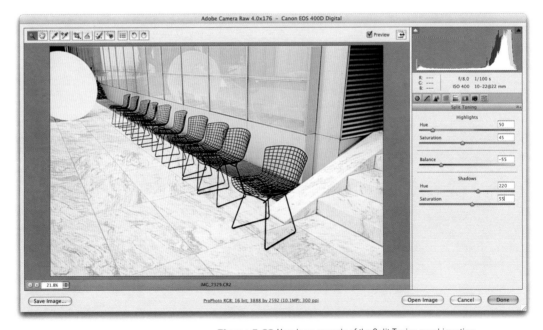

Figure 5.28 Here is an example of the Split Toning panel in action.

## Lens Corrections panel

The Lens Corrections controls can help correct some of the
optical problems that are associated with digital capture. If
you inspect an image closely towards the edge of the frame
area, you may notice some color fringing, which will be
most apparent around areas of high contrast. This is mainly
a problem you get with cheaper lens optics used on some
digital cameras. The Chromatic Aberration controls should
be used with the preview image set to 100% and can help
remove any visible color fringing. The Red/Cyan Fringe
adjustment works by adjusting the scale size of the Red
channel relative to the Green channel and the Blue/Yellow
Fringe slider will adjust the scale size of the Blue channel
relative to the Green channel. The chromatic aberration
controls are also available in the Lens Correction filter.

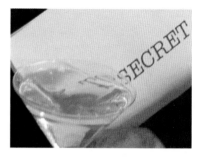

**Figure 5.29** If you hold down the ⌥ *alt*
key as you make adjustments to the Red/Cyan
Chromatic aberration controls you can hide the
Blue/Yellow color fringing. Do the same with the
Blue/Yellow Chromatic aberration controls to
hide the Red/Cyan color fringing.

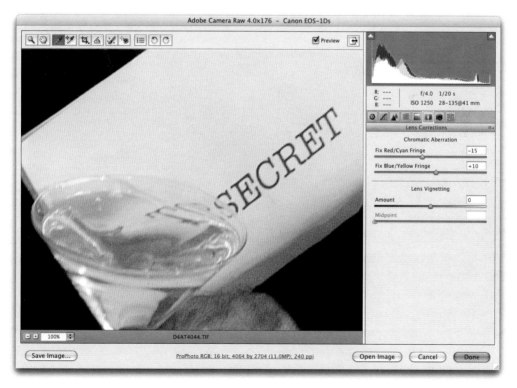

**Figure 5.30** The Camera Raw Lens Corrections panel controls.

## Vignette control

With some camera/lens combinations you may see some brightness fall-off to occur towards the edges of the picture frame. This will result in the corners being more darkly exposed compared to the center. This is a problem you are more likely to encounter with wide angle lenses, and you may notice the deficiency if the subject features a plain evenly-lit background. The Amount slider can be used to correct for this by lightening the corners relative to the center of the photograph and the Midpoint slider can be used to offset the fall-off. As you increase the Midpoint value, the exposure compensation will be accentuated more towards the outer edges. Or, you can use the Vignette controls to create a darkening vignette effect as is shown below.

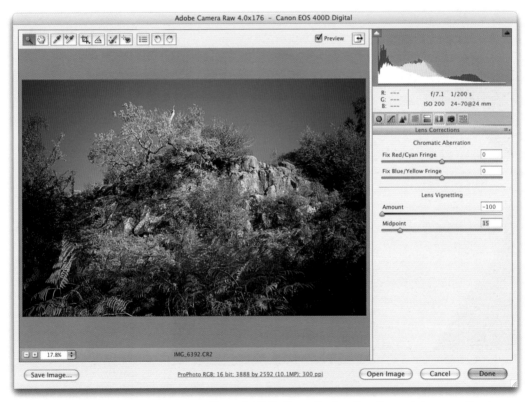

**Figure 5.31** The Camera Raw Lens Corrections controls were used here to deliberately darken the corners of the photograph.

## Camera Calibration panel

Camera Raw is the product of much camera testing and raw file analysis that was carried out by Thomas Knoll at Adobe. Test cameras were used to build a two-part profile of each camera sensor's spectral response under standardized tungsten and daylight balanced lighting conditions. And from this, the Camera Raw processor is able to calculate a pretty good color interpretation under these lighting conditions, and beyond, across a wide range of color temperatures. This method may not be as accurate as having a proper profile built for your camera, but to be honest, profiling a camera is something that can only really be done where the light source conditions are always the same, because you would otherwise need to reprofile the camera every time the lighting was changed.

The Calibrate panel controls provide a mechanism for fine-tuning the color adjustments in Camera Raw so that you can address any slight differences between your camera and the ones Thomas used to test with, and customize the Camera Raw output to produce a custom calibration for each individual camera. This system of calibration does require a little extra effort to set up, but it is worth doing if you want to fine-tune the color calibration for each individual camera that you shoot with.

You also have to bear in mind that many of the default Camera Raw settings were achieved through testing a limited number of cameras. And it has been reported by some that there can be a discernible variation in color response between individual cameras. It was as a result of testing a wider pool of cameras that Thomas Knoll decided to update the default settings for certain camera makes and provided a new v 3.0 default camera profile (in addition to keeping the legacy profile available for use).

In the early days of Camera Raw I used to shoot a Gretag Macbeth ColorChecker chart and use a visual color comparison technique with a synthetic ColorChecker chart to adjust the Calibrate settings. It was all very complex! But fortunately there is now an easier way to calibrate your camera equipment.

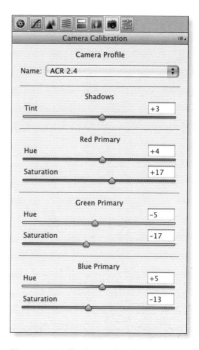

**Figure 5.32** The Camera Raw Calibrate panel controls are used to fine-tune the Camera Raw color interpretation. The Camera Profile setting at the top can offer a choice of camera profile settings. The reason for this is that some of the original Camera Raw profiles that came with Camera Raw did not necessarily reflect the best average chip performance of the supported cameras. So some camera profiles have been updated and made available as ACR 3.0 profiles. These profiles will be better than the ACR 2.4 setting, but the older profile is still there so as to not cause conflict for those users who wish to continue using this profile with their pre-saved calibrations.

### ACR compatible cameras

The list of cameras compatible with the latest version of Camera Raw can be found at the Adobe website by following this link: www.adobe.com/products/photoshop/cameraraw.html.

275

## The ACR Calibrator process

The script will run through a series of steps, in which the raw image containing the color checker chart will be opened many times using different settings and measure the results. This process can take a very long time to complete, which is why it is important to keep the bit depth at 8-bits per channel and the image size small. It will also help if you hide all the palettes first before you run the script.

## *The ACR Calibrator script*

If you are interested in achieving consistent color within a studio environment, then Camera Raw calibration is well worth doing. The easiest solution is to shoot a Gretag Macbeth ColorChecker chart under standard lighting conditions and then run the ACR Calibrator script that was created by Tom Fors (which I describe in the following steps). This will automatically measure the patches and generate a report with the calibration figures you need to enter into the Camera Calibration panel.

The ACR Calibrator script will work for Mac or PC with Photoshop CS, CS2 or CS3 and can be downloaded from the Chromoholics website at: http://fors.net/chromoholics/ The website also contains two short movies. There is one that shows you first how to install the ACR Calibrator script: http://fors.net/chromoholics/install/ and another with full instructions on how to use the ACR Calibrator script: http://fors.net/chromoholics/using/.

Once installed, the ACR Calibrator script will be available for use from the File ⇨ Scripts menu in Photoshop.

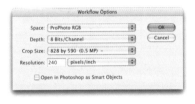

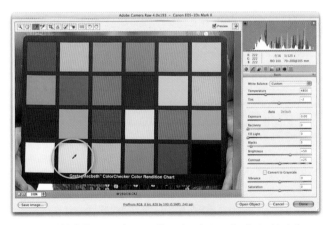

1 To use the ACR Calibrator script, you will need to photograph a Gretag Macbeth ColorChecker chart and open the raw file via the Adobe Camera Raw dialog in Photoshop. Use the white balance tool to measure the circled patch (next to the white patch). Next, crop the image tightly around the ColorChecker chart, go to the Workflow options and set the crop size to the smallest resolution possible and set the bit depth to 8-bits per channel. Now click Open to open the image in Photoshop.

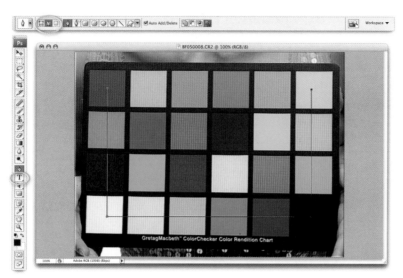

2 With the image open in Photoshop, select the pen tool with the Paths mode option selected in the Options palette. Click with the pen tool on the brown patch followed by the white patch, the black patch and lastly the blue-green patch. Now go to the File ⇨ Scripts menu and select the ACR Calibrator script. The script will automatically open the raw file many times over and gradually build a Calibrator status report in a new Photoshop document.

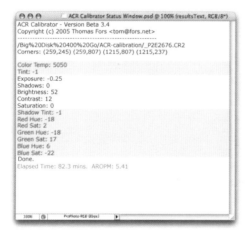

## Special Camera Raw settings

Apart from setting the bit-depth to 8-bit and the pixel dimensions to the smallest output size, there are no other settings you need concern yourself with. It does not matter if the auto settings are on in Photoshop CS3 or not and it does not matter which RGB output color space is selected.

3 Here is the ACR Calibrator Status Window after the script has run its full course. I have highlighted the calibration settings in yellow. You need to note these figures down, enter these in the Calibration panel in the Camera Raw dialog and save this as a custom calibration setting for your camera. You may also want to make a note of the Color temperature white balance and Tint settings and save these too as part of your custom calibration setting.

277

## Using Camera Calibration to distort colors

The Camera Calibration panel is really intended for fine-tuning the color calibration of a camera and get the Camera Raw processed colors to match as closely as possible to the colors in the original scene. But one of the interesting things you can also do with the Calibrate panel is to deliberately mess up the colors in an image to create unusual color effects.

To achieve the results you see here I mostly adjusted the color Hue and Saturation sliders in the Calibrate panel, taking the sliders to their extremes and linking these adjustments with modifications to the White Balance, Temperature and Tint sliders. If you check the panel settings you can see which values were used in the Calibrate panel. If you find a calibrate setting that you like and would like to reuse on other images, then it would be a good idea to follow the instructions coming up in the section on Camera Raw presets and save these as custom settings.

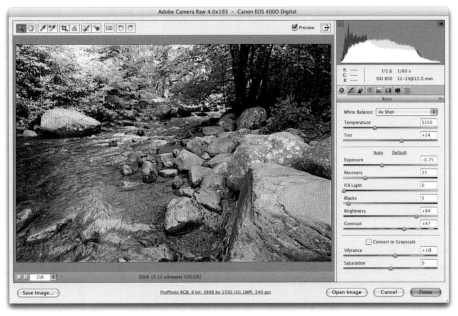

**Figure 5.33** This shows the normal version of the image using the As Shot settings before I played around with the Calibrate settings.

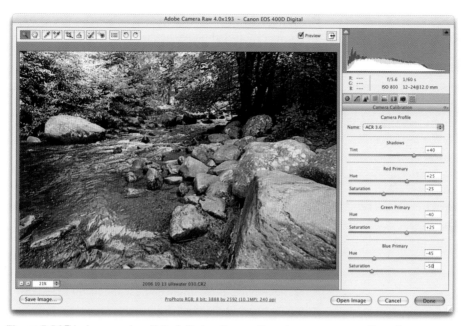

Figure 5.34 This shows a version with the Calibrate settings used to produce a cross-processed type effect.

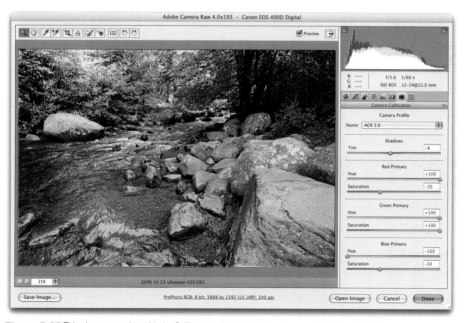

Figure 5.35 This shows a version with the Calibrate settings used to produce a color infrared effect.

## Retouch tool tips

The Show Overlay box can be used to turn the retouch circle viewing on or off, which can help when previewing the retouched results, as well as allowing you to retouch the image without seeing the retouch circles. You can remove individual retouch circles by selecting them and hitting the *Delete* key. Or, you can click on the Clear All button to delete all retouch circles. But note that the Preview button will not allow you toggle previewing the effects of the retouching. The Preview option toggles the visibility of the current panel settings.

## Retouch tool

To retouch spots and blemishes via the Camera Raw interface, you should select the retouch tool (B) from the tools section and ideally work on the image at a 100% magnification. Whenever the retouch tool is active you will see a control panel expand so you can set the spot radius size for the Retouch tool mode. In Spot mode, the retouch tool will behave like a cross between the spot healing brush and the clone stamp in Photoshop. It will carry out a straight forward clone of the image with a soft feathered edge circle, automatically selecting the area to sample from. In Heal mode, the retouch tool will behave more like a cross between the spot healing and normal healing brush in Photoshop, where it will auto-select an area to sample from and blend the sampled data with the surrounding data outside the spotting circle. In either case, you can click to select an applied clone circle and use the menu to switch from one mode to the other.

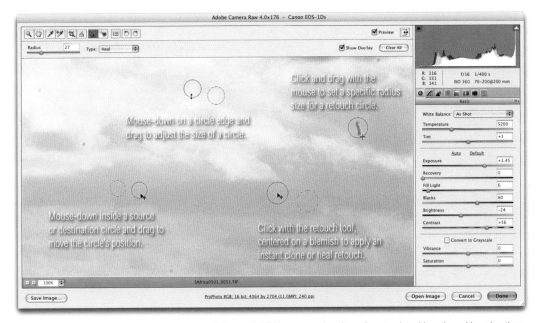

**Figure 5.36** This screen shot shows the retouch tool in action, with explanations of how to apply and modify the retouch spot circles.

## Red eye removal

The remove red eye tool is useful for correcting photographs taken of people where the direct camera flash has caused the pupils to appear bright red. To use this tool, open up an image that needs to be retouched, select the red eye removal tool and mouse drag over the eyes that need to be adjusted. In the example shown here, I dragged the mouse to roughly select an eye in this picture. As I did this, Camera Raw was able to detect the red eye areas that needed to be retouched and automatically adjusted the marquee size to fit. The tool sliders can be used to fine-tune the Pupil Size area that you want to correct as well as the amount you want to Darken the pupil by. You can revise the red eye removal settings by clicking on a rectangle to reactivate it, or use the D key to remove individual red eye corrections. If you don't like the results you are getting, you can always click on the Clear All button to delete the red eye retouching and start over again.

### Synchronized spotting

Note, if you are working in multiple image mode in Camera Raw, it is possible to select several images and simultaneously spot them all together at the same time!

### Keeping the sensor clean

Dust marks are the bane of digital photography and ideally you want to do as much as you can to avoid dust or dirt getting onto the camera sensor. I have experimented with various products and find that the Sensor Swabs used with the Eclipse cleaning solution from Photographic Solutions Inc (www. photosol.com) are reliable products. I use these from time to time to keep the sensors in my cameras free from marks.

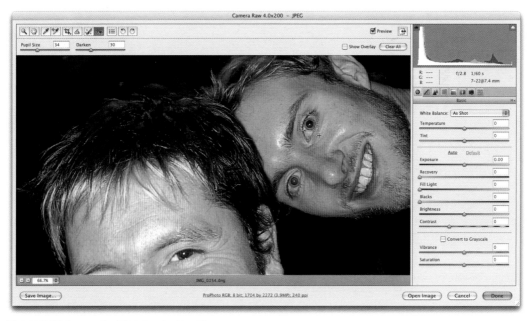

**Figure 5.37** An example of the red eye tool in action.

## Removing a crop

To remove a crop, open the image in the Camera Raw dialog again, select the crop tool and choose Clear Crop from the menu. Alternatively, you can hit *Delete* or simply click outside of the crop in the gray canvas area.

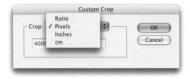

**Figure 5.38** The Custom Crop settings.

## Camera Raw cropping

You can crop an image in Camera Raw before it is opened in Photoshop. Camera Raw cropping is limited to cropping within the bounds of the image area and is non-permanent. The crop will be applied when the image is opened and also updated in the Bridge thumbnail and preview. The Camera Raw straighten tool can initially be used to measure a vertical or horizontal angle and apply a minimum crop to the image, which you can then resize accordingly. If you save a file out of Camera Raw using the Photoshop format, there will also be an option to preserve the cropped pixels. One of the useful tips I learnt from Bruce Fraser was how you can use the Custom Crop settings to create a crop size using the pixels units and create a custom size output that matches the size required for a specific layout, or one that exceeds even the standard output sizes available in the Workflow Options.

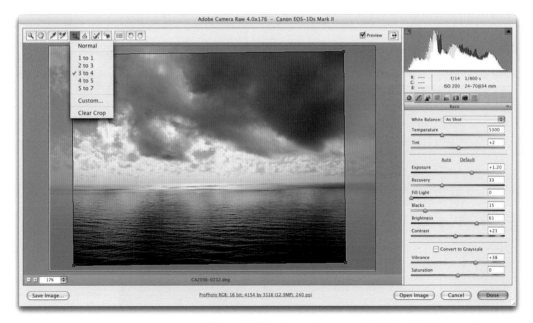

**Figure 5.39** The Camera Raw crop tool sub options include a range of preset crop proportions where you can add your own custom presets by clicking on the Custom... item in the menu shown here. The crop units can be adjusted to crop according to the aspect ratio (the default) or by pixels, inches or centimeters.

## Presets panel

In the Presets panel, you can click on the New Preset button to save the current Camera Raw settings as a new custom preset. Mouse down on the Camera Raw menu (circled) and you will see the menu shown below in Figure 5.40. 'Image Settings' will be whatever the current Camera Raw settings are for the image. This might be the default settings or it might be a custom setting that you created when you last edited the image in Camera Raw. The 'Camera Raw Defaults' will reset the default settings in all the panels and apply whatever the white balance setting was at the time the picture was captured, while the 'Previous Conversion' will apply the Camera Raw settings that were applied to the previous saved image. If you proceed to make any custom changes while the Camera Raw dialog is open then the Settings will change to display 'Custom Settings'.

### New Camera Raw defaults

The Save New Camera Raw Defaults option will make the current Camera Raw settings sticky every time from now on when Camera Raw encounters a new file. This includes images processed by Bridge. So for example, if you were working in the studio and had achieved a perfect Camera Raw setting for the day's shoot, you could make this the new Camera Raw default setting and all subsequent imported images will use this setting by default. At the end of the day you can select Reset Camera Raw defaults to clear this behavior and restore the default Camera Raw settings.

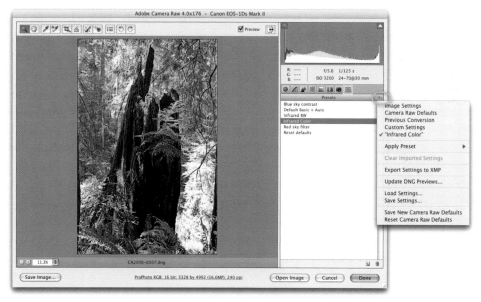

**Figure 5.40** When the Presets panel is selected, you can add Camera Raw settings as new presets, for use on other images. In the example shown here, I selected an Infrared Color preset which was saved using the settings shown in Figure 5.35 on page 279. If you mouse down on the Camera Raw menu (while in any panel view) you can access all the Camera Raw image settings described in the main text.

## Export settings to XMP

In the Camera Raw preferences there is an option to save image settings in the XMP data. In the case of most file formats, including DNG, it means that when this option is checked, the image settings information will automatically be written to the XMP space in the file header. In the case of proprietary raw files, it would be unsafe for Camera Raw to edit an unknown file format, so the information is stored using XMP sidecar files that accompany the image whenever you use Bridge (or Lightroom) to move the raw files from one location to another. If the Save images in XMP option is checked, Camera Raw will export the XMP data anyway. If this setting is not selected, you can use the Export Settings to XMP option to manually export the XMP data with selected images.

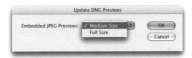

Figure 5.41 DNG files will store a JPEG preview of how the processed image will look and when you are editing DNG images via Camera Raw, there is a Camera Raw preference to update the DNG previews automatically. If this option is disabled, you can manually update the JPEG previews by selecting 'Update DNG Previews' from the Camera Raw menu.

## Saving and applying presets

To save a preset, go to the Camera Raw fly-out menu and choose Save Settings... Or, if you are in the Presets panel, click on the Add Preset button to create a new Camera Raw preset. A preset can be one that is defined by all camera raw settings, or it can be one that is made up of a subset of settings (as shown in Figure 5.42). Either way, a saved preset will always appear listed in the Presets panel. To apply a preset to an image, either go to the Camera Raw menu and choose Load Settings... Or, go to the Presets panel and just click on a setting that you want to apply to the image. And to remove a preset setting, go to the Presets panel, select it and click on the Delete button.

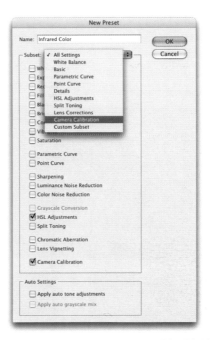

Figure 5.42 The dialog shown here is the New Preset dialog. It is identical to the one seen when you choose Save Settings... You can choose to save All Settings to record all the current Camera Raw settings as a preset. You can select a subsetting selection such as: Basic, or HSL Adjustments, or manually check the items that you would like to have included in the subset selection that will make up the saved Camera Raw preset.

## Copying and synchronizing settings

If you have a multiple selection of images in the Camera Raw dialog, you can make a selection of images from the filmstrip or click on the Select All button to select all images, then any adjustments you make to the selected image will be simultaneously updated in all the other pictures as well. Alternatively, if you make adjustments to a single image, then include other images in the filmstrip selection and click on the Synchronize... button, this will pop the Synchronize dialog shown in Figure 5.43. Select the specific settings you wish to synchronize and click OK. The Camera Raw settings will now synchronize to the currently selected image. You can also copy and paste the Camera Raw settings via Bridge. Select an image and choose Edit ⇨ Apply Camera Raw Settings ⇨ Copy (⌘ ⌥ C _ctrl_ _alt_ C). Select the image or images you wish to paste the settings to and choose Edit ⇨ Apply Camera Raw Settings ⇨ Paste (⌘ ⌥ V _ctrl_ _alt_ V).

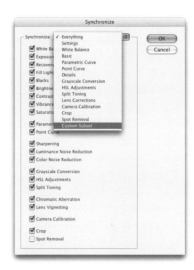

**Figure 5.43** When the Synchronize options dialog box appears you can select a preset range of settings to synchronize or make your own custom selection of settings to synchronize between the currently selected images.

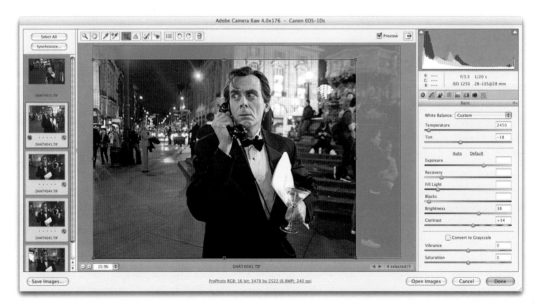

**Figure 5.44** In this example, I made a selection of images via the Filmstrip, clicked on the Synchronize button, which opened the dialog shown in Figure 5.43.

## Other HDR applications

All those special effects used in movies such as *Jurassic Park* used a 32-bit color space to render the computer-generated characters and make them interact convincingly with the real world film footage. So 32-bit image editing is useful in creating realistic animated special effects. The way this is usually done is to record what is known as a lightprobe image of the scene in which the main filming takes place. A lightprobe is an omnidirectional HDR image which can consist of a sequence of six or seven overlapping exposures shot using a 180 degree fisheye lens pointed in opposite directions. A basic lightprobe can be a series of photographs of a mirrored sphere taken with a normal lens. The resulting lightprobe image contains all the information needed to render the shading and textures on a computer generated object with realistic-looking lighting.

32-bit rendering is applicable to the computer games industry. The military and aeronautics industries are also particularly interested in the potential to render more realistic looking virtual landscapes for simulation training. A wireframe landscape designed on a computer can be made to respond dynamically to different programmed lighting environments.

Paul Debevec is a leading expert in HDR imaging. His website www.debevec.org contains much interesting information on HDR and its various applications.

## 32-bit editing and High Dynamic Range

Photoshop will support 32-bit images and offer a limited range of editing controls such as Layers and Painting to those who have purchased the extended version of Photoshop CS3. For many years now we have been used to editing images with a fixed exposure in 8-bit or 16-bit per channel mode and preparing them for print. However, a 32-bit color space has the potential to contain deep-bit detailed tonal information, because an HDR format image in 32 bit uses floating point math calculations (as opposed to regular whole numbers) to describe everything from the deepest shadows to the brightness of the sun. The 32-bit mode is therefore using a completely different type of image mode to describe the luminance values in an image.

A 32-bit file will be four times bigger than a standard 8-bit per channel image and can only originate from a high dynamic range capture device or be manufactured from a composite of camera exposures, as described over the following pages, using the Merge to HDR option. High Dynamic Range (HDR) imaging is not big yet, but it is predicted that digital cameras will soon start to feature HDR capture capabilities. Such cameras may not even need an exposure setting, because a single standard HDR exposure will be capable of capturing everything! Exposure decisions could then be made on the computer after the picture has been taken. That is the vision for the future of HDR stills photography.

## Merge to HDR

HDR cameras are not common yet but, in the meantime, Photoshop can simulate HDR capture by using the Merge to HDR feature to combine two or more images captured at different exposures with a normal digital camera and blend the selected images together to produce a 32-bit high dynamic range image. You can then convert this 32-bit HDR file into a 16-bit per channel or 8-bit per channel low dynamic range version which you can then edit normally in Photoshop. The HDR conversion dialog provides several methods for converting the merged exposure file, the most useful of which are probably the Exposure and Gamma and the Local Adaptation method.

To use Merge to HDR, you need to think about making some bracketed exposures. Ideally, the camera should be mounted on a tripod, but if your digital camera has fast burst capture with auto bracketing, you can often get away with hand holding the camera. However, the subject matter must be perfectly still, as you won't be able to merge photographs where the subject is moving. The exposure bracketing should be between 1 and 2 stops apart and the auto exposure set to aperture priority so that the aperture remains fixed and only the exposure times vary.

### Really still, still life

The Merge to HDR dialog can automatically align the images for you. But it is essential that everything else remains static. For example, the aperture must remain fixed, because if you bracket your images using the lens aperture, the depth of field will vary between each exposure. This will prevent you from achieving smooth, HDR merged images.

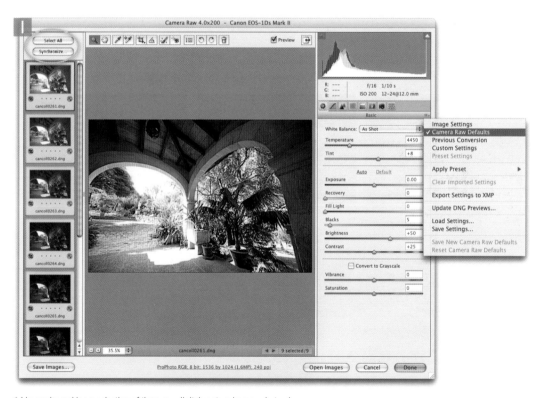

**1** I began by making a selection of three raw digital capture images shot using different time exposures set at one stop or more apart. It is important that all auto adjustments are switched off. In this example, I made sure that Camera Raw Defaults was applied to the first image and synchronized this setting across all the selected images.

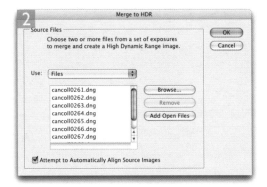

2 One can either go to the Bridge menu and choose Tools ⇨ Automate ⇨ Merge to HDR or go to the File menu in Photoshop and choose Automate ⇨ Merge to HDR. In this example I clicked on the Browse button and navigated to select all the images shown at Step 1. Ideally, you should plan to capture your HDR merge images with the camera firmly secured on a tripod and use a cable release. You will notice that there is an automatic alignment feature in the Merge to HDR dialog. This means that you might just get away shooting the HDR merge images with a hand-held camera using an auto bracket setting. Again, remember that the aperture must remain fixed and you only want to adjust the time exposure. Try setting the camera to the aperture priority exposure mode and the bracket function to shoot three or more exposures at 1–2 stops apart.

3 After you click OK, the Merge to HDR dialog will attempt to display the merged HDR image. This is impossible to do on a standard computer monitor, so set the slider beneath the histogram to preview 'slices' of the HDR image (I have shown here how the preview will look at three different slider settings). At this stage you can deselect or select the source image thumbnails on the left to see how this will affect the merged HDR picture.

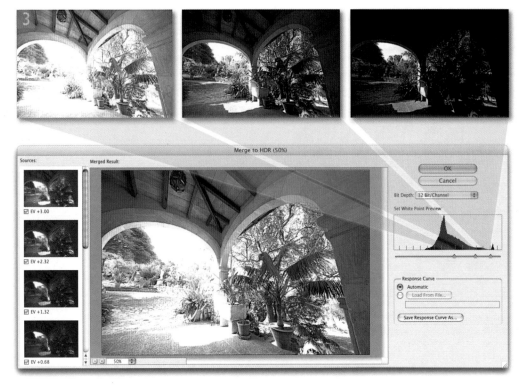

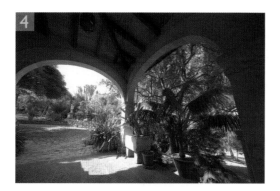

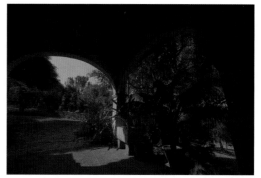

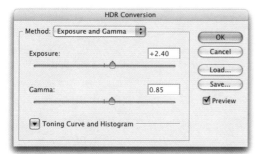

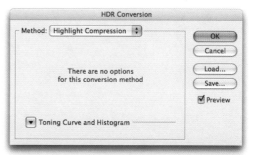

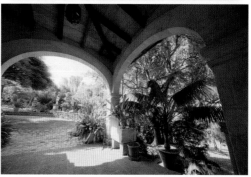

4 After you have chosen the desired images to blend as a merged HDR, you can click OK to render a 32-bit per channel HDR composite image, which can be saved as a Portable Bit Map (.pbm) master image. If you wish to convert this HDR format image and compress the high dynamic range to create a normal Photoshop image, then choose a lower bit depth in the Merge to HDR dialog and click OK. Or, if you are editing an opened 32-bit image, go to the Image menu and choose Mode ⇨ 16 bits (or 8 bits) per channel. This will pop the HDR conversion dialog shown here, which provides four methods for converting the image data. Exposure and Gamma has two slider controls. You can use the Gamma slider to (effectively) reduce or increase the contrast and the Exposure slider to compensate for the overall exposure brightness. These controls are rather basic, but they do allow you to create a usable conversion from the HDR image data, which of course can then be further modified using the image adjustment controls in Photoshop. The Highlight Compression simply compresses the highlights, preserving all the highlight detail. It can render good midtones and highlights at the expense of losing detail in the shadows. The Equalize Histogram option attempts to map the extreme highlight and shadow points to the normal contrast range of a low dynamic range Photoshop image, but this will usually make a rather blunt conversion.

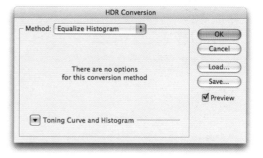

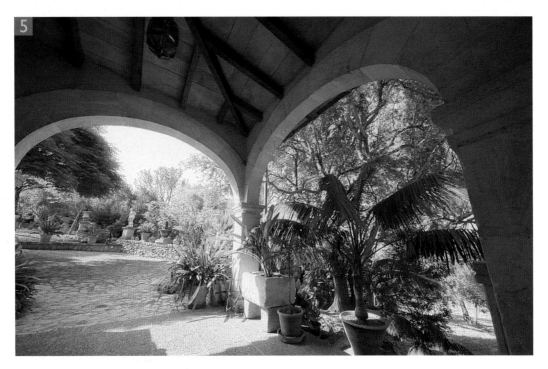

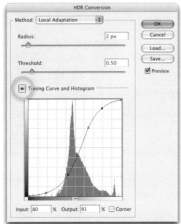

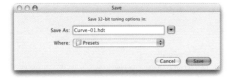

**5** The final method is called Local Adaptation. And you will notice that the controls here bear some similarity to those found in the Shadow/Highlight image adjustment dialog. It is best to start with a low Threshold setting of 0.5 and then adjust the Radius slider to determine the ideal radius setting that will produce a reasonably good looking conversion. You can then switch to adjusting the Threshold slider again to fine-tune the adjustment, but take care to make sure that you don't create any ugly haloes around the high contrast edges. If you now click on the disclosure triangle in the HDR Conversion dialog, this will display the Toning Curve and Histogram. You can now treat this as a Curves adjustment tool with which you can create a tone enhancing contrast curve that will be applied during the HDR conversion. This curve can also be saved as a Toning Curve preset for use with other HDR image conversions. Click OK and Photoshop will apply whichever conversion method you have selected and create a finished image like the one shown here. It has to be said that HDR merged images can sometimes look pretty freaky because the temptation is, as shown here, to try to squeeze a wide dynamic range scene into a low dynamic range print. Just because you can preserve a complete tonal range does not mean you must always represent it in print.

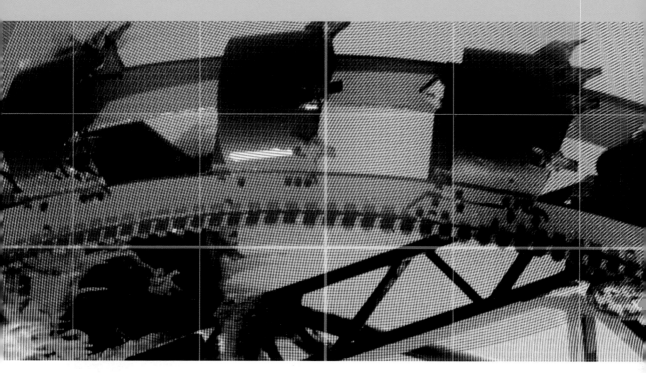

**Chapter 6**

# Fine-tuned Image Corrections

W e have so far looked at how to apply global edits to pixel images such as scanned TIFFs or JPEGs and the alternative route for processing raw images (as well as non-raw images) via Camera Raw. In Chapter 4, I mentioned that regardless of whether you used Camera Raw or not, it would still be important to master the use of the basic image adjustment tools such as Levels and Curves. This is because in this chapter we are now going to focus on how to fine-tune the appearance of an image. I will show you how to apply localized image corrections through the use of image adjustment layers and layer masks as well as some of the other ways you can make selective tone and color image adjustments.

## Screen redraw times

One potential drawback is that by having a lot of adjustment layers present this may slow down the screen preview. This slowness is not a RAM memory issue, but to do with the extra calculations that are required to redraw the pixels on the screen.

## The dodge and burn tools

Although there are tools in Photoshop called dodge and burn, they are not really suitable for the types of dodging and burning that photographers wish to achieve when working with Photoshop. This is not to say that the dodge and burn tools serve no use. They are just not ideal for this type of photographic retouching. I therefore recommend you use the adjustment layer method described here.

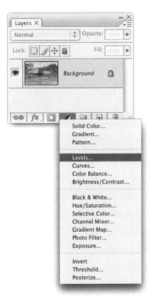

**Figure 6.1** The easiest way to add a new adjustment layer is to mouse down on the button shown here in the Layers palette.

# Adjustment layers

Nearly all the image adjustments you see listed in the Image ⇨ Adjustments menu can also be applied as adjustment layers via the Layer menu or Layers palette (see Figure 6.1). Adjustment layers offer the ability to apply multiple image adjustments and/or fills to an image and have these changes remain 'dynamic'. In other words, an adjustment layer is an image adjustment that can be revised at any time – adjustment layers enable the image adjustment processing to be deferred until the time when the image is flattened. Adjustment layers always have an active layer mask, which means that whenever an adjustment layer is active, you can paint or fill using black to selectively hide the adjustment effect, and paint or fill with white to reveal. Adjustment layers are savable in the Photoshop native, TIFF and PDF formats, they add very little to the overall file size and best of all, provide limitless opportunities to edit and revise the adjustments that are made to an image.

If you want to dodge or burn a photograph, i.e. make a localized correction to darken the sky or lighten someone's face, then the best way to do this is by using a masked adjustment layer. In the technique shown here, I added an adjustment layer that darkened the image as a whole and then filled the adjustment layer mask with black to hide the layer adjustment and painted (or in this case, partially filled) the adjustment layer mask with white to selectively apply the image adjustment layer to the photograph.

Working with adjustment layers is by far the best way to shade or lighten an image. This is because you have the freedom to re-edit the adjustment layer to make the adjustment lighter or darker. And you can edit the mask associated with the adjustment to redefine the areas you want to adjust. In the following example I show you how to use a Levels adjustment layer to create a darkening vignette, but you could also use a Curves adjustment layer. Either technique will work just as well here.

## Adjustment layer dodging

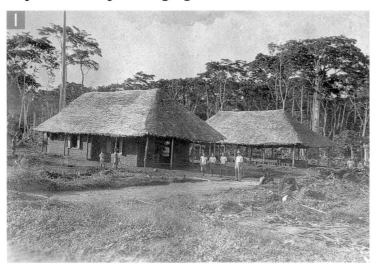

1 Here is a faded photograph from my father's archives when he lived and worked in what was then known as the Belgian Congo. You will notice that the photograph is slightly faded towards the edges and in need of a little repair work.

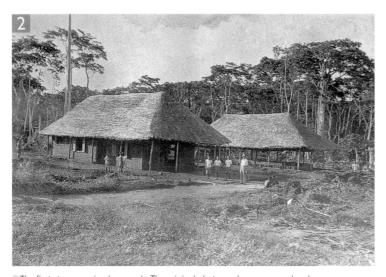

2 The first steps are simple enough. The original photograph was scanned and brought into Photoshop in 16-bits per channel mode. This enabled me to make some tonal corrections to enhance the contrast, minimizing the loss of levels information. I also used the clone stamp and spot healing brush to remove some of the dust and scratch marks.

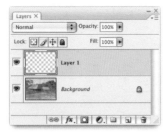

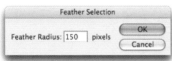

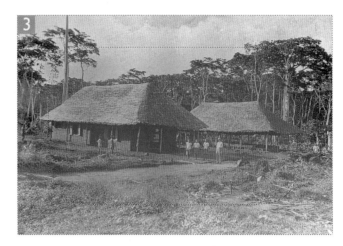

**3** I carried out all the retouching on an empty new layer and cloned some elements of the foreground to fill in the bottom left corner where there was some missing detail. I then wanted to apply a darkening vignette to burn in the corners. I made a rectangular selection and feathered the selection using Select ⇨ Feather, entering a feather radius of 150 pixels. I then inverted the selection (the selection is shown here as both a selection and Quick Mask).

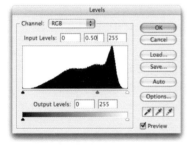

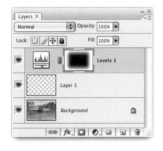

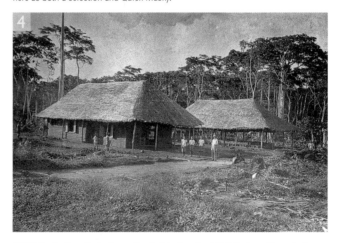

**4** With the feathered selection active, I clicked on the Add Adjustment Layer button in the Layers palette and selected a Levels adjustment. This did two things. It added a new Levels adjustment layer to the top of the layer stack and converted the active selection into a mask, masking the adjustment I was about to make. In this step you can see that I applied a Levels adjustment that darkened the outer edges.

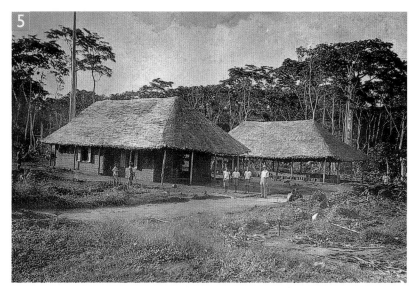

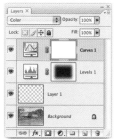

5 And finally, I added a Curves adjustment layer to create a warm sepia toning effect (see Chapter 9 to find out how to apply coloring effects using adjustment layers).

## Multiple adjustment layers

You can add as many adjustment layers as you like and preview how an image will look with combinations of two or more adjustment layers and see how these will affect an image before you apply them. You can have several adjustment layers in a file and choose to readjust the settings as many times as you want. It is possible therefore, to keep changing your mind and keep making changes to an adjustment layer without ever compromising the quality of the image.

The chief advantages of adjustment layers are therefore: the ability to defer image adjustment processing and the ability to edit the layers and make selective image adjustments. But when you add multiple adjustment layers to an image, it is wrong to assume that when flattened, the cumulative adjustments will somehow merge to become a single image adjustment. When you merge down a series of adjustment layers, Photoshop will apply them sequentially as if you had made a series of normal image adjustments.

### Grouped adjustments

If you place your image adjustment layers inside a layer group you can use the layer group visibility to turn multiple image adjustments on or off at once.

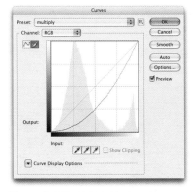

Figure 6.2 The Multiply blend mode calculated as a curve.

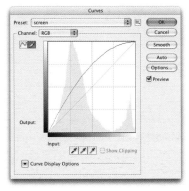

Figure 6.3 The Screen blend mode calculated as a curve.

## Blend mode adjustments

You can lighten or darken an image by adding an adjustment layer above the Background layer (or at the top of the layer stack) and simply change the blend mode to Screen or Multiply. You don't need to make any image adjustments, just add an adjustment layer (any will do) and change the layer blending mode. You could achieve the same type of result by duplicating a Background layer and changing the blend mode, but it is pointless to do so as you end up with an image that is twice the file size, whereas adding an adjustment layer will normally increase the file size by just a few kilobytes.

This technique of adding a neutral adjustment layer and changing the blending mode offers a useful shortcut route for lightening or darkening an image. On a side note here, a Multiply or Screen blend mode is effectively nothing more than a Curves adjustment setting. Figures 6.2 and 6.3 show the curves calculated from a Multiply and Screen mode adjustment at 100%.

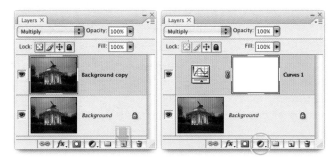

Figure 6.4 Here are two Layer palette views. In the one on the left I dragged the Background layer down to the New Layer palette button to make a duplicate layer and changed the layer blending mode from Normal to Multiply. When the image was saved, the file size doubled to 64 MB. In the example on the right, I added a neutral adjustment layer. In this example I clicked on the Add Adjustment layer button and selected Curves. A Curves dialog appeared and I clicked OK without making an adjustments to the curve. I then changed the adjustment layer blend mode from Normal to Multiply. Both methods produced identical results, but in the adjustment layer example, the file size was increased by just 57 kilobytes.

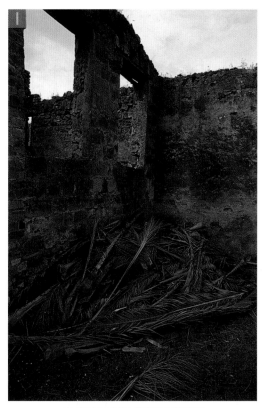

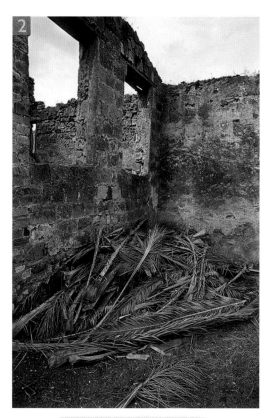

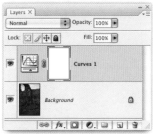

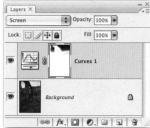

**1** You can use the layer blending modes as an alternative method to lighten or darken an image. In this example I had a dark image that needed to be made brighter. I went to the Layers palette and added a new adjustment layer. It does not particularly matter which. In this example I happened to choose Curves.

**2** When I changed the adjustment layer blending mode to Screen, the result was the same as if I had made a copy of the Background layer and set it to Screen blend mode. Screening will make the image lighter and Multiply will make the image darker. I then added a gradient to the adjustment layer using the default foreground/background colors. This partially hid the adjustment layer and retained some of the original darker tones at the top of the picture. I also used the paintbrush with white as the foreground color to edit the layer mask contents.

297

## Repeated adjustments warning

It is important to stress here that the color data in an image can easily become lost through repeated image adjustments. Pixel color information will progressively become lost through successive adjustments as the pixel values are rounded off. This is one reason why it is better to use adjustment layers, because you can keep revising these adjustments without damaging the photograph until you finally decide to flatten the image.

## *Luminosity and Color blending modes*

The problem with using Normal mode tone adjustments is that as you use Levels or Curves to adjust the tonal balance of a picture, the adjustments you make will simultaneously affect the color saturation as well. In some instances this might be quite desirable. For example, whenever you start off with a flat image that requires a major Levels adjustment, the process of optimizing the shadows and highlights will leave you with a nice bright-looking picture with increased contrast and more saturated color. This can be considered to be a good thing. But if you are carrying out a careful tone adjustment and want to manipulate the contrast or brightness without affecting the saturation, changing the blend mode to Luminosity can isolate an adjustment so that it only targets the luminosity values.

This is where using adjustment layers can come in useful, because you can easily switch the blend modes for any adjustment layer. In the example shown here, a curves adjustment was used to lighten the rocks and add more contrast to the sky. If this adjustment is carried out in the Normal mode, it will have the effect of increasing the color saturation as well. If the curve is applied using a Luminosity blend mode, the saturation will remain unaffected. As a matter of fact, I use the luminosity blend mode nearly every time I add a Levels or Curves adjustment layer to an image, especially if the tones and colors have already been optimized for contrast and color. This is because whenever I add localized corrections I definitely don't want these adjustments to further affect the saturation of the photograph.

Similarly, if you are using an image adjustment to alter the colors in a photograph, you will want the adjustment to target the color only and leave the luminance values as they are. So whenever I make a color correction using Levels, Curves, Hue/Saturation, or any other method, I will very often change the adjustment layer blend mode to Color.

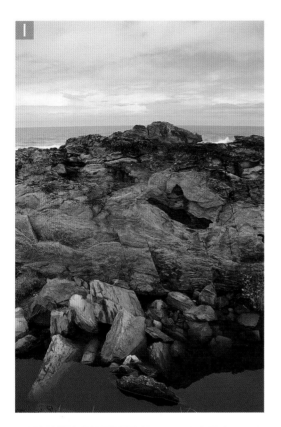

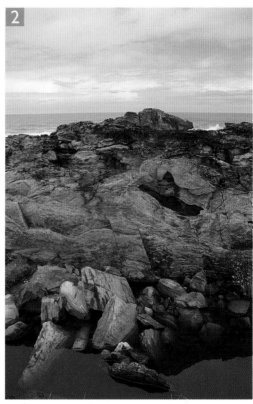

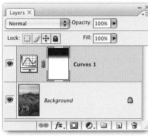

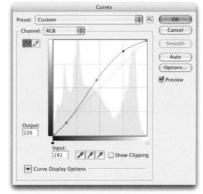

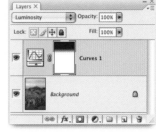

1 When you increase the contrast in an image using a Curves adjustment, you will also increase the color saturation.

2 In this example I applied a Curves adjustment as an adjustment layer and changed the blending mode to Luminosity. This effectively increased the contrast in the original scene, but without increasing the color saturation.

## Color Temperature

Color Temperature is a term that links the appearance of a black body object to its appearance at specific temperatures, measured in degrees Kelvin. Think of a piece of metal being heated in a furnace. At first it will glow red but as it gets hotter, it emits a yellow and then a white glow. Indoor tungsten lighting has a low color temperature, a more orange color. Sunlight has a higher color temperature and emits a bluer light.

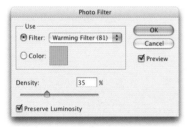

# Fine-tuned color adjustments

## Photo Filter

One of the advantages of shooting digitally is that most digital cameras will record a white balance reading at the time of capture and this information can be used to automatically process an image that is more or less color corrected. This can be done either in-camera or by using the 'As Shot' white balance setting in Camera Raw when processing a raw capture image. But if you are shooting with color film, then the only way to compensate for fluctuations in the color temperature of the lighting is to use the right film (daylight or tungsten balanced) and, if possible, use the appropriate color compensating filters.

But you can also crudely adjust the color balance in Photoshop by using the Photo Filter adjustment, which can be found in the Image ⇨ Adjustments menu and Layers palette image adjustment layer menu. The Photo Filter adjustment offers a preset range of filter colors but, if you click on the color button, you can select any color you like (after clicking on the color swatch) and adjust the Density to modify the filter's strength.

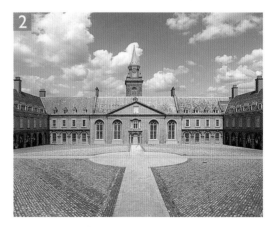

**1** This photograph was shot using 35 mm transparency daylight film, balanced for a color temperature of 5500 K. The color temperature was clearly higher when the photograph was taken, hence the blue cast.

**2** To improve the photograph, I chose Image ⇨ Adjustments ⇨ Photo Filter. By mousing down in the Filter pop-up menu, I could select a preset filter color to apply to the image. In this case, I chose a Warming Filter (81) at a density setting of 35%.

## Arbitrary Map mode curve editing

If you click on the Arbitrary Map mode button in the Curves dialog, you can sketch in the grid area with the pencil cursor to create a freehand curve map shape. The initial results are likely to be quite repulsive, but click on the Smooth button a few times and the curve becomes less jagged and the tonal transitions will then become more gentle. Another example of an Arbitrary Map mode curves adjustment can be found in Chapter 9 on darkroom effects.

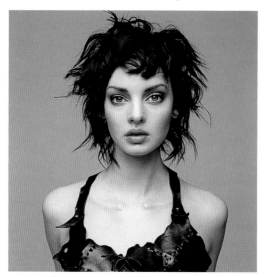
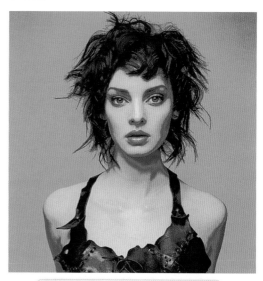
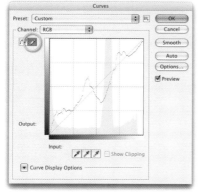
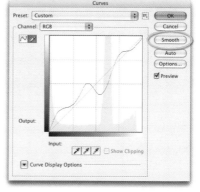

Figure 6.5 If you click on the Arbitrary Map button in the Curves dialog, you can draw a freehand curve shape like the one shown here. Click on the Smooth button to produce a gentler effect.

Client: Anita Cox Salon. Model: Sorcha, Bookings.

## Matching color and lighting across images

The Match Color image adjustment can be used to sample and match the colors from one image to another or match the color of a specific object from another shot in the same series. For example, one can use Match Color to ensure that an important product is always reproduced the same in different shots throughout a publication. Or you can use it to sample and match colors within the same image. Let me illustrate the last example by taking a photograph used for a ballet poster and match the colors from the dress of the ballerina with the pyjamas of the two dancers.

The Match Color adjustment works by taking the image data from the sample image or sample selection area and converting this to a separate high-precision perceptual color

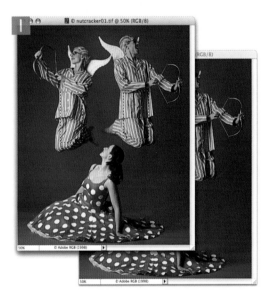

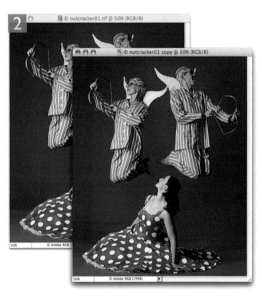

**1** The first step is to create a duplicate of the master image. This is because one needs to have an image to sample colors from and an image to apply the correction to. In the original image window I have made a marquee selection of the pyjama colors that I want to sample from in the original image window.

**2** In the duplicate window I made a selection of the ballerina's blue dress. We now have an active selection in both window views. I selected the copy image window, the one with the ballerina selection and chose Image ⇨ Adjustments ⇨ Match Color.

Photograph: Eric Richmond.

space made up of Luminance and two color components. Match Color aims to transfer the image statistics taken from the source image or selection area and then apply them to the active target image or selection area so that eventually the colors in the target will match the colors sampled from the source.

Match Color can also work quite effectively if you have two images taken of the same subject and you simply want to match the lighting color between the two images. It is less good at matching dissimilar photographs, because the reference source needs to have something in common with the target.

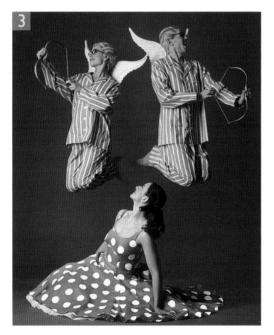

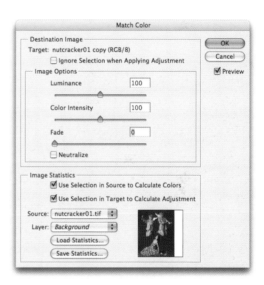

3 There are two sections in the Match Color dialog. The upper section allows you to control the color conversion settings. The lower section is where we can select the source for the Color Match conversion. I moused down and selected the original image window as the source. Notice that we have the two options above checked here. Use Selection in Source to Calculate Colors and Use Selection in Target to Calculate Adjustment. If both these boxes are checked you will then see a preview of the calculated adjustment in the target document window. When I did this the color of the dress matched the color of the pyjamas.

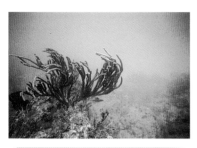

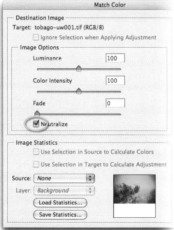

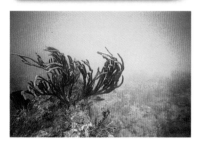

Figure 6.6 The Match Color image adjustment is also a useful image correction tool in its own right. In this extreme example, I used the Match Color adjustment with the Neutralize option checked (circled), to help reduce the color cast in this underwater photograph.

## Match Color settings

You can also save Match Color statistics as Match Color settings (which will have a .sta extension) so that you can load saved Match Color statistic settings for use on other images. After you have established the Source and Target image settings, the Match Color Image Options will allow you to modify the Color Match result. The Luminance and Color Intensity sliders will prove useful here in allowing you to fade the amount of the adjustment or compensate the color intensity to get an ideal color match between two images. As you will have seen in the previous step-by-step example, it often helps to make a selection of the areas of interest in both the source and target images. In the case of a source image, you will need to check the Use Selection in Source to Calculate Colors option. In the case of a destination image, you will need to check the Use Selection in Target to Calculate Adjustment option.

## Match Color auto adjustments

The Match Color image adjustment can also function as an auto color correction tool for images that have a heavy color cast. And as you can see in Figure 6.6, Match Color can be quite effective at removing a deep blue/cyan cast from an underwater photograph. If you use Match Color in this way, I would suggest that you either fade the Match Color adjustment using the Color blend mode or create a duplicate of the Background layer, apply Match Color to this layer and set the layer blend mode to Color. Note that using Match Color to auto-correct images with heavy casts can result in images that have less overall saturation, so you may sometimes want to add a Hue/Saturation layer to boost the saturation a little.

## Coloring effects with Match Color

One can also use the Match Color adjustment in a creative way to sample colors from a source image, such as one that is already open in Photoshop, and apply these to another completely different image. This technique can produce interesting but often weird and unusual-looking results.

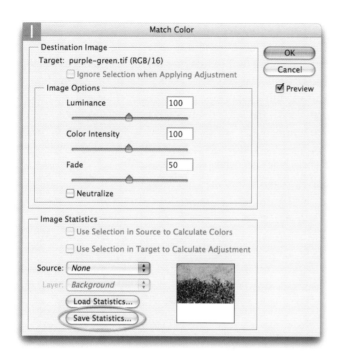

### Creating a Color Match library

If you like the idea of using this technique then you should perhaps consider creating your own library of Match Color statistics settings. Open up a bunch of images and save out different Match Color settings which you can then call upon at any time to apply to an image or a selection within an image.

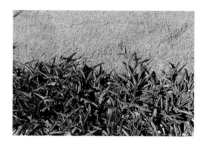

**purple-green.sta**

1 Match Color can be used as a tool for applying creative color effects. I opened an image in Photoshop, chose Image ⇨ Adjustments ⇨ Match Color and clicked on the Save Statistics button to save a Match Color statistics setting.

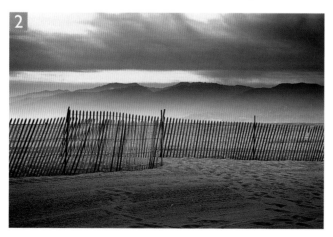

2 I then opened the image shown on page 165, opened the Match Color dialog again and clicked on the Load Statistics... button. I selected the previously saved Match Color setting, set the Fade to 50% and clicked OK.

## Color replacement tool

The color replacement tool is suitable for use as a color aware painting tool for making localized color changes. The steps shown here were done using the Color mode. This modifies the pixels, replacing the color and saturation with that of the foreground color, but the Hue and Saturation modes are also useful if you want to modify these color components individually.

Sampling: Once

Sampling: Continuous     Sampling: Background swatch

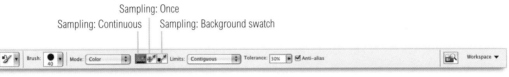

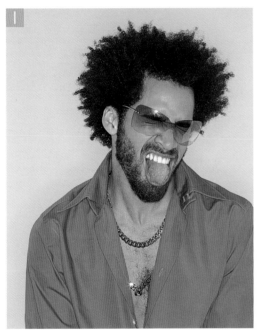

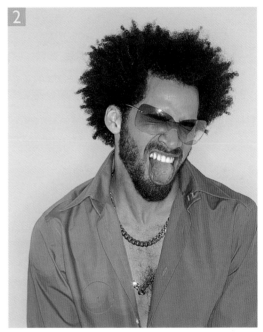

1 There are various ways one can change the color of an object. The color replacement tool offers a simple easy-to-use solution. I began by selecting it from the Tools palette (you will find it grouped with the paint brush and pencil tool).

2 I wanted to change the color of the purple shirt. I double-clicked the Foreground color in the Tools palette. This opened the Color Picker dialog and I selected a dark yellow as the new foreground color. The color replacement brush was set to work in Color mode with the sampling set to Once, which meant that the brush would start replacing the color based on the color of the pixels I clicked on first.

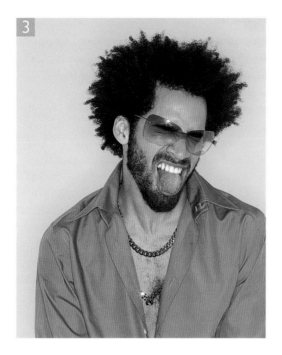

Client: Anita Cox salon.

**3** The color replacement tool limits in the Options palette were set to Contiguous. This meant that I was able to use the brush to click and paint over the left-hand side of the shirt in one action. Because the shirt was undone, there were no contiguous pixels to allow me to carry on painting the other side of the shirt. So I clicked again and painted with the brush to complete the color replacement.

As was explained in Chapter 4, you can also use the Hue/Saturation image adjustment to make selective color corrections. In this example, I added a new Hue/Saturation image adjustment layer, selected Reds from the Edit pop-up menu and adjusted the red component of the underlying image such that the skin tones were made more yellow and less saturated.

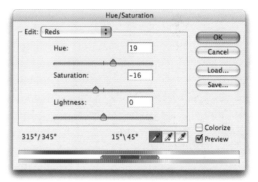

In Sample Once mode, the color replacement will be based on where you first click and only the pixels within the specified tolerance will be modified. As with the magic wand, the tolerance setting determines the tonal range of pixels that will be modified. In Continuous mode, the sample source is updated as you drag through the image. In some instances this mode can produce smoother results, but as you drag take care that the cursor cross-hair doesn't stray outside the area you are modifying.

Limits can be set for the color replacement too. In this example the Contiguous mode limits the tool's application to the pixels that are within the tolerance range and are also adjacent to each other. In Discontiguous mode you can paint beyond isolated groups of pixels. If you refer back to the forest images on page 175, you would need to use the color replacement brush in Discontiguous mode in order to bring about a similar color transformation of all the leaves.

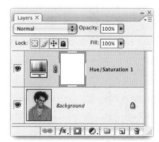

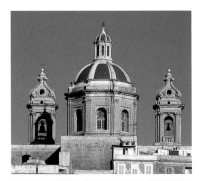

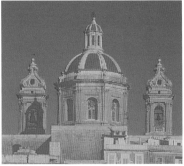

## Color Range

The Color Range is not an image adjustment tool, but a color-based selection tool. Where the magic wand creates selections solely based on luminosity, the Color Range option creates selections that are based on color values which are similar to the sample pixel color. And the beauty of Color Range is that you can dynamically adjust the tolerance amount within the dialog. The only drawback is that a Color Range selection tool can only be used to make discontiguous selections. But it is possible to make a selection first of the area you wish to focus on and then choose Color Range to make a color range selection within the selection area.

To make a Color Range selection, first choose Select ⇨ Color Range. To add a color to a Color Range selection, select the Add to Sample eyedropper and click in the image window to add. To subtract from a selection, click on the Subtract from Sample eyedropper and click in the image to select the colors you want to remove from the selection. And then adjust the Fuzziness setting to adjust the tolerance of the selection to increase or decrease the number of pixels that will be selected. The selection preview in the document window can be None (the default) or Quick Mask (as shown in Figure 6.8) or Grayscale or Matte color. The Grayscale is a really useful preview mode if you want to get a nice large view in the document window of what the Color Range/mask will look like.

Among other things, you can use the Color Range command to make a selection based on out-of-gamut colors. This means you can use Color Range to make a selection of all those 'illegal' RGB colors outside the CMYK gamut and apply corrections to these pixels only. This task is made easier if you feather the selection slightly and hide the selection edges (View ⇨ Hide Extras). Then choose View ⇨ Gamut Warning. Adjustments can be made using the Selective Color or Hue/Saturation commands. Local areas may also be corrected with the sponge tool set to Desaturate.

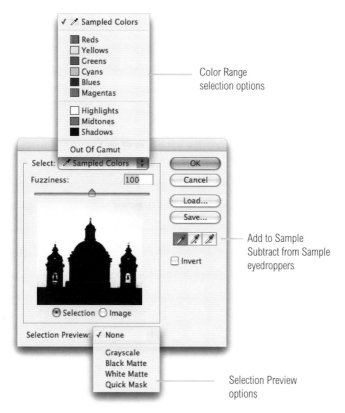

Color Range
selection options

Add to Sample
Subtract from Sample
eyedroppers

Selection Preview
options

**Figure 6.8** The Color Range dialog with expanded menus showing the full range of options that are available. The Grayscale preview mode is especially useful if you find the small Color Range dialog preview too small.

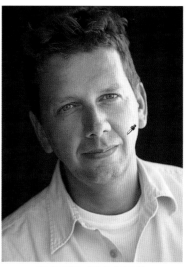

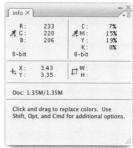

**Figure 6.9** When you are retouching a portrait, you can use the Info palette CMYK readout numbers to help judge if the skin tones are the right color. Set the palette options to display RGB and CMYK readouts. Using the eyedropper, Caucasian skin tones should have roughly a third or a quarter as much cyan as magenta and slightly more yellow than magenta. Black skin tones should be denser, have the same proportion of cyan to magenta, but usually a higher amount of yellow than magenta and also some black.

## Replace Color

The Replace Color command is really like a combination of the Select ⇨ Color Range and Hue/Saturation command. With Replace Color, you can select a color or range of colors, adjust the fuzziness of your selection and apply the Hue/Saturation adjustments to those selected pixels only. Alas, the selection made this way is not savable. The Replace Color command has its uses. For example, if you want to correct out-of-gamut colors, before converting to CMYK, then you could use the Replace Color adjustment to adjust the out-of-gamut preview image.

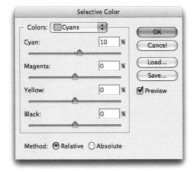

Figure 6.10 The Selective Color dialog.

## Selective Color

The Selective Color command is more suited for adjusting CMYK images. It allows you to selectively fine-tune the color balance in the additive and subtractive primaries, blacks, neutrals and whites. Unlike the Hue/Saturation image adjustment, the Selective Color adjustment has fixed settings for selecting the reds, greens, blues, cyans, etc. Selective Color may sometimes be useful for tweaking CMYK images, but you are otherwise better off using the Hue/Saturation image adjustment when editing RGB images. A Relative percentage change will proportionally add or subtract. So if you have a cyan value that is currently 40%, adding a Relative 10% will equal 44%. Adding an Absolute 10% percentage change will make the new value 50%.

## Adjusting out-of-gamut colors

If the colors in an image appear oversaturated and likely to clip when converted to CMYK, try creating a new window view of the image and choose View ⇨ Gamut Warning. Then use the Hue/Saturation adjustment. As you bring the colors back into gamut, the gamut warning will disappear, indicating the image colors are now in gamut.

The problem with the gamut warning is the way it displays the out-of-gamut colors as in or out using a solid color. A color that is only slightly out of gamut will be highlighted the same as a color that is extremely out of gamut. For this reason, I prefer to use the soft proofing in Photoshop on a good quality display to judge if an image will print successfully.

## The essential adjustment tools

As you can see, there are a lot of tools to choose from in the Image ⇨ Adjustments menu. But a lot of these are essentially doing the same thing. In many cases all you are using is a different type of interface to manipulate the image pixels. And you will also have learnt which ones are in fact the most essential. There are still a few image adjustment tools that I have not had a chance to focus on yet, but will do so over the next few chapters.

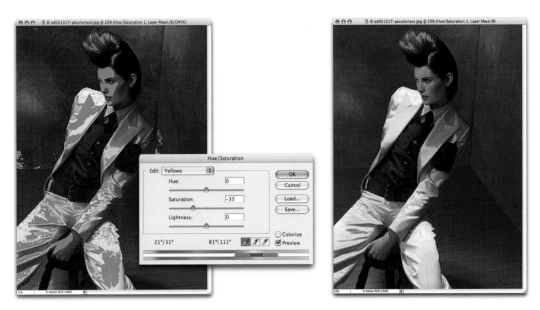

**Figure 6.11** Out-of-gamut color correction can be achieved using the Hue/Saturation adjustment to selectively (and smoothly) adjust the out-of-gamut colors. The Gamut warning shown here will also help indicate which colors remain out of gamut. Gamut warning tells you what is out of gamut, but not by 'how much'. It is therefore of limited use. Soft proofing, which is covered in Chapter 13, is a better solution.

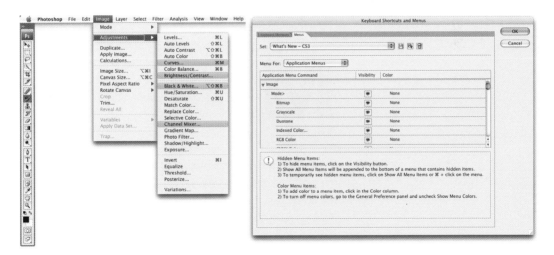

**Figure 6.12** You can customize the way the Photoshop menus are displayed. You can use the Edit menu to open the Keyboard Shortcuts and Menus dialog shown here and create your own custom menu layouts in which important tools are color coded and less important items can be hidden. In this example I went to the Window ⇨ Workspace menu and selected the What's new in Photoshop CS3 Workspace setting.

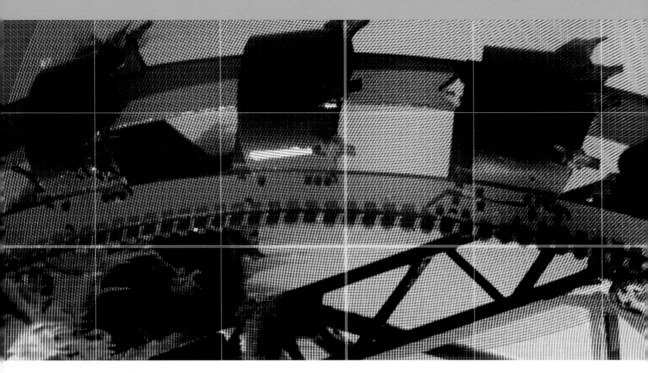

**Chapter 7**

# Image Retouching

**M**ost photographers will be drawn to
Photoshop's potential as a tool for
retouching photographs. As my colleague
Jeff Schewe likes to say: 'you know why
Photoshop is so successful? Because reality sucks!'
Well, that's Jeff's viewpoint, but then he does come
from a background in advertising. Other photographers,
like Stephen Johnson, are wary of doing anything to a
photograph that might change or misrepresent what they
photographed originally. The techniques described in this
chapter will teach you some of the basic techniques you
will need to learn, such as how to spot a photograph and
remove artifacts like dust spots, before going on to explore
some of the more advanced techniques that can be used to
clean up and repair damaged photographs.

## Basic cloning methods

The clone stamp tool and healing brush are the most useful tools to apply at the beginning of a retouch session. Both tools work in a similar way. Hold down ⌥ alt and click to select a source point to clone from. Release the ⌥ alt key and move the cursor over to the point where you want to clone to and click or drag with the mouse. If you have the tool set to aligned mode, this will establish a fixed relationship between the source and destination points. If the tool is set to non-aligned mode then the source point will remain fixed, returning to that spot after each application of the clone stamp brush. I usually find it more convenient to use the clone stamp tool in aligned mode and the healing brush in non-aligned mode. This is because when I use the clone stamp I like to preserve the relationship between the source and destination points, apply a few clones, then sample a new source point and continue cloning other parts of the photograph.

Whenever I clone over an area where there is a gentle change in tonal gradation, it will be almost impossible to disguise my retouching work, unless the point I am sampling from and the destination point match exactly in hue and lightness. So in these situations I will be better off using the healing brush. And for healing brush work I usually prefer to use the non-aligned mode because this will allow me to choose a source point that contains optimum information with which to repair a particular section of the photograph and I can keep referencing the same source point as I apply the healing brush.

As with all the other painting tools, you can change the brush size, shape and opacity to suit your needs. When you are working with the painting tools you may find it useful working with different combinations of brush settings, but this doesn't necessarily always apply when working with the clone stamp and healing brush. For clone stamp work you will typically want to stick to using fine to medium-sized brushes with a soft or semi-soft edge, and for healing brush work you need to always use a hard edged brush shape.

### All Layers option

The All Layers and Current & Below options are useful if you want to make sure that your retouching is always stored on a separate layer. With the All Layers option in use, you can carry out all your spotting or healing brush retouching on an empty new layer and the All Layers option will sample from the layers below and above the current layer. If you select the Current & Below option, Photoshop will only sample from the layers below the current layer. This is useful because it means you can have an active adjustment layer in place above the layer you are doing the retouching on and it won't affect the pixel sampling.

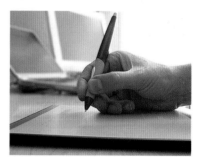

**Figure 7.1** If you are carrying out any type of retouching work which relies on the use of the paint tools, a pressure sensitive tablet and pen, such as the Wacom™ shown here, are an absolute must.

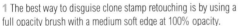

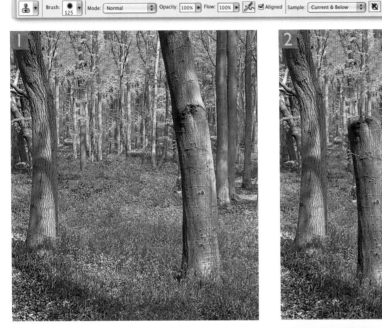

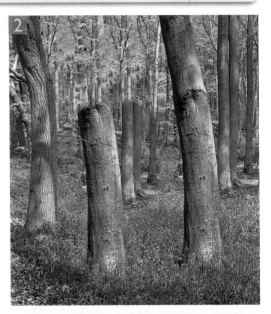

**1** The best way to disguise clone stamp retouching is by using a full opacity brush with a medium soft edge at 100% opacity.

**2** By adding a new layer above the Background layer I was able to keep all the clone retouching on a separate layer. The Aligned box is normally checked by default in the Options palette. I used the ⌥ *alt* key to set the sample point at the base of the tree trunk on the left and then moused down in the image to the left of the source point and dragged upwards to paint a cloned copy of the tree trunk. Photoshop will retain this relationship for all subsequent brush strokes with the clone stamp tool until a new source and destination are created.

**3** When the Current & Below option is selected in the Options palette, Photoshop will sample data from the current layer and all layers below as if they were a single flattened layer.

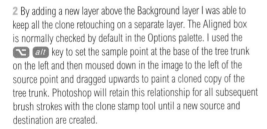

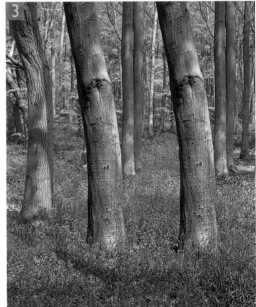

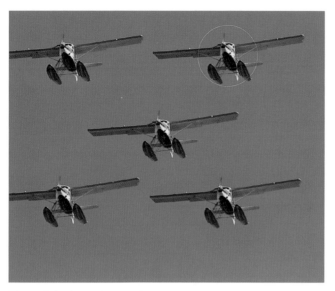

**Figure 7.2** When you have the clone stamp tool selected and the Aligned box in the tool options is unchecked, the source point will remain static and each application of the clone stamp will make a copy of the image data from the same original source point.

## Clone stamp brush settings

I mostly always leave the opacity set to 100%. Cloning at less than full opacity usually leads to tell-tale evidence of cloning. Where the film grain in the photograph is visible, this can lead to a faint overlapping grain structure, making the retouched area look slightly blurred or misregistered. When smoothing out skin tone shadows or blemishes, I will occasionally switch to an opacity of 50% or less. Retouching light soft detailed areas means I can get away with this. Otherwise stick to 100%. And for similar reasons, you don't want the clone stamp to have too soft an edge; ideally make the clone stamp brush shape have a slightly harder edge.

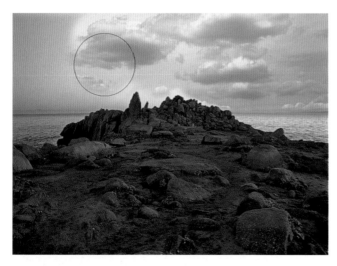

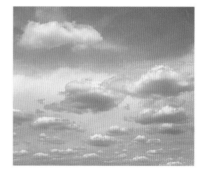

**Figure 7.3** You can sample the sky from one image window and copy it to another separate image using the clone stamp. Just ⌥ *alt*-click with the clone stamp in the source (sky) image, then select the other image window and click to establish a cloning relationship between the source and destination images.

## Replacing film grain

You may encounter a problem if the photographic original contains noticeable film grain. To counteract this it may help to apply a small amount of noise after you have applied the Dust & Scratches filter. Add enough noise to match the grain of the original (usually around 2–3%). This will enable you to better disguise the history brush retouching.

## Alternative history brush spotting technique

This spotting method has evolved from a technique that was first described by Russell Brown, Senior Creative Director of the Adobe Photoshop team. It revolves around using the Remove Dust & Scratches filter, which is found in the Filter ➪ Noise submenu. If this filter is applied globally to the whole image, you will end up with a very soft-looking result. You are actually only meant to apply this filter selectively to the damaged portions of a picture in Photoshop. The technique shown here has the advantage of applying the filtered information via the history brush such that only the pixels which are considered too dark or too light will be painted out. This modified approach to working with the Dust & Scratches filter avoids destroying the tonal values in the rest of the picture.

As you can see, this technique works well when you have a picture that is very badly damaged and where using the clone stamp would be a very tedious process. What is really clever is the way that the Lighten and Darken blend modes are used to target which pixels are repaired from the stored Dust & Scratches history state.

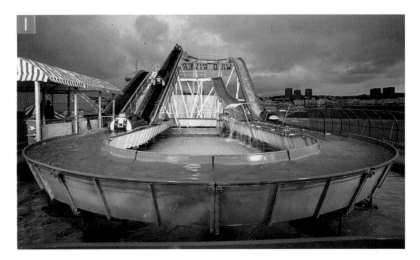

**1** This photograph serves as a good example with which to demonstrate the history brush spotting technique, as there are a lot of hair and scratch marks that are clearly visible in this picture.

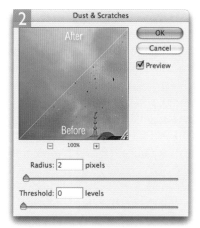

**2** I went to the Filter menu and chose Noise ⇨ Dust & Scratches. I checked the Filter dialog preview and adjusted the Amount and Threshold settings until I could verify that most of the dust marks would be removed. I clicked OK to apply the filter to the image.

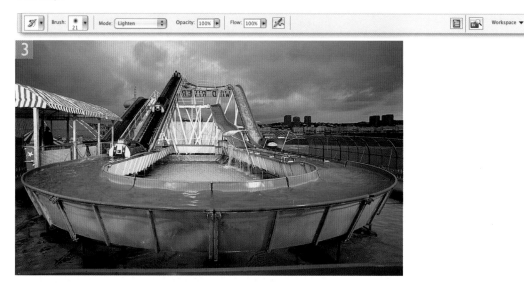

**3** I then went to the History palette and clicked on the previous unfiltered image history state, but set the history brush source to paint from the filtered version. I selected the history brush and changed the history brush blending mode in the tool Options bar to Lighten. As I painted over the dark spots, the history brush would lighten only those pixels that were darker than the sampled history state. All other pixels remained unchanged. I continued using the history brush in this way. To remove the light spots, I changed the tool blending mode to Darken and painted with the history brush as before, to remove the light blemish marks.

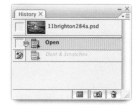

## Healing brush settings

The default mode for the healing brush has the Aligned box unchecked. This makes sense, because when you are using the healing brush to retouch texture from one area to another, you ideally want to sample from the same source point.

## Heal using 'All Layers'

When the Current & Below or All Layers option is selected in the healing brush tool options you can carry out all the healing brush work on a separate layer.

## Healing brush

The healing brush is used in the same way as the clone stamp tool, although it is important to stress that the healing brush is more than just a super clone stamp and it has its own unique characteristics. So although it is similar to the clone stamp, you will need to take these differences into account and adapt the way you work with it. To begin with, you establish a sample point by [⌥] [alt]-clicking on the portion of the image you wish to sample from. Release the [⌥] [alt] key and move the cursor over to the point where you want to clone to and click or drag with the mouse to carry out the healing brush retouching.

The healing brush performs its magic by sampling the texture from the source point and blending the sampled texture with the color and luminosity of the pixels that surround the destination point. For the healing brush to work it reads the pixels within a feathered radius that is up to 10% outside the perimeter of the healing brush cursor area. By reading the pixels that are outside the brush cursor area, the healing brush is able (in most cases) to calculate a smooth transition of color and luminosity within the area that is being painted. It is for these reasons that there is no need to use a soft edged brush, since you will always get more controlled results through using a hard edged brush.

Once you understand the fundamental principles behind the workings of the healing brush, you will come to understand why it is that the healing brush will sometimes fail to work as expected. You see, if the healing brush is applied too close to an edge where there is a sudden shift in tonal lightness then the healing brush will attempt to create a blend with what is immediately outside the healing brush area. So when you retouch with the healing brush you need to be mindful of this phenomenon, but there are things you can do to address this. For example, you can create a selection that defines the area you are about to start the retouching on and constrain the healing brush work to inside the selection area.

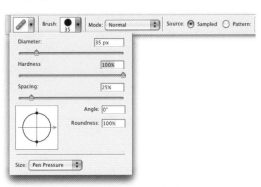

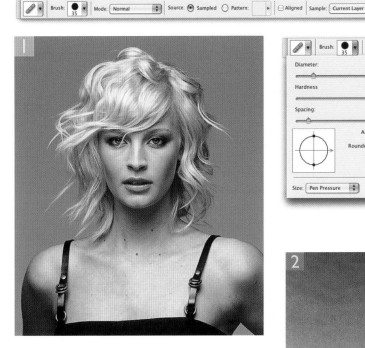

**1** The healing brush retouching can be carried out on the Background layer, on a copied Background layer or an empty new layer. In this example, I selected the healing brush from the Tools palette and edited the brush style to create a hard edged brush. The brush blending mode should be Normal, the Source radio button checked and ideally the Aligned box left unchecked.

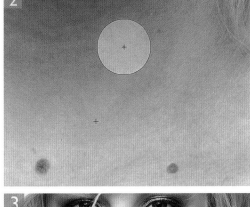

**2** To use the healing brush, ⌥ alt-click to define the source point, which in this example was a clean area of skin texture. You are now ready to retouch with the healing brush. In the example shown here, I simply clicked on the blemishes to remove them with the healing brush. If you are using a pressure sensitive tablet as an input device, then the default brush dynamics will be size sensitive. You can use light pressure to paint with a small brush, and use heavier pressure to get a full-sized brush.

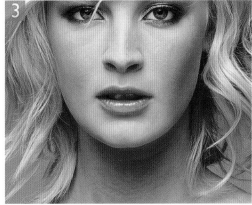

**3** I continued using the healing brush to complete the skin tone retouching. In this example I sampled one pixel source point for the chest and neck areas and another to retouch the face.

Client: Thomas McMillan.
Model: Sophie Boeson @ Models One.

## Better healing edges

Since the healing brush is blending around the outside edge, you can improve the healing effect by increasing the outer circumference. The following technique came via Russell Brown, who informs me that he was shown how to do this by an attendee at one of his seminars.

If you change the healing brush to an elliptical shape, you will tend to produce a more broken-up edge to your healing work and this will sometimes produce an improved healing blend. There are two explanations I have for why this works. Firstly, a narrow elliptical brush will inevitably produce a longer perimeter to the painting edge. This means that more pixels are likely to be sampled when calculating the blend. The second thing you will notice is that when the healing brush is more elliptical, there is a randomness to the angle of the brush. Try changing the shape of the brush the way I describe. As you start using an elliptical-shaped brush, you will see what I mean.

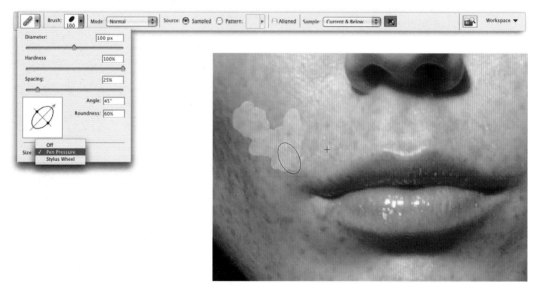

**Figure 7.4** To adjust the shape and hardness of the healing brush, select the healing brush tool and mouse down on the brush options in the tool Options bar. Set the hardness to 100% and drag the elliptical handles to make the brush shape more elliptical. Notice also that if you are using a Wacom tablet or other pressure sensitive input device, the brush size is linked by default to the pen pressure.

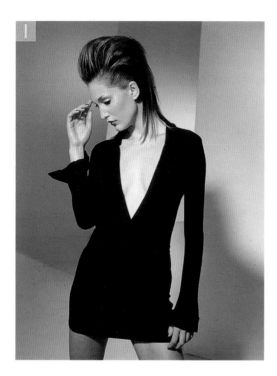

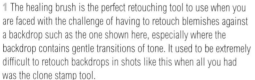

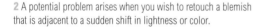

**1** The healing brush is the perfect retouching tool to use when you are faced with the challenge of having to retouch blemishes against a backdrop such as the one shown here, especially where the backdrop contains gentle transitions of tone. It used to be extremely difficult to retouch backdrops in shots like this when all you had was the clone stamp tool.

**2** A potential problem arises when you wish to retouch a blemish that is adjacent to a sudden shift in lightness or color.

**3** In this picture you can see that even if you use the healing brush with a small hard edged brush, the brush may pick up the darker tones of the model's dress and you will get to see the ugly-looking shading shown here.

**4** The answer to the problem is to make a preselection of the area you wish to heal (with maybe some minimal feathering) and thereby restrict the extent to which the healing brush tool analyzes the surrounding pixels.

Client: Anita Cox. Model: Steph at IMG.

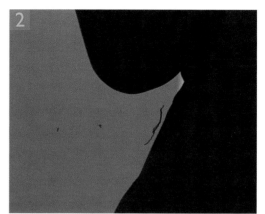

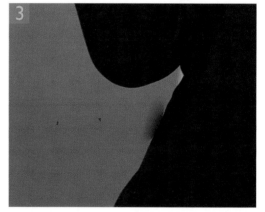

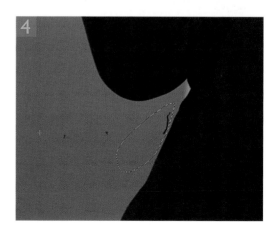

## Default healing tool

The spot healing brush is the default healing tool in Photoshop, so the first time you select it and try to use the ⌥ alt keys to establish a source point to sample from, you will be shown a warning dialog explaining there is no need to create a sample source with this tool. It will offer you the option to switch to using the normal healing brush instead.

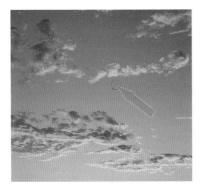

**Figure 7.5** In Proximity Match mode, the spot healing brush works by searching automatically to find the best pixels to sample from to carry out a repair. It is a good idea when using this tool to retouch larger areas, and for the brush direction to be coming from the side that contains the most suitable texture to make the sample. This will give the spot healing brush a better clue as to where to sample from.

## Spot healing brush

The spot healing brush was added in Photoshop CS2 and is a healing tool that was originally found in Photoshop Elements 3.0. The spot healing brush may not be quite as versatile as the healing brush, but in many ways is a lot easier to use. All you have to do is select the spot healing brush and click on the marks or blemishes you wish to remove and the spot healing brush will automatically sample the replacement pixel data from around the area you are trying to heal.

The spot healing tool has two basic modes of operation. The Proximity Match mode is analyzing the data, around the area where you are painting, to identify the best area to sample the pixel information from. It then uses the pixel data that has been sampled in this way to replace the defective pixels beneath where you are painting. You can use the spot healing brush to click away and zap small blemishes, but when you are repairing larger areas in a picture you will usually obtain better results if the brush size used is smaller than the defective area. And because the brush is intelligently looking around for the good pixel data to sample from, it is best to apply brush strokes that drag inwards from the side where the best source data exists (see Figure 7.5).

The Create Texture mode works in a slightly different fashion. The spot healing tool will read in the data surrounding the area you are attempting to repair. As you do this it will generate a texture pattern from the sampled data. So the main difference is that Proximity Match is repairing and blending with actual pixels, while Create Texture is repairing and blending using a texture pattern that has been generated on-the-fly.

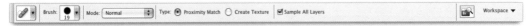

**Figure 7.6** The spot healing brush Options palette.

### Clone and healing sample options

The sample options in Photoshop CS3 allow you to choose how the pixels are sampled whenever you use the clone stamp or healing brushes. The Current Layer option will sample the contents of the current layer only, ignoring all other layers. The Current & Below option (see Figure 7.7) will sample the current layer and all layers below, ignoring all the layers above it. The All option will sample all visible layers in the layer stack, including those that are above the current layer. But if the Ignore adjustment layers button (circled) is turned on, Photoshop will ignore the effect adjustment layers are having on the image.

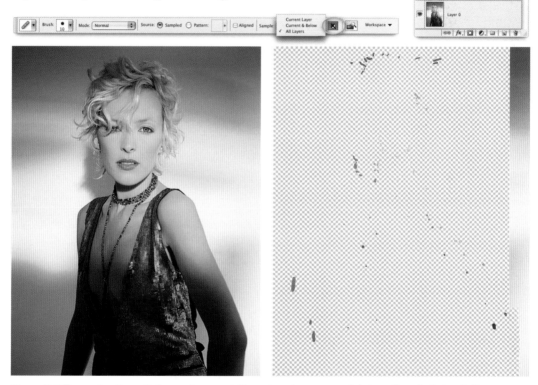

**Figure 7.7** The sample options will allow you to carry out all your clone stamp and healing brush work to an empty new layer. The advantage of this is that you can keep all your retouching work separate and leave the original Background layer untouched. In this example, the All Layers option allowed me to sample from layers above and below. Because the Ignore Adjustment Layers option was checked. Photoshop ignored the effect any adjustment layers would have on the sampled pixels.

Hair: James Bacon for Andrew Collinge Hairdressing. Finalist 'North West' British Hairdressing Awards 2006.
Model: Grethe @ FM.

## Overlay blend modes

You can adjust the opacity of the Clone Source overlay and change the blend mode as well. In some instances you may find it useful to work with the Difference blend mode at 100%. The Difference blend mode will show a solid black preview when identical pixels are in register.

## *Clone Source palette*

The Clone Source palette is useful for photographic retouching mainly because it allows you to see a preview of the alignment of the pixels that you are about to paint with. All the other features, such as the multiple sample points, are really of more use for people working in video editing, where it is desirable to store multiple clone sources when you want to clone in exact registration from one frame to another across several images in a sequence.

**1** Here is a photograph in which there is a litter bin that I wish to remove. But the tricky thing here is that the bin is just in front of a circular alcove, and this would normally make it less easy to remove. But not so if you use the new Clone Source palette controls.

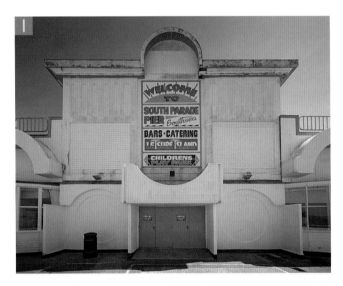

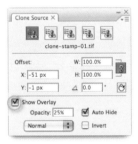

**2** To start with, I wanted to remove the bottom of the bin. This could be done normally by placing the source point for the clone stamp on the edge of the black line and estimating where to click with the clone stamp so that you can continue painting along the line 'in register'. By using the Clone Source palette, I can now switch on the Show Overlay option and adjust the opacity, so that with the Auto Hide option turned on as well, when I release the mouse, I get to see a ghost image preview of how the pixels will be painted at the destination point. This takes away all the guesswork and makes it much easier to paint with the clone stamp in perfect alignment with the underlying image.

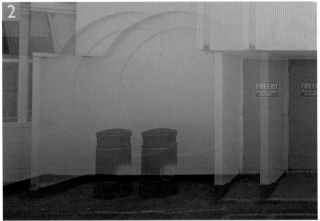

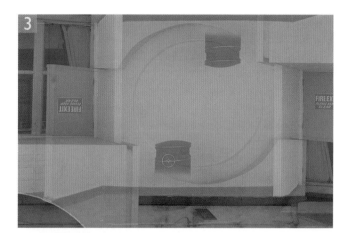

**3** I now switched tools and selected the healing brush. And this time I went to the Clone Source palette and set the clone source angle to be 180° relative to the destination. This meant that when I sampled using the pixels from the top right corner of the curve, the preview showed a 180° rotated preview of where the pixels would be painted at the destination point. Again, the overlay was very important because I could use it to precisely align the preview with the image below, so that the edge of the circle was precisely aligned.

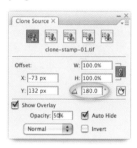

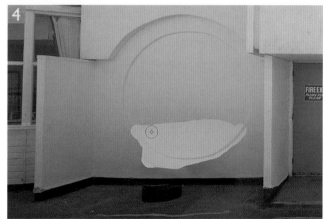

**4** Here is a screen shot showing the healing brush in action. Because I had the Auto Hide option checked still, the overlay was temporarily hidden as I painted.

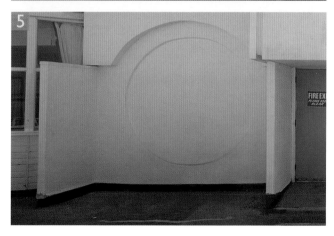

**5** And here is the final result, in which I only had to carry out some minor extra retouching in order to tidy up the remaining parts of the picture.

## Source and Destination modes

In Destination mode you can drag the selection area with the patch tool to a new destination point and Photoshop will perform a healing blend calculation to merge the sampled patch area with the underlying pixels in the new area of the image. In Source mode you can drag the selection area with the patch tool to a new destination point to select the pixels that will replace those in the original source selection area. The Use Pattern button in the Options bar for the patch tool will let you fill a selected area with a preset pattern using a healing type blend.

## Patch tool

The patch tool uses the same complex algorithm as the healing brush to carry out its blend calculations, but the patch tool uses selection-defined areas instead of a brush. When the patch tool is selected, it initially operates in a lasso selection mode that can be used to define the area to patch from or patch to. For example, you can hold down the ⌥ *alt* key to temporarily convert the tool to become a polygonal lasso tool with which to draw straight line selection edges. You don't actually need the patch tool to define the selection; any selection tool or selection method can be used to prepare a patch selection. Once you have made a selection, select the patch tool to proceed to the next stage. As with the healing brushes, the patch tool has to work with either the Background layer or a copied pixel layer. One of the nice features of the patch tool is the way that the selection area in Source and Destination mode will preview the image as you drag to define the patch selection.

**1** The patch tool works in a way that is similar to the healing brush. Using the picture opposite, I can show you how the patch tool can be used in Source mode to cover up the metal staples that are holding the large pot together. When you select the patch tool you can use it just like the lasso tool to loosely define a selection area. For example, you can use the ⌥ *alt* modifier key to temporarily switch from free form lasso to polygonal lasso selection drawing mode. Or you can use any other preferred selection method (it really doesn't matter at this stage) as you prepare the image for patching.

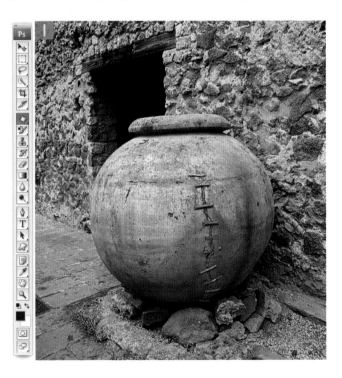

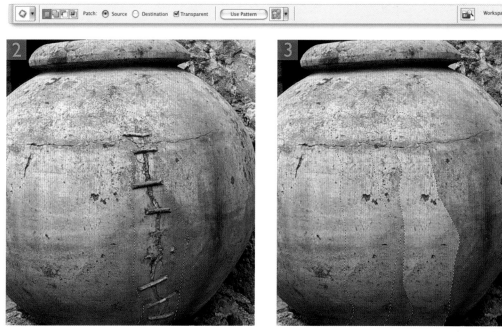

2 Having defined the selection for the area I wanted to patch, I made sure that the patch tool was selected in the Tools palette and dragged inside the selection to relocate it on an area of texture on the pot that I wished to sample from.

3 As I released the mouse, Photoshop began to calculate a healing blend, analyzing the pixels from the source area I had just defined and used these to merge seamlessly with the pixels in the original selection area.

4 If the patch/healing process has been successful, you should see an almost completely smooth join. The pixels that you select to be sampled from in the patch process will adjust their luminosity and color to blend with the pixels in the original defined area, to match the lighting and shade, etc. However, you won't always get a 100% perfectly convincing result. In the example used here, I made a couple of attempts at patching the staples before finding a patch selection that worked well. Furthermore, you have to beware of any repeating patterns giving away the fact that the image has been cloned. I finished retouching this photograph by applying a few healing brush strokes to remove those tell-tale signs.

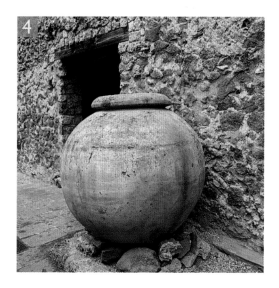

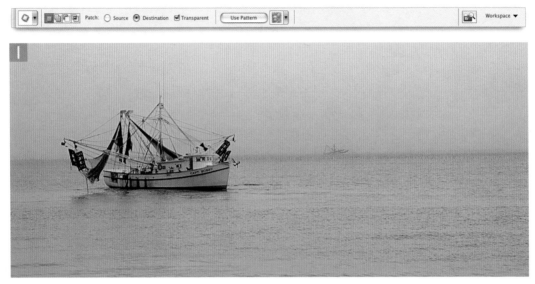

1 The patch tool uses the same blending calculations as the healing brush to perform its blend calculations. In this image I wanted to demonstrate how you can use the patch tool in Destination mode to make a duplicate of this fishing boat.

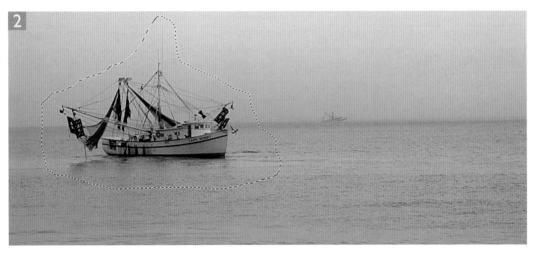

2 I used the patch tool to define a rough selection outline of the boat. In use, the patch tool is just like the lasso tool; you can use the ⌥ alt modifier key to draw straight line points. If you prefer you can use any other selection tool such as the magic wand or convert a pen path into a selection.

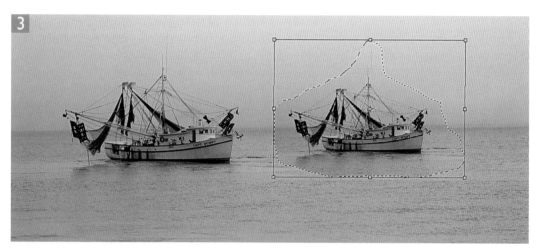

**3** I made sure that Destination was selected in the Options bar. When the selection was complete, I used ⌘ ⌥ T ctrl alt T, which copied the pixel selection and added the free transform bounding box to the selected pixels. I then dragged the transform to a new location. In this example I dragged the transform across to the right, aligned the center point to the horizon and held down the Shift ⌥ Shift alt keys to scale the transform down in size to make the second boat smaller and appear to be further away in the distance.

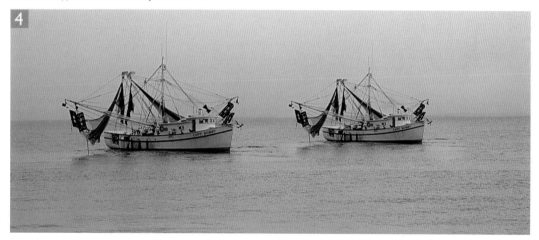

**4** I then hit Enter to OK the transformation. After that I moused down with the patch tool inside the selection area and moved the selection very slightly. If you follow these steps precisely and release the copied selection, the patch tool will calculate how to merge the dropped selection with the underlying pixels. This will produce a smooth-looking blend with the surrounding sky and sea area. The patch tool works well with a subject such as this, because the sea and sky provide a fairly even backdrop for the pixels to blend smoothly.

Photograph: Thomas Fahey.

## Healing brush modes

The healing brush offers a choice of blending modes. The Replace mode is identical to the clone stamp tool, except it allows you to merge film grain more reliably and smoothly around the edges of your brush strokes. The other healing brush blending modes can produce different results, but in my opinion they won't actually improve upon the ability of the healing brush in Normal mode, since the healing brush is already utilizing a special form of image blending to perform its magic.

## Healing brush strategies

You can also use a Pattern preset as the source for the healing brush or patch tool by choosing a preloaded preset or creating one of your own. The Filter ➪ Pattern Maker is ideal for this purpose as you can sample from just a small area of useful texture in an image and use the Pattern Maker to create a randomly generated pattern source that can be used to apply a smoothly blended texture over a larger area of the picture using the healing brush. The following example illustrates how you can use the healing brush and patch tool to solve a rather more complex retouching problem. Although the healing brush and patch tool are natural candidates to use here, I needed to plan carefully how they would be used, as I also needed to rely on the clone stamp tool to do some of the preparation work, in particular where the edges of the selection to be healed extend to the edge of the document bounds.

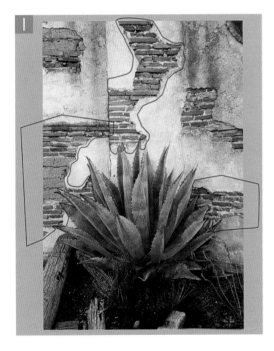

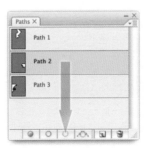

1 Let us consider how we would go about covering up all the exposed bricks in the picture opposite, so as to match the remaining plaster work. Some of these areas are too large to use the patch tool in one operation. Notice how I prepared three paths, to define some of the areas to be repaired, that closely followed the outline of the cactus leaves. These will be used in the following steps. To begin with though, I converted Path 2 into a selection by dragging the Path 2 palette icon down to the Make Selection button in the Paths palette.

**2** I then used this selection to copy the pixels to make a new layer. Choose: Layer ⇨ New ⇨ Layer via Copy (⌘ J ctrl J). I clicked on the Lock Transparency box in the Layers palette and selected the clone stamp, and was then able to clone some of the pixels in the image to provide a wall textured border edge on the left and the right. I did this in order to provide the healing brush or patch tool some edge pixels to work with. If you don't do this, Photoshop will try to create a patch blend that merges with the cactus leaf colors.

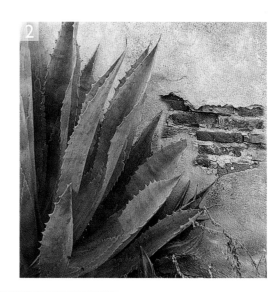

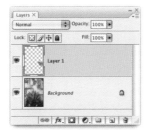

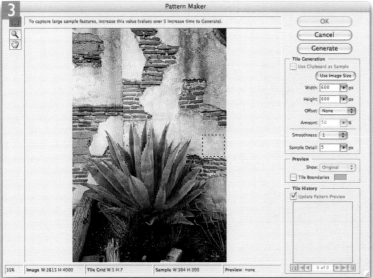

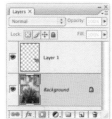

**3** I could have tried selecting the healing brush and attempted to sample some of the plaster texture to fill in the remaining gap. In this and the other sections I wanted to repair, the area to be covered up was so large that I decided to create a new pattern based on a small selection of the image. I made the Background layer active and chose Pattern Maker from the Filter menu. I then marquee selected a small area as shown here.

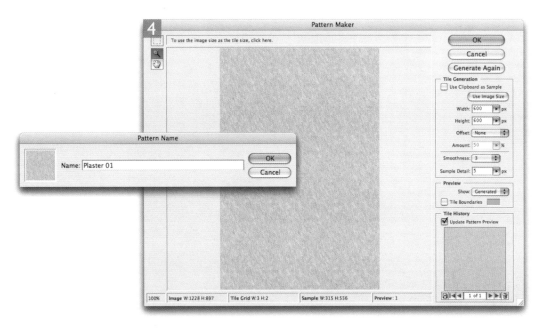

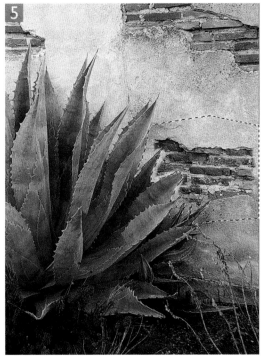

**4** I made the tile area fairly large (600 pixels square in this example) and I set the Smoothness setting to 3. If I clicked on the Generate button at the top of the dialog, the Pattern Maker would generate a randomized pattern that is a wraparound texture, the result of which is previewed in the dialog. I didn't need to click OK as this would apply the texture as a fill to the current image. Instead I clicked on the Save Preset Pattern button at the bottom of the dialog. Once I had named the new pattern, it would become appended to the other Pattern presets and it was then safe for me to click the Cancel button to return to the main image.

**5** I then activated Layer 1 again, selected the patch tool and drew a rough selection of the plaster wall area I had just prepared as shown in this close-up image.

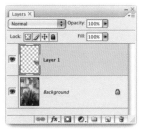

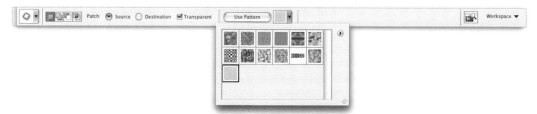

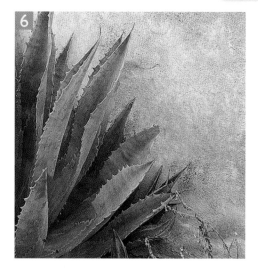

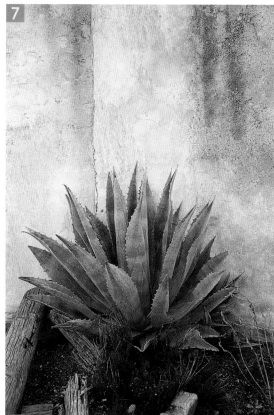

**6** I selected this new custom pattern in the patch tool options, then clicked the Use Pattern button. As you can see, Photoshop was able to calculate a perfectly smooth blend, and this was achieved using a texture pattern that had been synthesized in Photoshop.

**7** I repeated these steps on the other parts of the photograph so that eventually I ended up with the finished result shown here.

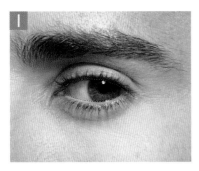

1 To add contrast to the eyes, select the lasso tool and draw a selection around the outline of the eyes (hold down **Shift** to add to a selection). To feather the selection choose Select ⇨ Feather and enter a radius of 2 pixels.

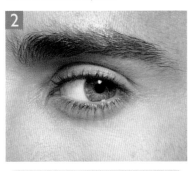

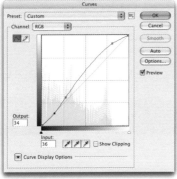

2 Apply either a Curves adjustment or add a Curves adjustment layer and draw a lightening curve to add lightness to the eyes but keep the tone in the dark areas of the pupils the same.

## Retouching portraits

The eyes are always the center of attention in a portrait. If the eyes are sharp then the rest of the photograph will appear to be in focus, even if you have a shallow depth of field and the eyes are the only thing that are sharp!

So what do you do if the eyes don't look sharp? I sometimes like to use the PhotoKit Sharpener plug-in (a demo is available on the DVD) to apply a gentle capture sharpen to the image at the beginning of a retouching session. And if that is not enough, I will then also add a creative sharpener (with the same plug-in). This is returned in the form of a masked layer. If you don't wish to use the Sharpener plug-in, the other alternative is to copy the Background layer to make a new layer, apply a heavier than normal sharpen and add a layer mask using ⬚ *alt* and clicking on the Make layer mask to hide the layer contents. Then paint with a white brush on the layer mask to selectively reveal the extra-sharpened layer. In some cases you can resort to using even more extreme measures to enhance the sharpness. You can actually draw the sharpening edges yourself. This is described in the step-by-step tutorial on the page opposite.

## Adding lightness and contrast to the eyes

If you lighten the eyes too much they will look unnatural. Worse still, if you overdo the lightening and make them too white, the whites of the eyes will appear without any detail on the page and print as paper white. I use a fairly simple method for lightening the eyes which is based on making a feathered selection of the whole eye area and apply a Curves adjustment to the eyes. Now you could just select the whites of the eyes and lighten these areas on their own. That works too, but I find that by applying a Curves adjustment to the whole eye, I can anchor some points in the curve to make the iris go darker or lighter. Or, I can add more contrast in the shadows to make the pupils darker. This is just as effective as selecting the whites only but you have simultaneous control over the lightness of the iris and pupils.

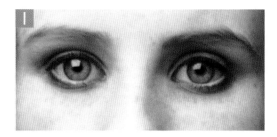

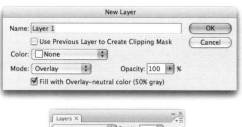

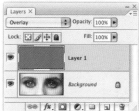

1 You can sharpen the eyes manually by adding a neutral Overlay blend layer. In this example, I held down the ⌥ *alt* key as I clicked the New Layer button in the Layers palette. This applied a new layer via the New Layer dialog box. I chose Overlay as the blend mode and then checked the box that says Fill with Overlay-neutral color (50% gray).

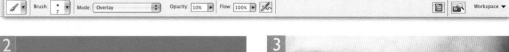

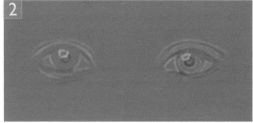

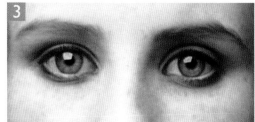

2 To sharpen the eyes, I made sure the neutral gray layer was the one that was active. I selected the paintbrush tool and changed the brush blend mode to Overlay and reduced the Opacity to 10%. I then used a Wacom pen and tablet to gently apply paint strokes to the neutral gray layer, following around the contours of the eyes. I used black as the foreground color to add emphasis to the dark outlines such as the edges of the pupils. I then exchanged the foreground color to white (which can also be done by hitting the ⓧ key) to add emphasis to the light areas such as the catch light reflection in the eye.

    Alternatively, you could use the dodge and burn tools to add contrast to the features. Select the burn tool and set the Range to Midtones. Use the burn tool as before to darken the dark line edges and hold down the ⌥ *alt* key to make the burn tool temporarily become a dodge tool and use this to lighten the lighter edges.

3 You won't normally see the neutral gray layer as shown in the previous illustration (to take the screen shot I turned off the visibility of the Background layer). But what you should see as you paint on this layer is a gradual increase in apparent sharpness to the eyes and other parts of a picture you wish to enhance using this technique.

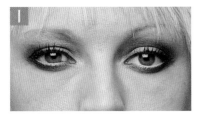

1 In this close-up view you can see that the model's right eye has some burst blood vessels. Fortunately the model is looking straight to camera and we can easily make a repair by copying across pixel data from the good eye.

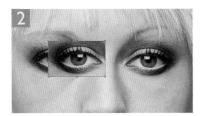

2 I made a selection of the other eye and used the ⌘ J ctrl J shortcut to copy as a new layer and then used Edit ⇨ Transform ⇨ Flip Horizontal to match it to the other eye.

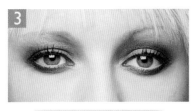

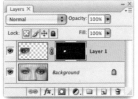

3 I ⌥ alt -clicked the Add Layer Mask button to add a filled layer mask to 'hide all' on the layer. I selected the paintbrush and with white as the foreground color gradually painted back in the good eye layer to repair the bloodshot area.

## Repair work using a copied selection

Another way to repair an image is to copy a selection of pixels sampled from another part of the picture or a separate image even. Back in the mists of time before there were layers in Photoshop, you could duplicate a selection to make it a temporary layer by ⌥ alt dragging inside a selection with the move tool. Well, you can still do this in Photoshop, but overall you will usually find it more practical to copy the selection contents as a new layer. To do this, make a selection and then use Layer ⇨ New ⇨ Layer via Copy, or use the keyboard shortcut ⌘ J ctrl J. This will copy the selection contents as a new layer. Once you have duplicated the selection contents as a new layer you can use the copied layer to cover up another portion of the image by dragging it across with the move tool and transforming the layer as necessary.

In the step-by-step example that is shown here on the left, I wanted to cover up the burst blood vessels in the model's right eye. I made a simple rectangular selection over the good eye, copied the contents to a new layer and transformed the new layer by flipping it horizontally. The add layer mask step is important. Note that when you add a layer mask and fill or paint with black, you are not deleting the image data but are merely hiding the layer contents. In this example the layer mask allowed me to initially hide all of the copied layer and then selectively paint back in, with white as the foreground color, the bits that I wanted to reveal. In the example shown here, I could paint in over the eye to replace the damaged areas only. One of the things you have to be careful of when retouching the eyes in this way is to make sure that you preserve the catch light reflections in the eyes, because if you were to flip the catch lights as well, your subject could end up looking cross-eyed!

## Removing stray hairs

As a fashion and beauty photographer I usually do all I can to make sure the hair is looking good at the shooting stage. But there will always be some stray hairs remaining. I do like to use the healing brush as much as possible. But as I pointed out earlier, the healing brush is not an ideal tool when painting up against areas where there is a sudden change in tone. In most instances, I find it preferable to retouch the hair with the clone stamp tool. I use a Wacom pen stylus and a custom setting where the brush size is a round brush with a size of around 10 pixels with opacity and brush size linked to the amount of pressure applied. I have found this to be a useful brush setting for cloning hair strands and painting new strands of hair. The brush size can then be modified and made larger or smaller using the square bracket keys on the keyboard. Using the clone stamp tool in this way I can clone out cross-hairs, remove intricate strands of hair and paint new strands that match the texture and color of the existing hair.

If you are retouching fine strands of hair, pay careful attention to where the strands of hair originate, the direction they are flowing in and where they meet up with or cross over other strands of hair. A clumsy retoucher may simply lop off loose strands without regard to whether this leaves the hair looking natural or not. At times, it is like sorting through a mass of electric cable, making sure that you don't cut the hair off at the root and leave the rest of the hair just floating there! When I am asked to tidy up fluffy loose hairs, I approach the task in gradual stages, gradually thinning out the hair rather than cutting it all off. This is because it would look unnatural to see a soft textured hairstyle suddenly change into a perfectly smooth outline. To keep the hair looking real I try to leave some stray hairs in the picture. Sometimes I will begin by erasing the loose hairs around the hair outline and actually paint in some loose stray hairs afterwards (using the clone stamp tool configuration in Figure 7.8). Doing so enables me to obtain a more natural look to the hair.

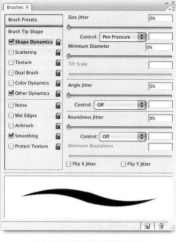

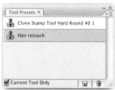

**Figure 7.8** When using the clone stamp tool to retouch hair strands, I use a special preset setting. The brush size is around 10 pixels. And the Shape Dynamics and Other Dynamics (Opacity) are linked to the pen pressure of the Wacom pen.

## Coloring hair roots

Here is a two-step process that can help correct dark roots in a picture. Firstly, make a copy of the Background layer. This allows you to fade out or selectively mask the work that is done on this layer. Select the paintbrush and choose the Color blend mode. Hold down the ⌥ *alt* keys to sample a color from the lighter hair area. Now paint over the darker hair roots using the paintbrush in Color mode. This painting step applies the correct color to the roots. To make the hair look lighter, change the paintbrush blend mode to Soft Light. Sample a light hair color again and paint over the roots once more with the paintbrush tool. This should do a good job of coloring the hair without destroying the contrast in the hair texture. To restore contrast, add an empty new layer mask. Reset the paintbrush blend mode back to Normal and apply fine black paint strokes to the layer mask to hide parts of the new layer.

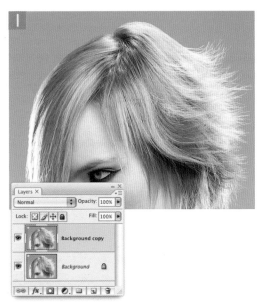

**1** To disguise the hair roots that were showing, I duplicated the Background layer, selected the brush tool and changed the brush blending mode to Overlay.

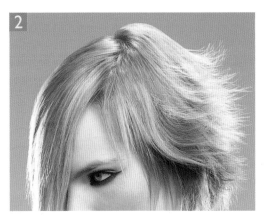

**2** I held down the ⌥ *alt* key to sample a color from some of the lighter hair area and gently painted over the dark hair areas where the roots were showing most. This colorizes the hair. I then changed the brush blend mode to Color and painted some more, gently adding more lightness to the hair. It sometimes helps to add a layer mask to the Background copy layer and paint thin brush strokes to restore some of the hair shadows and achieve a smoother blend with the rest of the hair.

## Red eye correction

Red eye in portraits is caused when the flash source is used too close to the lens axis and the pupils of the eye are wide open. One way to avoid this happening is to set your camera flash to Red eye mode (if available). The camera will usually pop a single or short series of flashes just before firing the main camera flash exposure. Failing that, the new red eye tool can be used to correct the picture in Photoshop afterwards.

The Pupil Size setting should be adjusted depending on the pixel dimensions of the image you are working on. And the Darken amount can be adjusted according to the lightness of the red eye in the shot, although you will find that the default settings tend to work just fine in the majority of cases. But now in Photoshop CS3 of course, Camera Raw features a really good red eye removal tool (see page 281) that in many ways is more sophisticated than the one described here.

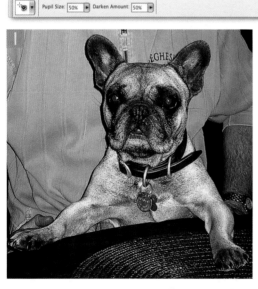

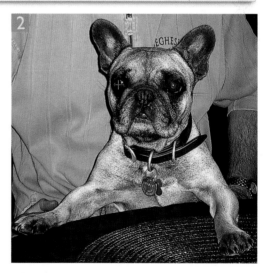

1 The red eye tool is very easy to use and effective at removing red eye from portraits shot with a direct flash.

2 The default tool settings should be OK to start with. To use the tool just click on the red area of the eye. Photoshop will automatically calculate how to remove the red cast and darken the pupils.

## Disguise your retouching

The basic rule of retouching should be to disguise your work so that whatever corrections are made to a photograph, it is not immediately apparent that the picture has been retouched. If you are working for a fashion client they are usually looking for image perfection. Although I may sometimes employ a lot of Photoshop wizardry in order to satisfy the client, I feel it is important to fade out the retouching and let some of the original blemishes show through. My preference is to retouch the skin enough to clean up blemishes and smooth the tonal shading, and do this without hiding the underlying skin texture. I achieve this by nearly always reducing the opacity of the layer that contains all the retouching work.

## Beauty retouching

I have included in this chapter a mixture of Photoshop retouching techniques that would be useful for photographers and have selected a few specific Photoshop retouching tasks that demand a special approach, like how to retouch areas where there is not enough information to clone from. In the following example, I show how to retouch using the paint brush and where it is important to carefully disguise your retouching.

There are many different types of skin and the skin texture varies a lot on different parts of the body. If you examine the face, neck, arms, etc., in close-up you will notice that each area has a different skin texture. For example, the skin under the eyes will have a coarse goose bump texture. The forehead will generally be very smooth (apart from any lines). The cheeks will also be smooth, but slightly pitted with pores. And if you are retouching a female portrait you may notice fine downy hair. As you move down towards the neck area the texture of the skin changes to become more coarse again. It is important to pay close attention and carefully choose your source point for the skin whenever you are cloning or healing a portrait.

## Brush blending modes

The painting and editing tools can be applied using a variety of blending modes which are identical to those you come across in layers and channel operations. You could try experimenting with all the different tool blending mode combinations but I wouldn't advise you do so, as it is unlikely you will ever want to use them all. I reckon that the following modes are probably the most useful: Screen, Multiply, Lighten, Darken and Color when combined with the paint brush, blur and gradient tools.

Painting in Color mode has many uses. Artists who use Photoshop to colorize scanned line art drawings will regularly use the Color and other blending modes as they work. Painting using the Color blending mode is also ideal for hand coloring a black and white photograph.

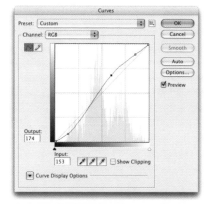

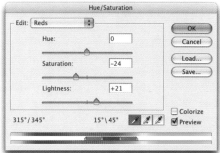

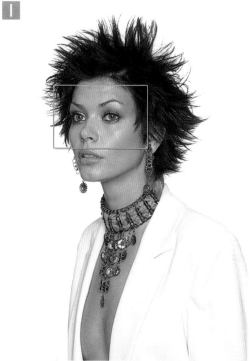

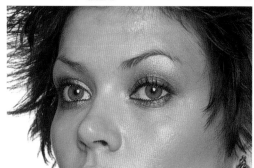

**1** The first thing to retouch here are the eyes, which I nearly always want to lighten to some extent. I used the lasso tool to draw around the outline of the eyes. This selection does not have to be perfect – a reasonably steady hand is all you need! After that I went to the Select menu and chose Feather... and entered a feather radius of 1 or 2 pixels. After making the selection and feathering it, I moused down on the Adjustment Layer button at the bottom of the Layers palette and selected Curves. This will automatically add a Curves adjustment layer with a layer mask based on the selection just made. I normally apply a curve that will lighten the whites of the eyes and also increase the contrast between the whites and the iris. I also added a Hue/Saturation adjustment layer to target the Reds and gently reduce the saturation of the red veins in the eyes. I then 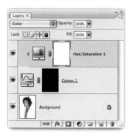 *alt*-clicked between this and the Curves adjustment layer in the Layers palette to create a clipping group with the eye lightening adjustment layer. When you create a clipping group in the Layers palette, the clipped layer will be displayed indented with a downward pointing arrow (as shown in the Layers palette screen shot right).

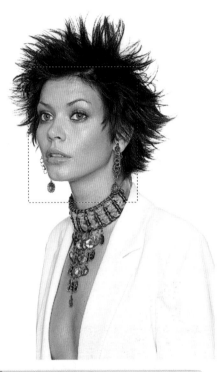

**2** I next wanted to concentrate on retouching the face. This was done by marqueeing the head and making a new layer via copy (⌘ J / ctrl J). This enabled me to modify the pixels on a separate layer, without permanently altering the background layer. Mistakes are easily made and this way I can always revert to the before version and compare the retouched layer with the original version of the image.

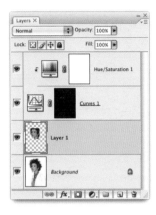

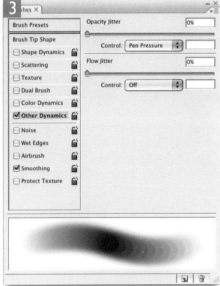

**3** I do much of my beauty retouching using the brush tool on this copied layer. I prefer to use a pressure sensitive stylus and pad such as the Wacom™ Intuos™, because this allows me a much finer degree of control than I can get with a normal mouse. Whenever you select a painting type tool you can select from a number of options from the Brushes palette that will enable you to determine what aspects of the brush behavior will be governed by the way you use the pressure sensitive stylus. Photoshop will not just be aware of the amount of pressure you apply with the stylus. If you are using the Wacom™ Intuos™, Photoshop is now able to respond to input information such as the barrel rotation of the stylus, the angle of tilt or the movement of the thumbwheel (if you have one). In the example shown here I have checked the Other Dynamics checkbox and selected Pen Pressure from the Control menu. You can lock these brush attribute settings so that they stay fixed whenever you change brush presets.

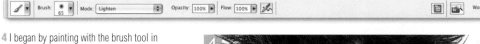

**4** I began by painting with the brush tool in Lighten mode. When the brush tool is selected, you can sample a flesh tone color by ⎇ *alt*-clicking to sample a color within the image. I then brushed lightly over the darker areas of the face such as underneath the eyes, which will lighten the darker areas. When using Lighten mode, only the pixels that are darker than the sampled color will be replaced. It is also a good idea to always keep resampling new colors as you paint.

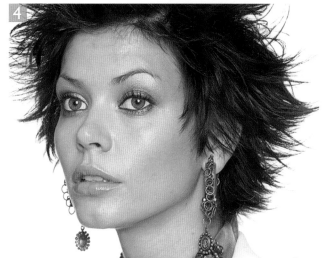

**5** I continued painting like this in Lighten mode to smooth other areas of the face. Where there were some shiny highlights, I switched to using the brush tool in Darken mode. I sampled a new color that was a touch darker than the highlights and painted over these areas to remove the shine. When using Darken mode, only the pixels that are lighter than the sampled color will be replaced. At this stage I will retouch at 'full volume' so to speak. Some fashion photographers quite prefer the super-retouched effect. Others argue that too much retouching will make the model's skin look more like a plastic doll rather than that of a real woman. It is up to you, but I usually prefer to fade the opacity of the retouched layer. Try reducing the layer opacity down to somewhere between 45 and 85%. Doing so will restore more of the original skin texture and the final retouched result will look a lot more convincing.

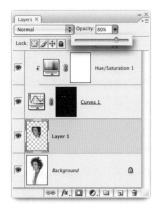

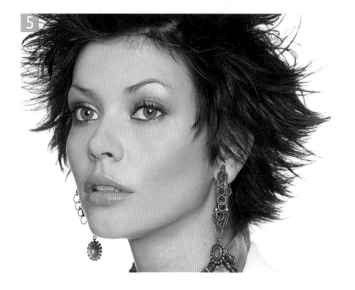

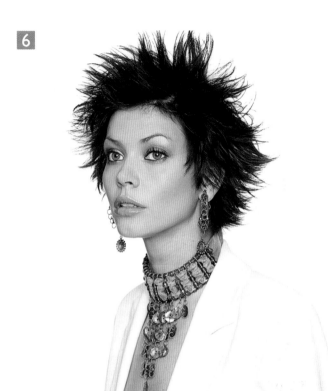

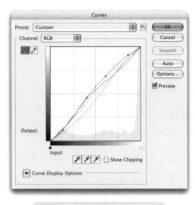

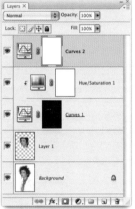

**6** Finally, I introduced a Curves adjustment to increase the contrast in the Red and Green color channels and decreased the contrast in the Blue color channel, to add a subtle cross-processing type of effect to the photograph.

Client: Andrew Price Salon.
Model: Lisa Moulson at MOT models.

## Retouching portraits

Beauty retouching is about enhancing the makeup and the smoothness of the lighting on the face in a fashion/beauty photograph. Portrait retouching requires a fairly similar approach to getting rid of the blemishes and enhancing the skin texture of the subject. But I find that portrait retouching requires a more subtle approach as you don't really want to always reduce the lines and wrinkles quite so much when retouching portrait photographs. It is interesting how there has been quite a backlash in recent years, with many celebrities reacting against pictures where their faces (and bodies) have been retouched out of all recognition. In Figure 7.9 below I have shown an example of a classic portrait where the retouching is more restrained. Facial wrinkles can be removed by using the dodge tool set to Midtones or Shadows and applied with a smallish soft edged brush at low opacity of around 5%. After gently brushing with the dodge tool, you will notice how the lines start to disappear.

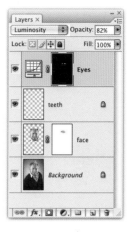

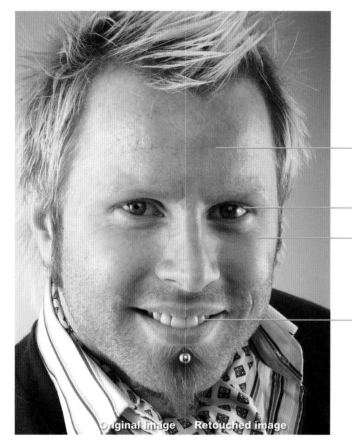

Healing brush used to cover up forehead lines. A layer mask used to fade out some of the retouching.

Eyes lightened using a Curves adjustment layer set to Luminosity mode.

Lines knocked back using the dodge tool set to 5% opacity and Shadows mode.

Teeth lightened slightly by making a selection outline of the teeth, copying to a new layer, setting the layer locking to Lock Transparency and painting over the teeth with the paint brush using a light tooth color set to Lighten bend mode.

**Figure 7.9** Here is a fairly straightforward retouching exercise, where I mostly used the healing brush to clone areas of skin texture to cover up minor blemishes. The healing brush work was all done to a new layer, so that I could add a layer mask later and fade out some of the retouching by painting on the layer mask with black using a light brush opacity. This allowed me to bring back some of the wrinkles in the skin and thereby avoid the complete 'botox' look.

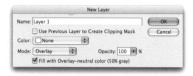

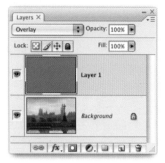

## Adding Noise

As well as removing noise you sometimes need to actually add more noise instead. When you use Photoshop to retouch a photograph you may at times find yourself painting with what might be called pure pixels. If you are cloning pieces from one part of the picture to another then you are probably not going to run into too many problems. But if you use the paint brush tool and apply gradients or blurs to parts of a photograph, there can be a mismatch where the smoothness of the pixels painted using Photoshop does not match the inherent texture of the rest of the image. You should therefore consider selectively adding noise whenever you add a gradient or paint with Photoshop. Note that Add Noise options are already included in a lot of Photoshop features such as the Brush options, Gradient Fill layers and the Lens Blur filter.

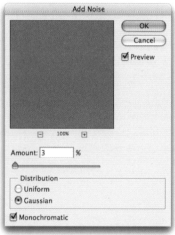

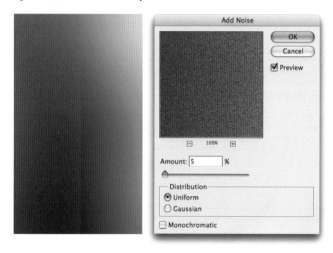

**Figure 7.10** To add noise on a separate layer, ⌥ *alt*-click the Add New Layer button in the Layers palette. This will pop a New Layer dialog. Select Overlay as the blending mode and you will notice that you can now check the Fill with Overlay-neutral color (50% gray) box below. In this blending mode the layer will have no visible impact on the underlying layers. But if you filter the layer and add noise, you can create a film grain layer. Try adding a layer mask to this layer to selectively add or remove the noise.

**Figure 7.11** Gradient banding is a common problem in Photoshop. Banding can occur whenever you apply a heavy blur filtration. It can also sometimes appear on gradient fills. The Gradient options include a Dither mode and this will help somewhat. However, the best way to hide banding is to apply a small amount of noise, using the Noise ⇨ Add Noise filter. The Gaussian option will produce a more irregular distribution of noise. The example here shows a noticeably banded gradient with and without the noise being added. The Noise filter is well worth remembering any time you wish to hide banding or make Photoshop painting work appear to merge better with the grain of a scanned original.

## Blurring along a path

Some Photoshop tools are more suitable for retouching work than others. The blur tool is very useful for localized blurring as you can use it to soften edges that appear unnaturally sharp. You can use Photoshop paths to apply a stroke using any of the Photoshop tools (see Figure 7.12). If you are working with selections then a selection can be converted to a path (use the current selection or load a selection – go to the Paths palette options and choose Make Work Path). For example, if you want to soften the outline of an image element and have a matching selection saved, convert this to a path, select the blur tool and choose Stroke (Sub) Path from the Paths palette. You could use the sharpen tool to sharpen along an edge, but it does have a tendency to produce unpleasant artifacts and I don't really recommend you to use it. If you wish to apply localized sharpening, then I suggest you follow the instructions that were described at the end of Chapter 4.

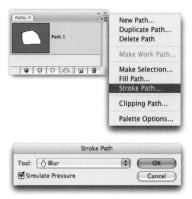

Figure 7.12 To stroke a path in Photoshop, create a closed or open path and go to the Paths fly-out menu and select the Stroke Path... option. Select the tool you wish to stroke with in the Stroke Path dialog. Now click OK and the path will be stroked with the selected tool using the currently selected brush setting for the chosen tool.

## Smudging pixels

The smudge tool is a paint smearing tool and it is important to recognize the difference between this and the blur tool. While the blur tool is best suited for merging pixels, the smudge tool is more of a painting tool. It can be used either for blending in a foreground color or 'finger painting' or, in other words, smearing pixels across an image. Smudge strokes created with the smudge tool do tend to look odd on a photographic image unless you are trying to recreate the effect of Instant Polaroid smearing. A better smudge tool is the super putty plug-in which is part of the Pen Tools suite freely distributed by Wacom. Some retouchers like to use the smudge tool to refine mask channels, working in Quick Mask mode, and the smudge tool set to Finger Painting to drag out mask pixels to follow the outline of hair strands. I tend to stick with the brush tool and use this in conjunction with a pressure sensitive graphic tablet device. Under the Other Dynamics options you can use a low stylus pressure to produce faint brush strokes. And under the Size Dynamics you can set the Size control to be linked to the stylus pressure.

### Rotate in perspective

If you have a copied selection active in Vanishing Point you can, if you wish, move the cursor outside the selection area to rotate the contents.

# Vanishing Point

The Vanishing Point filter provides a modal dialog in which you can define the perspective planes in an image and then use the tools available inside the Vanishing Point dialog to carry out basic retouching work that will match the perspective of the picture. You can make a selection within the Vanishing Point preview area and clone the selection contents within one or more predefined plane areas.

You can paste the contents of a selection and align it in perspective with the target image. And you can also apply the clone stamp in Healing or Non-healing modes, or paint with the paintbrush in perspective.

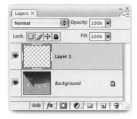

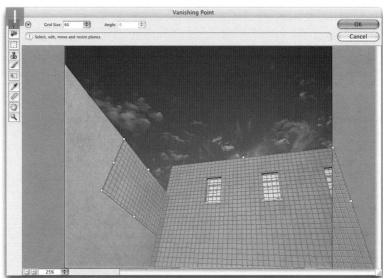

Original photograph: Jeff Schewe.

**1** Before commencing any Vanishing Point work, it is a good idea to create an empty layer first and make it active before choosing Vanishing Point from the Filter menu. The next task is to define the planes of perspective using the create plane tool. I clicked to set four points to define the first plane of perspective, using visual clues in the picture as a guide (hold down X to temporarily double the preview magnification). Once the first four points have been set, a blue grid will appear within the plane. A blue grid means you have described a good perspective plane. A red or yellow grid will indicate that this does not meet the criteria of a good grid plane. I could then resize the grid by dragging on the side or corner handles. The grid size can be adjusted via the control settings at the top, and the individual grid corners can be realigned by using the edit plane tool **V**. I then created a second plane to define the perspective of the left-hand wall, by **⌘** *ctrl* dragging the side handle on the left side of the first plane.

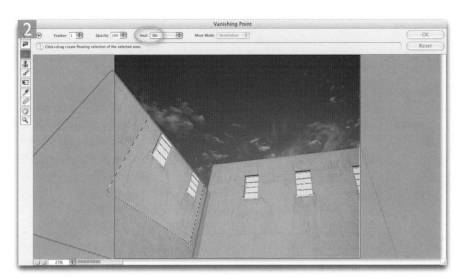

**2** After the two planes of perspective had been defined, I dragged with the marquee tool ⓜ to define the two windows on the right-hand wall and held down the ⌘ ⌥ *ctrl* *alt* key as I dragged from inside the marquee selection, to copy the selection and place it on the left-hand wall. As I did this the windows snapped to the predefined perspective plane of the second wall. Notice that before I commenced copying the selection contents, the Heal option was switched to On (circled).

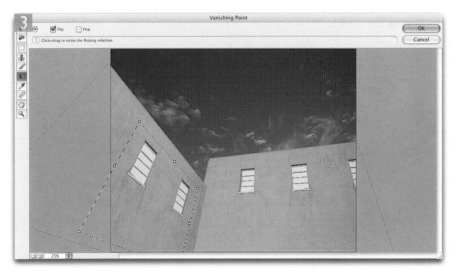

**3** Because the Heal option was switched on, the area surrounding the window frames blended smoothly with the other wall. But the perspective of the windows themselves was wrong. So before I clicked outside the marquee selection to flatten the contents, I selected the transform tool ⓣ and this changed the control options view at the top of the Vanishing Point dialog so that I could check the Flip option (to flip the selection contents from left to right). I then clicked OK to apply the filter.

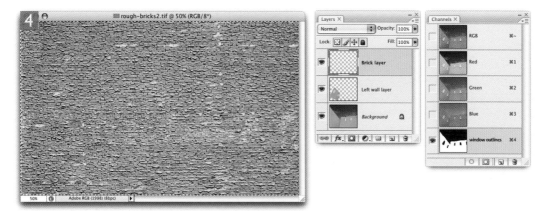

**4** I opened a photograph taken of a brick wall and made a Select ⇨ All of the contents (⌘A *ctrl* A). Back in the original image, I added a new empty layer, loaded a pre-made selection of the walls that masked the two windows and chose Vanishing Point from the Filter menu again.

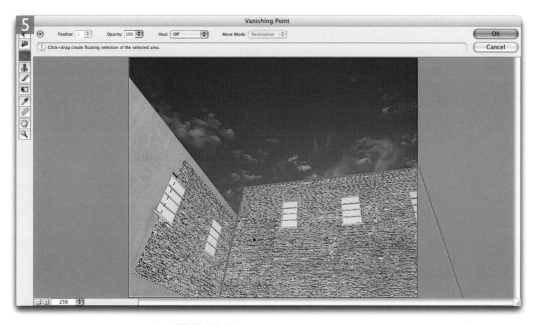

**5** I used ⌘ V *ctrl* V to paste the selection contents. The selection containing the brick wall image could then be dragged across to the perspective plane area, and as I did so the selection contents snapped to the perspective of the wall, leaving the windows visible. The selection contents had not been flattened yet, so I could ⌥ *alt* drag the selection to copy it and drag across to fill more of the wall area and copy the brick selection around the corner and onto the other wall. I could then keep on ⌥ *alt* dragging to make more copies of the brick wall to fill both walls.

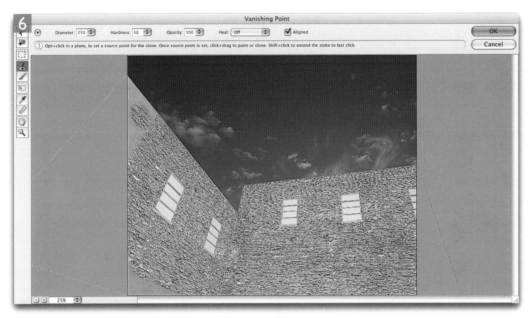

**6** To fill the walls with bricks completely I also selected the stamp tool **S** and used it with Heal set to Off, to clone the bricks in perspective to fill in the gaps.

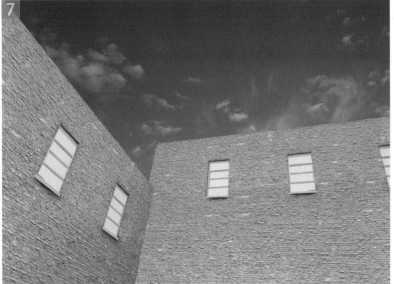

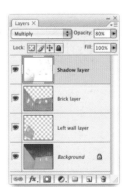

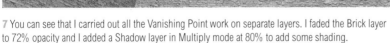

**7** You can see that I carried out all the Vanishing Point work on separate layers. I faded the Brick layer to 72% opacity and I added a Shadow layer in Multiply mode at 80% to add some shading.

## Rendering options

People have long asked for angled guides in Photoshop. With Vanishing Point, you can now create an empty new layer, launch Vanishing Point, use the Create Plane tool to create a perspective plane and go to the Vanishing Point options menu (circled below in Figure 7.13) and choose Render Grids to Photoshop. This will draw the guides shown in the preview on the empty layer. Likewise, you can use the Render Measurements option to do the same with the recorded measurements.

## Vanishing Point planes and measurements

This latest version of Vanishing Point offers two new features that will make this plug-in tool more useful. To start with you can now drag off new planes using a custom angle. For example, in Figure 7.13 below, the interior has a sloping wall. One can now adjust the planes so as to accurately follow all the angled surfaces of the room. So long as you get the initial plane description completely accurate, you should find that the consecutive planes will match the remaining perspective planes in the scene. And now when you clone or copy objects in Vanishing Point you will notice that you can paint or paste continuously around the corners of a plane, as shown in Figure 7.15.

If you happen to have the extended version of Photoshop CS3, you can make a calibration measurement along a line on one of the planes and from this be able to make further measurements of objects on associated planes. So for example, in Figures 7.14 and 7.15, one could create a calibration measurement based on the known height of a room, and from that work out the distances and sizes of some of the objects in the room.

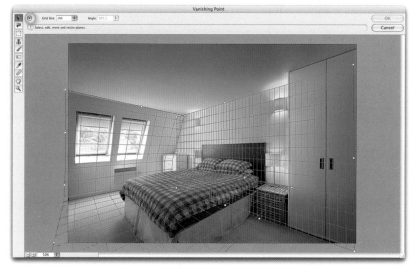

**Figure 7.13** Vanishing Point in Photoshop CS3 will allow you to describe planes that are at any combination of angles.

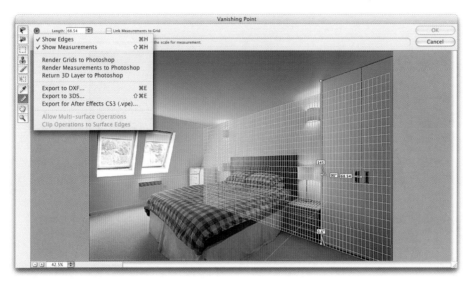

**Figure 7.14** The measurement tool in Vanishing Point can be used to make comparative measurements in a perspective plane. In the example shown here, if I know the height from the floor to the ceiling I can draw a measurement line along the vertical axis and enter a unit value that corresponds with the known height of the room. Once I have done this, I can use the measurement tool to calculate other measurements relative to the first measurement.

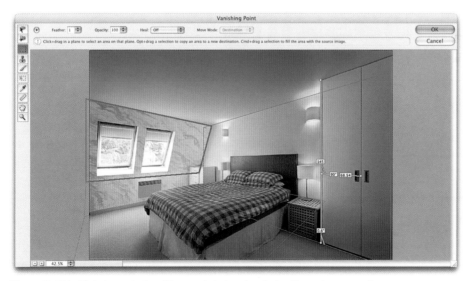

**Figure 7.15** In this last example, I used the same technique described on the previous pages of making a mask selection of the wall with the windows, opened Vanishing Point and pasted a selection of a texture pattern. Note how you can now place a texture across more than one plane at a time.

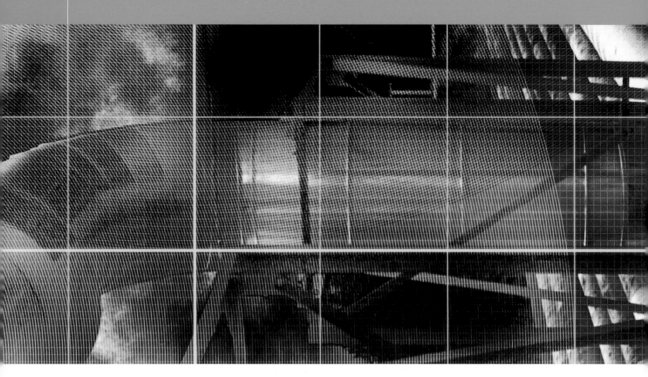

# Layers, Selections and Masking

F or a lot of people the real fun starts when you can use Photoshop to swap parts of one photograph with another and make composite photographs using different image elements. This chapter explains the different tools that can be used in montage work. I will suggest some strategies for shooting pictures with a view to making a composite image which will also serve as a neat introduction to the use of layers in Photoshop. Later we will be looking at some of the other tools and methods that can be used to isolate picture elements from photographic images. But to begin with, let us focus on some of the basic principles of how to make a selection and the interrelationship between selections, alpha channels, masks, Quick Mask mode and paths.

## Selections and channels

When you read somewhere about masks, mask channels, image layer mask channels, alpha channels, quick masks and saved selections, they are basically all the same thing: either an active, semipermanent or permanently saved selection.

### Selections

There are many ways you can create a selection in Photoshop. You can use any of the main selection tools, the Select ⇨ Color Range command, or convert a channel or path to a selection. When you use a selection tool to define an area within an image, you will notice that the selection is defined by a border of marching ants. Selections are only temporary though. If you make a selection and accidentally click outside the selected area with the selection tool, it will disappear. Although you can restore the selection with an Edit ⇨ Undo command (⌘ Z ctrl Z ).

During a typical Photoshop session, I will draw basic selections to define the areas of the image where I want to carry out image adjustments and afterwards deselect them. If you end up spending any length of time preparing a selection then you will usually want to save the selection as an alpha channel (also referred to as a 'mask channel'). To do this, choose Save Selection from the Select menu.

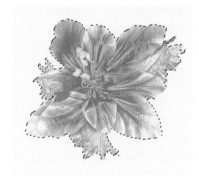

**Figure 8.1** A selection is represented in Photoshop using marching ants.

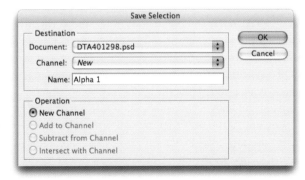

**Figure 8.2** To save a selection as a new alpha channel you can choose Select ⇨ Save Selection and select the New Channel button option.

## Recalling the last used selection

The last used selection will often be memorized in Photoshop. Choose Select ⇨ Reselect to bring back the last used selection.

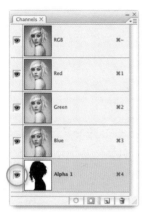

**Figure 8.3** When you save a selection it is added as a new alpha channel in the Channels palette. An alpha channel can be viewed by clicking on the channel name. If you click on the empty space next to the channel (circled), you can preview an alpha channel as if it were a quick mask.

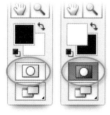

**Figure 8.4** The Quick Mask mode option is in the Tools palette just below the foreground/background swatch colors. Shown here are the two modes: Selection mode and Quick Mask mode. You can switch between these two modes by clicking on the button that I have circled here. And you can change the Quick Mask color settings by double-clicking this button.

The Save Selection dialog box will ask if you want to save as a new selection. Doing so creates a brand new alpha channel. If you check the Channels palette, you will notice the selection appears there labeled as an alpha channel (#4 in RGB mode, #5 if in CMYK mode). To reactivate this saved selection, choose 'Load Selection' from the Select menu and select the appropriate channel number from the submenu, or ⌘ *ctrl*-click the alpha channel in the Channels palette. You can also create a new alpha channel by clicking on the Make New Channel button at the bottom of the Channels palette and fill the empty new channel with a gradient or paint in the alpha channel with a painting tool using the default black or white colors. This new channel can then be converted into a selection.

In marching ants mode, a selection is active and available for use. All image modifications made will be effective within the selected area only. But remember, selections are only temporary and can be deselected by clicking outside the selection area with a selection tool or by choosing Select ⇨ Deselect (⌘ D *ctrl* D).

## Quick Mask mode

You can also preview and edit a selection in Quick Mask mode where the selection will be represented as a transparent colored mask overlay. To switch to Quick Mask mode from a selection, click the Quick Mask icon in the Tools palette (see Figure 8.4) or use the keyboard shortcut Q to toggle between the Selection and Quick Mask mode. To revert from a quick mask to a selection, click the selection icon in the Tools palette or press V again. Whether you are working directly on an alpha channel or in Quick Mask, modifications can be carried out using any of the fill, paint or even selection tools. You can also use any combination of Photoshop paint tools, or image adjustments to modify the alpha channel content. If the Quick Mask color is too similar to the subject image, double-click the Quick Mask icon, click on the Color box in the opened dialog and choose a different color from the Color Picker. If you simply want to temporarily hide the distraction of the marching ants, then use ⌘ H *ctrl* H.

## Modifying selections

You can modify the content of a selection using the modifier key methods discussed earlier in Chapter 2 (see pages 60–61). Just to recap, you hold down the *Shift* key to add to a selection, hold down the ⌥ *alt* key to subtract from a selection and hold down the ⌥*Shift* *alt Shift* keys to intersect a selection as you drag with a selection tool. The magic wand is a selection tool too, but all you have to do is to click (not drag) with the magic wand, holding down the appropriate key(s) to add or subtract from a selection. Note also that if you are working with the lasso or marquee tool and either of these tools is still selected, placing the cursor inside the selection and dragging moves the selection boundary position, but not the selection contents.

## Alpha channels

Note that an alpha channel is effectively the same thing as a mask. A selection can be stored as a saved selection by converting it to become a new alpha channel. To do this choose Select ⇨ Save Selection. An alpha channel can also be converted back into a selection by choosing Select ⇨ Load Selection. Alpha channels are stored as extra channels in the Channels palette in sequence below the main color channels. Just like a normal color channel, an alpha channel can contain up to 256 shades of gray in 8-bits per channel mode or up to 32,000 shades of gray in 16-bits per channel mode.

When an alpha channel is selected and made active, it can be viewed on its own as a grayscale mask and can be manipulated almost any way you want inside Photoshop. An alpha channel can also effectively be viewed in a 'Quick Mask' type mode. To view and edit an alpha channel in this way, make the alpha channel active and then click on the eyeball icon next to the composite channel, which is the one at the top (see Figure 8.3). You will then be able to edit the alpha channel mask with the image visible through the mask.

### Reloading selection shortcuts

To reload a selection from the saved mask channel, go to Select ⇨ Load Selection. ⌘ *ctrl*-clicking a channel is the other shortcut for loading a selection and by extension, combining ⌘ ⌥ channel # *ctrl* *alt* channel # (where # equals the channel number) does the same thing. Alternatively you can also drag the channel icon down to the Make Selection button in the Channels palette.

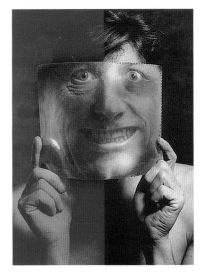

**Figure 8.5** The right half of the image shows a feathered selection and the left half the Quick Mask mode equivalent display.

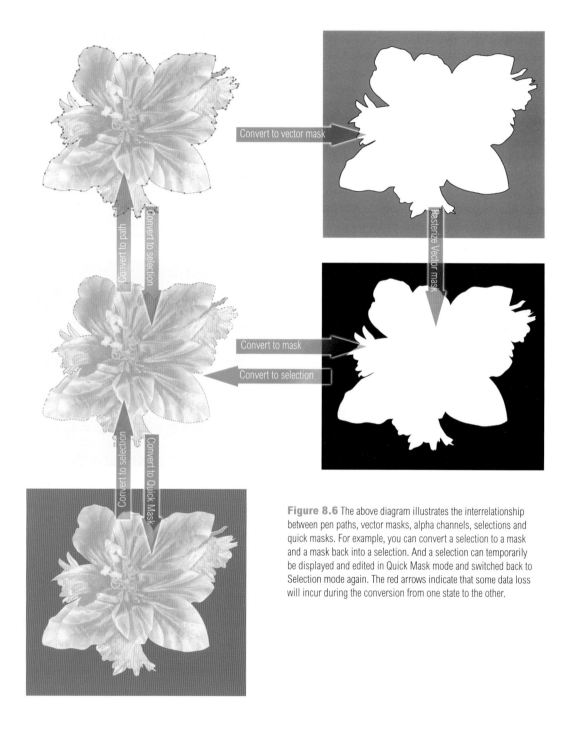

Convert to vector mask

Convert to path

Convert to selection

Rasterize vector mask

Convert to mask

Convert to selection

Convert to selection

Convert to Quick Mask

**Figure 8.6** The above diagram illustrates the interrelationship between pen paths, vector masks, alpha channels, selections and quick masks. For example, you can convert a selection to a mask and a mask back into a selection. And a selection can temporarily be displayed and edited in Quick Mask mode and switched back to Selection mode again. The red arrows indicate that some data loss will incur during the conversion from one state to the other.

## Selections, alpha channels and masks

As was pointed out at the beginning of this chapter, there is always an intertwined relationship between selections, quick masks and alpha channel masks. This interrelationship also extends to the use of vector paths and vector masks. The accompanying diagram in Figure 8.6 illustrates these relationships more clearly.

Starting at the top left corner, we have a path outline that has been created with the pen tool in Photoshop. A pen path outline can be saved as a path and an active path can be used to create a vector mask, which is a layer masked by a pen path mask (see pages 363, 374 and 418). And a vector mask can be rasterized to make a layer mask (a layer that is masked by an alpha channel). Meanwhile, a pen path can be converted to a selection and a selection can be converted back into a work path. If we start with an active selection, you can view and edit a selection as a quick mask and a selection can also be converted into an alpha channel and back into a selection again.

When preparing a mask in Photoshop, most people will start by making a selection to define the area they want to work on and save that selection as an alpha channel mask. This will allow you to convert the saved alpha channel back into a selection again at any time in the future. The other way to prepare a mask is to use the pen tool to define the outline first and then convert the pen path to a selection. If you think you will need to reuse the pen path again, such as to convert to a selection again at a later date, then it is worth remembering to save the work path as a named path via the Paths palette.

The business of using vector masks and layer masks is covered in more detail later on. But basically, a vector mask is a pen path applied to a layer which defines what is shown and hidden on that layer. And a layer mask is an alpha channel applied to a layer which defines what is shown and hidden.

### Converting vectors to pixels

In Figure 8.6 I mention that some of the conversion processes will incur a loss of data. This is because when you convert vector data to become a pixel-based selection, what you end up with is not truly reversible. Drawing a pen path and converting the path to a selection is a very convenient way of making an accurate selection. But if you attempt to convert the selection back into a pen path again, you will not end up with an identical path to the one that you started with. Basically, converting vectors to pixels is a one-way process.

Converting a vector path into a pixel-based selection is a good thing to do, but you should be aware that converting a pixel-based selection into a vector path will potentially incur some loss of data. More specifically, a selection or mask can contain shades of gray, whereas a pen path merely describes an outline where everything is either selected or not.

## Smoothing a selection

If you make a selection using the magic wand or Color Range method, the chances are that the selection is not as smooth as you might think. You will mostly notice this when you view such a selection in Quick Mask mode. The Smooth option in the Select ⇨ Modify submenu addresses this by enabling you to smooth out the pixels selected or not selected to the level of tolerance you set in the dialog box.

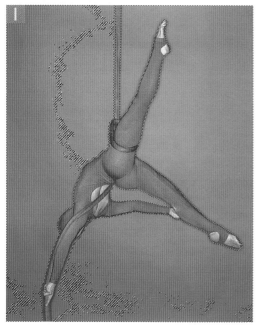

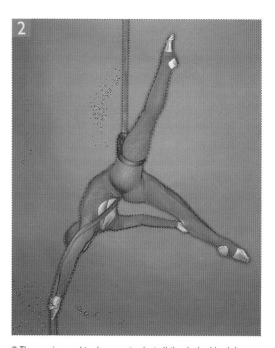

**1** The objective here was to make a simple soft edged selection based on tonal values and change the color of the background slightly. I used the magic wand tool to make a selection of the backdrop. A tolerance setting of 25 was used. I enlarged the selection locally by choosing Select ⇨ Grow. Note that the amount of growth is governed by the tolerance values linked to the magic wand tool options.

**2** The magic wand tool may not select all the desired backdrop pixels. I chose Select ⇨ Modify ⇨ Smooth, and entered a Radius value of between 1 and 16. The selection is now a lot smoother. Smooth works like this: if the Radius chosen was 5, Photoshop will examine all pixels with an 11 x 11 pixel block around each pixel. If more than half are selected, any stray pixels will be selected as well. If less than half are selected, any stray pixels will be deselected.

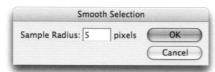

**3** With the selection satisfactorily complete, I hid the selection edges (View ⇨ Hide Extras) and opened the Hue/Saturation dialog box. Adjust the Hue and Saturation sliders to color the selected area.

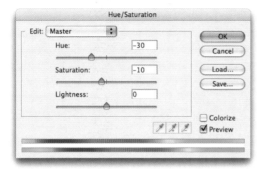

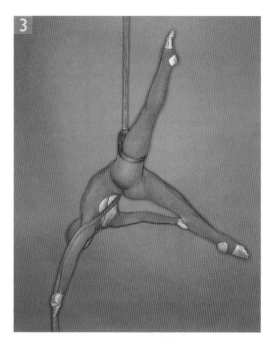

Photograph by Eric Richmond.

## Expanding and shrinking selections

To expand or shrink a selection, choose Select ⇨ Modify ⇨ Expand/Contract. Selections can be modified up to a maximum of 100 pixels. Other options include Border and Smooth. To see how these work, make a selection and choose one of the Modify options from the Select menu. Enter various pixel amounts and inspect the results by switching from Selection to Quick Mask mode. The border modifications are rather crude, but they can sometimes be improved by applying feathering or saving the selection as a channel and applying the Gaussian Blur filter. To see the Border selection command in use, check out the matte removal tutorial on pages 414–15.

But beware, there is an inherent flaw in Photoshop that creates angled corners when you use Select ⇨ Modify ⇨ Expand Selection. The most accurate way to expand an active selection is to choose Select ⇨ Transform Selection, and use the bounding box handles to scale a selection more accurately.

### Grow and Similar

The Grow and Similar options enlarge the selection using the same criteria as with the magic wand tool, regardless of whether the original selection was created with the wand or not. To determine the range of color levels to expand the selection by, enter a tolerance value in the Options palette. A higher tolerance value means that a wider range of color levels will be included in the enlarged selection.

The Select ⇨ Grow option expands the selection, adding contiguous pixels, i.e. those immediately surrounding the original selection of the same color values within the specified tolerance. The Select ⇨ Similar option selects more pixels from anywhere in the image of the same color values within the specified tolerance.

## Feather shortcut conflict?

The Select ⇨ Feather keyboard shortcut is ⌘ ⌥ D ctrl alt D. If you are using Mac OS X then it is possible that this keyboard shortcut will instead toggle Showing/Hiding the Dock. To get around this, go to the System Preferences and choose Keyboard & Mouse ⇨ Keyboard Shortcuts and deselect the Automatically Show/Hide the Dock shortcut.

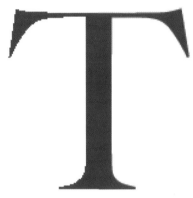

**Figure 8.7** The above illustration shows a graphic where the left half is rendered without anti-aliasing and the right half uses anti-aliasing to produce smoother edges.

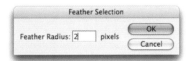

**Figure 8.8** If you want to soften the edges of a selection, then use Select ⇨ Feather and enter the desired feather radius.

## Anti-aliasing and feathering

All selections and converted selections are by default anti-aliased. A bitmapped image consists of a grid of square pixels. Without anti-aliasing, a diagonal line would be represented by a jagged sawtooth of pixels. Photoshop gets round this problem by anti-aliasing the edges, which means filling the gaps with in-between tonal values. All non-vertical/horizontal sharp edges are rendered smoother by the anti-aliasing process. So wherever you encounter anti-aliasing options, these are normally switched on by default. And there are only a few occasions when you may wish to turn this off.

Sometimes you may have an 8-bit image which resembles a 1-bit data file (say an alpha channel after you have applied the Threshold command) which needs to be anti-aliased. The best way to do this is to apply a Gaussian Blur filter to the mask, using a radius of 1 pixel. If it is just a small portion of a channel mask that requires smoothing, you can use the blur tool to lightly soften the edge.

To soften a selection edge, go to the Select menu, choose Feather and enter a pixel radius. A low pixel radius of between 1.0 or 2.0 is enough to dampen the sharpness of a selection outline, but there are times when it is useful to select a much higher Radius amount. For example, in Chapter 6 on pages 293–295, I used the rectangular marquee tool to define a rectangular selection. I then feathered this selection by 150 pixels, inverted the selection and applied a Levels adjustment through the feathered selection to create a vignette that darkened the outer edges of the photograph.

## Smoother selection edges

When you are doing any type of photographic retouching it is important to always keep your selections soft. If the edges of a picture element are defined too sharply, it will be more obvious to the viewer that a photograph has been retouched or montaged. The secret of good compositing is to avoid creating hard edges and keep the edges of your picture elements soft so they merge together more smoothly.

## Photoshop paths

The selection tools are nice and easy to use and many people will quite happily use a combination of, say, the magic wand and Quick Mask to generate a selection of an outline. But if you are editing anything other than low resolution images there will be times when the standard selection tools just won't be able to provide the precision you are after. In these circumstances you really will need a more accurate way to define an outline. This is where the pen tools and Photoshop paths come in.

The magic wand may do a fine job on tutorial-sized files, but is not a method that translates well to working on bigger images. If you are planning to work with large files, you will mostly find it quicker to draw a path and convert this to a selection rather than relying on the selection and paint tools alone. The magnetic tools fall halfway between. They are cleverly designed to automate the selection process, but there is usually no alternative available but to manually define the outline with a path.

### Selections to paths

An active selection can also be converted to a path by clicking on the Make work path from selection button at the bottom of the Paths palette. Alternatively, choose the Make work path option from the Paths palette fly-out menu.

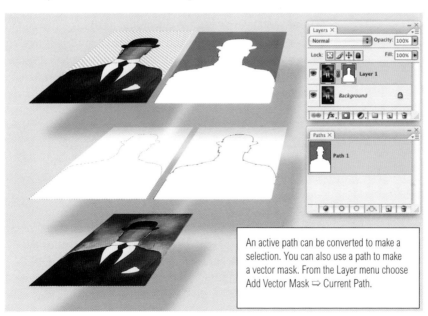

An active path can be converted to make a selection. You can also use a path to make a vector mask. From the Layer menu choose Add Vector Mask ⇨ Current Path.

**Figure 8.9** A current path can be converted to a selection or loaded as a vector mask to hide the contents of a layer.

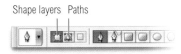

Shape layers  Paths

**Figure 8.10** The Shape layers mode is the default setting in the pen tool options. But I usually recommend that you click on the Paths mode button to set this as your new default.

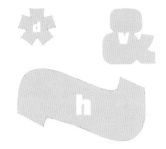

**Figure 8.11** The path tutorial file which can be found on the CD-ROM.

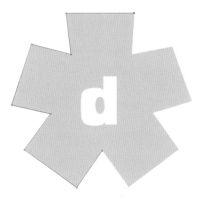

**Figure 8.12** Simply click with the pen tool to create straight line segments.

## Creating a path

A work path can be created in Photoshop using the pen tool and there are two main ways of making a path. In Paths mode a 'work path' is created and the subsequent work path (whether it is closed or not) can then be converted to a foreground fill, stroke or a selection by dragging the path down to the appropriate button at the bottom of the Paths palette. In Shape layers mode you can create a filled object defined by the path that is filled with the current foreground color. An active 'current' path can also be converted into a vector mask which will mask the contents of a layer using the path.

## Drawing paths with the pen tool

Unless you have had previous experience working with a vector-based drawing program like Freehand or Adobe Illustrator, the concept of drawing with the pen tool will probably be unfamiliar to you. It is difficult to get the hang of at first, but I promise you it is well worth mastering the art of drawing with the pen tool. It is a bit like learning to ride a bike, once you have acquired the basic skills, it will all start to fall into place. Paths are useful in several ways: either applying a stroke with one of the paint tools, for saving as a clipping path, or defining a complex shape, which can be converted to a selection or applied as a vector mask to mask a layer.

## Guidelines for drawing pen paths

We shall start with the task of following the simple contours illustrated in Figure 8.11 (you will find a copy of this image in a layered Photoshop format on the CD). This Photoshop file contains saved path outlines of each of the shapes. The Background layer contains the basic image and above it there is another layer of the same image but with the pen path outlines and all the points and handles showing. Make this layer visible and fade the opacity if necessary so that you can follow the handle positions when trying to match drawing the path yourself. Start at kindergarten level with the letter 'd'. If you mastered drawing with the polygon lasso tool, you will have no problem doing this. Click on the corner points one after another until you reach the point where you started to draw the path. As you approach this point with the cursor you will notice a small circle appears next to the cursor, which indicates you are now able to click (or drag) to close the path. Actually this is better than drawing with the polygon lasso, because you can now zoom in if required and precisely reposition each and every point. Hold down the ⌘ *ctrl* key to temporarily switch the pen tool to the direct selection tool and drag a point to realign it precisely. After closing the path, hit ⌘ *Enter* *ctrl* *Enter* to convert the path to a selection and click *Enter* on its own to deselect the path.

Now try to follow the letter 'h'. This will allow you to concentrate on the art of drawing curved segments. Observe that the beginning of any curved segment starts by dragging the handle outward in the direction of the intended curve. To understand the reasoning behind this, imagine you are trying to define a circle by following the imagined edges of a square box containing the circle. To continue a curved segment, click and hold the mouse down while you drag to complete the shape of the end of the last curve segment and predict the initial curve angle of the next segment. This assumes the next curve will be a smooth continuation of the last. Whenever there is a sharp change in direction you need to make a corner point. Convert the curved segment by holding down the ⌥ *alt* key and clicking on it. Click to place another point. This will create another straight segment as before in the 'd' example. Hold down the ⌘ *ctrl* key to temporarily access the direct selection tool which can be used to reposition points. When you click a point or segment with this tool, the handles are displayed. Adjust these to refine the curve shape.

The 'v' shape will help you further practice making curved segments and corner points. A corner point should be placed whenever you intend the next segment to break with the angle of the previous segment. In the niches of the 'v' symbol, hold down the ⌥ *alt* key and drag to define the predictor handle for the next curve shape.

**Figure 8.13** To draw a curved segment, instead of clicking, mouse down and drag as you add each point. The direction and length of the handles define the shape of the curve between each path point.

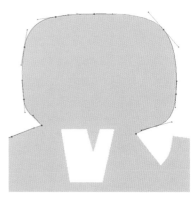

**Figure 8.14** When you create a curved segment the next handle will continue to predict a curve, continuing from the last curved segment. To make a break, you need to modify the curve point, converting it into a corner point. To do this, hold down the ⌥ *alt* key, click on the path point or click and drag to create a new predictor handle going off in a new direction.

### Editing path segments

You can edit a straight line or curved segment by selecting the direct selection tool, clicking on the segment and dragging. With a straight segment the anchor points either end will move in unison. With a curved segment, the anchor points remain fixed and you can manipulate the shape of the curve as you drag with the direct selection tool.

So, to edit a pen path, you use the ⌘ *ctrl* key to temporarily convert the pen tool to the direct selection tool, which you use to click on or marquee anchor points and reposition them. And you use the ⌥ *alt* key to convert a curve anchor point to a corner anchor point and vice versa. If you want to convert a corner point to a curve, ⌥ *alt* +mouse down and drag. To change the direction of one handle only, ⌥ *alt* drag on a handle. To add a new anchor point to an active path, simply click on a segment with the pen tool. To remove an anchor point, just click on it again.

### *Rubber Band mode*

As you read on in this chapter you will notice there are a number of occasions where I find it necessary to use the pen tool to define an outline and then convert the pen path to a selection. In the end, the pen tool really is the easiest way to define many outlines and create a selection from the path. One way to make the learning process somewhat easier is to switch on the Rubber Band option which is hidden away in the pen tool Pen Options. In Rubber Band mode, you will see the segments you are drawing take shape as you move the mouse cursor, and not just when you mouse down again to define the next path point. As I say, this mode of operation can make path drawing easier to learn, but for some people it can become rather tiresome to use after you have got the basic hang of how to follow a complex outline using the various pen tools.

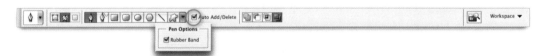

**Figure 8.15** The easiest way to get accustomed with the ways of the pen tool is to go to the Pen Options in the Options bar, mouse down on the Pen Options options and check the Rubber Band box.

# Layers

Layers play an essential role in all aspects of Photoshop work. Whether you are designing a web page layout or editing a photograph, working with layers lets you keep various elements in a design separate from each other. Layers allow you the opportunity to construct an image in stages and maintain the flexibility to make any editing changes you want at a later stage.

To rename a layer in Photoshop, simply double-click the layer name. To duplicate a layer, drag the layer icon to the New Layer button. To discard a layer, drag the layer icon to the Delete button in the Layers palette. There is also a delete Hidden Layers command in both the Layers palette submenu and the Layer ⇨ Delete submenu.

The Photoshop Layers feature has evolved in several stages over the years and Photoshop CS2 onwards includes new methods for selecting multiple layers and linking them together. But first let's look at the different types of layers that you can have in a Photoshop document.

## Image layers

The most basic type of layer is an image layer which is used to contain pixel information only. Using either the Layer menu or the Layers palette fly-out, layers can be duplicated from one file to another, either individually, in multiples or as Groups. The same applies when dragging and dropping a layer or layers from one file to another. And this can be assisted by the use of the *Shift* key to ensure they are centered with the destination file. New empty image layers are created by clicking on the New Layer button in the Layers palette (see Figure 8.19). Layers can also be created by copying the contents of a selection from another image layer within the same document. Choose Layer ⇨ New ⇨ Layer via Copy, or use the keyboard shortcut *⌘ J* *ctrl J*. This will copy the selection contents, duplicating them to become a new layer in register with the image below. Alternatively you can cut and copy the contents from a layer by choosing Layer ⇨ New ⇨ Layer via Cut or use the *⌘ Shift J* *ctrl Shift J* keyboard shortcut.

### Deleting multiple layers

You delete multiple layers quite easily. Use *Shift* click or *⌘* *ctrl* to select the layers or layer groups you want to remove and then press the Delete Layer button at the bottom of the Layers palette.

### Layer number limits

You can add as many new layers as you like to a document up to a maximum limit of 8000 layers.

### Layer visibility

You can selectively choose which layers are to be viewed by selecting and deselecting the eye icons. And in Photoshop, you can choose to make the switching of Layer visibility on and off an undoable action, in which case it becomes a recorded action within History. This is carried out within the History Palette Options.

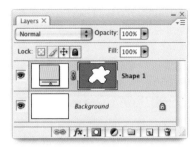

Figure 8.16 The pen tool and shape tools include a Shape layer mode button for creating shape layer objects defined by a vector path created using either of these tools.

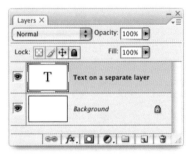

Figure 8.17 Text layers are created whenever you add type to an image. Text layers allow you to re-edit the typed content at any time.

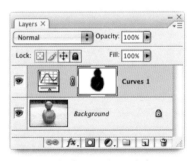

Figure 8.18 Adjustment layers don't contain pixels or vector objects. They are image adjustments that can be strategically placed within an image to apply image adjustments to individual or multiple layers. But like other layers, you can mask the contents and adjust the blending mode and layer opacity.

## Shape layers

Shape layers is a catch-all term to describe a non-pixel layer where the layer is filled with a solid color and the outline is defined with a vector mask and/or a layer mask. A shape layer is created whenever you add an object to an image using one of the shape tools, or draw a path in the Shape layer mode, or when you add a solid fill layer from the adjustment layer menu. Figure 8.16 shows an example of a shape layer, that is basically a solid fill layer masked by a vector mask.

## Text layers

Text layers, like shape layers, are also vector based. Type faces are essentially made up of vector data which means they are resolution independent. When you select the type tool in Photoshop and click or drag with the tool and begin to enter text, a new text layer will be added in the Layers palette. A text layer is symbolized with a capital 'T'. When you hit *Return* to confirm a text entry, the layer name will display the initial text on that layer, making it easier for you to locate. Note also that double-clicking the text layer icon will highlight the text within your image.

## Adjustment layers

Adjustment layers are image adjustments that are added in the form of a layer where you can toggle an adjustment layer on or off by clicking the layer eyeball icon. One of the chief advantages of working with adjustment layers is that you can re-edit the adjustment settings at any time and they also have a built-in layer mask that will allow you to use the paint or fill tools to selectively apply the image adjustments to an image.

## Layers palette controls

The blending mode options determine how a selected layer will blend with the layers below, while the opacity controls the transparency of the layer contents and the Fill opacity slider controls the opacity of the layer contents independent of any layer style (such as a drop shadow) which has been applied to the layer. And next to this are the various layer locking options. Most of the essential layer operation commands are conveniently located in the Layer palette fly-out options. And at the bottom of the palette are the layer content controls for layer linking, adding layer styles, layer masks, adjustment layers, new groups, new layers as well as a Delete Layer button.

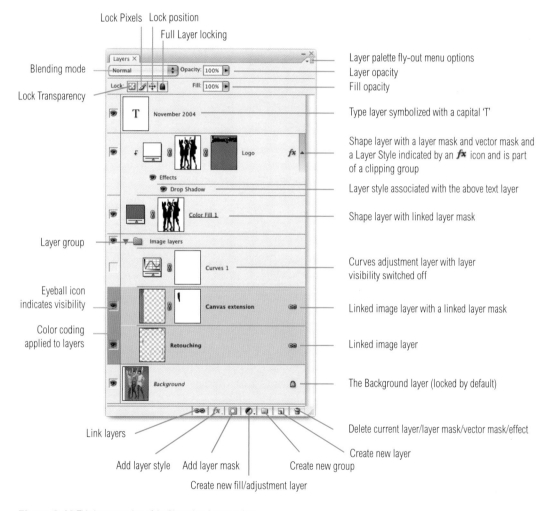

Lock Pixels   Lock position

Full Layer locking

Blending mode

Lock Transparency

Layer palette fly-out menu options

Layer opacity

Fill opacity

Type layer symbolized with a capital 'T'

Shape layer with a layer mask and vector mask and a Layer Style indicated by an *fx* icon and is part of a clipping group

Layer style associated with the above text layer

Shape layer with linked layer mask

Layer group

Curves adjustment layer with layer visibility switched off

Eyeball icon indicates visibility

Linked image layer with a linked layer mask

Color coding applied to layers

Linked image layer

The Background layer (locked by default)

Link layers

Delete current layer/layer mask/vector mask/effect

Create new layer

Add layer style   Add layer mask

Create new group

Create new fill/adjustment layer

**Figure 8.19** This is an overview of the Photoshop Layers palette.

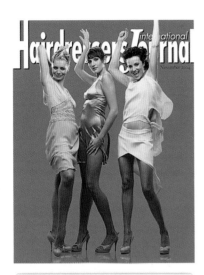

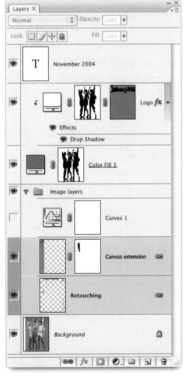

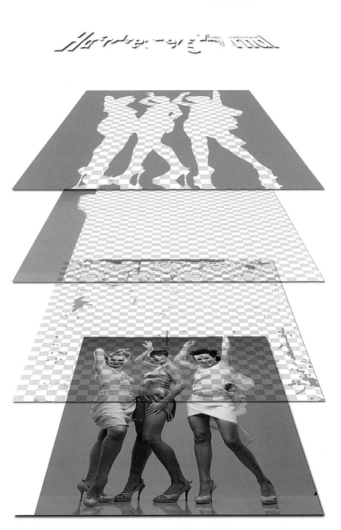

**Figure 8.20** Here is an expanded diagram of how the layers in a magazine cover image file are arranged inside Photoshop, one on top of the other. The checkerboard pattern represents transparency and the layers are represented here in the order they appear in the Layers palette.

Client: Goldwell Professional Haircare.

# Masking layers

You can hide the contents of a layer either wholly or partially by adding a layer mask, a vector mask or both. Layer masks are defined using a pixel-based mask, while vector masks are defined using path outlines. Masks can be applied to any type of layer: image layers, adjustment layers, type layers and shape layers. Click once on the Add Layer Mask button to add a layer mask, and click a second time to add a vector mask (in the case of shape layers a vector mask is created first and clicking the button will then add a layer mask). The most important thing to remember about masking in Photoshop is that whenever you apply a mask you are only hiding the contents and are not deleting anything. By using a mask to hide rather than erase unwanted image areas, you can go back and edit the mask at a later date. Or if you make a mistake when editing the layer mask, it is easy to correct mistakes – you are not limited to a single level of undo.

## Adding a layer mask

Click once on the Add Layer Mask button to add a layer mask to an image layer, type layer or shape layer (when you add an adjustment layer or fill adjustment layer a layer mask will be added automatically). The layer mask icon will appear next to the layer icon and a dashed stroke surrounding the icon will tell you which is active.

To show or hide the layer contents, first make sure the layer mask is active. Select the paintbrush tool and paint with black to hide the layer contents and paint with white to reveal.

To add a layer mask based on a selection, highlight the layer, make the selection active and click on the Add Layer Mask button at the bottom of the Layers palette, or choose Layer ⇨ Layer Mask ⇨ Reveal Selection. To add a layer mask to a layer with the area within the selection hidden, ⌥ alt-click the Layer Mask button in the Layers palette or choose Layer ⇨ Layer Mask ⇨ Hide Selection.

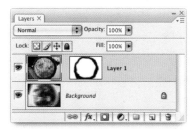

**Figure 8.21** The Layers palette view shown here contains two layers. The selected layer is the one highlighted in blue. The dashed border line around the layer mask icon indicates that the layer mask is active and any editing operations will be carried out on the layer mask only. There is no link icon between the image layer and the layer mask. This means that the image layer or layer mask can be moved independently of each other.

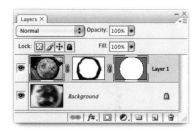

**Figure 8.22** In this next palette screen shot, the border surrounding the vector mask indicates that the vector mask is active and that any editing operations will be carried out on the vector mask only and not the image layer or layer mask. In this example, the image layer, layer mask and vector mask are now all linked. This means that if the image layer is targeted and you use the move tool to move it, the mask layers will move in unison.

## Adding an empty image layer mask

If you create an empty layer mask (one that is filled with white) on a layer, you can hide pixels in a layer using the fill and paint tools. To add a layer mask to a layer with all the layer remaining visible, click the Layer Mask button in the Layers palette. Alternatively, choose Layer ⇨ Add Layer Mask ⇨ Reveal All. To add a layer mask to a layer that hides all the pixels, ⎋ alt -click the Add Layer Mask button in the Layers palette. Alternatively, choose Layer ⇨ Add Layer Mask ⇨ Hide All. This will add a layer mask filled with black.

## Viewing in Mask or Rubylith mode

The small layer mask icon shows you roughly how the mask looks. But if you ⎋ alt -click the layer mask icon you can have the image window view switch to display the mask. And if you ⎋ Shift alt Shift -click the layer mask, the layer mask will be displayed as a Quick Mask type transparent overlay. Both these actions can be toggled.

## Copying a layer mask

You can use the ⎋ alt key to drag/copy a layer mask across to another layer.

## Removing a layer mask

To remove a layer mask, go to the Layer menu ⇨ Layer Mask submenu. There are now several options here: if you simply want to delete the layer mask, then select Delete. If you wish to remove the layer mask and apply it at the same time, then choose Apply. Or select the mask in the Layers palette and click on the Layers palette Delete button or drag the layer mask to the Delete button. A dialog box will appear asking do you want to Apply mask to layer before removing? Then click Discard to delete the mask, Cancel to cancel the operation, or Apply to apply the layer mask. To temporarily disable a layer mask, choose Layer ⇨ Layer Mask ⇨ Disable. To reverse this, choose Layer ⇨ Layer Mask ⇨ Enable. Also to temporarily hide the effect of a Layer mask, *Shift*-click the mask icon (when a layer mask is disabled it will be overlaid with a red cross). A simple click will restore the mask, but to restore a Vector mask you will have to *Shift*-click again. Or alternatively, *ctrl* right mouse-click the mask icon to open the full list of contextual menu options to apply, discard or disable the layer mask.

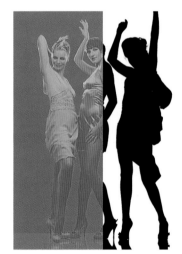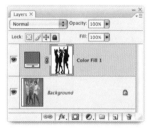

**Figure 8.23** Here is an example of how the image view will look if you ⎋ Shift alt Shift -click the layer mask (left) to display the layer mask in Quick Mask mode. And on the right, how it will look if you ⎋ alt -click the layer mask to view the mask in the image window. The layer mask can still be edited while it is viewed in these modes.

## Vector masks

A vector mask is just like an image layer mask, except the mask is described using a vector path instead. A vector mask can be edited using the pen path tools or the shape geometry tools. A vector mask is resolution-independent and can be transformed or scaled to any size without a loss in image quality. To add a vector mask from an existing path, go to the Paths palette, select a path to make it active, and choose Layer ⇨ Add Vector Mask ⇨ Current Path.

### Hiding/showing layer/vector masks

You can temporarily hide/show a layer mask by *Shift*-clicking on the layer mask icon. Also, clicking a vector mask's icon in the Layers palette hides the path itself. Once hidden, hover over it with the cursor and it will temporarily become visible. Click it again to restore the visibility.

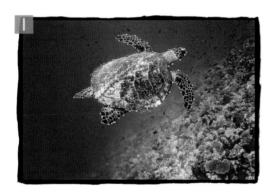

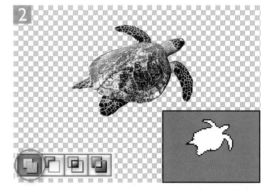

**1** A vector mask can be created from a currently active path such as the one displayed here. But the path mode will influence what is hidden and what is revealed when the path is converted into a vector mask.

**2** The path icon appearance will indicate the path mode. The gray fill in the path icon represents the hidden areas. So a path like the one shown here will have been created in 'add to path area' mode. When this mode is used to generate a vector mask, the outside areas will become hidden.

**3** If a path has been created in the 'subtract from path area' mode, the inside areas will become hidden when the path is used to create a vector mask. However, you can alter the path mode. Go back to Step 1. Select the path selection tool (the one immediately above the pen tool). Click on the path to make all the path points active and then select the pen tool and click on the 'add to path area' mode button in the Options bar to turn a path into an additive path. Or click on the 'subtract from path area' mode button to turn it into a subtractive path.

Photograph: Peter Hince.

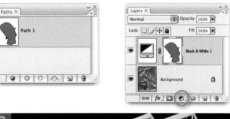

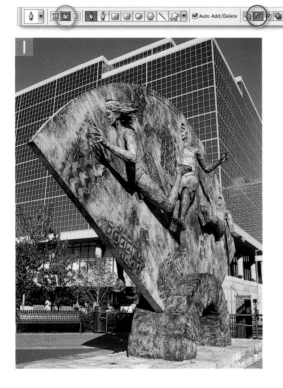

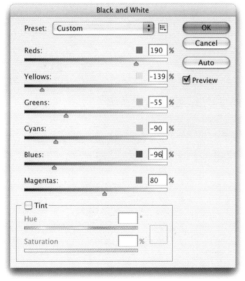

**1** I used the pen tool to define the outline of this park sculpture. Note that the pen tool has to be in path mode (circled in the Options bar). And because I wanted to create a path that selected everything outside the enclosed path, I checked the Subtract from Path Area button (circled in red) before I began drawing the path.

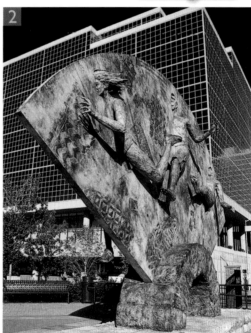

**2** With the work path active, I clicked on the New Adjustment Layer button in the Layers palette and selected Black and White. This added an adjustment layer with a linked vector mask. I used the Black and White dialog to make a black and white conversion of the areas selected by the vector mask. Note that you can use Layer ⇨ Change Layer Content to switch between different types of adjustment/fill layers. To edit a vector mask like this, you can use the direct path selection tool to manipulate the path outline.

# Working with multiple layers

Layers have become an essential feature in Photoshop and will enable you to do all kinds of complex montage work. But as layer features have evolved there has been an increasing need to manage layers more efficiently. When Photoshop CS2 was launched, a number of crucial changes were made to layers and some important alterations were made to the layer management, selection and linking processes. For some Photoshop users, the removal of the linking column was heresy. While I appreciate that this represented a big change to the Layers palette interface, I do not believe this did anything to harm or slow down the way we used layers in Photoshop.

## Layer group management

Multi-layered images can become extremely unwieldy to navigate when you have lots of layers all placed one above the other. Layers can be organized more efficiently by placing them in layer groups (previously known as sets). Layer groups use a folder icon and the general idea is that you can place related layers together inside a layer group folder. The layer group folder can then be collapsed or expanded. So if you have lots of layers in an image document, layer groups will make it easier to arrange your layers and make layer navigation much easier.

Layers groups can be made visible or invisible by clicking on the layer group eye icon. It is also possible to adjust the opacity and blending mode of a layer group as if it were a single layer, while the subset of layers within the layer group itself can all have individually set opacities and use different blending modes. You can add a layer mask or vector mask to a layer group and use this to mask the layer group visibility as you would with an individual layer.

To reposition a layer in the Layers palette, click on the layer and drag it up or down the layer stack. To move a layer into a layer group, drag it on top of the layer group icon or drag it into an expanded layer group. To remove a layer from a layer group, just drag the layer above or below its group in the stack.

## Nested layer groups

You can have a layer group (or groups) nested within a layer group up to three nested layer groups deep.

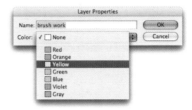

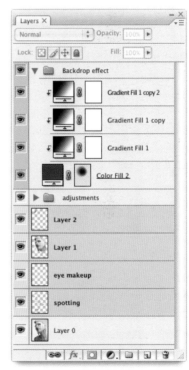

**Figure 8.24** Layers can be color coded. Choose Layer Properties from the Layers palette fly-out menu, or ⌘ *alt* double-click the layer (one layer at a time) and pick a color to identify each of the layers with.

## Group layer shortcut

Selected layers can be grouped together by choosing Layer ⇨ Group Layers or using the ⌘ G *ctrl* G shortcut.

Clicking on the Create a New Layer Group button in the Layers palette will add a new layer group above the current target layer. ⌘ *ctrl*-clicking on the Create a New Layer Group button will add a layer group below the target layer. ⌥ *alt*-clicking opens the New Group from Layers dialog. You can also lock all layers inside a layer group via the Layers palette submenu.

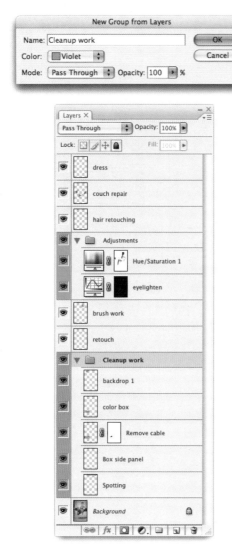

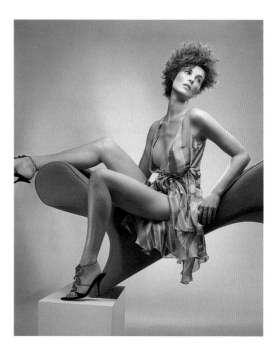

**Figure 8.25** When a Photoshop document ends up with this many layers, the layer stack can become extremely unwieldy. It is possible to organize layers within layer groups. All the basic cleanup work layers are grouped together in a single layer group. I was able to group them by *Shift*-clicking on the bottom five layers to make a multiple layer selection. I then chose New Group from Layers... from the Layers palette fly-out menu. I entered a name for the new group and selected a violet color to color code the layers within this group. The visibility of all layers in a group can be switched on or off and the opacity of the layer set group can be adjusted as if all the layers were a merged layer.

Client: Rainbow Room. Model: Nicky Felbert @ MOT.

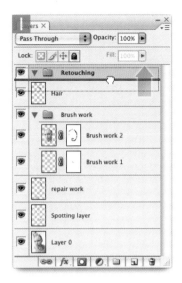

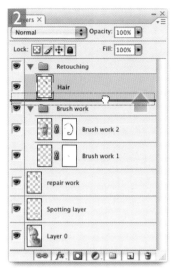

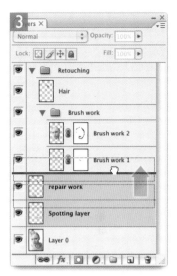

**1** Layers can be moved into a layer group by mousing down on a layer and dragging the layer into the desired layer group.

**2** The same method is used when you want to move a layer group within another layer group. Mouse down and drag to the position where you want it to be placed.

**3** You can also move multiple layers at once. Make a *Shift* select, or ⌘ *ctrl* layer selection and drag the selected layers into a layer group.

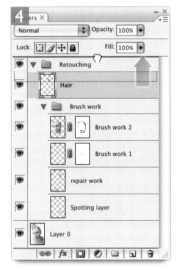

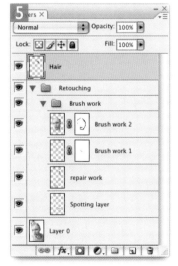

**4** To remove a layer from a layer group, just drag the layer out of the layer group until you see a bold line appear on the divider above or below the layer group.

**5** And here is a view of the Layers palette with the Hair layer now outside the retouching layer group.

## Move tool alignment options

The move tool Options bar now also integrates the alignment options that were previously only listed in the Layer menu. To find out more about layer alignment and distribution, refer to page 406.

## Layer selection and linking

When working with more than one layer you can choose to link layers together by creating links in the Layers palette. Multiple layers can be linked by first making a layer selection and then linking them together. Start by *Shift*-clicking on the layer names to select contiguous layers, or ⌘ *ctrl*-clicking to select discontiguous layers. At this point you can move, transform or group the layers as a group. But if you need to make this layer selection linking more permanent, then the layers can be linked together by clicking on the Link Layers button at the bottom of the Layers palette. When two or more layers are linked by layer selection or formal linking, any moves or transform operations will be applied to the linked layers as if they were one. But they still remain as separate layers, retaining their individual opacity and blending modes. To unlink a layer, select the layer and click on the link button to switch it off. Note that you can use the ⌘ ⌥ *A* *ctrl* *alt* *A* shortcut to select all layers (except a Background layer) and make them active.

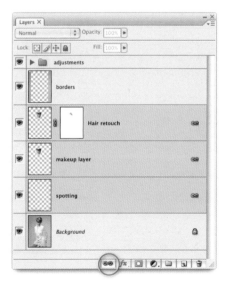

**Figure 8.26** To link two or more selected layers, click on the Link button at the bottom of the Layers palette.

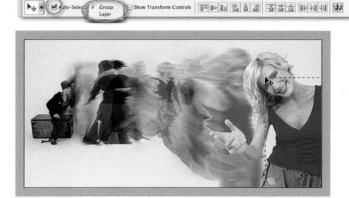

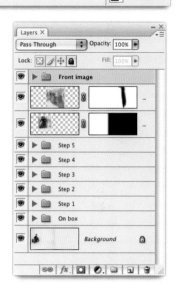

**Figure 8.27** Whenever the move tool is selected and the Auto-Select and Layer options are checked in the move tool options, you can auto-select a layer by just clicking in the image. If Auto-Select Layer is not checked, you can toggle this behavior by holding down the ⌘ *ctrl* as you click. When Auto-Select Layer is checked you can also marquee drag with the move tool from outside the document bounds to achieve a layer selection of all the layers within the marqueed area. But the move tool marquee must start from outside the document bounds, i.e. you must start from the canvas area inwards. If the Auto-Select and Group option is checked then only layer groups will be selected by this action. If unchecked, all layers that fall within the marqueed area will be selected.

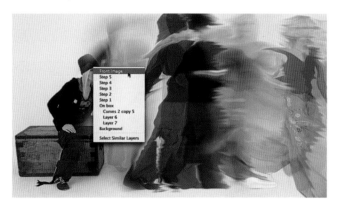

**Figure 8.28** When the move tool is selected, you can use the contextual menu to select individual layers. Mouse down on the image using *ctrl* right mouse-click to access the contextual menu shown here and click to select a named layer. The contextual options will list all of the layer groups in the document plus just those layers within the layer group immediately below the mouse cursor. The Similar Layers option is interesting because it will allow you to select layers that are of a similar kind, i.e. if a type layer is selected, the Similar Layers option will select all other type layers in the document.

Client: Hitachi/Ogilvy & Mather Direct.
Model: Lidia @ MOT.

## Layer mask linking

Layer masks and vector masks are by default linked to the layer content. If you move a masked layer, the mask moves with it, as long as no selection is active, then any movement or transformation of the layer content will be carried out independently of the associated mask. It is therefore sometimes desirable to disable the link between layer mask/vector mask and the layer it is masking. When you do this, any further movements or changes can now be applied to the layer or the layer/vector mask separately. You can tell if the layer or the layer/vector mask are selected, because a thin black dashed border will surround the layer or layer mask icon.

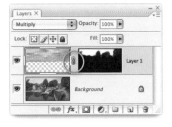

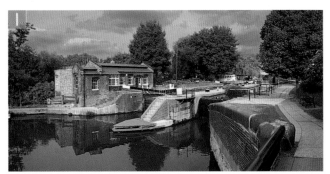

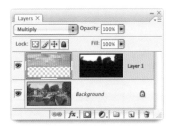

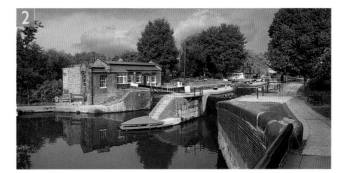

**Figure 8.29** This photograph contains a masked sky layer which is adding some dark clouds to the picture. The layer and layer mask would normally be linked. But if I click on the link icon between the layer and the layer mask, I can disable the mask and when the layer is made active I can move the sky layer independently of the mask.

## Layer locking

Photoshop layers can be locked in a number of ways. The layer locking options are to be found at the top of the Layers palette just below the blending mode options. To apply one of the locking criteria listed below to a layer, you need to select the layer first and then click on one of the Lock buttons. This action is toggled, so to remove locking, just click on the button again.

### *Lock Transparent Pixels*

When Lock Transparent Pixels is switched on, any painting or editing you do will be applied to the opaque portions of the layer only. Where the layer is transparent or semi-transparent, the layer transparency will always be preserved.

### *Lock Image Pixels*

The Lock Image Pixels option locks the pixels to prevent further editing. If you attempt to paint or edit a layer that has been locked in this way, you will see a prohibit warning sign.

### *Lock Layer Position*

The Lock Layer Position option will lock the layer position only. This means that while you can edit the layer contents, you are not able to accidentally knock the layer position with the move tool or apply a Transform command.

### *Lock All*

You can select combinations of Lock Transparent Pixels, Lock Image Pixels, and Lock Layer Position, but you can also check the Lock All option which will let you lock everything absolutely on a layer.

The above options mainly refer to image layers. With non-pixel layers you can only choose to lock the layer position or lock all.

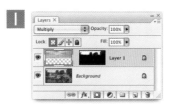

**1** This shows the Layers palette with a new image layer (Layer 1) above the Background layer. Lock Transparent Pixels will prevent you from painting in the layer's transparent areas accidentally.

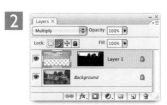

**2** Lock Image Pixels will preserve transparency and prevent you from accidentally painting on any part of the image layer, yet allow movement of the layer.

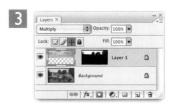

**3** Lock Layer Position will prevent the layer from being moved, while you can continue to edit the layer pixels.

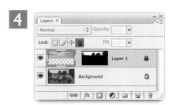

**4** The Lock All box will lock absolutely. The layer position will be locked, the contents cannot be edited. The opacity or blend modes cannot be altered, but the layer can be moved up or down the layer stack.

# Layer blending modes

The layer blending modes provide a mechanism for controlling how the contents of a layer blend with the layer or layers immediately below it, and these same blend modes can also be used to control how the paint and fill tools interact with the pixels they are painting. I have already mentioned a few of the blend modes that I use all the time, such as the Luminosity blend for blending adjustment layers without affecting the color component of an image. To help you learn and understand how the blend modes work, I have provided over the next few pages a summary of all the blend modes currently found in Photoshop CS3.

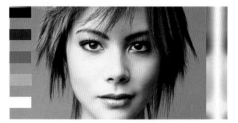 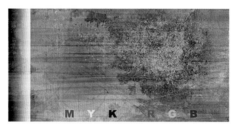

**Figure 8.30** The following pages illustrate all the different blending modes in Photoshop. In these examples, the photograph of the model was added as a new layer above the gray textured Background layer and the layer settings recorded in the accompanying palette screen shot.

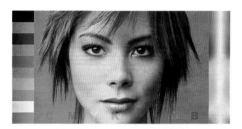

### Normal

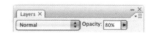

This is the default mode. Changing opacity simply fades the intensity of overlaying pixels by averaging the color pixels of the blend layer with the values of the composite pixels below (Opacity set to 80%).

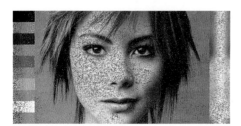

### Dissolve

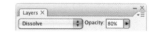

Combines the blend layer with the base using a randomized pattern of pixels. No change occurs when using Dissolve at 100% opacity. As the opacity is reduced, the diffusion becomes more apparent (Opacity set to 80%).

**Darken**

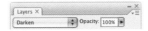

Looks at the base and blending colors and color is only applied if the blend color is darker than the base color.

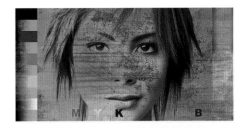

**Multiply**

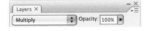

Multiplies the base by the blend pixel values, always producing a darker color, except where the blend color is white. The effect is similar to viewing two transparency slides sandwiched together on a lightbox.

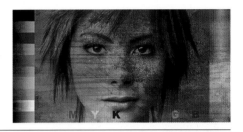

**Color Burn**

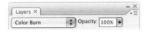

Darkens the image using the blend color. The darker the color, the more pronounced the effect. Blending with white has no effect.

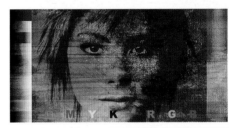

**Linear Burn**

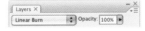

The Linear Burn mode produces an even more pronounced darkening effect than Multiply or Color Burn. Note that the Linear Burn blending mode will clip the darker pixel values. Blending with white has no effect.

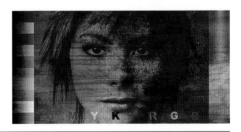

**Lighten**

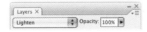

Looks at the base and blending colors and color is only applied if the blend color is lighter than the base color.

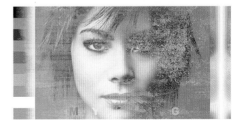

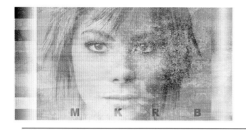

### Screen

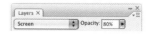

Multiplies the inverse of the blend and base pixel values together, always making a lighter color, except where the blend color is black. The effect is similar to printing with two negatives sandwiched together in the enlarger.

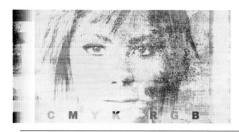

### Color Dodge

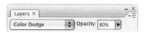

Brightens the image using the blend color. The brighter the color, the more pronounced the effect. Blending with black has no effect (Opacity set to 80%).

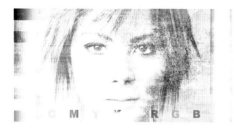

### Linear Dodge (Add)

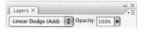

This blending mode does the opposite of the Linear Burn tool. It produces a stronger lightening effect than Screen or Lighten, but will clip the lighter pixel values. Blending with black has no effect.

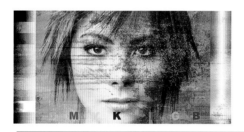

### Overlay

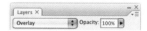

The Overlay blending mode superimposes the blend image on the base (multiplying or screening the colors depending on the base color) whilst preserving the highlights and shadows of the base color. Blending with 50% gray has no effect.

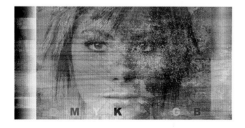

### Soft Light

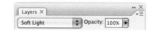

Darkens or lightens the colors depending on the base color. Soft Light produces a more gentle effect than the Overlay mode. Blending with 50% gray has no effect.

### Hard Light

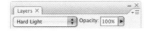

Multiplies or screens the colors depending on the base color. Hard Light produces a more pronounced effect than the Overlay mode. Blending with 50% gray has no effect.

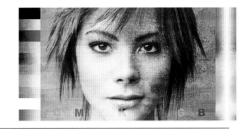

### Vivid Light

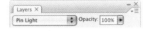

Applies a Color Dodge or Color Burn blending mode, depending on the base color. Vivid Light produces a stronger effect than Hard Light mode. Blending with 50% gray has no effect.

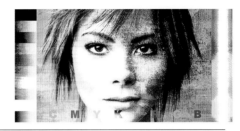

### Linear Light

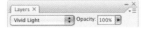

Applies a Linear Dodge or Linear Burn blending mode, depending on the base color. Linear Light produces a slightly stronger effect than the Vivid Light mode. Blending with 50% gray has no effect.

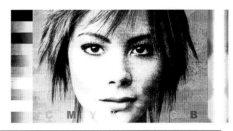

### Pin Light

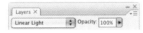

Applies a Lighten blend mode to the lighter colors and a Darken blend mode to the darker colors. Pin Light produces a stronger effect than Soft Light mode. Blending with 50% gray has no effect.

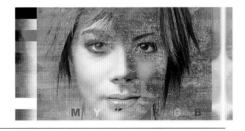

### Hard Mix

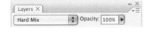

Produces a posterized image consisting of up to eight colors: red, green, blue, cyan, magenta, yellow, black and white. The blend color is a product of the base color and the luminosity of the blend layer.

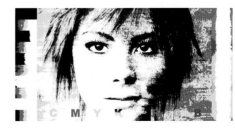

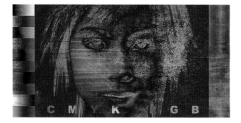

### Difference

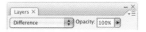

Subtracts either the base color from the blending color or the blending color from the base, depending on whichever has the highest brightness value. In visual terms, a 100% white blend value will invert (i.e. turn negative) the base layer completely, a black value will have no effect and values in between will partially invert the base layer. Duplicating a Background layer and applying Difference at 100% will produce a black image. Dramatic changes can be gained by experimenting with different opacities. An analytical application of Difference is to do a pin register sandwich of two near identical images to detect any image changes – such as a comparison of two images in different RGB color spaces, for example.

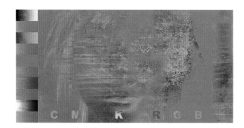

### Exclusion

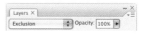

A slightly muted variant of the Difference blending mode. Blending with pure white will invert the base image.

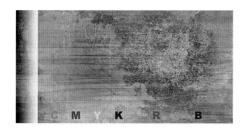

### Hue

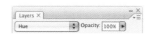

Preserves the luminance and saturation of the base image, replacing with the the hue of the blending pixels.

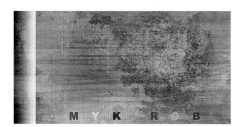

### Saturation

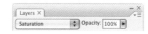

Preserves the luminance and hue of the base image, replacing with the saturation of the blending pixels.

## Color

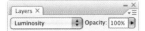

Preserves the luminance values of the base image, replacing the hue and saturation values of the blending pixels. Color mode is particularly suited for hand coloring photographs.

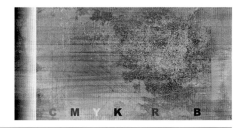

## Luminosity

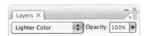

Preserves the hue and saturation of the base image while applying the luminance of the blending pixels.

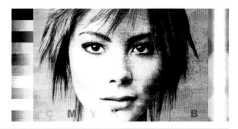

## Lighter Color

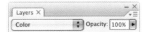

Lighter color is similar to the Lighten mode, except it works on all channels instead of working on a per-channel basis. When you blend two layers together, only the lighter pixels on the blend layer will remain visible.

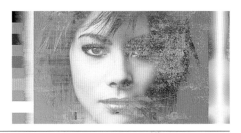

## Darker Color

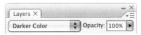

Darker color is similar to the Darken mode, except it works on all channels instead of working on a per-channel basis. When you blend two layers together, only the darker pixels on the blend layer will remain visible.

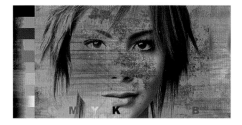

Client: Taylor Phillipps. Model: Tina at FM.

## Difference blend registration

The Difference blend mode has lots of potential for creating funky-looking images, which is shorthand for saying: if you think you are being original by using Difference mode when creating a digital art masterpiece, then think again.

But on a more serious note, the Difference blend mode is actually very useful as a tool for registering images or making visual analysis comparisons. If you have two supposedly identical layers and you set the upper one to Difference mode, the two should cancel each other out and all you will see is solid black. So let's say you want to test the effects of applying JPEG compression to an image. If you place one version as a layer on top of the other, the differences caused by the JPEG artifacting will be the only thing you can see in the image. Place an Invert adjustment layer above and you should see the differences even more clearly.

## Advanced Blending options

Layer groups allow you to group a number of layers together such that the layers contained within a layer group behave like a single layer. In Pass Through blending mode the layer blending passes through the set and the interaction is no different than if the individual layers were in a normal layer stack. However, when you select any of the other blending mode options, the layer group blending result will be equivalent to what would happen if you chose to merge all the layers in the current set to make them become a single layer and then set the blending mode.

Among the Advance Blending modes, the Knockout blending options enable you to force a layer to punch through some or all of the layers beneath it. A 'Shallow' knockout will punch through to the bottom of the layer set, while a 'Deep' knockout will punch through to just above the Background layer.

Layer styles are normally applied independent of the layer blending mode. When you check the Blend Interior Effects as Group box, such effects will take on the blending characteristics of the selected layer.

To put all this into practice, try opening the image shown on page 389 from the DVD and follow the steps outlined here. In particular, observe how the Blend Interior Effects as Group option works on Layer C which is using the Difference blending mode. When you check the Blend Interior Effects as Group option, the result will be the same as if you had first 'fixed' the interior layer style using the Normal blend mode and then changed the blend mode to Difference. Other aspects of the Layer Style blending options dialog box are covered in the Layers Styles section in the Photoshop for Photographers Help Guide, available from the DVD.

**1** The four letter layers shown here are grouped together in a layer group. Layer A is using the Multiply blending mode; B is using Overlay; C is using Difference; and D is using the Screen blending mode. The default blending mode of this layer group is Pass Through. This means that the layers in the layer group blend with the layers below the same as they would if they were in a normal layer stack.

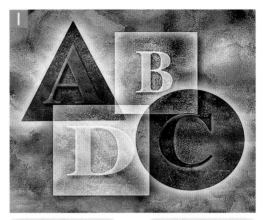

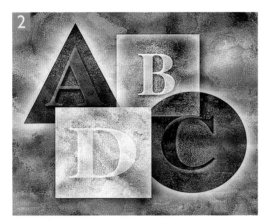

**2** If you select Layer D and double-click the layer to open the Layer Style dialog, you can alter the Advanced Blending options. The Knockout options allow you to 'punch through' the layers. A 'Shallow' knockout will punch through the three layers below it to just above the layer or layer group immediately below. A 'Deep' knockout will make the Layer D punch through all layers below it, straight down to the Background layer. Layer D now appears as it would if resting directly above the Background layer.

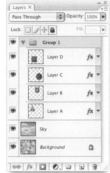
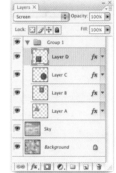

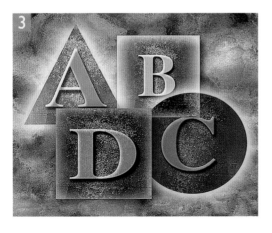

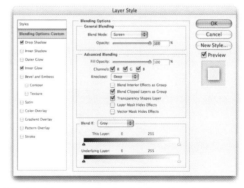

**3** The default layer group blend mode is Pass Through. If you change the layer group blending mode to anything else, the layers within the group will blend with each other as before, but will not interact with the layers underneath as they did in Pass Through mode. When the blend mode is Normal, the group layers appear as they would if you switched off the visibility of the Background layer.

389

## Smart Objects

One of the main problems you face when editing pixel-based layers is that every time you scale an image or the content of an image layer, you degrade the image slightly. And if you make cumulative adjustments, then the image quality will degrade quite rapidly. Creating a Smart Object from a layer or group of layers will enable you to carry out any editing on those layers within a separate document and they will from there on be 'referenced' by the parent document. The advantage of this is that once you have separated these layers from the parent document you can scale the Smart Object layer up and down in size, rotate it, distort it with the free transform or warp tool as many times as you like without degrading the original pixel data. Therefore, a Smart Object layer does in effect become a 'proxy' layer.

Smart Objects have been given a further boost in CS3. Now when you convert a layer or group of layers to a Smart Object, you can apply filters to them. Also coming up next, I will show you how it is now a lot easier to place a raw camera file as a Smart Object layer.

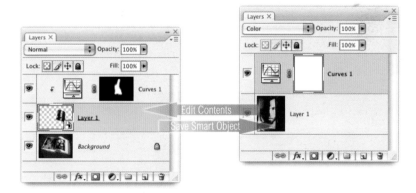

**Figure 8.31** You can promote a layer or group of layers to become a Smart Object. A Smart Object becomes a fully editable, separate document within a Photoshop document. The principal advantage is that you can repeatedly scale, transform or warp a Smart Object in the parent document without affecting the integrity of the pixels in the original Smart Object document.

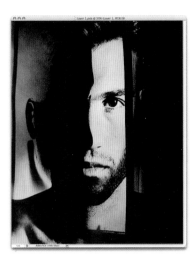

**1** Let's examine in more detail how you would use a Smart Object in Photoshop. Here is a photograph of a book that shows a couple of my promotional photographs and let's say I wanted to place the image on the right so that it matches the scale, rotation and warp shape of the photograph on the right-hand page.

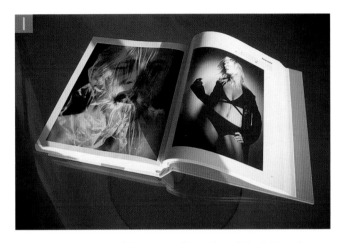

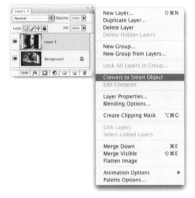

**2** I used the move tool to drag the photograph across to add it as a new layer and then went to the Layers palette options and chose Convert to Smart Object. This action would preserve all the image data on this layer in its original form. I then went to the Image menu and chose Free Transform. Because the layer boundary exceeded the size of the Background layer, I had to zoom out in order to access the corner handles of the Transform box.

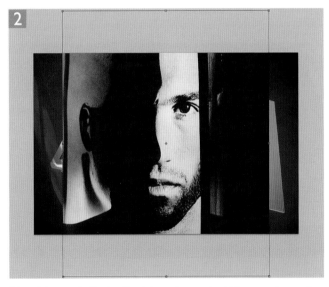

### Quick tip

In these situations it is useful to remember that you can use the ⌘ 0 ctrl 0 keyboard shortcut to quickly zoom out just far enough to reveal the transform bounding box handles.

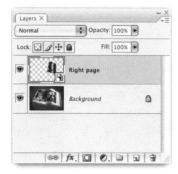

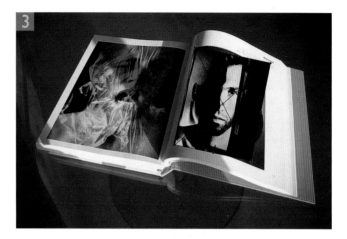

**3** I then scaled the Smart Object layer down in size so that it more closely matched the size of the photograph in the page. I also dragged the cursor outside the transform bounding box, so as to rotate the photograph roughly into position.

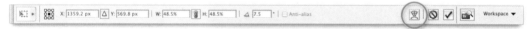

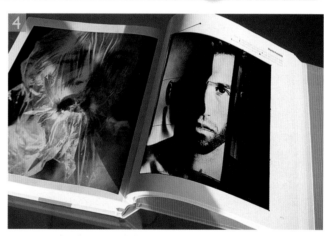

**4** After that, I clicked on the Warp button in the Options bar (highlighted above). This allowed me to fine-tune the position of the Smart Object layer, by using the corner curve adjustment handles to modify the outer envelope shape. I then moused down inside some of the inner sections and dragged them so that the inner shape also matched the curvature of the page.

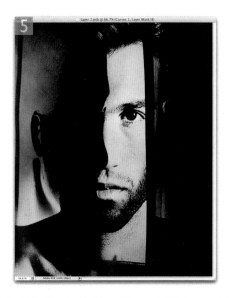

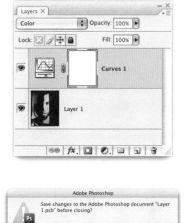

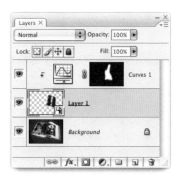

**5** I was able to edit the Smart Object layer. You can do this by going to the Layers palette fly-out menu and selecting Edit Contents. Or you can simply double-click on the Smart Objects icon in the Layers palette. In the example shown here, I added a Curves adjustment layer to turn the photograph blue. I then closed the window. As I did so this popped the prompt dialog shown here , reminding me to click Save in order to update the master Smart Object layer.

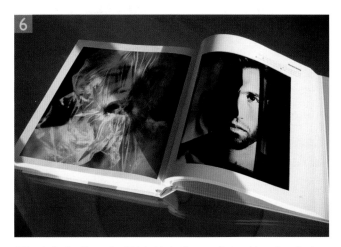

**6** Here is the final image in which I added a Curves adjustment layer in a clipping group with the Smart Object layer so that the shading matched that of the original photograph.

## Camera Raw Smart Objects

A Smart Object will store the raw pixel data within a saved PSD or TIFF image. This means that you can re-edit the raw data at any time. But it also means that a rendered pixel version of the Smart Object has to be stored as well. Documents that include Smart Objects can therefore have quite a large file size. The important thing to stress here is that this technique really applies to editing raw files only. In Photoshop CS3, you can use the Camera Raw plug-in to edit JPEG files. It is therefore theoretically possible to apply the technique shown here to JPEG images but it won't really bring you any real benefit compared to processing raw image files.

# Multiple raw conversions of an image

The Merge to HDR command provides an interesting first step into the world of high dynamic range photography. The chief disadvantage of working with Merge to HDR is that you have to remember to take sequential captures at the time of shooting and there must be absolutely no movement in the subject you are photographing.

To get the most out of your raw files it can sometimes be useful to make two or more conversions using Camera Raw, combine them together as layers in a single document then blend them to produce a composite image. One way to do this is to place a raw file as a Smart Object in Photoshop.

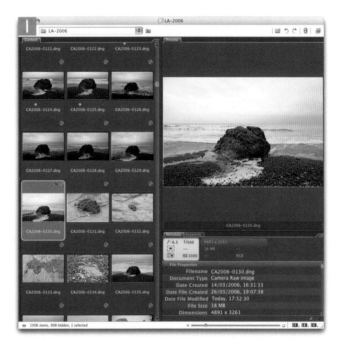

**1** To begin with I went to Bridge and selected out a raw image photograph that I wanted to edit and opened the image up via Camera Raw, using File ⇨ Open in Camera Raw... (⌘ R ctrl R).

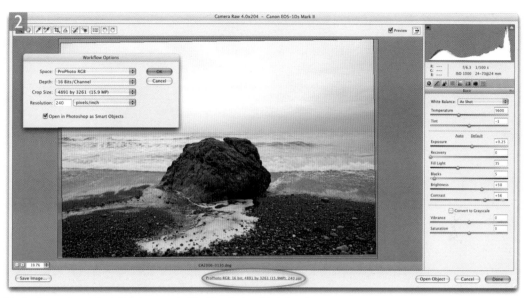

**2** In the Camera Raw dialog I clicked to open the Workflow Options (circled) and checked 'Open in Photoshop as Smart Objects'. I adjusted the Camera Raw settings to achieve the best brightness and contrast on the rocks and shoreline. Once I was happy with the settings, I clicked Done to open as a Smart Object in Photoshop.

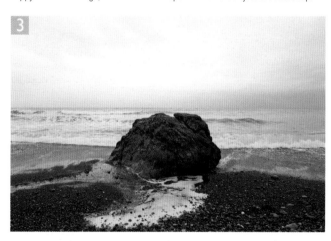

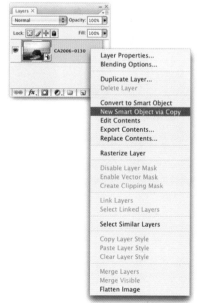

**3** Here is the processed image, placed as a single Smart Object layer in a new Photoshop document. I then wanted to create a new Smart Object layer of the same image where I could use new Camera Raw settings to adjust for the sky. To do this, I moused down on this first Smart Object layer while holding down the `ctrl` right mouse (to access the contextual menu shown here) and selected New Smart Object via Copy.

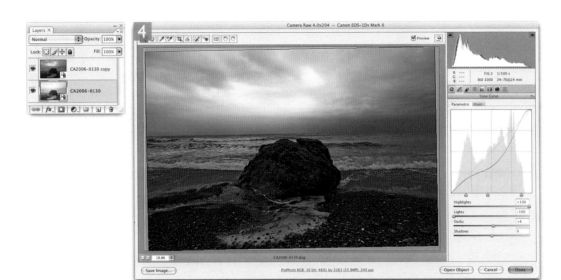

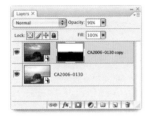

**4** This duplicated the Smart Object layer and allowed me to select Edit Contents from the Layers palette menu (which opened the Camera Raw dialog again) and used the Tone Curve panel controls to apply a darker image adjustment to bring out more detail in the sky. I clicked Done to OK the adjustment, which then updated the Smart Object copy layer in the master image document.

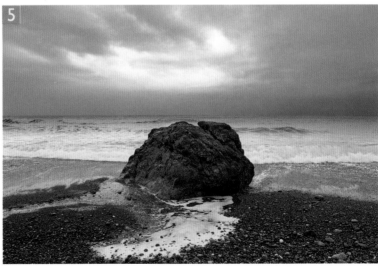

**5** Next, I added a layer mask to the Smart Object copy layer and applied a black to white linear gradient to create a fade between the two Smart Object layers and took the opacity of the layer down to 90%.

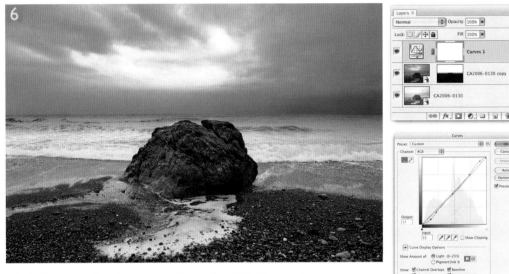

**6** For the final version shown here, I reopened the two Smart Object layers and checked the Convert to Grayscale option, to create monochrome renderings for both Smart Object layers. I added a Curves adjustment layer at the top of the layer stack to adjust the overall contrast of the combined Smart Object layers and add a sepia color tint to the picture.

## Place-A-Matic script

The steps I just outlined can be carried out more easily by running Dr. Brown's Place-A-Matic script for Bridge. You can download this script for free via the Russell Brown Show website. Go to: www.russellbrown.com and then go to the Photoshop Tips & Techniques section, scroll down to the Scripts section where you can download 'Dr Brown's Services' which, among other things, includes the Place-A-Matic script. Follow the installation instructions, and when you next launch Bridge you should see this appear as one of the new script options in the Tools menu. Basically, the Place-A-Matic script will automate almost all the steps I just described here over the last few pages and offer a quick way to create double raw settings conversions via Smart Objects. Note that you will still have to add a layer mask and decide for yourself how to blend the images.

## Smart Object layer blending

This technique can be adapted in various ways. You can use the layer blending options to change the layer blend mode or double-click the layer to open the Layer Style dialog where you can adjust the Blend if: This Layer options to adjust the transition between the two Smart Object layers.

## Layer blending to remove objects

Earlier in Chapter 1, I highlighted the Stacks feature as one of my favorite new techniques in Photoshop CS3. The Stacks feature was really designed as a tool for analytical work, where you can place a series of images together in alignment and apply a Stacks rendering to the layers and use this to process them in such a way that Photoshop will highlight the differences found between the layers, or as is shown here, blend the layers by analyzing the pixels on all the layers that are being processed within a stack, from the highest to the lowest and select the middle pixel value. This rendering process technique can be used to smooth out any differences between a group of layers that are processed as a stack.

So let's look at some of the various ways that stacks would actually be applied in real world situations. For scientists it might be useful to compare image captures to detect small differences between two or more digital images. Forensics users might also find the need to amplify minute changes in a series of images by using some of the various Stacks rendering algorithms to enhance such differences. Or, they might find the following creative technique useful when merging multiple images together to produce an image that represents a blend of all the common areas in a sequence of pictures. Pictures that have been shot using a high ISO video camcorder in low light conditions could be greatly enhanced using this technique to produce a single image with greatly enhanced image detail.

As I pointed out earlier in Chapter 5, a Median rendering is best at removing noise or blending images that have been shot hand held, or where you are trying to remove people moving through a shot. The Mean rendering works best when processing static shots. For example, astronomers could use a technique like the one shown here to combine a series of astronomy photographs but use a Mean rendering instead of a Median rendering to remove extraneous noise.

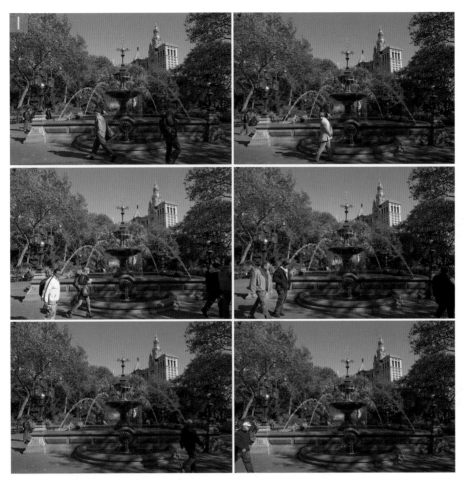

**1** Here is a sequence of photographs that were shot hand held over a time period of a minute or so. There were a lot of people walking in front of the fountain and I just made sure that I captured enough shots so that each portion of the picture had two or more frames where someone wasn't in front of the camera.

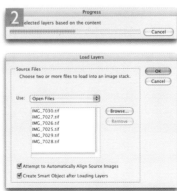

**2** I opened all of these photographs up in Photoshop and went to the File ⇨ Scripts menu to choose: Load Files into Stack. This opened the dialog shown here, where I chose Use: Open Files and checked the Attempt to Automatically Align Source Images and Create Smart Object after Loading Layers options.

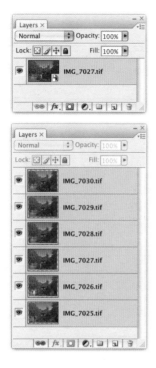

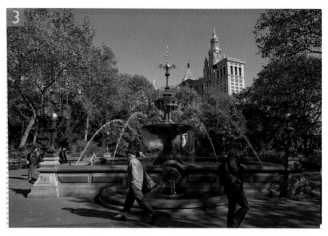

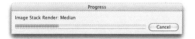

**3** Depending on how many pictures you have and how large they are, it may take a few minutes to process all the photographs. What you will end up with will be a new document with a Smart Object layer that contains all the previously open image documents as layers grouped within the Smart Object. If you double-click on the Smart Object icon you will see the full expanded list of layers contained in this Smart Object.

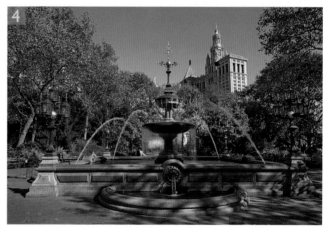

**4** And now for the clever part. If you have the Smart Object open, then make sure you close it again. You will want to start with the Smart Object selected (see the Layers palette top left). Go to the Layer menu and choose Smart Objects ⇨ Image Stack Mode ⇨ Median. Again, the Stacks rendering may take a little while to complete. In the result shown here, the Median rendering managed to blend the layers such that nearly all of the people in the merged picture disappeared completely.

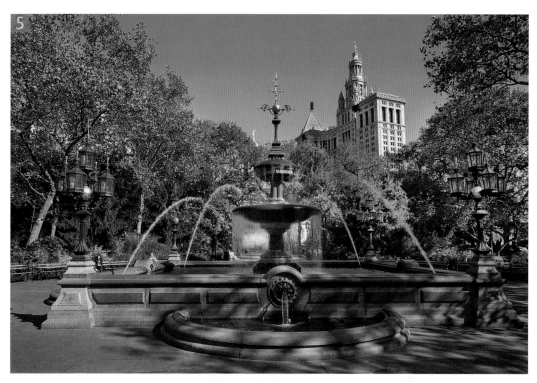

**5** The Image Stack median rendering did a pretty good job of removing the people, but there were still a few ghost outlines left. Obviously some people were having too good a time in the sun to want to move around much. Plus there were a few bits of rubbish and artifacts around the edges of the picture where the frames had overlapped. I tidied up the final picture by adding a little bit of spotting on a new layer and added some masked Curves adjustment layers to provide some dodging and burning to produce the final version shown above.

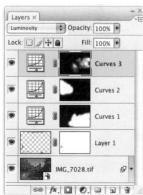

## Warp transforms

Photoshop also features a Warp transform mode. This tool is great for carrying out curved distortions on a layer in Photoshop and there was an example back on page 392 that showed you how to make use of this feature.

# Transform commands

The Image menu provides a choice of options in the Rotate Canvas submenu to rotate or flip an image. You use these commands to reorient a document where, say, a photograph had been scanned upside down.

The Transform commands can all be found in the Edit ⇨ Transform menu and these will allow you to apply transformations to individual or linked groups of layers. Select a layer or make a selection of the pixels that you wish to transform and choose either Edit ⇨ Transform or Edit ⇨ Free Transform (or check the Show Transform Controls box in the move tool Options palette). The main Transform commands include: Scale, Rotate, Skew, Distort and Perspective and these transformations can be applied singly or combined in a sequence before clicking *Enter* or *Return* or double-clicking within the Transform envelope to OK the transformation, which will be applied using the default interpolation method selected in the Photoshop preferences to calculate the new transform shape. You can apply any number of tweaking adjustments before applying the actual transform. A low resolution preview quickly shows you the changed image shape and at any time you can use the Undo command (⌘ *Z* *ctrl* *Z*) to revert to the last defined transform preview setting. And you can also adjust the transparency of a layer during mid-transform. The advantage of this is that a lot of folks like to use the Transform command to align layered images and having the ability to modify the opacity of the layer at the same time is very useful.

The Free Transform option is probably the most versatile of all and this is the one you will want to use most of the time. To access this, choose Edit ⇨ Free Transform or use the ⌘ *T* *ctrl* *T* keyboard shortcut and modify the transformation using the keyboard controls as indicated on the following pages. The Free Transform command is also available via the contextual menu. Just *ctrl* right mouse-click on a layer and select Free Transform.

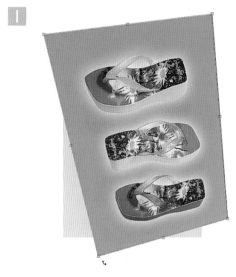

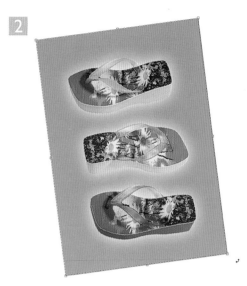

**1** You can rotate, skew or distort an image in one go using the Edit ⇨ Free Transform command. The following steps show you some of the modifier key commands to use to constrain a free transform adjustment.

**2** Place the cursor outside the bounding border and drag in any direction to rotate the image. Holding down the 𝘚𝘩𝘪𝘧𝘵 key as you drag constrains the rotation in 15 degree increments.

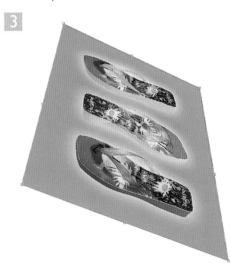

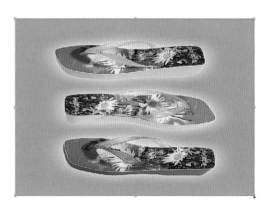

**3** Hold down the ⌘ ctrl key as you click any of the handles of the bounding border to perform a free distortion.

**4** If you want to constrain the distortion symmetrically around the center point of the bounding box, hold down the ⌥ alt key as you drag a handle.

403

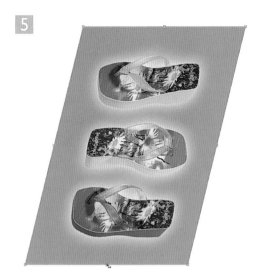

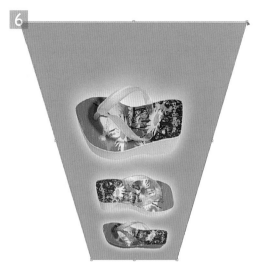

**5** To skew an image, hold down the ⌘ *Shift* *ctrl* *Shift* keys and drag one of the side handles.

Photograph by Davis Cairns. Client: Red or Dead.

**6** To carry out a perspective distortion, hold down the ⌘ ⌥ *Shift* *ctrl* *alt* *Shift* keys in unison and drag on one of the corner handles. When you are happy with any of the new transform shapes described here, press *Enter* or *Return* or double-click within the Transform envelope to apply the transform. Press *esc* if you wish to cancel.

## Smart Object mask solution

Another solution to the Smart Object plus mask transform problem is to place a Smart Object in a layer group and apply a layer mask to the Layer Group. If you now select the Layer Group and choose Free Transform, you can transform the mask and Smart Object in unison.

## Repeat Transforms

After applying a transform to the image data, you can instruct Photoshop to repeat that transform again by going to the Edit menu and choosing: Transform ⇨ Again (the shortcut is ⌘ *Shift* *T* *ctrl* *Shift* *T* ). The image transform will take place again on whatever layer is selected using the last remembered transform instruction. You can therefore apply a repeat transform to the same layer again or transform another existing layer. Where I find the Transform Again command to come in most use is when I need to repeat a precise transform on two separate layers.

The Transform Again command can also be regarded as a necessity when working on Smart Objects that have a layer mask applied to them. You see, there is currently no mask linking for Smart Objects, as you have with all other layers in Photoshop. Therefore, if you move or transform a Smart Object layer, you can use the Transform Again command to apply the same transformation to the mask layer as well.

## Numeric Transforms

When you select any of the Transform commands from the Edit menu or check Show Bounding Box in the move tool options, the Options palette will display the Numeric Transform commands shown below. The Numeric Transform options enable you to accurately define any transformation as well as choose where to position the centering reference point position. For example, the Numeric Transform is commonly used to change the percentage scale of a selection or layer. You just enter the scale percentages in the Width and Height boxes. If the Constrain Proportions link icon is switched off you can set the width and height independently. And you can also change the central axis for the transformation by repositioning the black dot (circled).

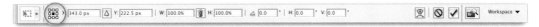

Figure 8.32 The Photoshop tool Options bar shown here in Transform mode.

## Transforming selections and paths

You can also apply transforms to Photoshop selections and vector paths. Make a selection and choose Select ⇨ Transform Selection (note, if you choose Edit ⇨ Transform, you will transform the selection contents of course). Transform Selection works just like the Edit ⇨ Free Transform command. You can use the exact same modifier key combinations to scale, rotate and distort the selection outline. Or you can use *ctrl* right mouse-click to call up the contextual menu of transform options. With Transform Selection, you can modify a selection shape quite effortlessly.

Whenever you have an active pen path the Edit menu will switch to Transform Path mode. You can use the Transform Path command to manipulate a completed path or a group of selected path points (the path does not have to be closed). But remember, you will not be able to execute a transform on an image on an image layer (or layers) until you have deselected all paths.

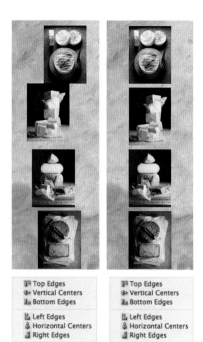

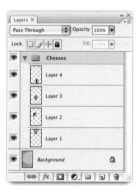

Figure 8.33 These linked layered images were arranged using the layer alignment feature. I chose Layer ⇨ Distribute Linked ⇨ Vertical Centers to evenly balance out the spacing and followed this with the Layer ⇨ Align Linked ⇨ Horizontal Centers. These alignments brought all the individual images horizontally centered around their common axis as shown in the above example.

Photographs: Laurie Evans.

## Transforms and alignment

Any transform you carry out can be repeated using the Edit ⇨ Transform ⇨ Again command (⌘ *Shift* *T* *ctrl* *Shift* *T* ). The transform coordinate change is memorized in Photoshop, so even if other image edits are carried out in between, the Transform ⇨ Again command will always remember the last used transform.

When more than one layer is present, the layer order can be changed via the Layer ⇨ Arrange menu, to bring a layer forward or back in the layer stack. In addition to this, two or more linked layers can be aligned in various ways via the Layer ⇨ Align Linked menu. The latter is a desirable feature for design-based work when you want to precisely align image or text layer objects in a design. The combination of repeat transforms and align layers also provides lots of interesting possibilities for making image patterns out of repeat transformations of a single element.

The alignment commands allow you to both distribute and align linked layers according to a number of different rules in the submenu list. To use this feature, first make sure the layers you want to align are all selected in the Layers palette, linked together, or in a layer group. The Distribute command evenly distributes the linked layers based on either the top, vertical central, bottom, left, horizontal central or right axes. So if you have several linked layer elements and you want them to be evenly spread apart horizontally and you want the distance between the midpoints of each layer element to be equidistant, then choose Layer ⇨ Distribute Linked ⇨ Horizontal Center. If you next want the layer elements to align, then go to the Layer ⇨ Align Linked menu. If the layers to be moved are linked, select the one to which you want the other layers to align. The other layer elements will always reposition themselves around the active layer.

Note here that all the Layer menu and Layers palette shortcuts are listed in a separate appendix which is available on the DVD as a PDF document.

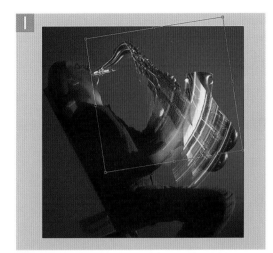

**1** Here I wanted to add more Motion Blur to the saxophone in this photograph. I began by making a mask of the saxophone instrument (which you can see in the Channels palette). I loaded this mask as a selection and used ⌘ J ctrl J to make a new copy layer from the background. I then selected Free Transform from the Edit menu, positioned the central axis point on the mouthpiece and dragged outside the bounding box to rotate the layer.

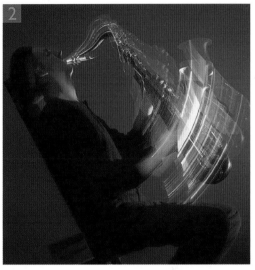

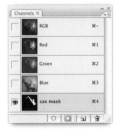 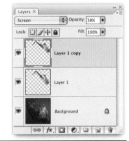

**2** I dragged the rotated layer to the New Layer button in the Layers palette to make a duplicate layer and chose Edit ⇨ Transform ⇨ Again command ( ⌘ Shift T ctrl Shift T ). This applied a repeat transformation. I then changed the blend mode of the two layers to Screen mode at 38%.

**3** To complete the effect, I chose Filter ⇨ Blur ⇨ Radial Blur and applied a Spin Blur to the first layer. Note that the blur center was offset roughly to where the mouthpiece was. I then applied the filter again ( ⌘ F ctrl F ) to the second layer.

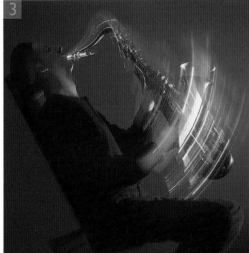

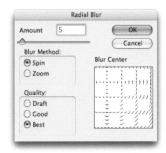

Photograph: Eric Richmond.

## Auto-Alignment

So far we have only looked at the use of the auto-alignment in Photoshop CS3 when auto-aligning images into an Image Stack. Let's now look at how to auto-align image layers in a document.

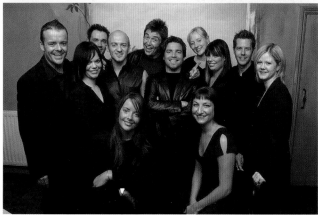

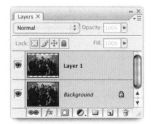

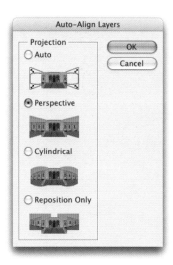

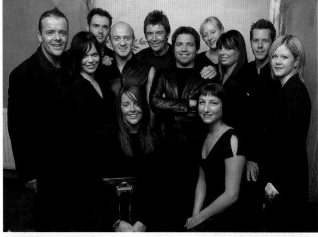

**1** Here are two photographs from a sequence of shots taken of a group portrait. Ideally, I wanted to combine the exposure at the top with the one below, where the two girls in the front looked more relaxed. To do this, I used the move tool (with the *Shift* key held down) to drag the lower photograph across to the top image to add it as a new layer in register with the one below. I then selected both layers and went to the Edit menu and chose Auto-Align Layers... I selected the Perspective option and clicked OK.

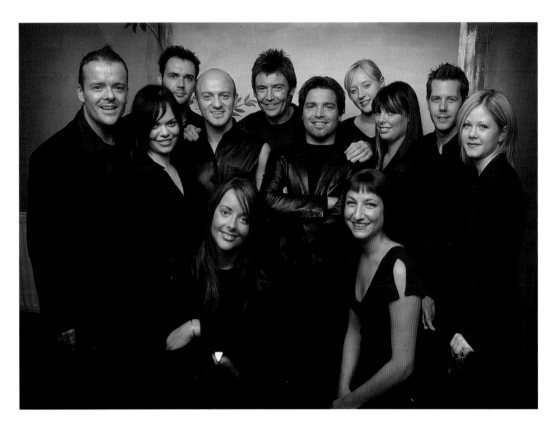

**2** After applying the Auto-Align command, the two layers should be in close register. In this example, the Auto-Align process enlarged the Layer 1 slightly, so that the people in the Layer 1 photograph matched the size of the people in the Background layer photograph. I then added a layer mask filled with black (🔲 *alt*-click the Add Layer mask button in the Layers palette.

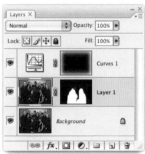

The interesting thing to note about the example used here is that the two photographs were taken from slightly different shooting angles and with different crops. But when the Auto-Align feature is used in the Perspective mode, it can do a really good job of aligning the images and getting them to match. If the photographs you are joining together were, for example, shot with the camera locked in position on a tripod, then you might find it better to use the Reposition Only alignment.

Client: Clipso

## Photomerge

The Photomerge command has been improved through the shared use of the new align content technology in Photoshop CS3. The difference between this and the Align Layers command is that you use Align Layers to align layers already in an image document. Photomerge is used to create an align layered image from a selected set of images. If you want to read more about the use of Photomerge, refer to Chapter 15 on automating Photoshop.

## Auto-Blend cut-outs

If you look closely at the way the Auto-Blend works, you will notice that when it analyzes the images, it adds a mask to each layer such that each area of the final composite is defined by a single portion from each layer. And the layers themselves are cut out using a jagged outline to break up the edges of each layer element. As a result of this, you should find that the combined Auto-Align and Auto-Blend, or full Photomerge process will usually produce a composite free of overlapping picture elements and fuzzy sections, like you can see in the Step 1 result opposite.

## *Auto-Blend layers*

The full auto-align process is carried out in two stages. So far we have looked at stage one, in which the Auto-Align Layers command is used to align selected layers, based on the image content and place them in register. An Auto-Blend Layers command can be used to complete the process, by intelligently analyzing the image and aggressively masking the individual layers to produce a composite in which the individual layers are all masked out like pieces of a jig saw puzzle. In the example shown on the opposite page, I used the Photomerge command settings shown in Figure 8.34 to merge a group of selected images using a Cylindrical layout, but without applying the 'Advanced Blending'. This allowed me the opportunity to apply some edits to the individual layers, before selecting the Edit ➪ Auto-Blend layers command to merge the layers together more smoothly. Note that the Photomerge command shown below in Figure 8.34 shares the same interface options as the Auto-Align Layers dialog. Basically, the Auto-Align Layers is just performing the layer alignment step that is part of a full Photomerge operation.

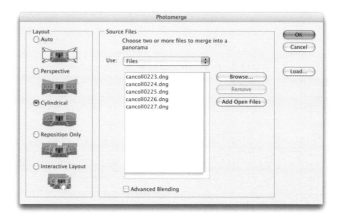

**Figure 8.34** Here is the Photomerge dialog showing the settings used to create the Photomerge composite shown in Step 1, opposite. The Cylindrical layout can be used to create a photomerge image in which the natural perspective lines are constrained to a cylindrical mapping. This is a useful layout mode to choose when merging images that make up an extreme wide-angle view.

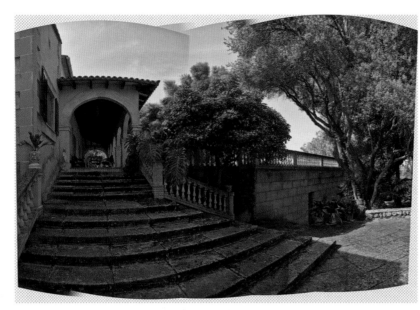

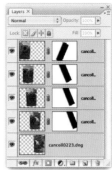

**1** As was mentioned in the text on the opposite page, there are times when it is more helpful to carry out a photomerge in stages. In this example, I used the Photomerge command to align the selected images, so that I could edit them individually first before blending them.

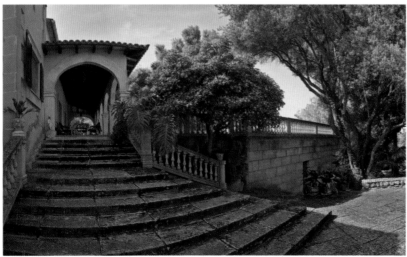

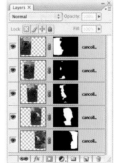

**2** Once I had edited the layers, I selected them all and chose Edit ⇨ Auto-Blend Layers to merge them and create the composite shown here (with a little extra work done to enhance the sky color).

### Matchlight software

Professional studio photographers may be interested in looking at the Matchlight system where you can place a special disk in a location scene and the software will be able to interpret the camera angle and lighting you need to use in the studio to match the outdoor location. For more information go to: www.gomatchlight.com.

### Masking programs and plug-ins

There are some third-party plug-ins which you might consider using as an alternative to the Photoshop methods described here. The most popular plug-ins are: Ultimatte Advantedge www.ultimatte.com and Extensis Mask Pro 3.0 www.extensis.com.

## Creating a montage

We have so far covered the basics of using selections, channels, pen paths and layers. Now we shall look at how these tools are put to use with some practical examples that demonstrate how I went about creating some composite images using layers in Photoshop.

The image selection is important because you want to make sure that the pictures you are about to combine into a composite image are able to match successfully. Care must be taken at the selection stage to check that the lighting conditions are similar and that the perspective will match. In the example shown on the page opposite this task is quite easy because I am combining two pictures that were shot outdoors with the sun coming from roughly the same direction. It also helps that the two pictures were both shot using a moderate wide-angle lens. If you want to be really precise then you may need to measure and match the camera height and angle. The colors may not match, but then that is a fairly easy thing to correct in Photoshop. If you want to achieve a realistic-looking join between two images, then the edges need to be made soft so that the two pictures blend together as smoothly as possible.

The next thing to do is to plan how to make the mask. Ask yourself how precise the mask needs to be. Could you, for example, get away with a simple magic wand or quick selection, or do you need to draw a pen path? As you will see later on in this chapter, I often like to inspect the individual color channels, copy the one with the most contrast and adapt the channel content to make a good mask. This can often cut out the need to draw a complex path. But alas, there are many times when drawing a pen path is the only way you can ever hope to accurately define the outline of an object. You could of course persevere with magic wand selections and edit such a selection using the paintbrush in Quick Mask mode. Occasionally I observe people preparing masks in Photoshop this way and I do find it really painful to watch because in the long run you will find drawing a pen path is nearly always going to be the quicker option by far.

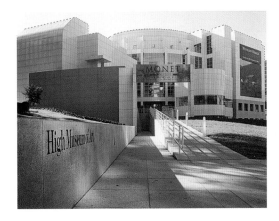

**1** I wanted to add a new sky to the picture shown here. Because the photograph was cropped quite tightly, I added extra white canvas to the top of the frame and began by making a selection of the sky area. A simple way of doing this is to select the magic wand tool, set the tolerance to around 12 and click in the sky area. You can see here an example of the selection saved as a new alpha channel mask. But my preferred method was to draw a pen path of the building, convert this to a selection and save as an alpha channel.

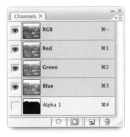
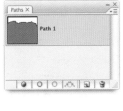

**2** I then looked for an image with an interesting sky, opened it, selected the move tool and dragged the beach image across to the museum image, to add it as a new layer. This new layer needed to be scaled up slightly, so I chose Edit ➪ Free Transform and dragged the corner handles so as to make the sky fit the width of the picture.

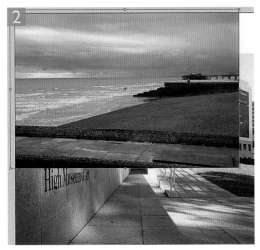

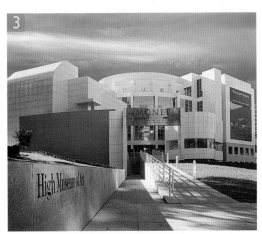

**3** Once I had scaled the sky to match the dimensions of the master image, it was time to cut out the sky, which I did by loading the mask I had created earlier. I activated the pen path and hit ⌘ *Enter* *ctrl* *Enter* to convert the path to a selection (alternatively, I could have ⌘ *ctrl*-clicked the alpha channel I had pre-saved to reload the selection). I then clicked on the Add New Layer Mask button at the bottom of the Layers palette to convert the selection to a layer mask, hiding all but the sky of Layer 1.

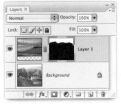

## Layer Matte commands

There are also some matting controls available in the Layer menu. One could use the Layer ⇨ Matting ⇨ Remove Black Matte command to remove all the stray black pixels. Likewise, the Remove White Matte command will remove the white pixels from a cut-out which was once against a white background. Where you have colored fringing, the Layer ⇨ Matting ⇨ Defringe command will replace edge pixels with color from neighboring pixels from just inside the edge. But the effectiveness of these is somewhat limited.

## Removing a matte color

If you use an anti-aliased selection to move an image element across to another image as a layer, the edge pixels may still contain some of the original background color. If the original picture has a black background, then some of the black matte pixels will appear as a black outline edge. The technique shown here is one based on a technique I once saw demonstrated by Greg Vander Houwen. The basic principle is that you can remove stray, spillover pixels from the edges of a layer by making a border selection of that layer and then copying some pixels from the layer below and sandwiching them on the layer above. The edge pixels are removed by selecting a layer blending mode which targets the edge pixels. To remove a black matte use Lighten, to remove white pixels try Darken.

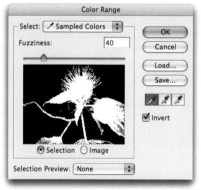

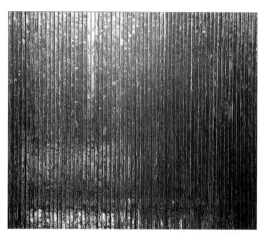

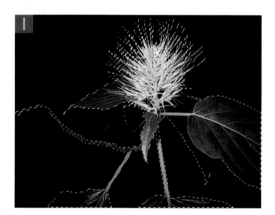

**1** I began by making a Color Range selection of the black area surrounding the flower. The Invert box was checked in the Color Range dialog, so this created an inverted selection that defined the flower's outline. The selection needed a little tidying up though, and I was able to do this in Quick Mask mode. I then selected the move tool and prepared to drag the selected pixel contents across to the other image shown here of the purple slatted glass.

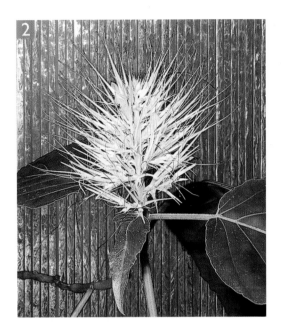

**2** Here is a close-up view of the flower placed as a new layer in the purple backdrop image. You will notice that a lot of black pixels have been carried over from the black background that surrounded the flower in the original image. One could try using the Layer ⇨ Matting ⇨ Remove Black Matte command to get rid of these black pixels, but it is not always as effective as one would like it to be.

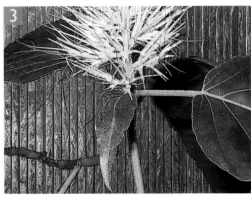

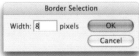

**3 |** ⌘ *ctrl*-clicked Layer 1 to load the flower as a selection again and then chose Select ⇨ Modify ⇨ Border... and entered a width of 8 pixels (the width will vary depending on the size of your image and transition width of the image borders). I then feathered the selection by 2 pixels.

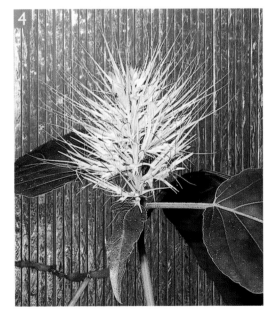

**4** With the border selection active I selected the Background layer and chose Layer ⇨ New ⇨ Layer via copy and then moved this Layer 2 to the top of the layer stack, above the flower. Now for the clever bit. Because I wanted to remove the black pixels, I changed the blend mode to Lighten. If I had wanted to remove white pixels, then I would select Darken mode. And finally I reduced the layer opacity slightly to 85%.

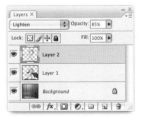

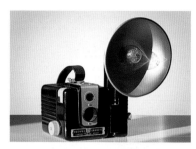

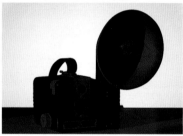

**Figure 8.35** One should always be on the lookout for any easy ways to create a mask. If, for example, you are shooting a still-life subject in the studio against a white backdrop you could try shooting an extra digital capture with the foreground lights switched off and this will give you an image that can quickly be converted into a mask.

Photo: Jeff Schewe.

## Cheating a mask

Do you really need to spend ages creating a mask in Photoshop? If you are a still-life studio photographer, the answer may be staring you in the face. Figure 8.35 gives you one example of a situation where a table top studio setup can allow you to cheat at creating a mask by simply turning off the foreground lights and making an additional exposure with a digital camera and using the silhouette image this creates as the basis for a mask. As long as you are using a digital camera to capture the two exposures and the camera is mounted on a tripod, the mask created here will be completely pixel accurate.

## Masking an object with a vector path

This next example shows you how I was able to prepare a silhouette mask based entirely on an outline made with the pen tool and how I then created a vector mask in Photoshop to cut out the airplane and place it against a sky image.

A pen path is the most sensible solution to use here because the object to be cut out had a smooth 'geometric' outline and the background behind the aircraft was very busy and contained a lot of intersecting lines. And also, with an image like this it would be almost impossible to separate the aircraft from the wall and girders behind using any other method than a pen path outline.

The Spirit of St Louis, flown by Charles Lindbergh, made the world's first solo transatlantic flight from the USA to Paris in 1927 and I photographed this historic aircraft inside the Washington DC National Air and Space Museum, Smithsonian Institution. The daylight coming in from the skylight above enabled me to produce a convincing composite when I blended the aircraft against an outdoor shot of a sky.

Spirit of St Louis: Pioneers of Flight Gallery. Reproduced courtesy of: National Air and Space Museum, Smithsonian Institution.

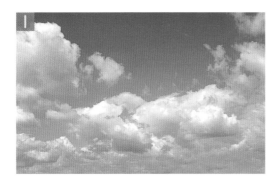

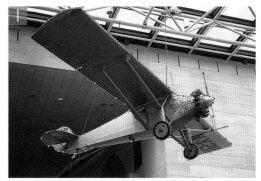

**1** Here are the two images: the sky background and the museum interior shot of the Spirit of St Louis. I selected the move tool from the Tools palette and dragged the St Louis image across to the sky image window, where it became a new layer (if the *Shift* key is held down, the new layer will be centered).

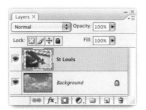

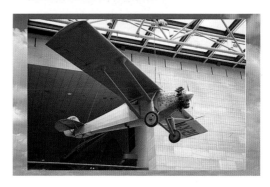

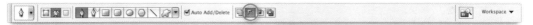

**2** I needed to isolate the aircraft from its surroundings. Because the subject had such a detailed background, there was no automatic way of doing this in Photoshop so, in this instance, the only solution was to draw a path. I magnified the image to view on screen at 200% and drew a path with the pen tool around the edges of the aircraft.

When the pen tool is selected, you can access all the other family of pen path modifying tools using just the *⌘* *ctrl* and *⌥* *alt* keys. Holding down the *⌘* *ctrl* key temporarily changes the pen tool to the direct selection tool. Holding down the *⌥* *alt* key temporarily changes it to the convert point tool. Clicking on a path adds a new point and clicking on an existing point deletes it. To make a hole in the work path, inside the outer edge, I clicked on the Subtract from Path Area mode button in the pen tool Options bar (circled).

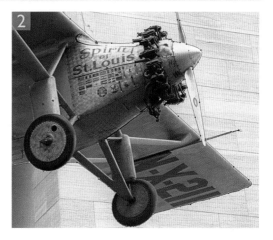

**Martin Evening**
**Adobe Photoshop CS3 for Photographers**

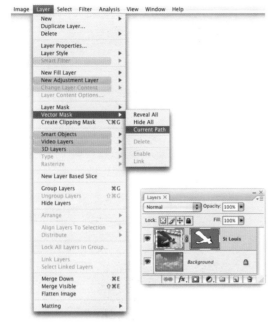

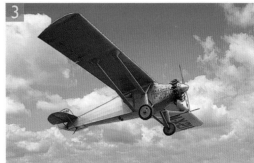

**3** When the path was complete, I made sure that the aircraft layer and path were both active. I went to the Layer menu and chose: Vector Mask ⇨ Current Path. This added a vector mask to the aircraft layer based on the active work path. The vector mask appeared linked alongside the aircraft layer.

**4** At this stage it was possible to reposition the aircraft if I wished, because the vector mask was linked to the layer image contents. Under close inspection, the aircraft appeared to have been reasonably well isolated by the path. However, where this is not the case, you can edit the vector mask outline using the usual pen path editing tools. If I group selected several of the path points around the wheel and moved them, you can see how the background is still visible and will show through the mask.

**5** Once I was happy with the way the vector mask was hugging the outline, I chose Layer ⇨ Rasterize ⇨ Vector Mask. This converted the vector mask into an image layer mask.

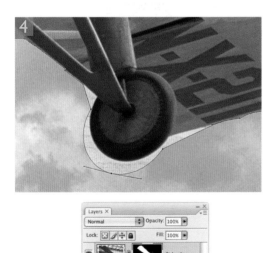

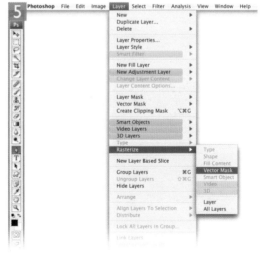

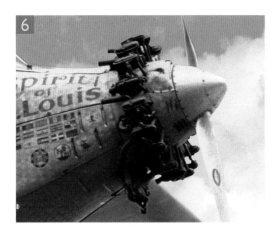

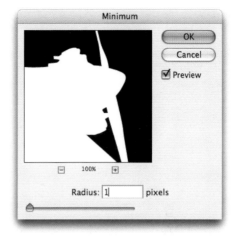

**6** I activated the image layer mask. I then went to the Filter menu and selected Other ⇨ Minimum and chose a 1 pixel Radius. This step effectively 'choked' the mask, making it shrink to fit around the edge of the masked object. Sometimes it helps to fade the last filter slightly using the Edit ⇨ Fade... command. Next, I applied a 1 pixel radius Gaussian Blur (you may wish to consider following this with an Edit ⇨ Fade... command, but it is not always absolutely necessary). I then applied a Levels adjustment to the mask. I chose Image ⇨ Adjustments ⇨ Levels, but kept the shadow point set where it was and adjusted the Gamma and Highlight sliders only. In effect what I did over these past few steps was to shrink the mask slightly, soften the edge and use the Levels adjustment to fine-tune the choke on the mask.

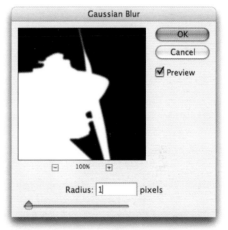

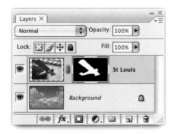

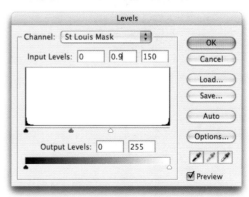

**7** The mask was mostly OK and only a couple of areas needed further improvement. I went to the History palette and reverted to the history state which was the one before I began adjusting the mask (it usually helps to have Allow Nonlinear History switched on in the History palette options). I then clicked on the history brush icon to the left of the fully modified mask history state and selected the history brush from the Tools palette. The image had now reverted to the unmodified layer mask state but, wherever I painted with the history brush, I could paint in the modified mask and vary the opacity of the history painting as I did so.

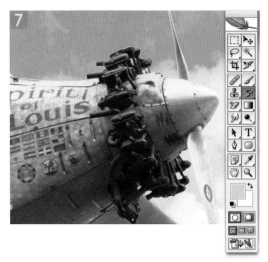

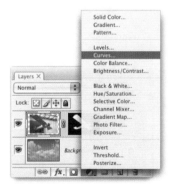 — Modified mask history state

**8** By this stage, the Spirit of St Louis appeared successfully cut out from its original museum surroundings. Because an image layer mask had been used to isolate the aircraft, no pixels had actually been erased and the mask could be edited at any time.

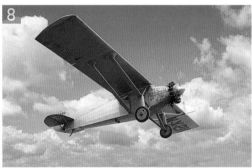

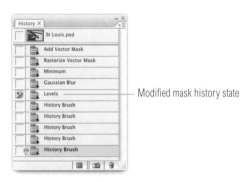

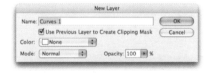

**9** I selected the aircraft layer again and ⌘ *alt* +moused down on the Adjustment Layer button in the Layers palette. I chose Curves and in the New Layer dialog box checked Use Previous Layer to Create Clipping Mask. This ensured that the following color adjustment would affect this layer only. The Curves adjustment made the aircraft slightly more blue and helped it blend more realistically with the color balance of the sky.

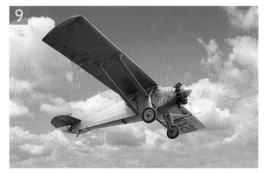

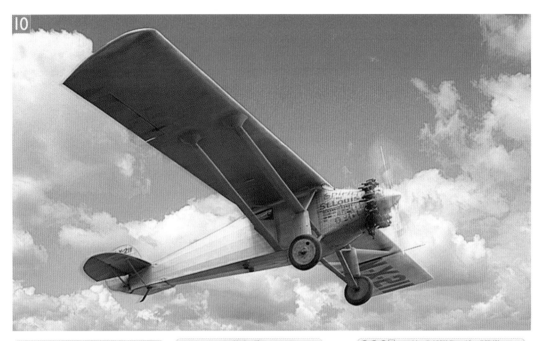

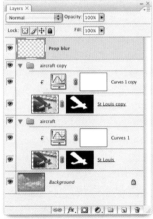

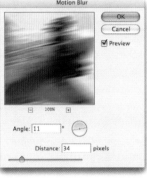

**10 |** *Shift* selected the St Louis layer and the Curves layer and selected Layer ⇨ Group Layers (⌘ G *ctrl* G). I then dragged the new layer group down to the Add New Layer button to duplicate the layer group. With the copied aircraft layer selected, I applied a Motion Blur to the layer. I then reduced the opacity to 80%. I had also prepared a spinning propeller image. I dragged this in as a separate layer and transformed it to match the scale of the aircraft. This final tweaking helped create the illusion of the Spirit of St Louis flying through the air. But, did they have high speed color film to record Charles Lindbergh's transatlantic flight in 1927?

## Keeping the edges soft

I have said it before, but it is worth repeating: retouched photographs will not look right if they have 'pixel-sharp' edges. A mask derived from a path conversion will be too crisp, even if it is anti-aliased. Whereas soft edged masks will usually create for a more natural-looking finish. So, either feather your selections before converting a selection to a mask or if you have a layer mask, try applying a little Gaussian Blur. You might find it helpful to use the blur tool to locally soften mask edges.

# Masking hair

Hair is one of the hardest things to mask successfully and if you are a people photographer who uses Photoshop to create montage images, you will readily appreciate the difficulty that is involved here. There is always a lot of discussion on the various Internet forums about this particular subject, so I know it is something that will interests a lot of photographers and Photoshop artists. The problem most people have is how to get rid of the trace pixels around the edges of the hair – these are always a sure giveaway that the picture has been comped together on the computer. What follows is a hair masking method which you can do in Photoshop without the need for any extra plug-ins and is a technique I find works well in most cases.

The first thing I would like to point out here is that for this technique to work, your model or subject must be photographed against a white or light colored backdrop. If you don't do this then you are just making the task a lot harder for yourself, so it is important that you plan ahead. All serious composite work is carried out against a plain backdrop. For example, the Ultimatte Advantedge software requires you shoot your subject against a blue or green backdrop. But in this example, I am going to show you how you can use a white backdrop.

The trick here is to make use of the existing color channel contents and to copy the information which is already there in the image and modify it to produce a new mask channel. So instead of attempting to trace every single strand of hair on a mask with a fine-tipped brush tool, you can save yourself a lot of time by making use of the information already contained in the color channels and use this to define the finely detailed edges. However, you will still find that the pen tool is useful for completing the outline around the smooth broad outline of the neck, shoulders and arms of the model's body.

**1** The following steps describe how I would go about photographing a model with a view to adding a new backdrop later. I normally plan my shoots to always photograph against a white background as this is the best way to mask the fine hair detail. In this example the background is not completely white, but there is certainly enough contrast between the hair and the backdrop for me to use the following technique to create a cut-out of the model and place her against a new backdrop image.

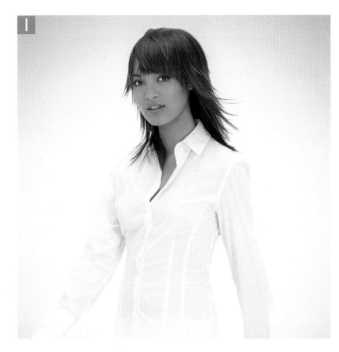

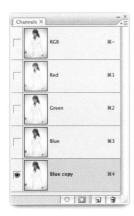

**2** I began by looking at the individual color channels and duplicated the one that contained the most contrast; in this case I decided that the Blue channel had the most contrast between the hair and the background. I duplicated the channel by dragging it to the New Channel button in the Channels palette. This created the new Blue copy channel shown active here.

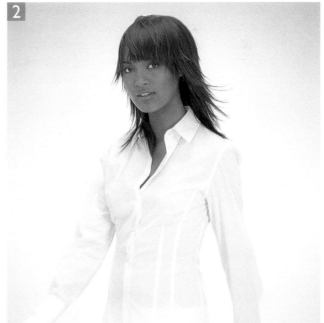

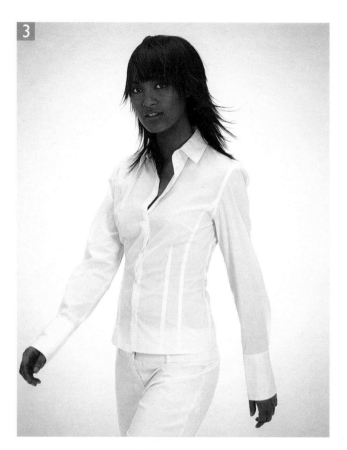

**3** The next few steps all took place on the Blue copy channel. I wanted to increase the contrast in this channel and make the hair darker. To do this, I went to the Image menu and chose Apply Image... As you can see in the dialog shown below, the Target channel was the Blue copy channel, the Source channel was also the same Blue copy channel and the blending mode was set to Multiply. So I was using the Apply Image to apply a Multiply blend mode on the alpha channel with itself. With Apply Image you can choose all sorts of channel blending combinations. Most of the time I use Apply Image in the Multiply and Overlay blending modes and will sometimes experiment with blending two different color channels with each other. The objective at this stage is to increase the contrast between the hair and background, by making use of the pixel information that is already present in the three color channels that make up this photograph.

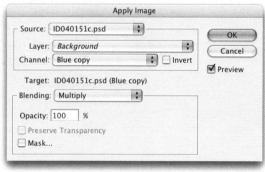

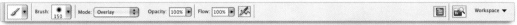

**4** Step 3 made quite a difference to the appearance of the mask channel and I now wanted to increase the contrast. To do this I used the paintbrush tool set to Overlay mode and switched between using black and white as the foreground colors. When using the Overlay blend mode, as you paint with white, paint is only applied to the light colored pixels. As you paint with black, paint is only applied to the dark colored pixels. Overlay is therefore a useful paint mode because you can paint quite freely using a large pixel brush to gradually build up the density around the dark hair strands without risk of painting over the light areas. I continued painting, taking care not to build up too much density on the outer hair strands. I should mention here as well that I prefer to paint using a pressure sensitive Wacom™ pen and tablet, with the pen pressure sensitivity for the Opacity switched on in the Brushes palette Other Dynamics options.

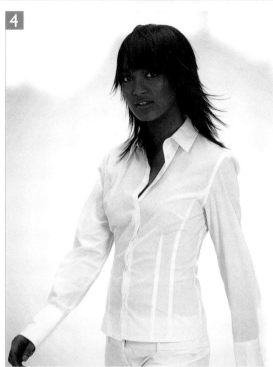

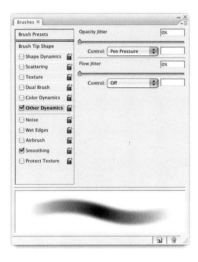

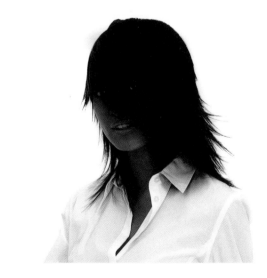

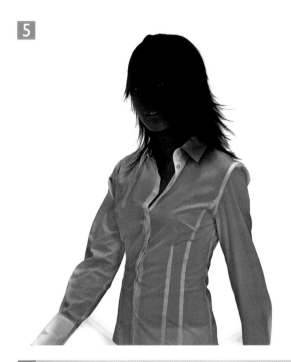

**5** The object at this stage is to create as much contrast as possible between the subject and the background. As well as using the Apply Image blend mode and the paint brush set to Overlay mode, you might like to try using the Shadow/Highlight adjustment to increase the density of the lighter pixels. I know this isn't what the Shadows/Highlight adjustment was intended for, but it really is a great tool for quick mask channel editing – give it a try next time. The trick here is to increase the Amount for the Highlights, adjust the Tonal Width to target the tones you want to darken, compensate with the Highlights Radius and tweak the result by taking the Brightness down and maybe adjust the Midtone Contrast as well.

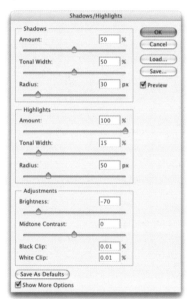

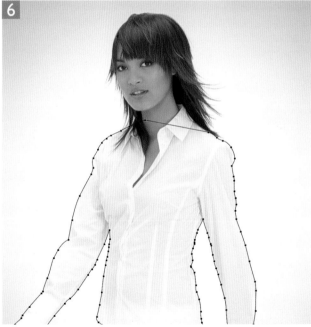

**6** The model's shirt was almost the same color as the backdrop so, in actual fact, the best way to isolate the rest of her body was to draw a pen path around the outline of her clothing.

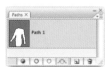

**7** I saved the Work path as a new path, called Path 1. I then converted this pen path to a selection by dragging Path 1 down to the Make Selection button in the Paths palette. I filled the selection with black, deselected the selection and used the paintbrush tool in Overlay mode again to paint over the rest of her face, to fill in the remainder of this mask channel.

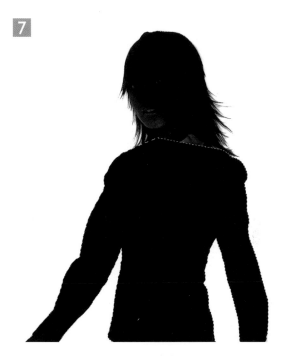

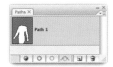

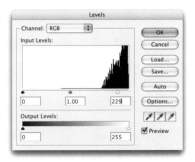

**8** With the mask complete I started putting it to use to clean up the background. I loaded the Blue copy channel as a selection (which selected the backdrop area only) and went to the Image menu to chose Adjustments ⇨ Levels. I applied a Levels adjustment to lighten the backdrop a little and create a nice white outline around the model. I then used the paint brush in Normal mode with white as the foreground color to paint the rest of the backdrop white. This is because it is not a good idea to be too heavy handed with the Levels adjustment. We want to use it enough to lighten the edges around the model, but no more than that. If I had lightened the backdrop further using Levels, I would have ended up destroying some of the fine hair strands.

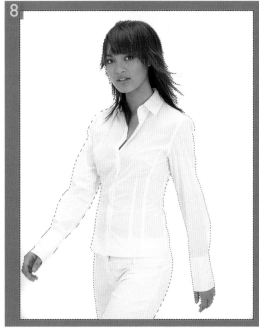

427

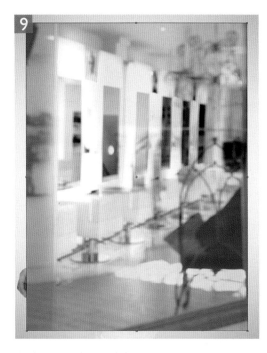

**9** It was now time to add a new backdrop. I opened up a new photograph of a salon interior, selected the move tool and dragged the backdrop image across to the model image window. This added the backdrop as a new layer. I kept the Layer 1 active and chose Edit ⇨ Free Transform and dragged the handles to scale the backdrop layer so that it filled the bounds of the underlying layer. When I was happy with the transformation I clicked OK.

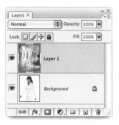

**10** I dragged the Green copy channel to the Load Selection button in the Layers palette and then clicked on the Add Layer Mask button (circled) in the Layers palette to convert the active selection to a layer mask. I also set the blending mode for Layer 1 to Multiply.

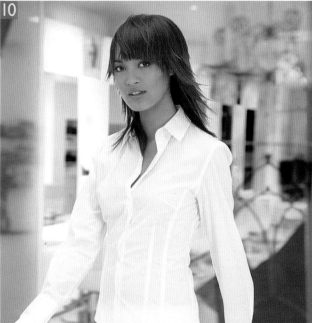

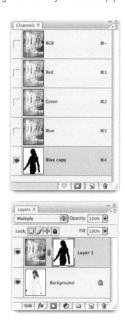

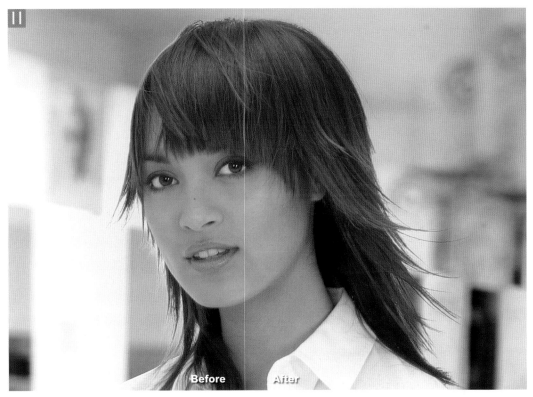

Before    After

**11** The layer mask based on the Blue copy channel punched a hole through Layer 1 and, by setting the layer blend mode to Multiply, this effectively 'projected' Layer 1 on top of the Background layer. As you can see, it is not a bad mask, but there are still some areas where we have white edges showing around the outline of the hair. The initial layer mask had worked reasonably well, but could still benefit from some fine-tuning. Earlier with the St Louis cut-out montage I showed you how to choke a mask using a combination of filters. Refine Edge allows you to do the same thing, but via a single dialog, and the above screen shot shows the picture before and after treatment.

Here is how it works. I made sure that the layer mask (not the layer image thumbnail) was selected and chose: Select ⇨ Refine Edge... and clicked on the Standard mask view (circled). You may initially see the hole in the mask displayed as white, but be patient while Photoshop calculates the mask and applies the mask transparently. And you will also want to hide the marching ants that will appear on screen by using ⌘ *H* *ctrl* *H*. I began by setting the Contract/Expand slider to choke the mask. Note that because the mask used here was hiding the selected layer, I actually needed to 'expand' the mask in order to shrink the size of the hole. Basically, drag the slider left or right to see what works best. I adjusted the radius, to smooth the edge transitions, and adjusted the Feather to help keep the mask edges looking soft.

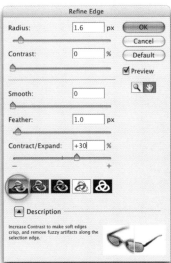

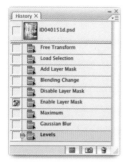

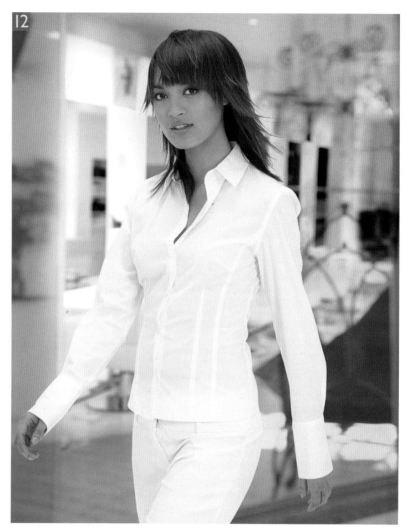

**12** Here is the completed version in which you can see a full length view of the model against the backdrop. One of the things that you have to look out for with this particular technique is that the modifications made to the layer mask, that are designed to improve the choke around the hair, may have a less desirable effect on the other areas of the image. What I suggest you do is analyze the whole of the outline to check the edges. Some portions may have looked better beforehand. To address this, I will select the History brush, set it to Normal blend mode and go to the History palette and set the source to the history state before I apply the Refine Edge treatment. And I then simply paint over the outline to restore the pre-treatment version (but make sure that the layer mask remains selected).

Client: Indola. Model: Pernille @ Storm

### *Masking tips*

I tried to show a varied combination of techniques in this last tutorial because I wanted to show how to mask a tricky subject in which it would be particularly difficult to mask out a white shirt from a white backdrop. This is a classic example of why pen tool skills are so important if you want to become an expert retoucher. But the main message I wanted to convey here is that it is always worth exploiting the channel content as much as you can as a shortcut to building an accurate mask that is based on the actual image content. As I showed in the tutorial, the tools I find useful here are the Apply Image command for building initial contrast by blending a channel with itself, or with a second channel. Changing the paint brush blend mode to Overlay is also a great tip for quick editing a black and white mask. And in recent years, I have found the Shadows/Highlight adjustment is perfect for then further improving the mask contrast.

### Refine Edge command

I am told that the Refine Edge command was actually based on my mask editing technique described in the Spirit of St Louis mask tutorial. In my opinion, the controls in Refine Edge now include everything you need to modify a layer mask edge. You can of course use Refine Edge via the Select menu or the Options palette (when a selection tool is active), but if you are preparing a selection in order to create a mask, it makes much more sense to use Refine Edge the way I have described on page 429, because this will allow you to preview the effects that the slider adjustments are having on the mask while it is active. As I mentioned earlier, when you use this method the initial preview may confuse you because after you click on the Standard mask view mode all you see is a white fill, but if you wait a few seconds, a transparent view will appear with marching ants active and you should use the ⌘ H ctrl H shortcut to hide the ants so that you can preview the mask properly.

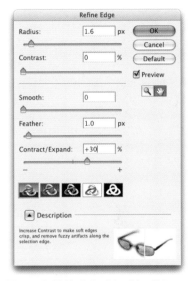

**Figure 8.36** The Refine Edge dialog. Note there is a Description section at the bottom of the Refine Edge dialog that helps explain what each of the controls do (summarized below).

**Radius**
Increasing the Radius will improve the edges in areas of soft transitions.

**Contrast**
This will make soft edges crisper and remove artifacts along the edges of a selection.

**Smooth**
This will help smooth out jagged selection edges (use Radius to help restore some of the detail).

**Feather**
This will uniformly soften the edge of the selection and help produce a soft edged mask.

**Contract/Expand**
This is the choke control and works like the Maximum and Minimum filters by shrinking or expanding a selection.

431

## Smoothing with Feather and Contrast

An alternative way to smooth a mask in Refine Edge is to use Feather and Contrast. The Smooth slider in Refine Edge is designed to smooth but without rounding out corners. If you want a more aggressive smoothing you can use Refine Edge's Feather and Contrast sliders. Simply increase Feather to blur the mask and then increase the Contrast to get back to the desired edge sharpness.

# Working with the quick selection tool

The quick selection tool is grouped with the magic wand in the Tools palette. I don't know about it being quick, but quick selection is certainly a more sophisticated kind of selection tool that has smart processing capabilities. You can use the quick selection tool to make a selection based on tone and color by clicking or dragging with the tool to define a portion of the image that you wish to select. You can then keep clicking or dragging to add to the selection without needing to hold down the *Shift* key as you do so. And you can subtract from a quick selection by holding down the ⌥ *alt* key as you drag. But what is clever about quick selection is that it remembers all the successive strokes that you make and this will provide stability to the selection as you add more strokes. So as you toggle between adding and subtracting, quick selection is temporarily storing these stroke instructions to help determine which pixels are to be selected and which are not. Sometimes you may find it can help if you make an initial selection and then apply a succession of subtractive strokes to define the areas you don't want to be included. You won't see anything happen as you apply these blocking strokes, but when you go on to select the rest of the object with the quick selection tool, you should find that as you add to a selection, the blocking strokes you applied previously will help prevent leakage outside of the area you wish to select. This aspect of quick selection behavior can help you select objects more successfully than was ever possible before with the magic wand. But as you make successive additive strokes to add to a selection and then erase these areas from the selection, you will have to work a lot harder going back and forth between adding and subtracting with the quick selection tool. In these situations it can be a good idea to clear the quick selection memory by using the 'double Q trick'. If you press the **Q** key twice, this will go to Quick Select mode and back to Selection mode again. The stroke constraints will be gone and you can then add to or subtract from the selection more easily since you have now cleared the quick selection memory.

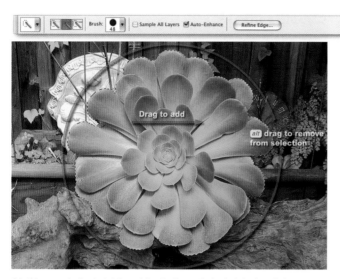

**1** In this example, I selected the quick selection tool, checked the Auto-Enhance edge option and dragged to make an initial selection of the plant interior. Then, with the ⌥ *alt* key held down, I dragged around the outer perimeter area to indicate the areas that were not to be included in the selection. I then continued clicking and dragging to select more of the plant leaves, while also ⌥ *alt* dragging outside to fine-tune the selection edge.

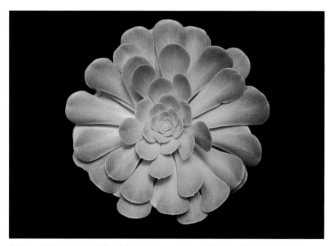

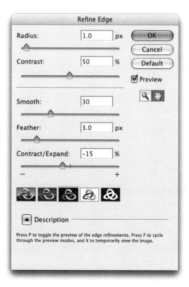

**2** I then clicked on the Refine Edge button and selected the 'on black' mask option to display the cut-out selection against a black background color. I contracted the selection slightly and applied a Smooth amount of 30 to smooth out the jagged edges. I found that by raising the Feather to 3 pixels and increasing the Contrast this was the right combination to get the selection outline I was after.

433

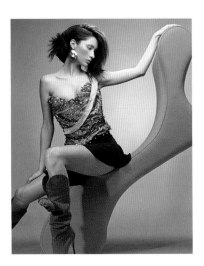

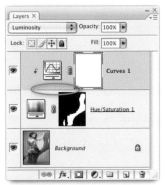

**Figure 8.37** In this example, I made a mask of the red chair and loaded the selection as a mask as I made a Hue/Saturation adjustment to change the color to match the backdrop. I then added a Curves adjustment layer which I wanted to share the same mask as the Hue/Saturation layer. Instead of reloading the selection and adding an identical mask, I created a clipping mask between the two adjustment layers.

Client: Rainbow Room.
Model: Jasmin Hemsley @ MOT.

## Clipping masks

Clipping masks enable you to mask the contents of a layer based on a mask that has already been applied to another layer. So if you have two or more layers that need to be masked identically, the most logical way to do this is to apply a mask to the first layer and then create a clipping mask with the layer or layers above it. Once a clipping mask has been applied, the upper layer or layers will appear indented in the Layers palette. You can alter the blending mode and adjust the relative opacity of the individual layers in a clipping mask, but the blending mode and opacity of the lower (masked) layer will continue to affect the blend and the opacity of all the layers that are in the clipping mask group.

The main advantage of using clipping masks is that whenever you have a number of layers that you require to share the same mask, you only need to apply a mask to the bottom most layer and when you make a clipping mask the layer (or layers) in the clipping mask group will all share that same mask. So for example, if you edit the master mask, the edit changes you make to that mask will be applied simultaneously to the layer (or layers) above it that are in the clipping mask group.

To create a clipping mask, make a *Shift* selection of the layers you want to group together and choose Layer ⇨ Clipping Mask ⇨ Create or *⌥* *alt*-click the border line between the layers (I have circled this region in Figure 8.37 opposite). This action will toggle creating and releasing the layers from a clipping mask. You can also use the keyboard shortcut *⌘* *⌥* *G* *ctrl* *alt* *G* to make a selected layer form a clipping mask with the layer below.

I use clipping masks a lot, but there is also another way that you can achieve the same kind of result and that is to make a selection of two or more layers and convert them into a layer group (Layer ⇨ Group Layers). With the layer group selected, click on the Add Layer Mask button in the Layers palette to add a layer mask to the group. If you now edit the layer mask for the layer group, you can simultaneously mask all the layer group contents.

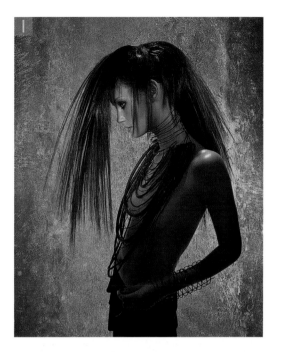

**1** If you check out the Layers palette below, you will notice that this is another example where a photograph was shot against white in the studio and a Backdrop layer was added on a separate layer above. The montage was created using the same steps described in the preceding tutorial.

**2** I wanted to add a gradient glow to make it look as if I had shone a light on the backdrop. I set white as the foreground color, selected the Backdrop layer and ⌥ *alt* moused down on the Add Adjustment Layer button at the bottom of the Layers palette, and selected Gradient from the pop-up menu. In the New Layer dialog, I checked: Use Previous Layer to Create Clipping Mask. I clicked OK and the Gradient Fill dialog appeared. I selected the foreground to transparency gradient, using a Radial gradient style. If you check the Layers palette again, you will notice that the Gradient layer appears indented, which signifies that it has formed a clipping mask with the layer below. I can remove the grouping by ⌥ *alt*-clicking on the line between the two layers.

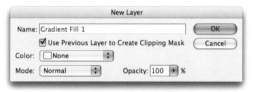

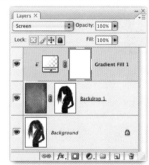

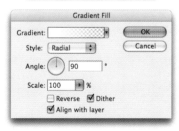

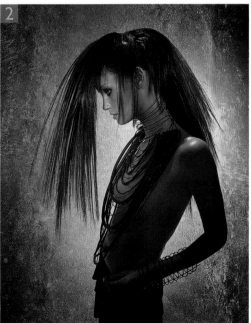

Client: JFK Hair. Model: Indriarty at Isis.

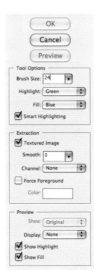

**Figure 8.38** The Extract filter options:

**Tool Options** Enter a value for the highlight or eraser brush size and choose a color for the Highlight and Fill displays. Smart Highlighting helps auto-detect the edges as you define a highlight edge.

**Extraction** The smoothness can be set anywhere between 0 and 100. If the preview shows an incomplete pixel selection, increasing the smoothness value will help rein in the remaining pixels. Force Foreground is useful where the object interior edge is particularly hard to define and the interior pixels are of a similar color value. Select the eyedropper tool to sample the interior color and check Force Foreground. Textured Image will take into account differences in texture as well as color.

**Preview** The view choices can be switched between the original image and the current extracted versions. The Show option allows you to choose the type of matte background to preview the extraction against. This can be the standard, transparent, Photoshop background pattern, gray, white, black or any other custom color.

# Extract filter

The Extract filter is able to intelligently isolate an object from its background. While automatic masking can sometimes make light of tedious manual masking, it can rarely ever be 100% successful. However, the enhancements added since the Extract filter made its first appearance in Photoshop certainly do make it a very workable tool and it includes the means to separate an object based on texture content as well as color. But you may find it helpful first to duplicate the layer you are about to extract before running the filter.

Choose Filter ⇨ Extract or the shortcut: ⌥ ⌘ X ［alt］［ctrl］［X］. The active layer will be displayed in the Extract dialog window. You then define the outline of the object using the edge highlighter tool. This task is made easier using the Smart Highlighting option, which is like a magnetic lasso tool for the Extract filter. Smart Highlighting will work well on clearly defined edges and can be temporarily disabled by holding down the ⌘ ［ctrl］ key as you drag. You need to highlight the complete edge of the object first (excluding where the object may meet the edge boundaries) and then fill the interior with the extract fill tool (clicking again with the fill tool will undo the fill). The Extract filter eraser tool can be used to erase highlight edges and when using the edge highlighter tool you can toggle between highlighting and erasing by holding down the ⌥ ［alt］ key. When the edges and interior fill are completed, click on the Preview button to see a preview of the extraction, or click OK to make an immediate extraction. The edge touchup tool can be used inside the preview window to add definition to weak edges, adding opacity where it sees transparency inside the edge and removing opacity outside of this edge. The cleanup tool will merely erase transparency from the extraction or restore erased transparency when you ⌥ ［alt］ drag. As you define the highlight edge, wherever possible, you want to select a small-size brush and aim to draw a narrow edge. Where there is an overlap between the object you want to extract and the background, you will want to draw a wider edge.

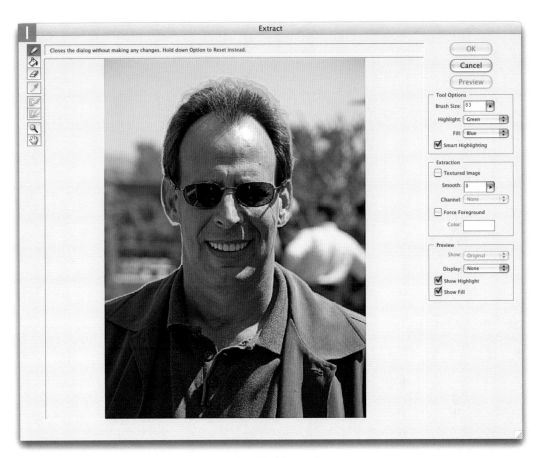

**1** Here is an example of where I wanted to make a cut-out of my friend Steve and remove him from the distracting elements in the background. I began by dragging the Background layer to the Make New Layer button in the Layers palette (this duplicated the Background layer). I then chose Filter ⇒ Extract. I selected the edge highlighter tool and started to draw around the edges of Steve's shoulders. You want the highlight edge to overlap the foreground and background areas, but the highlight edge must form a complete enclosure (you can ignore where the object meets the image boundaries). Notice that I had checked the Smart Highlighting box; this can make the edge drawing a little easier. The Smart Highlighting mode works in a similar way to the magic lasso and magic pen tool – it forces the edge highlighter tool to 'hug' the sharp edges as you draw. If you use a pressure sensitive pen, as you apply more pressure, you will produce a thicker edge.

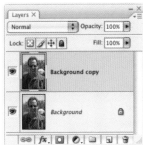

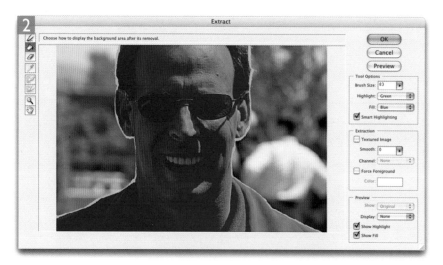

**2** When I had finished drawing the outline, I checked the result carefully and used the eraser tool to delete any parts where the edge was untidy and then selected the fill tool to click inside the outline and fill the interior.

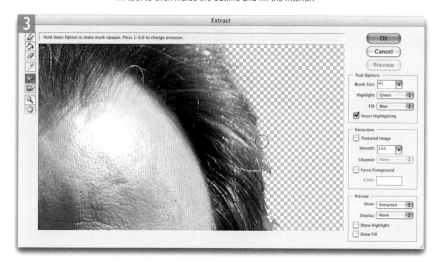

**3** To test the potential success of the extraction, I clicked on the Preview button. This applied the extraction to the image in the preview window only, but before doing that, I set the Smooth setting to 100. While in Preview mode, you can edit the edges using tools within the Extract dialog. Here, I selected the cleanup tool and used it to erase unwanted pixels and held down the ⌥ *alt* key to restore the pixels so far erased by the extraction. I also used the edge touchup tool to follow the edges, which adds opacity where the tool sees transparency inside the edge and removes opacity outside the edge.

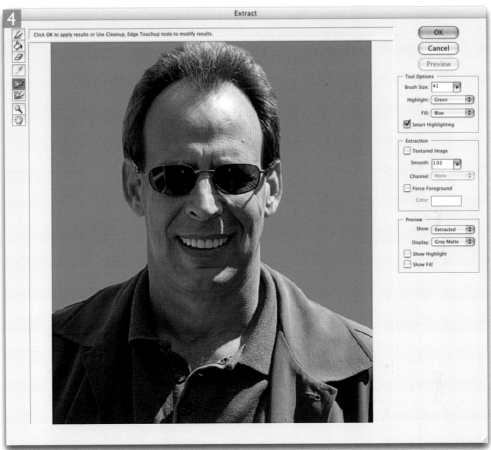

**4** While in Preview mode, it is worth spending time alternating between the cleanup tool and edge touchup tool to refine the edge. I suggest switching the Preview Display mode from transparency to Gray matte (and maybe the Black or White mattes as well), to check how the edges are looking.

I then clicked OK to permanently apply the extraction to the Background copy layer. If for some reason I needed to go back to the original version, it was still available in the layer below. But more usefully, one can use the History palette to restore any detail that shouldn't have been erased during the extraction. Go to the History palette, set the History State to the one before the Extraction as the history source and use the history brush to paint those pixels back in. If you still need to erase more pixels, I recommend selecting the background eraser tool (which is described in the Photoshop for Photographers Help Guide, available on the DVD). Set the background eraser tool to Find Edges mode, click on a sample area to define the pixel colors you want to erase and paint around the outside edge.

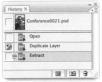

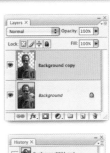

439

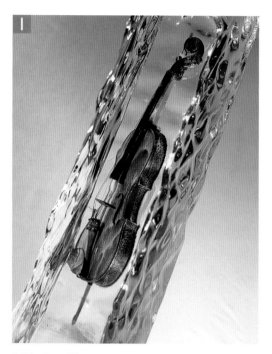

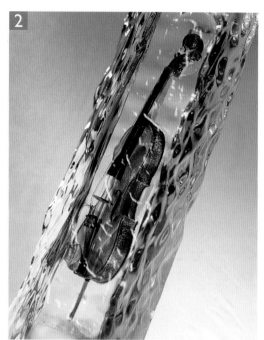

**1** Using Layer Effects, you can create and save layer styles that can be used in Photoshop to paint a texture. This illustration shows a violin trapped in a block of ice. I added an empty new layer and applied a layer style I had created called waterdroplet. You will find the waterdroplet layer style on the CD. To load this style on your system, simply double-click the layer style and Photoshop will do the rest for you.

**2** For the water droplet style to work effectively, I had to take the layer fill opacity down to 0%. As I painted on the empty new layer with the brush tool, I was effectively able to paint using the layer style effect and create the translucent melted ice effect you see here. The Style is one that I created myself but it was based on the steps outlined by Greg Vander Houwen. If you still have Photoshop CS, you can access a PDF that includes Greg's great Rain Drop tutorial via the Photoshop CS Welcome screen.

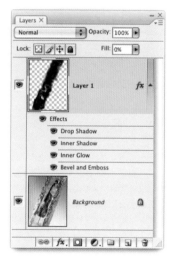

Client: The South Bank.
Photograph: Eric Richmond.

## Layer Styles

Layer Styles enable you to apply various layer effects linked to any of the following types of layer: a type layer; an image layer; or a filled layer masked by a vector mask or layer mask.

### Applying layer styles to image layers

You can sometimes choose to apply layer effects and styles to image layers and use the layer at zero fill opacity to paint in certain textured effects. The example on the opposite page shows how I went about using a waterdrop layer style to add a molten ice texture to a photograph.

Layer effects work in the same way as adjustment layers do: they create a live preview of the final effect and only when you flatten down the layer are the pixels modified and the effect becomes fixed. Layer effects are not scalable in the same way as image data is. If you resize an image the layer effect settings will not alter to fit the new image size; they will remain constant. If you go to the Layer menu and choose Layer Style ⇨ Scale Effects, you will have the ability to scale the effects up or down in size.

If you need to work with real layers, you can rasterize a layer style by using the Create Layers option. Go to the Layer menu and choose Layer Style ⇨ Create Layers. This will deconstruct a layer style into its separate components placing the newly created layers in a clipping mask above the target layer.

Layer effects and styles can be shared with other layers or files. Select a layer that already has a style applied to it. Go to the Layer Styles submenu and choose Copy Layer Style, then select a different layer and choose Paste Layer Style from the same submenu. Alternatively you can ⌥ alt drag on the *fx* icon to copy the entire layer style from one layer to another. And if you don't wish to copy the complete layer style, you can ⌥ alt drag to copy just a single effect between layers.

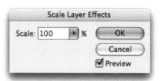

**Figure 8.39** When making a change to the image size, the layer styles will not adjust proportionally. If it is important that you retain the exact scaling, choose Layer ⇨ Layer Style ⇨ Scale Effects and enter a scale percentage which most closely matches the percentage change in image size.

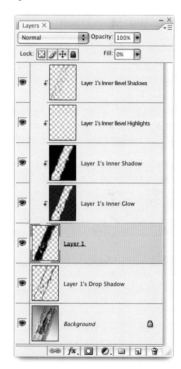

**Figure 8.40** Many Layer Styles (but not all) can be deconstructed into a series of layers. Choose Layer ⇨ Layer Style ⇨ Create Layers. Here is an example of how the layer effect applied on the page opposite would look if broken down in this way.

## Complete guide to layer effects

If you load the Photoshop for Photographers Help Guide that is on the DVD, there is a Layer Effects section that gives a complete description of all the different layer effects you can access in Photoshop. Most of these are of more interest to graphic designers but some, like the steps shown here, can be useful for photographers who use Photoshop.

## Adding glows and shadows

The steps shown here demonstrate how Photoshop's layer effects can be put to use to create glows and shadows in a photograph. One of the chief advantages of using layer effects in this way is that you can adjust the glow/shadow settings and revise the effect at any time. The object you wish to add the effect to must of course be on its own layer and the effectiveness of this technique is dependent on having a well-defined cut-out for the layered image. If there are some stray color pixels, you may wish to remove the matte colors first by choosing Layer ⇨ Matting ⇨ Remove Black/White Matte.

**1** This layered composite image features a cut-out image of a model, placed as a layer above a neutral gray-filled Background layer.

**2** In this next step, I wanted to create an outer glow effect around the model. I first made a duplicate of Layer 1 by dragging it down to the Make New Layer button in the Layers palette. The Fill opacity for this duplicate layer was set to 0%. I then moused down on the Add Layer Style button and selected the Outer Glow layer effect. The settings used are shown here. I set the Opacity to 85%, changed the glow color from yellow to white and added 3% Noise. The glow effect was mostly determined by how I adjusted the Elements settings. The Spread setting should ideally be kept quite low, while you can use the Size slider to adjust the width of the glow effect.

**3** The shadow effect was achieved using the same layer structure as the outer glow technique. In this next step I double-clicked the Effects Layer to open the Layer Style dialog again. I changed the color from white to black and the blending mode from Screen to Multiply and set the Opacity to 40%. All the other settings remained the same as before, and the outer glow suddenly becomes an outer shadow. You may want to fine-tune the layer contents in order to achieve a better blend between the shadow effect and the subject. In this example, I ⌘ ctrl clicked on the Layer 1 Copy layer to load the opaque layer contents as a selection and then clicked on the Add Layer Mask button to convert the selection to a Layer Mask. These simple steps produced a smoother blend between the layer contents and the shadow effect. If required, you could also manipulate or paint on the layer mask to tidy up any gaps between the subject and the shadow effect.

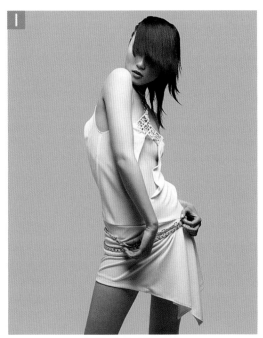

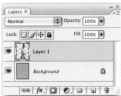

Client: Russell Eaton. Model: Gina Li @ Premier.

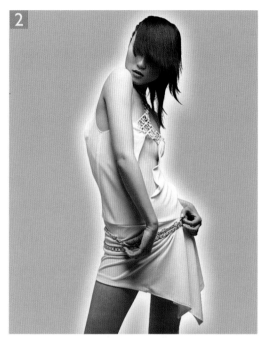

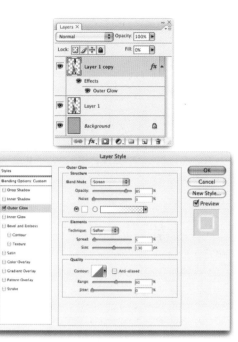

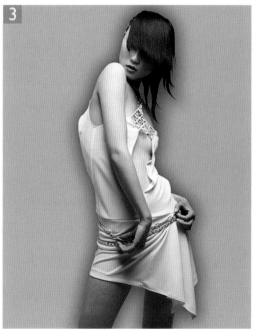

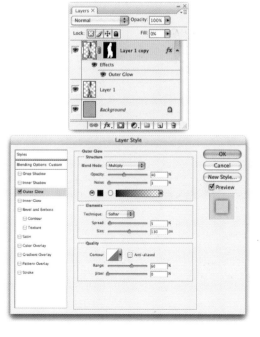

443

### Editing layer effects

Double-clicking the layer or anywhere in the layer effect list will reopen the Layer Style dialog.

### Layer what?

It is unfortunate that Photoshop uses mixed terminology to describe layer effects and layer styles. Naturally, this can lead to confusion, because a layer style can be both an individual layer effect and a combination of layer effects. Meanwhile, the Photoshop User Guide and Help menu refer to the individual effects as layer effects, even though the Layer menu, Layers palette and Layer Effect dialog refer to them as layer styles.

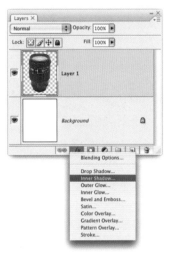

**Figure 8.41** A layer effect can be applied to an image, shape or type layer by mousing down on the Add a Layer Style button in the Layers palette. When you add a new layer effect an italicized *fx* icon will appear next to the layer name in the Layers palette.

## *Inner shadows*

Layer Styles enable you to apply various layer effects linked to any of the following types of layer: a type layer; an image layer; or a filled layer masked by a vector mask or layer mask. A Layer Style is made up of individual layer effects which are accessed via the Layer menu or by clicking on the Add a Layer Style button at the bottom of the Layers palette. Layer effects can be applied individually or as a combination of effects to create a layer style and these can be saved by clicking in the empty space area of the Styles palette. As with the adjustment layers, layer styles will always remain fully editable. When you add a new layer effect, the Layer Style dialog will open to let you adjust the settings and create the desired layer effect. After adding a layer effect, an italicized *fx* symbol will appear in the layer caption area and next to that a disclosure triangle. When you click on this disclosure triangle, an indented Effects layer will appear below containing an itemized list of the individual layer effects used to create the master layer style and allow you to control the visibility of the individual effects.

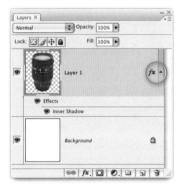

**Figure 8.42** If you click on the disclosure triangle next to the *fx* icon, an indented list of the effects making up the layer style will show below. These appear in the same descending order that the layer effects appear in the Layer Styles dialog. Each effect can be made visible or invisible by toggling the eye icon next to it in the Layers palette. Or you can hide all of the effects at once by clicking on the eye icon next to 'Effects'.

## Spot color channels

Spot colors can be added to images as part of the graphic design when you need to add a specific process color in addition to the standard CMYK printing inks. Photoshop is able to simulate the effect of how a spot color will reproduce in print and how a special color overlay will interplay with the underlying image. Spot colors include a wide range of industry standard colors. The colors available can include those found in the CMYK gamut, but also a whole lot more that are not, including metallic 'specials' (manufacturers' printed book color guides are an accurate reference for how the color will print). Spot colors are mostly used where it is important that the printed color conforms to a known standard and for the printing of small point size type and graphics in color.

### Spot color limitations

A four-color process mix can be used when printing larger sans-serif type using large point sizes, but not for fine type and line diagrams, as the slightest misregistration could make the edges appear fuzzy when printed.

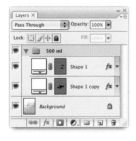

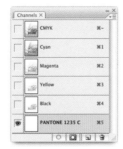

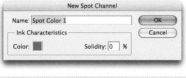

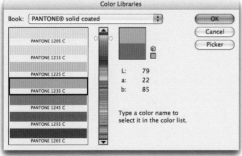

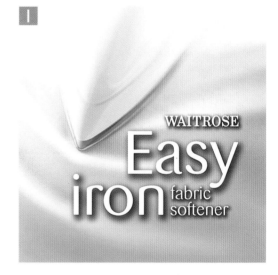

**1** A spot color channel is used to add a fifth color to a CMYK file. The master image contained some shape layers based on artwork supplied by the designer, to which I added a drop shadow effect. To add the spot color channel, I went to the Channels palette flyout menu and chose New Spot Channel... This popped the New Spot Channel dialog. I clicked on the swatch color to open the Color Picker and then clicked on a button marked Color Libraries. A quick way to select a known Pantone reference color is to rapidly type in the Pantone reference number.

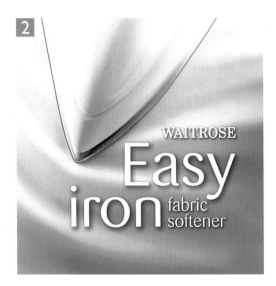

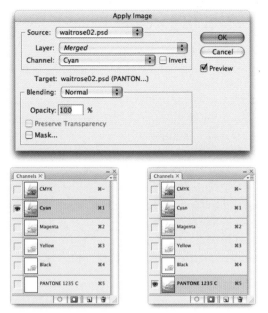

**2** I wanted to use the new spot color to add color to the fabric, but not to the iron. I drew a path to define the area outside the iron, made an inverse selection and feathered the selection. I activated the new spot channel and used Image ⇨ Apply Image to blend the selected Cyan channel contents into the spot color channel using a Normal blend.

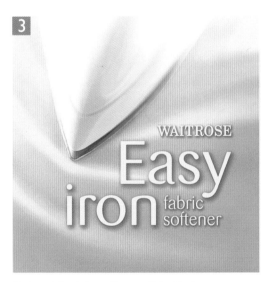

**3** Meanwhile, with the selection still active in the Cyan channel, I hit ⌥ *alt* delete to fill the selected area with white. I then did the same thing in the Magenta channel as well. There now remained a CMYK full color image of the iron, but the fabric and lettering outside of the iron was now using the yellow, black and spot color channels only. To preview all of the color channels combined, I clicked on the composite channel and the spot color channel eyeball icons. The client wanted the drop shadow lettering to predominantly use the spot color ink. I therefore had to make an inverted selection of the iron in the Black channel and apply a Levels adjustment to substantially lighten the lettering in the Black channel. And here is a screen shot of the image which shows the final result after I had basically taken the image information from the darkest channel (the cyan channel) and copied this over to the new spot color channel.

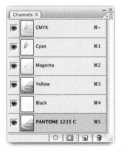

Photograph: Laurie Evans. Designer: Richard Lealan.
Client: Waitrose Limited.

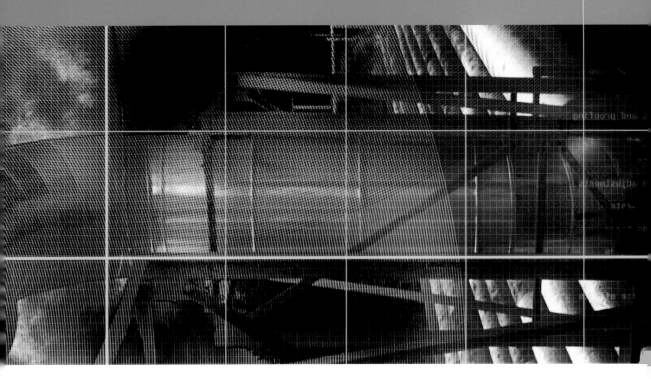

# Chapter 9

# Darkroom Effects

**T**he ability to duplicate traditional darkroom techniques in Photoshop will be of particular interest to photographers. This chapter shows you how to use Photoshop as your digital darkroom and how to replicate in Photoshop some traditional photographic effects such as solarization, split tone printing, cross-processing and diffusion printing.

We shall start by looking at the different ways that you can convert a color image to monochrome. The distinction between shooting black and white or color is not always fully appreciated, because how you light and color compose a shot can often be determined by whether it is intended for color or monochrome. However, in the digital age, everything is captured in RGB color and if you want a black and white image, your best bet is to do the monochrome conversion in Photoshop and not 'in camera'.

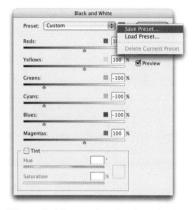

Figure 9.1 Once you have found a setting for a Black & White adjustment that you would like to use again, you can choose Save Preset... and save this as a named setting. The slider settings used here were saved as a 'Red Contrast' preset.

### Slider adjustments

The Black & White slider adjustments will, for the most part, manage to preserve the image luminance range without clipping the shadows or highlights, until you apply extreme negative or positive weightings to two or more sliders.

### Lab color conversions

Another way to convert a color image to monochrome is to do an RGB to Lab color mode conversion, copy the Luminosity channel, convert back to RGB and choose Edit ⇨ Paste. There is nothing necessarily wrong with this method, but it is not much better than converting an image to grayscale and then back to RGB mode again. The techniques I describe here are far more versatile.

# Black and white from color

When you change a color image from RGB to Grayscale mode in Photoshop, the tonal values of the three RGB channels are averaged out, usually producing a smooth continuous tone grayscale. The formula for this conversion roughly consists of blending 60% of the Green channel with 30% of the Red and 10% of the Blue. The rigidity of this color to mono conversion formula limits the scope for obtaining the best grayscale conversion from a scanned color original. The same would apply if you were to simply desaturate the image, or make a Lab mode conversion and use the Luminosity channel. In each of these cases you are not really helping yourself to make full use of the information contained in the image.

Black and white film emulsions will also interpret a color scene using a standard formula. So in a way, these too are like rigid grayscale conversions. Except you may be familiar with the concept of using strong colored filters over the lens in black and white photography and how this technique can be used to emphasize the contrast in certain areas, like add more contrast to a sky. Well, the same principle can apply when you use Photoshop to convert an image from color to black and white, because if you always capture the original scene in color, you will have three different grayscale versions of the original scene and these can be blended together in different ways. In Photoshop CS3 there are now at least two new ways that you can convert a color image into black and white. Earlier in Chapter 5, I introduced the new Camera Raw Grayscale Mix controls and showed how you could use the eight color sliders to alter the makeup of a grayscale mix conversion. These same controls are also available in Photoshop as a Black & White image adjustment that can be applied to an image either directly, or as an adjustment layer. The advantage of working with the Black & White adjustment is that you can quickly convert an image to black and white by adding an adjustment layer and have the option to play with the blending modes to refine the black and white conversion.

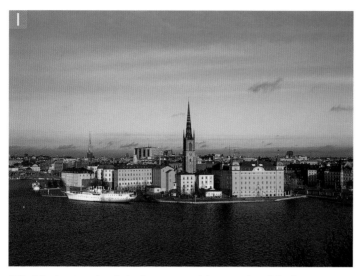

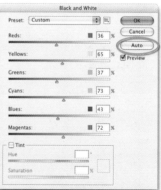

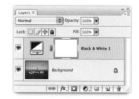

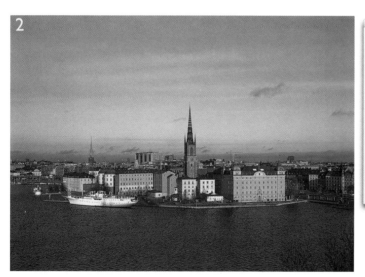

**1** The following steps show the basic new approach for converting a full color original photograph like the one shown here, into black and white.

**2** The new Black & White image adjustment can either be applied directly by going to the Image ⇨ Image Adjustments menu or, as I have done here, by adding an adjustment layer. For this step, I clicked on the Auto button, which will apply an auto setting for the sliders based on an analysis of the image color content.

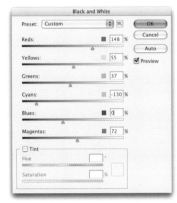

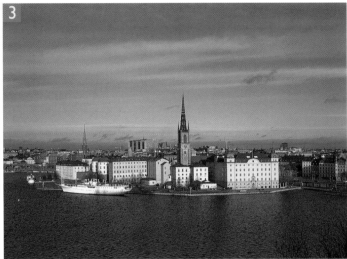

3 The Auto setting may give you an acceptable black and white conversion. But, if not, then you can adjust the sliders manually to achieve a better result. In this example, I increased the weighting for the Reds slider, and reduced the weighting for the Cyans and Blues sliders.

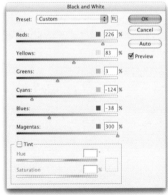

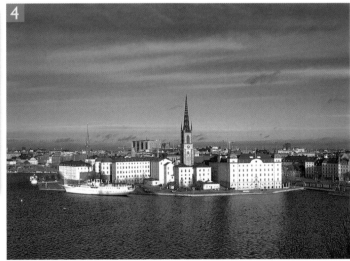

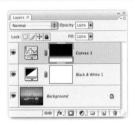

4 Lastly, I went for an even stronger conversion to produce more contrast between the building and the sky by reducing the Cyans and Blues sliders further and adding more weighting to the Reds and Yellows. I also added a gradient modified Curves adjustment layer to lighten the water in the foreground.

## Split color toning

Although the Black & White adjustment contains a toning option, it can only apply a single color balance adjustment. But it is usually nice to have the ability to apply a split tone coloring to a photograph and the simplest way to do this is to use the Color Balance adjustment. I am normally inclined to disregard use of Color Balance adjustments. But in situations such as this, the simple controls in Color Balance are quite adequate for the job of coloring a monochrome image that is in RGB mode. The Color Balance controls are really quite intuitive: if you want to colorize the shadows, click on the Shadows radio button and adjust the color settings. Then go to the Highlights and make them a different color and so on. I always apply these coloring effects by using an adjustment layer set to the Color blend mode.

## Color blend mode

You will notice that I regularly use the Color blend mode when applying adjustment layers that are intended to color an image. The advantage of using the Color blend mode is that you are able to alter the color component of an image without affecting the luminosity. This is important if you wish to preserve more of the tone levels information.

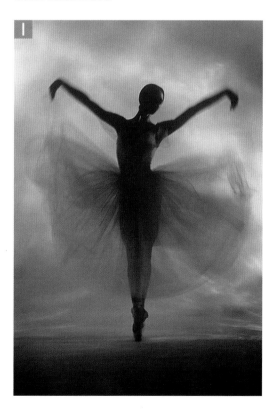

**1** I started with a grayscale image and converted it to RGB color mode. Alternatively, you could take an RGB image and convert it to monochrome using the Black & White image adjustment. I then added a Color Balance adjustment layer to colorize the RGB/monochrome image. To do this, I chose New Adjustment Layer... from the Layers palette fly-out menu and selected Color Balance. I clicked on the Shadows button and adjusted the sliders to apply a magenta cast to the shadows.

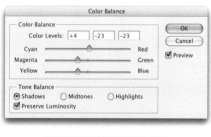

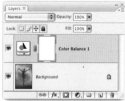

Photograph: Eric Richmond.

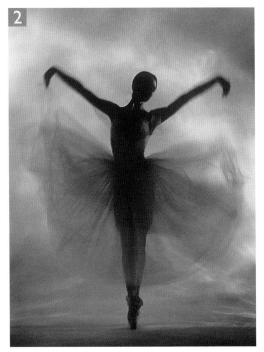

**2** I then clicked on the Midtones button and adjusted the color sliders to produce a green/blue color balance for the midtone values. You will notice that I had Preserve Luminosity checked. This helps prevent the image tones from becoming clipped.

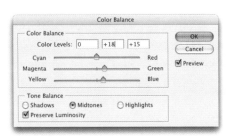

**3** Finally I clicked on the Highlights button and applied a sepia cast to the highlights. I also set the adjustment layer blending mode to Color, which also helped to preserve the image luminance information. To further modify the Color Balance toning, try varying the opacity of the adjustment layer.

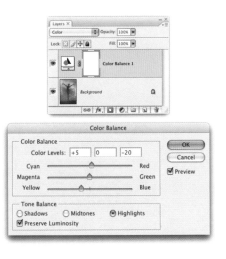

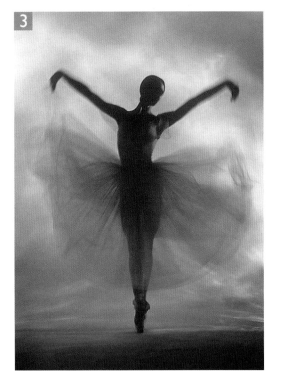

## *Adjustment layer split toning*

The Color Balance method is reasonably versatile, but very often I will use two Curves adjustment layers and take advantage of the Layer Style blending options to create a split tone coloring effect. The advantage of this method is that one can adjust the layer opacity and Layer Style blending modes of each individual layer and this will offer more flexible options for coloring the shadows and highlights.

## Camera Raw black and white

Despite the inclusion of the new Black & White image adjustment and the fondness I have for the Photoshop techniques shown here, the best tools for black and white conversion and split color toning are now to be found in the new Camera Raw dialog, which will also process JPEG, TIFF and PSD files (providing the PSD contains a saved flattened composite).

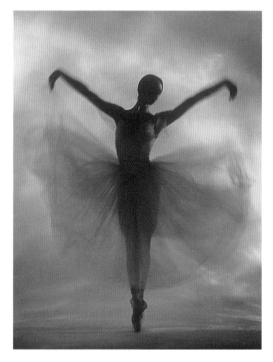

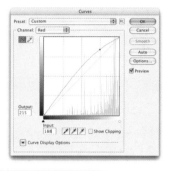

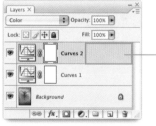

Double-click in this area of the layer to open the Layer Style dialog.

**Figure 9.2** In this last example, I added two Curves adjustment layers. The lower Curves layer colors the image blue, while the top one colors it red. If I double-click the upper Curves layer, this will pop the Layer Style dialog shown below. If I ⌥ alt-click on the divider triangle in the blend layer options, I can separate these dividers and split them in two. As I adjust them, I can control the amount of split between the two color adjustments.

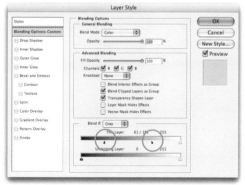

Photograph: Eric Richmond.

# Black and white solarization

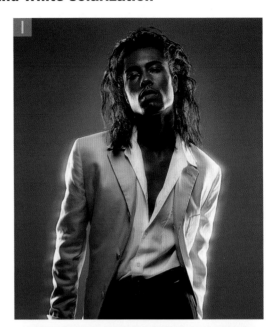

**1** This original photographic technique is associated with the artist Man Ray and is achieved by briefly fogging the print paper towards the end of its development. The digital method described here uses the Curves adjustment and allows some degree of control, because you can experiment with different curve point shapes to create different solarization effects and you could also consider using a layer mask as well, to selectively mask the adjustment. I began with an image in RGB mode, went to the Layers palette and added a new Black & White adjustment layer.

**2** I adjusted the individual sliders to vary the black and white mix that was used to produce the monochrome conversion. I didn't aim for a particularly extreme adjustment, I just lightened the reds and yellows so that the skin tones were rendered lighter.

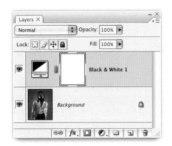

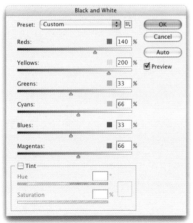

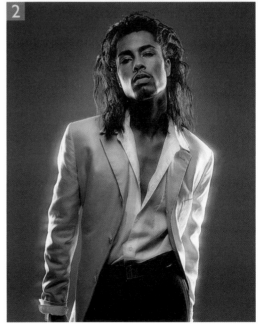

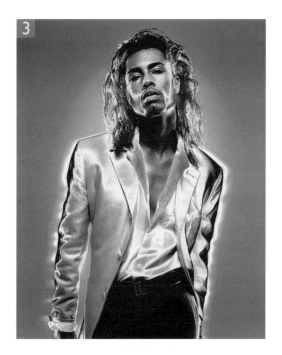

**3** Next, I added a Curves adjustment layer above the Black & White layer, selected the arbitrary map tool (circled) and drew an inverted V. The easiest way to do this is to first click in the bottom left corner and then hold down the *Shift* key as you click to add the top middle point and, lastly, the bottom right point on the curve. This will produce the solarizing effect curve shown here.

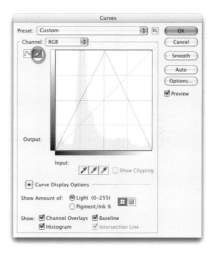

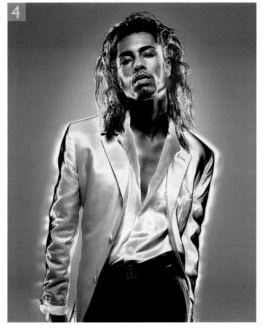

**4** I then added a second Curves adjustment layer and started experimenting with some different split tone color toning effects using the technique described on page 453. The other interesting thing you can do here is to double-click the Black & White layer and readjust the channel settings one more time. As you do this you will notice how it is possible to apply subtle changes to the solarization effect.

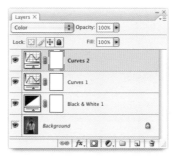

Client: Anita Cox. Model: Sze Kei.

## Deficiencies of grayscale printing

A black and white image can be reproduced a number of ways in print. If you are working from a basic 8-bit grayscale image, this will have a maximum of 256 brightness levels. A practical consequence of using basic 8-bit grayscale files for print is that as many as a third of the tonal shades will get lost during the reproduction process and this is why images reproduced from a grayscale file can look extremely flat when printed, especially when compared alongside a CMYK printed image. Adding two or more printing plates will dramatically increase the range of tones that can be reproduced from a monochrome image. The fine quality black and white printing you see in certain magazines and books is often achieved using a duotone or conventional CMYK printing process.

## Duotone mode

A duotone is a grayscale image printed using two printing plates (a tritone uses three and a quadtone four). To create a duotone image your image must first be in grayscale before you convert it to Duotone mode (Image ⇨ Mode ⇨ Duotone). The Ink Color boxes display a Photoshop preview of the ink color with the name of the color (i.e. process color name) appearing in the box to the right. Normally the inks are ordered with the darkest at the top and the lightest inks at the bottom of the list. The graph icon to the left is the duotone curve box. The duotone curve box is opened by double-clicking the graph icon and when it is open you can specify the proportions of ink used to print at the different brightness levels of the grayscale image. You can change the shape of the curve to represent the proportion of ink used to print in the highlights/midtones/shadows.

The only file formats (other than Photoshop) to support duotones are EPS and DCS. So save using these when preparing an image for placing in either an InDesign or QuarkXPress document. Duotones are really a special printing mode which is used in commercial printing only. You can use the Duotone mode to produce split tone color effects of monochrome images, but you will need to convert them to RGB or CMYK mode if you wish to make any other type of print. Remember as well that if any custom ink colors are used to make the duotone, these need to be specified to the printer and this will add to the cost of making the separations if CMYK inks are already being used in the publication. Alternatively you can take a duotone image and convert it to CMYK mode in Photoshop. This may well produce a compromise in the color output as you will be limited to using the CMYK gamut of colors.

There are a number of Duotone presets (plus tritones and quadtones) to be found in the Photoshop Goodies folder. Experiment with these by clicking the Load... button in the Duotone dialog box and locating the different preset settings.

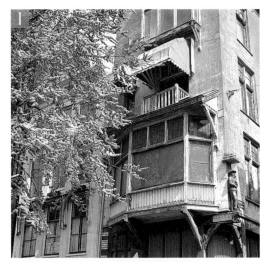

**1** The grayscale display in Photoshop is foremost based on the assumption that you want to see a representation on screen of how the grayscale file will print. Go to the Color Settings and select the anticipated dot gain for the print output. This will be the Photoshop grayscale workspace that all new documents will be created in or be converted to. If you are working on a grayscale image that is intended for screen-based publishing then go to Window ➪ Proof setup and select the Windows RGB preview.

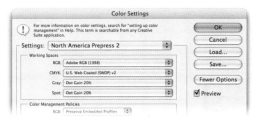

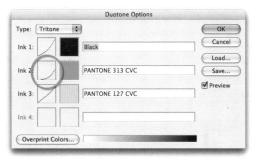

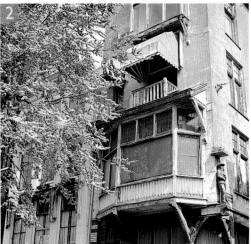

**2** When the Preview is checked in Duotone Options, any changes you make to the duotone settings will immediately be reflected in the appearance of the on-screen image. In the example shown here, a custom color tritone was selected and the component ink colors are displayed with the darkest color at the top. If I double-click the cyan color graph icon, this will open the Duotone Curve dialog. The duotone curve is similar to the image adjustment curves, except a little more restrictive in setting the points. The color ramp in the duotone dialog reflects the tonal transformation across an evenly stepped grayscale ramp and you can specify the ink percentage variance at set points along the horizontal axis.

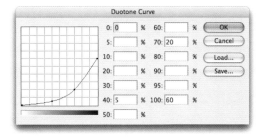

## Color Infrared film emulsions

Color infrared film emulsions are predominantly sensitive to infrared radiation. Vegetation in particular reflects a lot of infrared light which is beyond the scope of human vision. Hence, green foliage will appear very bright and almost iridescent when captured on infrared film.

## Infrared film simulation

I first invented the following technique some eight years ago when I was asked to come up with different ways to convert a color image to black and white. Since then I have had the opportunity to refine the steps used and make some improvements. And now that you can do layered editing in 16-bit per channel mode, one can achieve much smoother results by following the steps shown here.

**1** This photograph of a Japanese garden is in RGB mode and is a good one for demonstrating the infrared technique, which is basically an extension of the color to monochrome technique using the Black & White adjustment. As you can see, there are a lot of green leaves in the picture and the aim of this technique was to lighten the leaves and apply a slight glow to them. The following steps required some extreme image adjustments, and so I felt it was important to keep the image in 16-bit per channel mode throughout. I began by copying the Background layer.

**2** The next step was to add a Black & White adjustment layer. Now if I want the green colors to appear the lightest (because of all the green foliage) then I have to somehow boost the lightness in the greens and other colors that are close to green. The maximum setting allowed for any color weighting is +300%, so to get the effect I was after I set the Greens to +300 and the Yellows and Cyans to +150.

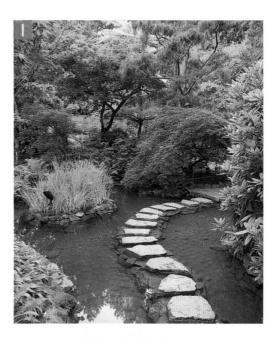

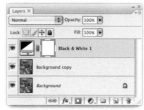

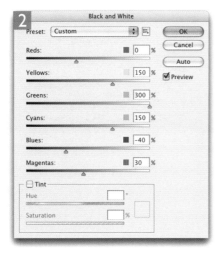

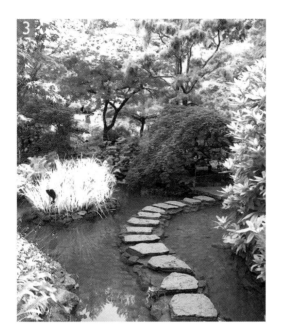

**3** I now wanted to add some glow to the foliage. It is important that the underlying image has remained in RGB (because it is the adjustment layer which is making the monochrome conversion). In this step I made the Background copy layer active and then went to the Channels palette, highlighted the Green channel and applied a Gaussian Blur filtration to that channel only. The amount used here was 5 pixels, but you might want to apply more for a more diffuse effect.

**4** I followed this with an Edit ⇨ Fade Filter command, reducing the blur to a 25% opacity and changed the blend mode to Screen.

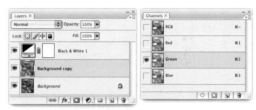

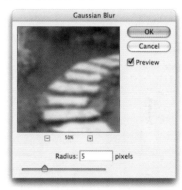

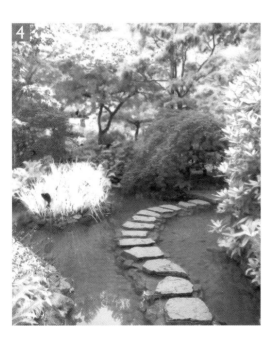

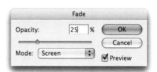

**5** The picture now looked rather light and the highlight areas
were probably burnt-out. To address this, I first made sure I
could view the Histogram palette so that I could see a levels view
that represented a composite view of the image. I then applied a
Levels adjustment that was sandwiched between the Background
copy and the Black & White adjustment layer. As I adjusted the
levels settings it was important that I referred to the histogram that
was displayed in the Histogram palette instead of the one in the
Levels dialog to gauge how to set the levels. In this example, I set
the Highlight Output slider to 214, to retain more highlight detail.

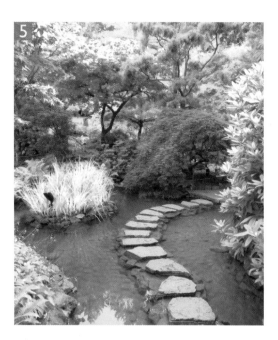

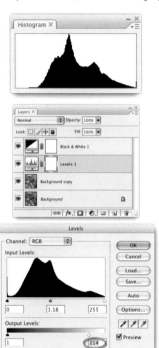

**6** To further simulate the infrared emulsion, one could also add
some Gaussian noise to the Background copy layer, or add a grain
layer using the technique shown on page 346.

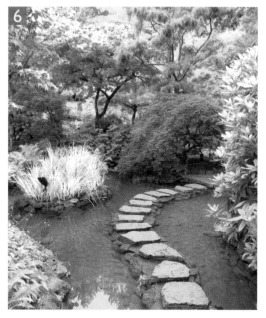

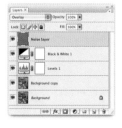

# Coloring effects

## Cross-processing

The cross-processing technique has long been popular among fashion and portrait photographers who are fond of distorting colors and bleaching out the skin tone detail. There are two basic cross-processing methods: E-6 transparency film processed in C-41 chemicals and C-41 negative film processed in E-6 chemicals.

You can simulate cross-processing effects quite easily in Photoshop and do so without the risk of 'overdoing' the effect or losing important image detail. The technique shown over the next two pages aims to replicate the cross curve effect you typically get when using a C-41 film processed in E-6. In this example you will notice how I manage to make the shadows go blue, while the highlights take on a yellow/red cast. The technique outlined here is another of those which I have adapted over the years and this most recent update is I think more flexible. As with all the other coloring effects described in this chapter, the main coloring adjustments are applied as adjustment layers using the Color blend mode. This will help preserve the original luminosity, but if you want to simulate the high contrast cross-processed look, then use the Normal blend mode instead and, in addition to this, you might want to consider deliberately increasing the contrast in the RGB composite channel as well (this will also boost the color saturation). The other thing you can do to adapt this technique is to explore alternative color channel adjustments and try using different color fills and layer opacities.

## Lab Color effects

This is not a cross-processing effect per se, but this technique sure can mess with the colors in your images in some pretty interesting ways. I would suggest that this effect is best applied to medium or high resolution images and that the source image should be fairly free of artifacts. I found that you can also create some interesting variations if you invert the colors while the image is at the Lab mode stage.

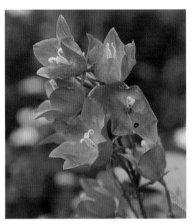

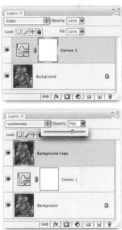

**Figure 9.3** One way to preserve the luminosity in an image is to always set a 'coloring' adjustment layer to the Color blend mode. Some techniques described in this chapter involve a series of extreme image adjustments or multiple adjustment layers. Therefore, there is always the potential risk that if you are not careful, you will lose important highlight and shadow detail. A solution to this is to make a copy of the original Background layer and place it at the top of the layer stack, and set the layer blending mode to Luminosity. This will produce the same result as setting a single adjustment layer to Color mode, but by adjusting the layer opacity this will restore varying amounts of the original image luminance.

461

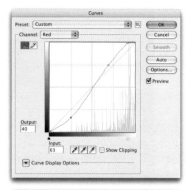

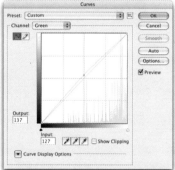

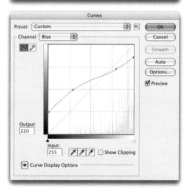

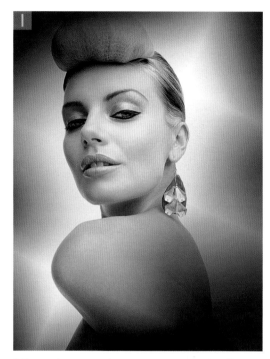

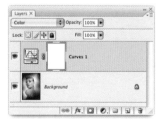

**1** Here are the steps used to create a cross-processing effect that simulates C-41 film processed in E-6 chemicals. You can adapt this technique by using different channel Curve adjustments and using different fill colors. To start with I added a Curves adjustment layer which was set to the Color blend mode. I then adjusted the curves in the individual color channels as shown in the screen shots on the left.

Model: Lucy Edwards @ Bookings.

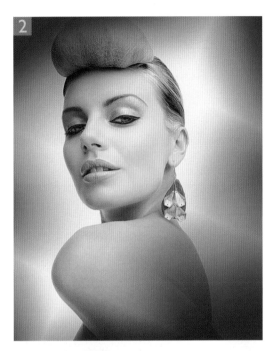

**2** The Curves channel adjustments applied in Step 1 added a blue/cyan cast to the shadow areas and added a red/yellow cast to the highlights. Because the Curves adjustment layer was set to the Color blend mode, the luminosity was unaffected.

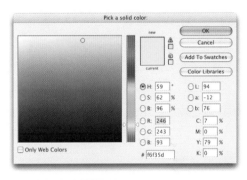

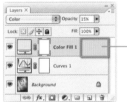

Double-click in this area of the layer to open the Layer Style dialog.

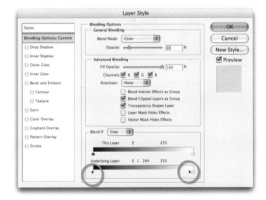

**3** I then added a Color Fill layer which was also set to Color mode, set the opacity to 15% and selected a strong yellow fill color. I then double-clicked the Fill layer and adjusted the Underlying layer blend options. I ⬚ _alt_-clicked on the Underlying Layer shadow point triangle slider and dragged to separate the dividers and split them in two. I dragged the right-hand shadow slider across to the right. This created a transitional blend between the underlying layer and the fill yellow layer above.

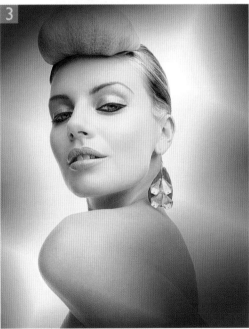

**1** Here is another type of Photoshop cross-processing effect for RGB images. It involves the use of the Lab Color mode to enhance the image colors and then pasting the enhance color version as a new layer in the original RGB image. To start with I opened an RGB image and created a duplicate copy by choosing Image ⇨ Duplicate...

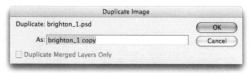

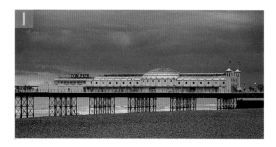

**2** I converted the duplicate image to Lab Color mode by choosing Image ⇨ Mode ⇨ Lab Color. The Lab Color image contains a Lightness channel with **a** and **b** color channels. I went to the Channels palette and selected the **a** channel first and expanded the channel contrast by choosing Image ⇨ Adjustments ⇨ Equalize. This produced the extreme color shift shown in the image here. I then clicked on the Lab composite channel in the Channels palette (it is essential you remember to do this so that all three channels are selected again) and copied the enhanced image across to the original image as a new layer. You can do this by either choosing Select ⇨ All and copying and pasting the image contents. Or, you can select the move tool and drag the Lab image across to the original RGB version. Make sure that you hold down the *Shift* key as you do so. A *Shift* drag will ensure that the layer is centered when you let go of the mouse. There is no need to worry about the color space mismatch. Photoshop will automatically convert the file back to RGB mode again as you make the copy and paste.

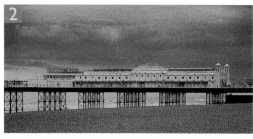

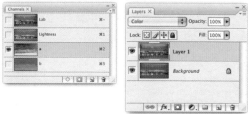

**3** I set the new layer blend mode to Color and the layer opacity to 30%. This Lab coloring technique can sometimes generate harsh pixel artifacts, so I chose Filter ⇨ Blur ⇨ Gaussian Blur and applied a 2.5 pixel Radius to soften the image layer slightly. Because the new layer is using the Color blend mode, this blurring will not affect the sharpness of the image luminosity.

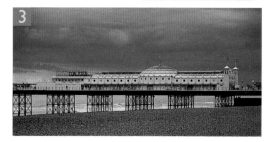

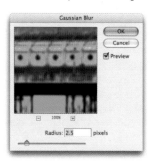

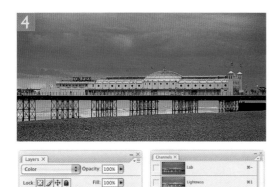

**4** I returned to the Lab copy image and went back a couple of steps in the History palette to the original unmodified state and selected the **b** channel this time. I then repeated the steps described in Step 2. I applied an equalize image adjustment and then copied the newly enhanced composite Lab image across to the original RGB version, this time bringing it in as Layer 2. And, as before, I set the blend mode to Color, the opacity to 30% and applied a Gaussian Blur to the new image layer.

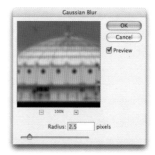

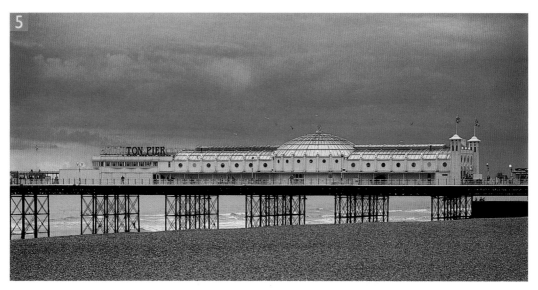

**5** Here is the finished result. As you can see, when using the Lab Color process described here, you can end up with two brightly colored, semi-transparent layers. The fun starts when you adjust the relative opacity of each and experiment with different amounts of opacity in these two layers.

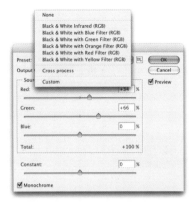

Figure 9.4 Channel Mixer settings can be saved as presets. Note the Black and White conversion presets that are in Photoshop CS3.

## Channel Mixer color adjustments

The Channel Mixer will let you achieve the sort of coloring effects that could once only be done with the Apply Image command. The Channel Mixer is an interesting image adjustment tool because it alters the image by swapping color channel information, sometimes producing quite unique and subtle color adjustments which cannot necessarily be achieved with any of the other color adjustment tools. Before the advent of the Black & White adjustment, you could have used the Channel Mixer to make Monochrome adjustments and you will notice some legacy presets are supplied via the Preset menu. The steps shown here suggest some of the ways you can use Channel Mixer to produce unusual color effects.

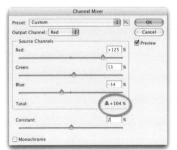

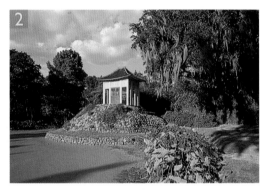

1 This image is correctly color balanced, but suppose I wanted to create a warm sunlit version? One answer would be to adjust the overall color balance by applying a curves correction. The Channel Mixer, however, offers a radically different approach, it allows you to mix the color channel contents.

2 In the Channel Mixer settings shown below, I boosted the Red channel to 125%, mixed in a little of the Green channel and subtracted 34% from the Blue channel. Notice how when the Red, Green and Blue channel percentages were added up, they were close to 100%. Where they exceed this, a warning sign appears.

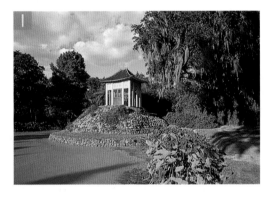

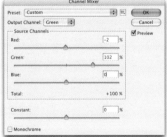

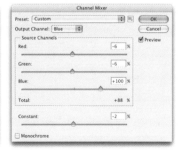

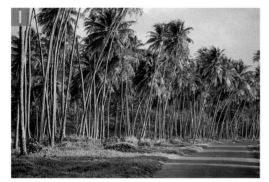

**1** If you are feeling adventurous then you can achieve some really quite wild coloring effects with the Channel Mixer. But I suggest you should tame the effect by sandwiching the Channel Mixer adjustment layer between the Background layer and a copied Background layer set to Luminosity mode (see page 461).

**2** In this first example, I set the Channel Mixer blending mode to Darken and adjusted the individual color channel Channel Mixer settings as shown below. Because the Background copy layer is set to Luminosity, you can make quite extreme adjustments without losing luminosity detail. You also have to be very patient when making adjustments via the Channel Mixer, because leaving aside the Constant slider, there are nine sliders you can adjust! The settings used here enabled me to produce a rich color distortion effect.

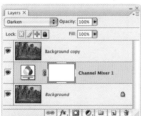

**3** The Darken mode produced an interesting result, but you may want to also experiment with all the other blend modes. This variation was achieved by changing the blend mode to Exclusion and taking the Channel Mixer layer opacity down to 50%.

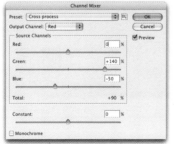

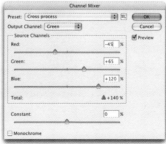

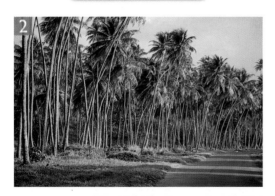

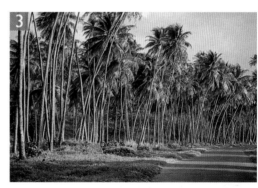

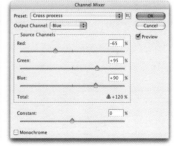

### PhotoKit Color plug-in

Some of the effects shown in this chapter such as the split toning, cross-processing and color overlays are all available in the form of an automated plug-in called PhotoKit Color. One reason for the plug is that I did design all the coloring effects myself. You can download a 7-day demo from the Pixel Genius website: www.pixelgenius.com.

## Color overlays

Another method for colorizing an image is to add a solid color fill layer from the adjustment layer menu in the Layers palette and set the layer blending mode to Overlay, Color or Soft Light mode. The Overlay blend mode will produce the most intense-looking results; when selecting a color from the Color Picker, it is best to choose a fully saturated color from the top right corner and reduce the opacity of the fill layer afterwards to around 10–30%. The Color blend mode can work fine with any color, but by selecting a more saturated color you will have more options at your disposal. The Soft Light blend mode provides a more gentle blend and is the one used in the accompanying steps to simulate using a color gradient to make the sky in the photograph appear more blue.

**1** In this example I wanted to add a blue gradient to the top of the picture to enhance the sky and add a dash of blue. This is effectively a Photoshop technique for adding a blue gradient filter. I began by adding a new fill color layer using a bright blue color and set the Color Fill layer blend mode to Soft Light.

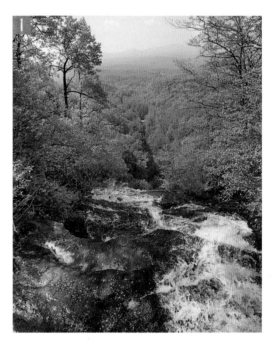

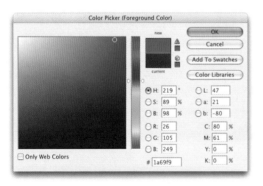

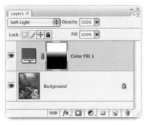

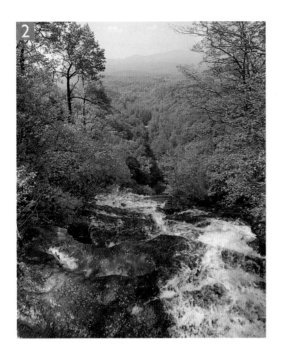

**2** With the Color Fill layer active, I selected the gradient tool and with the foreground/background colors set to their defaults, dragged downwards around the middle of the picture to add a gradient to the Color Fill layer mask. I then double-clicked the Color Fill layer to open the Layer Style dialog and adjusted the layer blending option for 'This Layer' as shown below. To separate the triangle sliders, I ⌥ alt-clicked on the shadow point triangle slider and dragged to separate the dividers and split them in two.

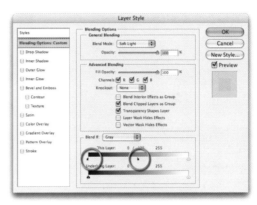

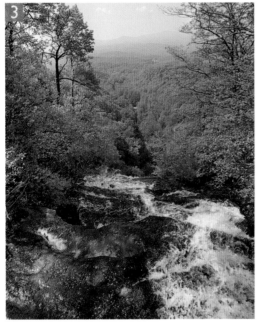

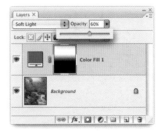

**3** The above Layer Style adjustments produced a smoother blend of the blue color fill with the sky and trees, but I felt that the color was too strong. To address this, I went to the Layers palette and reduced the Color Fill layer opacity to 60%.

## Hand coloring a photograph

The Color overlay blend mode is probably the simplest one to use when hand coloring an image, but what follows shows a more advanced technique that I use when adding a specific color.

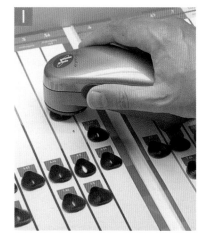

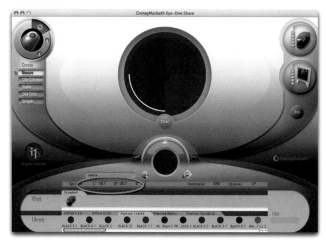

**1** This first step revolves around the use of the Gretag MacBeth Eye-One spectrophotometer to measure a precise color. I then used the measured reading to create a color swatch that can be used in Photoshop. But the steps after this will still work if you resort to guessing the color or are given a specific color swatch reference to work with. I used the Eye Share software to record color from some hair swatch colors and made a note of the Lab Color values.

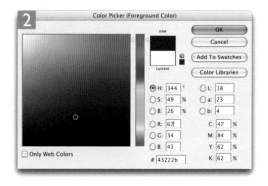

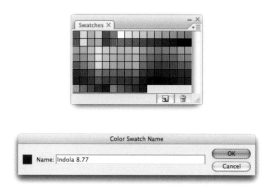

**2** I then opened the Color Picker in Photoshop and entered these (rounded up) Lab Color values in the Lab coordinates. I clicked OK and then clicked in an empty space in the Swatches palette to save and name the new swatch, ready for use at the next step.

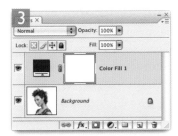

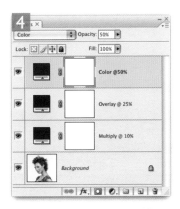

**3** It is at this point that I should acknowledge the photographer, Jim Divitale, who devised the following multi-layered coloring technique. The foreground color should have the desired swatch color loaded. I then added a new Color Fill layer in the Layers palette using this color. Now, at this point, you might find it helpful to create a new action and hit the Record button to record the following steps as a Photoshop action. Start by copying the Color Fill layer two times.

**4** Now set the uppermost Color Fill copy layer to Color mode @ 50% opacity. Click on the middle layer and set the blend to Overlay mode @ 25% and lastly go to the original layer, set that to Multiply blend mode @ 10%.

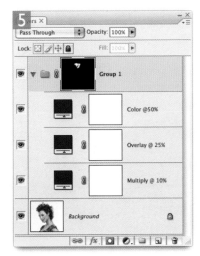

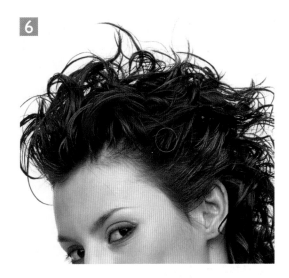

**5** I *Shift*-clicked the three layers to select them and chose New Group from Layers... from the Layers palette fly-out menu. I then *alt*-clicked on the Add a Layer Mask button in the Layers palette to add a layer mask filled with black, which will hide the layer group contents.

**6** If you have been recording all this as an action, you can press the Stop button now. When you have completed these steps you can paint with white on the layer group's layer mask to simultaneously reveal all three layers in the group. The blend and opacity modes for the three layers are just a suggestion. Feel free to readjust the opacity settings as desired.

Client: Indola. Model: Lisa Maria @ Take 2.

## Gradient Map coloring

The Gradient Map adjustment will map the colors in an image based on a gradient. Some examples of this are shown below, where the most effective way to do this is by using a reduced layer opacity and changing the layer blend mode.

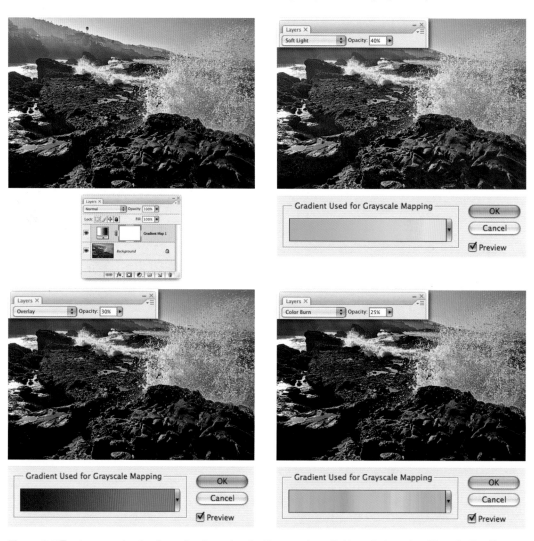

**Figure 9.5** The above examples show how various types of gradient layers can be applied to a color image by adding a Gradient Map adjustment layer and how the original photograph can be colored in many different ways. Even the use of Noise gradients can produce some interesting results, although it pays to fine-tune the smoothness and shape of the gradient using the gradient edit options.

## Adding a border to an image

Here is a simple two step technique for adding a new border to an image in Photoshop.

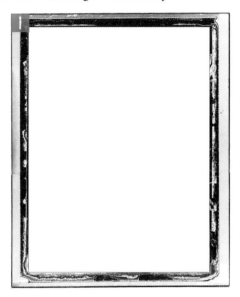

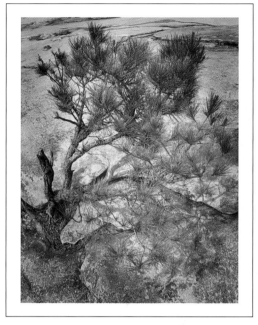

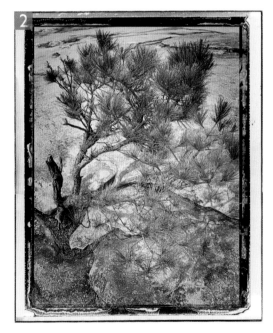

**1** We have here top left, a scan that was made from a print of a Polaroid™ processed border and above, a black and white image where I had enlarged the canvas size to include a wide white border. I selected the move tool and dragged the Polaroid™ scan image across to the black and white image, to add it as a new layer.

**2** I then changed the blending mode of the Polaroid layer to Multiply. This made the border layer merge with the underlying layer. Once I had done this, I selected the Edit ⇨ Free Transform to scale the layer to neatly overlay the image below. Lastly I added a Curves adjustment layer to colorize the image to create a gold color tone effect.

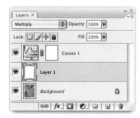

## Softening the focus

A quick way to soften the focus in a photograph is to duplicate the Background layer and use Filter ⇨ Blur ⇨ Gaussian Blur to blur the image. You can then use one of the methods described below to modify the soft focus effect. You can reduce the layer opacity as necessary to restore more of the original image sharpness. And if you add a layer mask to the layer you can fill or add paint to the mask and apply the soft focus effect selectively.

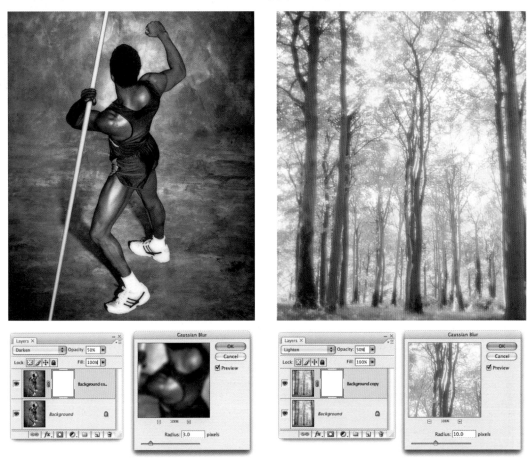

**Figure 9.6** In the javelin thrower example, I applied a Gaussian Blur filter to a Background copy layer and set the layer blend mode to Darken at 50%. This method simulates diffusion darkroom printing. With the forest scene I applied a greater amount of blur and set the layer to Lighten blend mode, also at 50%. This produced a soft focus lens effect.

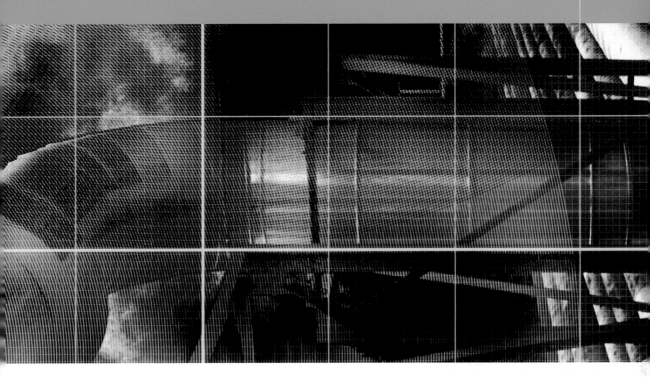

**Chapter 10**

# Photoshop Filters

One of the key factors attributed to Photoshop's success has been the program's support for plug-in filters. A huge industry of third-party companies has grown in response to the needs of users wanting extra features within Photoshop. Since this book concentrates mainly on what is in the Photoshop program itself, rather than trying to cover all the hundred or more filters that are available in the program, I have concentrated here on just those filter effects I believe are useful for photographic work. This chapter therefore focuses mainly on the filters that are really useful for everyday production and creative output, and also suggests ways that you can use the new Smart Filters feature to extend your filtering options.

## RGB only filters

You will notice that most of the effects filters work in RGB mode only. This is because they can have such a dramatic effect on the pixel values, and they would easily send colors way out of the CMYK gamut. So to unleash the full creative power of Photoshop plug-ins, this is a good argument for having to work in RGB mode and convert to CMYK later.

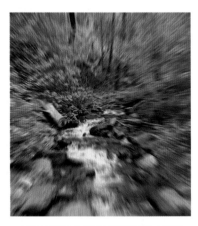

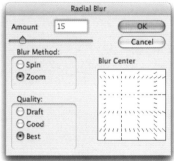

**Figure 10.1** When using the Radial Blur filter in Zoom mode, you can drag the center point to match the center of interest of the image you are about to filter.

# Filter essentials

Most of the Photoshop filters provide a preview dialog with slider settings that you can adjust. Some of the more sophisticated plug-ins (such as Liquify) are like applications operating within Photoshop. These have a modal dialog interface, which means that whenever the filter dialog is open, Photoshop is pushed into the background and this can usefully free up keyboard shortcuts. With so many effects filters to choose from in Photoshop, there is plenty enough to experiment with. The danger is that you can all too easily get lost endlessly searching through all the different filter settings. There is not enough room here to describe every Photoshop filter, but we shall look at a few of the ways filters can enhance an image, highlighting the more useful creative filters plus a few personal favorites.

# Blur filters

There are many ways you can blur a photograph in Photoshop. And each of these filters is able to blur an image differently. You don't really want to bother with the basic Blur and Blur More filters, but what follows is a brief description of the blur filters you will find useful.

## Gaussian Blur

The Gaussian Blur is a good general purpose blur filter which can be used for many purposes from blurring areas of an image to softening the edges of a mask.

## Radial Blur

Radial Blur does a very good job of creating blurred spinning motion effects. For example, the Spin blur mode can be used to add movement to a car wheel, where you wish to convey faster motion, while the Zoom blur mode can do a neat simulation of a zooming camera lens. This may appear to be a very sluggish plug-in, but it is after all carrying out a major distortion of the image. For this reason you are offered a choice of render settings. For top quality results, select the Best mode. If you just want to see a quick preview of the whole image area, select Draft.

**1** I opened the image shown here, went to the Filter menu and chose Convert to Smart Filters. This converted the Background layer to a Smart Object. I then selected a Radial Spin blur from the Filter ⇨ Blur submenu, using Best mode. I repositioned the center of the blur to roughly align with the top of the hydrant.

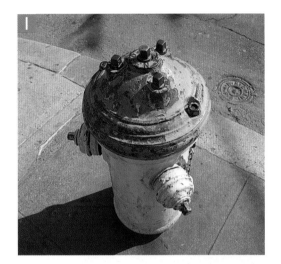

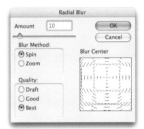

**2** I wanted to remove some of the Spin blur from the center of the image, so I clicked to select the Smart Filters layer mask and added a black to white radial gradient to the mask, where black was the foreground color, and dragged outwards from the center. This masked the effect of the Smart Filter layer.

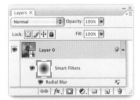

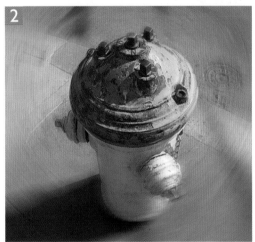

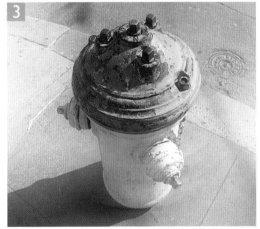

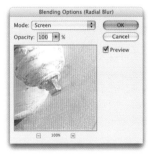

**3** With Smart Filter layers you can re-edit the filter at any time (such as reposition the center for the Radial Blur. If you double-click the Filter settings button, this will open the Blending Options for the filter. Here is a variation using a Screen blend fade.

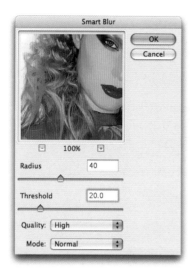

**Figure 10.2** The Smart Blur filter.

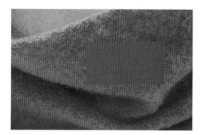

**Figure 10.3** The Average Blur can be used to merge the pixels within a selection to create a solid color which can then be used to take a sample color measurement of the average color within that selection area.

## Smart Blur

This filter blurs the image while at the same time identifying the sharp edges and preserving them. When the settings are pushed to the extremes, the effect becomes very graphic and can look rather ugly. In some ways its function mimics the Median Noise filter and is another useful tool for cleaning up noisy color channels or artificially softening skin tones to create an airbrushed look. When retouching with this tool you could apply the Smart Blur to a copied layer and then lower the opacity.

## Average Blur

The Average Blur simply averages the colors in an image or a selection. At first glance it doesn't do a lot, but it is a useful filter to be aware of. Let's say you want to analyze the color of some fabric to create a color swatch for a catalog. The Average filter will merge all the pixels in a selection to create a solid color and you can then use this to sample with the eyedropper tool and create a new Swatch color.

## Motion Blur

The Motion Blur filter can be used to create an effective impression of blurred movement. Both the blurring angle and length of blur (defined in pixels) can be adjusted and the blurring spreads evenly in both directions along the axis of the angle set. Let's suppose you want to offset the blur so that it appears to be trailing behind an object. Well, there is an example of this on page 421 where the blur was applied to a duplicate layer and the blurred layer shifted with the move tool to one side of the subject. In the example on the page opposite, I used the Motion Blur filter to add more general blurred movement to the photograph of a ballerina.

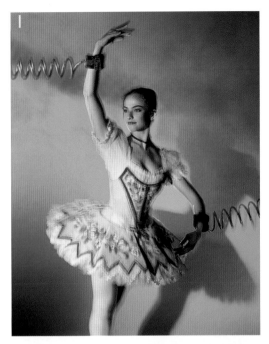

**1** This photograph already has a little Motion Blur where the subject was moving slightly during the camera exposure. In this example I wanted to add the appearance of some extra motion using Photoshop's Motion Blur filter. I began by selecting the Background layer and choose Convert for Smart Filters from the Filter menu.

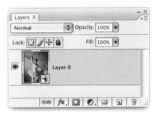

**2** I then chose Filter ⇨ Blur ⇨ Motion Blur and applied a 90 pixel blur at an angle of minus 8°. This of course blurred the entire layer, but it is quite easy to now mask the effect of the filter. I clicked on the Smart Filters layer mask, selected the paintbrush tool, set Black as the foreground color and painted over the layer to reveal more of the unblurred layer below. The trick here is to paint with a large soft edged brush so as to maintain a soft transition between the two layers around the outline of the subject.

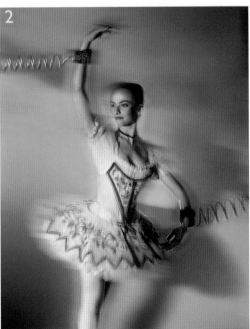

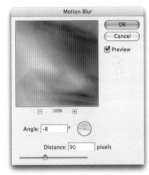

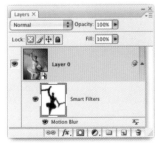

Photograph: Eric Richmond.

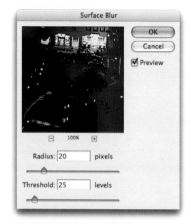

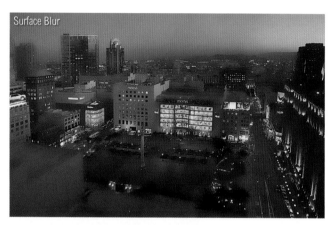

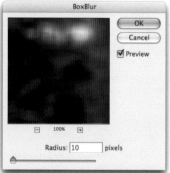

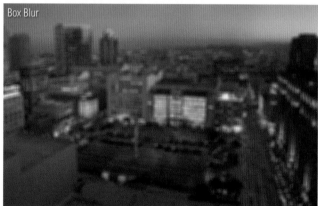

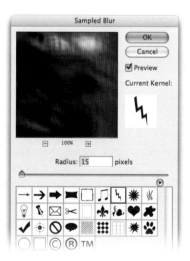

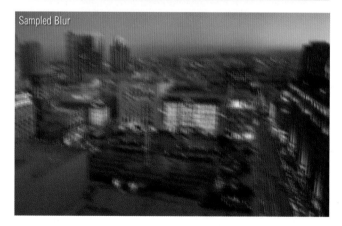

**Figure 10.4** The new Photoshop blur filters.

## Surface Blur

This might be considered an edge preserving blur filter. The Radius adjustment is identical to that used in the Gaussian Blur filter. The higher the Radius, the more blurred the image will become. But it is the Threshold slider that determines the weighting given to the neighboring pixels and whether they become blurred or not. Basically, as you increase the Threshold this will extend the range of pixels (relative to each other) that become blurred. So as you increase the Threshold, the flatter areas of tone are the first to become blurred and the high contrast edges will remain less blurred (until you increase the Threshold more).

## Box Blur

The Box Blur uses a fairly simple algorithm to produce a square shape blur. It is a fairly fast filter and could be useful for creating special effects.

## Sampled Blur

The Sampled Blur filter allows you to specify any shape you like as a kernel for creating the blur effect and adjust the blur radius accordingly. At the bottom of Figure 10.4 you will see that I selected a lightning bolt shape which enabled me to simulate a camera shake effect with this filter. The Sampled Blur is no match for the power of the Lens Blur filter, but is nonetheless a versatile and creative tool.

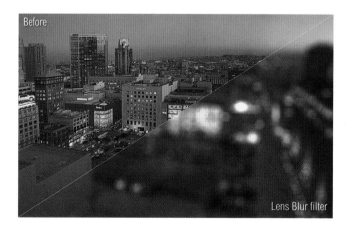

### Fade command

Filter effects can be further refined by fading them after you have applied a filter. The Fade command is referred to at various places in the book (you can also fade image adjustments and brush strokes, etc.). Choose Edit ⇨ Fade Filter and experiment with different blending modes. The Fade command is almost like an adjustment layer feature, but without the versatility and ability to undo later. It makes use of the fact that the previous undo version of the image is stored in the undo buffer and allows you to calculate many different blends but without the time-consuming expense of having to duplicate the layer first. Having said all that, history offers an alternative approach whereby if you filter an image, or make several filtrations, you can return to the original state and then paint in the future (filtered) state using the history brush or make a fill using the filtered history state (providing Non-linear History has been enabled).

Figure 10.5 The best way to learn how to use the blur filters discussed here and the Lens Blur filter on the following page is to experiment with an image like the one shown here, which is available on the DVD. In this night-time scene there are lots of small points of light; you can use this image example to get a clear idea of how the Specular Highlights and Iris controls work, and how they will affect the appearance of the blur in the photograph.

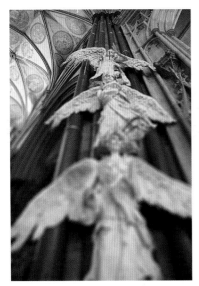

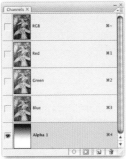

Figure 10.6 In this example, I created a linear gradient mask channel called Alpha 1, where the gradient went from white to black. I then loaded the Alpha 1 channel in the Lens Blur filter dialog to use this as a depth map. With the Alpha 1 channel selected, I could adjust the Blur Focal Distance slider to determine the point where the image would remain sharp and the Lens Blur would not affect this portion of the image. But there is an even easier way to do this. You can just click anywhere in the image to decide which point you would like to keep sharp (in the above image example, I clicked on the angel at the top of the pillar to make her sharp). The out of focus effect will fade out gradually based on the gray values in the Depth Map channel source.

## Lens Blur

If you want to make a photograph appear realistically out of focus, it is not a simple matter of making the detail softer. Consider for a moment how a lens works. The camera lens will focus an object to form an image made up of circular points on the film/sensor surface. When the radius of these points is very small, the image is considered sharp. When the radii are large, the image will appear to be out of focus. It is particularly noticeable the way bright highlights blow out when this happens and how you can see the shape of the camera lens iris in the blurred highlight points. The Lens Blur filter has the potential to mimic the way a camera lens forms an optical image. The best way to understand how it works is to look at the shape of the bright lights in the night-time scene in Figure 10.5 which shows an image before and after I had applied the Lens Blur filter. You will also find this image on the DVD.

### *Depth of field effects*

You can also create a mask to define the areas where you wish to selectively apply the Lens Blur. This will allow you to create shallow depth of field effects. In the Lens Blur dialog you can then load this mask under the Depth Map section in order to define the plane of focus.

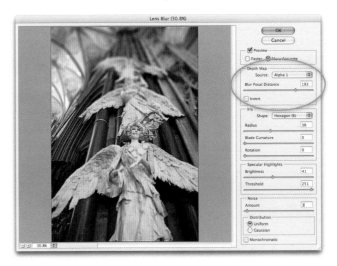

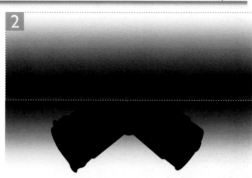

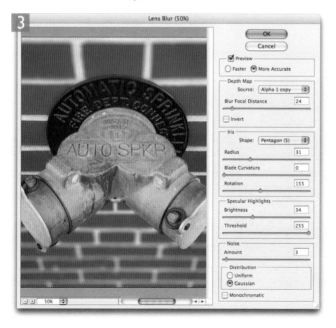

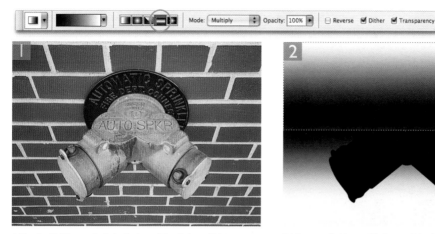

**1** The Depth Map controls in the Lens Blur dialog will let you simulate a shallow depth of field focus effect. The image shown here is a good choice to demonstrate this with because the wall is photographed at an oblique angle and starts off with everything in sharp focus, which is one of the pluses (and minuses) of using a compact digital camera! I first drew a pen path to define the outline of the hydrant, I hit ⌘ Enter ctrl Enter to convert the path to a selection, and then clicked on the Save Selection as a Channel button in the Channels palette.

**2** I then needed to modify the mask to define a depth of field map. I selected the gradient tool in reflected gradient mode (circled) and set the tool blend mode to Multiply mode and dragged vertically from the center. To get the fade at the top, I kept the gradient tool in reflected mode and changed the blend to Normal mode. I made a rectangular marquee selection of the top half of the picture, selected the gradient tool again and dragged vertically from the middle again (as shown above).

**3** I then chose Filter ⇨ Blur ⇨ Lens Blur. I went to the Depth Map section and moused down on the Channel source menu and selected the channel I had just created, which in this case was named: Alpha 1 copy. If you try this out for yourself, try adjusting the Blur Focal Distance slider to adjust the amount of blur that is applied to the areas that are selected (and partially selected) by the Depth Map Source channel.

## Applying Lens Blur to a composite image

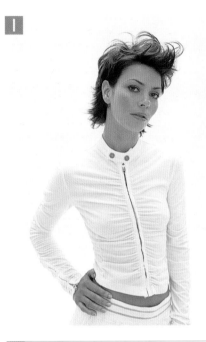

**1** I wanted to blend this photograph of the model with a New York street scene. The model has been lit so that the lighting matches the outdoor daylight. But if I merge the two images together as they are, the background detail would be too distracting.

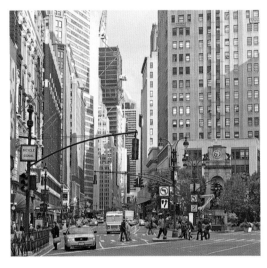

**2** I dragged the street image over to add as a new layer above the Background layer of the model and chose Convert for Smart Filters from the Filter menu. But before applying a filter, I then created a new alpha channel and added a gradient like the one shown here.

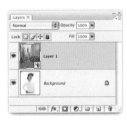

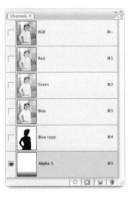

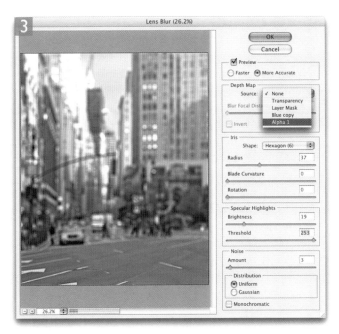

3 To make the background appear out of focus, I selected the New York street, Smart Filter layer and chose Filter ⇨ Blur ⇨ Lens Blur. I first adjusted the Specular Highlights Threshold setting, bringing it down just enough until the highlights started to bloom. I then adjusted the Specular Highlights Brightness setting to create the desired amount of lens flare. The Iris Radius controls the width of the blur and the effect of this adjustment will be particularly noticeable in the specular highlights. Further adjustments can then be made to the iris shape such as the blade curvature of the iris and the rotation. These minor tweaks allow precise control over the iris shape. And lastly, I went to the Depth Map section and selected the Alpha 1 channel, that was created in Step 2. With the Blur Focal distance left at zero, this created a depth of field effect in which less lens blurring was applied to the foreground portion of the backdrop image.

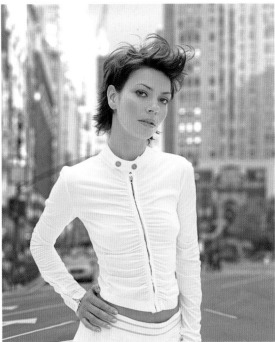

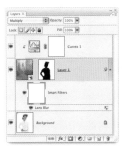

4 I blended the two images together using the montage technique described in Chapter 8. As you can see in the Layers palette dialog, the street scene image is hidden by a mask I had prepared earlier and is blended with the Background layer using the Multiply blend mode. I also added a Curves adjustment layer which was grouped with the street image layer beneath it. The Curves adjustment was added in order to lighten the blurred layer and match the lightness of the model in the picture.

Client: Reflections.
Model: Lisa Moulson @ MOT.

### Smart Filters/Smart Objects

When you go to the Filter menu and choose Convert for Smart Filters, you are basically doing the same thing as when you create a Smart Object. So if a layer or group of layers have already been converted to a Smart Object, there will be no need to choose Convert for Smart Filters.

### Smart Filter benefits and cons

The benefit of Smart Filtering is the ability to re-edit the filter settings, which is especially useful where you don't always get a preview of how a filter effect will look. But on the downside, Smart Filter layers make the file size increase dramatically and can really slow down the Photoshop editing process.

# Smart Filters

New to Photoshop CS3 is the Smart Filters feature. This is something that Photoshop users have been requesting for many years, but now that we have Smart Filters, I do wonder just how many people will be using this feature on a regular basis. But I have managed to provided a couple of examples in this chapter (as well as earlier in the book) to show where I do find this to be of real use. For example, Smart Filters can be particularly useful when working with the blur type filters because you may very often want the ability to re-edit the blur amount. In the previous example, where I had applied a Lens Blur filter to the Backdrop layer, it was particularly useful to apply this as a Smart Filter. You can switch filtering effects on or off, combine two or more filter effects and mask the overall Smart Filter combination. The blending options also allow you to control the opacity and blend modes for individual filters. On page 479, I showed how you could use the Smart Filter mask to selectively paint out a filter effect. And as I have shown below in Figure 10.7, you can also group one or more layers into a Smart Object and filter the Smart Object layer.

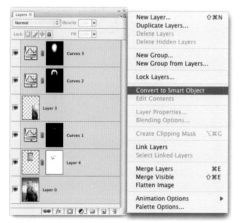
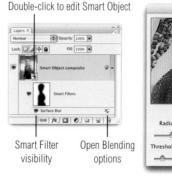
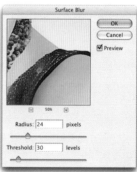

**Figure 10.7** You can make a selection of more than one layer in a document and convert these into a Smart Object. From there you can add filter effects that will be applied as Smart Filters to a composite version of all the selected layers. And the multi-layered image can still be accessed and edited by double-clicking the Smart Object icon in the image thumbnail.

## Lighting and rendering

Rendering processes are normally associated with 3D design programs, yet Photoshop has hidden powers itself when it comes to rendering 3D shapes and textures. Some of these filter effects will utilize texture maps, a number of which are preloaded in the Application Presets folder when you install Photoshop.

### Fibers filter

The Fibers filter can be found in the Filter ⇨ Render menu. In some ways it is similar to the Render Clouds filters. It can generate abstract fiber patterns which could be useful if you wanted to artificially create a natural-looking fibrous texture.

### Lighting Effects

When used properly, the Lighting Effects filter is an occasionally useful Photoshop tool for generating textures, 3D objects or lighting fills. The Lighting Effects filter has been around for a long time in Photoshop, and the tiny preview desperately needs to be updated to match the preview size area of the other modal dialogs. But apart from the lack of a decent preview, you can still put it to some good uses. Over the next few pages I will show you how the Lighting Effects filter can be used to render a theatrical-looking curtain from an ordinary pair of drapes and make it look as if they have been lit from below by a row of footlights. In this tutorial I am also able to show how you can use one of the image color channels to act as a texture map so that the lighting appears to enhance the texture of the curtain material.

### Missing 3D Transform

The 3D Transform filter is no longer installed as standard in Photoshop. It hasn't been completely dumped; it is there on the Photoshop application resource disk and you can install it by simply copying it across to the Photoshop plug-ins folder.

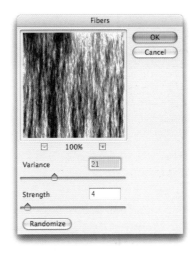

**Figure 10.8** The Fibers filter.

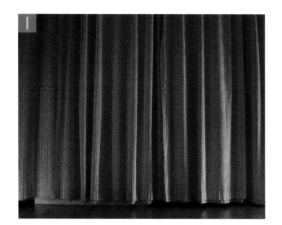

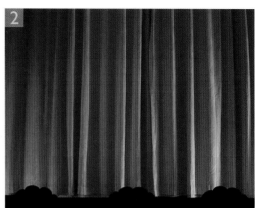

**1** In this example I wanted to use a photograph taken of some light colored drapes and use the Lighting Effects filter to apply some rendered lighting to help make them look more theatrical.

**2** I Applied Convert to Smart Filters to the Background layer, to prepare them for Smart Filtering, and placed an image layer above it that added a stage footlights silhouette shape.

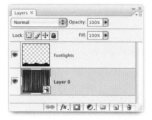

**3** I selected the Smart Object layer and chose Filter ⇨ Render ⇨ Lighting Effects. I started off by applying a single spotlight to the middle of the image layer. The preview is really tiny compared to most other Photoshop filters, but you can just about see the outcome of the effect in the preview area. You can set the color of each individual light by clicking on the color swatch, which will open the Color Picker. The light I have selected here is a Spotlight effect and you can drag on the center spot or on any of the four handles to reposition the light source and adjust the width of the light spread. When I use this filter, I usually adjust the positioning and handles first and then adjust the Intensity and Focus settings to establish the desired lighting characteristics. After that I will go to the Exposure slider to fine-tune the brightness of the lighting and finally adjust the Ambience slider to increase or decrease the ambient lighting effect.

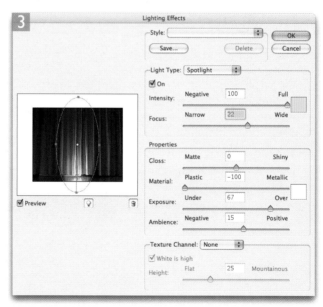

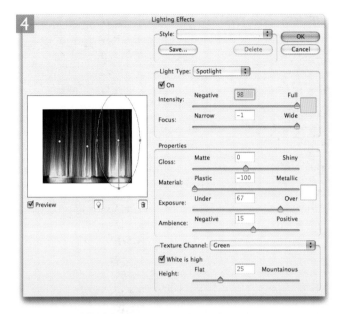

4 To add more lights, you can either drag from the light bulb icon (circled) up into the preview area or ⌥ alt drag on one of the existing lights to make a copy of the light. As you can see here, I copied the first light twice to create a triple uplighting effect. If you create a lighting effect like this and would possibly like to reuse it, then you can click on the Save... button to save this combination as a new Lighting Effect preset.

One of the unique (and rather clever) things you can do in the Lighting Effects dialog is to utilize a color channel or alpha channel as a texture map. In the dialog shown here you will notice that I selected the Green channel as a Texture Channel. The White is high checkbox was checked and I set the texture height setting to 25%. A higher amount will produce a more pronounced texture.

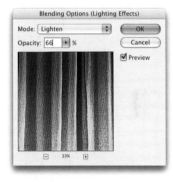

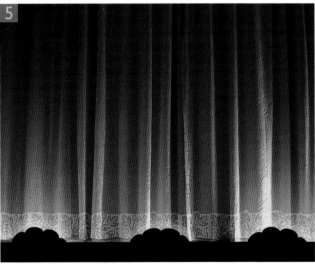

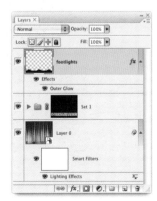

5 Here is the finished result in which the plain drapes have been dramatically lit using the Lighting Effects filter. I double-clicked on the Lighting Effects settings icon to open the Blending Options, where I set the Opacity to 66% and the blend mode to Lighten. To complete the scene, I selected the footlights layer and added an outer glow layer effect to add a little extra atmosphere to the rendered scene plus I added a patterned gilt decoration.

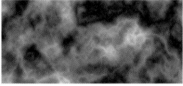

Figure 10.9 Examples of the Render ⇨ Clouds filter (top) and the Render ⇨ Difference Clouds filter (bottom).

## Clouds and Difference Clouds

This filter generates a cloud pattern that fills the whole image (or selected area), based on the foreground and background colors. The cloud pattern alters each time the filter is applied, so repeated filtering ( ⌘ F  ctrl F ), for example, will produce a fresh cloudscape every time. If you hold down the ⌥  alt key whilst applying the Cloud filter, the effect is magnified. The Difference Clouds filter has a cumulative effect on the image. Applying it once creates a cloud pattern based on the inverse color values. Repeating the filter produces clouds based on the original colors and so on... although after each application of the filter the clouds will become more contrasty.

**1** Here is an interesting way you can use the Clouds filter to create a rough edged border. I opened an image, added an empty new layer and chose Select ⇨ All, followed by Select ⇨ Modify ⇨ Border, and entered a pixel value that was large enough to create a suitable sized border.

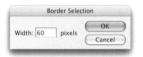

**2** I then feathered the selection by a much smaller percentage. In this example I created a 60 pixel border selection and feathered it by 10 pixels. I reset the foreground/background colors, went to the Filter menu and choose Render ⇨ Clouds.

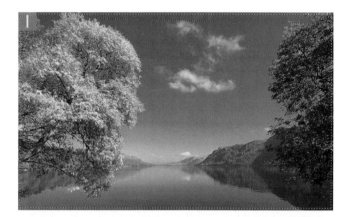

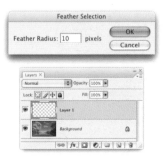

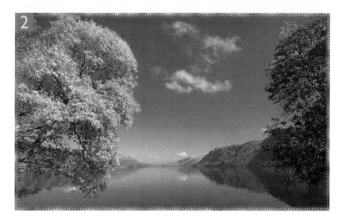

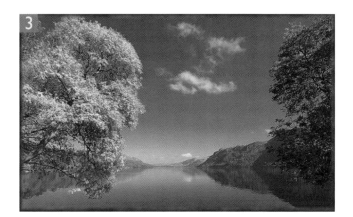

**3** I added another empty new layer and, with the selection still active, filled the selection with black and set the blend mode to Multiply.

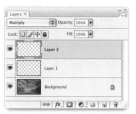

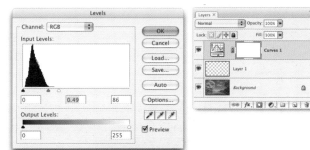

**4** I then deselected the selection, merged these two layers, and changed the blend mode of this merged layer also to Multiply mode and applied an extreme Levels adjustment that would harden the edges of the border. And finally, I added a Curves adjustment layer at the top of the layer stack to add a split tone color effect.

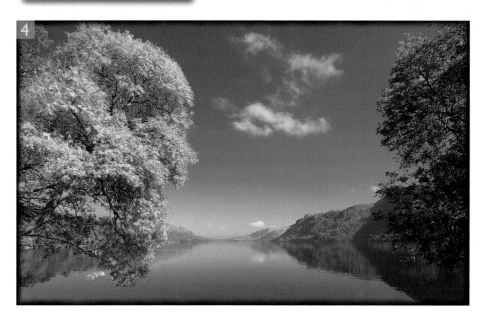

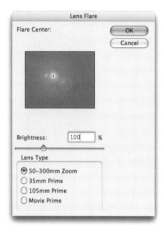

## Lens Flare

The Lens Flare filter is a little overused perhaps but, nevertheless, the Lens Flare filter is ideal for adding realistic-looking lens flare effects to computer rendered images, applying the ghosting type of patterns that are normally associated with camera lens flare. But instead of applying the lens flare directly to the Background layer, I prefer to add a new layer filled with neutral gray set to Overlay mode and apply the Lens Flare filter to this layer only. This allows me the option of repositioning the flare effect afterwards. Another approach is to apply the filter to a black fill layer and set the blending mode to Screen.

**1** To add a new layer filled with a neutral blending gray, I ⌥ *alt*-clicked on the New Layer button in the Layers palette, selected the Overlay blend mode and then checked the Fill with Overlay Neutral Color (50%) checkbox.

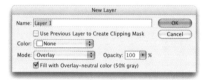

**2** I then applied the Lens Flare filter. The position of the lens flare center point can be adjusted in the dialog preview. If you ⌥ *alt*-click in the preview box, this will call up the Precise Flare Center dialog, where you can set precise mouse coordinates for where to center the lens flare effect.

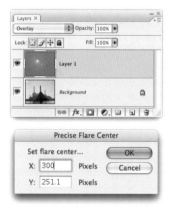

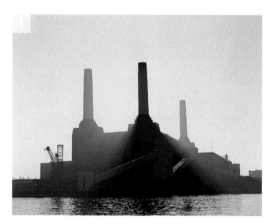

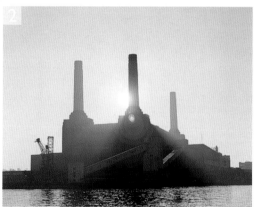

# Pattern Maker

The Pattern Maker is a creative tool that you can use to generate random abstract patterns that are based on a sampled image, either a whole image or a selected area. It is useful for creating interesting textures that can be saved as custom Pattern presets but, more specifically, it can be used to generate texture patterns that can be used to convincingly fill parts of an image. The Pattern Maker was shown being put to use in Chapter 8, where I created a stone wall texture pattern that could be used in conjunction with the healing brush to cover up an area with a texture that matched the surrounding wall texture.

Pattern Maker tools: marquee selection; zoom; hand

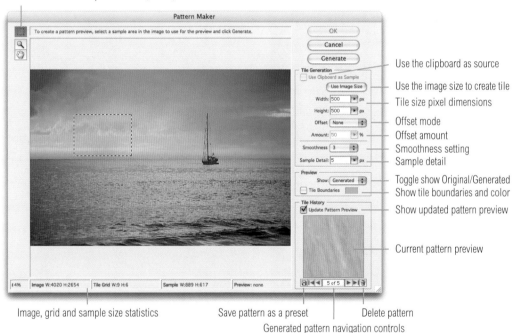

Use the clipboard as source
Use the image size to create tile
Tile size pixel dimensions
Offset mode
Offset amount
Smoothness setting
Sample detail
Toggle show Original/Generated
Show tile boundaries and color
Show updated pattern preview

Current pattern preview

Image, grid and sample size statistics          Save pattern as a preset          Delete pattern
Generated pattern navigation controls

**Figure 10.10** The Pattern Maker dialog controls. You can generate a pattern based on either the actual image size or a tile area of specified pixel size. If you wish, the generated tiles can be offset either horizontally or vertically by a set percentage amount. Increasing the smoothness will produce better results, but take longer to process. Increasing the sample detail will preserve more recognizable detail. A lesser amount will produce more abstract results. Check the Save Preset Pattern button at the bottom of the palette if you want to save a generated pattern to the Pattern Presets. For as long as the dialog is open, you can keep generating new presets, review their histories using the navigator buttons and delete or retain them as necessary.

## Displacement rules

The Displace filter must use an image saved using the native Photoshop file format, which will act as a displacement map when calculating the displacement. Black (0) will produce the maximum negative displacement shift and white (255) will produce the maximum positive shift, while gray (128) will produce no displacement. If a displacement map image file contains more than one channel, the first channel will determine the horizontal displacement and the second channel will control the vertical displacement.

# Pixel distortions and corrections

In the following sections we will be looking at the various ways you can distort an image or make lens distortion corrections in Photoshop.

## Displace filter

The Displace filter is not the most intuitive of filters but is still quite invaluable if you need to distort any type of layer so as to appear to match the shape or texture of the underlying layers. The effect works well with text effects and where the displacement map you use has been softened beforehand. You will find a large number of displacement maps contained on the Adobe Photoshop disk and these can be loaded to generate all types of surface texture patterns.

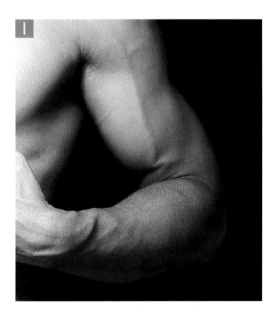

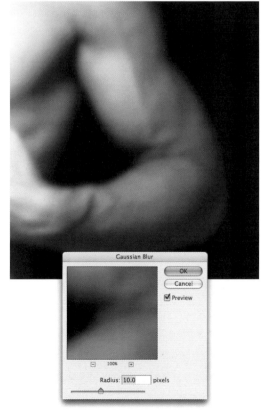

**1** I wanted to add a tattoo to the arm of this model. This needed to be done in several stages. To start with I made a duplicate of the color image by choosing Image ⇨ Duplicate. I then converted the duplicate image to Grayscale mode, applied a 10 pixel Gaussian Blur to this grayscale version and saved this duplicate version of the image to the desktop, where it would be easy to locate again later on. It is important to note here that the image was in grayscale and saved in the native Photoshop (PSD) file format.

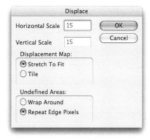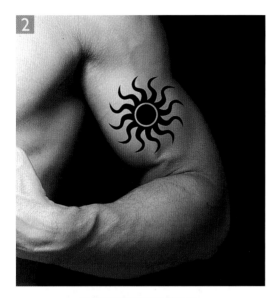

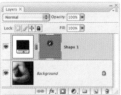

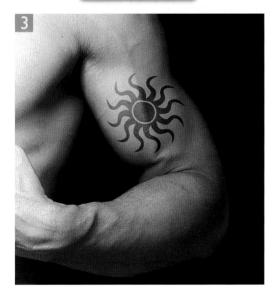

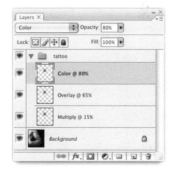

**2** I closed the blurred grayscale version, returned to the master image and added a shape layer of the desired tattoo and positioned this over the arm. I was now ready to displace the tattoo layer. I went to the Filter menu and chose Distort ⇨ Displace... Now, because the layer I was about to filter was a vector layer, a dialog popped asking if I would like to rasterize the shape layer. I clicked OK. The Displace dialog allowed me to set the displacement amount for the horizontal and vertical axes. You don't always want to get too carried away with entering high amounts here. Start off with 10 and try redoing the displacement again using higher values if you feel this is necessary.

The Displacement Map settings won't make any difference in this instance because the pixel dimensions of the map I was about to use matched the image exactly. After I had clicked OK in the Displace dialog, I was asked to select the displacement map. This is where the saved grayscale image comes in. I located the grayscale map that had been saved earlier to the desktop and clicked Open to select it.

**3** In the final image you can see how the shape has been displaced and appears to follow the contours of the arm. To achieve the blended result you see here I duplicated the newly displaced layer twice and adjusted the blend modes and layer opacities as shown here: the top layer used Color mode @ 80%; the middle layer Overlay mode @ 65%; and the lower layer was set to Multiply mode @ 15%.

## Chromatic aberration and Vignetting

Some lenses will suffer from other kinds of optical defects as well. For example, chromatic aberration can sometimes be noticed along high contrast edges. You can now remove these quite easily using the two chromatic slider controls in the Lens Correction dialog. You may sometimes notice a darkening vignette towards the edges of a picture when you are shooting with an ultra wide-angle lens. The Vignette controls allow you to compensate for this as well. Or if you prefer, you can use them to introduce a vignette even. These topics are also covered on pages 273–274.

## Set Lens Default

If the image you are editing contains EXIF metadata describing the lens, focal length and f stop used, you can click on the Set Lens Default button to archive the settings used. These will be available in the future as a Lens Default option in the Settings menu.

## Edge pixels

As you apply the Lens Correction, the curvature and shape of the image will change. The Scale slider will crop the picture as you apply a correction. If you prefer not to do this there is the problem of how to render the outer pixels. The default setting uses the Edge Extension mode to extend the edge pixels. This may be fine with skies or flat color backdrops, but is otherwise quite ugly and distracting, although having extended pixels will make it easier to apply the healing brush in these areas.

# Lens Correction

Photographers are always striving for optical perfection but sadly not all lenses are capable of delivering the goods. The Lens Correction filter was a new addition to Photoshop CS2 and it offers several ways you can correct images that suffer from different types of optical distortion.

The most obvious forms of distortion are the pin cushion and barrel lens effects which are all too common a problem when shooting with lower quality lenses. You can use the distort tool to drag toward or away from the center of the image to adjust the amount of distortion in either direction. Or you can use the Remove Distortion slider, which I find offers more precise control.

The rotate tool can be used to straighten photographs. Drag with the tool on the preview to define what should be a correct horizontal or vertical line and the image will rotate to align correctly. You can also adjust the rotation in the Transform section. Try clicking in the Angle field (circled) and use the up and down arrow keys to nudge the rotation in either direction by small increments.

The grid pattern will prove really useful for helping you to judge the alignment of the image. But better still, you can use the move grid tool to shift the placement of the grid. And the grid controls at the bottom of the Lens Correction dialog will enable you to adjust the grid color and dynamically adjust the grid spacing, plus toggle showing or hiding the grid.

The Transform controls let you adjust the vertical and horizontal perspective. These offer an immense amount of control to correct the perspective view of a photograph such as the vertical perspective keystone effect you get when pointing the camera up to photograph a building. Or, the horizontal perspective you get when photographing a subject from the side instead of dead center. You should only need to use these controls where you need your subject to appear perfectly square on to the camera, such as in architectural photography.

Lens Correction tools: distort tool; rotate tool; move grid tool; hand tool; zoom tool              Lens Correction preset settings

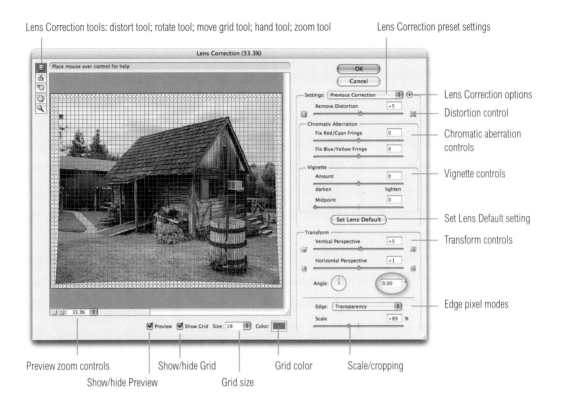

Lens Correction options

Distortion control

Chromatic aberration controls

Vignette controls

Set Lens Default setting

Transform controls

Edge pixel modes

Preview zoom controls      Show/hide Grid        Grid color    Scale/cropping

Show/hide Preview        Grid size

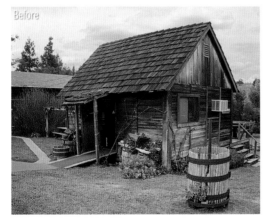

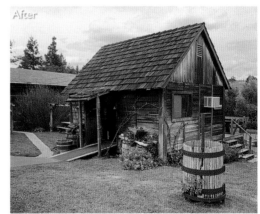

**Figure 10.11** The Lens Correction filter was applied to the before image to correct for a barrel type lens distortion and I aligned the vertical lines of the building to the grid in the dialog shown above. The Lens settings (excepting the Transform settings) can be saved as presets via the Lens Correction options to the designated Settings folder. These presets can be associated with the lenses that you use most often and if saved to the correct folder will appear listed in the Lens Correction Settings menu.

## Liquify tools

### 🐾 Warp tool (W)

Provides a basic warp distortion with which you can stretch the pixels in any direction you wish.

### ✎ Reconstruct tool (E)

Used to make selective undos and restore the image to its undistorted state.

### 🌀 Twirl tool (R)

Twist the pixels in a clockwise direction. Hold down the ⌥ alt key to switch tool to twirl in a counterclockwise direction

### 🌸 Pucker tool (P)

Shrinks pixels and produces an effect similar to the 'Pinch' filter.

### 🔷 Bloat tool (B)

Magnifies pixels and is similar to the 'Bloat' filter.

### ❖ Push left tool (S)

Shifts the pixels at 90° to the left of the direction in which you are dragging.

### 🔲 Mirror tool (M)

Copies pixels from 90° to the direction you are dragging and therefore acts as an inverting lens.

### ≋ Turbulence tool (A)

Produces random turbulent distortions.

### 🖌 Freeze mask tool (F).

Protects areas of the image. Frozen portions are indicated by a Quick Mask type overlay. These areas will be protected from any further liquify distortion tool actions.

### 🖌 Thaw mask tool (T)

Selectively or wholly erase the freeze tool area.

### 🔍 Zoom tool (Z)

Use to magnify or zoom out

### ✋ Hand tool (H)

Scroll the preview image.

## Liquify

The Liquify filter is designed to let you carry out freeform pixel distortions. When you choose Filter ➪ Liquify or use the ⌘ Shift X ctrl Shift X shortcut, you are presented with what is called a modal dialog, which basically means you are working in a self-contained dialog with its own set of tools and keyboard shortcuts, etc. It is therefore operating like a program within the Photoshop program. To use Liquify efficiently, I suggest you make a marquee selection first of the area you wish to manipulate before you select the filter. And once the dialog has opened, use the ⌘ 0 ctrl 0 shortcut to enlarge the dialog to fit the screen.

Basically, you will select one of the Liquify tools to manipulate the image preview and when you are happy with your liquify work, click Enter to OK the pixel manipulation and this will calculate and apply the liquify adjustment to the main image.

The Liquify tools are all explained in the column on the left and the chart in Figure 10.12 also summarizes the effect each of these tools will have on an image. The easiest tool to get to grips with is the Warp tool, because you simply click and drag to push the pixels in the direction you want them to go in. But I also like working with the Push Left tool, because it allows me to carry out some bold warp adjustments (see page 503). Note that when you drag with this tool it shifts the pixels 90° to the left of the direction you are dragging in. When you ⌥ alt drag with this tool, it will shift the pixels 90° to the right of the direction you are dragging in.

The pucker tool is sometimes useful for correcting over distorted areas and squeezing the pixels inwards again. The reflection tool is perhaps the most unwieldy of all, copying pixels from 90° to the direction you are dragging and therefore acting as an inverting lens (which if you are not careful will easily rip an image apart). And apparently, some retouchers who work on adult magazines are very fond of the turbulence tool, for reasons that are beyond me and it is inappropriate to enquire further!

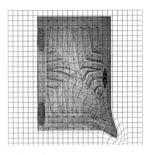

Warp tool

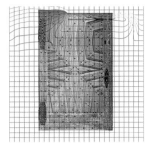

Reconstruct tool

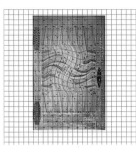

Twirl clockwise tool

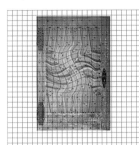

Twirl counterclockwise tool

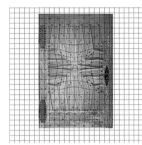

Pucker tool

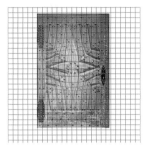

Bloat tool

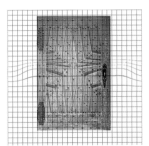

Push left tool

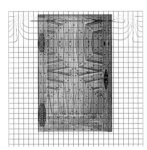

Mirror tool

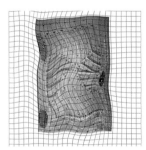

Turbulence tool

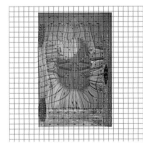

Freeze mask tool

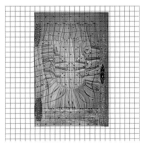

Thaw mask tool

**Figure 10.12** These illustrations give you an idea of the range of distortion effects that can be achieved using the Liquify tools described on page 498.

## One step at a time

The key to working successfully with the Liquify filter is to use gradual brush movements to build up a distortion. This is why I prefer to set the Brush Pressure at an extremely low setting and use a Wacom pad to apply the liquify brush strokes, with the Stylus Pressure option selected.

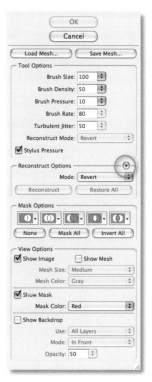

**Figure 10.13** The Liquify dialog options. The Reconstruct Options referred to in Figure 10.14 caption are shown circled here.

## Liquify tool controls

Once you have selected a tool then you will want to check out the associated tool options which are located to the right. All the tools (apart from the hand and zoom tool) are displayed as a circular cursor with a cross-hair in the middle. The tool options will be applied universally to all the tools and these options include: Brush Size, Brush Density, Brush Pressure and Brush Rate. If you mouse down on the double-arrow icon next to the field entry box, this will pop a dynamic slider which you can use to adjust the tool option setting. You can also use the square bracket keys [ ] ] to enlarge or reduce the tool cursor size. And the rate of increase/decrease can be accelerated by holding down the *Shift* key. I highly recommend that you use a pressure sensitive pen and pad such as the Wacom system and if you do so, make sure that the Stylus Pressure option is checked and set the brush pressure to around 10% (or less even). The Turbulent Jitter control is only active when the turbulence tool is selected. In this context the jitter refers to the amount of randomness that will be introduced in a turbulence distortion applied with this tool.

## Reconstructions

Next we have the Reconstruct Options. The standard mode is Revert and if you apply a Liquify distortion and click on the Reconstruct button, the image will be restored to its undistorted state in stages each time you click on the button (while preserving any areas that have been frozen with the freeze tool). If you click on the Restore All button the entire image will be restored in one step (ignoring any frozen areas). The default Revert mode will produce scaled reversions that return you to the original image state in the preview window. There are some alternative options which are more relevant once you have created a frozen area. For example, the Rigid mode provides one-click reconstruction. Stiff, Smooth and Loose provide varying speeds of continual reconstruction, producing smoother transitions between the frozen and unfrozen areas as you revert the image. You can use *esc* or ⌘ *.* *ctrl .* to halt the reconstruction at an intermediate stage. But avoid applying a second click, as this will exit the Liquify dialog and you will lose all your work! Another way to reconstruct the image is to click on the options triangle in the Reconstruct Options and select one of the options. This will pop a dialog control like the one shown in Figure 10.14, which will allow you to use a slider to determine what percentage of reconstruction you would like. The image reconstruction can also be achieved by using the reconstruct tool to selectively restore the image.

## Mask options

The mask options can utilize an existing selection, the layer transparency or layer mask as the basis of a mask to freeze and constrain the effects of any liquify adjustments. The first option is Replace Selection and this will replace any existing freeze selection that has been made. The four other options allow you to modify an existing freeze selection by adding to, subtracting from, intersecting or creating an inverted selection. You can click on the buttons below to clear all freeze selections by clicking None, choosing Mask All to freeze the entire area, or choosing Invert All to invert the current frozen selection.

### Multiple undos in Liquify

Don't forget that you also have multiple undos at your disposal while inside the Liquify dialog. Use ⌘ Z ctrl Z to undo or redo the last step; ⌘ ⌥ Z ctrl alt Z to go back in history and ⌘ Shift Z ctrl Shift Z to go forward in history.

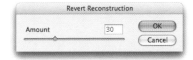

**Figure 10.14** You can control the exact amount by which an image is reconstructed to its original state by going to the Reconstruct Options and selecting the desired reconstruction mode.

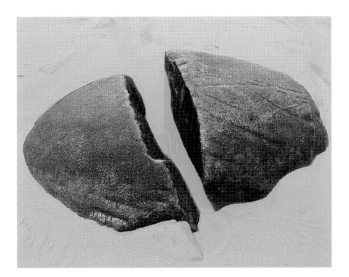

**Figure 10.15** Freeze masks can be used to protect areas of a picture before you commence doing any liquify work. In the example shown here a freeze mask was loaded from a layer mask. When you freeze an area in this way it is protected from subsequent distortions so you can concentrate on applying the Liquify tools to just the areas you wish to distort. The frozen mask areas can be unfrozen by using the thaw mask tool.

## Predetermined distortions

In the main text I refer to the use of a 'target distortion guide'. Let's say you have a predetermined idea of what the final distortion should look like. You can create an empty layer, draw the distortion on this layer and use the Show Backdrop options discussed here to select that specific layer and have the ability to switch the guide Layer visibility on or off.

## Liquify and Smart Filters

Note that the Liquify filter cannot be applied to a Smart Object as a Smart Filter.

## View options

The freeze mask can be made visible or hidden using the Show Mask checkbox in the View options, where you can also set the color of the mask.

The mesh grid can be displayed at different sizes using different colors and this will give you an indication of the underlying warp structure and readily help pinpoint the areas where a distortion has been applied. You can use the checkboxes in this section to view the mesh on its own or have it displayed overlaying the liquify preview image.

The Show Backdrop option is normally left unchecked. If the Liquify image contents are contained on a layer, then it is possible to check the Show Backdrop option and preview the liquified layer against the Background layer, all layers or specific layers in the image. Here is how this option might be used. Let's say that you want to apply a liquify distortion to a portion of an image and you are starting out with just a flattened image. Make a selection of the area you wish to work on and make a copy layer via the selection contents using ⌘ J *ctrl* J . As you apply the Liquify filter you can check the Show Backdrop checkbox and set the mode to Behind. At 100% opacity the Liquify layer will cover the Background layer completely, but as you reduce the opacity you will be able to preview the effect of your liquify distortion at different opacity percentages. This technique can prove useful if you wish to compare the effect of a distortion against the original image or a target distortion guide.

## Saving the mesh

If you are working on an extremely large image then it may take a long time to carry out a liquify distortion. This is where the Save and Load mesh options can help. If you carry out your liquify distortions on a scaled-down version of the master image first, you can save the mesh as a separate file. Open up the master file later, load the mesh you saved and apply it to the master image. On page 504 I have provided an example of where a mesh should be saved and reused on a second image layer.

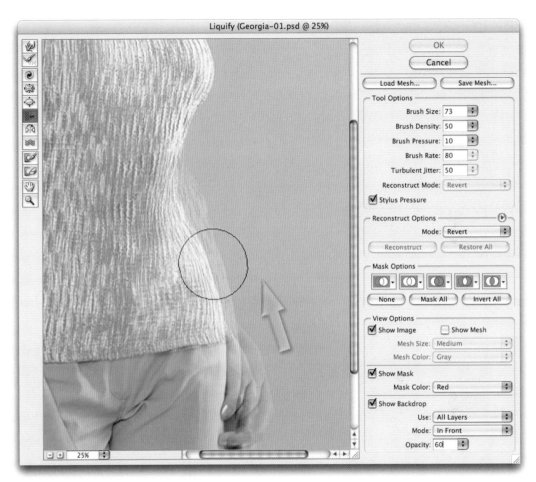

**Figure 10.16** The shift pixels tool is great for slimming down waists. The pixels will be shifted to the left of the direction you drag with the tool. In this example the pixels were shifted inwards to the left as I dragged in an upward direction. If I drag downwards they would be shifted to the right. Because the Backdrop option is selected in the Preview options, you can see an overlaying preview of the undistorted version. If you have more than one layer selected, you can select a specific layer to preview your distortion against.

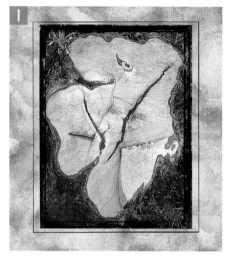

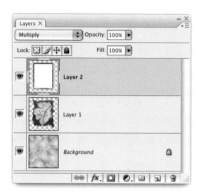

**1** It is possible to imitate a Polaroid™ film emulsion transfer with the Liquify filter. The image shown here has a Background layer, a tree stump image layer and, above this, an independent Polaroid™ emulsion border layer set to Multiply blend mode.

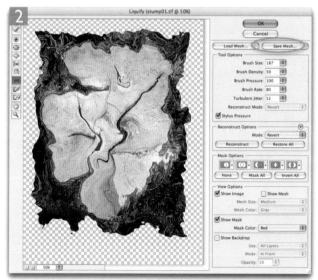

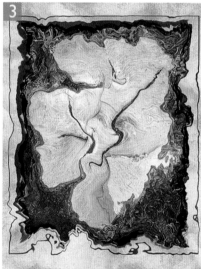

**2** I activated the tree stump image layer and chose Liquify from the Filter menu. I mainly used the turbulence tool plus the clockwise and counterclockwise twirl tools to create the distortions that you see here. I then clicked on the Save Mesh button to save the distortion so that it could be reused.

**3** I then selected Layer 2 (which was the border image in Multiply mode) and opened Liquify again. This time I clicked on the Load Mesh button and loaded the recently saved mesh, applying an identical distortion to produce the result shown here.

## Filter Gallery

To use the Filter Gallery, select an image, choose Filter Gallery from the Filter menu and click on various filter effect icons, revealed in the expanded filter folders. The filter icons provide a visual clue as to the outcome of the filter. As you click on it the filter effect can be previewed in the preview pane area. This in itself is a huge improvement as you can preview a much bigger area now. As you can see in Figure 10.17, you can combine more than one filter at a time and preview how they will look when applied in sequence. To add a new filter, click on the New Effect Layer button at the bottom. As you click on the effect layers you can edit the individual filter settings. To remove a filter effect layer, click on the Delete button.

Filter Gallery preview

Collapse/expand filter effects    Filter effect settings

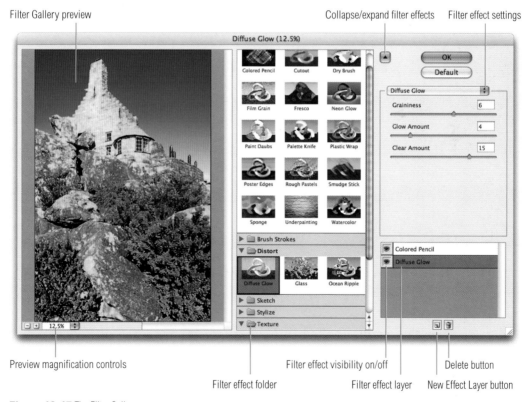

Preview magnification controls

Filter effect folder

Filter effect visibility on/off

Filter effect layer

Delete button

New Effect Layer button

**Figure 10.17** The Filter Gallery.

## Warp transforms

The Warp transform command is not actually a filter but it does provide a perfect solution for all those Photoshop users who have longed for a means to carry out direct, on-canvas image warping. The Warp command is therefore more like an extension of the Free Transform command and in fact the two are both quite nicely integrated. If you select the Free Transform option from the Edit menu you can click on the Transform/Warp mode button to toggle between the Free Transform and Warp modes. The beauty of this is that you can combine a free transform and warp distortion into a single pixel transformation. If you are familiar with the Smart Object feature, which is discussed in detail in Chapter 8, then you will realize that the Warp command can carry out non-destructive distortions to single layers or multiple layers at once.

When a Warp option is selected you can control the shape of the warp envelope using the bezier handles at each corner of the warp envelope box. The box itself contains a 3×3 mesh and you can mouse down and drag within any of the nine warp sectors, and drag with the mouse to fine-tune the warp. What is really great about this command is the way that you can make the warp overlap on itself, as shown on the following page.

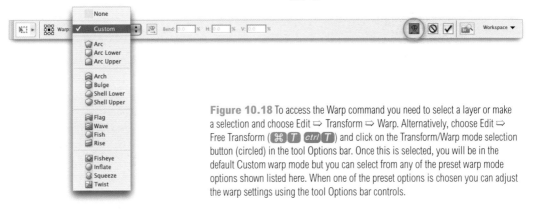

**Figure 10.18** To access the Warp command you need to select a layer or make a selection and choose Edit ⇨ Transform ⇨ Warp. Alternatively, choose Edit ⇨ Free Transform (⌘ T ctrl T) and click on the Transform/Warp mode selection button (circled) in the tool Options bar. Once this is selected, you will be in the default Custom warp mode but you can select from any of the preset warp mode options shown listed here. When one of the preset options is chosen you can adjust the warp settings using the tool Options bar controls.

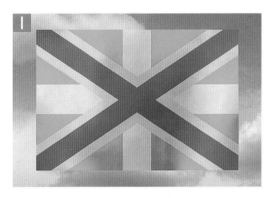

**1** The easiest way for me to illustrate the power of the new Warp command is to create a made-up flag and use the custom warp controls to distort the flag shape to make it appear to be flapping in the wind. This flag is supposed to represent the nation of CMYK color. Am I suggesting here that some diehard CMYK advocates may be living in a world of their own? Of course not.

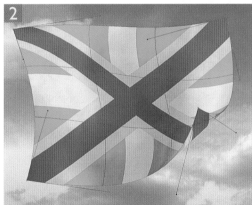

**2** I went to the Edit menu and selected Edit ⇨ Transform ⇨ Warp. The default option is the custom mode. Alternatively, I could have chosen Edit ⇨ Free Transform and clicked on the Warp mode button in the tool options. In custom warp mode you have access to the bezier control handles at the four corners of the warp bounding box and these can be adjusted in the same way as you would manipulate a pen path to control the outer shape of the warp. One can then click inside any of the nine sectors and drag with the mouse to manipulate the image as if you were stretching the image on a rubber sheet.

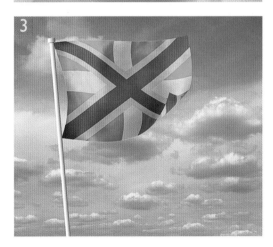

**3** You will notice how I was able to twist the warp so that the flag was twisted in on itself to reveal the reverse side of the flag. To complete the picture I added a shading layer set to Overlay mode which had a layer mask based on a selection of the warped flag layer. And finally, I added a flag pole.

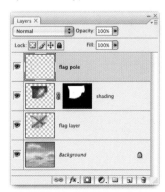

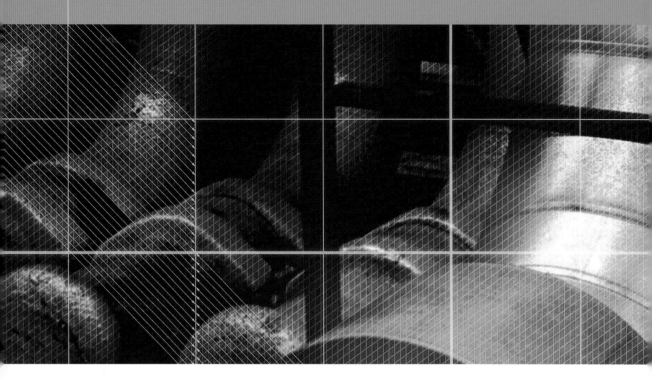

# Chapter 11

# Image Management

One of the consequences of working with digital images in Photoshop is that you will soon find yourself struggling to cope with an ever-growing collection of image files. In order to do this, you usually need something more than the system folder browser to preview the files on your computer system. At a minimum you need some kind of file browser program that will allow you to preview images easily, choose which ones you want to open in Photoshop and carry out basic file management tasks such as rating the images you like most and adding metadata. Operating systems may in future offer better image browsing tools and on the PC platform it is interesting to note how the latest Vista operating system contains a photo browser that offers improved image navigation for photographers.

In the meantime, there are several dedicated file browser programs on the market that will help you manage your images better such as iView Media Pro™, Extensis Portfolio™ and PhotoMechanic™. But iView is more than just a File Browser; it is also a sophisticated database cataloging program that will allow you to manage your images efficiently and quickly. And more recently, we have seen the emergence of digital photography workflow programs such as Apple's Aperture™ and Adobe Photoshop Lightroom™, which are designed to provide a complete workflow management solution from digital raw processing through to image library management.

Bridge is included with Photoshop and also as part of the Creative Suite package and is best described as a standard file browser program. It may not be as sophisticated as some of the other programs I have mentioned, but it does provide you with a direct way to manage your photographs via Photoshop and Adobe Camera Raw. On the plus side, Bridge comes free, it integrates nicely with Adobe Camera Raw and contains most of the tools you need to import, raw process and manage your images. Plus it can work with the automation tools in Photoshop, such as the image processor, Contact Sheet and Web Photo Gallery features. Bridge CS3 now has a more functional interface and there have been some significant innovations. On the down side, Bridge doesn't necessarily do these things as well or as fast as some of the other programs I mentioned. For example, although there is a new Import Photos feature, you can't import and rename more than one set of images at a time. And it still takes the same length of time as it did before to generate contact sheets or Web Photo Galleries. Inputting metadata and keywords remains an awkward process and despite the increased importance of Smart Objects, there is no direct and easy way to open a raw image as a Smart Object in Photoshop (there is a way, but it's well hidden). However, there are some great third-party scripts out there which fill in some of these gaps and most of these can be downloaded for free.

## Bridge origins

The File Browser made its first appearance in Photoshop 7.0 as an integrated feature in Photoshop. Bridge evolved as a stand-alone application and came with the CS2 suite. The Bridge program allows you to inspect and compare images at a full screen resolution, make picture selection edits, sort images using different criteria and conduct image searches based on things like the file name or metadata content (more of which later).

## Bridge and Camera Raw

Bridge integrates smoothly with the Adobe Camera Raw plug-in, to let you work directly with your raw image files within Photoshop (assuming your camera's raw format is supported).

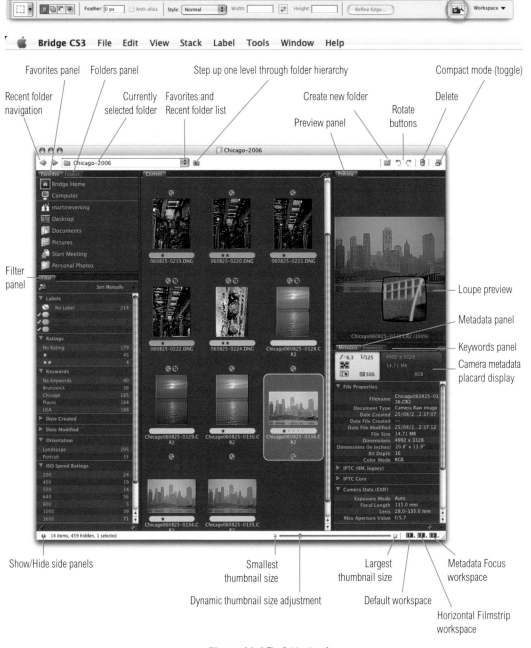

Favorites panel   Folders panel          Step up one level through folder hierarchy                    Compact mode (toggle)

Recent folder              Currently   Favorites and                              Create new folder            Delete
navigation                 selected folder   Recent folder list                                       Rotate
                                                              Preview panel        buttons

Filter
panel

Loupe preview

Metadata panel

Keywords panel

Camera metadata
placard display

Show/Hide side panels                           Smallest              Largest           Metadata Focus
                                                thumbnail size        thumbnail size    workspace

                         Dynamic thumbnail size adjustment        Default workspace

                                                                          Horizontal Filmstrip
                                                                          workspace

**Figure 11.1** The Bridge interface.

# Launching Bridge

To launch Bridge you need to click on the Go to Bridge button icon 📷 which is always present in the Photoshop CS3 Options palette. Clicking this button will launch Bridge and open a window like the one shown in Figure 11.1 that will display the contents of the folder you last visited. You can also launch Bridge by choosing File ⇨ Browse... or by using the ⌘ ⌥ O ctrl alt O or ⌘ Shift O ctrl Shift O shortcuts. To open an image, simply double-click a thumbnail and the image will open in Photoshop. If you want the Bridge window to close as you open the image, then hold down the ⌥ alt key as you double-click. Now if you refer back to Chapter 5, you will note how opening Camera Raw files can vary depending on how the preferences are configured. When you double-click on a raw camera file thumbnail, or multiple thumbnails in Bridge, this will normally open images via the Adobe Camera Raw dialog hosted in Photoshop. And if you go to the File menu in Bridge and choose Open in Camera Raw... ( ⌘ R ctrl R ) the images will open via the Camera Raw dialog hosted in Bridge. The subtle distinctions between which application hosts Adobe Camera Raw are elaborated on in Chapter 5, but essentially a double-click will open a raw file via Camera Raw in Photoshop. And if you hold down the Shift key as you double-click, you can open a raw image by passing the Camera Raw dialog.

## Rotating the thumbnails and preview

You can apply 90° rotations via the Rotate commands in the Bridge Edit menu or use the following keyboard shortcuts: ⌘ [ ctrl [ will rotate a thumbnail anti-clockwise and ⌘ ] ctrl ] will rotate a thumbnail clockwise. Alternatively, you could use the Rotate buttons at the top of the Bridge menu. Note that it is the thumbnail and preview images that are rotated, and that the rotation of the image only takes place when you come to open the image.

## Open anything

Well almost anything... The key thing about Bridge is that it's an open dialog for all the programs in the Adobe Creative Suite. And you are not just limited to opening documents in the CS3 Creative Suite. For example, you can even open things like Word documents in the Word program via Bridge. And you can drag and drop documents from the Bridge window to an external folder or vice versa.

## Return to Photoshop

The same command you use to go to Bridge, ⌘ ⌥ O ctrl alt O, can be used when you wish to return to Photoshop.

## Adding new folders

New folders can be added by choosing New Folder from the File menu in Bridge ⌘ Shift N ctrl Shift N or ctrl right mouse-click in the Content area and choose New Folder from the contextual menu.

## Automatic Bridge launch

Bridge can be set to open immediately after launching Photoshop; set this in Photoshop's preferences.

## Most recent folders

The Bridge program maintains a list of most recently visited folders to enable fast and easy access. The default number is 10, but you can make this any number you want. The Favorites section contains checkboxes that allow you to select which items you want to have appear in the Favorites palette.

## Bridge preferences

The Bridge preferences are located in the Edit menu in Windows and the Bridge menu in Mac OS X.

### General preferences

The first section contains the Appearance controls where you can adjust separately the brightness for the general interface or the image content and preview area. The Behavior section will let you make Adobe Photo Downloader launch by default whenever a new camera card is inserted (or if the camera is connected to the computer directly). The Double-click Edits Camera Raw settings in Bridge option allows you to override the default behavior and forces Bridge to be the program that always hosts the Camera Raw plug-in. Lastly, the Reset button can be used to reset all the alert warning dialogs in Bridge.

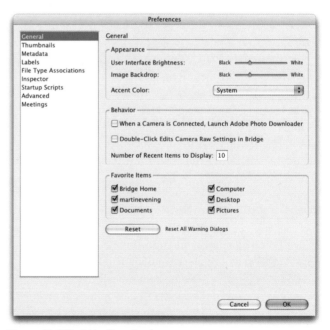

**Figure 11.2** The Bridge General preferences.

## Thumbnails preferences

Now that Adobe Camera Raw can process JPEG and TIFF files as well as raws, there is a preference that allows you to make Adobe Camera Raw the default editor for such files whenever you double-click to open them. Thumbnails can be generated as Quick Thumbnails for faster preview generation, High Quality thumbnails (but slower), or only generate a high quality preview when you actually click on a file to view it.

In the Details section you can choose to have additional lines of metadata appear beneath the thumbnails in the content area. In Figure 11.4 you can see an example of a thumbnail where three additional items of information are displayed below the thumbnail. The Show Tooltips option is useful if you want to learn about each section of the Bridge interface. And it does also allow you to read long file names in the Bridge content area more easily. But overall, it does tends to become rather irritating after a while.

### Limiting preview generation

It can take a long time for Bridge to generate preview images of large image files. If you have the Maximize PSD Backwards Compatibility preference turned on (see page 117) the layered PSD files will generate a composite image layer when saved. This will certainly reduce the time it takes to build each preview in Bridge. If you limit the file size for rendering previews using 'Do not process file larger than: x MB' this will also help speed up the time it takes to build a cache of previews of very large files.

### Thumbnails only

You can use the ⌘ T ctrl T keyboard shortcut to toggle hiding and showing the text information that appears below the image thumbnails in the content area.

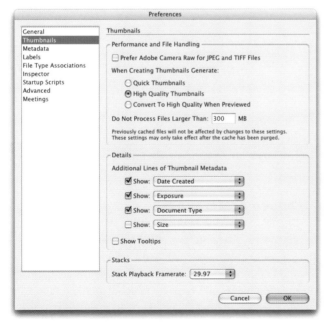

**Figure 11.3** The Bridge Thumbnails preferences.

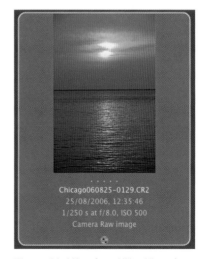

**Figure 11.4** Up to four additional lines of metadata can be added beneath the thumbnails in Bridge.

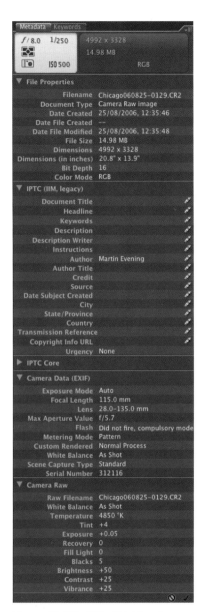

Figure 11.5 The Bridge Metadata preferences.

## Metadata preferences

The metadata preferences in Bridge will let you decide which metadata items are displayed in the Bridge Metadata panel. You can uncheck individual metadata sections or items so as to reduce the amount of information that is displayed. If you keep the Hide Empty Fields box checked, then a metadata item will only appear listed if it contains actual data. The Metadata placard shows a visual display of the main camera EXIF metadata, as it might appear in the LCD display of a digital camera.

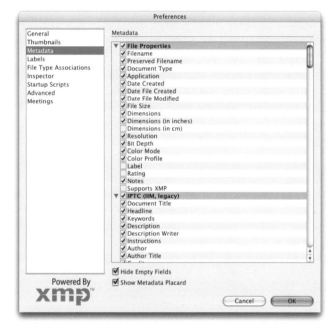

Figure 11.6 The Bridge Metadata preferences.

## Advanced preferences

The Enable Color Management option will affect whether the previews are generated correctly or not. I can't think of any good reason why you should not have this option turned on at all times. Only when this option is enabled, will the thumbnails and Preview panel display provide a reliable guide as to how the colors in an image will look when it is opened in Photoshop.

Bridge by default uses hardware acceleration to drive the graphics display. But if you are working with an underpowered graphics card you may find it better to check Use Software Rendering and relaunch Bridge.

The International section allows you to regionalize Bridge for international languages and for use with international keyboard designs. Note that the changes applied here only come into effect on restart.

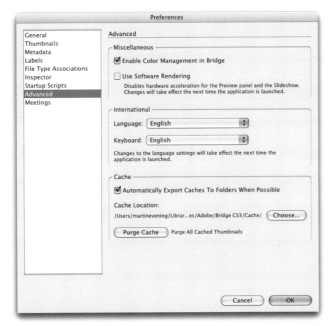

**Figure 11.7** The Bridge Advanced preferences.

## Bridge color accuracy

The Enable Color Management option is a little misleading here since, if Bridge color management were disabled, you would see a very different outcome compared to what actually happens when the Enable Color Management in Bridge option is unchecked. For example, if color management in Bridge were turned off and this matched the way the Photoshop color settings work when color management is turned off, we should be seeing a noticeable difference in the way wide gamut RGB images are displayed in Bridge. But we don't and the difference is only slight. It appears that this option is really more of a 'true color' preview option and when disabled it will allow Bridge previews to be rendered slightly faster, but at the expense of previews being less accurate. If you are doing photographic work, I suggest you should have color management enabled everywhere in all your Adobe applications, including this option that has been added to Bridge CS3.

## Cache management

From the moment you open an image folder in Bridge, the program sets to work, building the thumbnails and previews, reading in the image file metadata as it does, taking into account things like: Camera Raw information, image rotation instructions, file rating and labeling.

This is quite a lot of information that Bridge has to process. If it is your intention to use Bridge to manage large collections of images, especially large numbers of raw files, you really do need a fast computer, or Bridge

IMG_7356.CR2          IMG_7356.xmp

**Figure 11.8** If the Camera Raw preferences are set to save .xmp files as sidecar files, you will see sidecar files like this appear alongside a raw image file that has been modified via Bridge.

Adobe Bridge Cache.bc        Adobe Bridge Cache.bct

**Figure 11.9** If the Bridge preferences are configured to use a distributed cache, cache files like the two shown here will automatically be added as Bridge inspects each folder.

## XMP and Sidecar files

The file-specific information that can generally be read by other programs, such as the custom IPTC metadata and Camera Raw settings (which only other Adobe programs can read) are normally stored in the file header XMP space. However, because proprietary raw files are an unknown entity it is only safe to store such data within a separate XMP sidecar file that will travel with the raw file when it is moved from one folder to another and get renamed if the original master gets renamed.

will appear frustratingly slow. The information that is built up during this process is stored in the form of 'cache data'. The Bridge cache has two components: the image metadata and thumbnail cache. Every time you open a folder in Bridge it will check to see if there is an image cache located somewhere, such as the Application Support/ Adobe/Bridge/Photoshop CS3 folder. If a cache is present, the inspected folder will display the archived thumbnails, previews and metadata instantaneously. This works fine so long as the folder is being inspected on the computer that created it and the folder name has not changed since the cache was created. If these two conditions are not met, then Bridge will have to start all over again and build a new cache. Now if you are editing a bunch of raw files, the information you added before, such as the rotation, image rating and Camera Raw adjustments, will not have been saved in the image files because most raw file formats cannot be edited (an exception being the new Adobe DNG format). So obviously, it is very useful to preserve the cache information wherever possible.

This is why it is a good idea to set the Cache preferences so that Bridge will distribute the cache files whenever possible. Bridge will then automatically update the cache by adding the two cache data files within the same image folder. The advantage of doing this is that it does not matter how you may rename the folder later, the folder image cache will still be recognized. This is especially important if you are about to share a folder of images you have edited in Bridge with another Bridge user (note: a Bridge cache will not be recognized by the older Photoshop File Browser), or you are about to archive the pictures you have edited to a CD or DVD disc. This ensures that the cache data will always be preserved. Sometimes a cache may appear out of date and require a forced update. To do this, go to the Tools menu and choose the Build Cache for Subfolders option. This will force Bridge to prioritize building a cache for not just the current targeted folder, but can also include all the subfolders as well. You won't have to visit them each in turn.

## Slideshow view

The Bridge Slideshow feature could be considered a useful tool for making neat-looking presentations. But I think you will find that the Slideshow viewing mode also offers a very suitable, clear interface in which to edit your pictures, devoid of all the clutter of the Bridge window. In Figure 11.11, the Bridge Slideshow is shown displayed in Full Screen mode. You have access to all the usual image rating controls, so one can sit back to review and edit a collection of pictures and use just the arrow keys 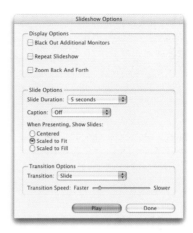 to progress through the shots, and use the ▣ key to increase the star rating and use the ▣ key to decrease the star rating. And a single click with the apostrophe key can be used to toggle adding or subtracting a rating. Go to the View menu and choose Slideshow Options... for further Slideshow settings, including the new slide transitions and zoom options.

**Figure 11.10** The Slideshow Options dialog, which includes a choice of slide transition options.

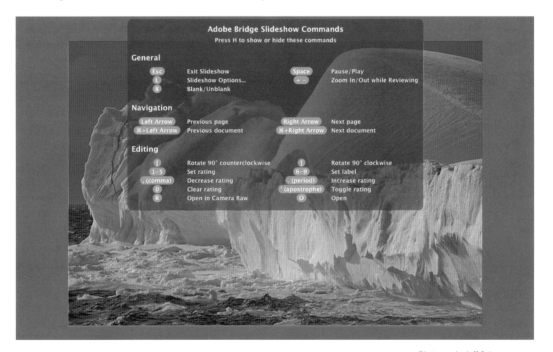

**Figure 11.11** The Bridge window contents can be previewed in Slideshow mode by choosing View ⇨ Slideshow ⌘ L *ctrl* L. You can now use the + – keys to zoom in and out during playback.

Photograph: Jeff Schewe.

## Deleting contents

The (Delete) key can be used to delete selected images. If you click (Delete) or click on the Delete button ( ) in Bridge, this will pop a dialog asking if you want to send a file to the trash directly. This action will remove the thumbnail from the Bridge window and send the original file to the Trash (Mac) or Recycle bin (PC). Even so, a file won't be permanently deleted until you empty the contents of the Trash (Mac)/ Recycle bin (PC) at the operating system level. If you use ⌥ (Delete) (alt) (Delete), rather than proceed to the delete message, this will 'mark' an image as being a reject. You can then use the Filter panel to select the 'mark as rejected' images only and delete as required. Note that you can only delete a folder that is empty.

## Stacking images

You can use the Stack menu in Bridge to group files into stacks. In Figure 11.13 you can see an example where some of the files have been grouped in this way. To use this feature, select two or more files, go to the Stack menu and choose Group as Stack (⌘ G ctrl G). This will group the images and indicate them as a stack with a number showing how many files are included in the stack. To ungroup the images from a stack, use: ⌘ Shift G ctrl Shift G. To expand a stack use: ⌘ ➡ ctrl ➡. To collapse the stack again use: ⌘ ⬅ ctrl ⬅. And if you want to expand all stacks use: ⌘ ⌥ ➡ ctrl alt ➡. If you want to collapse all stacks use: ⌘ ⌥ ⬅ ctrl alt ⬅.

# Arranging the Bridge contents

You can customize the visibility and arrangement of the various panels and customize the Bridge layout to suit your individual requirements. For example, you can click on one of the workspace buttons in the bottom right corner of the Bridge interface and switch from the default workspace to a Filmstrip or Metadata Focus workspace. Or, you can set about creating your own custom workspace layout. Go to the Window menu and you can highlight a panel item to toggle making it either hidden or visible. Now mouse down on a panel and try dragging it to a new position or grouping arrangement in either the left or right side panel areas. If you double-click on a panel divider (as shown in Figure 11.13) you can collapse all the panels in that section. And if you click on the Show/Hide panels tab in the bottom left corner or hit the (Tab) key, you can toggle collapsing or revealing both side panels at once. The panel sizes can be adjusted in height by dragging the horizontal panel dividers and you can double-click a Panel tab to quickly collapse the panel contents to show the tab only. Double-clicking the Panel tab will expand the panel contents to their former size. You can also rearrange the thumbnails that are in the Content panel by dragging them to a new position with the mouse. This will change the sort order to custom and this new sort order will remain sticky until such time as you change the sort order again.

You can save the layout of a custom workspace setting and assign a keyboard shortcut for quick retrieval in the future, or assign it to one of the three numbered presets in the bottom right corner. This is done by mousing down on a preset number (circled in Figure 11.13) and selecting a custom workspace setting.

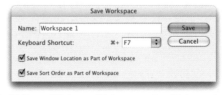

**Figure 11.12** Choose Window ⇨ Workspace ⇨ Save Workspace to save a custom Bridge layout and assign a hot key shortcut.

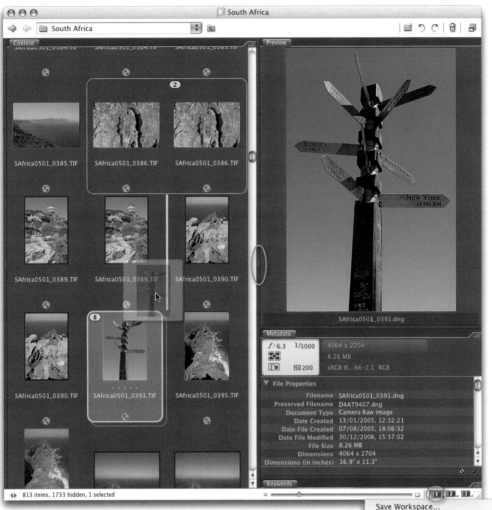

**Figure 11.13** The panel arrangements within Bridge can all be customized to suit your own preferred way of working. The thumbnails can be moved around within the content area, as if you were editing photographs on a lightbox. If you double-click on a Panel tab, such as I have done here with the Keywords panel, this will collapse the panel, hiding its contents. The panel sizes can be adjusted by dragging on the vertical and horizontal dividers, and if you double-click on the divider bar (circled) you can toggle showing and hiding the side panel sections. In this example, you can see how some of the images had been grouped into stacks and the Preview panel has been expanded so that we get to see a large preview of the selected thumbnail or thumbnails if more than one image is selected in the Content panel.

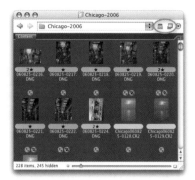

**Figure 11.14** To shrink the size of a Bridge window, click on the Switch to Compact Mode button. Click on the button again to restore the window to the original view mode and size. If you click on the button to the left, you can compact a window to ultra-compact mode. Note that a Compact mode Bridge window will always remain in the foreground, in front of any documents or other programs, by default. This behavior can be altered though. Go to the compact Bridge fly-out menu and deselect 'Compact Window Always on Top'.

## Customizing the panels and content area

Let's now take a look at how the Bridge interface is structured. The Bridge window interface consists of three adjustable sections and these are used to contain the individual Bridge panels, with a main Content panel that is always visible. All the individual panels can be adjusted vertically as well as horizontally and placed in any section of the Bridge interface. The Content panel has a Thumbnails and a Details viewing modes and you can switch between these by going to the View menu in Bridge. By combining and adjusting the various panels with these two Content panel viewing modes, it is possible to achieve a wide variety of different work space layouts. In Figure 11.15 below you can see a bare bones layout of the Bridge interface, where the Content panel only is visible in the middle. In Figure 11.16 you can see a Bridge layout where the content area remains in the Thumbnails view mode and I have made the Favorites, Metadata and Keywords panels visible. And in Figure 11.17, the Content area view mode has been switched to display the contents in Details mode.

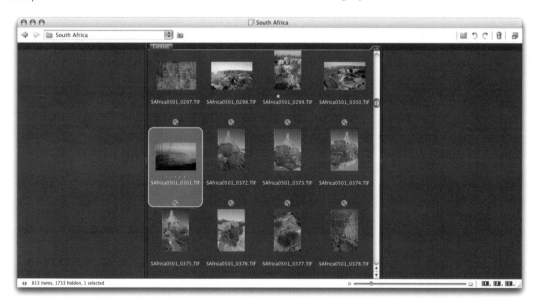

**Figure 11.15** Here is a basic view of the Bridge interface where you can see the three panel sections and just the Content panel is visible (you can't hide the Content panel).

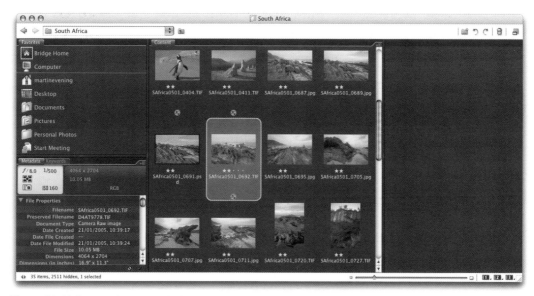

**Figure 11.16** One can make more panels visible by going to the Window menu in Bridge and highlighting the ones you wish to add (those panels that are already visible will have a tick mark next to them.

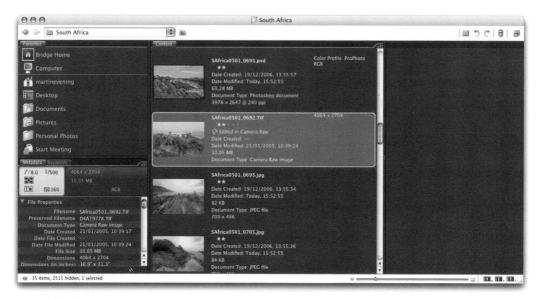

**Figure 11.17** The Details view mode will display the image thumbnails in the Content panel in a list view, accompanied by basic metadata information.

## Custom workspaces

The preset workspace keyboard shortcuts range from ⌘ ctrl + F1 to F6. You can customize the Bridge layout to suit your own way of working, create your own custom workspace settings and assign these shortcuts. Choose Window ⇨ Workspace ⇨ Save Workspace... The saved setting will then appear in the Workspace menu.

## Selecting a Bridge workspace

Bridge CS3 ships with several preset workspace settings that can be accessed by going to the Window ⇨ Workspace menu. The Light Table layout (⌘ ctrl + F2) is useful should you wish to maximize the Content panel size so that it fills the screen. The Horizontal Filmstrip (⌘ ctrl + F6) is great for editing landscape images, because you can use the left and right keyboard arrows to navigate through the filmstrip and see a nice large preview. And the Vertical Filmstrip workspace (⌘ ctrl + F6) is therefore a useful navigation workspace for portrait images. These work spaces provide nice simplified Bridge layouts that are ideal for navigating images. Look closely and you will notice that the Content panel has a fly-out menu that will force the contents to scroll vertically or horizontally. Or you can set this to Auto and Bridge will work out which direction to scroll the thumbnails in. This is useful to know when creating your own layout designs.

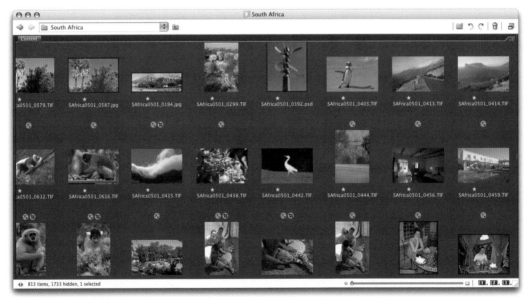

**Figure 11.18** Here is a view of a Bridge window configured using the Light Table workspace preset, which can be accessed via the Window Workspace submenu or by using the ⌘ F2 ctrl F2 keyboard shortcut.

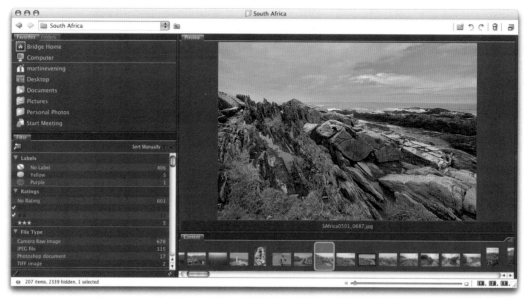

**Figure 11.19** The Horizontal Filmstrip workspace combines a large Preview panel
with a narrow Content panel running along the bottom.

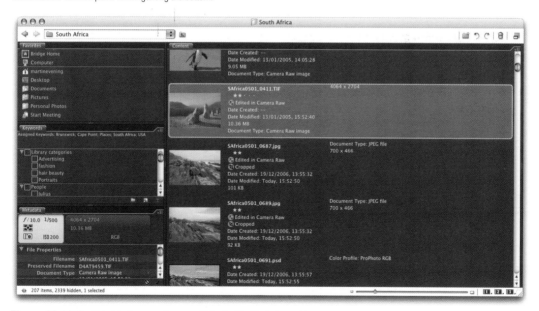

**Figure 11.20** The Metadata Focus workspace will display the Content panel in
Details view mode with the Favorites, Keywords and Metadata panels on the left.

## Multiple displays

Choose Window ⇨ New Synchronized Window (⌘ ⌥ N ctrl alt N) and you can have synchronized windows working across two monitor displays. For example, you could have one window displaying a full screen preview and the other window displaying the Folders and Content panels.

## Working with multiple windows

You can have multiple window views open at once, which means you can now access more than one folder of images at a time, without having to use the Folders panel or window navigational buttons to navigate back and forth between different image collections. Having multiple windows also makes it easier to make comparative editing decisions when reviewing a collection of images (see Figure 11.21 below).

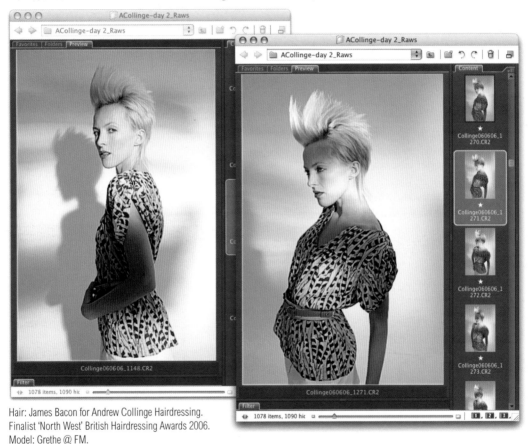

Hair: James Bacon for Andrew Collinge Hairdressing. Finalist 'North West' British Hairdressing Awards 2006. Model: Grethe @ FM.

**Figure 11.21** Bridge will let you have multiple Bridge windows open at once. In the arrangement shown here, I pointed both windows at the same source folder of images. But I configured them differently so that the first window focused on displaying a favorite image nice and big in the Preview panel, while the second window was configured using the Filmstrip Focus preset workspace (choose Window ⇨ Workspace ⇨ Filmstrip Focus or use ⌘ F5 ctrl F5) with the filmstrip set to display vertically. I was then able to navigate through the image thumbnails and compare alternative shots with the one displayed in the first window.

# Bridge panels

## Folders panel

The Folders panel can display a list tree view of the folder contents on all the drives currently connected to the computer. Folders listed here can be expanded or collapsed, allowing you to inspect their contents. Should a CD/DVD/ external drive or other removable volume fail to appear, you may need to refresh the Folders panel contents which can be done by using the fly-out menu or `ctrl` right mouse-clicking and selecting 'Refresh', or by the `F5` keyboard shortcut. When you highlight a folder in the Folders panel, all the files in that folder will be displayed as icons in the content area on the right. Note that Bridge is only able to create a preview of image files it already understands or has a file import plug-in for. As this is happening, Bridge will write a folder cache of all the image thumbnails and previews, which is stored in a central folder located on the hard disk; although, as was pointed out on pages 515–516, you can configure the Bridge preferences so that the cache information is exported locally to the image folder at the same time. This saved cache should make the thumbnails appear quicker the next time you visit a particular image folder. Incidentally, it is a good idea to switch on the backward compatibility option in the main Photoshop preferences, as this will speed up the writing of the thumbnail cache file. If a folder contains a cache that was exported from Bridge CS2 or earlier, Bridge CS3 will be able to read it, but earlier versions of Photoshop will not be able to interpret Bridge CS3 cache files.

## Favorites panel

The Favorites panel provides a set of shortcuts to various folder locations, such as the Desktop or Pictures folder. The items that appear in Favorites can be edited via the Bridge preferences and you can also add your own Favorites by dragging a folder from the Content panel over to the bottom of the Favorites list.

## Cache building routines

When you point Bridge at a folder of images it will speedily generate low res thumbnails and, when that is done, a second pass will add higher resolution data.

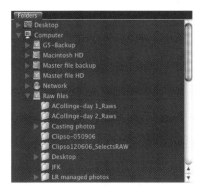

**Figure 11.22** The Folders panel displays a complete list view of all the folders in your main hard drive and any mounted disks. Bridge will allow you to drag and drop folders with ease within the content area and folders panel areas, as well as drag directly to external folders.

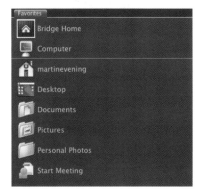

**Figure 11.23** The Favorites panel contains a list of starting points to ease Bridge navigation.

## Rotating loupe

When you work with the loupe tool and drag it to the corner of a preview image you may sometimes see the loupe spin round to reveal the corner details of an image.

## Preview panel

The preview panel can now display a preview of a selected image at any screen resolution size you want. The colors in the preview will provide a reliable preview of how the image will appear when opened via Camera Raw or Photoshop (see page 515) and the preview redraw speed in the Preview panel should be quite fast if you are using the default graphics hardware accelerated setting in the Bridge preferences. In Figure 11.24 below you will notice how when more than one image is selected via the content area the Preview panel is able to display several images at once, (up to a maximum of nine images).

You can also use the Preview panel to carry out close-up inspections of a previewed image using the new loupe tool. If you click anywhere in the Preview panel, this will reveal a loupe magnifying glass adjacent to the point where you clicked, displaying that particular section of the preview image at a 1:1, actual pixels view. You can then use the ➕➖ keys to zoom in (up to 800%) or zoom out again. To close, click inside the loupe, and to reposition, simply click anywhere inside or outside the loupe and drag with the mouse. To compare close-up details in two or more images at once, hold down the ⌘ *ctrl* key as you click inside the second image.

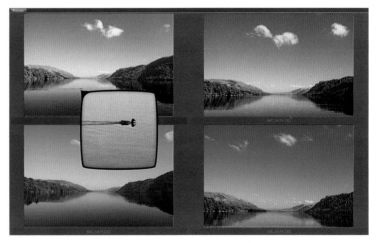

**Figure 11.24** The Preview panel, showing a loupe close-up view of an image.

## Metadata panel

The metadata information is divided into several sections. The File Properties lists the main file statistics such as file name and size etc. The IPTC sections are used to hold the file-specific metadata information and are all editable (the pencil icons will indicate which metadata items you can edit). To do so, mouse-click the field next to the metadata heading and type in the data you wish to enter. The remaining sections will probably depend on how you have configured the Metadata preferences in Figure 11.25. Some of these items are specific to other CS3 suite programs, or specialist users. You can use the preferences to check which items you want to see displayed in the Metadata panel.

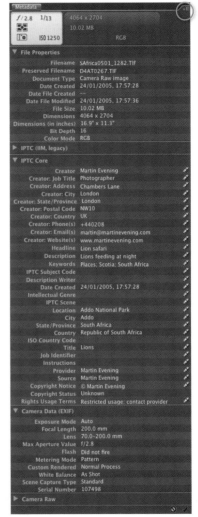

Figure 11.26 The Metadata panel is able to display all the metadata contained in an image file. The metadata sections can be compacted to make viewing easier and the IPTC fields can all be edited. You can also increase the font size in the Metadata panel via the panel fly-out menu. This will make it easier for typing into the metadata and for locating existing entries more accurately.

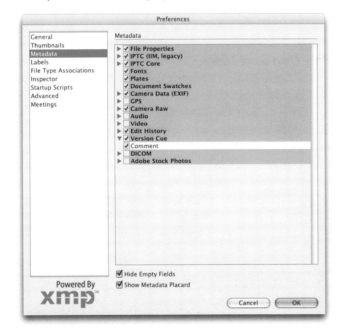

Figure 11.25 If you mouse down on the Metadata panel options (circled in Figure 11.26), you can open the Bridge preference dialog for the Metadata display content. Each metadata item has a checkbox against it. This allows you to show or hide individual items. And since it is unlikely that you will really want to see or use all the metadata items listed here, you can deselect the information items you don't need. If the Hide Empty Fields box is checked, the checked items will only be displayed in the Metadata panel if there is an accompanying data entry. But the main ones you will want to use will be the EXIF Camera Data, Camera Raw data, and the Edit History log.

## Metadata everywhere

Metadata usage is commonplace on the Internet. Enter a search term into any search engine and within seconds web link suggestions will appear on the screen. Web designers add metadata tags to the header section of websites and this will enable search engines to catalog them more effectively. Parents and schools use metadata to filter out the web content that children can access. MP3 players use metadata to categorize your music collections. Metadata is used in all sorts of ways and if anything, we seem to have too much metadata out there, because web search engines often offer you thousands of possible links, when you would rather have your choice narrowed down to a smaller selection. The trick is for distributors to provide metadata that is useful and for retrieval systems to intelligently sort through the metadata.

**Figure 11.27** Here is an example of the File Info dialog, shown here displaying the Description information. To save you time when filling out the editable sections of File Info dialog, you can mouse down on the little fly-out menu buttons next to each field entry and select from a list of previously entered metadata entries. In this example, I circled in blue the Keywords metadata options.

## Image metadata

Maybe you are wondering what all the information in the Metadata panel is useful for. Well, for quite a lot actually, especially if you are running a photography business or are an amateur who shoots a lot of digital photographs. Metadata is usually defined as being 'data about data' and the concept of metadata is one you should already be quite familiar with. Librarians use metadata to classify and catalog books in a library, where in the old days one would be accustomed to using index cards to do a search by an author's name or by the book's title. Everything is now computerized of course and with a computerized system it is possible to record so much more information about a file and use this information to carry out sophisticated searches and cross-reference one file with another.

## File Info metadata

The File Info dialog shown in Figure 11.27 has been around since the early days of Photoshop, but it seems that until recently few people had bothered using it. The File Info dialog is designed to let you inspect all the metadata relating to an image document as well as edit the

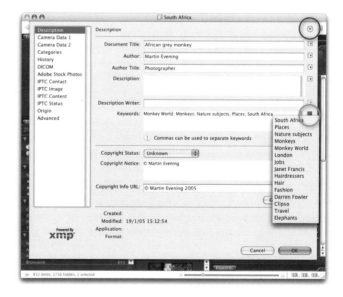

IPTC image metadata that relates to the picture content. Photoshop has always supported the information standard developed by International Press Telecommunications Council (IPTC), which was designed to help classify and label images and text files using metadata. In previous versions of Photoshop, you could access the File Info via the File menu and use it to title an image, add the name of the author, add keywords and inspect the camera capture metadata. File Info is still in the Photoshop File menu, but if you highlight an image, or group of images in Bridge, you can access File Info via the Bridge File menu, or by using the default keyboard shortcut: ⌘ ⌥ Shift I
ctrl alt Shift I . The File Info dialog will then appear as a sheet that drops down from the title bar. The File Info dialog contains seven sections, some of which are editable, such as the Description and IPTC sections shown in Figure 11.27. Other sections, such as the camera EXIF metadata, provide information only. You can use File Info with single or multiple image selections to edit the IPTC metadata, add your name as the author, mark the images as being copyrighted, add a copyright notice, etc. Marking an image as being copyrighted in the File Info has the extra advantage of adding a copyright symbol to the title bar of your image window whenever anyone opens it in Photoshop.

After configuring the File Info settings you can then save them as a metadata template. One could begin by selecting an image, enter some basic custom metadata such as author name, copyright tag, etc. and follow this by mousing down on the File Info fly-out menu and choosing Save Metadata Template... This template can then be used to apply your author details to images singly or in batches to other images, without having to always type in the same data over and over again. In Figure 11.28, I named a template 'London studio work' and clicked Save. Once I have saved a custom metadata template in this way, I can select other images, make an image selection in Bridge and choose a pre-saved template from the Append Metadata or Replace Metadata menus in the Tools menu.

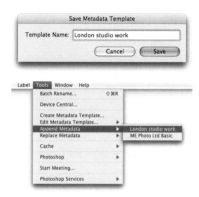

**Figure 11.28** You can configure the File Info dialog and create a custom metadata template containing the metadata items you might wish to regularly apply to collections of images. If you go to the File Info options (circled in red in Figure 11.27) you can choose Save Metadata Template... and name the template as shown here. Once you have done this you can apply this template to other images by choosing it from the Tools ⇨ Replace Metadata/Append Metadata menu. Replace Metadata will substitute all pre-existing metadata with that in the template. Append metadata is the safer option since it will only add to the metadata that is already embedded in the image file.

## Future uses of metadata

It is quite scary to consider the number of freely distributed digital images out there that contain no information about the contact details of the person who created the image. Imagine a scenario in the future where metadata can be used to embed important information about usage rights. Imagine also that a third-party developer could service a website that allowed interested purchasers to instantly discover what specific exclusive usages were currently available for a particular image? You could even embed a self-generating invoice in the image file. If someone tried to strip out the metadata, you could use an encrypted key embedded in the file to re-import the removed metadata, and/or update specific metadata information. I predict that metadata will offer tremendously powerful advantage to individual image creators who wish to distribute their creative work more securely over the Internet and profit from legitimate image rights purchases.

## Other types of metadata

Metadata comes in many forms. In the early days of digital camera development, the camera manufacturers jointly came up with the EXIF metadata scheme for cataloging camera information. You may find it interesting to read the EXIF metadata that is contained in your digital camera files. It will tell you things like what lens setting was used when a photo was taken and the serial number of the camera. This could be useful if you were trying to prove which camera was used to take a photograph when there were a lot of other photographers nearby trying to grab the same shot and also claiming authorship. The EXIF metadata can describe everything about the camera's settings, but the EXIF schema cannot be adapted to describe anything but camera data information. In 2001, Adobe announced XMP (eXtensible Metadata Platform), which to quote Adobe: 'established a common metadata framework to standardize the creation, processing and interchange of document metadata across publishing work flows'. Adobe has already integrated the XMP framework into Acrobat, InDesign Illustrator and Photoshop. XMP is based on XML (eXtensible Markup Language) that is the basic universal format for using metadata and structuring information on the Web. Adobe has also made XMP available as an open-source license, so it can be integrated into any other system or application. Adobe's enormous influence in this arena means that XMP has now become a common standard in the publishing and imaging industry. Adobe and also third-party companies are now able to exploit the potential of XMP to aid file management on a general level and for specific needs such as scientific and forensic work.

Some of the metadata items that can be listed in the File Info and Metadata panel include things like GPS metadata, where if GPS coordinates happen to be embedded in a file, you can cross-reference these with another application such as Google Earth. Other items have specific uses such as the DICOM metadata which is used for storing important medical information in medical images.

### Edit History log

If the History Log options are enabled in the General preferences, an edit history can be recorded in either the file metadata, as a separate text file log, or both. The edit history has many potential uses. An edit history will record how much time was spent working on a photograph and could be used as a means of calculating how much to bill. In the world of forensics, the history log could be used to verify how much (or how little) work was done to manipulate an image in Photoshop. And the same arguments can apply to validating images that are used to present scientific evidence.

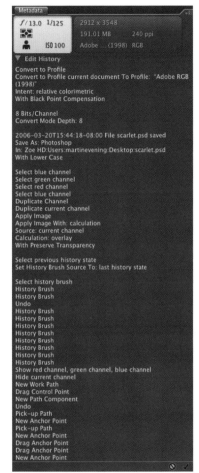

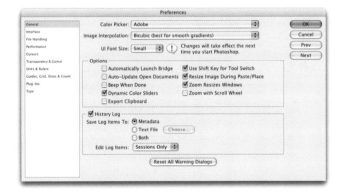

**Figure 11.29** For a history log to be recorded, the History Log option must first be checked in the Photoshop General preferences. A history log can be saved to the file metadata, as a text log file, or as both. The Edit log items can be recorded as session information only, concise (as shown in Figure 11.30) or as a verbose record of what was done to a file in Photoshop.

In the case of images that have been processed via the Adobe Camera Raw plug-in, the Camera Raw metadata section will store a record of the Adobe Camera Raw (or Lightroom) settings used.

And lastly, there may be hidden metadata that won't show up in any metadata inspector. This could be things like camera manufacturer EXIF metadata containing proprietary information that only the camera manufacturer's software has access to.

**Figure 11.30** If the history log options have been configured in the Photoshop General preferences, the history log content can record: sessions only (such as the time a file was opened and closed); a concise log listing of what was done in Photoshop; or as shown here, a detailed log will include a comprehensive list of the settings applied at every step. If you choose to embed the history log in the file metadata, the Edit History log can be viewed via the Bridge Metadata panel.

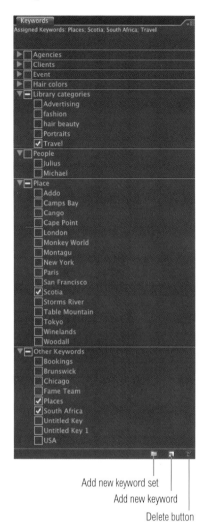

Add new keyword set
Add new keyword
Delete button

**Figure 11.31** The Keywords panel can be used to assign keywords to one or more images at a time. It can also provide feedback on the keywords already assigned. In the example shown here I have highlighted an image and I can see that four keywords have been assigned, telling me that it is a travel photograph that was taken in South Africa at a location called Scotia. Some of these keywords appear in the Bridge established hierarchy. Those listed under 'Other Keywords' were added by an external program.

# Keywords panel

Keywording provides a way to group and organize images within Photoshop. By using keyword tags to describe the image content, you can catalog files so that you can find images more quickly when filtering images via the Filters panel or conducting a search with the Find command.

It is best to add keywords as new images are added to the computer image collection. For example, if you refer back to the File Info dialog shown in Figure 11.27, you can see how it would be possible to create a metadata template where multiple keyword terms are listed within the template, and this can then be saved and applied to select groups of images in Bridge. For example, every time you shoot a particular sporting event you might want to have a template that applies relevant metadata that you always need for such jobs, such as the name of the stadium and home team. When you add metadata terms via File Info, each keyword must be separated by a semi colon (;). This is important for making sure the keywords are separated. If you add keywords in this way, they will appear listed in alphabetical order in the Keywords panel shown in Figure 11.31. In this example you can see some newly added keywords grouped under 'Other Keywords'. The Keyword panel provides some basic organization by allowing you to group keywords into single hierarchy sets. You would normally create a keyword category first, such as 'People' or 'Places'. To add a new keyword, click inside an existing Keyword set (or create a new set), click on the New Keyword button at the bottom of the panel and type in a new name for the keyword you want to add. To assign keywords to one or more images, you need to make your image thumbnail selection from within Bridge, then go to the Keyword panel and click on the empty square to the left of the desired keyword. This method will allow you to assign one or more keywords to multiple images at once.

Keywording information entered in Bridge can normally be read by other metadata aware programs. However, because the keyword hierarchy organization in Bridge is limited, keyword hierarchy is not preserved when reading in keyword metadata added in other programs.

# Managing images in Bridge

The effort put in to adding basic metadata and keyword information can in the long run make your life much easier. Because, if you don't categorize your photographs in this way you can soon end up feeling frustrated as the number of photographs stored on the computer system continues to grow. The Bridge tools are designed to help you get started with the cataloging work and put the metadata information to use when applying filtered searches.

Let's consider how metadata information is used to manage music files. A program like iTunes will update its music database automatically. Insert a CD into your computer and a program like iTunes will query an online database, downloading the album title, artist, track listings and genre of music. This is a good example of metadata in action, and how it can be used to help you manage your music collections as easily as possible. When you are converting music files to an MP3 format, the cataloging is effortless because it can take place in the background automatically. But when you want to catalog image files, you will have to input the metadata manually yourself.

So far in this chapter I have described some of the ways you can go about adding metadata in Bridge and how the metadata information can be organized. Although Bridge has the means to be an image asset manager, it does lack the sophistication of a fully dedicated asset management program like iView™ or Adobe's new Lightroom program. To be honest, I don't use Bridge a great deal these days. This is mainly because I find Lightroom is better suited for most of my needs. It allows me to import camera files exactly the way I want and it has a better and more versatile library management interface for editing and managing the metadata. If you are serious about library management and cataloging your images, you may want to try this program out, or else consider some of the other popular products such as iView Media Pro™ or Apple Aperture™. But where I do still find Bridge to be useful is as a straightforward image browser rather than as a library management program.

## Adobe Photoshop Lightroom

A lot of people have been asking: if I have Photoshop and Bridge, why do I need Lightroom? Especially since Lightroom incorporates all the adjustment tools that are in the latest version of Camera Raw. I suppose the best answer is to point out that Lightroom is a workflow program that allows you to manage your images efficiently all the way from import through to web or print output. For some people, the combination of Bridge and Camera Raw will provide them with all the tools that they ever need to manage their pictures and work with Photoshop. For amateurs and professionals who are looking for a faster and more streamlined approach for their image processing and management, then Lightroom will be the answer. Although I do still use Bridge for some file browsing tasks, I find that I now mostly use Lightroom because it is a very stable application. It integrates smoothly with Photoshop and offers some rather nice and unique approaches to image processing that you won't find in any other program. Overall, I find I can work much faster and more efficiently using Lightroom.

## Photo Downloader in Bridge

You can import images into Bridge via the new Photo Downloader, which was discussed earlier on in Chapter 5 on pages 232–236.

## Universal rating methods

You are not limited to using the rating controls just within Bridge. The rating keyboard shortcuts described here work equally well when you are reviewing your images in the Camera Raw dialog or the Slideshow viewing mode.

## Canceling and turning off labels

The labeling controls have a toggle action. For example, if you select an image and use ⌘ 6 ctrl 6 to label it red, you can use the same keyboard shortcut to cancel the label color. You can also turn off the labeling by selecting No Label from the Label menu.

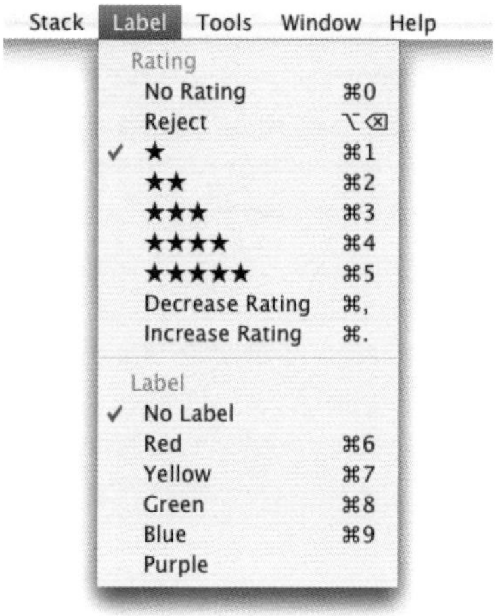

| Stack | **Label** | Tools | Window | Help |
|---|---|---|---|---|

| Rating | |
|---|---|
| No Rating | ⌘0 |
| Reject | ⌥⌫ |
| ✓ ★ | ⌘1 |
| ★★ | ⌘2 |
| ★★★ | ⌘3 |
| ★★★★ | ⌘4 |
| ★★★★★ | ⌘5 |
| Decrease Rating | ⌘, |
| Increase Rating | ⌘. |
| **Label** | |
| ✓ No Label | |
| Red | ⌘6 |
| Yellow | ⌘7 |
| Green | ⌘8 |
| Blue | ⌘9 |
| Purple | |

**Figure 11.32** Image ratings and labels can be applied via the Label menu in Bridge, or by using the keyboard shortcuts described in the main text. You can also mark an image as being a reject (see page 518). This is not the same as deleting, you are simply labeling it as a potential delete image.

## Image rating and labeling

One of the main tasks you will want to carry out in Bridge is to rate the images, selecting those that you like best from the rejects and sort them into groups. The Bridge program provides two main ways to categorize your images. In the Label menu you can apply ratings to an image in the form of stars, going from one to five. This image rating system allows you to apply cumulative ratings to the images you like and it is probably more useful to get to know the keyboard shortcuts which range from ⌘ 1 ctrl 1 to ⌘ 5 ctrl 5, when applying ratings to images. But you can also use ⌘ . ctrl . to increase the rating by one star, or use ⌘ , ctrl , to decrease the rating for an image. This makes it easier for you to focus all your attention on the images as you use the ← → arrow keys to progress from one picture to the next and work with either of the above rating keyboard shortcut methods to mark the shots that you like. In addition to this you can still use the ⌘ ctrl +' (apostrophe) keyboard shortcut as a simple binary rating system that will allow you to add or remove a single star rating from an image. How you use the ratings is up to you, but generally it is a good idea to be sparing with your ratings. Unrated images can be the rejects, while one and two stars can be used to mark the images you like best. And three stars upwards should be reserved for those pictures that are really special.

Color labels can be used to signify other things. Author Peter Krogh in his *DAM book*, suggests that labels can be used to apply negative ratings, where a zero star represents an image that has been inspected but rated neutral, a red label means yet to be rated, a yellow label means it's an out-take and a green label means 'trash me'. And a wedding photographer might use color labels to quickly separate out shots according to the location they were shot in. It is a simple matter of selecting the individual or multiple images you would like to label and then choosing a color from the list in the Label menu. Or, you can use the keyboard shortcuts that range from ⌘ 6 ctrl 6 for red, to ⌘ 9 ctrl 9 for blue. You can also use ctrl right mouse to apply label colors via the contextual menu.

## Sorting images in Bridge

You can change the order in which the images are displayed in the Content panel by going to the View ⇨ Sort menu and selecting a new sort criteria and choosing whether you want to see the images displayed in ascending or descending order. As we come on to looking at methods for filtering the images displayed in the Bridge Content panel, you will see how combining the filtering with the Sort options is perfect for organizing how the thumbnail images will be arranged in the Content panel.

## Refreshing the view

If you alter the contents of a volume or folder at the System level, outside Bridge, then the Bridge Folder panel and content area won't always know to update the revised volume or folder contents. If you ever need to refresh the view in Bridge, use this menu item or the **F5** keyboard shortcut.

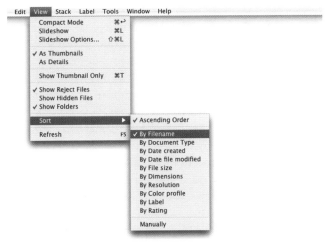

**Figure 11.33** The Sort menu options allow you to arrange the displayed thumbnail images by ascending or descending order using any of the criteria listed in the menu. Normally this is left at the default 'By Filename' setting, but if you selected By Date file modified the images would be displayed in the order of which ones were most recently edited.

## Filtering images

Of all the new features in Bridge CS3, the Filter panel has the most potential for making your workload easier. The Filter panel will allow you to see and choose single or cumulative, multiple criteria by which to filter the images that are displayed in the content area. When managing large folders or hierarchies of folders, the filtering controls can really make it easier to narrow down an image search.

## Filtering shortcuts

The following shortcuts can be used to filter images in the Content panel:

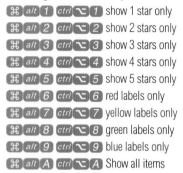

⌘ alt 1 ctrl ⌥ 1 show 1 star only
⌘ alt 2 ctrl ⌥ 2 show 2 stars only
⌘ alt 3 ctrl ⌥ 3 show 3 stars only
⌘ alt 4 ctrl ⌥ 4 show 4 stars only
⌘ alt 5 ctrl ⌥ 5 show 5 stars only
⌘ alt 6 ctrl ⌥ 6 red labels only
⌘ alt 7 ctrl ⌥ 7 yellow labels only
⌘ alt 8 ctrl ⌥ 8 green labels only
⌘ alt 9 ctrl ⌥ 9 blue labels only
⌘ alt A ctrl ⌥ A Show all items

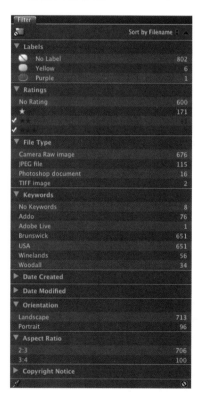

**Figure 11.34** The Filters panel.

## *Filter panel*

The Filter panel displays all the options that are available for filtering the images currently in the Content panel. These are grouped into sections and as soon as you click on any item listed in the Filter panel, the contents of the Content panel will be filtered accordingly. For example, in Figure 11.34, you can see how Bridge was pointed at a large folder of images where the files in that selection were labeled using yellow and purple and the ratings ranged from no rating to three stars. In this example, I clicked on the two star and three star items in the Filter panel, which filtered the images so that only those images with two or three stars were displayed in the Content panel. Similarly, I could have gone to the Keywords section and clicked on one or more of the keyword tags listed there and made a filtered selection that was based on a combination of certain keywords, but contained only those images with a two or three star rating. But wait, there's more... In the Filter panel you can filter images by other criteria such as: by file type, date created/modified, image orientation, speed ISO rating, camera serial number or copyright notice. And within the Filter panel you also have direct access to the Sort menu as well, so you can filter and sort all within the one panel.

You can also use the keyboard shortcuts that were in Bridge CS2, which allowed you to filter by label or rating. But these do work slightly differently now. You also have a flatten view control where if you point Bridge at a folder that contains a nested group of subfolders and click on the Flatten View button (🗁) at the top of the Filter panel, this will populate the Content area with a flattened view of the contents of all the subfolders in that particular folder. This in my opinion is a really useful way to get an overview of the subfolder contents without having to navigate through each subfolder in turn to see what is in there. The only downside to flatten view mode is that you will temporarily lose track of which master folder you are inspecting, but this can be restored by clicking on the Flatten View button to restore the unflattened view mode again.

## Image searches

You can search for images using specific criteria. In my line of work I regularly carry out model castings where I add the details of the name of the model and the agency into the Description metadata. Over the course of several months I can build up a collection of hundreds of model images. If I ever need to conduct a search for a particular model, I can go to the Edit menu in Bridge, choose Find... ⌘ F ctrl F and search for all images that match the name of the person I am searching for (see Figure 11.35). A Bridge search can be limited to a single folder, or made to include all subfolders. So choose carefully which folder you point Bridge at and whether the subfolder option needs to be checked or not before conducting a search. If Bridge has not had a chance to cache the files in all folders yet, select the Include Non-Indexed files option, but this will make for slower searches.

## Search criteria

The search criteria can be almost anything you want. The source folder will default to the folder you are viewing in the front most Bridge window. But you can select other folders to look in and in some cases it will be necessary to select a folder that contains a lot of subfolders and make sure that the Include All Subfolders option is checked. The search criteria can be adapted in many ways. For example you can include search terms where you ask Bridge to search for files that exclude specific criteria.

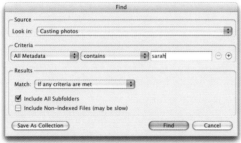

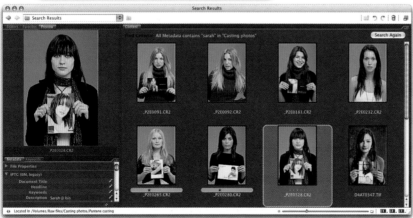

**Figure 11.35** In this example I chose Find... from the Bridge Edit menu, selected All Metadata for the criteria to search by and entered the first name of the model I was looking for. Note that I asked the search to include all subfolders in the Casting Photos folder. The image files that matched the search criteria were displayed in a temporary, virtual folder called Search Results.

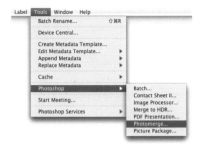

Figure 11.36 The Photoshop Automate menu is available from the Tools menu in Bridge.

## Bridge automation

The Photoshop Automate features can all be accessed directly in Bridge by choosing Tools ⇨ Photoshop and selecting one of the options from the submenu. To apply a Photoshop action to a group of images, make a selection of images in Bridge, choose Tools ⇨ Photoshop ⇨ Batch... and configure the dialog to run a batch action processing routine on the selected photos. So for example, if you want to create a web gallery from a selection of images in Bridge, make a filtered selection of images, arrange the order you want the pictures to appear in, and choose the Web Photo Gallery option from the Tools ⇨ Photoshop menu. You can read more about this and all the other automation features in Chapter 15 on automating Photoshop.

### Renaming schemes

The renaming scheme you use can be anything you choose. There are no hard and fast rules. But whatever method you decide to use, it should be done with a view to the future and should avoid the possibility of you creating file names that overlap with other files. I prefer to adopt a naming scheme where a short text description (such as the client name or an abbreviation) is followed by the date shot, using the YYMMDD format, followed by a four digital serial number.

## Renaming images

To rename an image in Bridge, just click and hold the mouse down on the file name and then type in a new one. To batch rename a selection of images, choose Batch Rename... from the Tools menu, which will open the Batch Rename dialog shown in Figure 11.37. You can rename the files in the same folder or rename and move them to a new (specified) folder. In the New Filenames section you can configure the file renaming structure by clicking on the plus buttons to add new components to the file renaming structure. Note that when you mouse down on a renaming component there will often be further options that you can choose from.

In the example shown here, the first field was set as a Text entry, in which I entered the word 'Casting', followed by an underscore. Next, I chose a YYMMDD Date Time setting based on the date the file was created. This was followed by another text underscore and lastly, a four digit serial number that started with the number '1' (if I had wanted the serial number to begin at a number other than 0001, I could enter a new number to start the sequence from). Note there is no need to enter a file extension at the end, because Bridge will do so automatically.

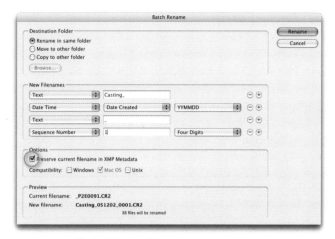

Figure 11.37 The Batch Rename dialog will also let you preserve the current file name and copy the files to another folder as you rename them.

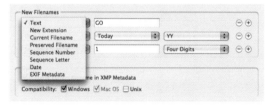

Figure 11.38 Lots of extra options become available as you mouse down on the pop-up menus. Selecting the Preserved Filename will restore the original file name, providing the box circled in Figure 11.37 is checked.

## Applying Camera Raw settings

You can use the Edit ➪ Develop Settings menu in Bridge to apply a saved Camera Raw preset setting to selected images or choose Previous Conversion, to apply the last used Camera Raw setting. The settings listed here will be like the ones you also see listed in the Camera Raw Preset panel (see page 283).

You can also use this menu to copy and paste settings from one file to another, or better still work with the keyboard shortcuts. Use ⌘ ⌥ C ctrl alt C to copy a setting and ⌘ ⌥ V ctrl alt V to paste. The Clear Settings command will remove any applied develop settings and reapply the default Camera Raw settings.

### Editing the Batch renaming fields

In the Batch Rename dialog, the default mode settings are configured to do nothing at all, but once you start editing the pop-up menus, you will discover that the renaming options are quite extensive. You can select items such as Text, where you can enter your own text data. You can also incorporate the original file name in parts of the new name, which will make a lot of people I know very happy.

### Undoing a Batch Rename

If you inspect the Batch Rename options closely you will notice there is an option to preserve the original file name. So if you do slip up for some reason, Bridge and Photoshop CS3 are able to locate and reassign the original name to the file. But, and it's a big but, this will only be possible if you remember to check the box that says: Preserve current filename in XMP Metadata.

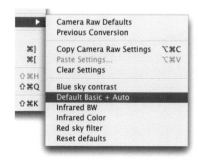

Figure 11.39 The Bridge Edit ➪ Develop Settings submenu.

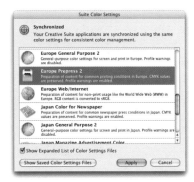

### Photoshop Services

The Tools ⇨ Photoshop Services submenu will allow you to connect to various online ordering services, such as Online Print Services, for which you will have to register first. There is an example of one such service on page 658.

# Bridge extras

Photoshop CS3 can be purchased as a stand-alone program or as part of the CS3 Creative Suite package. And Bridge is included with both packages, but you will only get to see certain extra items, such as the Color Management Suite synchronization and Bridge Home if you purchase the CS3 Suite package. But everyone will be able to access Adobe Stock Photos as well as the Adobe Connect Start Meeting feature from the Favorites panel.

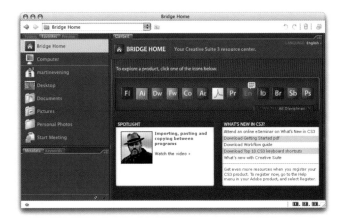

# Backing up your data

When managing your digital images, the most important thing is to make sure you have a backup procedure in place that can be relied upon in the event of a disaster, such as a hard drive failure or theft of a computer. If you don't have too big an image library, this could be achieved quite simply by having a single hard drive connected to the computer that you can backup your files to. At a more advanced level, you could invest in a mirrored RAID storage system where the data is mirrored across two or more drives of equal capacity. If one of the drive units were to fail, the data is protected on the backup drive, so you can simply replace the defective drive and the data is mirrored across to the replacement drive again. But be warned that mirroring the data in this way is still not entirely foolproof. However you choose to backup your data, the following points should be borne in mind.

Scheduled backups are most important because it is useful to have a buffer between the contents that are on the current working drives and the backup versions. It is all too easy to delete a file or discover you need to revert to an earlier version of a file. If you make a mistake on a mirrored RAID system, the mistake will be mirrored to the other drive. But if you also maintain a copy on a separate backup drive system, there should always be a recent backup copy of the data ready for you to access.

Hard drives can provide storage space that is fast, cheap and high capacity. But they can still be vulnerable to things like a virus attack. It may take a while to burn copies of your data to CD or DVD, but while such media may not be completely infallible, your data won't be vulnerable to virus attacks.

Where do you store the backup data? If you keep the backup data on separate hard drives, it is not too difficult to keep these backup drives stored in a safe location away from the computer, such as in a fire proof safe, or off-site somewhere. For absolute security, some people backup all their data over a fast Internet connection to a remote server.

## DVD storage

Recordable DVD drives have become increasingly popular and are often supplied as standard with some computer models. Recordable DVD discs are capable of storing 4.7 GB of data. But again, to be realistic, I would knock that figure down to something more like 4.3 GB as the actual amount of data you can store on a disc. The only problem with a DVD (or CD) disc is that if it gets damaged you lose everything and that might mean losing a hefty chunk of valuable data. So make an extra backup copy of important data and archive this separately. Recordable discs also have a finite life-span. And who is to say if DVD, or the new Blu-ray standard, will not be superseded by some other form of recordable media requiring a different type of hardware device to read the data? Furthermore, if you archive raw camera files without converting them to the DNG format, will you always have the software to interpret these? In this industry a lot can happen in a matter of just a few years. For example, does anyone now remember Syquest disks?

## The DAM book

If you want to find out more about image management using Adobe Bridge and iView, I highly recommend that you read: *The DAM book, Digital Asset Management for Photographers* by Peter Krogh, ISBN 0-596-10018-3.

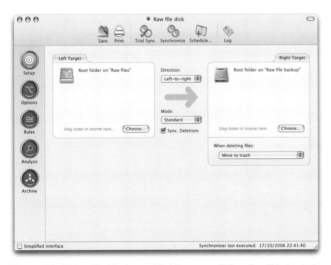

**Figure 11.42** As a Macintosh user, I find Chronosync™ from Econ™ technologies (www.econtechnologies.com) to be an indispensable tool for carrying out all my data backups.

## Fingerprint plug-ins

Software solutions have been developed to provide better data protection and security, giving suppliers of electronic data the means to identify and trace the usage of their intellectual property. These systems apply an invisible 'fingerprint' or encrypted code that does not spoil the appearance of the image but can be read by the detection software. The code must be robust enough to work at all usage sizes: from screen size to high resolution. They must withstand resizing, image adjustments and cropping. A warning message should be displayed whenever an image is opened up alerting the viewer to the fact that this picture is the property of the artist and a readable code embedded from which to trace the artist and negotiate a purchase.

Two companies have produced such encryption/detection systems: SureSign by Signum Technology and Digimarc by the Digimarc Corporation. Both work as plug-ins for Photoshop. They will detect any encrypted images you open in Photoshop and display a copyright detection symbol in the status bar alongside the file name. You have to pay an annual usage fee to Digimarc to register your individual ID (check to see if free trial period offers are in operation). Anyone wishing to trace you as the author, using the Photoshop Digimarc reader plug-in, will contact their website, input the code and from there read off your name and contact number. SureSign provide a unique author code plus transaction number. In my opinion, the latter is a more adaptable system.

## *Image protection*

Anyone who fully understands the implications of images being sold and transferred in digital form will appreciate the increased risks posed by piracy and copyright infringement. The music industry has for a long time battled against pirates duplicating original disks, stealing music and video sales. Digital music recordings on CD made this problem even more difficult to control when it became possible to replicate the original flawlessly. The issue of piracy is not new to photographers and image makers, but the current scale of exposure to this risk is. It includes not just us Photoshop geeks, but also anyone who has their work published or is interested in the picture library market.

To combat this problem, the first line of defense had been to limit the usefulness of images disseminated electronically by (a) making them too small in size to be of use other than viewing on a screen and (b) including a visible watermark which both identified the copyright owner and made it very difficult to steal and not worth the bother of retouching out. The combination of this two-pronged attack is certainly effective but has not been widely adopted. The World Wide Web contains millions of screen-sized images, few of which are protected to this level. The argument goes that these pictures are so small and degraded due to heavy JPEG compression, what possible good are they for print publishing? One could get a better pirated copy by scanning an image from a magazine on a cheap flatbed scanner. Shopping is now replacing sex as the main focus of interest on the Internet, so screen-sized web images therefore do now have an important commercial value in their own right. Furthermore, the future success of digital imaging and marketing will be linked to the ability to transmit image data. The technology already exists for us to send large image files across the world at speeds faster than ISDN. Once implemented, people will want to send ever larger files by telecommunications. The issue of security will then be of the utmost importance.

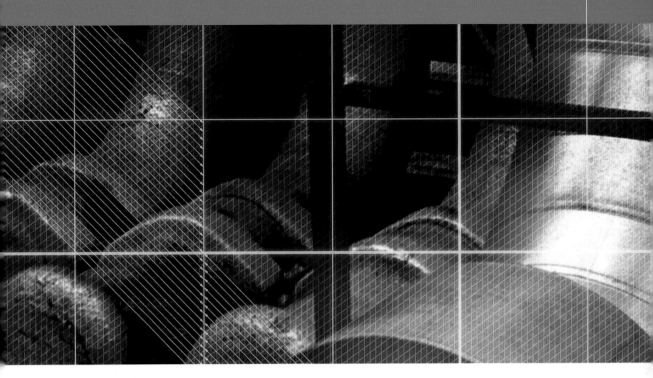

Chapter 12

# Color Management

Photoshop 5.0 was justifiably praised as a
ground-breaking upgrade when it was released
in the summer of 1998. The changes made to
the color management setup were less well
received in some quarters. This was because the revised
system was perceived to be extremely complex and
unnecessary. Some color professionals felt we already had
reliable methods of matching color and you did not need
ICC profiles and the whole kaboodle of Photoshop ICC
color management to achieve this. The aim of this chapter
is to start off by introducing the basic concepts of color
management. The first part will help you to understand the
principles of why color management is necessary. And then
we shall be looking at the color management interface in
Photoshop and the various color management settings.

## The need for color management

An advertising agency art buyer was once invited to address a meeting of photographers. The chair, Mike Laye, suggested we could ask him anything we wanted, except 'Would you like to see my book?' And if he had already seen your book, we couldn't ask him why he hadn't called it back in again. And if he had called it in again we were not allowed to ask why we didn't get the job. And finally, if we did get the job we were absolutely forbidden to ask him why the color in the printed ad looked nothing like our original photograph!

That in a nutshell is a problem which has bugged us all our working lives. And it is one which will be familiar to anyone who has ever experienced the difficulty of matching colors on a computer system with the original or a printed output. Figure 12.1 has two versions of the same photograph. One shows how the Photoshop image is previewed on the monitor and the other is an example of how a printer might interpret and reproduce those same colors when no attempt is made to color manage the image.

So why is there sometimes such a marked difference between what is seen on the screen and the actual printed result? Digital images are nothing more than just bunches of numbers and good color management is all about making sense of those numbers and translating them into meaningful colors at the various stages of the image making process.

## The way things were

Fifteen years ago, most photographers only used their computers to do basic administration work and there were absolutely no digital imaging devices to be found in a photographer's studio (unless you counted the photocopier). If you needed a color print made from a chrome transparency, you gave the original to the printer at a photographic lab and they matched the print visually to your original. Professional photographers would also supply chrome transparencies or prints to the client and the photographs then went to the printer to be digitized

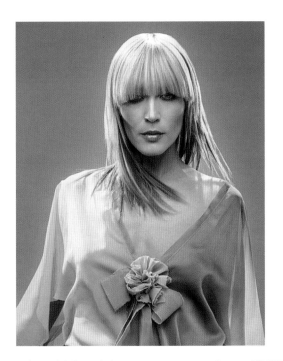 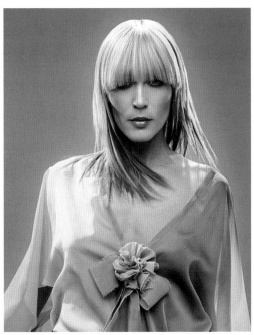

using a high-end drum scanner to produce a CMYK file. The scanner would be configured to produce a CMYK file ready to insert in a specific publication. And that was the limit of the photographer's responsibilities. If color corrections were required, the scanner operators would carry this out themselves on the output file.

These days a significant number of photographers, illustrators and artists are now originating their own files from digital cameras, desktop scanners or directly within Photoshop. This effectively removes the repro expert who previously did all the scanning and matching of the colors on the press. Therefore, there is no getting away from the fact that if you supply digital images to a printer, you will be deemed responsible should any problems occur in the printing. This may seem like a daunting task, but with Photoshop it is not hard to color manage your images with confidence.

**Figure 12.1** The picture on the left shows how you would see the Photoshop image on your screen and the one on the right represents how that same image might print if sent directly to a printer without applying any form of color management. This is an actual simulation of what happens when raw RGB data is sent without any form of compensation being applied to balance the output to what is seen on the screen. You might think it is merely a matter of making the output color less blue in order to successfully match the original. Yes, that would get the colors closer, but when trying to match color between different digital devices, the story is actually a lot more complex than that. The color management system that was first introduced in Photoshop 5.0 will enable you to make use of ICC profiles and match these colors from the scanner to the screen and to the printer with extreme accuracy.

Client: Russell Eaton. Model: Lidia @ M&P.

## Why not all RGB spaces are the same

Go into any TV showroom and you will probably see rows of televisions all tuned to the same broadcast source but each displaying the picture quite differently. This is a known problem that affects all digital imaging devices, be they digital cameras, scanners, monitors or printers. Each digital imaging device has its own unique characteristics. And unless you are able to quantify what those individual device characteristics are, you won't be able to communicate effectively with other device components and programs in your own computer setup, let alone anyone working outside your system color loop.

Some computer monitors will have manual controls that allow you to adjust the brightness and contrast (and in some cases the RGB color as well), so we have some element of basic control there. And the desktop printer driver software will also probably allow you to make color balance adjustments, but is this really enough though? And if you are able to get the monitor and your printer to match, will the colors you are seeing in the image appear the same on another person's monitor?

## RGB devices

Successful color management relies on the use of profiles to describe the characteristics of each device such as a scanner or a printer and using a color management system to successfully translate the profile data between each device in the chain. Consider for a moment the scale of the color management task. We wish to capture a full color original subject, digitize it with a scanner or digital camera, examine the resulting image via a computer screen and finally reproduce it in print. It is possible with today's technology to simulate the expected print output of a digitized image on the display with remarkable accuracy. Nevertheless, one should not underestimate the huge difference between the mechanics of all the various bits of equipment used in the above production process. Most digital devices are RGB devices and just like musical instruments, they all possess unique color tonal properties, such that no two devices are always identical or will be able to reproduce color exactly the same way as another device can. Nor is it always possible to match in print all the colors which are visible to the human eye. Converting light into electrical signals via a device such as a CCD chip is not the same as projecting pixels onto a computer screen or reproducing a photograph with colored ink on paper.

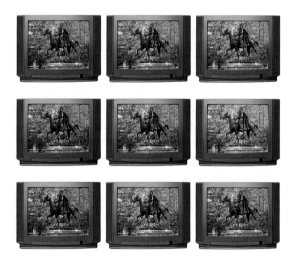

**Figure 12.2** All digital devices have individual output characteristics, even if they look identical on the outside. In a TV showroom you will typically notice each television displaying a different colored image.

## The versatility of RGB

A major advantage of working in RGB is that you can access all the bells and whistles of Photoshop which would otherwise be hidden or grayed out in CMYK mode. And these days there is also no telling how many ways a final image may end up being reproduced. A photograph may get used in a variety of ways, with multiple CMYK separations made to suit several types of publications, each requiring a slightly different CMYK conversion because CMYK is not a 'one size fits all' color space. High-end retouching for advertising usage is usually done in RGB mode and a large format transparency output produced. That transparency can be used as an original to be scanned again and converted to CMYK but the usual practice is to use the transparency output for client approval only. The CMYK conversions and film separations are produced working directly from the digital file to suit the various media usages.

Photographers are mainly involved in the RGB capture end of the business. The proliferation of Photoshop, plus the advent of high quality desktop scanner and digital cameras, means that more images than ever before are starting out in and staying in RGB color. This is an important factor that makes color management so necessary and also one of the reasons why I devote so much attention to the managing of RGB color, here and elsewhere in the book. But if professional photographers are more likely to supply a digital file at the end of a job, how will this fit in with existing repro press workflows that are based on the use of CMYK color? Although digital capture has clearly taken off, the RGB to CMYK issue has to be resolved. If the work you create is intended for print, the conversion of RGB to CMYK must be addressed at some point and so for this important reason, we shall also be looking at CMYK color conversions later on in this chapter.

### Color management references

If your main area of business revolves around the preparation of CMYK separations for print, then I do recommend you invest in a training course or book that deals with CMYK repro issues. I highly recommend the following books: *Real World Color Management* by Bruce Fraser, Chris Murphy and Fred Bunting. *Color Management for Photographers* by Andrew Rodney and *Getting Colour Right, The Complete Guide to Digital Colour Correction* by Neil Barstow and Michael Walker.

### Color vision trickery

They say that seeing is believing, but nothing could be further from the truth, since there are many interesting quirks and surprises in the way we humans perceive vision. There is an interesting book on this subject titled *Why We See What We Do*, by Dale Purves and R. Beau Lotto (Sinauer Associates, Inc). And also a website at www.purveslab.net, where you can have a lot of fun playing with the interactive visual tests, to discover how easily our eyes can be deceived. What you learn from studies like this is that color can never be properly described in absolute mathematical terms. How we perceive a color can also be greatly influenced by the other colors that surround it. This is a factor that designers use when designing a product or a page layout. You do it too every time you evaluate a photograph, probably without even being aware of it.

## Beyond CMYK

There are other types of output to consider, not just CMYK. Hexachrome is a six-color ink printing process that extends the range of color depth attainable beyond conventional limitations of CMYK. This advanced printing process is currently available only through specialist print shops and is suitable for high quality design print jobs. Millions have been invested in the four-color presses currently used to print magazines and brochures, so expect four-color printing to still be around for a long time to come, but Hexachrome will open the way for improved color reproduction from RGB originals.

Photoshop supports six-color channel output conversions from RGB, but you will need to buy a separate plug-in utility like HexWrench. Spot color channels can be added and previewed on screen: spot color files can be saved in DCS 2.0 or TIFF format. Multimedia publishing is able to take advantage of the full depth of the RGB color range. If you are working in a screen-based environment for CD, DVD and web publishing, RGB is ideal. And with today's web browsers, color management can sometimes be turned on to take full advantage of the enhanced color control these programs can now offer.

## Output-centric color management

Printers who work in the repro industry naturally tend to have an 'output-centric' view of color management. Their main concern is getting the CMYK color to look right on a CMYK press. But the printer can color correct a CMYK image 'by the numbers' if they wish. Take a look at the photograph of the young model in Figure 12.3. Her Caucasian flesh tones should at least contain equal amounts of magenta and yellow ink, with maybe a slightly greater amount of yellow, while the cyan ink should be a quarter to a third of the magenta. This rule will hold true for most CMYK press conditions. The accompanying table compares the CMYK and RGB space measurements of a flesh tone color. However, you will notice there are no similar formulae that can be used to describe the RGB pixel values of a flesh tone. If you were to write down the flesh tone numbers for every RGB device color space, you could in theory build an RGB color space reference table. And from this you could feasibly construct a system that would assign meaning to these RGB numbers for any given RGB space. This is basically what an ICC profile does except an ICC profile may contain several hundred color reference points. These can then be read and interpreted automatically by the Photoshop software and give meaning to the color numbers.

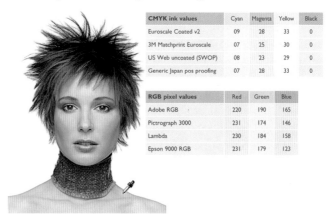

| CMYK ink values | Cyan | Magenta | Yellow | Black |
|---|---|---|---|---|
| Euroscale Coated v2 | 09 | 28 | 33 | 0 |
| 3M Matchprint Euroscale | 07 | 25 | 30 | 0 |
| US Web uncoated (SWOP) | 08 | 23 | 29 | 0 |
| Generic Japan pos proofing | 07 | 28 | 33 | 0 |

| RGB pixel values | Red | Green | Blue |
|---|---|---|---|
| Adobe RGB | 220 | 190 | 165 |
| Pictrograph 3000 | 231 | 174 | 146 |
| Lambda | 230 | 184 | 158 |
| Epson 9000 RGB | 231 | 179 | 123 |

**Figure 12.3** The tables shown here record the color readings in RGB and CMYK color spaces of a typical Caucasian flesh tone. As is explained in the text, while the CMYK readings are all fairly consistent, this is not the case when you try to compare the RGB values.

# Profiled color management

The objective of profiled color management is to use the measured characteristics of everything involved in the image editing workflow from capture to print and to reliably translate the color at every stage. In a normal Photoshop workflow, the color management process begins with reading the profiled RGB color data from the incoming file and if necessary converting it to the current Photoshop RGB work space. While the image is being edited in Photoshop the RGB work space image data is sent to the computer display and converted on-the-fly to the profiled monitor space so that the colors are viewed correctly. When the image is finally output as a print, the RGB work space data is converted to the profile space of the printer. Or, you might carry out an RGB to CMYK conversion to the CMYK profile of a known proof printer.

A profile is therefore a useful piece of information that can be embedded in an image file. When a profile is read by Photoshop and color management is switched on, Photoshop is automatically able to find out everything it needs to know in order to manage the color correctly from there on. Note that this will also be dependent on you calibrating your monitor, but essentially all you have to do apart from that is to open the Photoshop Color Settings from the Edit menu and select a suitable preset such as the US Prepress Default setting. Do this and you are all set to start working in an ICC color managed workflow.

Think of a profile as being like a postcode (or ZIP code) for images. For example, the address label shown in Figure 12.4 was rather optimistically sent to me at 'Flat 14, London', but thanks to the postcode it arrived safely! Some labs and printers have been known to argue that profiles cause color management problems. This I am afraid is like a courier company explaining that the late delivery of your package was due to you including a ZIP code in the delivery address. A profile can be read or it can be ignored. What is harmful in these circumstances is an operator who refuses to use an ICC workflow. If you feel you are getting the runaround treatment, it may be time to change labs.

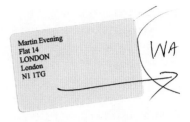

**Figure 12.4** Even if you have never been to London before, you know it's a fairly big place and 'Flat 14, London' was not going to help the postman much to locate my proper address. However, the all-important ZIP code or postcode was able to help identify exactly where the letter should have been delivered. An image profile is just like a ZIP code – it can tell Photoshop everything it needs to know about a file's provenance.

## Translating the color data

One way to comprehend the importance of giving meaning to the numbers in a digital file is to make a comparison with what happens when language loses its meaning. There is an excellent book by Lynne Truss called *Eats, Shoots & Leaves: The Zero Tolerance Approach to Punctuation*. It is partly a rant against poor punctuation, but also stresses the importance of using punctuation to assign exact meaning to the words we read. Remove the punctuation and words will easily lose their true intended meaning. Another good example is the way words can have different meanings in other languages. So a word viewed out of context can be meaningless unless you know the language that it belongs to. For example, the word 'cane' in English means 'dog' in Italian.

## Color Management Modules

The International Color Consortium (ICC) is an industry body that represents the leading manufacturers of imaging hardware and software. The ICC grew out of the original Color Consortium that was established in 1993 and has been responsible for extending and developing the original ColorSync architecture to produce the standardized ICC format which enables profiles created by different vendors to work together. All ICC systems are basically able to translate the color gamut of a source space via a reference space (the Profile Connection Space) and accurately convert these colors to the gamut of the destination space. At the heart of any ICC system is the Color Management Module, or CMM, which carries out all the profile conversion software processing. Although the ICC format specification is standardized, this is one area where there are some subtle differences in the way each CMM will handle the data. In Photoshop you have a choice of three CMMs: Adobe Color Engine (ACE), Apple ColorSync or Apple CMM. And there are other brands of CMM that you can use as well. But this really need not concern most Photoshop users. The default CMM used in Photoshop is Adobe (ACE) and I recommend that you leave this as set.

## The Profile Connection Space

If the CMM is the engine that drives color management, then the Profile Connection Space, or PCS, is at the hub of any color management system. The PCS is the translator that can interpret the colors from a profiled space and define them using either a CIE XYZ or CIE LAB color space. The Profile Connection Space is an interim space. It uses unambiguous numerical values to describe color values using a color model that matches the way we humans observe color. You can think of the PCS as being like the color management equivalent of a multilingual dictionary that can translate a language into any other language.

If an ICC profile is embedded in the file, Photoshop will recognize this and know how to correctly interpret the color data. The same thing applies to profiled CMYK files as well. Photoshop uses the monitor display profile information to render a color correct preview on the monitor screen. It helps to understand here that in an ICC color managed workflow in Photoshop, what you see on the monitor is always a color corrected preview and you are not viewing the actual file data. So when the RGB image you are editing is in an RGB work space, such as Adobe RGB, and color management is switched on, what you see on the screen is an RGB preview that has been converted from Adobe RGB to your profiled monitor RGB via the PCS. The same thing happens when Photoshop previews CMYK data on the screen. The Photoshop color management system calculates a conversion from the file CMYK space to the monitor space. Photoshop therefore carries out all its color calculations in a virtual color space. So in a sense, it does not really matter which RGB work space you edit with. It does not have to be exactly the same as the work space set on another user's Photoshop system. If you are both viewing the same file, and your displays are correctly calibrated and profiled, a color image should look near enough the same on both monitors.

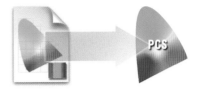

**Figure 12.5** A color management system is able to read the profile information from an incoming RGB file and behind the scenes it will build a table that correlates the source RGB information with the Profile Connecting Space values.

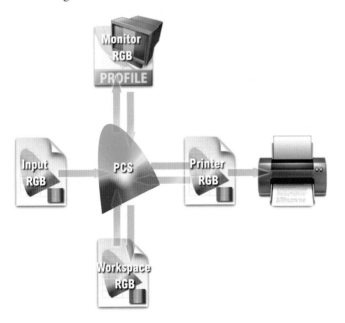

**Figure 12.6** Photoshop can read or make use of the profile information of an incoming RGB file and translate the data via the Profile Connecting Space and make an RGB to RGB conversion to the current RGB work space in Photoshop. As you work in RGB mode, the image data is converted via the PCS using the monitor profile to send a profile-corrected signal to the monitor display. When you make a print the image data is then converted from the work space RGB to the printer RGB via the PCS.

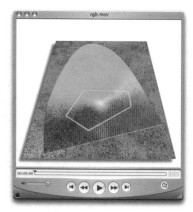

**Figure 12.7** The DVD accompanying this book contains a short movie which helps to explain the RGB space issue by graphically comparing some of the main RGB spaces.

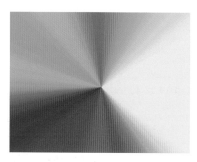

**Figure 12.8** A CMYK color space is mostly smaller than the monitor RGB color space. Not all CMYK colors can be displayed accurately due to the physical display limitations of the average computer monitor. This screen shot shows a continuous spectrum going through shades of cyan, magenta and yellow. The image was then deliberately posterized in Photoshop. Notice how the posterized steps grow wider in the Yellow and Cyan portions of the spectrum. This sample gradient pinpoints the areas of the CMYK spectrum which fall outside the gamut of a typical CRT monitor.

## Choosing an RGB work space

Although I highly recommended that you switch on the color management settings in Photoshop, you cannot assume that everyone else will. There are many other Photoshop users and color labs from the Jurassic era who are running outputs from files with Photoshop color management switched off and are not bothering to calibrate their displays properly.

If you are using Photoshop 6.0 or later it matters less individually which RGB color space you choose in the RGB setup, as long as you stick to using the same space for all your work. RGB to RGB conversions are not as destructive as RGB to CMYK conversions, but the space you plump for does matter. Once chosen you should not really change it. And whichever color work space you select in the RGB color settings, you will have to be conscious of how your profiled Photoshop RGB files may appear on a non-ICC savvy Photoshop system. What follows is a guide to the listed RGB choices.

### *Apple RGB*

This is the old Apple 13" monitor standard. In the early days of Photoshop this was used as the default RGB editing space where the editing space was the same as the monitor space. If you have legacy images created in Photoshop on a Macintosh computer using a gamma of 1.8, you can assume Apple RGB to be the missing profile space.

### *sRGB IEC-61966-2.1*

sRGB was conceived as a multipurpose color space standard that consumer digital devices could all standardize to. It is essentially a compromise color space that provides a uniform color space which all digital cameras and inkjet printers and monitors are able to match. sRGB aims to match the color gamut of a typical 2.2 gamma PC monitor. Therefore if you are opening a file from a consumer digital camera or scanner and there is no profile embedded, you can assume that the missing profile should be sRGB. It is an ideal color space for web design but unsuitable for photography or serious print work. This is mainly because the sRGB space clips the CMYK gamut quite severely and you will never achieve more than 75–85% cyan in your CMYK separations.

### ColorMatch RGB

ColorMatch is an open standard monitor RGB space that was implemented by Radius. ColorMatch has a gamma of 1.8 and is favored by some Macintosh users as their preferred RGB working space. Although not much larger than the gamut of a typical monitor space, it is at least a known standard and more compatible with legacy, 1.8 gamma Macintosh files.

### ProPhoto RGB

This is a large gamut RGB space that has the advantage of preserving the full gamut of raw capture files when converting the raw data to RGB. It is also suited for image editing that is intended for output to photographic materials such as transparency emulsion or a photo quality inkjet printer. This is because the gamut of ProPhoto RGB extends more into the shadow areas compared to most other RGB spaces, meaning better tonal separation in the shadow tones.

### Adobe RGB (1998)

Adobe RGB (1998) has become established as the recommended RGB editing space for RGB files that are destined to be converted to CMYK. For example, the Photoshop prepress color settings all use Adobe RGB as the RGB working space. Adobe RGB was initially labeled as SMPTE-240M which was a color gamut proposed for HDTV production. As it happens, the coordinates Adobe used did not exactly match the actual SMPTE-240M specification. Nevertheless, it proved popular as an editing space for repro work and soon became known as Adobe RGB (1998). I have in the past used Adobe RGB as my preferred RGB working space, since it is well suited for RGB to CMYK color conversions.

### The ideal RGB working space

If you select an RGB work space that is the same size as the monitor space, you are not using Photoshop to its full potential and more importantly you are probably clipping parts of the CMYK gamut. For many years I would have advised you to choose Adobe RGB as your work space, because it appeared to offer the best compromise between encompassing most of the CMYK gamut but without being so large as to be unwieldy. However, a few years ago I was in conversation with the late Bruce Fraser and he convinced me that cautionary warnings against ProPhoto RGB were perhaps a little overstated, even if you are going to end up converting a file from 16-bit to 8-bit RGB. So following Bruce's advice I mostly now use ProPhoto RGB as my principal RGB work space, although I would still strongly advise making the big tone edits in 16-bit before converting to 8-bit. The only other thing I would caution you on here is to never supply clients with ProPhoto RGB master files. If I ever send out RGB files, I make sure that I only release Adobe RGB or sRGB converted versions. If I am sending a file to someone who I believe is ICC color management savvy, I send them a profiled Adobe RGB version. If I am sending a file by email or to someone who may not understand color management, I always play safe and send them an sRGB version.

## Eyeball calibration

If you don't have a monitor calibration device, you can always build a profile for your monitor using a visual calibration method. You could, for example, use the Display Calibration Assistant that comes with the Mac OS X system. But the problem with relying on visual calibration is that because our eyes are so good at adapting to light, our eyes are poor instruments to use when calibrating a device like a monitor display

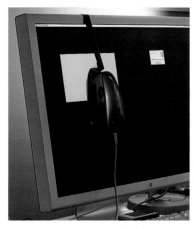

**Figure 12.9** Good color management is very much dependent on having your display calibrated and profiled. This should ideally be done using a hardware calibration device like the Gretag MacBeth Eye-One system.

## Profiling the display

The first step to making color management work in Photoshop is to calibrate and profile the screen display. This is by far the most important and essential first link in the color management chain. You can live without scanner profiling and it is not the end of the world if you can't profile every printer/paper combination. But you simply must have a well-calibrated and profiled display. It is after all the instrument you most use to make color editing decisions with.

In Chapter 3 I mentioned some of the equipment and software options that you can buy these days and showed a quick run through of how to calibrate a computer screen using a calibration device. I would strongly urge you to purchase a proper measuring instrument and use this to calibrate the display on a regular basis. A hardware calibration device combined with a dedicated software utility is the only way that you can guarantee getting good color from your system. This will enable you to precisely calibrate your display and build an accurate monitor profile. At the time of writing, I found four basic monitor profiling packages, which include a colorimeter and basic software program, all for under $300. Highly recommended is the basICColor Display and Squid combination. Then there is the Gretag MacBeth Eye-One Display 2 that comes with Eye-One Match 2 software, the Monaco Optix XR system and lastly the ColorVision Monitor Spyder and Spyder2Pro Studio. Of these I would probably recommend the Gretag MacBeth Eye-One Display 2, since I am very familiar with the (more expensive) Eye-One spectrophotometer system, which I use to calibrate and profile the display in my office. It is also an emissive spectrophotometer so I can also use it to build custom printer profiles. The units I have listed here (apart from the Eye-One) are all colorimeters so these can only be used for building monitor profiles. But they are usually regarded as being just as good as more expensive spectrophotometers for this type of task.

## Calibration and profiling

Profiling devices are attached to the screen via rubber suckers to a CRT, or hung over the edge of an LCD display using a counter weight that gently rests the calibrator against the surface. Don't use a calibrating device with suckers on an LCD as this will easily damage the delicate surface.

The software packages used will vary in appearance but they essentially all do the same thing. If you are using a CRT monitor it must be switched on for at least half an hour before you attempt to calibrate and profile it. The first stage is to calibrate the display to optimize the contrast and brightness. You should end up with a display luminance of around 85–110 cd/m². Most CRT monitors will allow you to manually adjust the individual color guns to help neutralize the screen. But on an LCD display all you can adjust is usually the brightness. Once this has been done you will want to lock down the hardware controls so they cannot be accidentally adjusted. This should be done before performing the calibration in which a series of colors will be sent to the screen and the measurements used to adjust the video card settings which will fine-tune the display to achieve optimum neutralization.

The second part is the profiling process. Once the screen has been calibrated a longer sequence of color patches will be sent to the screen and measured to build a profile describing how the neutralized screen displays these known colors. This data is collected together to build the profile. At the end you will be asked to name the profile and it should be automatically saved to the correct folder location and assigned as the new default monitor profile.

Some CRT monitor displays such as the Sony Artisan or Barco have built-in internal calibration mechanisms. You literally just switch them on and they self-calibrate to provide optimized performance. This takes a lot of the guesswork out of the calibration process.

Do remember that the performance of the display will fluctuate over time (especially a CRT display). It is therefore important to check and calibrate the monitor at regular intervals.

### Locating the display profile

On the Macintosh, the profile should automatically be saved in the Library/ColorSync/Profiles/Displays folder. On a PC, save to the Windows/System32/Spool/Drivers/Color folder.

### Monitor profile creation settings

Before you build a profile there are several option settings you have to decide upon. First there is the gamma space which I recommend should always be 2.2, even if it says somewhere that Macintosh users should use 1.8. The white point should be set to 6500 K. You may see 5000 K as the recommended setting, but your display will perform much better at 6500 K and is also closer to the native white point of most LCD displays (where possible select the native white point of your LCD). Select a small profile size for CRT profiles and large profile size for LCD profiles.

### LCD hardware calibration

Some high-end LCD displays are beginning to feature hardware-level calibration such as Eizo Coloredge and Mitsubishi Spectraview.

## Camera Raw profiling

As was explained in Chapter 5, the Camera Raw plug-in uses data accumulated from two sets of profiles which have been produced using daylight balanced and tungsten balanced lighting. This method of profiling works surprisingly well with most normal color temperature settings, but the data gathered is based on a small sample of cameras (sometimes just one!) and so cannot be regarded as offering absolute accuracy. It may be helpful to follow the calibrate procedure (described in the same chapter) to obtain improved color.

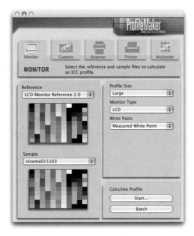

**Figure 12.10** ProfileMaker Pro™ interface.

## Profiling the input

Input profiling is possible but it is easier to do with a scanner than it is with a digital camera. To profile a scanner you need to scan a film or print target and use profile creation software such as Gretag MacBeth's ProfileMaker Pro™ program to read the data and build a custom profile based on readings taken from the scanned target. The target measurements are then used to build a profile that describes the characteristics of the scanner. This profile should be saved to the Macintosh Library/ColorSync/Profiles folder. Or on a PC, save to the Windows/System32/Spool/Drivers/ Color folder. It can then be incorporated into your color managed workflow to describe the image data coming into Photoshop (refer back to Figure 12.6). This can be done by selecting the profile in the scanner software or by assigning the profile in Photoshop as the file is opened.

Camera profiling is a lot trickier to do and few photographers feel it is something worth bothering with. This is because the camera sensor will respond differently under different lighting conditions and you would therefore need to build a new profile every time the light changed. This is not necessarily a problem if you are using a digital camera in a studio setup with a consistent strobe lighting setup. In these circumstances it is probably very desirable that you photograph a color checker chart and take measurements that can be used to create a custom input profile for the camera. The Gretag MacBeth Eye-One Photo system will offer camera profiling.

Overall, I would not stress too much about input profiles unless it is critical to your workflow that you have absolute color control from start to finish. For example, a museum photographer who is charged with photographing important works of art would absolutely want to profile their camera. But is it always necessary or desirable? The most important thing is to trust what you see on your monitor display and obtain good color management between the image displayed on the screen and what you see in the print.

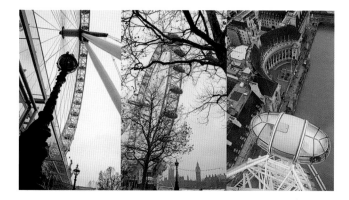

**Figure 12.11** Here are three photographs taken on and around the London Eye wheel. These pictures have each been processed using an incorrect white balance setting. In these examples, input color management becomes irrelevant. But it matters more how consistent the appearance is between the computer display and the print output.

## Profiling the output

Successful color management also relies on having accurate profiles for each type of media paper used with your printer. The printer you buy will come with a driver on a CD (or you can download one) and the installation procedure should install a set of canned profiles that will work when using the proprietary inks designed to be used in this device and with a limited range of branded papers. These tend to be OK in quality and will be enough to get you started. To get the best quality results I will use a test target like the one shown in Figure 12.12 and make a test print without color managing it. Once the test print has been allowed to stabilize, the target is measured the following day using the Gretag MacBeth Eye-One spectrophotometer (see Figure 12.13). The patch measurement results are then used to build a color profile for the printer. The other alternative is to take advantage of Neil Barstow's remote profiling service special offer which is available to readers of this book (see the Appendix).

If using custom printer profiles, you need one to be built for each printer/media combination. I believe it is well worth the expense since it is possible to achieve really excellent results. If you read through to the next chapter on print output, you will see that you can use a profiled printer to achieve good CMYK proofing even from a modestly priced printer, which comes close to matching the quality of a recognized contract proof printer.

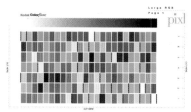

**Figure 12.12** This Kodak™ color target can be used to construct a color ICC profile. Neil Barstow of www.colourmanagement.net is offering a special discount rate to readers of this book (see Appendix for more details). A profile service company will normally supply you with instructions on how to print it out. When they receive your prints, they can measure these and email the custom ICC profile back to you. For more information on printing a profile test target, refer to Chapter 14.

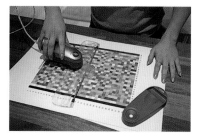

**Figure 12.13** Once a print profile has been printed out, the color patches can be read using a spectrophotometer and the measurements are used to build an ICC profile.

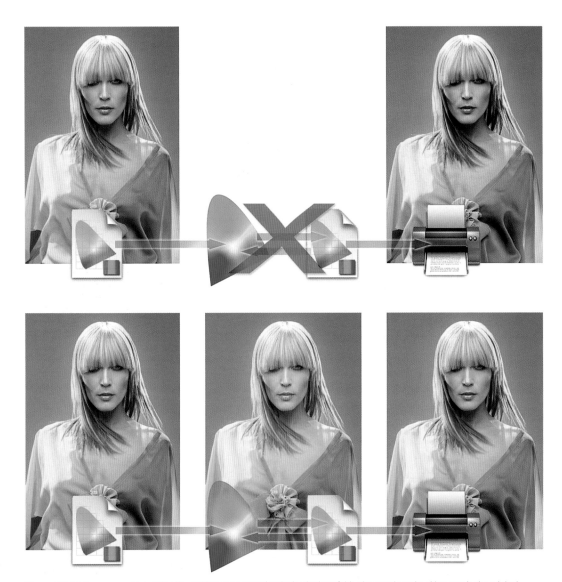

**Figure 12.14** Here we are reexamining the problem encountered at the beginning of this chapter where the skin tones in the original image printed too blue. In the upper workflow no printer profile is used and the image data is sent directly to the printer with no adjustment made to the image data. In the lower example we show how a profile managed workflow works. The profile created for this particular printer is used to convert the image data to that of the printer's color space before being sent to the printer. The (normally hidden) color shifting which occurs during the profile conversion process will compensate by making the skin tone colors more red, but apply less color compensation to other colors. The result is an output that more closely matches the original. This is a simple illustration of the ICC-based color management system at work. All color can be managed this way in Photoshop from capture source to the monitor display and the final proof.

## Photoshop color management interface

By now you should be acquainted with the basic principles of Photoshop ICC color management. It has become relatively easy to configure the Photoshop system. At the simplest level all you have to do is calibrate and profile your display and then go to the Photoshop Color Settings and select an appropriate prepress setting. This will switch on the Photoshop color management policies and be enough to get you up and running without the need to read any further. But if you are ready to discover more, then do read on.

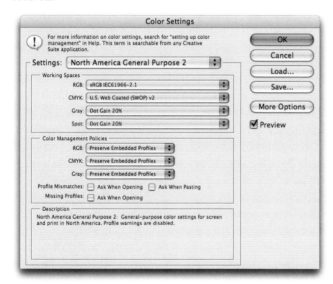

**Figure 12.15** All the Photoshop color settings can be managed from within the Photoshop Color Settings dialog. Photoshop conveniently ships with various preset settings that are suited to different Photoshop workflows. As you move the cursor pointer around the Color Settings dialog, help messages are provided in the Description box area below – these provide useful information which will help you learn more about the Photoshop color management settings and the different color space options.

### The Color Settings

The Color Settings are located in the Edit menu. Figure 12.15 shows the basic dialog controls and options. The first item you will come across is the Settings pop-up menu. Photoshop provides a range of preset configurations for the color management system and these can be edited to meet your own specific requirements. In Basic mode, the default setting will be some sort of General Purpose setting and the exact naming and subsequent settings list will vary depending on the region where you live.

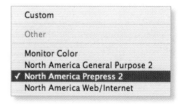

**Figure 12.16** The default settings are just defaults. I advise changing the setting to one of the prepress settings as this will configure Photoshop to use Adobe RGB as your RGB work space and switch on the Profile Mismatch and Missing Profiles alert warnings.

559

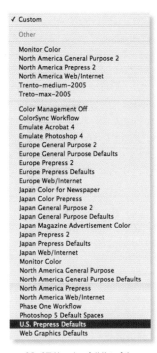

**Figure 12.17** Here is a full list of the preset settings (as seen when the More Options is selected). The General Purpose presets will preserve RGB profiles, but use sRGB as the RGB work space instead of Adobe RGB, and CMYK color management will be switched off. This is a little better than the previous Web Graphics default yet may help avoid confusion among novice users. In the basic Fewer Options mode, the choice will be restricted so that all you see will be the color settings for your geographical area.

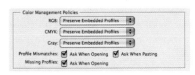

**Figure 12.18** The Color Management Policies, with the Profile Mismatch and Missing Profile checkboxes checked.

I would recommend that you follow the advice in Figure 12.16 and change this default to one of the prepress settings. So if Photoshop was installed on a European computer, you would select the Europe Prepress Default setting from this list. If a preset color setting says 'prepress', this will be the ideal starting point for any type of color managed workflow, especially if you are a photographer. That is all you need to concern yourself with initially, but if you wish to make customized adjustments, then you can select custom settings in the Working Spaces section below. For help selecting an ideal RGB work space, refer back to the section on RGB spaces on pages 552–553. The CMYK and Grayscale settings will be covered later.

### Color management policies

The first thing Photoshop does when a document is opened is check to see if an ICC profile is present. The default policy is to preserve the embedded profile information. So whether the document has originated in sRGB, Adobe RGB or ColorMatch RGB, it will open in that RGB color space and after editing be saved as such. This means you can have several files open at once and each can be in an entirely different color space. A good tip here is to set the Status box to show 'Document profile' (on the Mac this is at the bottom left of the image window; on a PC it is at the bottom of the system screen). Or, you can configure the Info palette to provide such information. This will allow you to see each individual document's color space profile.

### Profile mismatches and missing profiles

When there is a profile mismatch, Photoshop will warn you using one of the dialogs shown in Figure 12.19. Which of these you see will depend on the Color Settings. If you have a prepress setting selected, the Profile Mismatch and Missing Profile boxes will automatically be checked and the dialog that is shown when there is a profile mismatch will offer you a chance to convert the document colors to the current work space or discard the profile.

## *Preserve embedded profiles*

The default policy of Preserve Embedded Profiles allows you to use the ICC color management system straight away, without too much difficulty. So long as there is a profile tag embedded in any file you open, Photoshop will give you the option to open that file without converting it. So if you are given an Apple RGB file to open, the default option is to open it in Apple RGB and save using the same Apple RGB color space. This is despite the fact that your default RGB work space might be Adobe RGB or some other RGB color space. The same policy rules apply to CMYK and grayscale files. Whenever Preserve Embedded Profiles is selected, Photoshop will read the CMYK or Grayscale profile, preserve the numeric data and not convert the colors. And the image will remain in the tagged color space. This is always going to be the preferred option when editing incoming CMYK files because a CMYK file may already be targeted for a specific press output and you don't really want to alter those numeric color values.

**Embedded Profile Mismatch**

The document "DSC00334.JPG" has an embedded color profile that does not match the current RGB working space. The embedded profile will be used instead of the working space.

Embedded: sRGB IEC61966-2.1

Working: Adobe RGB (1998)

☐ Don't show again        Cancel        OK

**Embedded Profile Mismatch**

The document "DSC00334.JPG" has an embedded color profile that does not match the current RGB working space.

Embedded: sRGB IEC61966-2.1

Working: Adobe RGB (1998)

What would you like to do?
- ⦿ Use the embedded profile (instead of the working space)
- ○ Convert document's colors to the working space
- ○ Discard the embedded profile (don't color manage)

Cancel        OK

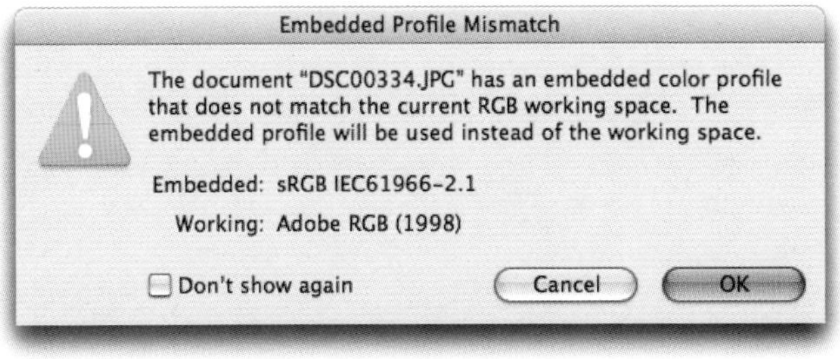

**Figure 12.19** If the Preserve Embedded Profiles color management policy is selected, this dialog will appear whenever there is a profile mismatch between the image you are opening and the current working space. When you see this dialog, click OK to open the image in its embedded color space. Click Don't show again if you don't wish to be reminded each time this occurs.

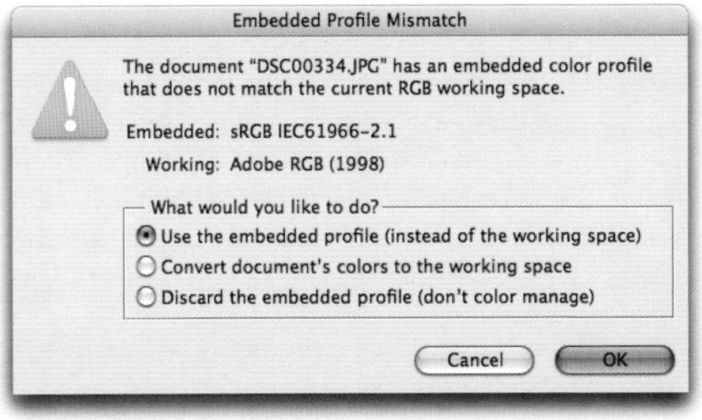

**Figure 12.20** If the Ask When Opening box is checked in the Profile Mismatches section (see Figure 12.18) then you will see a slightly different dialog like the lower one shown here. If the Ask When Opening option is checked, you can make a choice on opening to use the embedded profile, or override the policy and convert to the working space or discard the embedded profile.

Whatever you do, select one of these options and click OK, because if you click Cancel you will cancel opening the file completely.

### Include a 'Read Me' file

When you save a profiled RGB file, you might want to enclose a Read Me file on the disk to remind the person who receives the image that they must not ignore the profile information.

## *Convert to Working space*

If you select the Convert to Working space policy, Photoshop will automatically convert everything to your current RGB or CMYK work space. If the incoming profile does not match the work space, then the default option will be to carry out a profile conversion from the embedded profile space to the current work space. And when the incoming profile matches the current RGB, CMYK or grayscale work space, there is of course no need to convert the colors. Preserve Embedded Profiles is usually the safer option because you can't go wrong if you just click OK to everything. Convert to Working space can be a useful option for RGB mode because you may wish to convert all RGB images to your working space, but not for CMYK. For batch processing work I sometimes prefer to temporarily use a Convert to Working space RGB setting because this will allow me to apply a batch operation to a mixture of files in which all the images end up in the current RGB work space.

**Figure 12.21** If the Convert to Working RGB color management policy is selected, this dialog will appear whenever there is a profile mismatch between the image you are opening and the current working space. When you see this dialog, click OK to convert the document colors to the current color working space. Click Don't show again if you don't wish to be reminded each time this occurs.

**Figure 12.22** If the Ask When Opening box is checked in the Profile Mismatches section you will see the dialog shown here. You can make a choice on opening to convert to the working space, use the embedded profile, or override the policy and discard the embedded profile.

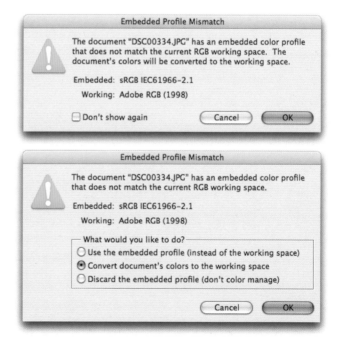

## Color Management Off

The other option is to choose Color Management: Off. When this option is selected Photoshop will appear not to color manage incoming documents. It will assume the default RGB or CMYK work space to be the source. If there is no profile embedded, then the document will stay that way. If there is a profile mismatch between the source and work space, the profile will be removed (with an alert warning pointing out that the embedded profile information is about to be deleted). But if the source profile matches the work space, there is no need to remove the profile, so in this instance the profile tag will not be removed (even so, you can still remove the ICC profile at the saving stage). So in this instance, Photoshop will still be color managing certain files and strictly speaking is not completely 'off'.

Turning the color management off is not recommended for general Photoshop work. So check the Color Settings to make sure you are not using one of the Web/Internet preset settings that will disable Photoshop's color management.

### When it is good to 'turn off'

Sometimes it is desirable to discard a profile. For example, you may be aware that the image you are about to open has an incorrect profile and it is therefore a good thing to discard it and assign the correct profile later in Photoshop. I would not recommend choosing Off as the default setting though. Just make sure you have the Color Management Policies set to Ask When Opening and you can easily intervene manually to discard the profile when using either of the other color management policy settings.

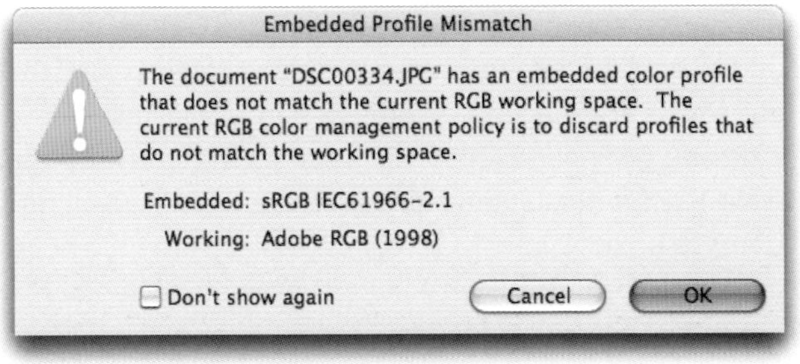

**Figure 12.23** If the Color Management Off policy is selected, this dialog will appear whenever there is a profile mismatch between the image you are opening and the current working space. When you see this dialog, click OK to discard the embedded profile. Click Don't show again if you don't wish to be reminded each time this occurs.

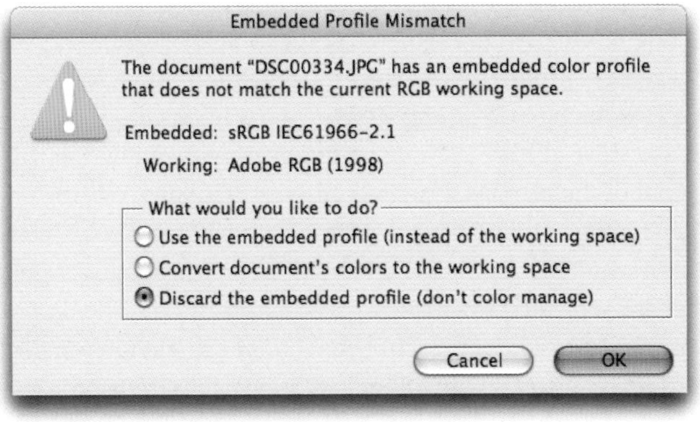

**Figure 12.24** If the Ask When Opening box is checked in the Profile Mismatches section you will see the dialog shown here. You can make a choice on opening to discard the embedded profile, use the embedded profile or convert to the working space.

## RGB to RGB conversion warning

A Convert to Profile is just like any other image mode change in Photoshop, such as converting from RGB to Grayscale mode, and it is much safer to use than the old Profile to Profile command in Photoshop 5.0. However, be careful if you use Convert to Profile to produce targeted RGB outputs that overwrite the original RGB master. Any version of Photoshop since version 6.0 will have no problem reading the embedded profiles and displaying the image correctly; and will recognize any profile mismatch (and know how to convert back to the original work space). But as always, customized RGB files such as this may easily confuse other non-ICC savvy Photoshop users. Not everyone is using Photoshop, nor does everyone have their color management configured correctly. Some RGB to RGB conversions can produce RGB images that look fine on a correctly configured system, but look very odd on one that is not (see page 570).

## Profile conversions

As you gain more experience you will soon be able to customize and create your own color settings. The minimum you need to know is which of these listed color settings will be appropriate for the work you are doing. And to help in this decision making, you can read the text descriptions that appear in the Description box at the bottom of the Color Settings dialog. For example, you might want to start by loading one of the presets present in the Color Settings menu and customize the CMYK settings to match the conditions of your repro output.

### Convert to Profile

Even if you choose to preserve the embedded profile on opening, it is useful to have the means to convert non-work space files to your current work space after opening. This is where the Convert to Profile command comes in, because you don't have to worry about remembering to convert the image on opening. The profile conversion can take place at any time, such as at the end of a retouch session, just before saving. Let's suppose we want to open an RGB image that is in Adobe RGB and the current working space is sRGB. If the Preserve Embedded Profile option is selected then the default behavior would be to open the file and keep it in Adobe RGB without converting. We could carry on editing the image in the Adobe RGB color space up until the point where it is desirable to carry out a conversion to another color space. To make a profile conversion, go to the Edit menu and choose Convert to Profile... This will open the dialog box shown in Figure 12.25. The Source space shows the current profile space and the Destination Space will most likely default to 'Working RGB', which in this case would be sRGB. But it will also contain a pop-up menu that will list all of the profiles available on your computer system (depending on how many profiles you have installed). The list of available profiles will be divided into several sections that are separated by dividers (see Figure 12.26). The first section starts with the default RGB, CMYK and Grayscale profiles. Below that are all the other available RGB profiles followed by the CMYK and lastly the Grayscale spaces.

The Convert to Profile command is also useful when you wish to create an output file to send to a printer for which you have a custom-built profile but the print driver does not recognize ICC profiles. For example, one of the printers I use is the Fuji Pictrograph. I have built a custom profile for this printer, but unfortunately there is no facility within the File Export driver to utilize the output profile. Therefore, I use the Convert to Profile command to convert the color data to match the space of the output device just prior to sending the image data to the printer to make a print.

Whenever you make a profile conversion the image data will end up in a different color space and you might see a slight change in the on-screen color appearance. This is because the profile space you are converting to has a smaller gamut than the one you are converting from. Whether an image is imported that is not in the working colour space or has been converted to one that is not, Photoshop appends a warning asterisk (*) to the color mode in the title bar (Mac) or status bar (PC).

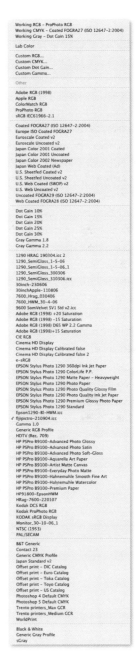

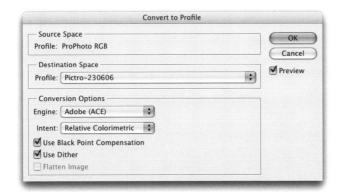

**Figure 12.25** Convert to Profile is located in the Edit menu and is similar to the old Profile to Profile command in Photoshop 5.0. The color management system in Photoshop 6.0 or later is different in that you don't need to carry out a profile conversion in order to correctly preview a file in Photoshop. It is nevertheless an essential command for when you wish to convert color data from one profile color space to another profiled space, such as when you want to convert a file to the profiled color space of a specific output device. In this example, I am using Convert to Profile to convert the RGB data from the source space to the profiled space of my Fuji printer.

**Figure 12.26** The profile list will display all the profiles that are available on your computer.

## Incorrect sRGB profile tags

Some digital cameras won't embed a profile in the JPEG capture files or, worse still, embed a wrong profile, yet the EXIF metadata will misleadingly say the file is in sRGB color mode. The danger here is that while you may select Adobe RGB as the RGB space for your camera, when shooting in JPEG mode, the camera may inadvertently omit to alter the EXIF tag which stubbornly reads sRGB.

This can be resolved by going to the Photoshop menu and choosing: Preferences ⇨ File Handling... If you check the Ignore EXIF Profile tag, Photoshop will always ignore the specified camera profile in the EXIF metadata and only rely on the actual profile (where present) when determining the color space the data should be in.

## *Assign Profile*

The Assign Profile command can be used to correct mistakes by assigning a profile to an image if one is missing, or removing an incorrect profile. When an image is missing its profile or has the wrong profile information embedded then the numbers are meaningless. The Assign Profile command allows you to assign correct meaning to what the colors in the image should be. So, for example, if you know the profile of an opened file to be wrong, then you can use the Edit ⇨ Assign Profile command to rectify the situation. Let's suppose you have opened an untagged RGB file and for some reason decided not to color manage the file when opening. The colors don't look right and you have reason to believe that the file had originated from the sRGB color space. Yet, it is being edited in your current Adobe RGB work space as if it were an Adobe RGB image. By assigning an sRGB profile, we can tell Photoshop that this is not an Adobe RGB image and that these colors should be considered as being in the sRGB color space. You can also use Assign Profile to remove a profile by clicking on the Don't Color Manage This Document button, which will allow you to strip a file of its profile. But you can also do this by choosing File ⇨ Save As... and deselecting the Embed Profile checkbox in the Save options.

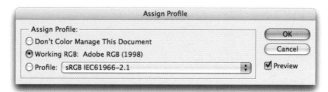

**Figure 12.27** The Assign Profile command is available from the Edit menu in Photoshop. Edit ⇨ Assign Profile can be used to assign a new correct profile to an image or remove an existing profile.

## *Profile mismatches*

One problem with having images with multiple color spaces open at once concerns the copying and pasting of color data from one file to another. Whenever you copy and paste image data, or drag copy an image with the move tool, it is possible that a profile mismatch may occur; although this will very much depend on how you have the Color Management policy settings configured in the Color Settings (see Figure 12.28). If the Profile Mismatches: Ask When Pasting box is unchecked in the Color Settings and a profile mismatch happens, you will see the dialog shown in Figure 12.29. This will ask if you wish to convert the color data to preserve the color appearance when it is pasted into the new destination document. If the Profile Mismatches: Ask When Pasting box is checked in the Color Settings, then you will see instead the dialog box shown in Figure 12.30. This dialog offers you the choice to convert or not convert the data. If you select Convert, the appearance of the colors will be maintained when you paste the data. If you choose Don't Convert the color appearance will change but the numbers will be preserved.

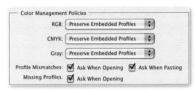

**Figure 12.28** The Profile Mismatches settings in the Color Management section of the Color Settings dialog will influence Profile Mismatch behavior.

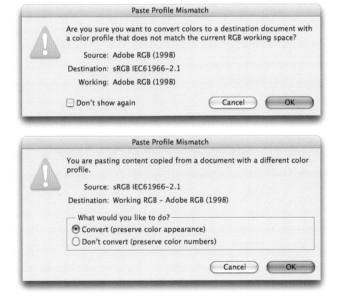

**Figure 12.29** If you attempt to paste image data from a document whose color space does not match the destination space, this dialog warning will appear, alerting you to the fact that there is a profile mismatch between the source and destination documents. If you click OK, Photoshop will convert the data and preserve the color appearance of the image data.

**Figure 12.30** If the Profile Mismatches: Ask When Pasting box is checked in the Color Settings dialog and you attempt to paste image data from a document whose color space does not match the destination space, this dialog warning will give you the option to Convert the colors (as in Figure 12.28 above), or Don't Convert and preserve the numbers instead.

## Color Settings save location

On Mac OS X, if Photoshop CS3 is installed for multi-users, the most likely path to save your settings to is: Users/Username/Library/Application Support/Adobe/Color/Settings folder. On a PC, save your settings to: Program Files/Common Files/Adobe/Color/Settings folder. The file will be appended with a .csf suffix.

## Saving a Color Setting

If you have configured the settings to suit a particular workflow, you can click on the Save... button to save these as a custom setting that will appear in the Color Settings menu the next time you visit the Color Settings dialog. When you save a setting you can enter any relevant comments or notes about the setting you are saving in the text box (see Figure 12.31). This information will then appear in the Color Settings dialog text box at the bottom. You might name the setting something like 'Client annual report settings' and so you might want to write a short descriptive note to accompany the setting.

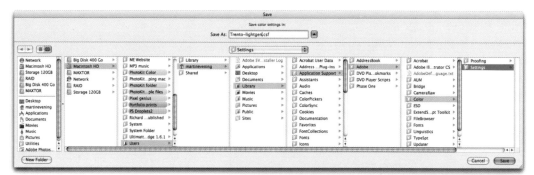

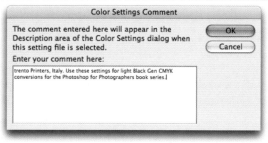

**Figure 12.31** Custom color settings can be loaded or saved via the Color Settings dialog. The relevant folder will be located in the Username Library/Application Support/Adobe/Color/Settings folder (Mac OS X) or Program Files/Common Files/Adobe/Color/Settings folder (PC). When you save a custom setting it must be saved to this location and will automatically be appended with the '.csf' suffix. When you save a color setting you have the opportunity to include a brief text description in the accompanying dialog. A Color Settings file can be shared between some Adobe applications and with other Photoshop users. The Mac OS X location of the settings file is user-specific, so the route is: Users/Username/Library/Application Support/ Adobe/Color/Settings folder.

## Reducing the opportunities for error

When you adopt an RGB space such as Adobe RGB as the preferred work space for all your image editing, you have to take into account that this might cause confusion when exchanging RGB files between your machine operating in a color managed workflow and that of someone who is using Photoshop with the color management switched off. When sending image files to other Photoshop users, the presence of a profile will help them to read the image data correctly. So as long as they have the Photoshop color settings configured to preserve embedded profiles (or convert to the working space) and their monitor display is calibrated correctly, they will see your photographs on their system almost exactly the way you intended them to be seen. The only variables will be the accuracy of their display calibration and profile, the color gamut limitations of the display and the environment it is being viewed in. Configuring the Color Settings correctly is not difficult to do, but the recipient does have to be as conscientious as you are about ensuring their monitor display is set up correctly. The situation has not been helped either by the way the default color settings have shifted about over the last seven versions of the program. The default settings in Photoshop CS3 use Preserve Embedded Profiles, but prior to that we had settings like 'Web Graphics' in which color management was switched off. Consequently, there are a lot of Photoshop users out there who have unwittingly been using sRGB as their default RGB work space and with color management switched off. And even when people do have the color management switched on, the monitors they are using may not have been profiled in months or are being viewed in a brightly lit room!

It is important to be aware of these potential problems because it is all too easy for the color management to fail once an image file has left your hands and been passed on to another Photoshop user. With this in mind, here are some useful tips to help avoid misunderstandings over color. The most obvious way to communicate what the colors are supposed to look like is to supply a printed output that

### Playing detective

How you deliver your files will very much depend on who you are supplying them to. I often get emails from readers who have been given the runaround by their color lab. One typically finds that the lab may be using a photo printer such as the Fuji Frontier which does not read incoming profiles and is simply calibrated to expect sRGB files. So far so good. As long as you send an sRGB file, you shouldn't have any problems. But if the color lab operator has Photoshop color management switched off, they will not know how to handle anything other than an incoming file that is in sRGB. If you were to supply them with an Adobe RGB file they won't read the profile and the colors will end up looking different in the final print. And then they blame the customer!

It helps to do a little detective work to ascertain the skill level of the recipient. The first thing you need to know is the color settings they are using. That will help you determine which RGB space they are using and whether the color management is switched on or off. The other thing to ask is 'do you have your monitor display calibrated and profiled?' And if the answer is yes, then ask how often they calibrate and profile their display. The answers to these questions will tell you quite a bit about the other person's system, how you should supply your files and also how accurately they should be able to judge the color on their monitor display. Basically, if you have any doubts, the safest option is to convert to sRGB.

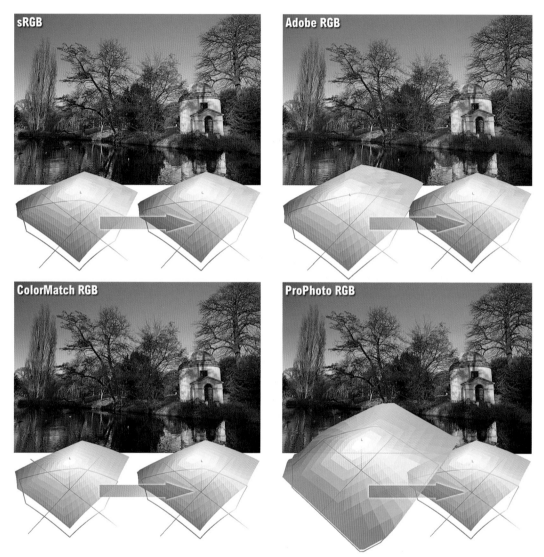

**Figure 12.32** The purpose of this illustration is to show what would happen if you submitted an RGB file to a Photoshop user who had their Photoshop system configured using sRGB as their RGB work space and with the color management policies set to ignore incoming profiles. The top left picture is the correct version and shows how the image would look if I supplied the image converted to the sRGB color space, anticipating that the other user was using this as their default RGB space. The remaining examples show how the same picture would look if I had supplied the same picture using different RGB spaces and the person receiving the file ignored the embedded profile. If the picture was delivered as an Adobe RGB file, the gamma would match but because Adobe RGB has a larger gamut than sRGB the colors would appear slightly desaturated. If I supplied a ColorMatch RGB file, sRGB would interpret this as a darker image because ColorMatch has a lower gamma of 1.8. And lastly, ProPhoto RGB has a much larger color gamut than Adobe RGB so the colors would appear even more muted when brought into sRGB without any color management.

shows what the photograph should look like. In fact this is considered routine when supplying images to a printer. If you are sending a file for CMYK repro printing then the file should be targeted to the CMYK output. Don't worry too much about what that means just yet, we will be covering this topic in the following chapter. But supplying a print is an unambiguous visual reference, which if done properly can form the basis of a contract between yourself, the client and the printer.

**Supplying a color proof**
To find out more about how to produce a proof print that is targeted to simulate a specific print output, you will find this topic is covered in the following chapter on pages 614–616.

If the person you are supplying the file to is in the same building or you are in regular contact with them, then you probably have a clear idea of how their system is set up. If they have Photoshop color management switched on, they can read any file you send them in any color space and it will be color managed successfully. But you cannot always make too many assumptions about the people you are sending image files to and so you should sometimes adopt a more cautious approach. I am often asked to supply RGB files as large JPEGs for initial approval by the client before making a finished print. In these situations I find it safer to supply a profiled sRGB image. I do this by choosing Edit ⇨ Convert to Profile... and selecting sRGB as the destination space. If the recipient is color management savvy, then Photoshop will read the sRGB profile and handle the colors correctly. If the recipient has not bothered to configure their color management settings then one can be almost certain that they are using sRGB as their default RGB work space. So in these instances, targeting the RGB colors to sRGB is probably the safer option. Figure 12.32 shows a comparison of how a single image that was edited using different RGB work spaces would look on a Photoshop system configured using a (non-color managed) Web Graphics default setting. In this example, the version that was converted to sRGB was the only one that stood a chance of being displayed correctly. I am certainly not advocating you use sRGB as your standard RGB work space, because it is still a poor space to use for photographic work. But it can be a useful 'dumbed down' space to use when communicating with unknown users.

## Grayscale for screen display

If you intend creating grayscale images to be seen on the Internet or in multimedia presentations, choose the Default Web Graphics color setting. The Grayscale work space will then be set to a 2.2 gamma space, which is the same gamma used by the majority of PC computer screens. The truth is, you can never be 100% sure how anybody who views your work will have their monitor calibrated, but you can at least assume that the majority of Internet users will have a PC monitor set to a 2.2 gamma.

## Macintosh gamma

The Macintosh 1.8 gamma setting should really be relegated to ancient history. The reason it exists at all is because in the very early days of the Macintosh computer and before ICC color management, a 1.8 gamma monitor space most closely matched the dot gain of the Apple monochrome laser printer.

## Custom Gray space settings

Figure 12.40 shows a range of dot gain values that can be used as a guide for different types of press settings. This is a rough guide as to which dot gain setting you should use on any given job. When the Advanced color settings option is checked you can enter a custom gamma value or dot gain curve setting (see 'Dot gain' on pages 579–580).

## Working with Grayscale

Grayscale image files can also be managed via the Color Settings dialog. The color management policy can be set to either Preserve Embedded Profiles or Convert to Grayscale work space and again the Ask When Opening box should be checked. If the profile of the incoming grayscale file does not match the current Gray work space, you will be asked whether you wish to use the tagged grayscale space profile, or convert to the current grayscale work space. If there is no profile embedded, you will be asked to either: 'Leave as is' (don't color manage), assign the current Gray work space or choose a Gray work space to assign to the file (and, if you wish, convert to the Gray work space).

If you examine the Gray work space options, you will see a list of dot gain percentages and monitor gamma values. If you are preparing grayscale images for display on a monitor such as on a website or in a multimedia presentation then you will want to select an appropriate monitor space setting such as Gamma 2.2 (see the sidebar: Grayscale for screen display). If you want to know how any existing prepress grayscale image will look like on the Web as a grayscale image, select the View ⇨ Proof Setup and choose Windows RGB or Macintosh RGB. You can then select Image ⇨ Adjust ⇨ Levels and adjust the Gamma slider accordingly to obtain the right brightness for a typical Windows or Macintosh display.

For prepress work you should select the dot gain percentage that most closely matches the anticipated dot gain of the press. It is important to note that the Gray work space setting is independent of the CMYK work space. If you want the Gray work space dot gain value to match the black plate of the current CMYK setting, then mouse down on the Gray setting and choose Load Gray... Now go to the Profiles folder which will be in the Library/Application Support/Adobe/Color/Settings folder on a Mac and in the Program Files/Common Files/Adobe/Color/Settings folder on a PC. Select the same CMYK space as you are using for the CMYK color separations and click the Load button.

## Advanced Color Settings

The advanced settings will normally remain hidden. If you click on the More Options button, you will be able to see the expanded Color Settings dialog shown in Figure 12.33. These advanced settings unleash full control over the Photoshop color management system. But do not attempt to adjust any of these expert settings until you have fully understood the intricacies of customizing the RGB, CMYK, Gray and Spot color spaces. I would suggest that you read through the remaining section of this chapter first before you consider customizing any of these settings.

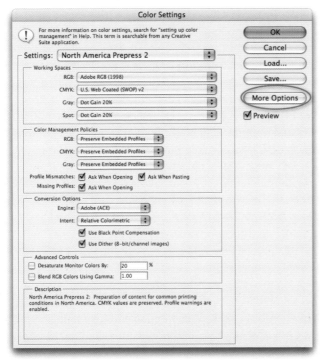

**Figure 12.33** The Photoshop Advanced Color Settings dialog. Clicking on the More Options button will unleash full control over all the Photoshop settings. The following sections of this chapter show how you can customize the color management settings in this advanced mode. Note that the button in this Color Settings dialog view will normally say 'Fewer Options'; I edited the screen shot to say 'More Options', simply to make it more obvious where to click.

## Black Point and Proof printing

You will want to use Black Point Compensation when separating an RGB image to a press CMYK color space. However, in the case of a conversion from a CMYK proofing space to an inkjet profile space, we must preserve the (grayish) black of the press and not scale the image (because this would improve the blacks). It is for these reasons that the Black Point Compensation is disabled in the Print with Preview dialog when making a proof print to simulate the black ink.

## Conversion options

You have a choice of three Color Management Modules (CMMs): Adobe Color Engine (ACE), Apple ColorSync or Apple CMM. The Adobe color engine is reckoned to be superior for all RGB to CMYK conversions because the Adobe engine uses 20-bit per channel bit-depth calculations to calculate its color space conversions.

## Black Point Compensation

This will map the darkest neutral color of the source RGB color space to the darkest neutrals of the destination color space. Black Point Compensation plays a vital role in translating the blacks in your images so that they reproduce as black when printed. As was explained in Chapter 4, there is no need to get hung up on setting the shadow point to anything other than zero RGB. It is not necessary to apply any shadow compensation at the image editing stage, because the color management will automatically take care of this for you and apply a black point compensation obtained from the output profile used in the mode or profile conversion. If you disable Black Point Compensation you may obtain deeper blacks, but you will get truer (compensated) blacks if you leave it switched on.

## Use Dither (8-bit per channel images)

Banding may occasionally occur when you separate to CMYK, particularly where there is gentle tonal gradation in bright saturated areas. Banding which appears on screen does not necessarily always show in print and much will depend on the coarseness of the screen used in the printing process. However, the dither option will help reduce the risks of banding when converting between color spaces.

## Rendering intents

The rendering intent will influence the way the data is translated from the source to the destination space. The rendering intent is like a rule that describes the way the translation is calculated. We will be looking at rendering intents in more detail on pages 584–587.

### Blend RGB colors using gamma

This item provides you with the potential to override the default color blending behavior. There used to be an option in Photoshop 2.5 for applying blend color gamma compensation. This allowed you to blend colors with a gamma of 1.0, which some experts argued was a purer way of doing things, because at any higher gamma value than this you would see edge darkening occur between contrasting colors. Some users found the phenomenon of these edge artifacts to be a desirable trapping effect. But Photoshop users complained that they noticed light halos appearing around objects when blending colors at a gamma of 1.0. Consequently, gamma-compensated blending was removed at the time of the version 2.5.1 update. But if you understand the implications of adjusting this particular gamma setting, you can switch it back on if you wish. Figure 12.34 illustrates the difference between blending colors at a gamma of 2.2 and 1.0.

### Desaturate monitor colors

The desaturate monitor colors option enables you to visualize and make comparisons between color gamut spaces where one or more gamut space is larger than the monitor RGB space. Color spaces such as Adobe RGB and Wide Gamut RGB both have a gamut that is larger than the monitor space is able to show. So turning down the monitor colors saturation will allow you to make a comparative evaluation between these two different color spaces.

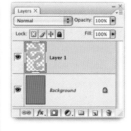

**Figure 12.34** In this test we have a pure RGB green soft edged brush stroke that is on a layer above a pure red Background layer. The version on the left shows the combined layers using the normal default blending. And the image on the right shows what happens if you check the 1.0 checkbox. The darkening around the edges where the contrasting colors meet will disappear.

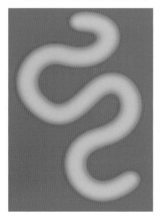

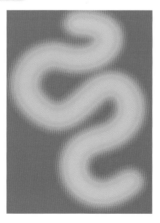

## *Customizing the RGB and work space gamma*

Expert users may wish to use an alternative custom RGB work space instead of one of the listed RGB spaces. If you know what you are doing and wish to create a customized RGB color space, you can go to the Custom... option in the pop-up menu and enter the information for the White Point, Gamma and color primaries coordinates. My advice is to leave these expert settings well alone. And do avoid falling into the trap of thinking that the RGB work space gamma should be the same as the monitor gamma setting. The RGB work space is not a monitor space.

Adobe RGB is a good choice as an RGB work space because its 2.2 gamma provides a more balanced, even distribution of tones between the shadows and highlights. These are the important considerations for an RGB editing space and remember, you do not actually 'see' Adobe RGB. The Adobe RGB gamma has no impact on how the colors are displayed on the screen, so long as Photoshop ICC color management is switched on. In any case, these advanced custom color space settings are safely tucked away in Photoshop and you are less likely to be confused by this apparent discrepancy between monitor gamma and the RGB work space gamma.

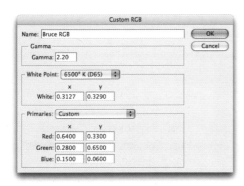
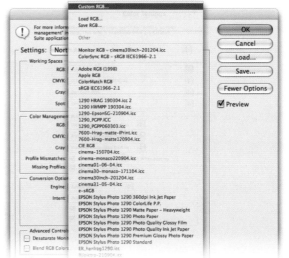

**Figure 12.35** The Custom RGB dialog. Use this option to create a custom RGB work space. The settings shown here have been named 'Bruce RGB', after Bruce Fraser who devised this color space as an ideal prepress space for Photoshop.

# RGB to CMYK

Digital scans and captures all originate in RGB but professional images are nearly always reproduced in CMYK. Since the conversion from RGB to CMYK has to happen at some stage, the question is: at what point should this take place and who should be responsible for the conversion? If you have decided to take on this responsibility yourself then you need to know something more about the CMYK settings. Because when it comes to four-color print reproduction, it is important to know as much as possible about the intended press conditions that will be used at the printing stage and use this information to create a customized CMYK setup.

## CMYK setup

If you examine the US prepress default setting, the CMYK space says U.S. Web Coated (SWOP). This setting is by no means a precise setting for every US prepress SWOP coated print job, because there can be many flavors of SWOP, but it does at least bring you a little closer to the type of specification a printer in the US might require for printing on coated paper with a web press setup. If you mouse down on the CMYK setup pop-up list, you will see there are also US options for web uncoated and sheetfed press setups. Under the European prepress default setting, there is a choice between coated and uncoated paper stocks, plus the latest ISO coated FOGRA27 setting. And then there is Custom CMYK... where you can create and save your custom CMYK profile settings.

## Creating a custom CMYK setting

Figure 12.36 shows the Custom CMYK dialog. This is better known as the familiar 'Classic' Photoshop CMYK setup. You can enter here all the relevant CMYK separation information for your specific print job. Ideally you will want to save each purpose-built CMYK configuration as a separate color setting for future use and label it with a description of the print job it was built for.

## Photoshop CMYK myths

There are some people who will tell you that in their 'expert opinion', Photoshop does a poor job of separating to CMYK. And I bet if you ask them how they know this to be the case, they will be stumped to provide you with a coherent answer. Don't let anyone try to convince you otherwise. Professional quality CMYK separations can be achieved in Photoshop. You can avoid gamut clipping and you can customize a separation to meet the demands of any type of press output. But the fact is that Photoshop will make lousy CMYK separations if the Photoshop operator who is carrying out the conversion has a limited knowledge of how to configure the Photoshop CMYK settings. For example, a wider gamut RGB space such as Adobe RGB is better able to encompass the gamut of CMYK and yield CMYK separations that do not suffer from gamut clipping. This is one big strike in favor of the Photoshop color management system. But CMYK is not a one-size-fits-all color space. CMYK conversions do need to be tailor-made for each and every job.

## Saving custom CMYK settings

The custom CMYK settings should be saved using the following locations: Library/ColorSync/Profiles/Recommended folder (Mac OS X). Windows/System32/Spool/Drivers/Color folder (PC).

## CMYK previews in Proof Setup

Once the CMYK setup has been configured, you can use View ⇒ Proof Setup ⇒ Working CMYK to apply a CMYK preview of what the image will look like after converting while you are still editing the image in RGB mode.

Once you have configured a new CMYK work space setting, this will become the new default CMYK work space that is used when you convert an image to CMYK mode. Altering the CMYK setup settings will have no effect on the on-screen appearance of an already-converted CMYK file (unless there is no profile embedded) because the CMYK separation setup settings must be established first before you carry out the conversion.

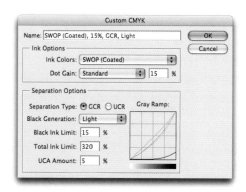

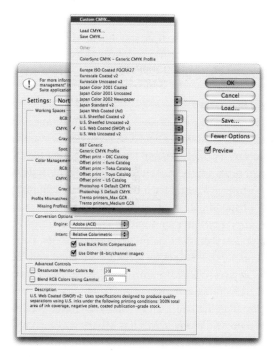

**Figure 12.36** When you select the Custom CMYK... option at the top of the pop-up menu list, this opens the dialog box shown above, where you can enter the specific CMYK setup information to build a custom targeted CMYK setting. If you have clicked on the More Options button, you will have a wider range of preloaded CMYK profile settings to choose from.

## *Ink Colors*

If you click on the Ink Colors menu, you can select one of the preset Ink Colors settings that are suggested for different types of printing. For example, European Photoshop users can choose from Eurostandard (coated), (uncoated), or (newsprint). These are just generic ink sets. If your printer can supply you with a custom ink color setting, then select Custom... from the Ink Colors menu. This will open the dialog shown in Figure 12.37.

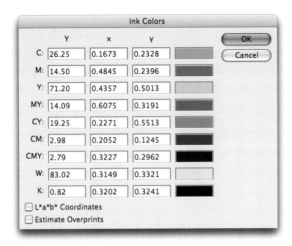

### Dot gain

Dot gain refers to an accumulation of factors during the
repro process that will make a dot printed on the page
appear darker than expected. Among other things, dot gain
is dependent on the type of press and the paper stock being
used. The dot gain value entered in the CMYK setup will
determine how light or dark the separation needs to be. If
a high dot gain is encountered, the separated CMYK films
will need to be less dense so that the plates produced will
lay down less ink on the paper and produce the correct-sized
printed halftone dot for that particular type of press setup.

You can see for yourself how this works by converting
an image to CMYK using two different dot gain values and
inspecting the individual CMYK channels afterwards and
comparing their appearance. Although the dot gain value
will affect the lightness of the individual channels, the
composite CMYK channel image will always be displayed
correctly on the screen to show how the final printed image
should look.

If you select the Dot Gain Curves option, you can
enter custom settings for the composite or individual color
plates. In the preparation of this book I was provided with
precise dot gain information for the 40% and 80% ink
values (these are shown in Figure 12.38).

### Advanced CMYK settings

There is not a lot you can do with the standard CMYK settings: you can make a choice from a handful of generic CMYK profile settings or choose Custom CMYK... If you check the More options box, you will readily be able to select from a more comprehensive list of CMYK profile settings in the extended menu, depending on what profiles are already in your ColorSync folder.

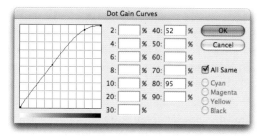

**Figure 12.38** If you select Dot Gain: Curves... from the CMYK setup shown in Figure 12.36, you will open the Custom Dot Gain dialog. If your printer is able to provide dot gain values at certain percentages, then you can enter these here. Dot gain may vary on each ink plate. If you deselect the All Same box, you can enter the dot gain for each individual plate. Note that when you select Custom Dot Gain... from the Grayscale work space menu, a similar dialog appears. If you are preparing to save a color setting designed for separating prepress CMYK and grayscale files, you will want to check that the black plate dot gain setting is consistent. Note that dot gain can vary for each plate and that the black plate dot gain may be slightly different.

## Gray Component Replacement (GCR)

The default Photoshop setting is GCR, Black Generation: Medium, Black Ink Limit 100%, Total Ink Limit 300%, UCA Amount 0%. If you ask your printer what separation settings they use and you are quoted the above figures, you know they are just reading the default settings to you from an unconfigured Photoshop setup and they either don't know or don't want to give you an answer. If you are creating a custom CMYK setting it is more likely you will want to refer to the table in Figure 12.40 for guidance. Or if you prefer, stick to using the prepress Adobe CMYK setting that most closely matches the output (such as: US Sheetfed/Web Coated/Uncoated, or European Pre-Press/Sheetfed/Web/Coated/Uncoated).

## Undercolor Removal (UCR)

The UCR (Undercolor Removal) separation method replaces the cyan, magenta and yellow ink in just the neutral areas with black ink. The UCR setting is also favored as a means of keeping the total ink percentage down on high-speed presses, although it is not necessarily suited for every job.

## Undercolor Addition (UCA)

Low key subjects and high quality print jobs are more suited to the use of GCR (Gray Component Replacement) with a small amount of UCA (Undercolor Addition). GCR separations remove more of the cyan, magenta and yellow ink where all three inks are used to produce a color, replacing the overlapping color with black ink. The use of UCA will add a small amount of color back into the shadows and is useful where the shadow detail would otherwise look too flat and lifeless. The percentage of black ink used is determined by the black generation setting (see below). When making conversions, you are better off sticking with the default GCR, a light to medium black generation with 0–10% UCA. This will produce a longer black curve and improved image contrast.

## Black generation

This determines how much black ink will be used to produce the black and gray tonal information. A light or medium black generation setting is going to be best for most photographic images. I would advise leaving it set to Medium and only change the black generation if you know what you are doing.

You may be interested to know that I specifically used a maximum black generation setting to separate all the dialog boxes that appear printed in this book. Figure 12.39 shows a view of the Channels palette after I had separated the screen grab shown in Figure 12.37 using a Maximum black generation CMYK separation. With this separation method only the black plate is used to render the neutral gray colors. Consequently, this means that any color shift at the printing stage will have no impact whatsoever on the neutrality of the gray content. I cheekily suggest you inspect other Photoshop books and judge if their palette and dialog box screen shots have reproduced as well as the ones shown in this book!

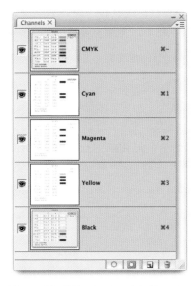

**Figure 12.39** Here is a view of the Channels palette showing the four CMYK channels after I separated the screen grab shown in Figure 12.37 using a Maximum black generation CMYK separation. Notice how all the neutral gray information is contained in the Black channel only. This is a good separation method to use for screen grabs, but not so for any other type of image.

| Separation settings | Ink colors | Separation method | Dot gain | Black generation | Black ink limit | Total ink limit | UCA |
|---|---|---|---|---|---|---|---|
| **US printing** | | | | | | | |
| Sheetfed (coated) | SWOP coated | GCR | 10–15% | Light/Medium | 95% | 320–350% | 0–10% |
| Sheetfed (uncoated) | SWOP uncoated | GCR | 15–25% | Light/Medium | 95% | 260–300% | 0–10% |
| Web press (coated) | SWOP coated | GCR | 15–20% | Light/Medium | 95% | 300–320% | 0–10% |
| Web press (uncoated) | SWOP uncoated | GCR | 20–30% | Light/Medium | 95% | 260–300% | 0–10% |
| Web press (newsprint) | SWOP newsprint | GCR | 30–40% | Medium | 85–95% | 260–280% | 0–10% |
| **European printing** | | | | | | | |
| Sheetfed (coated) | Eurostandard coated | GCR | 9–15% | Light/Medium | 95% | 320–350% | 0–10% |
| Sheetfed (uncoated) | Eurostandard uncoated | GCR | 15–25% | Light/Medium | 95% | 260–300% | 0–10% |
| Web press (coated) | Eurostandard coated | GCR | 15–20% | Light/Medium | 95% | 300–320% | 0–10% |
| Web press (uncoated) | Eurostandard uncoated | GCR | 20–30% | Light/Medium | 95% | 260–300% | 0–10% |
| Web press (newsprint) | Eurostandard newsprint | GCR | 30–40% | Medium | 85–95% | 260–280% | 0–10% |
| **Asian printing** | | | | | | | |
| Sheetfed (coated) | Toyo Inks coated | GCR | 8–15% | Light/Medium | 95% | 320–350% | 0–10% |
| Sheetfed (uncoated) | Toyo Inks uncoated | GCR | 15–25% | Light/Medium | 95% | 260–300% | 0–10% |
| Web press (coated) | Toyo Inks coated web offset | GCR | 12–20% | Light/Medium | 95% | 300–320% | 0–10% |
| Web press (uncoated) | Toyo Inks uncoated | GCR | 20–30% | Light/Medium | 95% | 260–300% | 0–10% |
| Web press (newsprint) | Toyo Inks uncoated | GCR | 30–40% | Medium | 85–95% | 260–280% | 0–10% |

**Figure 12.40** These separation guidelines reflect a typical range of settings one might use for each type of press output. These are guidelines only and reflect the settings you will already find in Photoshop. For more precise settings, consult your printer.

## Choosing a suitable RGB work space

The RGB space you choose to edit with can certainly influence the outcome of your CMYK conversions, which is why you should choose your RGB work space wisely. The default sRGB color space is widely regarded as an unsuitable space for photographic work because the color gamut of sRGB is in some ways smaller than the color gamut of CMYK and most inkjet printers. If you choose a color space like Adobe RGB to edit in, you will be working with a color space that can adequately convert from RGB to CMYK without any significant clipping of the CMYK colors. Figure 12.41 below highlights the deficiencies of editing in sRGB compared to editing in Adobe RGB.

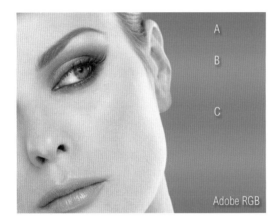

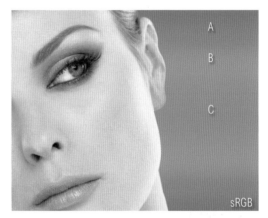

| CMYK Info (Adobe RGB) | A | B | C |
|---|---|---|---|
| Cyan | 97 | 75 | 95 |
| Magenta | 10 | 6 | 9 |
| Yellow | 96 | 8 | 5 |
| Black | 0 | 0 | 0 |

| CMYK Info (sRGB) | A | B | C |
|---|---|---|---|
| Cyan | 84 | 72 | 75 |
| Magenta | 18 | 7 | 10 |
| Yellow | 80 | 8 | 6 |
| Black | 1 | 0 | 0 |

**Figure 12.41** For the purposes of demonstrating the difference between two RGB color spaces. This example illustrates a Lab mode color image that was converted to CMYK once via Adobe RGB and once via sRGB. The color gradient was chosen to highlight the differences between these two RGB color spaces. The master image was converted to Adobe RGB and then to CMYK. A duplicate of the master was also converted to sRGB, and then to CMYK. As you can see, if you compare the separations shown above, the sRGB version is weaker at handling cyans and greens and there is also a slight boost in warmth to the skin tones.

**Which rendering intent is best?**

If you are converting photographic images from one color space to another, then you should mostly use the Relative Colorimetric or Perceptual rendering intents. Relative Colorimetric has always been the default Photoshop rendering intent and is still the best choice for most image conversions. I do also recommend that you use the Soft proofing method, described in the following chapter, to preview the outcome of any profile conversion and check to see if a Relative Colorimetric or Perceptual rendering will produce a better result.

# Rendering intents

When you make a profile conversion such as one going from RGB to CMYK, not all of the colors in the original source space can be expected to have a direct equivalent in the destination space. RGB is mostly bigger than CMYK and therefore those RGB colors that are regarded as 'out of gamut' will have to be translated to their nearest equivalent in the destination space. The way this translation is calculated is determined by the rendering intent. A rendering intent can be selected in the Color Settings to become the default rendering intent used in all color mode conversions. But you can override this setting and choose a different rendering intent when using Edit ⇨ Convert to Profile, or View ⇨ Proof Setup ⇨ Custom.

## Perceptual

Perceptual (Images) rendering is an all-round rendering method that can also be used for photographic images. Perceptual rendering compresses the out-of-gamut colors into the gamut of the target space in a rather generalized way, while preserving the visual relationship between those colors, so they do not become clipped. More compression occurs with the out-of-gamut colors, smoothly ramping to no compression for the in-gamut colors. Perceptual rendering provides a best guess method for converting out-of-gamut colors where it is important to preserve tonal separation. But Perceptual rendering is less suitable for images where there are fewer out-of-gamut colors.

## Saturation (Graphics)

The Saturation rendering intent preserves the saturation of out-of-gamut colors at the expense of hue and lightness. Saturation rendering will preserve the saturation of colors making them appear as vivid as possible after the conversion. This is a rendering intent best suited to the conversion of business graphic presentations where retaining bright bold colors is of prime importance.

### Relative Colorimetric

Relative Colorimetric is the default rendering intent utilized in the Photoshop color settings. Relative Colorimetric rendering maps the colors that are out of gamut in the source color space (relative to the target space) to the nearest 'in-gamut' equivalent in the target space. When doing an RGB to CMYK conversion, an out-of-gamut blue will be rendered the same CMYK value as a 'just-in-gamut' blue. Out-of-gamut RGB colors will therefore be clipped. This can be a problem when attempting to convert the more extreme range of out-of-gamut RGB colors to CMYK color. But if you are using the View ⇨ Proof Setup ⇨ Custom to call up the Customize Proof Condition dialog, you can check to see if this potential gamut clipping will cause the loss of any important image detail when converting to CMYK with a Relative Colorimetric conversion.

### Absolute Colorimetric

Absolute Colorimetric maps in-gamut colors exactly from one space to another with no adjustment made to the white and black points. This rendering intent can be used when you convert specific 'signature colors' and need to keep the exact hue, saturation and brightness, like the colors in a commercial logo design. This rendering intent is seemingly more relevant to the working needs of designers than photographers. However, you can use the Absolute Colorimetric rendering intent as a means of simulating a target CMYK output on a proofing device. Let's say you make a conversion from RGB to CMYK using either the Relative Colorimetric or Perceptual CMM and the target CMYK output is a newspaper color supplement printed on uncoated paper. If you use the Absolute Colorimetric rendering intent to convert these 'targeted' CMYK colors to the color space of the proofing device, the proofer will reproduce a simulation of what the printed output on that stock will look like. Note that when you select the Proof option in the Photoshop print dialog, the Absolute Colorimetric rendering is applied automatically to produce a simulated proof print.

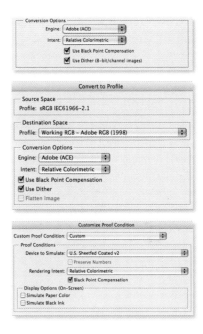

**Figure 12.42** The default rendering intent is set by choosing More Options in the Color Settings dialog and mousing down on the Intent menu in the Conversion Options. This default setting can be overridden when using the Convert to Profile command. You can also change the rendering intent in the Custom Proof dialog. This allows you to preview a simulated conversion without actually converting the RGB data.

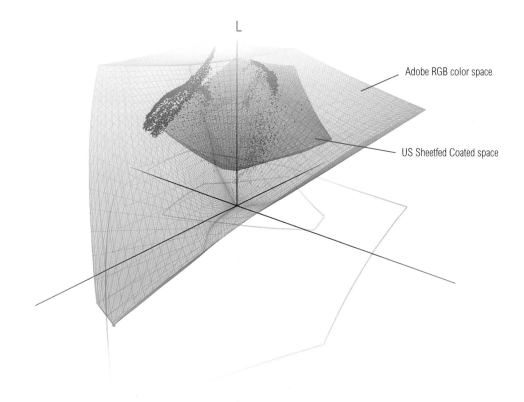

Adobe RGB color space

US Sheetfed Coated space

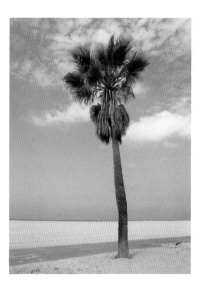

**Figure 12.43** To illustrate how the rendering intent can influence the outcome of a color mode or profile conversion I used Chromix ColorThink 2.1.2 to help me create the diagrams shown on these two pages. The above diagram shows the Adobe RGB color space overlaying a US Sheetfed Coated CMYK color space. As you can see, Adobe RGB is able to contain all the colors that will be squeezed into this smaller CMYK space. The photograph opposite has been plotted on this diagram so that the dots represent the distribution of RGB image colors within the Adobe RGB space.

When the colors in this image scene are converted to CMYK, the rendering intent will determine how the RGB colors that are outside the gamut limits of the CMYK space will be assigned a new color value. If you look now at the two diagrams on the opposite page you will notice the subtle differences between a relative colorimetric and a perceptual rendering. And I have highlighted a single blue color in each to point out these differences. The upper example shows a relative colorimetric rendering. You will notice that the out-of-gamut blue colors are all rendered to the nearest in-gamut CMYK equivalent. Compare this with the perceptually rendered diagram below and you will see that these same colors are squeezed in further. This rendering method will preserve the relationship between the out-of-gamut colors but at the expense of producing a less vibrant separation.

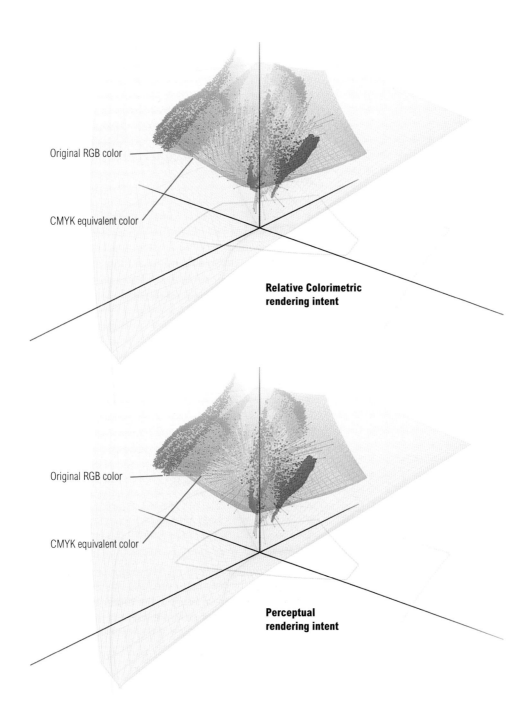

Original RGB color

CMYK equivalent color

**Relative Colorimetric
rendering intent**

Original RGB color

CMYK equivalent color

**Perceptual
rendering intent**

## CMYK to CMYK

It is not ideal for CMYK files to be converted to RGB and then converted back to CMYK. This is a sure-fire way to lose data fast! I always prefer to keep an RGB master of the image and convert to CMYK using a custom conversion to suit each individual print output. Converting from one CMYK space to another is not really recommended either, but in the absence of an RGB master, this will be the only option you have available. Just specify the CMYK profile you wish to convert to in the Convert to Profile dialog box. Remember, the Preserve Embedded Profiles policy will ensure that tagged incoming CMYK files can always be opened without converting them to your default CMYK space (because that would be a bad thing to do). This means that the numbers in the incoming CMYK files will always be preserved, while providing you with an accurate display of the colors on the screen.

## Lab Color

The Lab Color mode is available as a color mode to convert to via the Image ⇨ Mode menu and the Convert to Profile command, but does not use embedded profiles. Lab Color mode is assumed to be a universally understood color space, and it is argued by some that saving in Lab mode is one way of surmounting all the problems of mismatching RGB color spaces. You could make this work, so long as you didn't actually do anything to edit the image while it was in Lab mode. But overall, I would not really advise it. In fact, these days I see little reason to use the Lab Color mode for anything in Photoshop. Now, a few people did take me to task over these comments that were made in the previous edition of the book, so I suppose I should clarify my views. In the early days of Photoshop I would use Lab mode to do things like sharpen the Luminosity channel only, but in my view this, and the other Lab mode tricks I had learnt, soon became redundant as Photoshop started introducing things like layer blending modes and people devised better ways to apply image sharpening, such as the Bruce Fraser techniques I described earlier in Chapter 4.

## Info palette

Given the deficiencies of the color display on a monitor, such as its limited dynamic range and inability to reproduce colors like pure yellow on the screen, color professionals will often rely on the numeric information to assess an image. Certainly when it comes to getting the correct output of neutral tones, it is possible to predict with greater accuracy the neutrality of a gray tone by measuring the color values with the eyedropper tool. If the RGB numbers are all even, it is unquestionably gray (in a standard/linearized RGB editing space such as Adobe RGB). Interpreting the CMYK ink values is not so straightforward. A neutral CMYK gray is not made up of an even amount of cyan, yellow and magenta. If you compare the Color readout values between the RGB and CMYK Info palette readouts, there will always be more cyan ink used in the neutral tones, compared with the yellow and magenta inks. If the CMY values were even, you would see a color cast. This is due to the fact that the process cyan ink is less able to absorb its complementary color – red – compared to the way magenta and yellow absorb their complementary colors. This also explains why a CMY black will look reddish/brown, without the help of the black plate to add depth and neutrality.

## Keeping it simple

Congratulations on making it through to the end of this chapter! Your head may be reeling from all this information about Photoshop color management. But successful color management does not have to be complex. Firstly, you need to set the Color Settings to the prepress setting for your geographic region. This single step will configure the color management system with the best defaults for photographic work. The other thing you must do is to calibrate and profile the monitor. As I said before, if you want to do this right, you owe it to yourself to purchase a decent colorimeter device and ensure the monitor display is profiled regularly. Do these few things and you are most of the way there to achieving reliable color management.

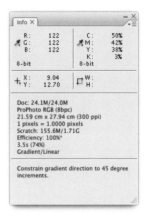

**Figure 12.44** When you are editing an RGB image, the Info palette readings can help you determine the neutrality of a color. If the RGB values are all equal, and the RGB color space you are editing in is one of the standard linear spaces, such as Adobe RGB, sRGB or ProPhoto RGB, etc., then the even RGB numbers will equal gray. But notice how the corresponding CMY numbers are not all even. A greater proportion of cyan ink is required to balance out with the magenta and yellow inks to produce a neutral gray color in print.

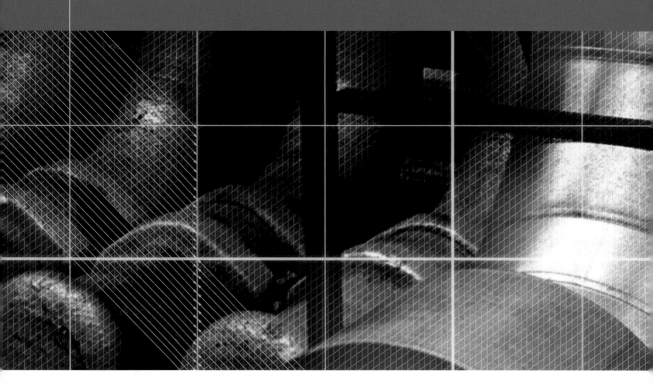

**Chapter 13**

# Print Output

The preceding chapter considered the issues of color management and how to maintain color consistency between digital devices. This chapter will deal with the process of making prints from your images. The standard of output available from digital continuous tone and inkjet printers has improved enormously over the last decade. There are so many print methods and printer models to choose from, so it is therefore important to understand what the strengths and weaknesses are of each. To start with you need to consider your main print output requirements. Are you looking for speed, volume printing or a high quality final art finish? And do you require your print output to form the basis of a repro contract print?

## Inkjet printers

Inkjet printers now dominate the printing market and are especially popular with photographers who are using Photoshop. Inkjet printers come in all shapes and sizes from small desktop devices to huge banner poster printers that are the width of a studio.

Inkjet printers work by spraying very fine droplets of ink as the head travels back and forth across the receiving media/paper. The different tonal densities are generally created by varying the number of evenly-sized individual droplets and dithering their distribution. Hence the illusion of a lighter tone is represented using sparsely scattered ink dots. The more recent printers are also able to produce variable-sized droplets. The Epson Stylus Photo models use six color inks and these are capable of producing an even smoother continuous tone output. The six color inkjets use additional light cyan and light magenta inks to render the paler color tones. The print output is still CMYK (or CcMmYK to be more accurate), but looks smoother because you have less noticeable dot dithering in the lighter areas. But the print times are also slower than the non-Stylus Photo models.

Inkjet printers are used for all sorts of printing purposes. An entry-level inkjet can cost as little as $150 and is suitable for anything from office letter printing to outputting photographs from Photoshop. And you don't have to spend much more than a few hundred dollars to buy an A4 or A3 printer that is capable of producing photo-realistic prints. Later on in this chapter I will discuss how it is possible to use a printer like this to produce acceptable guide prints for CMYK press color matching.

Although inkjets are CMYK (or CcMmYK) color devices, they work best when they are fed RGB data. This is because a lot of these printers use Quartz rendering (Mac) or GD (PC) drivers as opposed to PostScript. These print drivers can't understand CMYK. So if you send CMYK data to the driver it will convert the data from some form of generic CMYK to RGB before converting the data again to its own proprietary CMYK color.

### Inkjet origins

The first inkjet devices were manufactured by IRIS and designed for commercial CMYK proof printing on a limited range of paper stocks. It was largely due to the experimentation of country rock musician and photographer Graham Nash that the IRIS evolved to become an inkjet printing device suitable for producing fine art prints. This costly venture began in the early nineties and was to revolutionize the world of fine art printing thanks to these pioneering efforts. The IRIS printer stopped production in 2000 and its successor is the IXIA from Improved Technologies. The IRIS/IXIA is still favored by many artists, but in the last decade companies like Epson, Hewlett-Packard (HP) and Roland have developed high quality wide-format inkjet printers that are suitable for large format printing, including fine artwork applications.

The revolution in inkjet technology began at the high-end with expensive wide-format printers, but the technology soon diffused down to the desktop. Epson was one of the first companies to produce affordable high quality desktop printers. And Epson has retained its lead in printer and consumables technology, always coming out with new and better printers, inks and papers, although companies like Canon and Hewlett-Packard are now beginning to regain their slices of the printer market with printers to rival Epson's continuing dominance.

## Branded consumables

The inkjet manufacturers like to sell their printers cheaply and then make their profit through the sales of proprietary inks designed for their printers. If you care to read the small print, using anything but the manufacturer's own inks may void the manufacturer's guarantee. But this should not necessarily discourage you from experimenting with other ink and paper combinations and apparently this situation is being legally challenged in the USA. It has to be said that the number of ink and paper products you can buy these days is quite bewildering. But overall, I recommend that you mostly stick to using the proprietary brand inks for the best quality results.

## Hewlett-Packard Z series

The Z series printers include two 12-ink color models. These printers have an incredibly wide color gamut which is achieved by the addition of red, green and blue inks.

If you perform the color management in Photoshop and disable the printer color management, it is also possible to produce what is known as a cross-rendered CMYK guide print from an RGB file, using the Proof Setup dialog to specify a CMYK space to proof with.

### The ideal inkjet

Your first consideration will probably be the print size and how big you need your prints to be. Most desktop inkjet printers are able to print up to A3+ (13" × 19"), while the Epson 3800 can print up to A2 (16.5" × 23.5") size. The wide-format printers like the Epson 9600 and 10600 can print up to 44" wide and the Hewlett-Packard printers as wide as 96". The Hewlett-Packard Z series also has built-in Gretag Macbeth calibrators that can help maintain closed-loop color accuracy. The bigger printers are designed to be freestanding and therefore require a lot of office space. Wide-format printers are suitable for all commercial purposes and are particularly popular with fine art photographers who need to produce extra-large exhibition quality art prints.

### Photographic print quality

Almost any inkjet printer can give you acceptable print quality, but some printers are definitely more suited to photographic quality printing than others. The Epson Stylus Photo range of printers are marketed as a good choice for photographic print output because they use specially formulated inks and print with six or more ink colors, which can yield superb results. Printers like these and others can also be adapted to take third-party inks that are specially formulated for black and white or archival printing. The Epson 3800 printers are suitable for archival printing and have an extra light black ink which also makes this an almost ideal printer for black and white work, as is the more robust Epson 4800, which offers bigger ink cartridges. In recent years, Hewlett-Packard has ramped up its range of photo printers. The PhotoSmart 9180 is a personal favorite because it is simple to set up and also features a built-in calibration device.

## Image permanence

The permanence of an inkjet print will be determined by a variety of factors. Mostly it is down to the combination of the inks and media that are used to produce the print, followed by the environment in which a print is kept or displayed and whether it has been specially treated to prevent fading. Light remains the biggest enemy though. If prints are intended for long-term exhibition, then you have to make sure that you use a suitable ink and paper combination, and that the prints are displayed behind UV filtered glass and sited so they are not exposed to direct sunlight every day.

## Inks and media

To start with I recommend that you explore using the proprietary inks and papers that are 'officially' designated for use with your printer. Firstly, it should be pointed out that the manufacturing engineers have designed these ink and paper products expressly for their printers and, secondly, the printer companies will usually supply canned profiles which, although not perfect, can be very useful at getting you an approximately matching print (providing you use their ink and paper of course). And thirdly, if you stick to using proprietary inks and papers at the beginning there are fewer variables for you to worry about when you are learning how to print from Photoshop.

There are two types of inks used in inkjet printers. Dye inks were once the most popular because they were capable of producing the purest colors. But the dye molecules in such inks were also known to lack stability. This means they were prone to deteriorate and fade when exposed to prolonged intense light exposure, high humidity or reactive chemicals. Pigment-based inks have a more complex molecular structure and as a result are less prone to fading. But pigmented inks have traditionally been considered less vivid than dye inks and have a restricted color palette (the color gamut is smaller).

Some modern inks use a hybrid combination of dyes and pigments. Some of these specially formulated

### Wilhelm Imaging Research

Henry Wilhelm has conducted much research into the various factors that affect the permanence of inkjet prints. The Wilhelm Imaging Research website contains print permanence reports for several printers. Henry has also coauthored a book: *The Permanence and Care of Color Photographs: Traditional and Digital Color Prints, Color Negatives, Slides, and Motion Pictures*, which offers a definitive account on the subject. For more information go to: www.wilhelmresearch.com.

### Third-party delays

As new printers come to market it can take a while for third-party companies to devise their own ink sets. One reason for this is the way that recent inkjets have smart chips fitted to the ink cartridges. These are meant to alert the print driver when they are low on ink, but they are also harder to copy. Third-party manufacturers have to devise a way to reverse-engineer their cartridges so as to work with the newer printers.

## Inkjet economies

Ink cartridges don't come cheap and once you get into serious print making, you will soon get through a lot of expensive cartridges. I don't recommend you economize by buying ink refill kits as these are very messy to use. In the long run it can work out more economical if you buy a printer that uses single ink cartridges with higher ink capacities (don't forget there are some places where you can recycle your used cartridges). Another solution is to invest in a continuous inkflow system (CIS). These can be bought as kits which you use to modify your printer. In place of the normal ink cartridges, you have a special cartridge that links to separate ink reservoirs that can feed a continuous flow of ink to the printer head. The advantages are that you don't have to keep replacing ink cartridges and it is more efficient and economical to run. Companies supplying continuous inkflow systems include: Lyson, NoMoreCarts CIS, MIS Cobra CFS, Camel Ink Systems CRS and MediaStreet Niagra II Continuous Ink Flow System.

## Optimizing the printer

Neil Barstow is a UK-based color management consultant who offers a CD containing a manual and test files to help you optimize your printer settings. For more information on this and his UK-based color consultation services, go to: www.colourmanagement.net.

Neil is able to offer an introductory discount on his consultancy services to readers (see the special offers section at the back of this book).

pigment-based ink and paper combinations will produce bright prints that also have exceptional image permanence. When using the correct paper and inks, the life expectancy is predicted to be over 100 years and may be as long as 200 years with certain paper combinations.

## Third-party inks

These are mostly designed for the Epson printers and even then you will find that not all printer models are supported. Lyson make a range of inks for both color and black and white printing. The Lyson Fotonic color inks are designed to provide increased image permanence and in some instances actually have a slightly larger gamut than the standard Epson inks. Whenever third-party inks are used, you will almost certainly want to have custom profiles made for each ink and paper combination. To work with third-party inks and papers a user must first optimize the printer settings.

A lot of photographers like to use the special black ink sets such as the Lyson Quad Black and Small Gamut (SG) inks, MIS Quadtones, MIS Variable Mix (VM) Quadtones and Lumijet Monochrome Plus monochrome inks. These black ink sets can be used with four- or six-color printers in place of the usual color inks. They print overlaying inks of varying gray lightness in place of the usual CMYK inks and have the potential to make rich-toned fine-art prints with good image permanence on a variety of paper surfaces. When ordering ink supplies you need to make sure that the cartridges are compatible with the printer and, if using a custom profile, are of the same type. But the paper can be equally critical. The premium glossy and semi-gloss paper is a popular choice for photographers as these papers match the quality of a normal photographic print surface and the print longevity when used with Epson 4000 is estimated to be up to 60 years. A lot of photographers and artists have enjoyed experimenting with various fine-art paper stocks. When these are combined with the right types of ink, it is possible to produce prints that can be expected to last even longer.

# Print sharpening

Earlier in Chapter 4, I outlined some of the ways you could go about pre-sharpening an image to optimize it for input. This type of sharpening is best thought of as corrective sharpening. The aim here is to sharpen the photograph just enough so as to compensate for the loss of sharpness that is a natural consequence of the capture process. Output sharpening is a different matter. Any time you output a photograph to be printed – either in a magazine, on a bill board, or when you send it to a desktop printer – it will always benefit from a significant amount of pre-sharpening. Some output processes may incorporate some automatic output sharpening, but most don't. It is therefore a good idea to always include an output sharpening step just before you make any kind of print. The question next is how much should you sharpen? The following steps show a simple sharpening routine that is ideal for print output.

## High Pass filter edge sharpening

The technique described over the page is one of several that were devised by Bruce Fraser for his Photokit Sharpener product. The settings shown here would be suitable for a making a medium-sized print at 300 pixels per inch on a typical inkjet printer, using glossy paper. But if one wanted to adapt this for other print resolutions and output devices, you would need to do what Bruce and Jeff Schewe did, and carry out a lot of research, testing the action settings with different paper types and sizes, and at different print resolutions, and modify the steps and settings used.

The sharpening technique shown here will produce quite aggressive sharpening, but the only way to effectively judge the correct amount of sharpening to apply for output is to evaluate the printed output. You cannot rely on the screen to be your guide, because the amount of sharpening that is required to make a decent-looking print will look awful when viewed on the display. You can try reducing the document zoom level to 50% or 25% to get a better impression of what the printed image will look like, but even so the only way to truly judge is by making a print.

## Real World Sharpening

If you want to find out more about Bruce Fraser's writing on sharpening and output sharpening, I can again recommend his book: *Real World Sharpening with Adobe Photoshop CS2*. ISBN: 0-321-44991-6. Bruce is sadly no longer with us, but the techniques in his book, although described for Photoshop CS2, are still completely valid when working with Photoshop CS3.

## Judge the print, not the monitor

It is difficult to judge the correct amount to sharpen an image for a print output when you are using a monitor to preview the image. At a normal viewing distance, the human eye can resolve detail to around 1/100th of an inch. So if the image you are editing is going to be printed from a file with a resolution of 300 pixels per inch, the edges will need a 3 pixel Radius if they are to register as sharp in print. When an image is viewed on a monitor at 100%, this kind of sharpening will look oversharp and quite ugly, because at a 100% screen view you are viewing the image much closer up than it will actually be viewed when printed. This is why it is better to prejudge the output sharpening at a lower zoom percentage such as 50% or 25% even.

## Printing resolution

Inkjet printers will typically allow you to print using a range of DPI settings. With the Epson printers, some people advise you to use a pixel resolution that is a divisible number of the print head resolution.

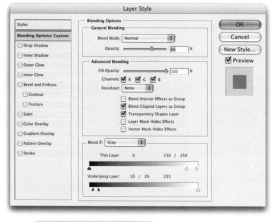

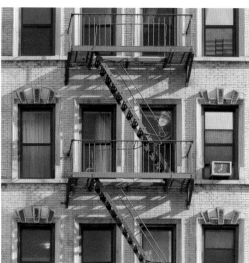

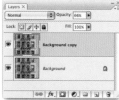

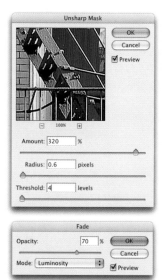

**1** The Bruce Fraser output sharpening method described here is the basis for sharpening an inkjet print on glossy paper at 300 ppi. You begin by making a duplicate copy of the Background layer and set the layer opacity to 66%, and double-click on the duplicate layer to open the layer blending options and make the Blend If sliders match the settings shown here.

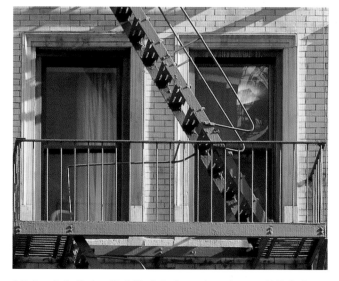

**2** Next, apply the Unsharp Mask filter to the layer using an Amount of 320, Radius of 0.6 and Threshold of 4. Then choose Edit ⇨ Fade, change the blend mode to Luminosity and reduce the opacity to 70%.

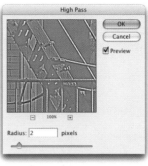

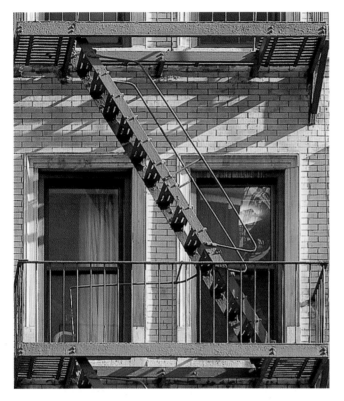

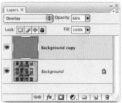

**3** Now change the Layer blend mode from Normal to Overlay and apply the Other
⇨ High Pass filter, using a Radius of 2 pixels. Note that the sharpening layer
can be increased or decreased in opacity or easily removed so that the underlying
Background layer remains unaffected by the sharpening steps.

## Making a print

There have been a few changes made to the print routines
in Photoshop CS3. What we have now is a Page Setup...
menu (⌘ Shift P ctrl Shift P) for setting up the printer
and paper settings and a Photoshop application Print...
menu item (⌘ P ctrl P) that will now take you
directly to the Photoshop Print dialog (formerly known
as Print with Preview). The Print One Copy command is
there should you wish to make a print using the current
configuration for a particular image, but wish to bypass the
print dialogs. But do heed my warnings about print settings
not always being sticky!

## Saving print presets

To help minimize print setup errors, it is often worth creating print presets. Apply all your page setup and print settings first, then pull down the Print Presets menu (see page 605), choose Save As… from the bottom, and name it appropriately.

## Page Setup

The first thing you need to do is go to the Page Setup dialog and make sure the right printer is selected (you may have to do this each time in Mac OS X). Choose a paper size that matches the paper you are about to print with and choose the right orientation: either portrait or landscape.

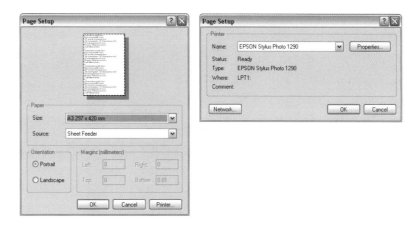

**Figure 13.1** On a PC computer, go to the File menu and choose: Page Setup... In the main Page Setup dialog you will want to click on the Printer... button to select which printer model you want to print to. Click OK and this will return you to the Page Setup dialog again where you can select the paper size, print feed method and print orientation: Portrait or Landscape.

## Scale setting in Page Setup

Although the Mac OS X Page Setup dialog will allow you to adjust the print scale size, I don't advise you to use this – either here or in the Photoshop Print dialog – unless you absolutely must. It is always much better to resize the image in Photoshop first and print at a 100% scale size.

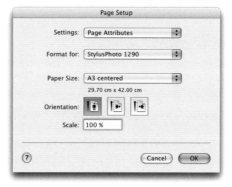

**Figure 13.2** On Macintosh OS X, again go to the File menu and choose: Page Setup... Where it says: Format For, select the printer you want to print to and then select the paper size and print orientation: Portrait or Landscape.

### Ensuring your prints are centered

We would all love Photoshop printing to be simpler, but unfortunately there are no easy solutions and this is not necessarily all Adobe's fault either. The problem is that you have a multitude of different printer devices out there and in addition to this, you have two main types of operating systems, each of which has their own protocols as to how the system print dialogs should be organized.

Making sure a print is centered is just one of several problems that require a little user intervention. If you center a print in the Photoshop Print dialog and yet it does not print centered, this is probably due to the default margin settings being uneven. The reason for this is that some printers require a trailing edge margin that is wider than all the other margins. But as I have shown below, you can overcome this by creating your own custom paper sizes and margin settings.

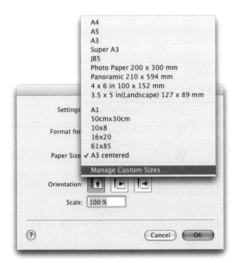
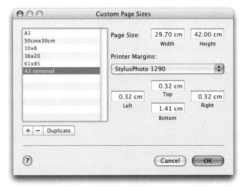

**Figure 13.3** On Mac OS X, go to the Page Setup menu and choose Manage Custom Sizes... In the Custom Page Size dialog check out the margin width for the bottom trailing edge margin for the selected printer. If you want your prints to be centered when printing landscape or portrait, all you have to do is to adjust the Top margin width so that it matches this bottom measurement. Set a Width and Height for the new paper size and save this as a new paper size setting and add 'centered' so you can easily locate it when using the Page Setup dialog.

## Output options

To apply some of the Output options mentioned here, you must be using a PostScript print driver and you should also allow enough border space surrounding the print area to print these extra items.

For example, when the Include Vector Data option is unchecked, it will rasterize the vector layer information, such as type at the image file resolution. However, if it is checked, it will rasterize the vector information such as type much crisper at the full printer resolution, provided that you are outputting from a PostScript RIP.

## Freeform placement on the page

When the bounding box is made visible, you can drag the box and box handles to visually arrange the page position and scale. If a selection is active before you select Print Options and Print Selected Area is checked, the selected area only will be printed.

## Photoshop Print dialog

When you choose Print... from the File menu, Photoshop CS3 now takes you by default to what I prefer to describe as the Photoshop Print dialog (as opposed to the System Print dialog). This dialog used to be known as Print with Preview and it has since undergone a major overhaul to provide better settings control and a larger color managed print preview. But first we shall look at the Output settings.

## *Output settings*

To adjust the Output settings, make sure that Output is selected from the top menu. The Printer model you selected in Page Setup will be visible in the Printer menu and below that you will see a Page Setup... button. You could, if you like, bypass going to Page Setup and access everything via this Photoshop Print dialog. Although, if you are using a PC, the Page Setup will now take you directly to the system print dialog, because you have already chosen a printer model and the paper size, and orientation controls will also be available in the system print dialogs. Oh boy, see my comments on the previous page about the operating systems forcing the print pipelines to be so different and confusing.

When the Center Image box is deselected and the Show Bounding box is enabled, you can position an image anywhere you like, by dragging inside the preview area. Or, you can position the image by entering in measurements for the Top and Left margins. In the Scaled Print Size section, if the image overflows the currently selected page size, you can choose Scale to Fit Media, which will automatically resize the pixel resolution to fit the page (the Print resolution PPI will adjust) and you can also enter a specific Scale percentage, or Height and Width for the image. But as I pointed out on page 598, it is not really a good idea to resize the image via the Print dialog if you can help it.

On the right, you can select any extra items you wish to see printed outside the image area. The Calibration Bars will print an 11-step grayscale wedge on the left and a smooth gray ramp on the right. If you are printing CMYK separations, tint bars can be printed for each plate color and the Registration Marks will help a printer align the separate plates. The Corner and Center Crop Marks will indicate where to trim the image and the Bleed button option lets you set how much to indent these crop marks by. Checking the Description box will print any text that was entered in the File ⇨ File Info box Description field and check the Labels box to have the file name printed below the picture. Click on the Background... button to print with a background color other than paper white. For example, when sending the output to a film writer, you would choose black as the background color. Click on the Border... button to set the width for a black border, if desired. But be aware that setting the border width can be an unpredictable business. If you set too narrow a width, the border may print with an uneven width on one or more sides of the image.

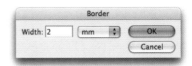

**Figure 13.4** The Border option will allow you to add a black border and choose the size.

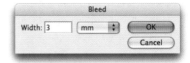

**Figure 13.5** The Bleed option will work in conjunction with the Corner Crop Marks option and determine how far to position them from the edge of the printed image.

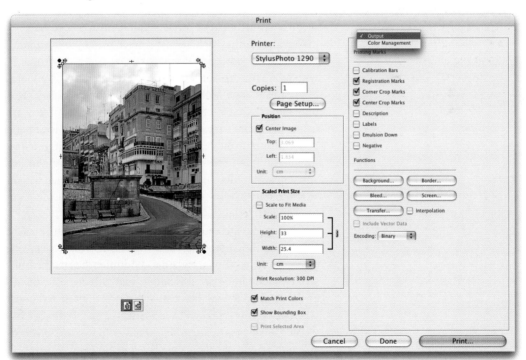

**Figure 13.6** The Photoshop Print dialog, showing the Output options.

601

## About the print dialogs

The following dialogs include the Mac and PC instructions for the Epson 1290 inkjet printer settings. The Epson interface and main controls will be fairly similar for other makes of inkjet printers, but not identical. Figure 13.8 shows how I would go about making a print from an RGB image in Photoshop using one of the Epson 1290 printer profiles that were automatically loaded when I installed the Epson 1290 printer driver on my computer.

## Accessing canned printer profiles

A set of canned printer profiles should have been installed in your System profiles folder at the same time as you installed the print driver for your printer.

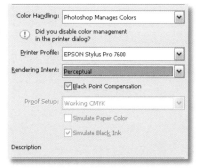

**Figure 13.7** If you are printing to an Epson printer on a PC and choose Photoshop Manages Colors, you will only be able to select the name of the printer from the profile list. Use the system print dialog to select the correct paper setting and this will be the same as selecting the printer paper profile as described for the Mac.

## Color Management

Now let's look at the Color Management settings for the Photoshop Print dialog. The source space can be the document profile (which in this case was ProPhoto RGB). If you click on the Proof button it will default to using the current CMYK work space, and later in this chapter I will be showing you how to use this feature.

Next we come to the Color Handling section. If printing from an RGB image, there are three options. No Color Management is used when printing out a target print for building a print profile (more of which later). The Printer Manages Colors option can be used if you want to skip to the system Print dialog and let the printer driver manage the color output. Or, the Photoshop Manages Colors option, which is shown in Figure 13.8, can be used. When this is selected you can use the Photoshop Print dialog to manage the print color pipeline and switch color management off in the system Print dialog. Mouse down on the Printer Profile menu and a long list of profiles will appear. Select the printer profile that matches the printer/paper you are about to print with. However, if you are using an Epson printer with a PC, the canned printer profiles will not be available to Photoshop within the application Print dialog; they can only be accessed via the Printer driver dialog. So if you are using an Epson printer with a PC computer, select the name of the printer from the Printer Profile menu. But if you have custom printer profiles available for your Epson printer, you can select these in the Printer Profile menu, just as you would on the Mac.

The Rendering Intent can be set to Perceptual, Saturation, Relative Colorimetric or Absolute Colorimetric. For normal RGB printing the choice boils down to the choice of two settings. Relative Colorimetric is the best setting to use for general printing, as it will preserve most of the original colors. Perceptual is a good option to choose when printing a richly colored image (or one with a lot of deep shadows) to a smaller gamut output space, such as a fine-art matte paper. Whichever option you choose, I would advise you to have Black Point Compensation

switched on, because this will map the darkest colors from
the source space to the destination print space. Black Point
Compensation will help preserve the darkest black colors
and maximize the full tonal range of the print output.
The Print dialog preview is also fully color managed.
Admittedly, the preview could have been a lot bigger,
but it does at least now give you some indication of how
a photograph will print. You will notice that as you pick
a printer profile or adjust the rendering intents, you can
preview on screen what the printed colors will look like
and, when proofing an RGB output in this way, you will
also be shown a preview that simulates the black ink and
paper white colors. This soft proofing option can be turned
off if you like by deselecting the Match Print Colors option.

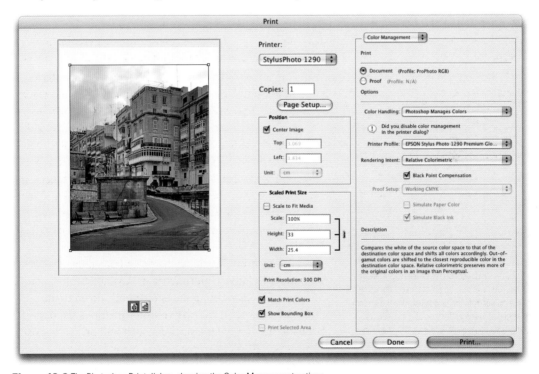

**Figure 13.8** The Photoshop Print dialog, showing the Color Management options.

## System Print dialog settings

Click Print... in the Photoshop Print dialog and you will be taken to either of the system print dialogs shown here, where you can configure the printer driver settings.

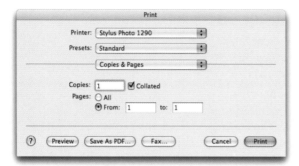

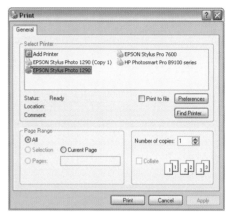

**1** No preset settings have been saved yet. In Mac OS X, mouse down on the Copies and Pages pop-up menu and choose 'Print Settings'. On a PC, select the printer and click on the Preferences... button to proceed to the next step.

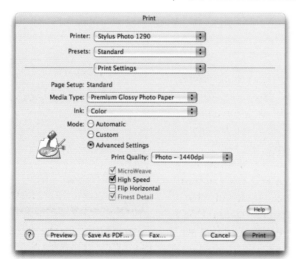

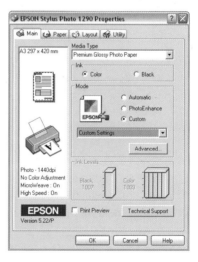

**2** Now select a media type that matches the paper you are going to print with. In Mac OS X, click on the Advanced Settings button and choose a print resolution (1440 dpi will produce nice smooth results). On a PC, first select the Media Type, click on the Custom button in the Printer Properties dialog and then click on the Advanced... button to proceed to the Advanced dialog settings.

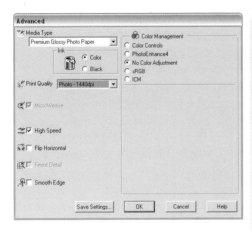
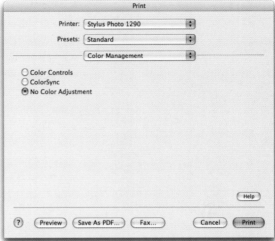

**3** In the Advanced section on a PC you can now set the print resolution quality. In the Color Management section click on the No Color Adjustment button. This is because you do not need to make any further color adjustments. The steps carried out at Step 2 will have established the Printer Profile setting in the PC print dialog. If using Mac OS X, go to the Color Management print settings option and click on the No Color Adjustment button. All you have to do now is click on the Print button at the bottom of the Mac dialog, or click OK in the PC Advanced dialog and wait for your image to print.

### System print dialog options

The system print dialog options will vary a lot from printer to printer as well as having Mac and PC variations. You may have a lot of options available to choose from and your printer driver may look quite different. But if you are using the Photoshop Print dialog to manage the colors, the main things to watch out for here is that you select the correct media setting in the print settings and that you turn off printer color management, which means selecting 'No Color Adjustment' in the Color Management section. Don't pay any attention to any of the other options you might see such as: 'EPSON Vivid' or 'Charts and Graphs'.

In the Print settings, a higher print resolution will produce marginally better-looking prints, but take longer to print. The High Speed option will enable the print head to print in both directions. Some people prefer to disable this option when making fine quality prints.

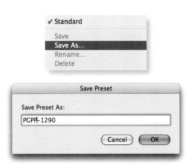

**Figure 13.9** Once you have established the print settings shown here for a particular printing setup, it makes sense to save these settings as a preset that can easily be accessed every time you want to make a print using the same printer and paper combination. It is also the only way for the settings to remain 'sticky'.

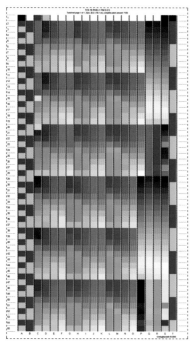

**Figure 13.10** Here is an example of a Gretag MacBeth color target which is used to construct an ICC color profile. A target file must be opened in Photoshop without any color conversion and the file sent directly to the printer, again without any color management and the print dimensions must remain exact. If it is necessary to resize the ppi resolution, make sure that the Nearest Neighbor interpolation mode is selected.

The print outputs are then measured using a reflective spectrophotometer and a profile built from these measurements. All you have to do is make a neutral path print, as shown on the following pages. A third-party profiling service such as Neil Barstow's (see the Special Offers page at the back of the book) will be able to supply you with the test chart and printing instructions. You mail the color management service provider a print and they will email a printer profile back to you.

## Building a custom printer profile

If you followed the previous steps carefully, then you should be getting the colors to match near enough what you are seeing on the monitor. And if not, then I suggest you check the calibration of your display and rebuild the monitor profile, although it is never possible to create a complete match between the display and the print, even under ideal light viewing conditions. But if you want to take your color management one step further, why not consider having a custom profile built for your favorite ink and paper combinations? Most of the canned inkjet printer profiles that I have come across are not that bad. They are able to get the colors to reproduce fairly well in print, but some do have a tendency to clog up the shadow detail. I would imagine that this is done deliberately to help improve the appearance of poorer quality images. But if you want to obtain the best results from your printer and have profiles made for non-regular ink and paper combinations then you need to have some custom printer profiles made.

If you don't have the necessary profiling kit and software, the most obvious thing to do is to contract the work out to a specialist service provider. For example, colourmanagement.net are offering a special coupon to readers of this book that will entitle you to a discount on their remote printer profiling services. Details of this offer are at the back of this book.

### *Printing a printer test target*

The next series of screen shots lead you through the steps to follow when printing out a target like the one shown in Figure 13.10. The important points to bear in mind here are that you must not color manage the target image. The idea is to produce a print in which the pixel values are sent directly to the printer without any color management being applied. The patch readings are then used to build a profile that will later be able to convert the image data to produce the correct-looking colors. The remaining Print dialog settings should be saved so that the same print settings can be applied as when you printed the test target.

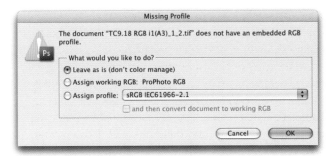

**1** Open a test chart file like the one shown in Figure 13.10. Such files are included as part of any print profiling package or supplied to you by the color management service provider. This file will have no embedded profile and it is essential that it is opened without making any conversions and is always printed at the exact same print size dimensions.

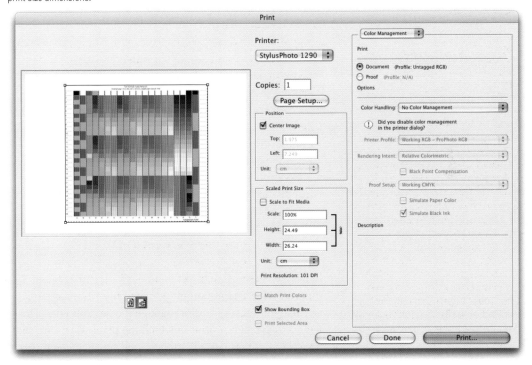

**2** Configure the Page Setup as shown earlier and choose File ➪ Print. The Print space should say Document: (Profile: Untagged RGB). The idea here is that you want to create a print output of the unprofiled data without applying any printer color management. In the Color Handling section, select the No Color Management option. Do not adjust the scale as it is very important this remains at 100%. When you have done this click Print...

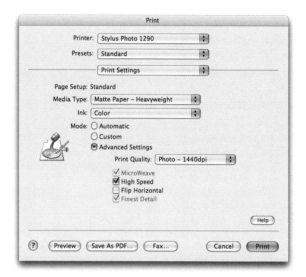

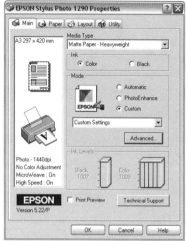

**3** In the Mac OS X Print settings section, choose the appropriate media type and the desired print resolution. In this example, I was building a profile for the Hahnemuhle Fine Art Rag paper, so I selected: Matte Paper – Heavyweight media type. On a PC, click the Custom button, choose a media type and click on the Advanced button.

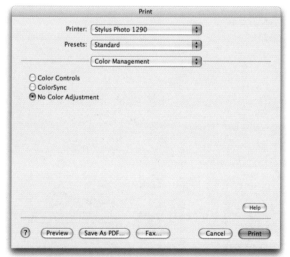

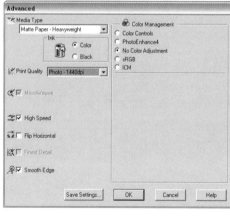

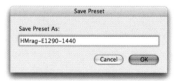

**4** On a Mac go to the Color Management and choose 'No Color Adjustment'. On a PC, go to the Advanced section, select the print quality resolution and in the color management section select 'No Color Adjustment'. However you need to configure these settings, they should now be saved as a named preset (in this example I named it as 'HMrag-E1290-1440'). This same setting should be used whenever you make a print using the custom profile.

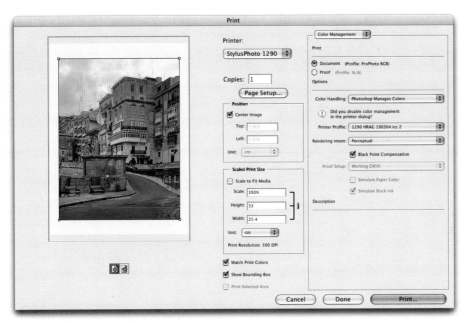

**5** The target print should stabilize for at least 24 hours before it can be measured and a profile built. This profile will be applicable for use with your printer, using the same ink sets and with the same media/paper type and print settings as were used to generate the printed target. The custom printer profile must be installed in the appropriate operating system ColorSync profiles folder. When you go to the Print dialog always choose Photoshop Manages Colors and select the custom profile as the Printer Profile.

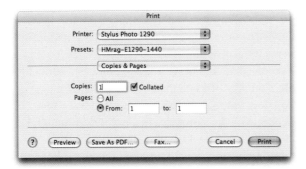

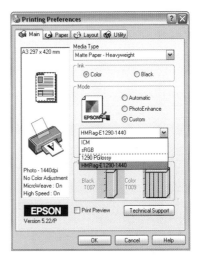

**6** When you go to the system Print dialog make sure you select the same preset setting that you saved when creating the target print (on a PC you need to click on the Preferences button to get to the dialog shown here). And that's it. Once you have established and saved the print settings and installed the printer profile correctly you only need to follow the two steps shown on this page each time you make a print.

## Installing custom printer profiles

The custom printer profiles should be saved using the following locations: Library/ColorSync/Profiles folder (Mac OS X), WinNT/System32/Color folder (2000), Windows/System/Color folder (PC).

## Inkjet papers

The optical brightener additives contained in many of today's inkjet papers can also bring about quite a noticeable shift in the way a print is perceived under different lighting conditions. If there is a high amount of UV light present the whites will look much brighter, but also bluer compared to a print that has been made using a paper stock such as GMG Premium Proofing papers, which are ideally suited for CMYK proof printing and viewed using controlled lighting with a color temperature of 5000 K.

## Output through a RIP

Some standard print drivers may use a mix of inks to print dark colors. But a good photo RIP like ColorBurst™ will use proper black generation (GCR) control to minimize color shifts in prints.

# Getting the most from your printer profiles

There is no such thing as a perfect color management workflow. Allowances will always need to be made for a small margin for error, but if you follow the guidelines carefully you should attain impressive results even from a modest desktop printer. And to fully appreciate the fruits of your labors you really need a calibrated light viewing box to view the prints correctly. Many inkjet prints take a while to dry after they come off the printer. A print produced on an older printer like the Epson 1290 can at first look quite green in the shadows, but after a few hours the ink colors will stabilize and the green cast eventually disappears. This is why you are often advised to wait at least 24 hours before measuring your printed target prints. Then there is the issue of what is commonly described as 'metamerism'. This refers to the phenomenon where when viewing under different lighting conditions, the ink dye/pigment colors will respond differently. This problem can be particularly noticeable when a monochrome image is printed using color inks. Although the color management can appear to be working fine when a print is viewed under studio lighting, if this environment is changed, and the print is viewed in daylight from a window, the print can appear to have a green cast. There was an example of this with the early Epson Ultrachrome 2000 printer where the pigment-based ink suffered from this green shift in daylight problem. The later Ultrachrome printers have almost managed to resolve this.

Even despite your best efforts to produce a perfect profile, you may just find that a specific color on the display does not match exactly. I sometimes see this happening with the skin tones in a portrait. Although I usually obtain a perfect match with a specific ink and paper profile combination, sometimes the printed result is just a fraction out on an item of clothing or in the skin tones, but every other color looks just fine. This could indicate that it is time to recheck the monitor calibration or it could be that you need to adjust the printer profile. If you know what you are doing it is possible to tweak profiles using a program like Gretag MacBeth's ProfileMaker Pro™. But I often just add a temporary Hue/Saturation adjustment layer using this to make a minor correction by targeting, say, the reds of the skin tones, and shift them to become 2–3% more yellow. But another more obvious reason why there may be a difference in the colors seen is that the color gamut of the printer is not as large as the gamut of the display on which you are viewing the image. This is where soft proofing can sometimes help you achieve more predictable results.

## Soft proofing via the display

When you carry out a color mode conversion or a Convert to Profile command, the color data is converted to the destination/device color space. When the file is in this new space, Photoshop will continue to color manage the image. If you are converting an RGB master to the CMYK work space, Photoshop will simulate the CMYK print output appearance on the monitor after the file has been converted to CMYK. But you don't have to completely convert an RGB image to CMYK in order to preview it in a CMYK color space. If you are editing an RGB master and go to the View ⇨ Proof Setup menu and select Working CMYK (which is the default setting), you can create a preview of how the colors would look if you converted from RGB to the working CMYK color space using the default rendering intent. This is known as soft proofing (a real proof is a hard copy print produced by a contract standard proof printer). If you choose the Custom... option you can select any profile space you want from the pop-up list in the Customize Proof Condition dialog and select different rendering intents.

The monitor will never be as accurate when it comes to showing how every CMYK color will reproduce, but it is usually close enough for carrying out all the preparation work, before reaching the stage where a final contract proof is demanded. Good quality displays such as the Eizo Color Edge CG 221 have larger color gamuts than most other monitors and are therefore particularly suited for soft proofing CMYK colors on the screen.

**Eizo ColorEdge™ displays**

Eizo is a Japanese company which produces a range of LCD displays, which includes the top of the range ColorEdge CG221 22" display. This monitor is the preferred choice of many high-end retouchers and the gamut of the screen is large enough to encompass the Adobe RGB color space, which in turn can be used to simulate quite accurately almost all the colors in a CMYK output.

## Proofing other output spaces

The Proof Setup is not just limited to CMYK output. You can use the Proof Setup to preview RGB conversions to RGB output devices or do things like preview how a prepress grayscale file will appear on a Macintosh or Windows RGB monitor. And you can load a custom profile for your printer to gain a more accurate preview of how an image will print. Each new window view can preview a different proofing setup. So, for example, you can create several new window views of the same document and compare the results of outputting to various types of press output directly on the display.

You can save a custom proof setting as a '.psf' file in the Users/Username/Library/Application Support/Adobe/Color/Proofing folder (Mac OS X), or the Program Files/Common Files/Adobe/Color/Proofing folder (PC). This saved proof setting will then be appended to the bottom of the list in the Customize Proof Condition dialog.

You don't have to keep returning to the Customize Proof Condition dialog. Once you have established a custom proof setting you can preview the colors in this space by simply choosing View ⇨ Proof Colors, or use the keyboard shortcut ⌘ Y ctrl Y to toggle the preview on and off. This keyboard shortcut makes it very easy for you to switch from normal to proof viewing mode. The document window title bar will also display the name of the proofing space after the color mode: RGB/Working CMYK.

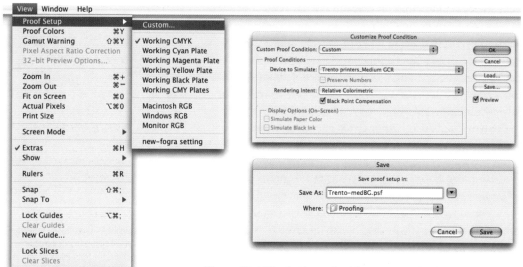

**Figure 13.11** Use the View ⇨ Proof Setup menu to select the device or color space you wish to soft proof with, whenever the Proof Colors command ⌘ Y ctrl Y is applied. If you click on Custom... this will take you to the Customize Proof Condition dialog, where you can select the profile of your printer or CMYK print output. In this example, I selected a custom CMYK setting for the book printers who are based in Italy.

## Display simulation options

When you select the Proof Colors option from the View menu, Photoshop takes the current display view and converts it on-the-fly to the destination color space selected in the Proof Setup. The data is then converted back to the RGB monitor space to form a preview using the relative colorimetric rendering intent and with black point compensation switched on. In simpler terms, the image you see on the display is effectively filtered by the profile space selected in the Customize Proof Condition dialog.

The Proof Colors view provides you with an advance indication of how a file might reproduce after it has been converted to CMYK (or any other print output space) and printed. The Proof Colors view may make the monitor image appear more muted, but it will more accurately reflect the appearance of the final print output. Even though the colors may look more flat, the image on the screen will still be optimized to the full contrast range of the display.

The Simulate Paper Color and Black Ink options enable you to achieve a more accurate simulation, one that takes into account the color of the paper and the black ink density. Simulate Paper Color will simulate how the whites in the image will appear, by simulating the color of the paper on the screen, and will use an absolute Colorimetric rendering to convert the proof color space data to the monitor space; it also simulates both the color of the paper and the black ink color density. However, the Paper Color simulation only works if the CMYK profile used is made on the actual paper stock used for printing, and only if this paper doesn't have too much optical brightener in it (otherwise the results will look bluish on screen). It is rather disappointing to see the display preview image deteriorate in front of your eyes in this way, so I follow Bruce Fraser's advice and try looking away from the display just prior to checking these press simulation settings.

The Simulate Black Ink option will simulate on screen the actual black density of the printing press by turning off the black point compensation in the conversion from the proof color space to the display color space, thus simulating the 'ink on paper black'.

## Preserve numbers

You use the Customize Proof condition to preview how a document will look before it has been converted to another color space. Preserve numbers can be useful for proofing how a CMYK file in a specific space will print if sent to a known CMYK space. By preserving the numbers you can simulate how a file will print before you consider re-separating it. And if the destination space is in the same color mode as the source space (i.e. RGB or CMYK), the Preserve Numbers box will allow you to preview how the image would look without a profile conversion.

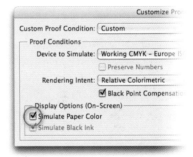

**Figure 13.12** The Display Options in the Customize Proof Condition dialog will allow you to achieve more authentic on-screen previews that take into account the density of the black in the final output being less black than the maximum black you see on the computer screen. When the Simulate Paper Color option is selected the screen image will simulate both the color of the paper stock and the black ink color. It is important to note here that while the Proof Condition settings for the Rendering Intent and Black Point Compensation have a bearing on a proof print output, the Simulate Paper Color and Black Ink options will only affect the screen preview.

## Realistic proofs

When you supply a CMYK proof you are aiming to show the printer how you envisage the picture should look in print. A proof is a print that has been produced using the same color gamut constraints as the halftone CMYK process. That way the printer will have an indication of what colors they should realistically be able to achieve.

## Supplying RGB files

Supplying RGB files instead of CMYK does work, but only so long as you supply the RGB files tagged with an ICC profile. Some people are doing this. But be warned, this method of supplying files for pre-press will only work if there is a clear agreed understanding that the recipient will be carrying out the conversion to CMYK and will ideally be given a CMYK proof print as a guide. If you send RGB files to a client, be careful to avoid any potential confusion down the line. Always inform them that the files are still in RGB mode.

## Contract proof versus aim print

The term 'aim' print most justly describes the appropriateness of a standard profiled inkjet output, when used as a guide for the designer or pre-press person who is determining how the colors in an image will reproduce when using CMYK inks on the actual press.

## Color proofing for press output

If you are supplying digital files for repro, then you will want to obtain as much relevant information as you can about the press, paper stock and print process that will be used to print a job. If the pre-press people you are communicating with are cooperative and understand what you are asking for, they may be able to supply you with a suitable proofing standard ICC profile, or they can provide you with information about the printing inks and other specifications used for the press. Go to the Edit ⇨ Color Settings ⇨ Working Space ⇨ CMYK ⇨ Custom CMYK dialog, and enter these settings as described in the previous chapter. Once you have saved this as a CMYK setting you can convert your RGB image to this custom CMYK color space and save it as a TIFF file.

A CMYK file on its own is not enough to inform the printer how it should be printed. It is standard procedure to supply a targeted CMYK aim print or proof along with the image, as this will provide a guide as to how you expect the picture to reproduce in print within the gamut of the specific CMYK print process. The term 'contract proof' is used to describe a CMYK proof that has been reproduced using an approved proofing device. These include the Epson x800 series with a good proofing RIP like the ColorBurst™ RIP. Kodak Approval™ is still much used, and perhaps to a lesser extent DuPont™ Chromalin™. Inkjet printers are essentially taking over the proofing industry, as many press houses move to Computer to Plate (CTP) technology, thus eliminating the need for film at the proofing stage. The contract proofing devices benefit from having industry-wide recognition, and if the proof that accompanies the file is generated using an approved contract device, a designer can use an aim print to pass off a job to the pre-press company handling the repro. A proof print is more likely to be accepted as a valid target print representing the colors that are achievable on the press.

## CMYK proofing with an inkjet

Even a humble inkjet printer is capable of producing 'targeted' CMYK prints that can be used as 'aim' prints or even as contract proofs (if produced via a RIP), because it is possible to simulate the restricted CMYK gamut of the press via the Photoshop Print dialog. Figure 13.13 shows the Photoshop print dialog for a ProPhoto RGB image. When the Proof option is selected as the Print space, the Proof Setup is invoked below and the default Proof Setup will use the current CMYK work space. The Photoshop Manages Colors option should be selected so that you can select a printer profile for the printer. In the Proof Setup you can then also select a saved Customize Proof Condition preset for the print process you wish to simulate (which includes the chosen rendering intent) and use the two checkboxes below to simulate the press conditions, using: Simulate Paper Color and Simulate Black Ink.

### Proof Setup presets

The complexities of configuring the Print with Preview dialog can be made easier if you choose to save the Customize Proof Condition settings as presets. That way you can quickly access the settings needed for simulated proof printing via the Proof Setup Preset menu in the Print dialog.

### Rendering intent grayed out

When Proof is selected as the source space, the Rendering Intent will be grayed out and the Black Point Compensation automatically switched off. This is because Photoshop will use the rendering intent that is applied in the custom proof setup.

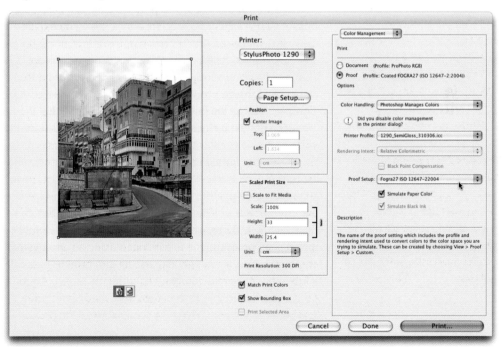

**Figure 13.13** Here, the Print dialog is configured for making a simulated CMYK print. After hitting Print, you would need to select the system print preset setting that matches the selected printer profile.

**Book resources**
If you want to learn more about printing from Photoshop, I can recommend some further reading: *Mastering Digital Printing* by Harald Johnson is a comprehensive title that does a good job of covering the subject of printing in extensive detail; *Real World Color Management* by Bruce Fraser, Chris Murphy and Fred Bunting; and also *Color Management for Photographers*, by Andrew Rodney. These are the industry bibles on the subject of color management and printing.

## *Simulation and rendering intents*

The aim here is to produce a print that simulates the output of a CMYK proof printer. We are configuring the Photoshop print dialog settings to utilize the Customize Proof Condition settings (which will already include the device to Simulate and the Rendering Intent) and then applying a further profile conversion from this proof setup space to the printer profile space. Photoshop makes it easy for you to select the right options so that you don't have to do anything more than decide whether you wish to simulate the black ink appearance only or simulate the paper color, in which case the simulate black ink will be checked automatically anyway. So by clicking on one or more of these buttons at the bottom, you can instruct Photoshop to work out for you how the data should be converted and sent to the printer to achieve the desired press simulation.

When Simulate Paper Color is selected, the whites may appear duller than expected. This does not mean the proof is wrong, rather it is the presence of a brighter white border that leads to the viewer regarding the result as looking inferior. To get around this try adding a white border to the outside image you are about to print. When the print is done, trim away the outer paper white border so that the eye does not get a chance to compare the dull whites of the print with the brighter white of the printing paper used.

When you hit the Print button, the same routine should be followed as usual. If you are using Photoshop to manage the colors, the system print settings should have the color management switched off and the Print Settings should match the paper type used or you should select the saved print preset that was created for use with the custom printer profile.

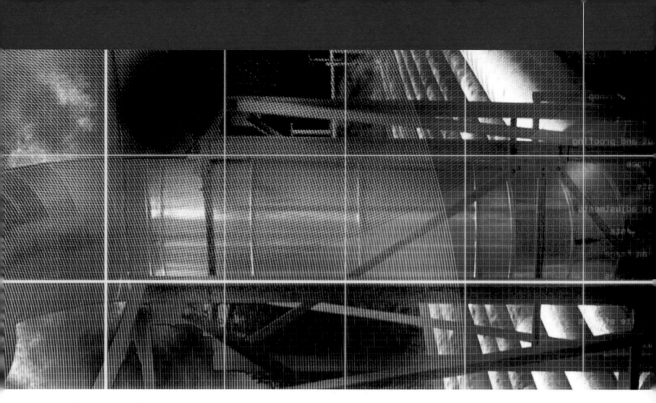

**Chapter 14**

# Output for the Web

The Internet is something most of us use every day and having the means to transmit images has become extremely important. There is the well-known saying 'a picture is worth a thousand words'. And it is so true – pictures allow us to communicate visually with clients, friends and family, in ways that words alone cannot. The most obvious advantage of sending or displaying images via the Web is its immediacy. Pictures can be sent around the world almost instantly and it is quick and easy to prepare an image to be distributed. The downsides are that, unlike producing a finished print, you have little or no control over the way the image is viewed by the recipient and the people you want to see your photographs must obviously have access to the Internet.

## Sending multiple images by email

Email programs can accept single or multiple attachments of any format, but not as a folder, unless it is compressed as an archive. And if the recipient is using an AOL account, do not send more than one image per email. Aladdin™ Software make the ubiquitous Stuffit™ program which is great for compressing files in his way. Although this originated for the Mac, it is available to Windows and handles ZIP compression as well as using its own proprietary format. It uses lossless compression and avoids the problem of Mac files appearing on Windows machines as two identically named files which contain the data and resource forks that constitute a Mac file.

A Stuffit archive will have a .sit extension, which requires expansion by Stuffit (which is incorporated into the Mac OS), but this can also be saved as a self-extracting archive. In this instance, the archive will bear the .sea extension and either WinZip or Stuffit can expand such Mac created archives. If the pictures in the source folder are JPEGs, then you will probably not notice a big difference in the final file size. But don't worry, this compression will not compromise the quality of the JPEG images any further.

# Sending images over the Internet

Let's look at the ways you can distribute images over the Web. In the past, people relied heavily on ISDN. But these days a fast Internet connection is all that most people need.

## Email attachments

With the increasing popularity of Broadband, cable and ADSL connections, you can effectively use a fast connection to the Internet to transmit and receive large files. The easiest way to do this is to send the files as attachments in an email. Email programs may differ, but most should let you simply drag a file from a folder on your computer into the body text area of an email. Click Send and you're done – the attached document will be distributed along with the text message in the email. It's relatively easy to do, but not completely flawless. There is no reliable way of knowing if the recipient's email program will be able to decode an attachment that has been sent from your email program. If you communicate using email this way, then you must remember to keep the attachments small. As a rule, I keep all attachments under 500 kilobytes (assuming the recipient also has a broadband type connection). I do like to check firstly, before sending anything bigger, to see if they mind receiving an attachment bigger than this. The Internet suffers quite enough already with bandwidth being consumed by unwanted junk emails. So don't add to the problem by sending large, unsolicited attachments. But if it is OK to send a big file, ask the recipient if there is a limit in place for the size of files they can receive in a single email, because if you exceed this, the email will only bounce back.

As long as you are aware of the parameters and restrictions of email programs and the possible limitations of the recipient's server, email can be an effective way to transfer smallish documents. Lots of people use email this way to share photographs. And the advanced email programs are also capable of displaying image file attachments within the body text area. But remember, this is by no means a foolproof way to send large images.

## Uploading to a server

With email you are sending a message that has the image embedded in it. Another alternative is to upload the image file to a server. You can then send an email that contains a clickable link that launches the recipient's web browser and this will take them directly to a page from where they can download the file. The advantage of this is that the email you send is small, as it only contains a text link to the server. There will be less risk of the email being rejected and if the person you are sending the email to needs to share the image with someone else, they only have to forward the message – they don't have to forward the entire image attachment all over again. But first you need to know how to upload to a server. If you connect to the Internet using a subscription service your Internet Service Provider (ISP) will most likely have provided you with a limited amount of server space that you can use to host your own website and upload files for others to download from in the way I described. If you don't have a subscription service or your ISP doesn't provide enough adequate server space, then you can always rent space from a company that maintains a dedicated server and provides web hosting. I use Image Access at www.image-access.net to host my websites and they provide me with all the server space that I require.

In Figure 14.1 I have provided some screen shots that show how I normally go about making an FTP connection to a server using the Fetch™ program on Macintosh OS X. To avoid having to re-enter the information each time you connect, it should be possible to save this information (along with the password if you wish) as a shortcut so that logging on to the server becomes almost as easy as opening a folder on your hard disk. I typically use the FTP software on a regular basis to upload image documents and Web Photo Galleries created in Photoshop. To give you an example of how I do this, I will create a document and make a connection to the server. The connection window opens, and this is like any other hierarchically structured folder. The main connection window will display the

### FTP software for Mac and PC

You will need File Transfer Protocol (FTP) software to upload documents to the server space. If using a Macintosh, I recommend using Fetch™: www.fetchsoftworks.com. If you are working on a PC, try using WS_FTP Pro www.ipswitch.com or Flash FXP™ www.flashfxp.com. All FTP software is more or less the same. To establish a connection you need to provide a link address to connect to the server. Next you need to enter your user ID and finally your password. If you are familiar with the steps required to configure your email account, you should already have the username and password information to hand. You may need to enter a subdirectory folder as well. If you have trouble configuring the connection, speak to your ISP. They are the best people to help you in these instances.

### Macintosh iDisk

Another option available to Macintosh users is iDisk. This is a Macintosh utility that has been enhanced for Mac OS X. iDisk is an online server space that you can use for off-site backup storage or as a space to place publicly accessible files and folders.

### Download a sample image file

I have uploaded a photograph to my server which you can access by typing in the following URL address in your web browser: www.martinevening.com/portraits/evening.pdf. This image document was saved as a Photoshop PDF file. You will probably be asked if you want to save the file to the desktop. Click Save and the file will start to download. The reason I saved this image as a Photoshop PDF was to demonstrate the security features that are available when using this format. To open the PDF file you will need to enter the password 'evening' when prompted.

website documents and subfolders. In here, I have created new subfolders with names like 'Locations', 'Travel' and 'Review'. I use these specific folders to upload the Web Gallery folders to so that they do not get mixed up with the folder structure of the main website. I will then double-click on a folder such as 'Review' to reveal the subfolder contents and then drag the Internet-ready file or folder across into this window. And that's it. The time this takes to accomplish will depend on the size of your file and Internet connection speed. To access these files, all you have to do is to supply people with a weblink such as the one in the accompanying sidebar. When they click on the link you give them, the file should start to download automatically to their computer.

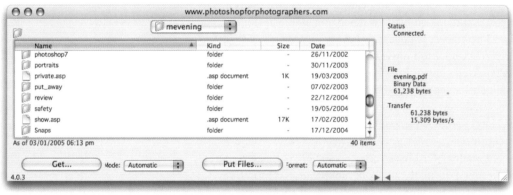

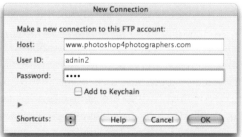

**Figure 14.1** The Fetch™ 4.0 FTP software interface, showing a new server connection being made.

## File formats for the Web

Now that we have covered the fundamentals of how to access a server and administer your allocated server space, let's look at preparing images to be displayed on the Web and take a look at the different file formats you can use and which are the best ones to choose in any given situation.

### *JPEG*

The JPEG (Joint Photographic Experts Group) format provides the most dramatic way to compress continuous tone image files. The JPEG format uses what is known as a lossy compression method. The heavier the compression, the more the image becomes irreversibly degraded. If you open a moderately compressed JPEG file and examine the structure of the image at 200%, you will probably notice that the picture contains a discernible checkered pattern of 8 × 8 pixel squares. This mosaic pattern will easily be visible at actual pixels viewing when using the heavier JPEG settings. The compression is more effective if the image contains soft tonal gradations as detailed images do not compress quite so efficiently and the JPEG artifacts will be more apparent. The JPEG format is mostly used for web design work, because a medium to heavy amount of JPEG compression can make most photographs small enough to download quickly over the Internet. Image quality is less of an issue here when the main object is simply to reduce the download times.

Photoshop compresses images on a scale of 0–12. A setting of 12 will apply the least amount of compression and give the highest image quality, while a setting of 0 will apply the greatest amount of compression and be the most lossy. When you choose to save as a JPEG, the document window preview will change to reflect how the compressed JPEG will look after it is reopened as a JPEG. The JPEG Options dialog box will also indicate the compressed file size in kilobytes and provide an estimated modem download time. This feedback information can be quite helpful. If you save a master file as a JPEG and then decide the file needs further compression, you can safely

### Keeping it small

Only one thing matters when you publish images on the Web and that is to keep the total file size of your pages as small as possible. The JPEG format is the most effective way to achieve file compression for continuous tone images. But graphics that contain fewer, distinct blocks of color should be saved using the GIF format. Some web servers are case sensitive and will not recognize capitalized file names. Go to the Photoshop Preferences menu ⇨ File Handling and make sure the Use Lower Case Extensions box is checked.

**Figure 14.2** Two JPEG images: both have the same pixel resolution and both have been saved using the same JPEG quality setting. Yet the Sahara desert image will compress to just 21 kilobytes, while the gas works picture is over three times bigger at 74 kilobytes. This is because it contains so much extra detail. The more contrasting sharp lines there are in an image, the larger the file size will be after compression. For this reason it is best not to apply too much unsharp masking to an image before you save it as a JPEG. If you are editing an image that is intended to go on a web page, you can deliberately apply blur to some of the less critical portions of an image to remove distracting detail and thereby reduce the JPEG size (check out the new Surface Blur filter shown in Chapter 10).

overwrite the last saved JPEG using a lower JPEG setting. It is possible to repeat saving in the JPEG format this way. For as long as the image is open in Photoshop, all data is held in Photoshop memory and only the version saved on the disk is degraded.

Once an image has been compressed using the JPEG format, it is not a good idea to repeatedly resave it as a JPEG, because this will only compound the compression already applied to the image structure. Unlike some programs, the JPEG compressor used in Photoshop converges, so that after repeated expansions and compressions using the same settings and without modifying the pixels, the data loss will be less and less with every save, to the point where there will be little or no

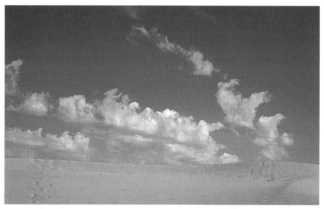

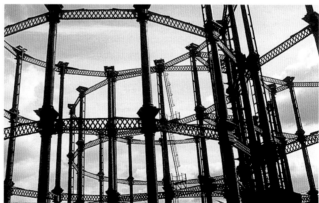

further loss. Your main uses for the JPEG format should be primarily to create smaller file size copies to conserve disk space, to ensure visitors to your website receive speedy downloads, and smaller email attachments. You normally want to compact a file in this way for inclusion on a web page, for faster electronic distribution, or saving a large file to a restricted amount of disk space. For example, an 18 MB, 10" × 8" file at 300 ppi resolution can be reduced in size to around 1 MB with hardly any degradation to the image quality. Some purists will argue that JPEG compression should never be used under any circumstances when saving a photographic image. It is true that if an EPS or TIFF file is saved with JPEG file compression there are some rare instances where this can cause problems when sending the file to some older PostScript devices. But otherwise, the image degradation is barely noticeable at the higher quality compression settings, even when the image is viewed on the screen in close-up at actual pixels viewing, never mind when it is seen as a printed output.

### *Choosing the right compression type*

As you can see in Figure 14.5, JPEG compression is a most effective way to reduce file size, but this is achieved at the expense of throwing away some of the image data. JPEG is therefore known as a lossy format. At the highest quality setting, the image is barely degraded and the JPEG file size is just 70 kilobytes, or 12% of its original size. If we use a medium quality setting the size is reduced further to just 18 kilobytes. This is probably about the right amount of compression to use for a photograph that is intended to be included in a typical web page layout. The lowest compression setting will squeeze the original 586 kilobytes down to under 7 kilobytes, but at this level the picture will appear extremely 'mushy' and it is best avoided.

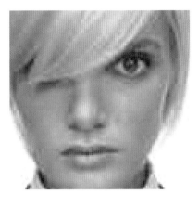

**Figure 14.3** This close-up view of the JPEG saved at the 10% Quality setting clearly reveals the underlying 8 × 8 pixel mosaic structure, which is how the JPEG compression method breaks down the continuous tone pixel image into large compressed blocks. At the higher quality settings you will have to look very hard to even notice any change to the image. Successively overwriting a JPEG image will degrade the image even further. However, if no cropping or image size change takes place, the degradation will only be slight. As a general rule always re-JPEG an image from an uncompressed master file.

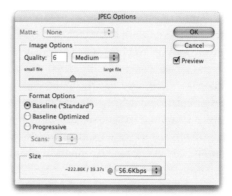

**Figure 14.4** The JPEG Options save dialog box. Baseline ('Standard') is the most universally understood JPEG format option and one that most web browsers will be able to recognize. Baseline Optimized will often yield a slightly more compressed sized file than the standard JPEG format and most (but not all) web browsers are able to read this correctly. The Progressive option creates a JPEG file that will download in an interlaced fashion, the same way you can encode a GIF file.

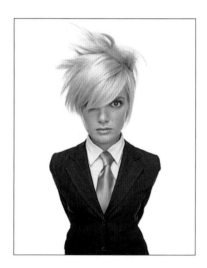

Client: Clipso. Model: Bianca at Nevs.

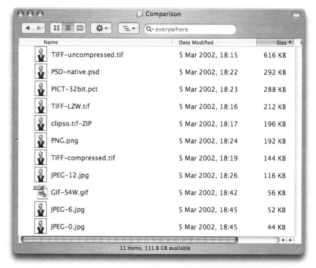

**Figure 14.5** Here we have one image, but saved eleven different ways and each method producing a different file size. The opened image measures 500 × 400 pixels and the true file size is exactly 586 kilobytes. The native Photoshop format is usually the most efficient format to save in because large areas of contiguous color such as the white background are recorded using a method of compression that does not degrade the image quality. An uncompressed TIFF format doggedly records every pixel value and is therefore larger in size. A compressed TIFF can be made smaller, but the save times are longer. Below that are the JPEG and GIF format versions which, as you can see, offer the most dramatic methods of compression.

## JPEG 2000

JPEG 2000 has more extensive features than a normal JPEG format. For example, you can save a 16-bit per channel image, which you can't do with an ordinary JPEG, and you can save alpha channels and paths, plus choose to preserve the camera EXIF and all other metadata when you save an image using this format. At one time it was thought that JPEG 2000 might be a better format for storing digital captures, but the advantages of shooting raw have clearly overtaken the JPEG 2000 specification. It is primarily a format that could be used for saving processed image files.

### JPEG 2000 compatibility

The JPEG 2000 plug-in is only available from the Bridge CS3 plug-ins folder. For instructions on how to use it in Photoshop CS3, refer to page 131. Only another Photoshop CS/CS2/CS3 user (or someone with the JPEG 2000 plug-in) can read files encoded in this format. Other programs may support it in the future, but for the time being, use with caution.

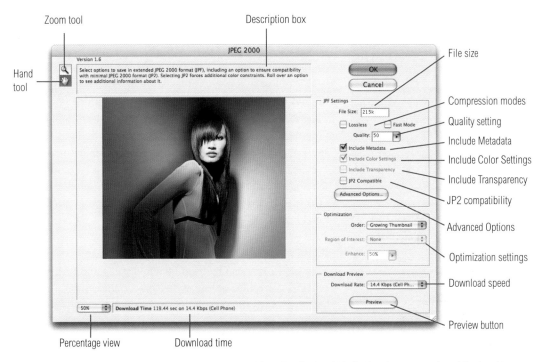

**Figure 14.6** The main controls are over on the right, starting with the File Size box. This displays the current projected file size of the compressed JPEG file, but you can also type in the desired file size and Photoshop will calculate a custom file compression to meet this target figure. Below that is the Lossless compression mode button which if checked will render a larger file size, but non-lossy JPEG. The Quality setting can be set anywhere between 1 and 100%, with 100% being the highest quality image setting. Notice how the Description box provides a commentary on the function of the other dialog items as you mouse over them. JPEG 2000 does not support layers, but if the base layer is a non-background layer and contains transparent pixels, checking the Include Transparency box will preserve the transparency. At one time this was thought useful for web designers once web browsers were able to recognize JPEG 2000 files, but in the meantime the PNG format has become the more commonly used file format where transparency is required in web graphics.

### GIF compression

You will find that when designing graphic images to be converted to a GIF, those with horizontal detail compress better than those with vertical detail. This is due to the GIF format using Run Length Encoding (RLE) compression.

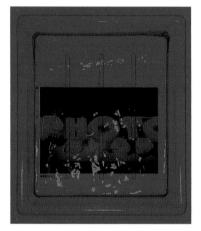

**Figure 14.7** The GIF file format is mostly used for saving graphic logos and typography. The picture shown here is one that was used for the cover design of an earlier edition of this book. But this is also a good example to illustrate the type of image that would be suitable for saving in the GIF format for use on a web page design. Note that the image contains a large amount of solid red and few other colors. This photograph was reduced in size to around 350 x 300 pixels. I then converted the image to Index Color mode using a palette of 16 colors. When the image was saved as a GIF it measured a mere 19 kilobytes.

## *GIF*

The GIF (Graphics Interchange Format) is normally used for publishing graphic type images such as logos. Some people pronounce GIF with a soft G (as in George) and others use a hard G (as in garage). Neither is right or wrong as both forms of pronunciation are commonly used. Or as Julienne Kost likes to say: 'it's pronounced, get a life!'

To prepare an image as a GIF, the color mode must be set to Indexed Color. This is an 8-bit color display mode where specific colors are 'indexed' to each of the 256 (or fewer) numeric values. You can select a palette of indexed colors that are saved with the file and choose to save as a CompuServe GIF. The file is then ready to be placed in a web page and viewed by web browsers on all computer platforms. Photoshop contains special features to help web designers improve the quality of their GIF outputs, such as the ability to preview Indexed mode colors whilst in the Index Color mode change dialog box, and an option to keep matching colors non-dithered. This feature will help you improve the appearance of GIF images and reduce the risks of banding or posterization. Be aware that when the Preview is switched on and you are editing a large image, it may take a while for the document window preview to take effect, so make sure that you resize the image to the final pixel size first.

## PNG (Portable Network Graphics)

This file format can be used for the display and distribution of RGB color files online and also available as a file format option in Save for Web. PNG (pronounced 'ping') features improved image compression and enables alpha mask channels (for creating transparency) to be saved with the image. Other advantages over JPEG and GIF are higher color bit depths, support for channels and limited built-in gamma correction recognition, so you can view an image at the gamma setting intended for your monitor. Newer versions of Netscape Navigator and Microsoft Internet Explorer web browsers will support the PNG format, as does Apple's Safari web browser program.

## Save for Web

The Save for Web option is included in the Save section of the File menu. This comprehensive dialog interface gives you complete control over how an image can be optimized for web use, offering a choice of JPEG, GIF, PNG-8 or PNG-24 formats. The preview display options include: Original, Optimized, 2-up and 4-up views. Figure 14.8 shows the dialog window in 2-up mode display. With Save for Web you can preview the original version of the image plus up to three variations using different web format settings. In the annotation area below each preview, you are able to make comparative judgements as to which format

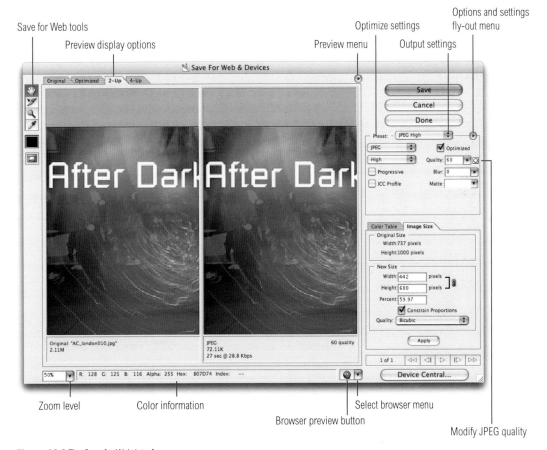

**Figure 14.8** The Save for Web interface.

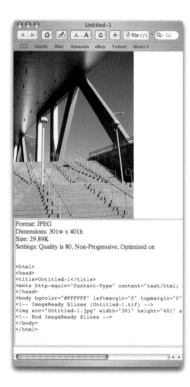

Format: JPEG
Dimensions: 301w x 401h
Size: 29.89K
Settings: Quality is 80, Non-Progressive, Optimized on

```
<html>
<head>
<title>Untitled-1</title>
<meta http-equiv="Content-Type" content="text/html;
</head>
<body bgcolor="#FFFFFF" leftmargin="0" topmargin="0"
<!-- ImageReady Slices (Untitled-1.tif) -->
<img src="Untitled-1.jpg" width="301" height="401" a
<!-- End ImageReady Slices -->
</body>
</html>
```

**Figure 14.9** When a browser window preview is selected, the default web browser program is launched and a temporary page will be created, like the one illustrated above. This will allow you to preview the Save for Web processed image as it will appear on the final web page. This is especially useful for checking if the RGB editing space used will be recognized differently by the browser. If you are relying on embedded ICC profiles to regulate the color appearance on screen, you can check to see if the profile is indeed being recognized by the selected web browser program.

and compression setting will give the best payoff between image quality and file size, and also determine how long it will take to download at a specific modem speed. Use the Preview menu to select from a list of modem and Internet connections on which these download times are based. You can also use the Preview menu list to select a preview setting and simulate how the web output will display on either a Macintosh display, a PC Windows display or with Photoshop compensation.

The Select Browser menu allows you to select which web browser to use when you preview a document that has been optimized for the Web (see Figure 14.9).

Photoshop provides an option for Progressive JPEG formatting. Most Netscape and Internet Explorer browsers support this enhancement, whereby JPEGs can be made to download progressively the way interlaced GIFs do. If you check the Optimize checkbox in the Save For Web & Devices dialog (see Figure 14.8) the optimize option can apply more efficient compression, but again is not generally compatible with older web browser programs. The quality setting can be set as Low, Medium, High, Maximum or it can be set more precisely as a value between 1 and 100%. Custom Save for Web output settings can be saved via the options fly-out menu, and the Blur control will allow you to soften an oversharpened original and obtain further file compression when using the JPEG format.

Next to the Quality setting is a small selection mask icon. Click on this icon to open the Modify Quality Settings. In the JPEG mode Save for Web dialog you can set zone optimized levels of compression based on the text layer/vector layer content or an alpha channel stored in the master document (see Figure 14.10), so that areas of important detail can have less JPEG compression applied to them. You can adjust the sliders to establish the range of JPEG compression from the total mask to no mask areas, and vary the softness of this transition. In Figure 14.10, the All Text Layers option is checked and you can see a preview of the mask based on the text layer in the Modify Quality settings dialog. A higher quality JPEG compression will therefore be applied to the text in the final JPEG output. In the Save for Web GIF format mode (discussed next), an alpha channel can also be used to zone optimize the color reduction and modify the dither settings.

The Save for Web dialog lets you save as: HTML and Images, Images only, or HTML only. The output settings let you determine the various characteristics of the Save for Web output files such as: the default naming structure of the image files and slices; the HTML coding layout; and whether you wish to save a background file to an HTML page output. Figure 14.9 shows an example of a temporary document window generated with the HTML code generated by Save for Web along with the HTML code in the format specified in the output settings.

The Image Size options are fairly similar to those found in the Image ⇨ Image Size dialog box. Just simply enter a new percentage to scale the image to and check what impact this will have on the file size (this will change the file size in all the optimized windows). An alternative approach is to select Optimize To File Size from the fly-out menu (see Figure 14.11). Use this to target the optimized file to match a specific kilobyte file size output and, if you wish, have Photoshop automatically determine whether it is better to save as a GIF or JPEG.

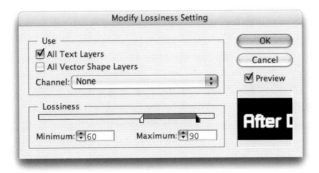

**Figure 14.10** Click on the button next to the Quality setting to open the Modify Quality Setting dialog. This will allow you to use an alpha channel to zone optimize the JPEG compression range or as shown above you can check the All Text Layers box to apply a higher quality compression setting to the text areas and a lower quality compression to the remaining image.

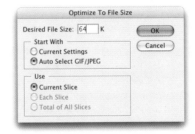

**Figure 14.11** Mouse down on the fly-out menu to access further optimization options such as the Optimize to File Size dialog shown here, where you can set the ideal file size to optimize the image to, or let Photoshop determine whether it would be more economical to save as a JPEG or GIF file.

## Web palette colors

The Web palette contains the 216 colors common to both platforms and is therefore a good choice for web publishing if viewers are limited to looking at the image on an 8-bit color monitor display. Now to be honest, restricting your colors to a Web palette should not really be that necessary these days, but the option is still there. However, the Web Snap slider will let you modify the color table by selecting those colors that are close to being 'browser safe' and making them snap to these precise color values. The Web Snap slider determines the amount of tolerance and you can see the composition of the color table being transformed as you make an adjustment.

## GIF lossy options

The Lossy option allows you to reduce the GIF file size by introducing file compression. This can be helpful if you have an overlarge GIF file. But too much compression will noticeably degrade the image until it looks like a badly tuned TV screen.

## GIF Save for Web

The GIF Save for Web options are also quite extensive. You have the same control over the image size and you can preview how the resulting GIF will appear on other operating systems and browsers – the remaining options all deal with the compression, transparency and color table settings that are specific to the GIF format. The choice of color reduction algorithms will allow you to select the most suitable 256 maximum color palette to save the GIF in. This includes the 8-bit palettes for the Macintosh and Windows systems. These are fine for platform-specific work, but such GIF files may display differently on the other system's palette. The Interlace option will add slightly to the file size, but is worth selecting – the image will appear to download progressively in slices. The Perceptual setting produces a customized table with colors to which the eye is more sensitive. The default Selective setting is similar to the Perceptual table, but more orientated to the selection of web safe colors. This is perhaps the best compromise solution to opt for now as every PC setup sold these days is able to display 24-bit color. The Adaptive table palette samples the colors which most commonly recur in the image. In an image with a limited color range, this type of palette can produce the smoothest representation using a limited number of colors. The diffusion dithering algorithm is effective at creating the impression of greater color depth and reducing any image banding, and the Dither slider allows you to control the amount of diffusion dithering. The Pattern and Noise options have no dither control. If the image to be saved has a transparent background, the Transparency option can be kept checked in order to preserve the image transparency in the saved GIF. To introduce transparency in an image you can select the color to make transparent using the eyedropper tool and then click inside the image preview area. The color chosen will appear selected in the color table. Select one or more colors and click on the Map Selected Colors to Transparent button in the Color Table. You can apply a diffusion, pattern or noise dither to the transparent areas, which will help create a smoother transparent blend in your GIF.

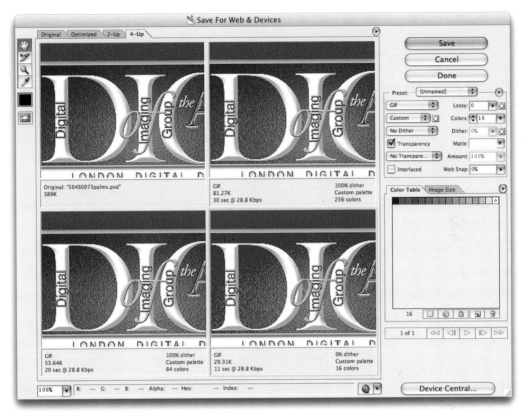

**Figure 14.12** The Save for Web interface showing GIF settings.     Design work: Rod Wynne-Powell.

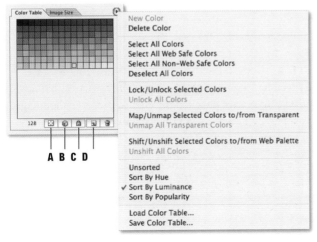

**Figure 14.13** The color table with Color palette fly-out menu shown.

A: Maps the selected color to transparency.
B: Shifts/unshifts selected colors to the Web palette.
C: Locks the color to the palette to avoid deletion.
D: Adds an eyedropper-selected color to the palette

## Device Central

The new Device Central application allows you to create and view image files for a variety of mobile devices, such as cell phone devices. If you go to the File menu and choose Device Central... this will open a dialog similar to the one below, where you can select a mobile device and click the Create button to create a new document with the correct pixel dimensions for the selected device. If you already have an image open, you can go to the Save for Web dialog and click on the Device Central... button which will then preview a resized image via the Emulator panel in Device Central. This will let you play around with the different settings to get an impression of how an image might look when displayed on one of the many mobile phone device presets that come with Device Central.

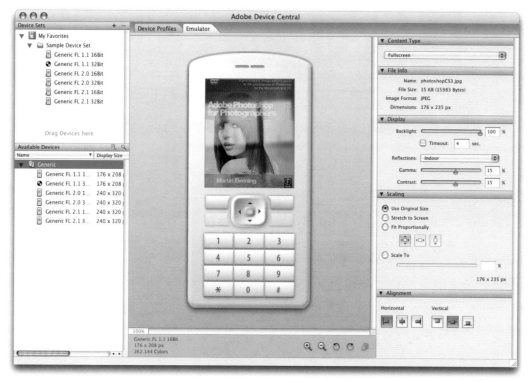

**Figure 14.14** An image of the cover design of this book is shown previewed here in the Device Central Emulator.

## Zoomify™ Export

There is a Zoomify™ Export option in the File menu with which you can create an output folder containing all the necessary components to produce zoomable image web pages. Visitors to pages created with the Zoomify export plug-in will be able to view the pages so long as they have an up-to-date Flash plug-in for their browser. Zoomify pages are ideal for portfolio presentations and commerce websites, where customers can easily view large images in close-up. If you go to the Zoomify website at www. zoomify.com, you can see some samples of customer sites where the export plug-in has been used.

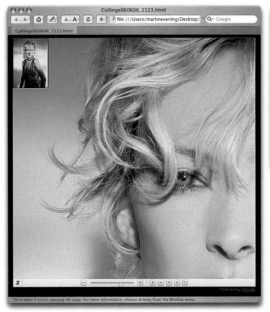

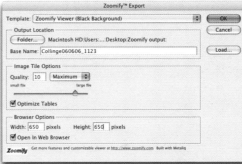

**Figure 14.15** Here is the Zoomify™ Export dialog box showing typical settings that might be used to create a zoomable image. The output will be a folder that contains all the necessary components to display a zoomable image. Once created, all you have to do is upload the folder to your website and add /foldername/ basefilename.htm/ to the usual URL weblink (note that the base file name referred to here is based on the image's file name). Visitors to such pages can left mouse-click on an area of interest to zoom in and ⌥ *alt*–click to zoom out. You can mouse down and drag to scroll, or use the navigator preview to select an area of interest to scroll to. According to the current information on the site, there are no usage fees or restrictions on usage of this plug-in.

## Adding a copyright watermark

Here is a technique that I devised a few years back for manually adding a copyright symbol to an image. With some patience and knowledge of Photoshop actions, you can record these steps as an action and use it to batch watermark images.

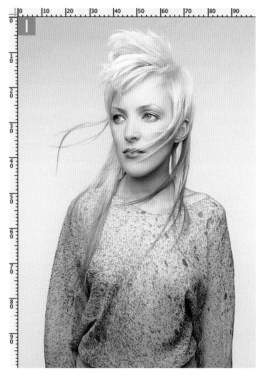

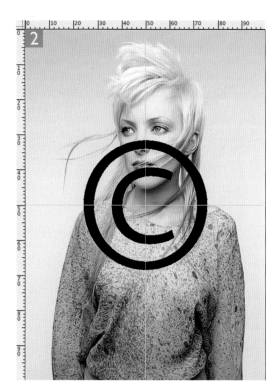

**1** The following steps show how to add a copyright symbol as a watermark. To start with I choose Rulers from the View menu; double-click either ruler and set the ruler units to Percentage.

**2** I dragged two guides out to intersect at 50%. I then selected the custom shape tool, went to the tool options and chose a copyright symbol from the default shapes list. I moused down on the point where the two guide lines intersected and dragged outwards. As I did so, I held down the 	⌥ *Shift* *alt* *Shift* keys to center and scale the shape as I dragged with the mouse.

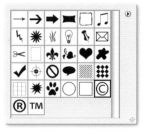

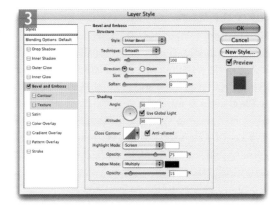

**3** In the Layers palette, I set the Fill opacity to 0% (the logo will disappear). I then double-clicked on the layer to open the Layer Style dialog and applied a Bevel and Emboss layer effect. The only adjustment I made in the Layer Style dialog was to reduce the Multiply opacity to 15%.

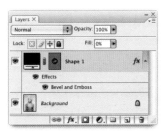

**4** Lastly, I saved the image as a PDF using the PDF security options to make the image password protected. To open the image in Photoshop, the recipient will need to know the relevant passwords. Once a user has successfully entered a password they will see the image in its layered form and can delete the watermark layer. Other copies made from this master file can serve as proof copies for use in page layouts or as a JPEG version on a website.

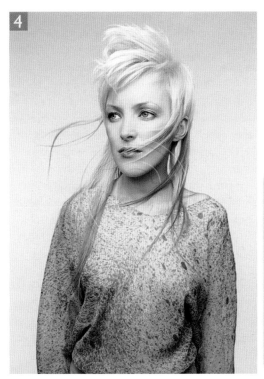

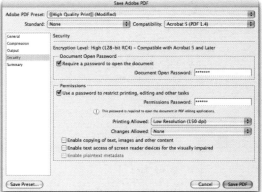

Client: Rainbow Room. Model: Grethe at FM.

## Web Photo Gallery creation

There are two ways to create a Web Photo Gallery. If you know the folder of images that you wish to create a gallery from, simply go to the File menu in Photoshop and choose Automate ⇨ Web Photo Gallery... Under Source images and select the folder of images you wish to process. Alternatively, you can use Bridge to make a custom selection of image and choose Tools ⇨ Photoshop ⇨ Web Photo Gallery... . Under Source images you will see that the source says: Selected Images from Bridge.

## Preparing RGB images for the Web

Web Photo Gallery will process any images you tell it to, resize and convert them to JPEGs and, if they are not in RGB mode, convert them to the current RGB work space. Now, if your RGB work space or the RGB space your RGB files are in is anything other than sRGB, then the galleries you create will most likely display the photographs rather differently in a web browser compared to the way you see them in Photoshop or Bridge. Unfortunately, Web Photo Gallery is not designed so that you can easily create web galleries in one simple step. In most cases you will want to run the Image Processor script (see page 656) first, which will allow you to batch process the selected images to create sRGB color versions in a new image folder. Once you have done this, you can then run Web Photo Gallery, using these images as the source. Pre-processing Web Gallery images in this way means they are more likely to be viewed the way you intended.

# Web Photo Gallery

The Web Photo Gallery feature can be used to process a folder of images and automatically generate all the HTML code needed to build a website complete with thumbnail images, individual gallery pages and navigable link buttons. This Photoshop feature can save you many hours of repetitive work. I use the Web Photo Gallery all the time, and it is a tool I have used a lot in the past.

Imagine you have a set of Photoshop images that need forwarding to a client or colleague. When you build a self-contained web photo gallery in Photoshop, the processed images and HTML pages are output to a destination folder. You can then upload this processed folder to your web server and simply pass the URL link on to the person who needs to see the photographs. For a quick reminder of how to do this, refer back to Figure 14.1. Drag the Web Photo Gallery processed folder across to the Server window and pass on the URL link via email. In the Figure 14.16 example, I decided to call the destination folder 'LTrain-2006' and placed it inside a folder called 'Snaps' on my server. I therefore appended '/Snaps/LTrain-2006/' to my normal website URL as the full URL for the recipient to follow. It is necessary to add a forward slash at the end of the URL link, because this indicates that 'LTrain-2006' is a folder containing a directory of files, but there is no need to add 'index.htm' after the forward slash because a web browser will by default always look for a file called 'index.htm' or 'index.html'.

The source can be any folder of images, regardless of whether they are in RGB or CMYK color mode, because Web Photo Gallery will convert all images to RGB anyway (see the sidebar on preparing RGB images for the Web). You can also access the Photoshop Web Photo Gallery directly from the Tools menu in Bridge. For example, in Figure 14.16 I made a selection of images within Bridge and used: Tools ⇨ Photoshop ⇨ Web Photo Gallery to create a gallery based on the Bridge selection. The image order can be changed by simply dragging the thumbnails in the Bridge window. When the Include all Subfolders box

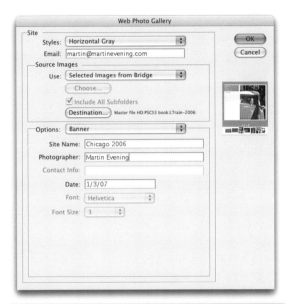

**Figure 14.16** The Photoshop Web Photo Gallery will let you save extra information such as your contact details and an active email address link. The security feature (see page 641) will enable you to apply a visible watermark to the gallery images that are created. This can be based on file data such as the file name, caption information, or alternatively you can enter some customized text.

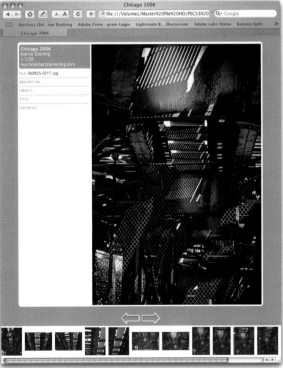

**Figure 14.17** Once the web gallery has been completed, it will automatically launch the completed pages in your default web browser, so you can preview the resulting pages offline before uploading them to a server.

## Designing your own templates

If you want to be really adventurous, then search the Adobe Photoshop Help database for information listed under: Customizing Web Photo Gallery Styles and using tokens in Web Photo Gallery styles. This will provide tips and instructions on how to write the HTML code from scratch. After you have completed the template output folder, you can further enhance the appearance of your gallery pages by importing them into a separate website editing program such as Adobe GoLive™ or Adobe Dreamweaver™.

is checked the subsets of folders can be processed too. It is not essential that you resize them to the exact viewing size, as the Web Photo Gallery options allow you to precisely scale the gallery images and thumbnails down in size while they are being processed.

There is now a choice of 20 template styles to choose from in Photoshop, a few of which are shown in Figure 14.18. Some of these templates have a simple HTML table design, while others utilize frames and basic JavaScript. These gallery styles can be customized to some extent by adjusting the Options settings, as described on the following pages. Because these templates vary a lot in their design, not all of the options settings will be recognized when you come to build a gallery. If you process a folder of images and are not sure about the look of the chosen layout, then try adjusting the Options settings or selecting an alternative Web Photo Gallery style. It is worth pointing out that if you have to redo a Web Photo Gallery because the banner title was incorrect or you want to change the contact details, make sure the 'Add Width and Height Attributes for Images' option is unchecked in the General settings each time you revisit the Web Photo Gallery settings and make changes to the Banner section or select a new template style. Photoshop will not need to reprocess all the image data and will instead recode the HTML. After a web gallery has been processed the settings used will be remembered the next time you use the Web Photo Gallery.

You can also create your own layout templates. Go to the Photoshop CS3/Presets/Web Photo Gallery folder and use the folders in there as a guide for designing your own customized HTML templates. One easy way of doing this is to make a copy of an existing WPG template, take a peek inside the template's images folder and open the various graphic elements in Photoshop. You can then create your own alternative graphic designs for things like the buttons and background patterns and save these, overwriting the previous image files, using the exact same file names. Give the modified template a new name and the next time you run the WPG, it will appear in the Styles pop-up menu.

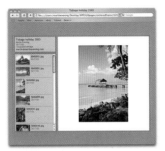

Centered Frame 1 Basic

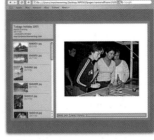

Centered Frame 1 Feedback

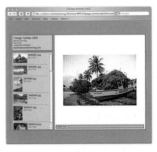

Centered Frame 1 Info Only

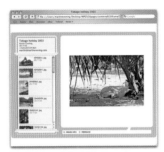

Centered Frame 2 Feedback

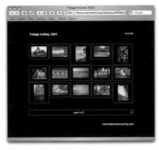

Dotted Border – White on Black

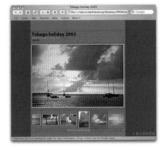

Flash – Gallery 2

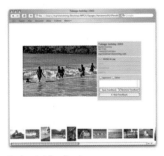

Horizontal Feedback

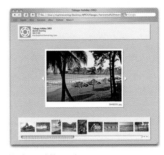

Horizontal Neutral

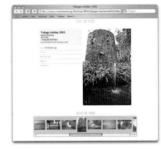

Horizontal Slideshow

**Figure 14.18** This shows you a few examples of the Web Photo Gallery templates in Photoshop CS3. These screen shots will give you a better impression of what the individual templates will look like rather than the tiny thumbnail displayed in the Web Photo Gallery dialog. These pages were mostly created using the default Web Photo Gallery color settings, so there is plenty of scope for you to produce your own customized Web Photo Gallery pages. The feedback templates allow visitors to mark favorite images, submit comments on individual photographs and send these back to you in the form of an email.

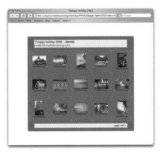

Table 2

## General

The Use UTF 8 Encoding option will apply to the URL only. If the Add Width and Height Attributes for Images is checked, Photoshop will be forced to reprocess every image every time you regenerate a web photo gallery, even if all you do is to change the Banner title. If I only make changes to the Banner information, or I want to choose a new gallery style, I will uncheck this option before clicking OK to generate a new Web Photo Gallery. The Preserve all metadata option will ensure that the metadata is not stripped out of the image files you create, but at the expense of making the gallery images bigger in size.

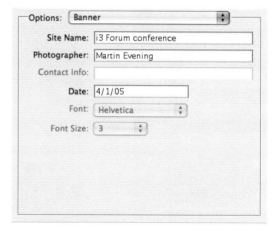

## Banner

Enter the name of your site in the Site Name field. The text entered here will appear in both the title bar and as a bold heading on the gallery pages. Type your name below, or to be more specific type something like 'Photography by:' followed by your name. Type in your contact details below, although only the Centered Frame, Horizontal Feedback and Horizontal Slideshow templates will use this data. Today's date will automatically appear in the Date Field and lastly you can customize the font type and font size used.

## Large Images

This lets you control the size and appearance of the main gallery images. You can determine whether the images need to be resized or not, the pixel dimension limits and the JPEG quality setting to use. Plus you can specify the number of pixels to add as a border. Many of the templates are capable of displaying image file metadata such as the Description (used to be Caption) and Copyright metadata. If the checkbox is enabled (and checked), this information is capable of appearing alongside or underneath each gallery image.

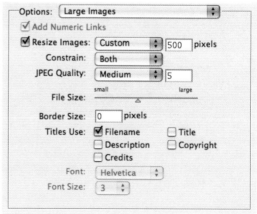

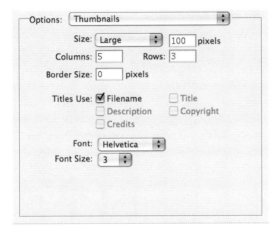

## Thumbnails

The thumbnails are smaller versions of the main image files that are used as a visual aid to navigation. The thumbnail size and appearance can be adjusted to suit your requirements. Obviously, the smaller the thumbnail size, the faster the gallery pages will load. Although there is a range of title options, you can normally have only the file name appear beneath a thumbnail.

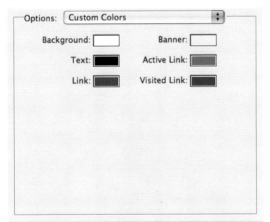

## Custom Colors

The Web Photo Gallery templates mostly use neutral color schemes. If you want to go more colorful, you can choose any colors you like for the background, banner headers and text. The link colors can also be changed so that they override the default colors used in some of the templates.

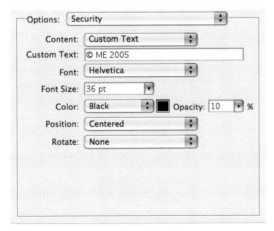

## Security

These settings let you place watermarks on the gallery images. If you select the Copyright setting, any copyright notice contained in the IPTC file info will automatically be used to watermark the image. Or you can select another type of text source from the Content pop-up menu, or enter custom text. Choosing the right font size will depend on the pixel width dimensions of your gallery images. A little testing is usually required here. If you check out the sample gallery page I created, the copyright notice opacity was set to 10%.

## Client feedback

Clients can use the feedback gallery interfaces to make image selections, add comments even and forward these as an email. At present, only the file names are used in the email to reference the selected photos, but the system still works a lot better than having someone write the image file names or model details down by hand and call you up on the telephone with their comments.

## Information and feedback

The feedback Web Photo Gallery templates utilize a JavaScript, which means that once a gallery has been built and uploaded to your server, visitors can use the website to send feedback comments back to you. For this to work you must remember to enter your email address in the main Web Photo Gallery dialog (see Figure 14.16). Whenever I conduct a model casting, I take digital shots and input the model's name and agency in the Description field of the IPTC Metadata pane in Bridge. This metadata information is then automatically stored in either the file header or an .xmp sidecar file. When I build a Web Photo Gallery and check the Description box under the options for Large Images, the model name and information will appear alongside each image in the final gallery.

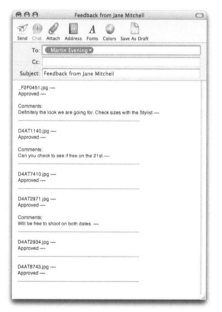
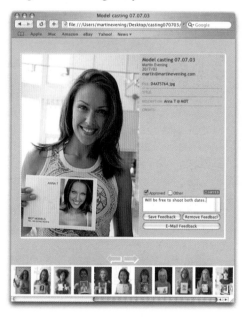

**Figure 14.19** Here is an example of a Web Photo Gallery created using one of the Feedback templates. I find these templates to be particularly useful when posting a collection of photographs taken from a model casting, or when I want to show a set of retouched photographs that require comments from a client. In this example, a client can visit a web gallery page, make a selection of the approved models, add a few comments and click on the Save Feedback button. Sending these comments as an email couldn't be simpler. All the client has to do is click on the Email Feedback button and enter their name. After that, Photoshop will launch the default email program and complete the email. All the client has to then do is add their comments and click 'Send'.

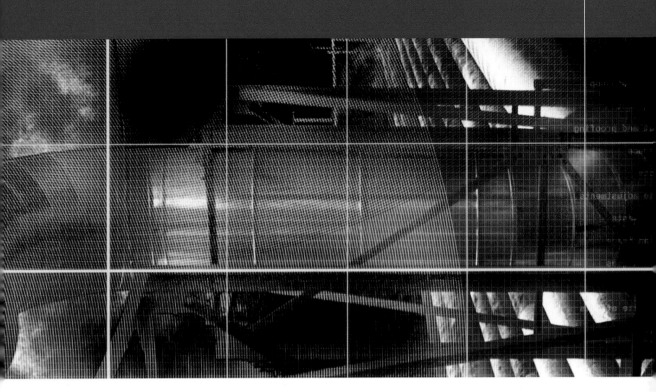

Chapter 15

# Automating Photoshop

**G**etting to know the basics of Photoshop takes a few months, while learning how to become fluent takes a little longer. One way you can speed up your Photoshop work is by learning how to use many of the keyboard shortcuts. There are a lot of them in the program and so it is best to learn these shortcuts a few at a time, and not try to absorb everything at once. Throughout this book I have often tried to indicate the Mac and PC key combinations for the various shortcuts that are available in Photoshop. And I have probably covered nearly all the keyboard shortcuts one might use on a regular basis. But there are even more shortcuts you can learn! Most of these are listed in the Shortcuts table PDF which is on the DVD that comes with the book, which you can also print out. Or, you can go to the Keyboard Shortcuts dialog in the Photoshop Edit menu.

## Table of Shortcuts

In earlier editions of this book I published a table that showed all the keyboard shortcuts in Photoshop. That table is still here, but it is now published as a PDF document on the DVD. There are two reasons for this. One is that Photoshop allows you to print your own summary of the keyboard shortcuts directly from the Keyboard Shortcuts manager dialog. But more importantly, there was so much new information that needed to be covered in this edition, we had to use all the space available to cover what is new in Photoshop CS3. This is why we decided to place the Shortcuts tables on the DVD instead.

## Contextual menus

A good many shortcuts are just a mouse-click away. Contextual menus are available throughout Photoshop. On a Macintosh you use *ctrl*-click and on the PC use a right mouse-click to open a contextual menu in an image document window or a Photoshop palette such as the Layers, Channels or Paths palette. For example, you can *ctrl* right mouse-click in the document window to access a list of all the menu options associated with the currently selected tool.

## Generating a shortcut summary

If you click on the Summarize... button, this will generate a document in an HTML format that summarizes all the shortcuts in this set. This summary can be printed out and used as a reference guide to all the available shortcuts.

# Custom keyboard shortcuts

The default keyboard shortcuts in Photoshop utilize just about all the key combinations that are available on a standard English language computer keyboard. For example, the Tools palette uses up every letter of the alphabet, you have the *⌘ ctrl* keys plus a letter, number or keyboard symbol, followed by the *⌘ Shift ctrl Shift* key combinations, the *⌘ ⌥ ctrl alt* combinations, and finally, a few key combinations that combine all three modifier keys, such as *⌘ ⌥ Shift ctrl alt Shift*.

Non-English language computer keyboards will differ. For example, keyboards produced for the Scandinavian countries will assign different special language symbols in place of the ones found on a US or British keyboard. In the past, this presented problems for non-English language Photoshop users, because things like the tilde key (~) wouldn't exist on certain keyboards. But the shortage of spare keyboard shortcuts has also limited the number of Photoshop functions that could have a keyboard shortcut.

When you use Photoshop CS or later, you can customize the keyboard shortcuts to suit your own way of working. Shortcuts that you find redundant can now be reassigned for the Photoshop commands you find more useful and modified shortcuts can then be saved as custom sets. But to start with, go to the Edit menu and choose Keyboard Shortcuts... (*⌘ ⌥ Shift K ctrl alt Shift K*). This will open the dialog shown in Figure 15.2, where you can select a preset setting such as 'Working with Type' or customize the current Shortcuts settings and create your own custom configurations.

The Palette shortcuts are grouped into: Application Menus, Palette Menus and Tools, so you can choose one of these to edit that particular section of the interface. The Application Menus and Palette Menus sets both contain subsets of items with expandable views. To create a new keyboard shortcut, click to select the menu item you wish to customize and hold down the keyboard key combination exactly as you would if you were using the keyboard shortcut. The keyboard shortcut will then appear in the

Shortcut column field of the item you are editing. You can also create more than one shortcut for each item. To do this, select an item in the list and click on the Add Shortcut button and enter a new shortcut just as you did before. When you are done, you can click on the Create New Set button. This will open the Save dialog box shown in Figure 15.1. Give the new set a name and save the new set to the Keyboard Shortcuts folder.

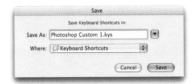

**Figure 15.1** The Keyboard Shortcuts Save set dialog. The default location for saving sets is the Keyboard Shortcuts folder in the Adobe Photoshop CS3 application folder.

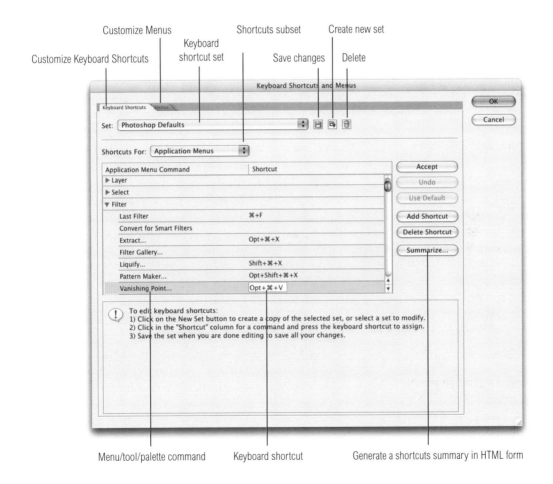

**Figure 15.2** The Keyboard Shortcuts dialog.

**Figure 15.3** As you edit the keyboard shortcuts, you will come up against the same problem that has long bugged the Photoshop engineers, and discover that many of the key combinations are already in use. When this happens, an alert message will appear at the bottom of the dialog telling you that the shortcut is already in use elsewhere. You can either undo the change or choose Accept. When you change the assigned shortcut the old shortcut will be removed from this set. If the Palette menu shortcut is also shared as a menu item, these changes will take place in both locations.

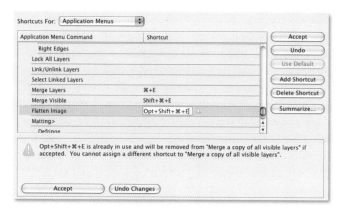

## Menu customization

You can access the Menu settings by clicking on the Menus tab, behind Keyboard Shortcuts, or by using the ⌘ ⌥ Shift M ctrl alt Shift M keyboard shortcut. You can choose to hide those menu options you never use and apply color coding to make more prominent the menu items you use most often. Photoshop CS3 ships with menu customization presets such as a What's New in Photoshop CS3 preset.

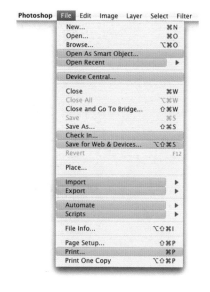

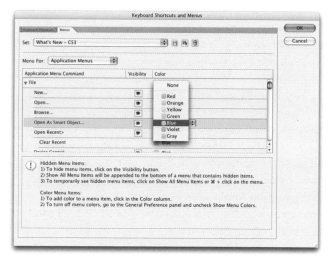

**Figure 15.4** The Photoshop menus can be customized by going to the Menus section. In the example shown here, I chose the What's New in Photoshop CS3 setting. This will highlight all the new Photoshop CS3 menu items in blue.

# Working with Actions

You can record a great many operations in Photoshop using what are known as Actions. Photoshop Actions are application scripts that you can use to record a sequence of events carried out in Photoshop. Actions that you record while working in Photoshop can then be replayed on other images. Actions can therefore save you the bother of laboriously repeating the same steps over and over again on subsequent images, as well as enabling you to batch process several images at once. Actions can also be saved within Action Sets and these can then be shared with other Photoshop users enabling them to replay the same sequence of Photoshop steps on their computer.

## Playing an action

The Actions palette already contains a set of prerecorded actions called Default Actions.atn. And if you go to the Actions palette fly-out menu you can load other sets from the menu list such as: Frames and Image Effects. To test these out, open an image, select an action from the menu and press the Play button. Photoshop will then apply the recorded sequence of commands to the selected image. If the number of steps in a complex action exceeds the number of available histories, there will be no way of completely undoing all the commands when the action has completed. So as a precaution, either take a Snapshot via the History palette or save the document before executing an action. If you are not happy with the result of the action, you can go back to the saved snapshot in History or revert to the last saved version. Photoshop Actions are normally appended with the .*atn* file extension and saved by default to the Photoshop Actions folder, inside the Photoshop Application Presets folder. But you can store them anywhere you like. And if you want to install an action you have downloaded or someone has sent to you, all you have to do is double-click it and Photoshop will automatically load the action into the Actions palette (and launch Photoshop in the process if the program is not already running at the time).

## Sourcing ready-made actions

When you first install Photoshop you will find some Actions already loaded in the Default Actions Set and you can load more by going to the Actions palette fly-out menu and clicking on one of the action sets in the list (see Figure 15.5). There are also many more Photoshop Actions that are freely available on the Internet. A useful starting point is the Adobe Studio Exchange site at: http://share.studio.adobe.com. This site contains a comprehensive list of actions, plug-ins and scripts, etc. Another is the Elated site: www.elated.com/actionkits/. Both these sites offer ready-prepared actions or sets of actions with examples of the types of effects achieved with them for you to freely download for use in Photoshop.

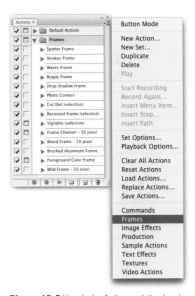

**Figure 15.5** Here is the Actions palette showing the palette fly-out menu options. You can add more action sets by selecting them from the list.

## Limitations when recording actions

Most Photoshop operations can be recorded within an action such as image adjustments, History palette steps, filters, and most tool operations in Photoshop. Tools such as the marquee and gradient fills are recorded based on the currently set ruler unit coordinates. Where relative positioning is required, choose the Percent units in Units & Rulers preferences before you begin recording. And avoid using commands which as yet cannot be recorded with an action. Certain operations like brush strokes (or any of the other painting tools) cannot be recorded as this goes beyond the scope of what can be scripted in Photoshop.

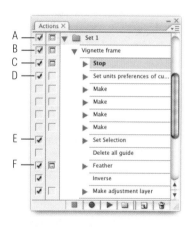

**Figure 15.6** Actions palette column icons.

A: The Set contains inactive operations.
B: The Action contains inactive operations.
C: Indicates the Action step is active and contains a Stop.
D: An active operation that has a dialog box.
E: An active operation with no dialog box.
F: An active operation with a Pause, which will open a dialog box.

## Recording actions

To record an action, open up a test image to work with. You may at this stage want to create a new action set to contain new actions. Next click on the New Action button icon at the bottom of the Actions palette. This will add a new action to the set. Give the action a name and then press the Record button. At this stage you can also assign a custom key combination using a combination of Function keys (*F1*–*F15*) with the *Shift* and *⌘* *ctrl* keys. You can then simply use the key combination to initiate running the action. Now carry out the Photoshop steps you wish to record and when finished click the Stop button.

Watch out for recording commands that rely on the use of named layers or channels that may be present in your test file, as these will not be recognized when the action is applied to a new image. Also try to make sure that your actions will not always be conditional on starting in one color mode only, or being of a certain size. If you intend recording a complex action, the best approach is to carefully plan in advance the sequence of Photoshop steps you intend to record. A Stop can be inserted in an action and this will always open a message dialog at a certain point during playback. It can include a memo to yourself (or another user replaying the action), reminding you of what needs to be done at a certain stage. Or if the action is to be used as a training aid, the message could include a teaching tip or comment. Actions are always created within sets and if you want to save an action, it has to be saved as a set. So if you want to separate an action to save on its own, click on the New Set button in the Actions palette to create a new set, drag the action to the new set, name the set and choose Save Actions... from the Actions palette fly-out menu (an action set must be highlighted, not an action). If you hold down the *⌘* *⌥* *ctrl* *alt* keys as you choose Save Actions... this will save the text descriptions of the action steps for every Photoshop action currently in the Actions palette. The following steps show you how to record a basic action.

**1** The Actions palette has been expanded here to list all the steps that make up an action I have named Vignette frame 15%. As a first step, I chose Show Rulers from the View menu. I *ctrl* right mouse-clicked a ruler and set the units to 'Percent'. By doing this, all positions were recorded, measured as a percentage of the document's dimensions. The recorded action will work effectively, whatever the size or proportions of an image.

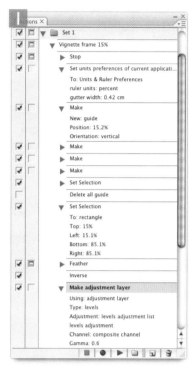

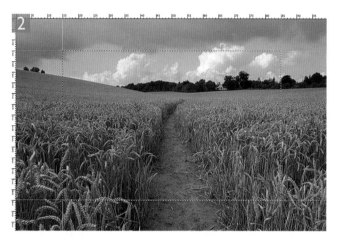

**2** I dragged ruler guides out from the rulers, placing four guides at 15% in from the edge. I then used these guides as a reference to draw a rectangular marquee and then cleared the guides afterwards to delete them. To create the vignette effect, I chose Feather from the Select menu and feathered the selection by 100 pixels, followed by an Inverse Selection.

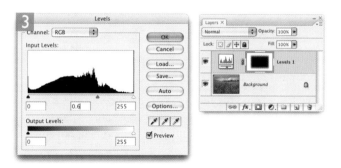

**3** I then clicked on the Add Adjustment layer button in the Layers palette and chose Levels. This step added an adjustment layer, automatically adding a layer mask at the same time, based on the current selection. So as I darkened the adjustment by dragging the Gamma slider to the right in Levels, only the outer areas were affected.

## Volatile actions

One thing you have to be aware of is that although actions will remain stored in the Actions palette after you quit Photoshop, a newly installed or created action can easily become lost should you suffer a computer or program crash before you quit. Photoshop Actions will also become lost if you trash the Photoshop preferences or uninstall Photoshop. It is therefore always a good idea to take the precaution of saving out any newly created or newly edited action sets so you don't lose them! These can be saved anywhere, but the Photoshop CS3/Actions/Presets folder is where the standard Action Sets are stored.

## Actions only record changed settings

One of the problems you commonly face when preparing and recording an action, is what to do if certain settings are already as you want them to be. Actions will only record a setting as part of an action if it actually changes. So, for example, you are recording an image size adjustment where you want the image resolution to end up at 300 pixels per inch, but the image is already defined in the Image Size dialog as 300 pixels per inch. In these situations, Photoshop does not record anything. To resolve these potential problems, you have to deliberately make the image size something else before you record the step, and then when you change the pixel resolution this will get recorded.

## Backgrounds and bit depth

Other action stoppers include the lack of a Background layer. There is not much you can do about this, but to convert the current base layer to a Background layer by choosing Layer ⇨ New ⇨ Background from Layer. Alternatively you can try making a flattened duplicate of the current image and then run the action. You may also want to check the bit depth of the image you are applying the action to. If the bit depth is 16 bit, not all Photoshop filters will work and you will need to convert the photograph to 8-bit per channel mode first.

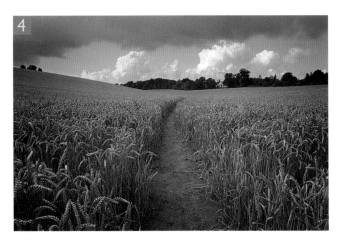

**4** When the recording is complete, you need to remember to click on the Stop button in the Actions palette. The action is now ready for testing. And when you have fine-tuned the actions as necessary, it is ready for use to apply as a single action or as part of a batch process operation.

## Troubleshooting actions

Check that the image to be processed is in the correct color mode. Many actions are written to operate in RGB color mode only. So if the starting image is in CMYK, the color adjustment commands will not work properly. Quite often, assumptions may be made about the image being flattened and having no layers. One way to prevent this from happening is to start each action by creating a new layer, then use Layer ⇨ Arrange ⇨ Send to Front, followed by a Merge Visible to layer command ( ⌘ ⌥ Shift E ctrl alt Shift E ). Some pre-written actions require that the start image fits certain criteria. For example, the Photoshop supplied Text Effect Actions require that you begin with an image that already contains layered text. If you have just recorded an action and are having trouble getting it to replay, you can inspect it command by command. Open a test image and expand the Actions palette to display all the items. Hold down the ⌘ ctrl key and click on the Play button. This will play the first command only. If there is a problem, double-click the command item in the list to rerecord it. Hold down the ⌘ ctrl key again and click on the Play button to continue.

## Action recording tips

Action recordings should be as unambiguous as possible. For example, if you record a step in which a named layer is brought forward in the layer stack, on playback the action will look for a layer with that name. Therefore, when adding a layer include naming the layer as part of the action. Do not use Layer 1, Layer 2, etc. This can only cause confusion with Photoshop's default naming of layers. And use the main Layer menu or Layer key command shortcuts to reorder the layer positioning. Doing so will make your action more universally recognized.

## Inserting menu items

There are some things which can be included as part of a Photoshop action that can only be included by forcing the insertion of a menu item. For example, Photoshop will not record zoom tool or View menu zoom instructions. But if you select Insert Menu Item from the Actions palette fly-out menu, as you record, you will see the dialog in Figure 15.7. The Menu Item dialog will initially say None Selected. If at this stage I choose a zoom command from the View menu, the instruction will now be recorded as part of the action, although frustratingly the image won't actually zoom in or out until you replay the action. I also use the Insert Menu Item to record opening dialogs that I regularly access, like the Web Photo Gallery. This saves me always having to navigate the File menu.

## Stop and pause

When editing an action, you can insert what is known as a Stop, which will allow you to halt the action process to display an alert message. This could be a useful warning like the one shown in Figure 15.8, which could be displayed at the beginning of the action playback. If you want to display a dialog setting during playback, insert a Pause by clicking in the blank space to the left of the action step (see Figure 15.6).

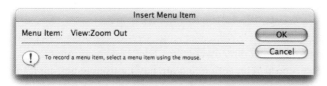

**Figure 15.7** The Insert Menu Item dialog will initially say None Selected. Select a menu item such as Window ⇨ Tile and click OK. When the Action is replayed the instruction will be included.

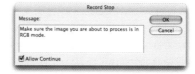

**Figure 15.8** The Record Stop dialog.

## Batch processing actions

One of the great advantages of Actions is having the ability
to batch process files. The Batch dialog can be accessed
via the File ⇨ Automate menu. And it can also be accessed
via the Tools ⇨ Photoshop menu in Bridge. You will need
to select an Action Set and Action from the Play section.
Then you need to select a Source and Destination. The
Source can be all currently open images, selected images
in the Bridge window or a designated folder, in which
case, you need to click on the Choose... button below
and select a folder of images. If you check the Override

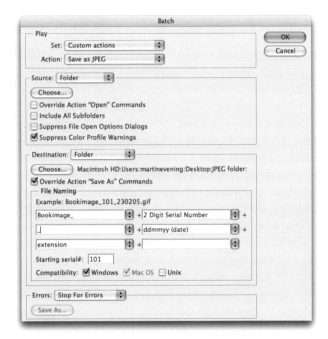

**Figure 15.9** An example of the Batch Action dialog set to apply a prerecorded
action. You can write your own fields. I have created a batch process where the image
will be renamed 'Bookimage_' followed by a two digit serial number, followed by an
underscore '_' the date expressed as: day; month; and year, followed by a lower case
extension. Note that the numbering has been set to start at '101'. So in this example
the file name structure will be something like: Bookimage_101_230205.gif. Note
also that the .gif extension is just there as an example to show that there will be an
extension appended to the file name. It won't actually be saved as a GIF. And the
Windows box has been checked to ensure file naming compatibility with PC systems.

Action 'Open' commands checkbox, Photoshop will only open and process images if the Action includes an Open command. And check the Include All Subfolders option only if you want to process all the subfolders within the selected folder.

Checking the Suppress Color Profile Warnings option will prevent the Missing Profile and Profile Mismatch dialogs appearing when you batch process images. If there is a profile mismatch, Photoshop will check what you did previously. If you previously chose to keep the image in its own profile space, then this is how the images will be batch processed. If there is no profile present, Photoshop will check to see if your previous preference was set to: Ignore, Assign a profile, or Assign and convert to the working space, and act accordingly.

The action you are using for the batch process may contain a Save or Save As command that uses a specific file format and format settings. This action step will also have recorded a Save destination. Now it might so happen that the Save destination is an important part of the action. But if the destination folder no longer exists, the action will fail to work. And besides, you can specify a destination folder within the Batch dialog. So in the majority of instances, if the action contains a Save instruction, I recommend you check the Override Action: 'Save As' Commands checkbox. And if the action does not contain a Save or Save As command, leave it unchecked.

The file naming options let you define the precise naming and numbering structure of the batch processed files. For example, the existing file document name can be made capitalized or use lower case type. Figure 15.9 shows the complete list of naming and numbering options (these are also used in the Create Droplet dialog). If a folder is selected as the destination, you have six editable fields at your disposal. You can use any combination you like, but the file extension must always go at the end. As you edit the fields, you will see an example of how the naming will work on a nominal image called MyFile.gif.

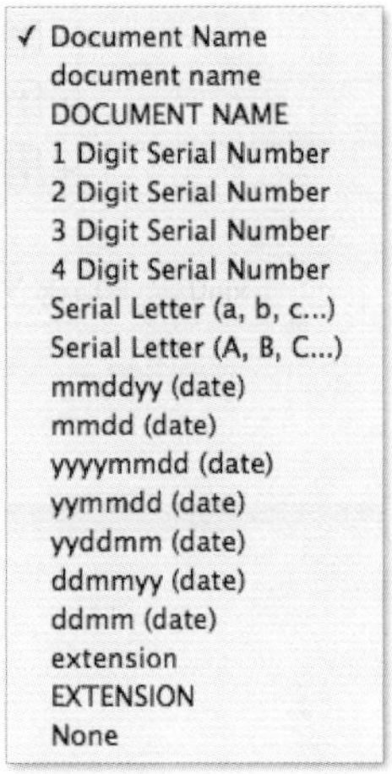

✓ Document Name
document name
DOCUMENT NAME
1 Digit Serial Number
2 Digit Serial Number
3 Digit Serial Number
4 Digit Serial Number
Serial Letter (a, b, c...)
Serial Letter (A, B, C...)
mmddyy (date)
mmdd (date)
yyyymmdd (date)
yymmdd (date)
yyddmm (date)
ddmmyy (date)
ddmm (date)
extension
EXTENSION
None

**Figure 15.10** The Batch interface naming and numbering options.

## Cross platform droplets

You can name a droplet anything you like, but to be PC compatible you should add a .exe extension. If someone sends you a droplet that was created using a PC, it can be made Mac compatible by dragging it over once to the Photoshop application icon.

## Creating a droplet

A Photoshop action can be converted into a self-contained application, known as a droplet, that can be saved outside Photoshop to somewhere useful, like the desktop. When you drag a document or a folder on top of a droplet icon it will launch Photoshop (if the program is not already running) and initiate a specific action sequence.

To make a droplet, go to the File ⇨ Automate menu and choose Create Droplet... Figure 15.12 shows the Create Droplet interface (the Create Droplet options are identical to those found in the Batch Actions dialog). Choose a location to save the droplet to and choose a destination folder for the droplet processed files. When you are finished, click OK. Droplets can play a useful role in any production workflow. They are effectively self-contained Photoshop batch processing routines. I have got into the habit of keeping a folder located on the desktop specifically designed to contain Photoshop droplets and their associated destination folders.

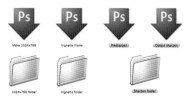

**Figure 15.11** When you drag and drop an image file on top of a droplet, this will launch Photoshop and perform a single or batch processing operation within the program. Droplets can perform Save and Close operations or save the processed results to an accompanying folder. I have an easily accessed folder on my main hard drive that contains dozens of droplets with their associated droplet folders.

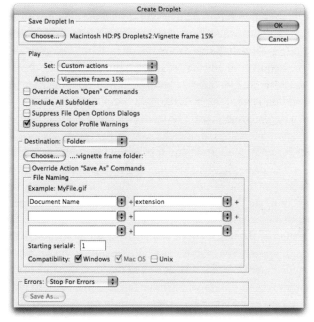

**Figure 15.12** The Create Droplet dialog.

# Scripting

One of the most neglected aspects of Photoshop has been the ability to write scripts to automate the program and do more than you can with Actions alone. For most of us, the prospect of writing scripts is quite scary, and I freely confess I am one of those who has looked at the scripting manuals and simply shuddered at the prospect of learning how to do such computer programming. But steps have been taken to make this stuff more accessible to the general user. You can start by referring to the Photoshop Scripting Guide and other PDF documents about scripting that can all be found in the Photoshop CS3/Scripting Guide folder. You can also download pre-made scripts from the Adobe Studio Exchange website: http://share.studio.adobe.com.

But to start with, go to the Scripts menu in the Photoshop File menu. There are a few sample Scripts here to experiment with. Among these is a script that will generate a Web Photo Gallery from the Layer Comps in a file. Back on pages 268 and 399 I showed examples of the load Files into Stack script, and in Figure 15.13 I have shown the interface for the Export Layers to Files script.

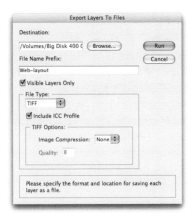

**Figure 15.13** An example of the Export Layers to Files script dialog from the Scripts menu in Photoshop.

## Script Event Manager

The Script Event Manager can be configured to trigger a Javascript or an action in Photoshop whenever a particular operation is performed. Below is a simple example of what can be done using scripting.

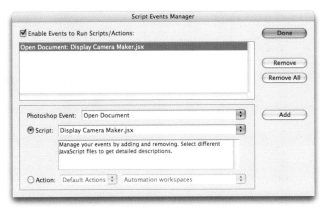

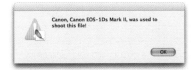

**Figure 15.14** The Script Event Manager is located in the File ⇨ Scripts menu. The dialog shown here is configured to trigger running a script that displays the name of the camera make whenever I open a Camera Raw file in Photoshop.

## Preparing JPEGs for the Web

When you are preparing images that are destined to be shared by email or published via the Web, the Image Processor is a handy tool to use because you can not only resize the images as part of the image processing, but you can instruct the Image Processor to convert the image from its current profile space to sRGB, which is an ideal RGB space for general purpose web viewing.

**Figure 15.15** The Image Processor (formerly known as Dr Russell Brown's Image Processor). This Scripting dialog can be configured to process single or multiple images, applying a Photoshop action, with the ability to add copyright info and save the files to a designated folder location in one or more of the following file formats: JPEG, PSD or TIFF. The destination folder will contain the processed images and these will be separated into folders named according to the file format used.

Once configured, you can click on the Save... button to save the settings and load them again at a future date.

## Image Processor

The Image Processor is located in the File ⇨ Scripts menu in Photoshop and can also be accessed via the Tools ⇨ Photoshop menu in Bridge. The Image Processor is a fine example of what Scripts can do when they are presented via an easy-to-use interface. The Image Processor basically allows you to select a folder of images (or use all open images) to process and select a location to save the processed files to. The Image Processor can then be configured to run a Photoshop action (if required) and save the processed files using either the JPEG, PSD or TIFF file formats. But it will also allow you to simultaneously process and save the files to more than one format at a time. So it is very handy if you wish to produce, say, a TIFF version at high resolution and a JPEG version ready to place in a web page design.

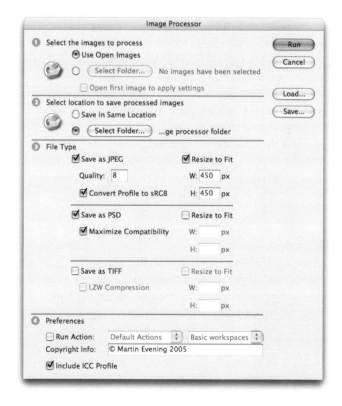

## Automated plug-ins

The Automation features described in this section are all
examples of Automated plug-ins. What distinguishes these
from normal plug-ins is that they enable Photoshop to
perform a complex set of procedures based on simple user
input. Some Automated plug-ins are like 'wizards' that
feature a step-by-step interface to guide you through various
options and help you produce the desired result. Adobe
has made Automated plug-ins 'open source', which means
it is possible for third-party developers to have the means
to build their own Automated plug-ins for Photoshop. I
believe that Pixel Genius (of which I am a co-founder) is so
far the only company who has made use of this feature in
Photoshop to produce the PhotoKit, PhotoKit Sharpener and
PhotoKit Color Automated plug-ins.

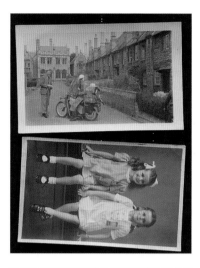

### Crop and Straighten Photos

This Automated plug-in is very straightforward to use,
if you have scanned images that need to be rotated and
cropped. Gang up several images on your scanner, scan the
pictures in as one image and choose Crop and Straighten
Photos from the Automate submenu (note, this option is not
available in Bridge). Photoshop will then create a rotated
and cropped copy version of each picture. It kind of works,
but only if the background has an absolutely solid color.
Crop and Straighten therefore works best when processing
scans of chrome transparencies and the border is deep
black. But otherwise it sometimes helps if you make a
selection around an individual image first.

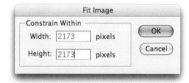

**Figure 15.16** The Crop and Straighten Photos
plug-in can be used to extract scanned photos
that need to be rotated and cropped.

### Fit Image

Fit Image... is a very simple Automated plug-in that
bypasses the Image ⇨ Image Size menu item. It is well
suited for the preparation of screen-based design work.
Enter the pixel dimensions you want the image to fit to, by
specifying the maximum pixel width or height. Note that
if you enter the same pixel dimensions for the width and
height, Fit Image can be used to batch process landscape
and portrait format images simultaneously.

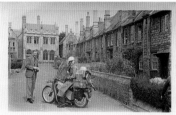

**Figure 15.17** The Fit Image dialog.

## Online printing

To launch Online printing, choose File ⇨ Print Online... and follow the dialog instructions to create yourself an account with one of the online print services available through Adobe. Selected images in Bridge can then be uploaded to your account folder with Ofoto™. From there on you can explore the various print options and finally place an order to have a print made and delivered. Online print services have become very popular in recent years, mainly due to the speed and popularity of broadband Internet services, making it easier to upload large image files. An online printing service can prove useful if you need to make enlargements bigger than your own printer can handle or if you wish to produce multiple print copies at a reasonable cost.

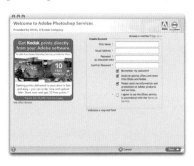

**Figure 15.18** The Online Print Services dialog.

## Picture Package

The Picture Package can automatically produce a picture package page layout based on one or more images. Figure 15.19 shows how you could have a combination of a single 5 × 7, with four smaller 2.5 × 3.5 sized images all oriented to fit within a single 10 × 8 print area.

Picture Package will normally generate a layout based on the frontmost image that is open in Photoshop. You can also select a specific file as the source or a folder, in which case a Picture Package will be created of every image in the folder, but this might take a long while to process.

If you double-click on any of the images displayed in the Picture Package layout preview, this will pop a Browse file dialog which will allow you to select an alternative image to replace one of the repeated images.

The Label section is useful if you wish to add, say, the file name or have the caption appear within the image area. For example, you could enter custom text, choose a low opacity and have it appear in the center of each image as a watermark (such as a copyright message). This labeling feature is still very limited as you cannot place the label outside of the image area (for example, just below each image). But you can now edit the layouts more easily.

The Picture Package Edit Layout dialog is shown in Figure 15.20. If you click on a template zone in the preview area an eight-handle bounding box will appear around the selected template zone, allowing you to edit the size and positioning of each zone. You also have the ability to delete or add more zones, and create templates using different page sizes. If you check the Snap To box in the Grid section this will display a grid, which will make it easy to ensure that the zones you place are all neatly aligned.

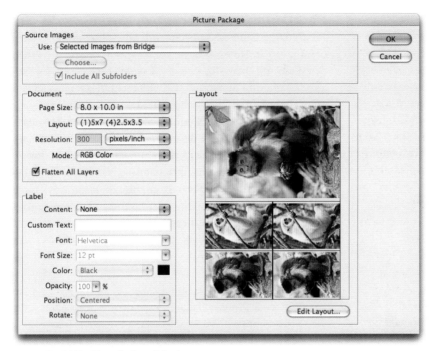

**Figure 15.19** The Picture Package dialog box.

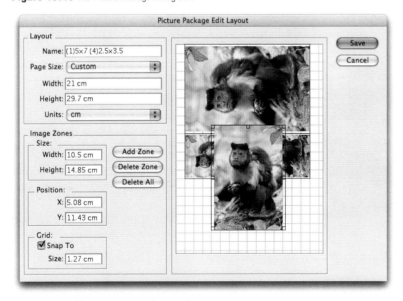

**Figure 15.20** The Picture Package layout editor.

## Photomerge made simpler

Those of you who are familiar with this feature will notice that the new Photomerge options will make it much easier to render a Photomerge image using one of the Auto options in the Photomerge dialog, which are shown in Figure 15.22. The Interactive layout mode is retained so that you can have full manual control over a Photomerge image.

## Photomerge in Interactive layout mode

Photomerge is mainly used for stitching photographs together to create panoramic compositions. There are other programs out there that can do the same kind of thing with varying degrees of success. But now with the improved auto-alignment in Photoshop CS3, I would consider the Photomerge feature to be among the best. I will often use Photomerge whenever I want to capture a view wider than the lens on my camera will allow. Photomerge will now work well in Auto or one of the other new modes, and there are examples of Photomerge being used in these ways on pages 10 and 411. But in this section I want to show you how to use Photomerge in the Interactive layout mode.

Photomerge tools    Work space area    Navigator

Lightbox area    Save Composition

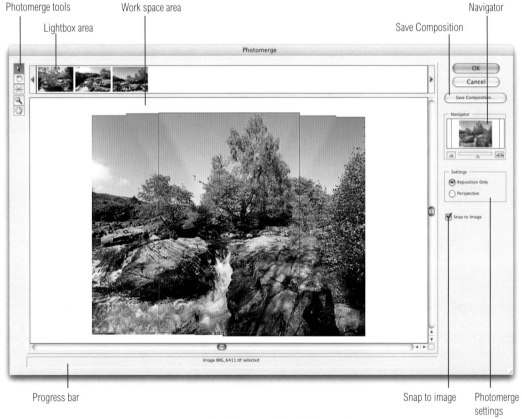

Progress bar    Snap to image    Photomerge settings

**Figure 15.21** The main Photomerge dialog.

You will generally get good results if you start with a simple composition that stitches together just a few shots rather than bombarding it with too many images. And before you shoot the photographs, set the exposure setting to manual so that the exposures are all consistent. And if you are shooting digitally, make sure that the white balance setting also remains the same (although if you shoot raw, you can apply a single white balance in the Camera Raw processing). The focal length must remain constant as well; do not attempt to zoom in or out as you are taking photographs. Wide-angle shots are more tricky to stitch together, so try to use a focal length that is equivalent to a 35 mm lens on a 35 mm camera, or longer.

There are two ways you can use Photomerge. The easiest way is to use Bridge to select the images you want to merge and choose Tools ⇨ Photoshop ⇨ Photomerge. The other way is to launch Photomerge from the File ⇨ Automate menu, and click on the Browse button in the introductory dialog to select a folder of images, or browse through the folders on your computer to add specific individual files you wish to merge together, or if the images you wish to merge are already open in Photoshop, select the Open Files option. If you then check the Blend images together option at the bottom, Photomerge will automatically attempt to join images together when it opens the Photomerge dialog shown in Figure 15.21.

**Photomerge photography tips**

If you are planning to capture a panoramic scene, then you need to make sure that all the images overlap sufficiently, by at least 15%. As you take your series of pictures, rotate the camera in gradual steps aiming to pivot the rotation around the center of the lens. And try to prevent the camera lens axis shifting about too much. You can do this by hand holding the camera but, to get the best results, you could consider using a tripod head like the Pan head from Manfrotto™ which, when used with the angle bracket clamp, will let you capture images that align more easily in Photomerge, as the center of rotation can be positioned accurately around the center of the lens axis.

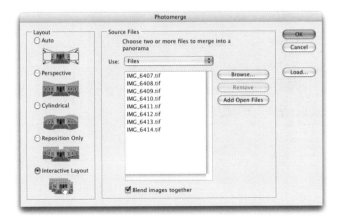

**Figure 15.22** The Photomerge opening dialog where you can select which images to process and choose from the different Photomerge modes. If you wish to load a pre-saved composition, there must be no images loaded in this dialog. Start with an empty dialog and click the Load... button. This will load the saved composition data and locate the associated source files.

**1** Although you can use the File ⇨ Automate menu in Photoshop, I find that the best approach is to make an edited selection of photographs via Bridge and choose Photomerge... from the Bridge Tools ⇨ Photoshop menu.

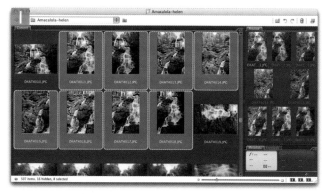

**2** The Photomerge dialog will list the photographs that have been selected and present a range of Photomerge options. For the following steps I chose to use the Interactive Layout option (the one selected at the bottom of the list of options).

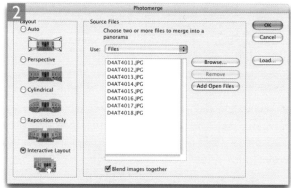

**3** As Photomerge launched it opened all of the images in sequence and attempted to auto-stitch the pictures together. As you can see here, Photomerge was able to work out how to assemble six of the eight shots in the work area all by itself. The two shots that wouldn't auto match were held in the lightbox area above. At this stage I was able to use the Navigator controls to zoom in and out of the work space area and scroll around the composition.

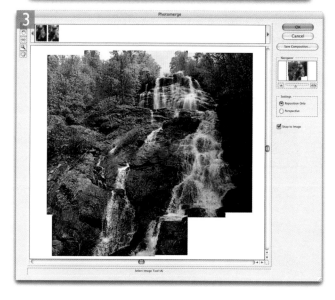

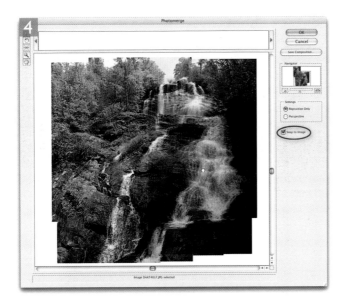

**4** To merge the remaining images held in the lightbox area, I made sure the Select Image tool was active and the Snap to Image box (circled) was checked. I clicked to select the images in the lightbox area and dragged them across into the work area. The image appeared semi-transparent where it overlapped the underlying composition. This enabled me to judge where to position it so that the image registers as closely as possible to the rest of the composition. If the image did not appear to match too well, I could have selected the rotate image tool and rotated it slightly until it did.

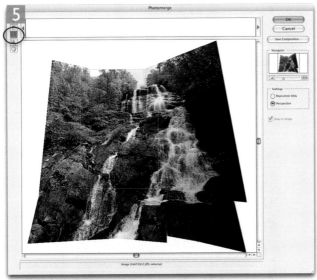

**5** Once all the image components were in place, I could try making further improvements. I clicked on the Perspective button in the dialog settings and Photomerge adjusted the composition preview, transforming each image component in order to achieve an improved composition perspective, centered around the currently active image. If the perspective needed adjusting, I could select the set vanishing point tool (circled) and click in the work area to set a new vanishing point. I then clicked OK to process the images and render a blended panorama photograph.

If at this stage I simply wanted to save the composition settings, I could click on the Save Composition button and name this as a saved Photomerge setting. To load a Photomerge setting, you can choose Photomerge from the Photoshop (not Bridge) File ⇨ Automate menu (see Figure 15.22) and click on the Load button in the opening dialog. Photomerge settings can be saved anywhere, but they may fail to work if the source folder name is changed.

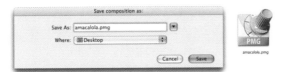

## Adding captions to the contacts

Check the Use Filename As Caption checkbox if you want the file name to appear below each picture. There is a small selection of fonts to choose from in point sizes going from 4 point up to 72 point.

## Contact Sheet II

The Contact Sheet II is able to take a folder of images or a selection of pictures from Bridge (or selected via the File ⇨ Automate menu in Photoshop) and combine them into a contact sheet. If there are more images in the folder than will fit a single page layout, then extra contact sheets will be produced. The Contact Sheet II dialog is shown in Figure 15.23. In the Document section you can define the contact sheet page size, color mode and pixel resolution. Below that is the Thumbnails section where you can set the number of rows and columns to be used in the layout. When the Use Auto-Spacing box is checked, Photoshop will position the contact sheet images as closely together as possible. But bearing in mind that some images may be in landscape and others in portrait mode, there will still be some gaps between each image. If the Rotate For Best Fit box is checked, Photoshop will ignore the orientation of images and lay them out to achieve the best fit on the page. This means you will end up with something that looks more like a normal film contact sheet.

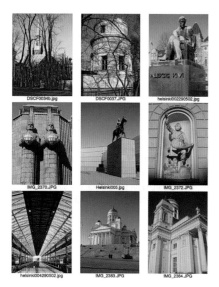

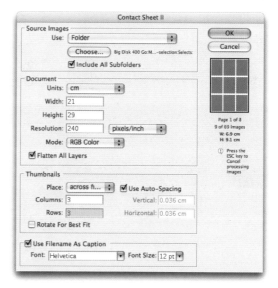

**Figure 15.23** With the Contact Sheet II feature you can automatically produce contact sheet prints that make the best use of the space on the page.

## Export Transparent Image and Resize Image

These last two Automation plug-ins are located in the Help menu. The Export Transparent Image Assistant interface starts by asking you whether the purpose of the final image is for print or online use. For example, if you want to make a transparent GIF and there is no selection currently active, it will tell you to cancel and make a selection first. From there on it will duplicate the current image and ask clearly put questions about the intended final output and guide you towards that desired goal. The Resize Image Assistant plug-in also has a clearly designed interface and takes the user step by step through the process of sizing an image for reprographic or online use (see Figure 15.25).

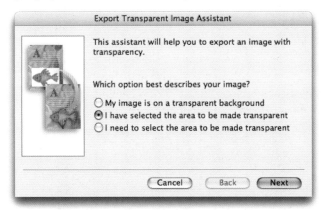

**Figure 15.24** The Export Transparent Image Assistant will require the image to be either against a transparent background, or you need to make a selection first of the area to be made transparent. The Export Transparency Assistant will then guide you to make a transparent GIF or PNG format image for the Web or a transparent image for print.

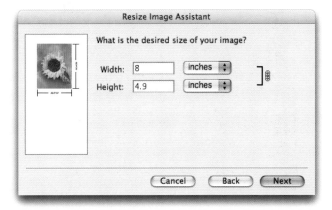

**Figure 15.25** The Resize Image Assistant can help you resize your images to the optimum resolution for multimedia or print output, based on the resolution of the print screen used. A warning may appear if the image is too small to be enlarged for print, which will suggest the image may need to be rescanned.

# Index

## Symbols

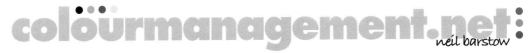

# colourmanagement.net
*neil barstow*

## Remote profiling for RGB printers

You have just been reading one of the best digital imaging books in the marketplace. Now you'll probably want to be sure your colour is as good as it can be, without too much back and forth when printing. Lots of print testing to achieve expected colour really does use up the ink and paper, but, more importantly it uses up the creative spirit. We'd like to offer you a deal on a printer profile. Just download the profiling kit from:
www.colourmanagement.net/profiling_inkjets.html.

The kit contains a detailed manual and colour charts. We ask you to print the charts twice, so we can compare the sets to check printer continuity. You post them to us.

We will measure both sets of charts using a professional auto scanning spectrophotometer. This result is then used within high-end profiling software to produce a 'printer characterisation' or ICC profile which you will use when printing. Comprehensive instructions for use are included.

You can read a few comments from some of our clients at:
www.colourmanagement.net/about.html.

Remote RGB profiles cost £95 plus VAT. For readers of 'Adobe Photoshop CS3 for Photographers', we are offering a special price of £50 plus VAT. If our price has changed when you visit the site, then we will give you 30 percent off.

**Coupon code: MEPSCS3-07**

We also resell the colour management gear that you need: profiling equipment, LCD displays, print viewers, RIPs, printers and consumables etc.
http://www.colourmanagement.net/profilegear.html.

## Consultancy services

Neil Barstow, colour management and imaging specialist, of www.colourmanagement.net, offers readers of this fine book a discount of 12.5% on a whole or half day booking for consultancy.  Subject to availability and normal conditions.

**Coupon code: MEPSCS3-07.**

Please note that the above coupons will expire upon next revision of Adobe Photoshop for Photographers. E&OE.

# Pixel Genius PhotoKit plug-in discounts
## www.pixelgenius.com

**PhotoKit**
**Analog Effects for Photoshop**
This Photoshop compatible plug-in is designed to provide photographers accurate digital replications of common analog photographic effects. PhotoKit is quick and simple and allows for a greatly enhanced workflow. Priced at $49.95.

**PhotoKit SHARPENER**
**A complete Sharpening Work flow for Photoshop**
Other products may provide useful sharpening tools, but only PhotoKit SHARPENER provides a complete image "Sharpening Workflow". From capture to output, PhotoKit SHARPENER intelligently produces the optimum sharpness on any image, from any source, reproduced on any output device. But PhotoKit SHARPENER also provides the creative controls to address the requirements of individual images and the individual tastes of users. PhotoKit SHARPENER is priced at $99.95.

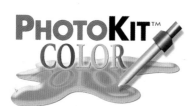

**PhotoKit Color**
**Creative color effects for Photoshop**
PhotoKit Color applies precise color corrections, automatic color balancing and creative coloring effects. This plug-in also provides a comprehensive suite of effects that lets you recreate creative effects like black and white split toning and cross processing. PhotoKit Color is priced at $99.95.

Pixel Genius is offering a 10% discount on any whole order, which must be placed from the Pixel Genius store at: www.pixelgenius.com. This is a one-time discount per email address for any order made from Pixel Genius. This coupon will not work on affiliate sites. Also it cannot be combined with other discounts or programs except for certain cross-sell items. Please note that this coupon will expire upon next revision of 'Adobe Photoshop for Photographers'.

**Coupon ID: PSFPCS3ME**